THE CAMBRIDGE COMPANION TO
KANT'S *CRITIQUE OF PURE REASON*

Immanuel Kant's *Critique of Pure Reason*, first published in 1781, is one of
the landmarks of Western philosophy, a radical departure from everything
that went before and an inescapable influence on all philosophy since its
publication. In this massive work, Kant has three aims. First, he constructs a
new theory of knowledge that delivers certainty about the fundamental
principles of human experience at the cost of knowledge of how things
are in themselves. Second, he delivers a devastating critique of traditional
"speculative" metaphysics on the basis of his new theory of knowledge.
Third, he suggests how the core beliefs of the Western metaphysical tradition
that cannot be justified as theoretical knowledge can nevertheless be justified
as objects of "moral faith" because they are the necessary conditions of the
possibility of moral agency. Kant started this third project in the *Critique of
Pure Reason*, but would go on to complete it in two other works, *Critique of
Practical Reason* and *Critique of the Power of Judgment*.

   The Cambridge Companion to Kant's "Critique of Pure Reason" is the first
collective commentary on this work in English. The seventeen chapters have
been written by an international team of scholars, including some of the
best-known figures in the field as well as emerging younger talents. The first
two chapters situate Kant's project against the background of Continental
rationalism and British empiricism, the dominant schools of early modern
philosophy. Eleven chapters then expound and assess all the main arguments
of the *Critique*. Finally, four chapters recount the enormous influence of
the *Critique* on subsequent philosophical movements, including German
Idealism and Neo-Kantianism, twentieth-century Continental philosophy,
and twentieth-century Anglo-American analytic philosophy. The book concludes with an extensive bibliography.

Paul Guyer is Professor of Philosophy and Florence R. C. Murray Professor in
the Humanities at the University of Pennsylvania, where he has taught since
1982. He is the author or editor of fourteen books on Immanuel Kant and
co–general editor of the *Cambridge Edition of the Works of Immanuel Kant*,
in which he has co-edited and co-translated the *Critique of Pure Reason*,
Critique of the Power of Judgment, and *Notes and Fragments*.

T0381866

The Cambridge Companion to

KANT'S
CRITIQUE OF
PURE REASON

EDITED BY

Paul Guyer

University of Pennsylvania

CAMBRIDGE
UNIVERSITY PRESS

CAMBRIDGE
UNIVERSITY PRESS

32 Avenue of the Americas, New York NY 10013-2473, USA

Cambridge University Press is part of the University of Cambridge.

It furthers the University's mission by disseminating knowledge in the pursuit of education, learning and research at the highest international levels of excellence.

www.cambridge.org
Information on this title: www.cambridge.org/9780521710114

© Cambridge University Press 2010

First published 2010

A catalogue record for this publication is available from the British Library

Library of Congress Cataloguing in Publication data

The Cambridge companion to Kant's Critique of pure reason / edited by Paul Guyer.
    p. cm. – (Cambridge companions to philosophy)
    Includes bibliographical references and index.
    ISBN 978-0-521-88386-3 (hardback)
    1. Kant, Immanuel, 1724–1804. Kritik der reinen Vernunft.   I. Guyer,
Paul, 1948–   II. Title.   III. Series.

    B2779.C25   2010
    121–dc22

2010017677

ISBN 978-0-521-88386-3 Hardback
ISBN 978-0-521-71011-4 Paperback

Contents

Contributors

R. LANIER ANDERSON is Associate Professor of Philosophy at Stanford University. He works in the history of late modern philosophy, with a primary focus on Kant, Nietzsche, and the Neo-Kantian movement. His recent papers include "It Adds Up After All: Kant's Philosophy of Arithmetic in Light of the Traditional Logic" (*Philosophy and Phenomenological Research*, 2004) and "Nietzsche on Truth, Illusion, and Redemption" (*The European Journal of Philosophy*, 2005). He is working on a book on Kant's analytic/synthetic distinction and its role in the critique of metaphysics entitled *The Poverty of Conceptual Truth*.

DANIEL DAHLSTROM is Chair and Professor of Philosophy at Boston University. His most recent publications include *Philosophical Legacies: Essays on Kant, Hegel, and Their Contemporaries* (2008) and a translation of Heidegger's first Marburg lectures, *Introduction to Phenomenological Research* (2006).

DINA EMUNDTS is Professor of Philosophy at the University of Konstanz, Germany. She is the author of *Kant's Übergangskonzeption im* Opus postumum (2004); editor of *Kant und die Berliner Aufklärung* (2000); and, with Rolf-Peter Horstmann, co-author of *G. W. F. Hegel: Eine Einführung* (2002).

MICHELLE GRIER is Professor of Philosophy at the University of San Diego. She is the author of *Kant's Doctrine of Transcendental Illusion* (2001).

PAUL GUYER is Professor of Philosophy and Florence R. C. Murray Professor in the Humanities at the University of Pennsylvania. He is the author of nine books on Kant, including, most recently, *Kant's*

System of Nature and Freedom (2005); *Values of Beauty* (2005); *Kant* (2006); *Kant's* Groundwork for the Metaphysics of Morals: *A Reader's Guide* (2007); and *Knowledge, Reason, and Taste: Kant's Response to Hume* (2008). He has edited numerous volumes on Kant, including *The Cambridge Companion to Kant* (1992) and *The Cambridge Companion to Kant and Modern Philosophy* (2006). Co–general editor with Allen Wood of *The Cambridge Edition of the Works of Immanuel Kant*, he translated the *Critique of Pure Reason* with Allen Wood (1998) and the *Critique of the Power of Judgment* with Eric Matthews (2000), and he edited Kant's *Notes and Fragments* (2005), which he translated with Curtis Bowman and Frederick Rauscher. He is at work on a history of modern aesthetics.

DESMOND HOGAN is Assistant Professor of Philosophy at Princeton University. His publications include "Noumenal Affection," *Philosophical Review* 118 (2009); "How to Know Unknowable Things in Themselves," *Noûs* 43 (2009); and "Three Kinds of Rationalism and the Non-Spatiality of Things in Themselves," *Journal of the History of Philosophy* 47 (2009).

ROLF-PETER HORSTMANN is Emeritus Professor of German Idealism at the Humboldt University, Berlin, and a regular visiting professor at the University of Pennsylvania. His books include *Ontologie und Relationen: Hegel, Bradley, Russell und die Kontroverse über interne und externe Beziehungen* (1984); *Die Grenzen der Vernunft: Eine Untersuchung zu Zielen und Motiven des Deutschen Idealismus* (1991); *Bausteine kritischer Philosophie: Arbeiten zu Kant* (1997); and, with Dina Emundts, *G. W. F. Hegel: Eine Einführung.* Among the many volumes he has edited are *Dialektik in der Philosophie Hegels* (1978) and *Transcendental Arguments and Science: Essays in Epistemology*, with Peter Bieri and Lorenz Krüger (1979).

A. W. MOORE is Professor of Philosophy at Oxford University. His publications include *The Infinite* (second edition, 2001); *Points of View* (1997); and *Infinite in Faculty, Noble in Reason: Themes and Variations in Kant's Moral and Religious Philosophy* (2003). He is the editor of *Meaning and Reference* (1993); *Infinity* (1993); and Bernard Williams's posthumous collection *Philosophy as a Humanistic Discipline* (2003). He is working on a book, *Making Sense of Things: The Evolution of Modern Metaphysics.*

KONSTANTIN POLLOK is Associate Professor of Philosophy at the University of South Carolina. He is the author of *Kant's Metaphysische*

Anfangsgründe der Naturwissenschaft: Ein Kritischer Kommentar (2001) and *Begründen und Rechtfertigen* (2009).

FREDERICK RAUSCHER is Associate Professor of Philosophy at Michigan State University. He is the author of many articles that focus on Kant's metaethics, particularly in relation to realism, naturalism, and evolution. He has also translated Kant's *Nachlaß* on ethics for *Notes and Fragments* and is translating and editing *Kant's Lectures and Drafts on Political Philosophy*, both for the Cambridge Edition of the Works of Immanuel Kant.

MICHAEL ROHLF is Assistant Professor of Philosophy at The Catholic University of America. He is the author of several articles on Kant.

LISA SHABEL is Associate Professor of Philosophy at The Ohio State University. She is the author of *Mathematics in Kant's Critical Philosophy: Reflections on Mathematical Practice* (2003).

ERIC WATKINS is Professor of Philosophy at the University of California, San Diego. His research has focused primarily on Kant's theoretical philosophy, placing a special emphasis on Kant's pre-Critical period and philosophy of science. He is the author of *Kant and the Metaphysics of Causality* (2005). He has edited *Kant and the Sciences* (2001) and edited and translated *Kant's Critique of Pure Reason: Background Source Materials* (2009).

KENNETH R. WESTPHAL is Professor of Philosophy at the University of Kent, Canterbury. His books include *Hegel's Epistemological Realism* (1989); *Hegel, Hume, und die Identität wahrnehmbarer Dinge* (1998); *Hegel's Epistemeology: A Philosophical Introduction to the Phenomenology of Spirit* (2003); and *Kant's Transcendental Proof of Realism* (2004). He is the editor of *The Blackwell's Guide to Hegel's Phenomenology of Spirit* (2009).

KENNETH P. WINKLER is Professor of Philosophy at Yale University. He is the author of *Berkeley: An Interpretation* (1989). His publications include *The Cambridge Companion to Berkeley* (2005) and an abridgment of Locke's *Essay Concerning Human Understanding* (1996). From 2000 to 2005, he was editor, with Elizabeth Radcliffe, of the journal *Hume Studies*. A collection of his papers, *Matters of Reason: Essays in Early Modern British Philosophy*, is forthcoming.

ALLEN W. WOOD is Ward W. and Priscilla B. Woods Professor at Stanford University. He was Isaiah Berlin Visiting Professor at Oxford University in 2005. He is the author of *Kant's Moral Religion* (1970, reissued 2009); *Kant's Rational Theology* (1978, reissued 2009); *Karl Marx* (1981, second edition 2004); *Hegel's Ethical Thought* (1990); *Kant's Ethical Thought* (1999); *Unsettling Obligations* (2002); *Kant* (2005); and *Kantian Ethics* (2008). He is Co–general editor of the *Cambridge Edition of the Works of Immanuel Kant*, in which he translated the *Critique of Pure Reason* with Paul Guyer (1998) and *Religion and Rational Theology* with George di Giovanni (1996). He is editing both Kant's *Lectures on Anthropology* for the Cambridge edition and *The Cambridge History of Philosophy 1790–1870*.

JULIAN WUERTH is Associate Professor of Philosophy at Vanderbilt University. He is the author of *Kant on Mind, Action, and Ethics* (forthcoming) and the co-editor of *Perfecting Virtue: New Essays on Kantian Ethics and Virtue Ethics* (forthcoming).

Abbreviations

Citations to Kant's texts are generally given parenthetically, although additional references are often included in the footnotes to the chapters. Two forms of citation are employed. Citations from the *Critique of Pure Reason* are located by reference to the pagination of Kant's first ("A") and/or second ("B") editions. All other passages from Kant's works are cited by the volume and page number, given by Arabic numerals separated by a colon, in the standard edition, of Kant's works, *Kant's gesammelte Schriften*, edited by the Royal Prussian, later German, then Berlin-Brandenburg Academy of Sciences, 29 volumes (Berlin: Georg Reimer, later Walter de Gruyter & Co., 1900–). Where Kant divided a work into numbered sections, his section number typically precedes the volume and page number. These references are preceded by a short title for the work cited, unless the context makes it obvious. All translations are from the *Cambridge Edition of the Works of Immanuel Kant* (1992–).

The following list, in alphabetical order, gives the short titles of Kant's works (with the date of original publication in parentheses) that are used throughout the volume.

Correspondence	Kant's correspondence, in volumes 10–13 of the Academy edition or in Zweig (see Bibliography)
Directions	*Concerning the Ultimate Ground of the Differentiation of Directions in Space* (1768)
Discovery	On a Discovery whereby any new *Critique of Pure Reason* is made superfluous by an older one (1790)
Dissertation	Inaugural dissertation *On the Form and Principles of the Sensible and Intelligible Worlds* (1770)
False Subtlety	*On the False Subtlety of the Four Syllogistic Figures* (1762)

FI	*First Introduction to the Critique of the Power of Judgment* (posthumous)
Groundwork	*Groundwork for the Metaphysics of Morals* (1785)
Judgment	*Critique of the Power of Judgment* (1790)
Living Forces	*On the True Estimation of Living Forces* (1747)
Logic	*Immanuel Kant's Logic: A Handbook for Lectures*, edited by G. B. Jäsche (1800)
Metaphysical Foundations or *MANW*	*Metaphysical Foundations of Natural Science* (1786)
Negative Magnitudes	*Attempt to Introduce the Concept of Negative Magnitudes into Philosophy* (1763)
New Elucidation	*A New Elucidation of the First Principles of Metaphysical Cognition* (1755)
Observations	*Observations on the Feeling of the Beautiful and Sublime* (1764)
Only Possible Argument	*The Only Possible Argument in Suppport of a Demonstration of the Existence of God* (1763)
Physical Monadology	*The Employment in Natural Philosophy of Metaphysics combined with Geometry, of which Sample I Contains the Physical Monadology* (1756)
Practical Reason	*Critique of Practical Reason* (1788)
Prize Essay	*Inquiry Concerning the Distinctness of the Principles of Natural Theology and Morals* (1764)
Progress	*What Is the Real Progress that Metaphysics Has Made in Germany Since the Time of Leibniz and Wolff*, edited by F. T. Rink (1804)
Prolegomena	*Prolegomena to any Future Metaphysics that Shall Come Forth as Scientific* (1783)
Pure Reason	*Critique of Pure Reason* (1781, 1787)
R	*Reflexionen* (Kant's notes and marginalia in volumes 14–20, 23 of the Academy edition)

PAUL GUYER

Introduction

I. THE EMERGENCE OF THE *CRITIQUE*

The *Critique of Pure Reason* by Immanuel Kant (1724–1804) is without
question one of the landmarks of the entire history of Western philosophy, comparable in its importance and influence to only a handful of
other works such as Plato's *Republic*, Aristotle's organon of logical
works, and Descartes's *Meditations on First Philosophy*. The *Critique*
was first published in 1781, after a decade of intensive preparation,[1] and
within a few years became the center of attention in German philosophy, and shortly after that in other European countries with advanced
philosophical culture such as Britain and France as well.[2] In the hope of

[1] Following the publication of his inaugural dissertation *On the Form and
Principles of the Sensible and Intelligible World* upon his appointment to
the chair in logic and metaphysics at the Prussian university in Königsberg
in 1770, Kant published almost nothing for the next decade as he devoted
himself entirely to the preparation of his *magnum opus*. Accounts of the
development of Kant's thought during that "silent decade" have been given
in Theodor Haering, *Der Duisburg'sche Nachlaß und Kants Kritizismus
um 1775* (Tübingen: J.C.B. Mohr, 1910); H.-J. De Vleeschauwer, *La
Déduction transcendentale dans l'Œuvre de Kant*, 3 vols. (Antwerp,
Paris, The Hague: De Sikkel, Champion, and Martinus Nijhoff, 1934–37),
especially volume 1, and the abridged translation of De Vleeschauwer's
work, *The Development of Kantian Thought: The History of a Doctrine*,
translated by A. R. C. Duncan (London, Edinburgh, etc.: Thomas Nelson
and Sons, 1962); W. H. Werkmeister, *Kant's Silent Decade: A Decade of
Philosophical Development* (Tallahassee: University Presses of Florida,
1979); Paul Guyer, *Kant and the Claims of Knowledge* (Cambridge:
Cambridge University Press, 1987), Part I; and Wolfgang Carl, *Der
schweigende Kant: Die Entwürfe zu einer Deduktion der Kategorien vor
1781* (Göttingen: Vandenhoeck & Ruprecht, 1989).
[2] As early as 1793, Karl Gottlob Hausius was able to publish a three-part
collection of *Materialen zur Geschichte der critischen Philosophie*
("Materials for the History of the Critical Philosophy") (Leipzig: Breitkopf,
1793). The *German Kantian Bibliography* that Erich Adickes published in
The Philosophical Review from 1893 to 1896, although originally intended
to catalogue works published up to 1887, stopped with no fewer than 2,832

I

clarifying some of the obscurity of the work and forestalling its misinterpretation, Kant issued a substantially revised edition of the work in 1787, in spite of his extensive agenda of other philosophical projects. That only intensified the debate about Kant's position, and ever since, students and scholars of Kant's philosophy have had to study the composite work that is the product of those two editions of the *Critique*.[3] The present *Companion* is designed to orient readers to the complex structure and arguments of the *Critique*, to the philosophical context within which it arose, and to the enormous influence it has had and continues to have on the subsequent history of philosophy.

Kant originally conceived of the work that he came to call the *Critique of Pure Reason* as the sole foundation that would be necessary before he

works by, on, or related to Kant published just by the time of Kant's death in 1804. The history of the early reception of Kant's work in Germany is told in Frederick C. Beiser, *The Fate of Reason: German Philosophy from Kant to Fichte* (Cambridge, MA: Harvard University Press, 1987). The history of the early reception of Kant's work in Britain has been told by René Wellek, *Immanuel Kant in England: 1793–1838* (Princeton: Princeton University Press, 1931).

[3] Beginning with Norman Kemp Smith's great translation of the *Critique* (1929, revised 1933), subsequent English translations (Pluhar, Guyer and Wood) have included all of the material from both editions of the *Critique*, and earlier translations (Meiklejohn, Max Müller), which were based on just one edition, have been updated with the material from the other edition (complete information on all these editions is provided in the Bibliography). Throughout the present volume, translations from the *Critique* are from the version published in *The Cambridge Edition of the Works of Immanuel Kant* – namely, Immanuel Kant, *Critique of Pure Reason*, edited and translated by Paul Guyer and Allen W. Wood (Cambridge: Cambridge University Press, 1998). This edition, like those of Kemp Smith and Pluhar, includes the original pagination of Kant's first ("A") and second ("B") editions, and passages are cited solely by those page numbers (an "A" page number if the passage is found only in the first edition, a "B" page number if it is found only in the second, and both "A" and "B" page numbers, separated by a slash, if the passage occurs in both editions. Other works are cited by an abbreviated title (the list of abbreviations precedes this Introduction) and the location of the passage by volume and page number in the standard German edition of Kant's published and unpublished works, *Kant's gesammelte Schriften*, edited by the Royal Prussian (subsequently German, then Berlin-Brandenburg) Academy of Sciences, 29 vols. (Berlin: Georg Reimer, subsequently Walter de Gruyter & Co., 1900–), the so-called "*Akademie* edition." The editions of Kant's three critiques in the *Akademie* edition are being updated as this *Companion* goes to press. Other recent German editions of the *Critique of Pure Reason* are also listed in the Bibliography.

could go on to provide detailed systems of theoretical and practical philosophy, which he called the "metaphysics of nature" and the "metaphysics of morals"[4] – as he conceived the work and even when he first published it, he clearly did not conceive of the two subsequent critiques that he would write, the *Critique of Practical Reason* (1788) and the *Critique of the Power of Judgment* (1790). In the ten known letters to his student Marcus Herz (1747–1803) that constitute Kant's progress reports on the first *Critique* during the "silent decade" of 1770 to 1780 during which he was working on it (Herz was a Jewish medical student in Königsberg who had enjoyed the honor of being Kant's "respondent" or spokesman at the public defense of his inaugural dissertation and who later became a prominent physician in Berlin), Kant tried out several names and descriptions for his project before settling on the one we know. In June 1771, he wrote to Herz that he was "now busy on a work which I call 'The Bounds of Sensibility and of Reason' [which] will work out in some detail the foundational principles and laws that determine the sensible world together with an outline of what is essential to the Doctrine of Taste, of Metaphysics, and of Moral Philosophy."[5] In his next letter to Herz, written on February 21, 1772, Kant repeated this title, though somewhat tentatively, now saying that it "might perhaps have the title, *The Bounds of Sensibility and Reason*," and made its all-encompassing ambition even clearer. He wrote:

I planned to have it consist of two parts, a theoretical and a practical. The first part would have two sections, (1) a general phenomenology and (2) metaphysics, but this only with regard to its nature and method. The second part would likewise have two sections, (1) the universal principles of feeling, taste, and sensuous desire and (2) the first principles of morality.[6]

---

[4] Kant would eventually fulfill his promise to provide these detailed works with the *Metaphysical Foundations of Natural Science* (1786), his derivation of fundamental propositions of Newtonian physics but also his own non-corpuscular theory of matter, and the *Metaphysics of Morals* (1797), divided into the *Metaphysical Foundations of Right*, his political and legal philosophy, and the *Metaphysical Foundations of Virtue*, his theory of ethical duties.

[5] Letter to Marcus Herz, June 7, 1771, 10:123; translation from Immanuel Kant, *Correspondence*, translated by Arnulf Zweig (Cambridge: Cambridge University Press, 1999), p. 127.

[6] Letter to Marcus Herz, February 21, 1772, 10:129; *Correspondence*, p. 132. Zweig translated the proposed title as "The Bounds of Sensibility and of Reason" in the letter of 1771 and "The Limits of Sensibility and Reason" in the letter of 1772, but Kant's key word in both titles is the same – namely, *Grenzen*, normally translated as "bounds" or "boundaries" and used, for example, to denote the demarcations between distinct political jurisdictions.

In spite of the fact that Kant then went on to confess that in his thought
on this grand project thus far he (along with all previous philosophers)
"had failed to consider ... the key to the whole secret of metaphysics ...
this question: What is the ground of the relation of that in us which
we call 'representation' to the object?"[7] Kant remained confident that
he would be able to publish the first part of the work, "which will deal
with the sources of metaphysics, its method and boundaries," within
three months! Almost two years later, however, at the end of 1773, he
wrote to Herz that "You search industriously but in vain in the book
fair catalog for a certain name beginning with the letter K" but that he
remained "obstinate in my resolve not to let myself be seduced by any
author's itch into seeking fame in easier, more popular fields, until
I shall have freed my thorny and hard ground for general cultivation";
yet he said "I still sometimes hope that I shall have the work ready
for delivery by Easter" – that is, in 1774.[8] But we know from our other
main source of information about Kant's progress on the *Critique* – a
group of sketches known as the *Duisburg Nachlaß*[9] – that Kant only
began to make headway on his question about the relation of the representation to the object around 1775, and thus three years after his
last letter to Herz, in a new letter from November, 1776, we find him
once again hoping to finish the work by the following Easter, thus by
1777. In this letter, although he does not tell Herz much about how
he is solving his question, Kant for the first time describes a work
that would have the structure of the work we have come to know. He
tells Herz:

As a matter of fact I have not given up hopes of accomplishing something in
the area in which I am working. People of all sorts have been criticizing me for the
inactivity into which I seem to have fallen for a long time, though actually I
have never been busier with systematic and sustained work since the years when
you last saw me. I might well hope for some transitory applause by completing
the matters I am working on ... But all these matters are held up by one major
object that, like a dam, blocks them, an object with which I hope to make a lasting
contribution and which I really think I have in my grasp. Now it needs only

[7] Letter to Marcus Herz, February 21, 1772, 10:130; *Correspondence*, p. 133.
[8] Letter to Marcus Herz from the end of 1773, 10:144–5; *Correspondence*,
p. 140.
[9] The *Duisburg Nachlaß*, a bundle of manuscripts that at one time belonged
to a family named Duisburg, provides the main source for the accounts of
Kant's development during the 1770s listed in note 1. The relevant texts,
Reflexionen 4674–4684 in the *Akademie* edition (volume 17), are translated in Immanuel Kant, *Notes and Fragments*, edited by Paul Guyer,
translated by Curtis Bowman, Paul Guyer, and Frederick Rauscher
(Cambridge: Cambridge University Press, 2005), pp. 157–77.

finishing up rather than thinking through. After I acquit myself of this task, which I am just now starting to do (after overcoming the final obstacles last summer) I seen an open field before me ... You know that it must be possible to survey the field of pure reason, that is, of judgments that are independent of all empirical principles, since this lies *a priori* in ourselves and need not await any exposure. What we need in order to indicate the divisions, boundaries, and the whole content of that field, according to secure principles, and to lay the road marks so that in the future one can know for sure whether one stands on the ground of reason or on that of sophistry – for this we need a critique, a discipline, a canon, and an architectonic of *pure reason*, a formal science, therefore, that can require nothing of those sciences already at hand, and that needs for its foundations an entirely unique technical vocabulary.[10]

Here, although without spelling out how he thinks he has finally begun to overcome the "final obstacles," Kant for the first time talks of a "critique" of "pure reason" and hints at two different aspects of such a "critique" – namely, that on the one hand it will have to *establish* that there is such a thing as *a priori* knowledge, knowledge that "lies *a priori* in ourselves and need not await any exposure from our experience," and on the other hand it will have to determine the *limits* of such knowledge, and thus establish once and for all the boundary between true reason (*Vernunft*) and mere sophistry (*Vernünftelei*). Finally, in August 1777, another nine months later, Kant elevates his new description of his project into its title. Here Kant says that he is slowly developing the idea for his entire system of philosophy, and that although "There is a stone that lies in the path of my completion of all these projects, the work I call my *Critique of Pure Reason*, ... all my efforts are now devoted to removing that obstacle and I hope to be completely through with it this winter."[11] But though Kant had now finally settled on the title for his work, it would in fact take him not one more winter but four more winters to finish the monumental work that he finally presented to the world at the Easter book fair of 1781 – and even then, as he would write Moses Mendelssohn (1729–1786) two years later, "although the book is the product of nearly twelve years of reflection, I completed it hastily, in perhaps four or five months, with the greatest attentiveness to its content but less care about its style and ease of comprehension."[12] Since no manuscript of the *Critique*, let alone a dated manuscript,

[10] Letter to Marcus Herz, November 24, 1776, 10:198–9; *Correspondence*, p. 160 (translation modified).
[11] Letter to Marcus Herz, August 20, 1777, 10:213; *Correspondence*, p. 164.
[12] Letter to Moses Mendelssohn, August 16, 1783, 10:345; *Correspondence*, p. 202. Kant had placed great hope in Mendelssohn's reception of the *Critique*, but Mendelssohn had pled that a "nervous indisposition" had rendered him incapable of serious philosophical work and that he was

survives, we have no way of knowing whether Kant thought about the *Critique* for twelve years and then wrote the whole book out in four or five months, or whether those months were how long it took him to make a final version of the book from materials he had been accumulating during his years of work.[13] But no matter how long it finally took Kant to write the book, both the importance of its contents and the difficulties of its comprehension have certainly challenged readers ever since.

2. THE AIMS OF THE *CRITIQUE*

Along with his numerous statements about his plans and hopes for his project during the years of its germination, Kant also made numerous programmatic statements about the aims of the book in its two editions and in numerous other publications beginning with his attempt to popularize his work, *The Prolegomena to Any Future Metaphysics* of 1783. They cannot all be considered here, certainly, but we can introduce Kant's aims for the book as it finally appeared by considering just a few. We have already seen that Kant's early letters to Herz suggested that the *Critique* would provide the foundations for both theoretical and practical philosophy, but that by the time of his 1776 letter to Herz it looks as if he has trimmed back his ambitions, and intends to accomplish only the twofold objective of both establishing and limiting the

now "dead to metaphysics." Kant responded that he found no sign of such an indisposition in Mendelssohn's own great work of 1783, *Jerusalem, or on Religious Power and Judaism*, but in any case made his comment about the hasty composition of the *Critique* and his lack of "care about its style and ease of comprehension" in order to place the responsibility for Mendelssohn's difficulty with the book on his own shoulders.

[13] The thought that Kant could not possibly have written the more than 800 pages of the *Critique* in four or five months and so must instead have used that time merely to assemble the book from materials produced over at least several years, with possible inconsistencies among them, is the premise of the so-called "patchwork theory" of the composition of the work. For advocacy of the patchwork theory, see Norman Kemp Smith, *A Commentary to Kant's 'Critique of Pure Reason'*, second edition (London: Macmillan, 1923), pp. xix–xxv; for rejection of the theory, see H. J. Paton, *Kant's Metaphysic of Experience*, 2 vols. (London: George Allen & Unwin, 1936), vol. I, pp. 38–46. I once heard the great Kant scholar Lewis White Beck elegantly argue that the truth or falsehood of the patchwork thesis was irrelevant to the question of whether the *Critique* contains any inconsistencies by saying that "A man who was inconsistent enough to have put together inconsistent manuscripts in four or five months would also have been inconsistent enough to have written inconsistent statements within four or five months" (personal recollection).

scope of *a priori* knowledge. In fact, the *Critique* as finally published focuses on the two goals of establishing that we do have *a priori* knowledge of the most general laws of nature coming from the structure of our own minds and of limiting the validity of such knowledge to the realm of objects that we can actually experience, but also aims, if not to establish the first principles of morality – that in the end would be left to subsequent works, the *Groundwork for the Metaphysics of Morals* of 1785 and the eventual second critique, the *Critique of Practical Reason* – then at least to carve out the conceptual space for a moral philosophy that in certain key ways would not be limited by what seem to be some obvious facts about human nature – the extent to which our behavior is driven by contingent desires – and even by the results of theoretical philosophy itself – the ubiquity of causal determinism in nature.

Kant's project in the *Critique of Pure Reason* is thus threefold: to establish that we know genuinely informative universally and necessarily true principles *about* our experience – in other words, that we possess what he calls "synthetic *a priori*" knowledge, synthetic because it goes beyond the mere analysis of concepts and *a priori* because universal and necessary truths cannot be known *from* ordinary experience, or *a posteriori*; to show that these principles do not yield theoretical *knowledge* about objects that we *cannot* directly experience, above all God and our own souls; and to show also that we still have room for rational *belief* about such objects insofar as those beliefs are required on *practical* grounds – that is, as conditions for the possibility of moral *practice* and even the moral transformation of the natural world rather than as conditions for the experience of the natural world. The first two of Kant's three objectives are suggested in a famous statement part way through the *Critique*, where he has essentially completed the first, constructive stage of his argument and is turning to the second stage, his critique of traditional metaphysics. Here he says that "the proud name of an ontology, which presumes to offer synthetic *a priori* cognitions of things in general in a systematic doctrine (e.g., the principle of causality), must give way to the modest one of a mere analytic of the pure understanding" (A 247/B 303): by an "analytic of the pure understanding" Kant means his constructive demonstration that certain principles are the absolutely indispensable conditions of the possibility of any experience of objects, even an experience of oneself;[14] by the

---

[14] This statement needs a qualification; as we will shortly see, Kant's account of the conditions of the possibility of experience also includes what he calls a "Transcendental Aesthetic" that demonstrates the synthetic *a priori* principles of sensibility as well as the much longer

"ontology" that must give way, he means the claim of traditional metaphysics to provide knowledge of things beyond our experience, such as God and an immortal soul, as well as knowledge of things that we do experience, such as objects in space and time, but knowledge of them as they are in themselves, independently of the way we experience them. The "analytic" of the understanding thus represents the first, constructive phase of Kant's project, and the critique of "ontology" the second, destructive phase. But then, in the Preface to the second edition of the *Critique of Pure Reason*, after Kant has already published the *Groundwork for the Metaphysics of Morals* and has realized that he next needs to write yet another foundational work in moral philosophy, the *Critique of Practical Reason* that was to appear the next year, Kant makes the further famous statement that

> I cannot even **assume God, freedom and immortality** for the sake of the necessary practical use of my reason unless I simultaneously **deprive** speculative reason of its pretension to extravagant insights; because in order to attain to such insights, speculative reason would have to help itself to principles that in fact reach only to objects of possible experience, and which, if they were to be applied to what cannot be an object of experience, then they would always actually transform it into an appearance, and thus declare all **practical extension** of pure reason to be impossible. Thus I had to deny **knowledge** in order to make room for **faith**. (B xxx)

Here Kant means that if we were to take the principles that govern our experience of nature to give us theoretical knowledge of all things as they are in themselves, then there would be no room for the ideas of God, freedom, and the immortality of the soul, all ideas that he takes to be vital to morality, because everything in our experience is finite, limited, and causally determined; but that if we recognize that these necessary facts about the objects of our experience, determined by the very conditions of the possibility of experience, are facts only about how things must appear to us, not how they must be in themselves independently of their relation to our knowledge of them, then there is at least room for us to believe about things as they are in themselves – above all, ourselves as we are in ourselves – what morality requires us to believe. In terminology that Kant would use in a later, unfinished work, an intended essay on the Berlin Academy of Sciences question "What Real Progress has Metaphysics made in Germany since the Time of Leibniz and Wolff?"

"Transcendental Analytic" that demonstrates the synthetic *a priori* principles of the understanding. But the statement quoted is not entirely misleading, since it is part of Kant's argument that the *a priori* principles of sensibility, or what he calls the "*a priori* forms of intuition," never give knowledge by themselves, but only in combination with the *a priori* principles of the understanding.

the "theoretico-dogmatic use of pure reason" must be limited at the second stage of his argument in order to make way for the possibility of the "practico-dogmatic" use of reason at the third stage.[15]

To be sure, Kant does not spend as much time in the first *Critique* on the positive, practical use of pure reason as he does on his critique of the attempted theoretical use of pure reason; he touches on it only briefly in one late part of the book, a chapter called the "Canon of Pure Reason," and only develops it fully in the second *Critique* that he initially did not intend to write at all; correspondingly, only one chapter of this *Companion* (Chapter 12) will discuss his account of the positive practical use of reason, while four Chapters (8 through 11) will discuss his critique of the "speculative" use of reason. Nevertheless, it is important to remember that in Kant's thought as a whole, if not in the *Critique of Pure Reason* by itself, his account of the positive, practical use of reason is at least as important as his constructive account of the conditions of possible experience and his destructive account of traditional theoretical or speculative metaphysics.

3. THE STRUCTURE OF THE *CRITIQUE* AND OF THIS *COMPANION*

The chapters that follow are divided into three groups. Chapters 1 and 2 of Part I, by Desmond Hogan and Kenneth Winkler, situate Kant's thought with respect to the two groups of philosophers that were most important for Kant, on the one hand the "rationalists" led by Gottfried Wilhelm Leibniz (1646–1716) and his followers Christian Wolff (1679–1754) and Alexander Gottlieb Baumgarten (1714–1762), and the "empiricists" John Locke (1632–1704) and especially David Hume (1711–1776). (The division of his predecessors into "rationalists" and "empiricists" was made canonical by Kant himself in "The History of Pure Reason" [A 852–5/B 880–3], where he also calls them "intellectual philosophers" or "noologists" on the one hand and "sensual philosophers" on the other.) Both Hogan and Winkler describe convergences as well as differences between Kant and the two main groups of his predecessors, Hogan showing how Kant obtained the very idea of *a priori* knowledge from the rationalists although he introduced his key distinction between analytic and synthetic *a priori* judgment (on which, more shortly) in criticism of them, and Winkler arguing that Kant obtained the idea of a "deduction" of key categories and principles

---

[15] See Kant, *What Progress has Metaphysics made in Germany since the Time of Leibniz and Wolff* (posthumously published in 1804, two months after Kant's death), 20:286–96.

from the empiricists, although again he introduced the key distinction between "physiological" or "empirical" and "transcendental" deductions in criticism of them. These two chapters provide an account of the ways in which Kant himself conceived of his transformation of modern philosophy.

The next eleven chapters of Part II (Chapters 3 through 13) describe and interpret each of the main sections of the *Critique* itself. An account of the structure of the *Critique* will help to follow the arc of argumentation described in these chapters. Kant introduced a great deal of original terminology into his book, but also borrowed much of its organization from philosophical practice in his time. The book has a Preface, completely rewritten for the second edition, and an Introduction, considerably expanded in the second edition, and is then unevenly divided into two main parts, "The Doctrine of Elements" and the "Doctrine of Method." In the Introduction, Kant states the goal of the constructive portion of his work – to demonstrate that we have synthetic *a priori* cognition, that is, knowledge that is universal and necessary yet genuinely informative, not merely definitional, in mathematics, in physics, and in philosophy itself (B 14–18). (Of course, Kant did not need any model for including an Introduction in his work!) The Introduction and its concept of synthetic *a priori* cognition are discussed by Lanier Anderson in Chapter 3.

The division between a Doctrine of Elements and a Doctrine of Method, however, was borrowed from the philosophy textbooks in Kant's time, especially logic textbooks,[16] and typically marked the distinction between the exposition of the main elements of logic, the rules for the formation of concepts, judgments, and inferences, and the illustration of the useful application of such rules. Kant included both his constructive account of the conditions of the possibility of experience and his critique of traditional metaphysics in his Doctrine of Elements and used his Doctrine of Method to comment on the differences between his own "transcendental" method of philosophy and the methods of traditional dogmatism and skepticism; to explain the difference between the methods of philosophy and of mathematics, which had been supposed to provide a methodological model for philosophy in the seventeenth and earlier eighteenth centuries; and to explain the difference between the doomed speculative or theoretical metaphysics and his own promising practical metaphysics. The last of these occurs in the second chapter of the Doctrine of Method, "The

---

[16] See Giorgio Tonelli, *Kant's Critique of Pure Reason within the Tradition of Modern Logic*, edited by David H. Chandler (Hildesheim: Georg Olms Verlag, 1994).

Canon of Pure Reason," while the first chapter of the Doctrine of
Method, "The Discipline of Pure Reason," explains the difference
between Kant's "transcendental" method and the methods of dogmatism, skepticism, and mathematics; the Doctrine of Method concludes
with two short chapters, "The Architectonic of Pure Reason" and the
even briefer "History of Pure Reason," already mentioned.

The Doctrine of Elements is approximately six times longer than the
Doctrine of Method (the former runs from A 19/B 33 to A 704/B 732, the
latter only from A 707/B 735 to A 855/B 883). The Doctrine of Elements
is itself divided into two even more disproportionate parts, on the one
hand the "Transcendental Aesthetic" which is only thirty pages in the
first edition (A 19–49) and forty in the second (B 33–73), and on the
other the "Transcendental Logic," which is well over six hundred pages
(A 50/B 74 to A 704/B 732). In these titles, Kant has borrowed the
traditional term "transcendental," which in medieval philosophy designated the most general determinations of being, to designate his own
conception of "cognition ... that is occupied not so much with objects
but rather with our *a priori* concepts of objects" (A 11/B 25) – thus he
has transformed the significance of the term from ontological to what
we would now call epistemological, although this term was not coined
for another hundred years. But the term "concept" in this statement has
to be taken broadly, since the reason for Kant's division of the Doctrine
of Elements into its two parts is precisely because in his view there are
not one but two sorts of fundamental components of all knowledge, on
the one hand sensory representations or "intuitions," or singular,
immediate representations of particular objects, and on the other hand
intellectual representations or "concepts," general and indirect representations of kinds of objects (see especially A 320/B 376–7); the argument of the *Critique* is then that there are *a priori* forms of intuition
and *a priori* forms of conceptualization, that all knowledge of objects of
experience involves both of these *a priori* forms of thought, and that the
mistakes of traditional theoretical or "speculative" metaphysics arise
when we attempt to gain knowledge of objects through *a priori* concepts alone without applying them to and restricting them by the
representations given by our senses with their own *a priori* forms
(although in the sphere of practice we *should* be guided by the ideas
of pure reason).

Kant names his discussion of the *a priori* forms of the representations
of the senses, or sensibility as he calls it, the "Transcendental Aesthetic,"
adapting the term "Aesthetic" from Alexander Gottlieb Baumgarten,
who had himself adapted it from the Greek word αισθησις (*aisthēsis*),
used, for example, by Plato to mean sense-perception, to designate a
"science of sensory cognition" that was supposed to comprehend the

general contribution of the senses to knowledge or "lower gnoseology" as well as the "theory of the liberal arts" (what we now mean by the term),[17] although as it turned out Baumgarten completed only the latter. Kant felt free to put the term to his own use because he thought that Baumgarten had failed to create a genuine *science* of the beautiful or of the fine arts; as he put it, Baumgarten's attempt at "bringing the critical estimation of the beautiful under principles of reason, and elevating its rules to a science," was "futile," because "the putative rules or criteria are merely empirical," and for this reason Baumgarten's term could instead be preserved "for that doctrine which is true science" – namely Kant's own "Transcendental Aesthetic" (A 21/B 35–6). In the Transcendental Aesthetic, Kant argues that all of our experience comes to us with spatial and temporal form, in the case of "outer sense" or our experience of objects other than ourselves, or with temporal form only, in the case of "inner sense" or our experience of our own subjective states (A 22/B 37), and then that we can have *a priori* knowledge of the structure of space and time and thus of the forms of all objects of sensibility, which must appear either in time alone or in space and time. Here is where Kant also introduces his notorious doctrine of "transcendental idealism," which is his view that our *a priori* knowledge of the necessity of space and time for experience and of their structure can be explained only by the supposition that space and time are *nothing but* the ways in which things appear to us, not things nor properties or relations of things as they are in themselves (A 26/B 42). The interpretation and validity of this doctrine, which Kant regards as the key to making room for the practical use of pure reason – above all, Kant thinks that if we need not and cannot assert that our souls are really in time, then we also need not assert that they are subject to causal determinism, and can therefore maintain the freedom of our wills – have proven controversial, to say the least.[18] Lisa Shabel provides an account and

[17] Alexander Gottlieb Baumgarten, *Aesthetica* (1750–58), Prolegomena, §1; in Baumgarten, *Ästhetik*, translated and edited by Dagmar Mirbach, 2 vols. (Hamburg: Felix Meiner Verlag, 2007), pp. 10–11. Baumgarten had originally introduced the term in his 1735 master's thesis, *Meditationes philosophicae de nonnullis ad poema pertinentibus/Philosophische Betrachtungen über einige Bedingungen des Gedichtes*, translated and edited by Heinz Paetzold (Hamburg: Felix Meiner Verlag, 1983), §CXVI, pp. 86–7; English translation by Karl Aschenbrenner, *Alexander Gottlieb Baumgarten's Meditations on Poetry* (Berkeley and Los Angeles: University of California Press, 1954).

[18] See especially Henry E. Allison, *Kant's Transcendental Idealism*, second edition (New Haven: Yale University Press, 2004), and in response, Paul Guyer, *Kant and the Claims of Knowledge* (Cambridge: Cambridge University Press, 1987).

assessment of Kant's arguments that we have *a priori* cognition of space and time and that this knowledge can only be explained by transcendental idealism in Chapter 4.

The second and much larger part of the Doctrine of Elements is the "Transcendental Logic." Here Kant intends the name "Transcendental Logic" to contrast with the traditional discipline that he calls "general logic." General logic "abstracts … from all content of cognition, i.e., from any relation of it to the object, and considers only the logical form in the relation of cognition to one another, i.e., the form of thinking in general" (A 55/B 79) – that is, in modern terminology general logic concerns the formal consistency of judgments and validity of arguments regardless of the truth of their premises, while transcendental logic does not "abstract from all content of cognition" but concerns the concepts and principles "by means of which we think of objects completely *a priori*" (A 55-7/B 79-81), or more precisely the *a priori* concepts and principles by means of which we think of all objects, whether empirical or otherwise. Transcendental logic is "a science, which would determine the origin, the domain, and the objective validity" of all cognition (A 57/B 81). Yet transcendental logic is formed along the guidelines of the traditional general logic. General logic throughout the Middle Ages and early modernity was divided into the three divisions of the logic of concepts, of judgments, and of inferences, the first of which concerned the rules for the proper definitions of concepts, the second the rules for properly formulated judgments, and the third the rules for valid inferences. Kant borrows this division, but with a twist. Thus he divides the Transcendental Logic into two main parts, the "Transcendental Analytic" and the "Transcendental Dialectic," and divides the Transcendental Analytic into two further parts, the Analytic of Concepts and the Analytic of Principles. The Analytic of Concepts comprises the derivation and deduction of the "pure concepts of the understanding" or the "categories," which are the *a priori* concepts, or even better the *a priori* forms for all concepts of objects, and are themselves derived from the "logical functions" of judgments or basic parts of judgments recognized in general logic and are the conditions that make it possible to apply judgments as analyzed by general logic to objects through well-formed concepts of objects (see especially A 79/B 104); the Analytic of Principles expounds the synthetic *a priori* principles that arise when the *a priori* concepts discovered and deduced in the Analytic of Concepts are applied to the spatial and temporal forms of our sensible representations or intuitions of objects in what Kant calls the "schematism" of the pure concepts of the understanding (A 137-47/B 176-87). The Analytic of Concepts and the Analytic of Principles constitute the heart of Kant's constructive theory of our synthetic *a priori* cognition of objects, and are the subjects of Chapters 5 through 7: in Chapter 5, Paul Guyer discusses Kant's derivation and deduction of the pure concepts of the understanding, the so-called "metaphysical" and "transcendental" deductions of the categories; in Chapter 6, Eric Watkins discusses the Analytic of Principles, especially the "Analogies of Experience," Kant's proofs of the principles of the conservation of substance, of the universal validity of causation, and of the universal validity of interaction as conditions of the possibility of making determinate judgments about temporal relations; and in Chapter 7, Dina Emundts discusses the "Refutation of Idealism" that Kant added to the Analytic of Principles in the second edition of the *Critique*, his attempt to refute Cartesian skepticism about external objects, as well as the concluding chapter of the Analytic of Principles, on the distinction between "phenomena" and "noumena," in which Kant emphasizes the restriction of the principles that have been proved to appearances ("phenomena") rather than things in themselves ("noumena").

Kant also calls the Analytic of Principles the "Transcendental Doctrine of the Power of Judgment" (e.g., A 148/B 187), and clearly means it to parallel the traditional logic of judgments just as the Analytic of Concepts had paralleled the traditional logic of concepts. However, in the second main part of the Transcendental Logic and its third part overall – namely, the Transcendental Dialectic – Kant does not build upon the traditional logic of *valid* inferences, but rather analyzes the *invalid* inferences that pure reason makes when it attempts to gain knowledge of things in themselves from the categories of the understanding alone, without taking into account that these categories yield knowledge only when they are applied to sensible intuitions, or representations of the senses (see especially A 338–40/B 396–98). Here is where Kant analyzes the failure of traditional speculative metaphysics, arguing that traditional proofs of the existence of our simple and immortal souls, of the existence of the world as a whole that is either finite or completely infinite in space and time, and of the existence of God all depend upon making inferences from the pure concepts of the understanding alone without regard to the limits of our sensible intuition, and fail for that reason.

In the Transcendental Dialectic, Kant diagnoses three groups of fallacious arguments: the "Paralogisms of Pure Reason" are arguments that our souls are simple and immortal substances (paralogisms are syllogisms that are fallacious because of an ambiguous term in the minor premise); the "Antinomies of Pure Reason" are arguments for contradictory positions on whether the world is finite or infinite in spatial and temporal extent and divisibility, on whether the world is an infinite

chain of events in which every cause is itself the effect of something
else or whether there is one or more uncaused cause of events in the
world, and on whether the world is nothing but a chain of contingencies
or whether there is a necessary ground for it; and the "Ideal of Pure
Reason" concerns the traditional arguments for the existence of God,
which Kant calls the "ontological" argument (the argument from the
concept of a perfect being to its existence), the "cosmological" argument (the argument from the existence of anything contingent to the
existence of a necessary being), and the "physico-theological" argument
(the argument from design in the world to a designer). In Kant's view,
these arguments are all fallacies arising from the assumption that if
something "conditioned is given, then so is the whole series of
conditions ..., which is itself unconditioned, also given (i.e., contained
in the object and its connection)" (A 308/B 364): the assumption that
the unconditioned is given when applied to the three fundamental
ideas of the subject, the world, and the ground of both gives rise to
the three "ideas" of the "absolute (unconditioned) **unity** of the **thinking
subject**" or soul, "the absolute **unity** of the **series** of **conditions of
appearances**" or the spatio-temporal world, and "the absolute **unity** of
the **condition of all objects of thought** in general" or God (A 334/B 391).
However, none of these ideas can yield actual knowledge, because in
Kant's view knowledge always requires sensible intuition as well as
concepts, and nothing unconditioned is ever given in sensible intuition –
everything given in intuition is always given in some region of space
and/or time, every region of space and time is always surrounded by
a larger one or divisible into a smaller one, thus is never unconditioned,
and therefore nothing unconditioned can be given in space or time.
The underlying strategy of Kant's generation of the "ideas of pure
reason" is diagnosed in Chapter 8 by Michael Rohlf, and then the
three classes of fallacious inferences to these ideas are analyzed in
Chapter 9, on the Paralogisms, by Julian Wuerth; Chapter 10, on the
Antinomies, by Allen Wood; and Chapter 11, on the Ideal of Pure
Reason, by Michelle Grier.

   The arguments that Kant criticizes in the Transcendental Dialectic
were arguments offered in the history of metaphysics from Aristotle
through the Middle Ages – for example, by Anselm and St. Thomas
Aquinas – to the early modern rationalists such as Descartes, Leibniz,
Wolff, and Baumgarten, although Kant's versions of the arguments
are sometimes idealizations that do not correspond exactly to any
particular historical antecedents. But for Kant these arguments were
more than just historical curiosities – if that was all they were, they
could have been dispatched much more quickly or just left to wither
away on their own. Rather, for Kant these arguments were inevitable,

natural illusions that can be avoided just as little as even an astronomer can avoid the impression that the moon is larger when it first rises (which is itself of course an illusion) than when it is at its peak in the nighttime sky (A 297/B 354), arising from an unavoidable tendency on our part to mistake reason's *task* always to *seek* for greater completeness in series of conditions for *knowledge* that the unconditioned is actually *given*. As Kant puts it, "the proper principle of reason in general (in its logical use) ... to find the unconditioned for conditioned cognitions ... cannot become a principle of **pure reason** unless we assume that when the conditioned is given, then so is the whole series of conditions ... which is itself unconditioned" (A 307–8/B 364), but we are not entitled to make that assumption. However, Kant also insists that although pure reason cannot *prove* that there is an immortal soul, a perfect and necessary God, and so on, neither can anything *disprove* these assumptions. Thus, the failure of pure reason's theoretical arguments still leaves room for the possibility of *belief* in immortality, freedom or spontaneous causation, and God if other grounds for such beliefs can be found; and transcendental idealism, with its distinction between how things appear and how things are in themselves, also leaves room for these beliefs even if they actually conflict with the character of appearance or our experience of the spatio-temporal world as expounded in the Transcendental Analytic. Moreover, Kant also holds that unless it can be proven otherwise, we are entitled to assume that "Everything grounded in the nature of our powers must be purposive and consistent with their correct use, if only we can guard against a certain misunderstanding and find out their proper direction" (A 643/B 671). This leads Kant to the third stage of the overall argument of the *Critique* – namely, his view that pure reason must not be merely a source of speculative fallacies, but must also have a positive use. In fact, Kant argues that the positive use of pure reason is twofold: on the one hand, he argues in an Appendix to the Transcendental Dialectic, reason's ideas of the unconditioned give rise to indispensable *regulative* principles for the conduct of scientific inquiry (e.g., A 680/B 708), and on the other hand, as he argues in the already mentioned "Canon of Pure Reason" in the Doctrine of Method, reason also gives rise to the unconditionally valid moral law, as a prescription of how the world *ought* to be rather than a description of how it actually is (A 807/B 835), as well as to beliefs on *practical* grounds that the conditions necessary for the possibility of rationally attempting to fulfill the moral law – namely, the existence of freedom, immortality, and God – obtain (A 811–19/B 839–47). In the *Critique of Pure Reason*, Kant calls these deliverances of reason "moral beliefs" (A 828/B 856) of merely "immanent use" (A 819/B 847); in the *Critique of Practical Reason* and subsequent works, he calls them "postulates of pure practical reason." The twofold positive use of reason is discussed by Frederick Rauscher in Chapter 12.

Our outline of the argument of the *Critique of Pure Reason* is now largely complete; there remains to mention only Kant's own account of the character of his constructive and critical argument, which he presents in the first chapter of the Doctrine of Method, and which is the focus of A. W. Moore's contribution in Chapter 13. Kant's characterization of his positive arguments in the Transcendental Analytic as "transcendental proofs" (e.g., A 786/B 814) has led to a recent debate on "transcendental arguments" as a distinctive method in contemporary philosophy, which Moore also discusses. And this leads us to Part III of this *Companion*, four chapters on the impact of the *Critique of Pure Reason* on the subsequent history of philosophy.

4. THE IMPACT OF THE *CRITIQUE OF PURE REASON*

The *Critique of Pure Reason* has had a nearly continuous impact on the subsequent history of philosophy, whether as an inspiration for views conceived of by their authors as refinements of the true "spirit" of Kant's philosophy or as a provocation for alternative approaches. For many of the most important philosophers since Kant, the *Critique* has been both a paradigm and a provocation. In Chapter 14, Rolf-Peter Horstmann discusses the reception of the *Critique* in the period of German idealism immediately following, beginning with its initial reception by Karl Leonhard Reinhold (1758–1823) and initial rejection by Friedrich Heinrich Jacobi (1743–1819), and continuing on to its transformations at the hands of Salomon Maimon (1752–1800), Johann Gottlieb Fichte (1762–1814), Friedrich Wilhelm Joseph Schelling (1775–1854), and Georg Wilhelm Friedrich Hegel (1770–1831). On Horstmann's account, these philosophers resisted above all Kant's restriction of theoretical philosophy to epistemology rather than ontology: they were not content to settle for Kant's practical rather than theoretical dogmatics, but instead attempted to restore to ontology the "proud name" that in Kant's view it had perforce surrendered to his own more modest "analytic."

In Chapter 15, Konstantin Pollok surveys the German movement of Neo-Kantianism, which began in the 1860s as a rejection of Hegelianism, and continued until the 1920s, when it fell victim to the existential phenomenology of Martin Heidegger. Pollok describes the two major schools of Neo-Kantianism: first, the Marburg school of Hermann Cohen (1842–1918), including Paul Natorp (1854–1924) and Ernst Cassirer (1871–1945), which was inspired by Kant's philosophical justification of the fundamental tenets of Newtonian physics to conceive of philosophy more generally as an analysis of the presuppositions of scientific, moral, and aesthetic practices reflecting the changes in the actual contents of such practices since Kant's time; and second, the Southwest (or Heidelberg or Baden) school of Wilhelm Windelband (1848–1915), Heinrich Rickert (1863–1936), and Emil Lask (1875–1915), which was inspired more by Kant's account of the positive practical use of reason to draw a distinction between considerations of fact and of value that have been influential in many quarters of twentieth-century thought.

In Chapter 16, on the reception of the *Critique* in twentieth-century Continental philosophy, Daniel Dahlstrom describes the reception of Kant by many German and French philosophers but focuses on Martin Heidegger's rejection of Neo-Kantian approaches to Kant in favor of his own transformation of Kant's theory of the conditions for judgments of time-determination into a phenomenology of the temporality of human existence.

Finally, in Chapter 17, Kenneth Westphal describes the enormous influence of Kant on twentieth-century Anglo-American ("analytic") philosophy through three case studies: he considers the great American pragmatist Clarence Irving Lewis (1883–1964), whose 1929 *Mind and the World Order*[19] introduced the contemporary idea of the "relativized *a priori*"[20] in lieu of Kant's own idea of the synthetic *a priori*; Peter Strawson (1919–2006), whose 1966 *The Bounds of Sense*[21] led to a great revival of interest in the *Critique* in Britain and America, although, as Westphal argues, Strawson's approach to Kant was influenced as much if not more by contemporary approaches to the theory of meaning rather than by Kant's own search for the conditions of the possibility of objective judgments; and Wilfrid Sellars (1912–1989), whose creative amalgam of influences from Kant, Wittgenstein, and others bore fruit in his highly original 1968 *Science and Metaphysics: Variations on Kantian Themes*,[22] as well as in his many papers and posthumously published lectures on Kant.

So now on to the *Critique*.

---

[19] Clarence Irving Lewis, *Mind and the World Order* (New York: Charles Scribner's Sons, 1929).

[20] Recently developed especially by Michael Friedman in *The Dynamics of Reason* (Stanford: Center for the Study of Language and Information, 2001), although Friedman emphasizes the influence of Hans Reichenbach (1891–1953) more than that of Lewis.

[21] P. F. Strawson, *The Bounds of Sense: An Essay on the* Critique of Pure Reason (London: Methuen, 1966).

[22] Wilfrid Sellars, *Science and Metaphysics: Variations on Kantian Themes* (London: Routledge & Kegan Paul, 1968).

Part I The Background to the *Critique*

1   Kant's Copernican Turn and the Rationalist Tradition

I. INTRODUCTION

The *Critique of Pure Reason* sets out to establish the sources, extent, and limits of *a priori* knowledge, with a view to ascertaining the prospects for metaphysics as a scientific enterprise. Kant defines *a priori* knowledge as knowledge that is "absolutely independent of all experience," and distinguishes it from empirical knowledge, whose sources lie in experience (B 2–3). The *Critique's* second edition frames its overarching goal as a general solution to the problem: How are synthetic judgments *a priori* possible? (B 19) This formulation, intended to express the work's focus on the problem of non-trivial *a priori* knowledge of objects, presupposes two important doctrines. Kant holds that the knowledge constituting the proper end of metaphysics is never mere empirical knowledge, even when the object of investigation is empirical reality. He also insists that substantive knowledge of objects does not find expression in merely analytic judgments – those in which the predicate "does not add anything" to the subject concept, but merely "breaks up" this subject concept into components "already thought in it" (A 6–7/B 10–11).

The *Critique's* epistemological investigation aims to "assure to reason its lawful claims, and dismiss all groundless pretensions, not by despotic decrees, but in accordance with reason's own eternal and unalterable laws" (A xi–xii). Kant employs "reason" in such contexts, in contrast to a narrower sense later introduced, as a general label for cognitive capacities underwriting *a priori* knowledge (A 11/B 24; A 305/B 363; A 323/B 380). His project of uncovering groundless pretensions to knowledge through reason issues famously in a rejection of a host of knowledge claims made by Descartes, Spinoza, and Leibniz. Because of this, Kant's great work is often viewed as fundamentally antagonistic to a Continental rationalist tradition that attained its pinnacle in these thinkers. Moses Mendelssohn, a committed follower of Leibniz, spoke memorably of the "all-destroying" Kant upon surveying the *Critique's* rejection of all theoretical proofs of the existence of God and the immortality of the soul, as well as its doctrine of ignorance of reality in itself.

The purpose of this chapter is to reconsider the novel explanation of *a priori* knowledge constituting the heart of the *Critique's* Copernican revolution in philosophy, as well as Kant's central objections to alternative explanations of such knowledge offered in the tradition. It will be helpful to begin by mapping some of the *Critique's* important philosophical continuities with rationalist predecessors, neglected by Mendelssohn, against which Kant's central epistemological innovation can stand out. A first point to underline is that the *Critique's* negative project of uncovering groundless pretensions to *a priori* knowledge is coordinated from the outset with its positive aim of "assuring to reason its lawful claims." Kant does not uphold a merely moderate rationalism, to use today's terms, in which *a priori* knowledge is restricted to logical principles and entailments. His position is extravagant by current epistemological standards; it reckons among our *a priori* possessions geometry and its full applicability to empirical reality, physical principles including the claim that action equals reaction in physical interactions, and metaphysical principles including the proposition that every event has a determining cause. Discussions of Kant's positive *a priori* knowledge claims tend to focus on his important differences with Hume. It is less often noted that his positive claims closely track so-called "rational knowledge" upheld in the main German schools of his day, and Kant underlines this connection by continuing to employ this standard designation (B 863–4; *Logic*, 9:22). His mature writings frequently present substantive *a priori* knowledge of nature as a "fact" to be explained, and the essential context here includes a broad consensus among German contemporaries regarding such possession. Kant frequently aligns himself with rationalist contemporaries on the possession issue. He is prepared, for example, to describe the causal principle defended by Leibnizian opponents as "so widely known and (with suitable restrictions) so patently obvious, that not even the weakest mind could believe itself to have made a new discovery with it" (*Discovery*, 8:247; B 4–5; A 783/B 811).[1]

Kant's firm conviction regarding possession of *a priori* knowledge in the fields of mathematics, physics, and metaphysics provides the

---

[1] Compare Kant's claim that Hume's skeptical challenge to the causal principle caused "no real trouble [to earlier philosophers], for sound common sense will always assert its rights in this domain" (*Prolegomena*, 4:351). Kant praises Hume for seeing that the causal principle is non-analytic, but adds that he was "very far from listening with respect to his [skeptical] conclusions" (*ibid.* 4:260). Kant's early works exhibit growing dissatisfaction with contemporary views on *sources* and *limits* of rational knowledge of nature, but never take a wholly skeptical position on possession of such knowledge.

backdrop for the *Critique's* claim to explain for the first time how such knowledge is possible. It is notable that Kant insists that relevant *a priori* knowledge in mathematics and physics is secure even without his explanation of its possibility. He writes that "pure mathematics and pure natural science would not have needed, for the purpose of their *own* security and certainty, a deduction of the sort that we have accomplished for them both" (*Prolegomena*, 4:327; A 237/B 296). The central purpose of the explanation, he explains, is not to correct a deficiency of *a priori* certainty in these sciences. It is to instruct us regarding the possibility of metaphysical knowledge more broadly by determining "how far (and why that far and not farther) reason is to be trusted" (*Prolegomena*, 4:351). Kant's insistence that possession of *a priori* knowledge does not depend on insight into its "only possible explanation" might seem surprising, and it would be peculiar if his main goal were rebutting skeptical attacks. It is hardly exceptional otherwise, since agreement regarding possession of knowledge often provides the context, in Kant's day and today, for disputes concerning its sources and justification. Kant can point, for example, to Leibniz's doctrine in the *New Essays* that rational certainty of mathematical truths is possible even without a full grasp of the reduction to the identities on which Leibniz, unlike Locke, takes such truths to rest.[2]

Aside from claims regarding possession of *a priori* knowledge, a further point of continuity with rationalist predecessors is visible in the role Kant envisages for *a priori* knowledge in the sciences. He believes that genuine science [*Wissenschaft*] offers explanatory insight exceeding what mere observation and organization of empirical particulars could justify. While such observation can reveal that a rule is observed in a certain set of data, reason desires to know *why* it is observed, and Kant accepts the view of Leibniz and Wolff that this demand of reason is only met by knowledge that the rule *must* obtain.[3] Though Kant sometimes speaks of purely empirical as well as rational sciences, he holds that only the latter are really deserving of the name – that "all *genuine* natural science requires a pure [*a priori*] part, on which the apodictic certainty sought by reason can be grounded" (*Metaphysical Foundations*, 4:468–9; *Logic*, 9:70–1).

[2] G. W. Leibniz, *New Essays on Human Understanding*, edited by Peter Remnant and Jonathan Bennett (Cambridge: Cambridge University Press, 1996), pp. 74–5, p. 413.
[3] Leibniz, *Monadology* §28, reprinted in Roger Ariew and Dan Garber, ed. and trans., *Leibniz: Philosophical Essays*, [AG] (Indianapolis: Hackett, 1989); *New Essays*, p. 80, 406; Christian Wolff, *Vernünfftige Gedancken von Gott, der Welt und der Seele des Menschen* [*German Metaphysics*], Halle 1719, §372.

As well as viewing the exhibition of necessity as a key aim of the scientific enterprise, Kant accepts Leibniz's position in the *New Essays* that the senses cannot "show necessity," and so knowledge that does exhibit it must be non-empirical. The *Critique's* claim that "experience teaches us that a thing is so and so, but not that it cannot be otherwise" (B 3) is at the very heart of Kant's mature philosophy, and it is often regarded as a crucial lesson from Hume. This is misleading, not only because Leibniz and Wolff agree on the point, but because its central application in the *Critique* echoes not Hume but Leibniz in upholding rational knowledge of nature. Kant begins the work by contending that "even among our experiences there are cognitions mixed in which must have their origin *a priori* ... because they allow us to say *more* about the objects that appear to the senses than mere experience would teach ... [resulting in] assertions containing true universality and necessity, the likes of which empirical cognition can never furnish" (A 2).[4]

The *Critique* sets out, then, by accepting the traditional rationalist doctrine that empirical reality is structured by necessities accessible to reason. We can know, according to Kant, that the internal angles of a perfectly planar empirical figure bounded by three perfectly straight lines *must* sum to two right angles, that action *must* equal reaction in physical interactions, and that an empirical event is preceded by something in accordance with which it *necessarily* follows. Kant's doctrine that such necessity provides a "sure criterion" of apriority is still widely misinterpreted today as an identification – and in post-Kripkean times, a conflation – of the necessary and the *a priori*. The *Critique* does not, however, assert that all metaphysically necessary truths are cognizable *a priori* – it rejects that claim. To take one important example, the proposition "God exists" is treated as metaphysically necessary if true, and it is regarded as true, but Kant holds that we cannot have theoretical *a priori* knowledge of this truth in principle.[5] His doctrine is rather that "if a judgment is thought together with its necessity," by which is meant *known* in a way that exhibits its necessity, it must be known *a priori*. The precise claim here requires care, since Kant sometimes maintains, following Leibniz, Wolff, and Georg Friedrich Meier, that there can be empirical, or as he says "historical," knowledge of necessary truths. In the usual example, such

[4] Compare *New Essays*, p. 80, 446, 455; Wolff, *German Metaphysics*, §371.
[5] See my *Rationalism and Causal Realism in Kant's Metaphysics*, unpublished Ph.D. dissertation, Yale University 2005, p. 187, 206; Nick Stang, *Kant's Modal Metaphysics*, unpublished Ph.D. dissertation, Princeton University 2008.

truths are learned from a third party or reliable source (A 836/B 864; *Logic*, 9:22; *Reflections on Logic*, R 1744, 16:99). What merely empirical sources will not supply, on the shared view of the schools, is knowledge including what Kant labels, not without ambiguity, "consciousness of necessity," and which he evidently understands, following Leibniz, as some grasp of the force of relevant necessities.[6]

We can note a final expression of Kant's proximity to Leibniz on the *a priori* in the dispositional model that both oppose to Locke's conception of "innate truth." Locke famously rejects innate truths, which he describes as "imprinted on the soul," on grounds that include an argument that paradigms are not universally accepted or even understood, while *"imprinting*, if it signify anything, [is] nothing else, but the making of certain truths to be perceived."[7] Leibniz rejects Locke's imprinting metaphor, defending instead an account of the mind as furnished with "inclinations, dispositions, tendencies, or natural potentialities" for rational knowledge. These dispositional features are compared, in a famous analogy, to the veins in a marble block that lend it to being worked into some figure. Just as the sculptor's labor remains essential to "uncover the veins, and clear them by polishing and by cutting away what prevents them from appearing," so *a priori* knowledge requires in addition to the mind's bare dispositional structure reflection upon its own thinking. It is through such reflection, Leibniz maintains, that "the mind is capable ... of finding [truths of reason] *within itself* ... though the senses are necessary to give the opportunity and the attention for this."[8] Kant accepts this dispositional model, asserting that *a priori* knowledge requires "absolutely no implanted or innate representations ... One and all ... the *Critique* considers them acquired" (*Discovery*, 8:221). What *is* needed, according to Kant, is a distinction between empirical ('derivative') and *a priori* ('original') acquisition. The latter is held to presuppose nothing innate except the formal ground or categorical basis of relevant representations. The representational ingredients of

---

[6] Kripke thinks that Kant holds that a proposition known to be necessary must be known *a priori* [*Naming and Necessity* (Cambridge, MA: Harvard University Press, 1980), p. 159]. I believe that passages that appear to support this reading are best interpreted as dealing with knowledge of necessity in Kant's thicker 'consciousness of' sense (contrast *Logic*, 9:22, 9:69). Compare Leibniz, *New Essays*, 85; Georg Friedrich Meier, *Auszug aus der Vernunftlehre* (Halle, 1752), I, 1, 18; Wolff, *Philosophia rationalis sive logica* (Frankfurt and Leipzig, 1740), §19.
[7] John Locke, *An Essay Concerning Human Understanding*, ed. P. H. Nidditch (Oxford: Clarendon Press, 1975), book I, ch. II, §5, p. 49
[8] *New Essays*, 79, 52.

a priori knowledge, and the knowledge itself, are viewed as first uncovered by reflection upon our thought on the occasion of encounters with objects (*Discovery*, 8:223; B 1).

On all of these points, then – the claim that we possess rational knowledge pertaining to empirical reality; the conception of the scientific enterprise as satisfying the demand for explanation by exhibiting necessity; the doctrine that necessity in the indicated sense establishes a priority; the dispositional approach to the *a priori* – Kant's mature thought remains very close to German predecessors, and in particular to Leibniz. I turn now to the central move with which Kant breaks decisively with all predecessors, before considering some classical puzzles presented by the innovation.

2. THE COPERNICAN TURN

Kant introduces the guiding idea of his Copernican revolution in philosophy, which is also his central departure from the tradition on *a priori* knowledge, as follows:

> Up until now it has been assumed that all our cognition must conform to the objects; but all attempts to find out something about them *a priori* through concepts that would extend our cognition have, on this presupposition, come to nothing. Hence let us once try whether we do not get farther with the problems of metaphysics by assuming that the objects must conform to our cognition, which would agree better with the requested possibility of an *a priori* cognition of them, which is to establish something about objects before they are given to us. (B xvi)

The development of this argument in the work itself moves from non-analytic *a priori* knowledge of objects to the conclusion that the objects known are not things as they exist wholly independent of the knowing mind. It employs a premise, which shows up at several key points, that the knowledge in question exhibits non-trivial constraints to which objects *must* conform, and we could not know such necessity to apply to wholly mind-independent entities (A 26/B 42; A 32–3/B 49; A 48/B 65; B 127; B 166–7). Kant concludes that knowledge exhibiting such necessities must pertain to things "conforming to our cognition," which is to say, to *appearances* of things to the subject.

In working out this central idea, the *Critique* traces *a priori* knowledge to two types of representational ingredients: singular representations or "intuitions" of space and time through which all objects are given, and a number of "concepts of the understanding" or "categories" through which objects are thought. In the Transcendental Aesthetic, Kant argues that our representations of space and time are themselves *a priori* and condition all experience, while underwriting non-trivial *a priori* cognition of objects of experience. Every object in space and time is known as bound, according to his analysis, by geometrical necessities and those of a "general theory of motion" held to "flow" from the represented character of space and time. Kant then applies his guiding thought that "if intuition must conform to the constitution of the objects [in themselves], I do not see how we could know anything of the latter *a priori*; but if the object (as object of the senses) must conform to our faculty of intuition, I have no difficulty in conceiving such a possibility" (B vii). He infers that the spatial and temporal form from which non-analytic *a priori* truths flow is the form of appearances; not of things as they are wholly independent of the subject (B 41; B 49).

Kant continues in the Transcendental Analytic with the claim that a number of fundamental concepts or "categories" including cause-and-effect and substance-and-accident are not themselves derived from experience, and are implicated in all of our knowledge of non-analytic necessities. These concepts are described as "self-thought *a priori* first sources of our cognition," which "contain the grounds of the possibility of all experience in general from the side of the understanding" (B 167–8). Applying his guiding idea, Kant infers that the application of these concepts grounding knowledge of non-analytic necessity must be to appearances, not to things in themselves. The argument again employs the premise that relevant necessities could not be known to pertain to reality as it exists wholly independent of the subject (B 126; B 167–8; *Correspondence*, 11:41).

Kant's strategy of accounting for knowledge of non-analytic necessity by restricting such knowledge to appearances structured by the mind's representational forms has attracted sharp criticism. Bertrand Russell famously objects that "the thing to be accounted for is our certainty that the facts *must always* conform to logic and arithmetic [etc]. To say that logic and arithmetic [etc] are contributed by us does not account for this. Our nature is as much a fact of the existing world as anything, and there can be no certainty that it will remain constant."[9] Charles Parsons and Philip Kitcher add that Kant's explanation of mathematical knowledge by restriction to objects structured by subjective forms fails, since careful examination of his proposal reveals that knowledge of the forms from which relevant truths

---

[9] Bertrand Russell, *The Problems of Philosophy*, reprinted in *Epistemology: Contemporary Readings*, ed. Michael Huemer (Routledge: London, 2002), p. 154. In fact, Kant's subjectivist theory of *a priori* knowledge is not intended to explain the possibility of *analytical* a priori knowledge.

supposedly flow is not prior to the mathematical knowledge to be explained. Kitcher concludes that Kant fails to justify his *a priori* knowledge claims, while Parsons argues that the Copernican proposal does not successfully "determine the boundaries of mathematical evidence."[10] The application of the Copernican model in the natural sciences attracts even harsher criticism: Kant's claim to know the *necessary* equality of action and reaction in physical interactions looks no less dubious for its restriction to mere appearances.[11] In general, philosophers sympathetic to the idea that the mind might grasp non-analytical necessities have often challenged Kant's claim that such knowledge must pertain merely to appearance, while those antecedently skeptical find plenty of resources to resist the *Critique's* claim that such knowledge presents 'no difficulty' once restricted in this way.

3. KANT'S EPISTEMOLOGICAL DICHOTOMY

We can make some headway in understanding Kant's Copernican proposal by turning to the central role in his argument of a supposedly exhaustive inventory of ways in which our representations could connect up with objects known through them. All non-trivial theoretical knowledge of an object, Kant maintains, must be grounded in a relation between a representation and its object that can come about in only two ways: "Either the object makes the representation possible, or the representation alone makes the object possible" (A 92/B 125–6; B 166; *Prolegomena*, 4:319; *Correspondence*, 10:130–1; R 4473).

On the typical presentation of the first mechanism, an object causes a representation in the knowing subject. Kant's Copernican turn rests on the contention that this first relation between object and representation could at best ground empirical knowledge of the object.[12] He

---

[10] Charles Parsons, "Infinity and Kant's Conception of the Possibility of Experience," *Philosophical Review* 78 (1964), p. 197; Philip Kitcher, "Kant and the Foundations of Mathematics," *Philosophical Review* 84:1 (1975), pp. 23–30.

[11] See *Metaphysical Foundations*, 4:546; compare Kant's *New System of Motion and Rest* (1758), 2:24–5. For detailed criticism, see Adickes, *Kant als Naturforscher*, 2 vols. (Berlin, 1924–25), vol. 1, p. 319.

[12] The first relation is not *sufficient* for empirical knowledge – the *Critique* famously denies any knowledge of things in themselves supposedly affecting the mind (A 30/B 45; on such noumenal affection, see A 42/B 59; A 494/B 522; A 566/B 594, 8:215). A central motive for this denial lies in Kant's explanation of *a priori* knowledge, which, in restricting space and time to subjective forms, restricts empirical knowledge to appearances.

infers that objects of which we have substantive *a priori* knowledge must be "made possible by our representations" in accordance with the second mechanism and in the sense already indicated; they must be viewed as mere appearances of things structured by forms contributed by the mind.

There is an intentional but subtle and sometimes overlooked asymmetry between Kant's two applications of his Copernican mechanism in explaining *a priori* knowledge. Its first application in the Transcendental Aesthetic argues from knowledge of necessities flowing from the represented character of space and time to the conclusion that space and time are merely subjective forms of inner and outer experience. The conclusion here includes a notorious and puzzling claim that things in themselves are *non*-spatiotemporal. As Kant puts it, "if we remove our own subject or even only the subjective constitution of the senses in general, then all constitution, all relations of objects in space and time, indeed space and time themselves, would disappear" (A 42/B 59; A 26/B 42; A 32–3/B 49). In the second case, objects of which we have theoretical non-analytic *a priori* knowledge involving the categories are described as mere appearances, not things in themselves. Kant does not draw the parallel conclusion that categories such as cause-and-effect do not apply to things in themselves. On the contrary, he carefully specifies that such categories "are not restricted in thinking by the conditions of our sensible intuition [space and time], but have an unbounded field" (B 166n; A 88/B 120; A 254/B 309).

This asymmetry proves of enormous significance, for Kant goes on to claim knowledge [*Wissen, Erkenntnis*] on practical grounds of the absolute freedom of the will, existence of God, and the immortality of the soul. These practically-grounded knowledge claims are made to rest on *non*-theoretical *a priori* warrants for applying categories to reality in itself (B xxvin; *Practical Reason*, 5:4, 30, 55, 121–148; *Judgment*, 5:469; *Progress*, 20:280, 300–01). Kant repeatedly insists, in addition, that the freedom whose reality is supposedly known on practical grounds is metaphysically impossible if space and time do apply to things in themselves: "If these intuitions [space and time] were not mere subjective forms of sensibility, but the things in themselves, actions would depend completely on the mechanism of nature, and freedom together with its consequence morality would be destroyed" (R 6343; B xxvii; A 536/B 564; *Practical Reason*, 5:95–7). Kant claims, in other words, that we know ourselves to be absolutely free on practical grounds, but we also know this freedom to depend metaphysically on the conclusion of the *Critique's* unusual and asymmetrical inference to the mere subjectivity of spatiotemporal form.

These peculiarities in Kant's application of his novel model of *a priori* knowledge look even more striking when we add a famous and influential objection to his central argument in the case of space and time. The objection challenges the *Critique's* inference from non-analytic *a priori* knowledge of spatiotemporal form to the non-spatiotemporality of things in themselves. Its proponents can grant that empirical encounters cannot produce knowledge that objects *must* conform to non-analytic constraints held by Kant to flow from spatiotemporal form. They can also allow, for argument's sake, the completeness of Kant's inventory of epistemological mechanisms. What follows, it seems, is that knowledge of relevant necessities does not "conform to the object" in the sense that it is not produced merely by empirical encounters with mind-independent reality. But the knowledge might presumably conform to this reality in a different sense: spatiotemporal form, and whatever necessities it imposes, might *apply* to things in themselves as well as appearances. Kant's argument does not merely deny the former "production-conformity" of knowledge of necessities. It also denies, without apparent justification, the latter "agreement-conformity." Generations of scholars have concluded that the *Critique* overlooks the intelligible possibility that spatiotemporality is the form both of appearance and of reality in itself.[13]

Though this old and resilient objection need not rest on a rejection of the completeness of Kant's inventory of epistemological mechanisms, it provides a natural occasion to question such completeness. The 'objectivist' models of *a priori* knowledge upheld by Kant's rationalist predecessors make use of mechanisms absent from his own list. The puzzles raised by his new model call for a closer look at the precise grounds of this omission.

4. KANT AGAINST THE TRADITION ON THE *A PRIORI*

Many of Kant's central objections to rationalist predecessors' theories of *a priori* knowledge can be reconstructed from scattered remarks directed against an influential mid-century German thinker, Christian August Crusius (B 167; *Prolegomena*, 4:319n; *Dreams*, 2:342; *Logic*, 9:21; *Correspondence*, 10:131; R 4275; R 4446; R 4473; R 4851). Crusius follows many philosophers of the modern period in viewing a broadly Augustinian divine illumination as the source of our

---

[13] For a discussion and influential defense of this "neglected alternative" objection, see Hans Vaihinger, *Commentar zu Kants Kritik der reinen Vernunft*, 2 vols. (Stuttgart: Spemann, 1881–92), vol. 2, pp. 144–150, 310.

non-empirical knowledge of mind-independent reality. His epistemology, labeled by Kant the "system of preformation," appeals in particular to two "material principles" of knowledge to supplement formal logical laws. A "Principle of Inseparability" asserts that what cannot be thought of as separated cannot really exist separately, and a "Principle of Noncombinability" asserts that what cannot be thought of as connected cannot really be connected.[14] The "unthinkability" referred to here is intended to pick out an extra-logical constraint on our thought, one the violation of which is experienced as a conflict with our "entire nature" as thinking beings. We are held to experience the constraint in question, for example, in judging that an event *must* have a determining cause, even though, as Crusius insists, no logical contradiction results from denying this.[15] The same material principles also serve as the source, along with formal logical laws, of all valid inference. Crusius locates the mark of a valid demonstrative inference in the unthinkability of the conjunction of premises and negation of the conclusion.[16] Only for a subset of "geometrical demonstration" does he identify such non–thinkability with logical inconsistency. He thus embraces logically ampliative demonstrative inference, a position comparable to that of Descartes and Locke, although opposed to Leibniz and Wolff.[17] Both in non-empirical judgment and in inference, his extra-logical thinkability test is presented as a reliable guide to extra-mental reality, and a source of certainty with regard to it.

Kant offers several objections to this model of *a priori* knowledge. He objects that Crusius's appeal to "thinkability" is indefinite outside of analytic contexts, that it thus fails to mark clear limits to knowledge, and that this in turn encourages "fanatical" speculation (*Prolegomena*, 4:319n; *Correspondence*, 10:131; B 167; *Logic*, 9:21; *Metaphysics von Schön*, 28:467). He also describes the proposal as resting on a "deceptive circle in the logical ordering [*Schlusreihe*] of our knowledge" (*Correspondence*, 10:131). This objection evidently echoes Antoine Arnauld's circle charge against Descartes's attempt to anchor the reliability of his "clear and distinct" perceptions in a non-deceiving God. Arnauld objects that the reliability to be

---

[14] Crusius, Christian August, *Entwurf der notwendigen Vernunftwahrheiten*, (Leipzig: Gleditsch, 1745), §15; *Weg zur Gewißheit* (Leipzig: Gleditsch, 1747) §259–61.

[15] *Entwurf*, §15, §31.   [16] *Weg zur Gewißheit*, §262, §521.

[17] Compare Descartes, *Rules for the Direction of the Mind*, in *Oeuvres de Descartes*, C. Adam and P. Tannery, eds. (Paris: L. Cerf, 1879–1913), hereafter (AT vol:page), (AT 10:368, CSM 1:14); contrast Leibniz, *New Essays*, 101, 361–8, 479–483.

demonstrated is already assumed in Descartes's proof that such a benevolent God exists; and Kant can likewise point to the fact that Crusius's proofs of a divine guarantor of the reliability of his principles rest on those very principles.[18] Kant concludes – and his own detailed critique of theoretical proofs of God's existence provides an important backdrop here – that the appeal to divinely implanted reality-tracking faculties amounts to a *deus ex machina* and "the destruction of all philosophy" (R 4473). These arguments provide the indispensable context for the *Critique's* assertion that appeal to an "implanted subjective necessity" to judge of mind-independent reality in certain ways could at best license the claim that "I am so constituted that *I* cannot think," for example, of a mind-independent event except as necessitated by a cause. This is held to fall short of the necessity we supposedly know to apply to *objects* in mathematics and the metaphysics of nature (B 167–8; A 48/B 65; *Correspondence*, 11:41; *Prolegomena*, 4:287).

Kant views his epistemological objections to preformation as extendable to the proposals of Plato, Descartes, and Malebranche (R 4275; R 4851; R 4894; *Correspondence*, 10:131, *Blomberg Logic*, 24:37). It is not at all clear that these objections defeat what still might appear a legitimate default assumption, namely, that non-analytic *a priori* knowledge viewed as antecedently secure should be held to pertain to reality in itself. What does seem clear, however, is that Kant's objections to preformation do not yet justify the *Critique's* puzzling inference from *a priori* knowledge of spatiotemporal form to the *mere* subjectivity of such form. It is one thing to challenge Descartes's conviction that his clear and distinct perceptions reliably track reality in itself. It is quite another to conclude, as the *Critique* most certainly does, that Descartes's supposed clear and distinct perceptions of space and time *mis*represent this reality.

A notable recent effort to bridge this apparent gap in Kant's argument has focused on his contention that we could not know that things in themselves *must* obey rules we know to govern things in space and time (A 48/B 65–6; *Prolegomena*, 4:287; B 167–8). Paul Guyer and James Van Cleve have suggested that this claim incorporates the proposition that reality in itself could at best be contingently governed by the rules in question. To complete the argument for the non-spatiotemporality of things in themselves, these interpreters ascribe to Kant the premise that knowledge of necessities governing

---

[18] Arnauld, *Fourth Set of Objections* (AT 7:214, CSM 2:150); Crusius, *Entwurf*, §33, §206.

things in space and time excludes such merely contingent agreement. If (1) the agreement between the spatiotemporal form of appearance and the form of reality in itself could be at best contingent, and (2) it could not be merely contingent, then it could not occur.[19]

The argument is valid, but both premises raise difficulties. If we substitute for the first the proposition that the agreement could be at best contingent as far as we know, the conclusion does not follow. While Van Cleve does not address the justification of the metaphysical contingency premise, Guyer concludes that Kant's argument is incomplete without such justification. The argument's second premise is also problematic. The necessity Kant understands to flow from the represented character of space and time is traditionally and naturally read as a conditional necessity: Necessarily, if something is in space and/or time, then it satisfies geometrical necessities and those associated with his "general theory of motion" (B 40–1; B 49). It is far from obvious why knowledge of such conditional necessity should be thought to exclude a merely contingent spatiotemporality of things in themselves. Indeed, Guyer infers that Kant is illicitly invoking a different necessity claim – that whatever is in space and time is necessarily in space and time. Such a premise would not, however, merely lack satisfactory justification. As Karl Ameriks argues, it contradicts Kant's official doctrine that objects encountered in experience are not, in themselves, spatiotemporal at all, and further that sensible forms through which we encounter empirical objects might conceivably have been different or absent (*Prolegomena*, 4:289; 4:350–1).[20]

While the suggested solution to the puzzle raised by Kant's inference to the mere subjectivity of spatiotemporal form thus faces difficulties, I believe that it is quite correct to propose that Kant's inference rests on a perceived conflict between necessity exhibited in supposed *a priori* knowledge and contingency attributed to reality in itself. By identifying the precise root of a suitable contingency in Kant's philosophy, we can shed further light on his necessity premise, and also suggest new responses to the problems thus far identified with his Copernican proposal.

---

[19] Paul Guyer, *Kant and the Claims of Knowledge* (New York: Cambridge University Press, 1987), pp. 354–69; also his *Kant* (New York: Routledge, 2006), pp. 64–65; James Van Cleve, *Problems from Kant* (New York: Oxford, 1999), pp. 34–37; compare Peter Strawson, *The Bounds of Sense* (London: Methuen, 1966), p. 60.

[20] Karl Ameriks, *Interpreting Kant's Critiques* (New York: Oxford University Press 2003), pp. 107–8.

5. KANT'S ROOT OF CONTINGENCY
AND THE COPERNICAN TURN

Leibniz's *Theodicy* (1710) defends a conception of the *contingent* as
that which has some alternative that is logically possible in itself.[21] The
aim of this defense is to square a contingency described as essential for
free agency with a commitment to the Principle of Sufficient Reason
(PSR), the principle that there is "no true or existent fact, no true
assertion, without there being a sufficient reason why it is thus and
not otherwise."[22] Leibniz's account of contingency allows him to
uphold the contingency of creation and of human action on the grounds
that "alternative sequences" of things are indeed internally consistent,
even while he insists that all such alternatives are excluded "with
certainty" by God's choice of the best world, in accordance with his
wisdom and the PSR.

Leibniz's defense of contingency met notable resistance in eighteenth-
century Germany, where many philosophers argued that his PSR in fact
entails a Spinozistic necessity of all things. In 1755, Kant upholds the PSR
in the created sphere, while maintaining that "infallible necessity"
within the world is indeed its consequence (*New Elucidation*, 1:396,
399, 403–4). Unpublished notes reveal, however, that Kant's position
on contingency has undergone a significant shift by the mid-
1760s. Alongside Leibniz's thin "internal" contingency of created substances and states given by the consistency of alternatives, Kant now
insists on the reality of "absolute" contingency (*schlechterdings
Zufälligkeit, omnimoda contingentia*), given by the conjunction of internal contingency and an absence of determining grounds (R 3717; R 4034;
R 4544; R 4693; R 5251). By the late 1760s, and consistently thereafter,
Kant ascribes such absolute contingency to all and only free acts of finite
rational agents. In a characteristic passage, he explains:

The proposition: everything which happens has a determining ground, that is,
something else which necessitates it, is the principle of the changes of all passive
substances [...] but *actions* [...] are not included under it [...] I now begin my
state as I wish. The difficulty here is not the possibility of the becoming but of
the grasping. The possibility of freedom cannot be grasped, because one cannot
grasp any first beginning [...] [For] reason comprehends [something] when it
cognizes it *a priori*, that is through grounds [...] Now first beginnings have no
[determining] grounds, thus no comprehension through reason is possible [...]
This is no objection, but a subjective difficulty. (R 4338)

[21] Leibniz, *Theodicy*, trans. E. M. Huggard (La Salle, IL: Open Court, 1985),
§§44–45, §§230–4.
[22] Leibniz, *Monadology*, §32.

Kant acknowledges that his new doctrine of absolute freedom introduces an essential theoretical unintelligibility into the world. There can be no full explanation as to why an absolutely free act is thus and not otherwise – such explanation would have to infer the act from a determining ground that is absent by hypothesis. Kant no longer follows Leibniz, however, in excluding absolute freedom on the grounds of its incompatibility with the PSR. Instead, he responds by effectively restricting the PSR, arguing that theoretical and practical grounds demand the ascription of absolute contingency to the free acts of finite rational agents (R 3855; R 4006; R 4058; R 4226; R 4334; R 4742; R 4961; R 5082; R 5552; *Pölitz Metaphysics*, 28:270, 332–3).

What light does this development shed on Kant's Copernican model of *a priori* knowledge? It was proposed earlier that the *Critique's* perplexing application of its new theory of the *a priori* in inferring the mere subjectivity of spatiotemporal form rests on a metaphysical contingency ascribed to reality in itself. I believe that this proposal is correct, and now suggest that the contingency premise at work here is the doctrine of absolute contingency to which Kant consistently subscribes from the mid-1760s.

One immediate objection to such a suggestion notes that Descartes and Crusius, unlike Leibniz and Wolff, agree that free acts possess the property of absolute contingency imputed by Kant.[23] We have already seen that Kant's epistemological objections to preformation systems of *a priori* knowledge among his predecessors do not seem to justify the *Critique's* inference to the *mere* subjectivity of spatiotemporal form. If Descartes and Crusius can accept Kant's contingency premise, we might wonder how it could fill the apparent gap in his argument.

The answer, I believe, lies in the crucial disagreement regarding the *content* of the non-analytic *a priori* knowledge needing explanation. Descartes and Crusius contend that *a priori* cognizable laws of motion leave room for a difference-making influence of absolutely contingent mental causes in the natural order. Whether Descartes conceives of mind–world action as the will changing the direction of bodies without affecting their overall quantity of motion (as Leibniz interprets him), or rather holds that his famous physical conservation laws simply do not apply to motions caused by minds (as Daniel Garber has argued), both he and Crusius reject a physical determinism in which the mind could at best overdetermine physical events. Leibniz and Wolff, by contrast, maintain that Descartes's interactionist theory

---

[23] Descartes, *Principles of Philosophy* I, 37, 41 (AT 8:18–20, CSM 1:205–6); letter to Mesland, 9 Feb 1645 (AT 4:173, CSMK 245); Crusius, *Entwurf*, §§ 82–84.

of mind–body action rests on an erroneous formulation of the laws of motion. Both view *a priori* cognizable laws of nature as imposing a fully deterministic order on physical reality.[24] While Kant sides from the mid-1760s with Descartes and Crusius regarding the absolute contingency of action, he agrees with Leibniz and Wolff on the determinism or "natural necessity" imposed by laws of motion cognizable *a priori*.[25]

As a consequence, Kant stands alone in facing a critical tension within his own theory of necessity and contingency. Unpublished reflections reveal that the problem exercises him intensively by the time he tells Mendelssohn in 1766 that "everything depends on seeking out the facts to the problem; *how is the soul present in the world, both to material natures and to others of its own sort*" (*Correspondence*, 10:71).[26]

This tension also reveals how Kant's doctrine of absolute contingency can explain the *Critique's* puzzling claim that necessities of geometry and of a "general theory of motion" flowing from the spatio-temporal form of empirical reality entail that such form is *not* that of reality in itself. Given Kant's insistence that the general theory of motion imposes fully deterministic order throughout the physical order,[27] his claim that things in themselves *could not be known* to be constrained by this doctrine of motion now immediately suggests an appeal to his absolute contingency premise. In particular, Kant's inference to the subjectivity of space and time from the premise that relevant necessities *could not be known* to govern things in themselves can be read as asserting that such knowledge is excluded by absolute contingencies at the level of reality in itself. This reading is consonant with Kant's consistent mature doctrine that if space and

---

[24] Leibniz, *Theodicy*, §60–61; Wolff, *German Metaphysics*, §761–4.

[25] See R 4058; R 4228; R 5997; R 6006; R 6317; R 6343; R 6349; R 6353; B xxvii; A 536/B 564; *Practical Reason* 5:95–7.

[26] "The greatest difficulty is this: how a subjectively unconditioned will can be thought in the nexus of efficient or determining causes" (R 3860, 1764–8; R 3922; R 4228; R 4334; R 4338; R 4742). "The principle of sufficient reason is the principle of order in the course of nature [...] If there is *only* nature, the series of [causal] connections is continuous" (R 5220; R 5997; R 5962; R 5978; R 6006).

[27] "Neither through a miracle, nor through a spiritual being can a motion be brought about in the world, without producing just as much motion in the opposite direction, thus in accordance with the laws of action and reaction ... Motions cannot begin by themselves, nor through something which wasn't itself in motion; and freedom and miracles are not to be met with among the phenomena" (R 5997, 1780s; B xxvii; A 536/B 564).

time did exist independently of the mind, there would be no absolute contingency in the world; rather, "actions would depend completely on the mechanism of nature, and freedom together with its consequence morality would be destroyed" (R 6343; B xxvii; A 536/B 564; *Practical Reason*, 5:95–7).

If a reading along these lines is correct, it can offer straightforward solutions to several classical puzzles presented by Kant's Copernican turn.[28] The traditional conditional interpretation of necessities that Kant associates with spatiotemporal form is retained: Necessarily, if something is given under the form of space and time, then it is governed by various mathematical and mechanical constraints. Contrary to Russell's charge, Kant's Copernican explanation of the *a priori* need not (and does not) assume that our nature is unchangeable. Even if spatiotemporal form is not the only possible form of experience, the conditional necessities that Kant associates with such form, plus his contingency premise, require the *Critique's* subjectivist explanation of knowledge of spatiotemporal form. We can also acknowledge Parsons and Kitcher's challenges to the *Critique's* account of mathematical necessities as "flowing" from a merely subjective spatiotemporal form and grasped by a mysterious insight. There remains an intelligible philosophical progression from Kant's pre-critical doctrine according to which rational knowledge in mathematics and mechanics rests on a supposed cognitive grasp of necessities flowing from spatiotemporal order viewed as a mind-*independent* order.[29] The *Critique's* asymmetrical application of its Copernican explanation in the cases of

[28] The argument sketched here passes over some important complications. For a fuller discussion, see Desmond Hogan, "Three Kinds of Rationalism and the Non-Spatiality of Things in Themselves," *Journal of the History of Philosophy*, July 2009.

[29] Kant's early works uphold the applicability of geometry to physical space against such opponents as Crusius, while claiming that "everything which belongs to motion can be made clear and intelligible to intuition" (*Negative Magnitudes* (1763), 2:194, 2:168; *New System of Motion and Rest*, 2:24–5; *Physical Monadology*, 1:478–9). That Kant sees insight into the mathematical structure of empirical reality as grounding rational knowledge of laws of motion is most explicit in the *Inaugural Dissertation's* assimilation of pure mechanics to pure mathematics. Kant writes that "pure mathematics deals with space in geometry and *time* in *pure mechanics,*" and further, "all observable events in the world, all motions and all internal changes necessarily accord with the *axioms which can be known about time*" (*Dissertation*, 2:402; compare *Metaphysical Foundations*, 4:470; *Prolegomena*, 4:321). The point is emphasized by Darius Koriako, *Kants Philosophie der Mathematik* (Hamburg: Felix Meiner Verlag 1999), p. 125.

space/time and the categories is no longer problematic but required: On the proposed reading, the explanation is motivated in part by a commitment to absolutely contingent causes not found in the order of appearance.

The interpretation can also perhaps resolve the best-known paradox in Kant's philosophy. This is the apparent incompatibility of the *Critique's* doctrine of ignorance of reality in itself and its metaphysics of space and time. The key point here, and one that offers important support for the proposal, is that Kant often expresses his absolute contingency premise as a denial of the *a priori knowability* of relevant features of reality. He writes, for example, that "reason comprehends [something] when it cognizes it *a priori, that is, through grounds* ... Now first beginnings *have no grounds*, thus no comprehension through reason is possible" (R 4338; R4180; *Pölitz Metaphysics*, 28:270). Something is known *a priori* in the sense at issue here when it is known through, in the sense of being inferable from, its cause or metaphysical ground. Such *a priori* knowability, central to the German rationalist tradition, presupposes the *existence* of a determining ground from which the relevant truth is inferable.[30] Kant's denial of the *a priori* knowability of "first beginnings" can for this reason express his metaphysical claim that such features *lack* determining grounds. If the *Critique's* doctrine of the unknowability of things in themselves incorporates denials of this kind, it is not merely compatible with Kant's conclusion regarding space and time; it can play a key role in the argument for that conclusion. Though a detailed discussion is not possible here, I have argued elsewhere that the *Critique's* noumenal ignorance doctrine does incorporate Kant's absolute contingency premise, and that this contingency premise is indeed implicit in the *Critique's* key claim that we could not know that things in themselves *must* obey rules known to govern things in space and time (A 32–3/B 49; A 48/B 65–6; B 167–8).[31]

Such an interpretation of Kant's Copernican theory of the *a priori* agrees with his own claim that "the origin of the critical philosophy is morality, with respect to the imputability of action" (*Nachlass*, 20:335; *Correspondence*, 12:257). Interpreters have given little weight to a number of important claims along these lines, including Kant's assertion that "the system of the *Critique of Pure Reason* turns on two cardinal points as a system of nature and of freedom, from which each leads to the necessity of the other (sic): the ideality of space and time

---

[30] Crusius, *Entwurf*, §38; Leibniz, *Theodicy*, §44.
[31] Hogan, Desmond, "How to Know Unknowable Things in Themselves," *Noûs* 43:1 (March 2009).

and the reality of the concept of freedom" (R 6353; R 6344; R 6349). The
general neglect of these striking claims has had three main explanations. The first is the obscurity in the emergence of Kant's libertarian
theory and in its presentation in the *Critique*. While Kant's position
on knowledge of absolute freedom in the period under consideration
remains a complex and thorny issue, several scholars have argued
that the textual evidence supports Kant's commitment to the demonstrability of such freedom both in 1781 and subsequently.[32]

A second important explanation for the neglect of the cited claims
is simply that Kant's austere epistemological explanation of non-
analytic *a priori* knowledge does not appear to invoke any premise related
to his doctrine of freedom. As we have just seen, attention to Kant's
utterances on *a priori* unknowability and absolute contingency removes
this impression. Finally, it is often thought that a role for freedom in
Kant's epistemological argument would conflict with his repeated
warnings that, in cases of conflict, deliverances of theoretical reason
trump conclusions assented to on grounds of their "inseparable connection" to morality (B xxviii–xxix; *Practical Reason*, 5:120). Setting aside
the possibility that Kant accepted the theoretical demonstrability of
absolute freedom in 1781,[33] his official position in later works is

---

[32] Kant upholds the theoretical demonstrability of absolute freedom both
before and after the appearance of the *Critique of Pure Reason* in 1781,
and the work itself contains a similar claim (A 546–7/B 574–5; *Pölitz
Metaphysics*, 28:268–9; R 5110; R 5203; R 5552, 8:13–14). While another
well-known passage of the *Critique* appears to deny the theoretical
demonstrability of absolute freedom (A 558/B 586), it is unclear on examination whether Kant means only to rule out some proofs (from "mere
concepts *a priori*"). In an undated marginal handwritten note to A 558,
Kant adds that freedom is demonstrable on moral grounds: "*Morality
is that which, if it is correct, positively presupposes freedom. If the
former is true, then freedom is proved.*" From the late 1780s, Kant claims
that absolute freedom is demonstrable *only* on such practical grounds
(references to practical proof are, however, seen earlier – see *Pölitz
Metaphysics*, 28:332–3; R 4156; compare Crusius, *Anweisung,
Vernünftig zu Leben* (Leipzig, 1744), §42). Kant's later works subscribe
to the view that an agent "judges that he can do something because he
is aware that he ought to do it and he *cognizes freedom within him*,
which, without the moral law, *would have remained unknown to him*"
(*Practical Reason*, 5:30). Kant continues to insist that we have *knowledge*
(*Wissen, Erkenntnis*) of absolute freedom, arguing that knowledge on
theoretical grounds does not exhaust our knowledge (*Practical Reason*,
5:4, 121; *Progress*, 20:310; *Judgment*, 5:469). For a classic discussion of
these developments, see Karl Ameriks, "Kant's Deduction of Freedom and
Morality," *Journal of the History of Philosophy*, 19 (1981), pp. 53–79.

[33] See note 32.

that such trumping would require a theoretical *demonstration* that absolute contingency does not exist at the level of ultimate reality. Kant's
own early attempts to furnish such demonstration, combined with his
analysis of similar efforts of Wolff, Baumgarten, and Eberhard, leave him
certain that the envisaged conflict will not materialize (*Discovery*,
8:193–8).

6. CONCLUSION

The *Critique's* revolutionary explanation of *a priori* knowledge challenges rationalist predecessors' upholding a more general competence
of human reason to know ultimate reality. Kant's opposition to these
predecessors rests on epistemological objections to justifications
appealing to divinely implanted principles, clear and distinct perception, intuitive understanding, vision in God, the Principle of Sufficient
Reason, and Platonic recollection. I have suggested that Kant's
replacement model of *a priori* knowledge is not itself fully intelligible
unless we give due consideration both to the specific content of the *a
priori* knowledge he views as flowing from spatiotemporal form, and
to the absolute contingency he upholds consistently from the mid-
1760s. This conclusion accords with Kant's well-known assertions
that his critical turn originated in struggles with conflicting claims
of reason (R 5037; *Correspondence*, 12:257–8). It also agrees with his
many claims that the historical development of reason from the despotic dogmatism of rationalist predecessors to the *Critique's* idealistic
explanation of *a priori* knowledge receives its most powerful impetus
not from the dissent and opposition of rival dogmatic systems but
from conflicts in the deliverances of reason itself (*Judgment*, 5:345; A
407/B 434; *Practical Reason*, 5:107; *Progress*, 20:327). That such deliverances can produce unshakable certainty in the *Critique's* striking
metaphysical conclusions is testimony to the persistently rationalist
orientation of Kant's mature thought.

2   Kant, the Empiricists, and the Enterprise of Deduction

I. DOGMATISM, SKEPTICISM, CRITIQUE

When Kant surveyed what the history of metaphysics had left behind, he saw a "stage of conflict" – a disconsolate landscape of edifices fallen into ruins (A 852–3/B 880–1).[1] Most of the wreckage, when new, had been the proud work of the philosophers Kant called "dogmatists." Kant never wavered in his admiration for their highest standards of construction: "the regular ascertainment of ... principles, the clear determination of ... concepts, the attempt at strictness in ... proofs, and the prevention of audacious leaps in inference" (B xxxvi). The

[1] References to works other than the *Critique of Pure Reason* are to volume and page number in *Kant's Gesammelte Schriften*, edited by the Prussian (later German) Academy of Sciences, 29 volumes (Berlin: Georg Reimer [later Walter de Gruyter], 1900–). Passages from the *Critique* are cited by page numbers in the first ("A") and second ("B") editions. All works by Kant are cited by their titles in the *The Cambridge Edition of the Works of Immanuel Kant*, from which I quote throughout; departures from those translations are noted. Passages from Locke's *Essay* are cited by book, chapter, and section; they are quoted as they appear in John Locke, *An Essay concerning Human Understanding*, edited by P. H. Nidditch (Oxford: Clarendon Press, 1975). Passages from Berkeley's *A Treatise concerning the Principles of Human Knowledge* are quoted as they appear in volume 2 of *The Works of George Berkeley, Bishop of Cloyne*, edited by A. A. Luce and T. E. Jessop (London: Thomas Nelson, 1949). They are cited by section number. Passages from Hume's *Treatise* and *Enquiry* are quoted as they appear in *A Treatise of Human Nature*, edited by David Fate Norton and Mary J. Norton (New York: Oxford University Press, 2000), and *An Enquiry concerning Human Understanding*, edited by Tom L. Beauchamp (New York: Oxford University Press, 1999); those from the *Treatise* are cited by book, part, section, and paragraph, and those from the *Enquiry* by section and paragraph. I also provide page numbers to the editions prepared by L. A. Selby-Bigge and P. H. Nidditch, which are still widely used. I cite them as "SBN": *A Treatise of Human Nature*, second edition (Oxford: Clarendon Press, 1978) and *Enquiries concerning Human Understanding and concerning the Principles of Morals*, third edition (Oxford: Clarendon Press, 1975).

failure of the dogmatists lay not in their manner of building, he thought, but in their decision to begin construction on what turned out to be uncertain ground.[2] They had neglected, he explained, to "prepare the field" (B xxxvi) – to conduct a "critique" or assessment of their own capacities.

The failure of the dogmatists was, in Kant's view, a failure of self-examination.[3] Socrates had long before insisted that the unexamined life is not worth living, but philosophical projects commencing with self-examination were especially characteristic of modernity. Descartes's *Meditations* is probably the best-known example. The confession of the Savoyard vicar in Rousseau's *Émile* – a book that, according to legend, kept Kant awake on the night he began to read it and at home to finish it up on the following day – is another. Like Kant, Rousseau's priest from Savoy had been disappointed by what "the philosophers" had to offer: "Far from ridding me of my vain doubts," he complained, they "multiplied the doubts that tormented me and failed to remove any one of them."[4] The priest resolved, in a passage recalling the *Meditations*, to follow "the Inner Light," and "to admit as self-evident all that I could not honestly refuse to believe, and to admit as true all that seemed to follow directly from this." "All the rest," he declared, he would leave "undecided." But he soon realized that these rules had first to be used to assess his own capacity for judgment:

But who am I? What right have I to decide? What is it that determines my judgments? ... I must ... first turn my eyes upon myself to acquaint myself with the instrument I desire to use, and to discover how far it is reliable. (p. 307)

That the mind is an instrument whose reliability calls for assessment was a longstanding theme in the literature of skepticism. But in the modern project of self-inspection, Kant's most decisive predecessors, as I believe he recognized, were the empiricists Locke and Hume. Locke

---

[2] There was, of course, at least one other problem: their lovingly constructed dwellings were being battered by dogmatists who took shelter in buildings of their own, and by skeptics with no fixed address. Against such assaults, better landscaping would be of little use. Perhaps in accord with this, Kant sometimes suggests that the dogmatists needed more modest designs, or juster estimates of the limits of their materials – faults he continues to represent, however, as failures of self-knowledge (A 707/B 735; see also *Perpetual Peace in Philosophy* 8: 416).

[3] At A 763/B 791, Kant says that "critique" has the power to "unhinge" the concepts of the dogmatist and "bring him to self-knowledge [*Selbsterkenntnis*]."

[4] *Émile* (New York: Barnes and Noble, 2005), p. 306.

introduces his *Essay concerning Human Understanding* by way of a brief *"History,"* a story of *"five or six Friends meeting at my Chamber, and discoursing on a subject very remote from* [human understanding]*,"* who *"found themselves quickly at a stand, by the Difficulties that rose on every side."* We know, from the report of one of Locke's friends, that the topic was morality and natural religion (religion, that is, insofar as it can be defended by reason). Then and there, Locke says, *"it came into my Thoughts, that we took a wrong course; and that, before we set our selves upon Enquiries of that nature, it was necessary to examine our own Abilities, and see, what Objects our Understandings were, or were not fitted to deal with"* (The Epistle to the Reader, p. 7 in Nidditch). Hume's philosophy is a more solitary expression of the same determination:[5]

I cannot forbear having a curiosity to be acquainted with the principles of moral good and evil, the nature and foundation of government, and the cause of those several passions and inclinations, which actuate and govern me. I am uneasy to think I approve of one object, and disapprove of another; call one thing beautiful, and another deform'd; decide concerning truth and falsehood, reason and folly, without knowing upon what principles I proceed. (*A Treatise of Human Nature* 1.4.7.12; SBN 270–1)

Like Locke's *Essay* and Hume's *Treatise*, Kant's *Critique of Pure Reason* is an essay in self-examination. It is a critique *of* pure reason in two different senses: Its *object* is pure reason – our "entire higher faculty of cognition" (A 835/B 863) – and its *agent* or *vehicle* is pure reason. It is, in the second sense, a critique *of* pure reason because it is a project that pure reason itself undertakes: an attempt, on the part of pure reason, to "measure *its own* capacity" (B xxii, my emphasis). The vehicle of Kant's *Critique* is a cognitive power that is not only pure, but strenuously and self-consciously systematic. For this reason, Kant hopes for greater success than was achieved by Locke or Hume. He pursues a characteristically empiricist goal, that of "limit[ing] all our speculative claims [to knowledge] merely to the field of possible experience," but he proposes to do so systematically rather than "by stale mockery at attempts that have so often failed, or by pious sighing over the limits of our reason" (A 395). Mockery (stale in substance, though fresh in expression) can be found in Hume (for example at *Treatise* 1.4.3.11; SBN 224–5); pious sighing can be found in Locke (for example, at *Essay*

---

[5] See also *Enquiry* 1.12 (SBN 12), where Hume stresses the importance of investigating "the nature of human understanding," in order to determine, "from an exact analysis of its powers and capacities," how far we can expect it to take us.

2.1.5). Instead of ridiculing those who have gone too far, or thanking God for what little knowledge we have, Kant sets out to draw precisely determined boundaries (A 395; see also B 423–4). He asks us to imagine that we are trapped within a shell. With us on the inside are the things we can know. Beyond us on the outside is a region of which we will remain forever ignorant. Instead of bumping up against the shell's inner surface here and there, Kant sets out to discover the equation that defines it. If he succeeds, he will know what it is we cannot know. And then we will know it too. But then, to borrow an observation made by Giorgio Agamben, "by knowing the unknowable, it [would not be] something about *it* we [would] know, but something about ourselves."[6]

Kant defines dogmatism in terms of its indifference or outright opposition to critique: It is, he says, "the dogmatic procedure of pure reason, **without an antecedent critique of its own capacity**" (B xxxv; see also A 3/B 7 and *On a Discovery* 8:226). For Kant, the most far-reaching instrument of antecedent critique is the activity he calls *deduction*. A deduction is an attempt to show that an idea or concept is one that is ours by right. In this chapter, I examine Kant's response to the empirical deductions he found in Locke and Hume, and survey the opening stages of Kant's argument that deductions from pure reason, prematurely dismissed by Hume, are indeed possible. Kant saw empiricism as an ancient and perpetually available philosophical tendency, but in this chapter I will fix my attention exclusively on Locke, Berkeley, and Hume, the early modern "British empiricists" most important, and most familiar, to present-day readers of the *Critique*. I will, however, touch on Berkeley only fleetingly, for two reasons: He had little or no influence on the conception or execution of Kantian deductions, and Kant saw him, for understandable reasons, not as an empiricist, but as a Platonist.[7]

In brief, the story I will be telling is this. Up to a point Kant admired Locke. He sympathized with what he saw as Locke's ambition: his hope of legitimizing concepts (including metaphysical concepts) by tracing them to their sources in experience. But he was persuaded by Locke's example, and even more by Hume's, that the empirical deduction of metaphysical concepts is a hopeless task. Hume was

---

[6] Giorgio Agamben, *Idea of Prose*, translated by Michael Sullivan and Sam Whitsitt (Albany: State University of New York Press, 1995), p. 34. The emphasis is mine.

[7] For discussion of Kant's reading of Berkeley see my "Berkeley and Kant," in Daniel Garber and Béatrice Longuenesse (eds.), *Kant and the Early Moderns* (Princeton: Princeton University Press, 2008), pp. 142–71 and 231–4.

important to Kant for two reasons. First, Hume seemed to show that the deduction of metaphysical concepts from pure reason is impossible. From this it seemed to follow that empirical deductions are our only hope. But, second, Hume's empirical deduction of the concept *cause* (a model, in Kant's view, for the empirical deduction of *any* metaphysical concept) failed to capture an essential ingredient of the concept – the very ingredient, ironically, that made it impossible (or so Hume thought) to deduce the concept from reason. What was needed, Kant concluded, was a new kind of deduction from pure reason, which he called *transcendental*.

I begin with a brief word about the vocabulary of empiricism and its transformation in the *Critique*.

2. THE VOCABULARY OF EMPIRICISM

The themes of this chapter are the origin and content of our ideas or conceptions, the range of their legitimate application, and the justification of the beliefs we form from them. I begin, however, with *words*: the words used by Locke, Berkeley, and Hume when they spoke of ideas or conceptions; the words chosen by their translators into German and by Locke's translator into Latin; the more elaborate vocabulary used by Kant himself; and some of the Latin words to which his vocabulary was carefully keyed. By coordinating the idioms of Kant and the empiricists, I hope to remove any doubt that when Kant speaks (in English translation following his own Latin equivalents) of *representations*, *intuitions*, *concepts*, and *ideas*, he is addressing many of the issues that the empiricists were addressing when they spoke simply of ideas.

Locke's philosophy was described by a hostile contemporary as "this new way of ideas," and ideas – together with the thoughts or propositions they make possible – are, in the *Essay*, Locke's constant preoccupation.[8] As the book begins, Locke actually apologizes to his readers for relying so often on the word *idea*, "it being that Term," he explains, that "serves best for whatsoever is the Object of the Understanding when a Man thinks," making it a convenient and close to unavoidable expression for "whatever is meant by *Phantasm, Notion, Species*, or whatever it is, which the Mind can be employ'd about in thinking" (1.1.8). Perhaps the *term* "idea" could have been avoided, as his small sample of a more scholastic vocabulary illustrates, but Locke was persuaded that in an essay on human understanding, ideas themselves

---

[8] The quoted words, from Bishop Edward Stillingfleet, are repeated by Locke himself in his first reply to the Bishop's criticisms, *The Works of John Locke* (London: Thomas Tegg, 1823), 4: 72.

could not possibly be set aside. For "since the Things, the Mind contemplates, are none of them, besides it self, present to the Understanding, 'tis necessary that something else, as a Sign or Representation of the thing it considers, should be present to it: And these are *Ideas*" (4.21.4). Ideas, as Locke explains here, are *representations*, and "representations" is exactly what Kant elected to call them: *Vorstellungen*, whose singular form, *Vorstellung*, was Kant's gloss on the Latin word *repraesentatio* (A 320/B 376) – the very word used by the German G. H. Thiele when, in 1741, he translated Locke's *Essay* into Latin.[9]

Neither Berkeley nor Hume followed Locke in his wide use of "idea." (Locke's indiscriminate use also made Kant uneasy: see A 319/B 376.) For Hume, the word covers only our less forceful perceptions, and not the lively perceptions – "impressions," as he called them – we have when we sense or feel (*Enquiry* 2.3 and 9; SBN 18 and 22); for Berkeley, although we have "ideas" of physical objects, we have "notions" rather than ideas of minds and their acts or operations (*Principles* 27, 140, 142).[10] I will, for the most part, ignore these departures in what follows.

Kant divides representations into three groups. *Intuitions* (*Anschauungen*, singular *Anschauung*, paired by Kant with the Latin word *intuitus* [A 320/B 377]) are singular representations that stand in an immediate relation to the objects they represent (A 320/B 377). *Concepts* (*Begriffe*, singular *Begriff*, paired by Kant with the Latin *conceptus* [A 320/B 377]) are general representations that relate to objects mediately, through "marks" or characteristics that can be shared by many things (A 320/B 377; see also A 19/B 33). (*Concept* or *Begriff* is sometimes applied more widely, to singular intuitions as well as to general concepts, but I will use "concept" only in the strict sense.) *Ideas* (*Ideen*, singular *Idee*, traced by Kant directly to Plato [A 313/ B 370]) are concepts that go "beyond the possibility of experience" (A 320/B 377) – meaning that they (or their objects) cannot even be *exhibited* in experience. "No appearance can be found," Kant writes, "in which [ideas] may be represented *in concreto*" – in the concrete, as

---

[9] John Locke, *De intellectu humano*, translated by G. H. Thiele (Leipzig: T. Georgi, 1741).

[10] Berkeley also claims that we have notions rather than ideas of relations, because all relations include "an act of the mind" (*Principles* 142). Kant's contemporary, J. N. Tetens, who was viewed by Kant as an empiricist (*Reflexionen* 18: 23), argues similarly that because a relation is "a superadded effect of the power of thought" [*eine hinzukommende Wirkung der Denkkraft*], its concept is not the effect of our power of representation [*vorstellenden Kraft*] (*Philosophische Versuche über die menschliche Natur und ihre Entwickelung*, two volumes (Leipzig: M. G. Weidmanns Erben und Reich, 1777), 1: 337).

realities in space and time (A 567/B 595). Intuitions are associated with *sense* or the mind's receptivity (A 19/B 33; A 51/B 75); concepts with the *understanding* or the mind's spontaneity (A 51–2/B 75–6); and ideas with *reason*. Ideas of reason include what Kant calls *ideals*. An ideal is an idea *"in individuo"* – an idea (or object) considered "as an individual thing" (A 568/B 596). There is, according to Kant, only "one single genuine ideal of which human reason is capable" (A 576/B 604), the idea of God. As the representation of an individual, the idea of God is in one way like an intuition, but unlike an intuition, the representation of God is not immediately related to its object. It represents God through its constituent concepts.[11]

This chapter will be confined to general concepts of the understanding. I will call them not only *concepts* but *ideas* and *conceptions*. The British empiricists sometimes use "conception" as a substitute for "idea," but I will understand a conception to be an idea that incorporates or conveys a certain degree of understanding – the kind of understanding we have when we appreciate the meaning of a word. When the characteristic claims of empiricism are applied to conceptions, they are, I think, more interesting and profound than they are when applied to ideas in Locke's broad sense. Are there, for example, "ideas" that take rise from experience alone? If ideas include brute sensations, as they do for Locke and Berkeley, I see no particular reason to deny it. But if conceptions are in question, a yes answer is more arresting – and more debatable. If a question is asked about conceptions, Locke, Hume, and Kant may all want to answer no. But they have different ways of arriving at this common answer.

In the 1757 German translation of Locke's *Essay*, the word "idea" is generally translated as *Begriff* (Kant's word for "concept") – a more appropriate choice than *Idee*, as the translator explains in a footnote, for what Locke has in mind.[12] *Begriff* is one of several words used for "idea" by J. C. Eschenbach in his 1756 German translation of Berkeley's *Three Dialogues*.[13] It is also the word used to translate "idea" in the

---

[11] See A 571–90/B 599–618 for Kant's elaborate construction of the idea of God, which differs markedly from the more streamlined empiricist constructions at *Essay* 2.23.33–5 and *Enquiry* 2.6.

[12] See the index under "Idee" and the explanatory footnote on p. 9 in *Herrn Johann Lockens Versuch vom Menschlichen Verstande* (Altenburg: Richter, 1757). From time to time, the word "idea" is translated as *Idee*, notably in passages where Locke is calling attention to the word itself.

[13] Johann Christian Eschenbach, *Sammlung der vornehmsten Schriftsteller die die Würklichkeit ihres Eignenkörpers und der ganzen Körperwelt Läugnen* (Rostock: A. F. Rose, 1756); Eschenbach also translates "idea" as *Gedanke* (or "thought") and *Vorstellung* ("representation").

1755 German translation of Hume's *Enquiry*.[14] When Kant speaks of representations (*Vorstellungen*) and concepts (*Begriffe*), then, he inserts himself into a discursive space already occupied by the empiricists.

3. THE ORIGIN AND CONTENT OF CONCEPTIONS; LOCKE AND EMPIRICAL DEDUCTION

The closing chapter of the *Critique*, "The History of Pure Reason," is the shortest one in the book, a placeholder for an amplified and properly documented history of reason's progress. Kant describes the chapter as a "cursory outline" of the disagreements behind "the most notable changes" or "revolutions" on the stage of conflict I described as I began (A 853/B 881). I will begin this section by explaining one of those disagreements. It concerns "**the origin** of pure cognitions of reason, whether they are derived from experience or, independent of it, have their source in reason" (A 854/B 882). "Empiricists" give the first answer; opposed to them are the "noologists," who give the second.

Empiricism is a stream with several cooperating currents. One is a tendency to trace the origin of conceptions to experience. I call this *origin-empiricism*. On the opening page of the Introduction to the second edition of the *Critique*, Kant accepts origin-empiricism in what might be called its *temporal interpretation*:

There is no doubt whatever that all our cognition begins with experience; for how else should the cognitive faculty be awakened into exercise if not through objects that stimulate our senses and in part themselves produce representations, in part bring the activity of our understanding into motion to compare these, to connect or separate them, and thus to work up the raw material of sensible impressions into a cognition of objects that is called experience? **As far as time is concerned**, then, no cognition in us precedes experience, and with experience every cognition begins. (B 1)

Temporally interpreted, origin-empiricism is the claim that experience always comes before the having of conceptions. This is one of the points made by Kant's repeated insistence, in works early and late, that there are no innate representations. For Kant, the word "innate" always

---

[14] *Philosophische Versuche über die menschliche erkenntnis von David Hume*, translated by J. G. Sulzer (Hamburg and Leipzig: G. C. Grund and A. H. Holle, 1755), and included among Kant's books (Arthur Warda, *Immanuel Kants Bücher* [Berlin: Martin Breslauer, 1922], p. 50). Moses Mendelssohn, writing a year after its publication, reports that "the German translation of this work is in everyone's hands" ("On Probability," p. 241 in *Philosophical Writings*, translated by Daniel O. Dahlstrom [Cambridge: Cambridge University Press, 1997]).

carries a contrast with "acquired"; he never wavers in his conviction that all representations, and in particular all conceptions, are acquired in time.[15] A more difficult question, raised directly by Kant as the passage from B 1 continues, is whether all of our conceptions are *caused* or *explained* by the experience they follow.[16] "Although all our cognition commences **with** experience," Kant cautions, "yet it does not on that account all arise **from** experience" (B 1). Here Kant is questioning whether origin-empiricism is true on what I will call its *causal interpretation*, and from now on it will be this causal interpretation, rather than the temporal one, that I will have in mind.

To accept origin-empiricism in its causal interpretation is to accept what John Campbell calls "the explanatory role of experience," according to which conceptions "are made available by our experience of the world."[17] This is not to say, as Campbell observes, that experience is "the only thing that has a role to play"; it is to say, more modestly, that it plays "some role."[18] But we can imagine a *radical* origin-empiricism that makes the more extreme claim.

[15] For a selection of passages that either reject innate representations or oppose them to acquired ones, see *Inaugural Dissertation* 2: 401 and 405; *Prolegomena* 4: 330; *On a Discovery* 8: 221, where Kant reports that "the *Critique* admits absolutely no implanted or innate *representations*," but "considers them [all] as *acquired*"; *On a Discovery* 8: 249; *Metaphysik L* 28: 33; *Metaphysik L₂* 28: 542; *Metaphysik Vigilantius* 29: 949 and 951; *Metaphysik Mrongovius* 29: 763; *Reflexionen* 4851 and 5637 (18: 8 and 275); and the letter to Kosman of September 1789 (10: 82). Although he rejects innate representations, Kant acknowledges that the mind has a wide range of innate powers. He describes the Transcendental Analytic as following the pure concepts back to "their first seeds and predispositions in the human understanding, where they lie ready, until with the opportunity of experience they are finally developed and exhibited in their clarity by the very same understanding" (A 66/B 91). The seed metaphor, which Kant repeats in the *Prolegomena* (4: 274), was a common nativist device, with deep roots in antiquity; Kant could have encountered it in Descartes or Leibniz. For a less metaphorical treatment of what he there calls the innate "ground" of pure representations and their "original" acquisition, see *On a Discovery* 8: 221–3.

[16] Even in the case of pure concepts, Kant writes, "we can search in experience, if not for the principle of their possibility, then for the occasional causes of their generation, where the impressions of the senses provide the first occasion for opening the entire power of cognition to them" (A 86/B 118).

[17] See John Campbell, "Berkeley's Puzzle," p. 128 in Tamar Gendler and John Hawthorne (eds.), *Conceivability and Possibility* (Oxford: Clarendon Press, 2002), pp. 127–43.

[18] See John Campbell, "Reply to Rey," *Philosophical Studies* 126 (2005), pp. 155–62, p. 162.

There are two aspects to the having of a conception: the very having of a conception, an aspect that all acts of conception have in common; and the content that differentiates one conception from another. According to origin-empiricism, experience is at least partly responsible for both. A second empiricist current is *content-empiricism*, the view that the content of any conception can be expressed, at least in part, in experiential terms.[19] Consider the following passage, where Berkeley explains what it means to say that a physical object *exists*:

> The table I write on, I say, exists, that is, I see and feel it; and if I were out of my study I should say it existed, meaning thereby that if I was in my study I might perceive it, or that some other spirit actually does perceive. There was an odour, that is, it was smelled; there was a sound, that is to say, it was heard; a colour or figure, and it was perceived by sight or touch. This is all that I can understand by these and the like expressions. For as to what is said of the absolute existence of unthinking things without any relation to their being perceived, that seems perfectly unintelligible. (*Principles* 3)

Origin-empiricism is a backward-looking view: it points to a cause from which a conception is thought to derive. Berkeley, in the quoted passage, is looking forward: assuming that the content of a conception lies in the difference it makes to the thoughts in which it figures, he tells us that the content of any existential thought regarding unthinking things can be spelled out, at least in part, in terms of the experiences we would have if the thought were true. At its most radical, content-empiricism is the view that the content of a conception is *exhausted* by its implications for experience.

---

[19] This is close to what Jonathan Bennett calls "concept-empiricism" or "meaning-empiricism" (*Kant's Dialectic* [Cambridge: Cambridge University Press, 1974], p. 27). Bennett writes that "Kant holds that a statement's meaning is a function of what it implies for actual and possible experience, and that a statement which has no such implications, no empirical cash value, means nothing." As an interpretation of Kant, this obviously goes too far – it seems to rob *God exists, I am transcendentally free*, and *I am immortal* of the meaning they must have if Kant is to succeed in his project of denying knowledge to make room for faith – but its first clause is a fair statement of a radical content-empiricism. The second clause in Bennett's statement is similar to the "principle of significance" that P. F. Strawson attributes to Kant. According to that principle, "there can be no legitimate, or even meaningful, employment of ideas or concepts that does not relate them to empirical or experiential conditions of their application" (*The Bounds of Sense* [London: Methuen, 1966], p. 16). As Strawson observes, this principle "is one with which empiricist philosophers have no difficulty in sympathizing" (p. 16). Like Bennett's concept-empiricism, it seems to rule out many claims that Kant regards as meaningful, a point Strawson considers, for example, on pp. 264–5.

Because origin-empiricism is a view about what causes content, and content-empiricism a view about the very nature of content, they are not the same.[20] But many philosophers suppose that to the extent experience accounts for content, that content must be articulable in experiential terms. The step from origin-empiricism to content-empiricism will seem especially compelling to anyone who accepts what might be called a "strong" conception of causation, according to which a cause explains its effect by making it intelligible. Descartes's doctrine that a cause must contain at least as much reality as its effect is the expression of a strong conception. If the effect contained more reality than the cause, the surplus reality of the effect would (Descartes fears) be unintelligible. Imagine now that we are origin-empiricists with regard to some conception. In that case, we believe that the content of a conception is to some extent caused by experience. Suppose further that we hold to a strong conception of causation. If we go on to deny content-empiricism – if we refuse to grant that the content caused by experience can be spelled out, to a corresponding extent, in the language of experience – it begins to look as if our candidate cause falls short of its alleged effect. For if the content possessed by the effect cannot be expressed in experiential terms, how can experience make it intelligible that the effect has that content? There will be an explanatory gap between the experience and whatever portion of a conception's content overflows the vocabulary of experience. The strong conception is relevant to empiricism because Locke for one seems to accept it, and Hume, though he officially denies it (advocating instead a conception of causation according to which even the richest conception, considered in itself, could be caused by absolutely anything, even by a puff of smoke that is altogether "content-free"), continues to rely on it – or so it seems to me – in his confidence that ideas are always caused by impressions that resemble them. I believe that a strong conception is also embraced by Kant; it leads him to conclude that to the extent a conception is caused by experience, its content cannot reach beyond experience.

Now the disagreement Kant describes between empiricists and noologists is, as he says, a disagreement concerning the origins of the "pure cognitions of reason." A "pure cognition of reason" is a representation destined for use in what Kant calls synthetic *a priori* judgments. Synthetic judgments are opposed to analytic ones:[21]

---

[20] Another reason they are not the same: there is no reason why conceptions with empirically articulable content could not sometimes be innate.

[21] Kant finds "a hint" of the distinction between analytic and synthetic judgments in Locke's remarks on affirmations of identity or diversity,

In all judgments in which the relation of a subject to the predicate is thought …
this relation is possible in two different ways. Either the predicate *B* belongs to
the subject *A* as something that is (covertly) contained in this concept *A*; or *B* lies
entirely outside the concept *A*, though to be sure it stands in connection with it.
In the first case I call the judgment **analytic**, in the second **synthetic**. (A 6–7/B 10)

A priori judgments are opposed to judgments that are empirical or
a posteriori: *a posteriori* judgments can be justified by experience,
while *a priori* judgments can only be justified by other means. The
marks of an *a priori* judgment are necessity and strict universality, as
Kant explains in the following passage:

Experience teaches us, to be sure, that something is constituted thus and so, but
not that it could not be otherwise. **First**, then, if a proposition is thought along
with its **necessity**, it is an *a priori* judgment; if it is, moreover, also not derived
from any proposition except one that in turn is valid as a necessary proposition,
then it is absolutely *a priori*. **Second**: Experience never gives its judgments true
or strict but only assumed and comparative **universality** (through induction), so
properly it must be said: as far as we have yet perceived, there is no exception to
this or that rule. Thus if a judgment is thought in strict universality, i.e., in such
a way that no exception at all is allowed to be possible, then it is not derived from
experience, but is rather valid absolutely *a priori*. … Necessity and strict universality are therefore secure indications of an *a priori* cognition, and also belong
together inseparably. (B 3–4)

In the view of the empiricist party to the disagreement described at
A 854/B 882, pure conceptions can be derived from an empirical or
"impure" source. This may look like a direct contradiction.[22] But it
is, perhaps, not a *direct* contradiction to suggest that a conception with
empirical origins, after being "elevated" by generalization or abstraction (29: 958–9), can figure in an *a priori* – or even synthetic *a priori* –
truth.

Kant's account of the disagreement between empiricists and noologists continues as follows:

Aristotle can be regarded as the head of the **empiricists**, Plato that of the **noologists**. Locke, who in recent times followed the former, and Leibniz, who

> such as *white is white*, or *white is not black*, and affirmations of
> coexistence, such as *gold dissolves in aqua regia* (*Prolegomena* 4: 270,
> where Kant refers to *Essay* 4.3.9 and following; see also *Reflexionen* 3738,
> 17: 278).

[22] And in his *Lectures on Metaphysics* (29: 958–9), Kant seems to say that it
is. But here, Kant (or his student note taker) papers over the crucial
distinction between judgments and the conceptions entering into them.
For remarks on Locke (and Hume) more attentive to this distinction, see A
95/B 127–8 (which should be read in conjunction with A 854/B 882).

followed the latter (although with sufficient distance from his mystical system), have nevertheless not been able to bring this dispute to any decision.[23]

Here Kant alludes to Leibniz's *New Essays on Human Understanding*, a commentary on Locke's *Essay*, in the form of a dialogue between Philalethes, a spokesman for Locke, and Theophilus, a spokesman for Leibniz. The *New Essays*, largely completed before Locke's death in 1704, were published only in 1765, decades after Leibniz's death, in the middle of Kant's own early career as a writer. Locke and Leibniz may have been distant figures, but for Kant and his German contemporaries, their voices were still resounding. "Although the author of the *Essay* says hundreds of fine things which I applaud," Leibniz writes of Locke in the Preface, "our systems are very different. His is closer to Aristotle and mine to Plato."[24] "Our disagreements," he continues,

concern points of some importance. There is the question whether the soul in itself is completely blank like a writing tablet on which nothing has as yet been written – a *tabula rasa* – as Aristotle and the author of the *Essay* maintain, and whether everything which is inscribed there comes solely from the senses and experience; or whether the soul inherently contains the sources of various notions and doctrines, which external objects merely rouse up on suitable occasions, as I believe and as do Plato and even the Schoolmen.

The dispute between Locke and Leibniz was an important landmark for Kant.[25] In Kant's view, Leibniz had succeeded in refuting Locke. As Kant writes in *On a Discovery*, p. 303, "Leibniz wanted to refute the empiricism of Locke. For this purpose examples taken from mathematics were well suited to prove such cognitions reach much further than empirically acquired concepts could do, and thereby to defend the *a priori* origin of the former against Locke's attacks."[26] Here, I think, Kant is

---

[23] *Critique*, A 854/B 882.
[24] I quote from the Preface in the translation by Peter Remnant and Jonathan Bennett, pp. 47–9.
[25] For evidence of the importance of the *New Essays* in Kant's eyes, see *Prolegomena* 4: 25, where Kant, in taking the measure of Hume's historical importance, refers to "the Essays of Locke and Leibniz." The *New Essays* was also an important landmark for Kant's contemporary Tetens; see his *Philosophische Versuche*, 1: 337 and 398. For a study of the early German reception of the *New Essays*, see Giorgio Tonelli, "Leibniz on Innate Ideas and the Early Reactions to the Publication of the *Nouveaux Essais* (1765)," *Journal of the History of Philosophy* 12 (1974), pp. 437–54.
[26] Leibniz appeals to the necessity of mathematical truths at many points in the *New Essays*, for example in the Preface, p. 50. In *Reflexionen* 5637 (18: 273), Kant writes that in view of the *a priori* character of mathematical cognition, "Locke, who earned almost too much honor after Leibniz had already refuted him, falls by the wayside."

reasoning as follows: the truths of mathematics are synthetic *a priori*; this is possible only if the content of their constituent conceptions reaches beyond experience; but their content can reach beyond experience only if the conceptions themselves do not originate in experience.[27] Leibniz may have refuted Locke, but he did not, in Kant's view, show where Locke went wrong. Nor did he give Locke's method the credit that in Kant's view it deserved.

Locke's *Essay* had, for Kant, been full of promise for metaphysics. "Once in recent times," he writes in the Preface to the first edition of the *Critique*, "it ... seemed as though an end would be put to all ... [metaphysical] controversies, and the lawfulness of all the competing claims would be completely decided, through a certain **physiology** of the human understanding (by the famous Locke)" (A ix). Kant is using the word "physiology" in a now-archaic sense that was familiar in the seventeenth and eighteenth centuries: the "physiology" of a thing was a study of its nature, often (but by no means always) an *empirical* study of its nature, of the sort announced in the title of Robert Boyle's *Certain Physiological Essays*.[28] Kant's admiration for the "physiology" of the *Essay* suggests that deriving ideas or concepts from experience was, for Kant, a way of credentializing them: a strategy for documenting their legitimacy. If this is correct, Kant was conceiving of Lockean "physiology" not only as an origin-empiricism, but as a content-empiricism: an empiricism that would give metaphysical terms an agreed-upon content or meaning, allowing metaphysical disagreements to be lawfully and peacefully resolved.

In other passages in the *Critique*, however, Kant holds the credentializing potential of Lockean physiology at arm's length, for example in a well-known passage that begins a long account of what Kant calls "deduction," comparing it to attempts to establish a legal entitlement:

Jurists, when they speak of entitlements and claims, distinguish in a legal matter between the questions about what is lawful (*quid juris*) and that which concerns the fact (*quid facti*), and since they demand proof of both, they call the

---

[27] For Kant, the origin of conceptions has justificatory bearing: a synthetic judgment can be justified *a priori* only if at least some of its constituent concepts are pure (*What real progress has metaphysics made?* 20: 346). By contrast, analytic judgments can be justified *a priori* even if all of their concepts are empirical. For further discussion, see *What real progress*, 20: 329, on "the despotism of empiricism."

[28] London: Henry Herringman, 1661. Kant's understanding of "physiology" is made explicit at A 845/B 873 and following, where it is identified with "the doctrine of nature." See also A 347/B 405, *Prolegomena* 4: 306, and *Metaphysik Mrongovius* 29: 764.

first, that which is to establish the entitlement of the legal claim, the **deduction**. We make use of a multitude of empirical concepts without objection from anyone, and take ourselves to be justified in granting them a sense [*Sinn*] and supposed signification [*Bedeutung*] even without any deduction, because we always have experience ready at hand to prove their objective reality. But there are also concepts that have been usurped, such as **fortune** and **fate**, which circulate with almost universal indulgence, but that are occasionally called upon to establish their claim by the question *quid juris*, and then there is not a little embarrassment about their deduction because one can adduce no clear legal ground for an entitlement to their use either from experience or from reason. (A 84–5/B 116–17; a *quid juris* is a question of right; a *quid facti* a question of fact.)

Present-day banks perform a task akin to deduction when they complete what nervous borrowers call a "title search." The search "clears" or establishes the title by showing that the present owner has an unencumbered right to sell the property. As the quoted passage concludes, Kant seems to distinguish between two kinds of deduction, one "from experience" and another "from reason." For some empirical concepts – but, I assume, only for some – labored deductions from experience are, it seems, unnecessary, because as Kant says, "we always have experience ready at hand to prove their objective reality." A quick glance is all it takes, it seems, to prove that my dog is really possible: my dog stands loyally "at hand," her evident existence testifying to her possibility. To prove a concept's objective reality is to prove that it has an object, or, more precisely, a *possible* object.[29] To be possible in the relevant sense,

---

[29] See, for example, *On a discovery* 8: 191, where the objective reality of a concept is equated with "the possibility that a thing with these properties can be given." An object that can be given is more than logically possible. Passages from the *Critique* conveying the same understanding include B 148 and B 194/A 155. When an object can be given "in some way," Kant explains in the latter passage, its concept has "significance and sense." For other passages along these lines, see A 156/B 195; B 268/A 220; B 288 and B 308, as well as *Metaphysik Vigilantius* 966–7 and 971. Kant's notion of objective reality is closely related to the traditional conception of a *real definition*. As Theophilus, Leibniz's representative, explains in the *New Essays*, the difference between real and merely nominal definitons "is that the real definition displays the possibility of the definiendum and the nominal does not" (p. 295 in the Remnant and Bennett translation). Kant himself writes that "a real definition would ... be that which does not merely make distinct a concept but at the same time its **objective reality**" (A 242). Objective reality also has close ties to the notion of *cognition*. "To **cognize** an object," Kant writes at B xxvi, "it is required that I be able to prove its possibility (whether by the testimony of experience from its actuality or *a priori* through reason)." "I can **think** whatever

the object must be more than logically possible or contradiction-free; it must, as Kant says, be *really* possible. When the object of a concept is really possible, the concept can enter into synthetic judgments whose truth or falsehood we can (at least in principle) determine. The real possibility of its object lends the corresponding concept (along, we can assume, with the attendant term) not only objective reality, but what the passage calls "sense" [*Sinn*] and "signification" [*Bedeutung*] or "significance." For Kant, "sense" or "significance" is not what we call "meaning"; it is, as he later explains, "objective significance," the signification of a possible object (A 197/B 242; A 240/B 299; B 302–3). Doubts about the sense or significance of the representation of my dog can, then, be quickly laid to rest, without the labor of deduction. All we need to do is look and see.

A deduction "from experience," or what Kant goes on to call an "empirical deduction," presumably calls for more than a quick inspection at what lies near at hand. It calls for reflective work, because it is an attempt to trace the origination of a concept that is itself the product of reflective work, as Kant indicates when he describes an empirical deduction as one showing "how a concept is acquired through experience *and reflection on it*" (A 85/B 117, my emphasis). In Locke's *Essay*, "reflection" generally functions as a label for the mind's notice of its own states and operations, but Kant is using it here, as he does elsewhere in the *Critique*,[30] to stand for the various operations by which the mind forms new concepts or ideas out of those that experience offers to it.[31] The mind "reflects" on the ideas it

I like," he continues, "as long as I do not contradict myself, i.e., as long as my concept is a possible thought, even if I cannot give any assurance whether or not there is a corresponding object somewhere within the sum total of all possibilities. But in order to ascribe objective validity to such a concept (real possibility, for the first sort of possibility was merely logical) something more is required" (B xxvi). Here "objective validity" [*objective Gültigkeit*] is serving as a synonym for "objective reality" [*objective Realität*]; elsewhere Kant distinguishes between them, as I will explain later.

30 For example, when Kant writes that "Locke totally **sensitivized** the concepts of understanding in accordance with his system of noogony (if I am permitted this expression), i.e., interpreted them as nothing but empirical or abstracted concepts of reflection" (A 271/B 327), he takes a concept "of reflection" to be one we arrive at by *reflecting and operating upon ideas*.

31 For an illuminating account of Kantian reflection, with very helpful comparisons to Locke, see Béatrice Longuenesse, *Kant and the Capacity to Judge: Sensibility and Discursivity in Kant's* Critique of Pure Reason, translated by Charles T. Wolfe (Princeton: Princeton University Press, 1998), pp. 111–27.

is given – gathers them up, so to speak – and then does something with them, its operations upon them also falling under "reflection" as I believe Kant understands it here. For Locke, these operations include discerning, combining, comparing, abstracting, and compounding (see *Essay* 2.12). When Kant writes that "a tracing of the first endeavors of our power of cognition to ascend from individual perceptions to general concepts is without doubt of great utility, and the famous Locke is to be thanked for having first opened the way for this" (A 86/B 119), it must be the Lockean operations of discerning, comparing, combining, abstracting, and compounding – or the mind's orchestration of these operations – that he has in mind. When Kant commends Locke, then, for opening the way for the empirical deduction or derivation of general concepts, he is presumably thinking of passages from the *Essay* such as the following:

The same Colour being observed to day in Chalk or Snow, which the Mind yesterday received from Milk, it considers that Appearance alone, makes it a representative of all of that kind; and having given it the name *Whiteness*, it by that sound signifies the same quality wheresoever to be imagin'd or met with; and thus Universals, whether *Ideas* or Terms, are made. (*Essay* 2.11.9)

This passage recounts a reflective task, one involving discerning, comparing, and abstracting, but is it responsive to the *quid juris*? Does it show, as Locke himself surely believes, that the concept *whiteness* is legitimate and its name indisputably significant? The question is even more pressing when compounding is involved. The idea of *dog*, as Locke repeatedly emphasizes, is our own workmanship (3.3.13, 3.6.37). But if it is "*made by the Mind*" (3.6.26), what right do we have to suppose it is (as Kant would say) objectively real?

Before we consider Kant's answer, I want to pause to note that in Kant's view, Locke cannot perhaps count as a radical origin-empiricist, simply because of his appeals to operations such as compounding.[32] In *What Real Progress Has Metaphysics Made in Germany?* Kant writes that "since compounding cannot fall under the senses, but has to be performed by ourselves, it belongs, not to the receptive nature of sensibility, but to the spontaneity of the understanding" (20: 275–6).[33] He

---

[32] For a more ambitious argument along these general lines, see Wayne Waxman, *Kant and the Empiricists: Understanding Understanding* (New York: Oxford University Press, 2005), pp. 167–73.

[33] See also the September 1789 letter to Kosmann, where Kant describes "a psychological deduction of our representations," in which they are regarded "as effects which have their cause in the mind where they are linked with other things" (10: 81–2, p. 321 in *Correspondence*).

makes the point only about compounding, but it applies no less tellingly to discerning, comparing, and abstracting, and it can be extended from Locke to Hume, who appeals to most of the same operations. For Locke, discerning, comparing, abstracting, and compounding all contribute to conceptual content, though it does not follow that these operations can endow a conception otherwise caused by experience with a content that reaches beyond it.

We can now return to our question: can a Lockean deduction answer the *quid juris*? As Kant proceeds to develop the analogy between philosophical and legal deduction, he seems to answer no:

Among the many concepts, however, that constitute the very mixed fabric of human cognition, there are some that are also destined for pure use *a priori* (completely independently of all experience), and these always require a deduction of their entitlement, since proofs from experience are not sufficient for the lawfulness of such a use, and yet one must know how these concepts can be related to objects that they do not derive from any experience. I therefore call the explanation of the way in which concepts can relate to objects *a priori* their **transcendental deduction**, and distinguish this from the **empirical deduction**, which shows how a concept is acquired through experience and reflection on it, and therefore concerns not the lawfulness but the fact from which the possession has arisen. (A 85/B 117)

A concept "destined for pure use *a priori*" is, as I have already suggested, one that figures in synthetic *a priori* truths. Kant *could* be speaking only of empirical deductions of concepts "destined for pure use *a priori*," in which case the passage would not be denying that empirical deductions of concepts with another, more modest destiny, such as *whiteness* or *dog*, are apt responses to the *quid juris*. But as the passage develops, it seems to be moving toward the broader point that Lockean deduction, though it can explain possession, can never establish right, even when the concept being examined is empirical:

Nevertheless, in the case of these concepts [with a pure use *a priori*], *as in the case of all cognition* [my emphasis], we can search in experience, if not for the principle of their possibility, then for the occasional causes of their generation, where the impressions of the senses provide the first occasion for opening the entire power of cognition to them and for bringing about experience. (A 86/B 118)

This sentence, which recalls Kant's observation that "although all our cognition commences **with** experience, yet it does not on that account all arise **from** experience" (B 1), comes shortly before Kant's tribute to Locke's pathbreaking "tracings." It is packed with allusions to earlier philosophy. The reference to the causes of a thing's "generation" recalls the scholastic distinction between the cause of a thing's very being and the less exalted cause of its coming to be. My parents, for example, are the causes of my coming to be, but they are not the originating and sustaining causes of my being, a role the scholastic philosophers reserved for God. An "occasional" cause is not a true or efficacious cause (though it is, according to occasionalist philosophers such as Malebranche, regularly mistaken for one), but a mere occasion on which the true cause (God again) exerts his power. Kant thereby places experience at two removes from the principle, whatever it may be, that is genuinely responsible for the content of conceptions. After commending Locke's pathbreaking efforts, Kant writes that

a **deduction** of the pure *a priori* concepts can never be achieved in ... [Locke's] way; it does not lie down this path at all, for in regard to their future use, which should be entirely independent of experience, an entirely different birth certificate than that of an ancestry from experience must be produced. I will therefore call this attempted physiological derivation, which cannot properly be called a deduction at all because it concerns a *quaestio facti*, the explanation of the **possession** of a pure cognition. It is therefore clear that only a transcendental and never an empirical deduction of them can be given, and that in regard to pure *a priori* concepts empirical deductions are nothing but idle attempts, which can occupy only those who have not grasped the entirely distinctive nature of these cognitions. (A 86–7/B 119)

Here Kant seems to be saying only that empirical deduction cannot answer the *quid juris* when it is raised with respect to concepts destined for "pure use." But he eventually concludes, I think, that no concept, not even the humblest empirical concept, can be certified – not, at least, in a fully satisfying way – by the means Locke makes available. Kant thinks it is a mistake to infer that a concept can be derived from experience from the bare fact that we encounter it in experience (A 94–5/B 126–7). Locke succumbs to what might be called the temptation of empiricism: to suppose that the content of a conception is explained by experience, or that its content is simply a matter of experience, because possession of the concept follows an experience in which the concept, or its object, seems to be present.

Two steps are required to reach the conclusion that no concept, not even an ordinary empirical concept, can be ratified by empirical deduction. One is an argument that the objective reality of empirical concepts depends on the objective reality of pure concepts. The other is an argument that the objective reality of pure concepts can never be established by empirical deduction. I will discuss the second step first; it was Hume who alerted Kant to its importance, interrupting his "dogmatic slumber" and giving "a completely new direction" to his research (*Prolegomena* 4: 260).

4. HUME AND THE TASK OF TRANSCENDENTAL DEDUCTION

I begin with a distinction that Kant does not make himself – between empirical *deduction* and empirical *derivation*.[34] In empirical *derivation*, an ordinary thinking subject derives an idea or conception from experience, perhaps by means of the Lockean operations I considered in the last section. Empirical *deduction* is the work of a philosopher who self-consciously re-enacts that derivation, and does so with an ulterior speculative motive – perhaps the motive of responding to the *quid juris*. An ordinary person has no special motive for deriving concepts from experience; when minds are making their way in the world, deriving concepts from experience is simply what they do. Ordinary derivation is, undeniably, at times a reflective activity, calling upon the mind's powers of recall, discernment, comparison, abstraction, and composition, but philosophical deduction is *doubly* reflective. It is a second-order activity in which a philosopher, with a theoretical aim in view, traces the process by which ordinary thinking subjects (including the theoretician, in his or her ordinary moments) arrive at their ideas. Locke and Hume agree that conceptions are empirically derived; when they reflect on the ordinary process of derivation, whether to explain how conceptions are arrived at or to settle doubts about their objective reality or content, they are engaged in the task of deduction. Empirical derivation and empirical deduction differ in their outcomes. The outcome of an empirical derivation is an idea or conception. The outcome of an empirical deduction – the outcome hoped for, at least – is a reassuring answer to the *quid juris*: good reason to believe that the conception in question is objectively real.

When Hume, then, traces ideas to resembling impressions, he is engaged in an empirical deduction that reproduces an earlier (or, perhaps, plots out a potential future) empirical derivation. His deductions have an ulterior motive: "by bringing ideas into so clear a light," he writes, "we may reasonably hope to remove all dispute, which may arise, concerning their nature and reality" (*Enquiry* 2.9; SBN 22). For Hume, to trace an idea to a resembling impression is to confirm what Kant calls its "sense and significance"; to quiet doubts concerning its "nature and reality" is to prove that it is, as Kant would say, objectively real. Impressions, for Hume, are the stuff of experience:

---

[34] For Kant, "empirical deduction" [*empirische Deduktion* (A 85/B 118)] and "empirical derivation" [*empirische Ableitung* (A 95/B 12)] seem to be alternate labels for the same activity.

the deliverances of "outward or inward sentiment" (*Enquiry* 2.5; SBN 19). They are the lively perceptions we have "when we hear, or see, or feel, or love, or hate, or desire, or will" (*Enquiry* 2.3: SBN 18). Because "all our ideas or more feeble perceptions are copies of our impressions or more lively ones" (2.5; SBN 19), we can expose a term as lacking "meaning or idea" by showing that there is no impression from which it has been (or could ever be) derived. But what about the derivation itself? If it is wrongly conducted, that will deal as costly a blow to a pretended idea as the absence of a founding impression. It seems important, then, for philosophers engaged in deduction to lay down rules for the conduct of derivations, and to show us that those rules, and the routines they define, are deserving of our trust. The success of any derivation depends not only on the raw materials but on the means, and we must be attentive to both.

But Hume's account of derivation is disappointingly casual. He seems to promise some strictness when he writes that although our thought seems, at first, "to possess ... unbounded liberty," it is "really confined within very narrow limits, and ... all this creative power of the mind amounts to no more than the faculty of compounding, transposing, augmenting, or diminishing the materials afforded us by the senses and experience" (*Enquiry* 2.5; SBN 19). But Hume leaves us wondering whether compounding, transposing, augmenting, and diminishing are operations that preserve objective reality. "When we think of a golden mountain," Hume writes, "we only join two consistent ideas, *gold*, and *mountain*, with which we were formerly acquainted. A virtuous horse we can conceive; because, from our own feeling, we can conceive virtue; and this we may unite to the figure and shape of a horse, which is an animal familiar to us" (2.5; SBN 19). Here Hume puts forward a crude account of objective reality: if the ideas or conceptions taken as input are objectively real (a fact established, I will assume for now, by bare impressions or simple experience) and at the same time mutually consistent, then any idea or conception compounded out of them will also be objectively real. This *seems* innocent enough, but it really tells us very little about the operation of compounding. I do not want to linger over this, however. I want instead to consider Hume's proudest attempt at an empirical deduction: his deduction of the concept *cause*. Here a new and potentially more disturbing operation plays a central role.

The concept of *cause* is the subject of *Enquiry* 4 and 7. Hume believes that it is part of the concept that a cause is necessarily connected with its effect (*Enquiry* 7.26–30 [SBN 73–8] and 8.25 [SBN 95–6] and even more explicitly at *Treatise* 1.3.2.11 [SBN 77]). This is a point with which Kant wholeheartedly agrees, for example at A 112, where he writes that "the concept of a cause brings the trait of necessity with it" (see also B 5). To clarify the concept of *cause*, then, Hume must clarify the concept of *necessary connection*. Unfortunately, "there are no ideas, which occur in metaphysics, more obscure and uncertain, than those of *power, force, energy,* or *necessary connexion*" (7.3; SBN 61–2). Reason alone cannot be the source of our idea of *cause* or *power* (7.8; SBN 64; see also T 1.3.3 and 1.3.14.5 [SBN 157]). "*Causes and effects are discoverable,*" after all, "*not by reason, but by experience*" (4.7; SBN 28). But reason or understanding can find no basis for the idea of necessary connection in our experience of things themselves. "Were the power or energy of any cause discoverable by the mind, we could foresee the effect, even without experience; and might, at first, pronounce with certainty concerning it, by the mere dint of thought and reasoning" (*Enquiry* 7.7; SBN 63). Reason or understanding, even with the assistance of experience, never enables us to foresee an effect with certainty. We therefore have no "idea of power, as it is in itself" (*Enquiry* 7.29; SBN 77). It follows, as Kant might put it, that there can be no deduction of *cause* from reason.

To "fix, if possible, [the] precise meaning" of *necessary connection*, and to "remove some part of that obscurity, which is so much complained of in this species of philosophy" (7.3; SBN 62), Hume appeals not merely to experience but also to a hitherto unrecognized operation of habit-formation and an attendant feeling:

The first time a man saw the communication of motion by impulse, as by the shock of two billiard-balls, he could not pronounce them to be *connected*; but only that it was *conjoined* with the other. After he has observed several instances of this nature, he then pronounces them to be *connected*. What alteration has happened to give rise to this new idea of *connexion*? Nothing but that he now *feels* these events to be *connected* in his imagination, and can readily foretell the existence of one from the appearance of the other. When we say, therefore, that one object is connected with another, we mean only, that they have acquired a connexion in our thought, and give rise to this inference, by which they become proofs of each other's existence. (7.28; SBN 75–6)

The operation is custom or habit, which gives rise to a "customary connexion in the thought or imagination between [an] object and its usual attendant" (7.30). We can agree, if only to advance the discussion, that the idea of *this object's following that object* is objectively real. We can even agree (again to advance the discussion) that the idea of *objects of one kind repeatedly following objects of another kind* is objectively real, even though it is a general idea. But what assurance do we have that the felt connection in our thought – or, to be more precise, the idea of that connection – is objectively real? Even if we allow that the compounding of ideas preserves objective reality, and that transposing, augmenting, and diminishing are either implicated in compounding or special forms of it, what reason is there to believe that the idea of a feeling that repeated pairings of objects trigger in us is a representation of something that can exist in the objects themselves? In the *Treatise*, Hume himself insists that we have every reason to think the opposite (1.3.14.19–28; SBN 164–9). In the *Enquiry*, he is less definite, but when he writes that "as we *feel* a customary connexion between the ideas, we transfer that feeling to the objects; as nothing is more usual than to apply to external bodies every internal sensation, which they occasion" (7.29), he seems to suggest that a process so undiscriminating cannot be trusted to supply ideas of how things themselves might be. Ideas arising in the way he describes are, he says explicitly, "inaccurate" (7.15; SBN 67), "uncertain," and "confused" (7.29; SBN 78), and as a result, the meanings of the words signifying them are "very loose" (7.29; SBN 78). So it looks as if Hume's fullest attempt at an empirical deduction either fails to deliver a yes answer to the *quid juris*, or delivers an emphatic no.

To Kant it seemed clear that Hume had substituted a feeling of expectation for what is, according to the concept of *cause*, an objective necessary connection – not a connection projected onto the cause and effect, but a connection holding between the cause and effect themselves. Hence in the *Prolegomena to Any Future Metaphysics*, Kant describes Hume as concluding that the concept of *cause* is a "bare fiction" without objective reality. Hume, he writes,

concluded that reason completely and full deceives herself with this concept, falsely taking it for her own child, when it is really nothing but a bastard of the imagination, which, impregnated by experience, and having brought certain representations under the law of association, passes off the resulting subjective necessity (i.e., habit) for an objective necessity (from insight). (4: 257–8)

If Hume gives us an empirical deduction of the concept of *cause*, it is a deduction, in Kant's view, that neither explains possession nor confers legitimacy. It does not explain the possession of "our" concept of cause, and the concept whose possession it does explain is not shown to be objectively real or legitimate. In Locke's *Essay*, empirical deduction had generally come to a happy conclusion. The concept deduced was not typically at odds with the concept awaiting deduction. Our impression of expectation or connection is itself the upshot of "experience," insofar as it arises out of experience and is itself introspectible, but it is not a matter of simple openness to the object to which it is applied. In applying it to an object, it seems that we intrude upon it. The impression is a function of *our* nature: of a necessity that is, as Kant observes, merely "subjective." If a concept is derived by custom or habit rather than "from insight," we have no reason to judge it objectively valid, and every reason to suspect that it is not.

It is important to understand the fundamental problem here: in the end, it does not lie with habit (or custom, or association) in particular, so much as with the appeal to a subjective feature of the human constitution whose objective bearing has yet to be established. Habit is, arguably at least, an "empiricist" mechanism because it is so closely attuned to experience: after repeatedly observing that thunder follows lightening, I come to expect the bang as soon as I see the flash. If such expectations had been built into the human frame – if they were "subjective predispositions for thinking, implanted in us along with our existence by our author in such a way that their use would agree exactly with the laws of nature along which experience runs" (B 167), making them what Kant goes on to describe as "a kind of **preformation-system** of pure reason" – the fundamental problem would remain. In that case, too, "all of our insight through the supposed objective validity of our judgments [would be] nothing but sheer illusion" (B 168), even though the underlying mechanism would be "nativist" rather than "empiricist."[35]

In the end, then, Kant concludes that because of its reliance on habit, Hume's empirical deduction of the concept of *cause* is not, in fact, a genuine deduction of our concept. The concept that Hume deduces from experience is not our own but another concept altogether. This verdict is delivered with greatest force in the *Critique of Practical Reason*, where Kant writes that Hume, taking the objects of experience to be things in themselves, rightly emphasized that "it cannot be seen why, because something A, is posited, something else, B, must necessarily be posited also" (5: 53). Hence "the concept was proscribed and into its place stepped custom in observation of the course of perceptions" (5: 53). The concept of cause is therefore an "illusion" according to Hume, but one that can be "excused insofar as the *custom* (a *subjective* necessity) of perceiving certain things or their determinations as often associated along with or after one another in their existence is insensibly taken for an *objective* necessity of putting such a connection in the objects themselves; and thus the concept of a cause is acquired surreptitiously and not rightfully – indeed, it can never be acquired or certified because it demands a connection in itself void,

---

[35] Although Kant's **preformation-system** of pure reason" (B 167–8) does not sound Humean to present-day ears, Kant may in fact have Hume in mind there. Kant's discussion of preformation recalls Hume's invocation of pre-established harmony at *Enquiry* 5.21.

chimerical, and untenable before reason, one to which no object can ever correspond" (5: 51). Hume, in effect, rejected the concept of cause (5: 12) because he realized (or perhaps without realizing it, showed) that it could not be *legitimately* derived from experience. Kant sums up his damning verdict in a single pregnant sentence: "Empiricism is based on a necessity *felt*, but rationalism on a necessity *seen*" (5: 13).[36] A rationalist about causation claims to see, in A or the concept of A, the inevitability of B. Hume says that B's inevitability cannot be seen in A, or in the concept of A, and so long as B and A are considered as things in themselves, Kant agrees. The only "necessity" left, for Hume, is the one we feel: the powerful expectation that B will follow A, based on the experience that it has reliably done so in the past.

It is in the light of these passages from the *Critique of Practical Reason* that we must read Kant's claim, in the *Prolegomena*, that Hume "was understood by no one" (4: 258):

One cannot, without feeling a certain pain, behold how utterly and completely his opponents, *Reid, Oswald, Beattie,* and finally *Priestley*, missed the point of his problem, and misjudged his hints for improvement – constantly taking for granted just what he doubted. ... The question was not, whether the concept of cause is right, useful, and, with respect to all cognition of nature, indispensable, for this Hume had never put in doubt; it was rather whether it is thought through reason *a priori*, and in this way has an inner truth independent of all experience ...: regarding this *Hume* awaited enlightenment. The discussion was only about the origin of this concept, not about its indispensability in use. (4: 258–9)

Hume did not doubt the indispensability of *cause*, but the concept he derived empirically was another concept altogether.

In concluding Section 2, I said that two steps were required to reach the conclusion that no empirical concept can be validated by empirical deduction. The second of those steps, to which I now turn, is the recognition that the objective reality of pure concepts can never be established by empirical deduction. Hume helped to bring Kant to this recognition and to persuade him of its importance. "I freely admit," Kant writes in the *Prolegomena*, "that the remembrance of David Hume was the very thing that many years ago first interrupted my dogmatic slumber and gave a completely different direction to my researches in the field of speculative philosophy" (4: 260). He then describes his response:

I tried first whether *Hume's* objection might not be presented in a general manner, and I soon found that the concept of the connection of cause and effect

---

[36] See also B 168, where Kant calls "subjective necessity" something "which must be felt."

is far from being the only concept through which the understanding thinks connections of things *a priori*; rather, metaphysics consists wholly of such concepts. I sought to ascertain their number, and as I had successfully attained this in the way I wished, namely from a single principle, I proceeded to the deduction of these concepts, from which I henceforth became assured that they were not, as *Hume* had feared, derived from experience, but had arisen from the pure understanding. This deduction, which appeared impossible to my sagacious predecessor, and which had never even occurred to anyone but him, even though everyone confidently made use of these concepts without asking what their objective validity is based on – this deduction, I say, was the most difficult thing that could ever be undertaken in metaphysics. (4: 260)

It is not easy to understand Kant's claim that the task of transcendental deduction "had never ... occured to anyone" but Hume. Kant's basic thought, I believe, is this: Hume was the first to search aggressively for the source of our right to believe that some A is necessarily connected to a B. He could not find that source in "pure understanding" as he understood it – that is, he could find it neither in the concepts of A and B, nor in A and B in themselves. (Here, the negative arguments of *Enquiry* 4 and 7 loom large.) Hume therefore attempted an empirical deduction of the concept, but he arrived instead at an empirical deduction of *another* concept, the concept of an A that as a matter of subjective fact, prompts expectations of a B. This was a poor substitute for the real thing. Whether or not he was aware of it, the lesson Hume taught is that a successful deduction of *cause* could be neither an empirical deduction nor a deduction "from pure understanding" *as he understood it*. It would have to be a deduction from pure reason or understanding of a radically new kind.[37] In the deductions from reason contemplated by Hume, the understanding tried to extract the concept of *cause* either from the concepts of A and B or, on the assumption that experience had acquainted it with A and B as they are in themselves, from the objects A and B. A Kantian transcendental deduction exhibits the concept of *cause* not as an element of A and B as they are in themselves, but as a necessary condition of the experience of A and B.[38] Thus Hume, of all Kant's predecessors, "came closest," as Kant says, to stating the

---

[37] For an indication that Kant takes his own deduction to be one from "pure understanding," see *Critique of Practical Reason* 5: 141.

[38] Kant says in the *Prolegomena* passage that Hume's problem can be generalized; he makes the same point in the *Critique*, where he mentions "the principle of persistence" as a principle raising the same basic problem raised by Hume (A 767/B 695; see also B 19–20 and especially B 127–8). Just as the concept of *cause* implies a necessary connection between two objects, the concept of *determination*, in Kant's view, implies a necessary connection between a determination and a substance. His main point in

general problem of pure reason, though he "did not conceive of it any-where near determinately enough and in its universality, but rather stopped with the synthetic proposition of the connection of the effect with its cause" (B 19–20).

I turn now to the remaining step toward the conclusion that no concept can be validated by empirical deduction, the argument that the objective reality of empirical concepts depends on the objective reality of pure concepts or categories. I will call this the thesis of *category-dependence*. In presenting this argument, I will be piecing together elements from Kant's Metaphysical and Transcendental Deductions.

One way of defending category-dependence would be to argue that if we analyze any empirical concept, we will find a pure concept hidden within. The concept *dog*, for example, will prove to be the concept of a *substance* with canine qualities, or the concept of an animal with a certain range of *causal powers*. Being a substance, or being a cause, will then be part of the very content of the concept *dog*. But Kant's argument does not proceed in this way. It moves indirectly from empirical concepts to pure concepts, by means of the notion of an *object*.

The argument begins with Kant's claim that all concepts are "predicates of possible judgments," (A 69/B 94), meaning that they are all capable of standing in the predicate position in judgments of the form "S is P." But concepts, as possible predicates, vary in their extension or range of application. In *all bodies are divisible*, the broader "concept of the divisible" is related to the narrower "concept of body" (Kant's own example at A 68/B 93), which can then stand in the same relation to the yet narrower concept of a metal (A 69/B 94). The concept of a metal can then serve, in turn, as the predicate in a judgment about pieces of gold. We then have a series of several judgments, whose predicates narrow in range as we descend:

All bodies are divisible.
Every metal is a body.
Every nugget of gold is a metal.

the *Prolegomena* passage is that such principles cannot be derived from concepts alone, or from objects as they are in themselves. But in *What real progress has been made in Germany since the time of Leibniz and Wolff?* Kant says that empiricism declares *all* metaphysical principles to be "a mere matter of custom" (20: 275). Yet *All change has its cause* is the only metaphysical principle Kant singles out by name there. Is he painting with too broad a brush, condemning all of "empiricism" for an appeal to custom found only in Hume? There is, in fact, a prominent appeal to custom in Locke – one that drew the disapproval of Leibniz (*New Essays* 217–18) – at *Essay* 2.23, in his account of the idea of *substance*, which may serve as another instance where empiricism turns to a "necessity felt."

Can we have a series of ever more specific predicates "all the way down"? The *Critique* contains a fascinating discussion of what Kant calls a "transcendental **law of specification**." It warns us against assuming that we have ever found a species that is "in itself the lowest" (A 655/B 683) – a species, that is, under which no lower species falls. But as Kant points out, this law "plainly does not demand an actual **infinity** in regard to the varieties of things that can become our objects" (A 656/B 684). In the end, according to Kant, our predicates will relate not only to other predicates but to objects. "Concepts, ... as predicates for possible judgments, are related to some representation of a still undetermined object" (A 69/B 94). To say that an object is undetermined is to say that it is awaiting determination by concepts. If it were not for the possibility of such objects, concepts would not have objective reality, as I defined that term earlier: their objective reality *just is* the real (and not merely logical) possibility of objects that conform to them.

It follows that for any concept to be objectively real, objects must be (really) possible. And in the Transcendental Deduction, Kant argues that no objects are really possible unless the categories apply to them. I cannot review the argument of the Deduction here. But its upshot is category-dependence: in order for an empirical concept to be objectively real, the categories must be objectively real, because if they were not, there would be no objects – no possible objects – in which the objective reality of even the most familiar concepts could be grounded. Kant states the thesis of category-dependence in many places. "If I take all thinking (through categories) away from an empirical cognition," he writes, "then no cognition of any object at all remains" (B 309). The categories contain the pure *a priori* conditions "of a possible experience and of an object of it" (A 96). They are "fundamental properties for thinking objects in general" (A 111), concepts without which "we cannot **think** any object" (B 165).

It seems, of course, that the empirical deduction of empirical concepts works perfectly well on its own. We wonder whether *dog* is objectively real, and a helpful friend simply brings a dog before us. When Kant says that the possibility of empirical concepts can be "cognized *a posteriori* and empirically," there is no doubt that he has such exchanges in mind (A 222/B 269–70). But when we are satisfied with an empirical deduction of this type (a *shallow* deduction, as it were), we are taking for granted the surroundings: it is true that *given all the concepts we already have*, nothing more than an experience of a dog is required to persuade us of the objective reality of the concept *dog*. But if we are asking a deep question about the origin of our concepts, it seems unhelpfully simple to reply by pointing to experience. Acquiring even a simple empirical concept depends on a great deal of stage-setting, and if we are inquiring, as origin-empiricists purport to do, into the deepest origins of our concepts, we need to consider how all of the needed props found their way on stage in the first place.

Kant sometimes distinguishes between *objective reality* and *objective validity*. When he does so, objective validity is represented as a more demanding notion: a concept is objectively real if and only if a corresponding object is really possible, while a concept is objectively valid if and only if objects can be thought or experienced only by its means (A 97; A 89–90/B 122; A 93/B 126; and A 111).[39] In the Transcendental Deduction, Kant argues that the categories are objectively valid in this demanding sense.

Kant has, in my view, only one notion of objective reality, but he thinks that objective reality can be proven or established in two different ways. The two ways are distinguished in the following passages:

> To **cognize** an object, it is required that I be able to prove its possibility (whether by the testimony of experience from its actuality or *a priori* through reason). (B xxvi)

> Invented concepts ... cannot acquire the character of their possibility *a priori*, like the categories, as conditions on which all experience depends, but only *a posteriori*. (A 222/B 269)

The first way, which is appropriate for empirical concepts, calls upon "the testimony of experience." Kant suggests in several places that the actual experience of an object can prove the objective reality of a concept. (This would be a shallow deduction.) The second quoted passage continues by saying that concepts whose possibility is proven *a posteriori* must be "given through experience itself." "Their possibility," he explains, "must be either cognized *a posteriori* and empirically or not cognized at all" (A 222/B 269–70). At B 308 he writes that "the possibility of a thing can never be proved merely through the non-contradictoriness of a concept of it, but only by vouching for it with an intuition corresponding to this concept."[40]

---

[39] "Objective validity" seems at times to be a simple substitute for "objective reality"; see B xxiv; A 156/B 195; A 311/B 368; and A 669/B 697. At other times, objective validity is identified with truth (for example at A 125 and A 788/B 816), but it is unclear whether truth in these passages means "agreement with the object" (A 157/B 197; A 820/B 848) or something more.

[40] I doubt that Kant really wants to require that the intuition correspond directly to the concept; I assume it would be enough, in accordance with the Postulates of Empirical Thinking, for the object of the concept to be connected to an intuition by causal laws (A 225/B 273).

The second way of establishing objectively reality is appropriate for pure concepts or categories. It is described in the following passsages:

> If there are pure *a priori* concepts, therefore, they can certainly contain nothing empirical; they must nevertheless be strictly *a priori* conditions for a possible experience, as that alone on which its objective reality can rest. (A 95)

> Experience ... has principles of its form which ground it *a priori*, namely general rules of unity in the synthesis of appearances, whose objective reality, as necessary conditions, can always be shown in experience, indeed in its possibility. (A 156–7/B 196)

It seems to me that in Kant's view, the only way of proving the objective reality of pure concepts is to establish their objective validity, in the demanding sense articulated earlier. To prove that a pure concept has a possible object, it must be shown that all possible objects conform to it, because the pure concept represents something that attaches to every possible object. The only way of showing that a concept making so bold a claim has a really possible object is to show that no possible object can exist without conforming to it. If I am right, the thesis of category-dependence can be restated as follows: the objective reality of empirical concepts depends on the objective validity of the categories.

If it is sound, the two-step line of reasoning I have attributed to Kant shows that origin-empiricism fails even where its success seemed most assured. It also suggests that pure understanding can arrive at striking conclusions by *a priori* means. This undermines *justification-empiricism*, a third empiricist current, which is the tendency to regard experience as our only resource, our ultimate resource, or by far our richest resource for the justification of what Kant calls synthetic judgments.[41] But the truths so justified have no application beyond the

---

[41] Both Locke and Hume are justification-empiricists in this sense. As Kant notes, Locke accepts the existence of some truths that he regards as necessary and *a priori* even though it is not a contradiction to deny them. But he thinks there are very few of them. In a passage from the *Essay* to which Kant directly points at *Prolegomena* 4: 270, Locke writes that our certain knowledge of the co-existence of one quality with another is "very narrow, and scarce any at all" (4.3.10) – words closely echoed by Kant. The examples Locke cites (see, for example, 2.13.2 and 4.8.2, 4, and 8) are perhaps more numerous than 4.3.10 suggests, but they are not numerous or interesting enough to serve as the subject matter of anything that could be dignified with the name of "metaphysics." In saying that all truths are either relations of ideas or matters of fact (*Enquiry* 4–12; SBN 25–6), Hume comes very close to saying that all synthetic truths are *a posteriori*. It is clear that neither Locke nor

limits of possible experience. This *empiricism of application*, a fourth empiricist current, is the "characteristically empiricist goal" I mentioned as I began.

5. CONCLUSION

I conclude by correcting an impression that I made as I began. Empiricism, in Kant's view, is not always as benign as my opening words doubtless suggested.

Kant's fullest illustration of the battleground of metaphysics is the Antinomies of Pure Reason. There "the side of **dogmatism**" (A 466/B 494) squares off against "the side of **empiricism**" (A 468/B 496), and if we take our practical interests to heart, there can perhaps be little doubt which way we should be leaning:

> That the world has a beginning, that my thinking self is of a simple and therefore incorruptible nature, that this self is likewise free and elevated above natural compulsion in its bodily actions, and finally, that the whole order of things constituting the world descends from an original being, from which it borrows all its unity and purpose connectedness – these are so many cornerstones of morality and religion. (A 466/B 494)

Empiricism, when it hardens (as it tends to) into dogmatic denial, "robs us of all these supports, or at least seems to rob us of them" (A 466/B 494), thereby bringing "irreparable disadvantage to the practical interests of reason" (A 471/499).

If, however, empiricists can rein in their dogmatic tendencies, they can perhaps join Kant in making room for faith (B xxx). In the following passage, Kant contemplates a skeptical empiricist:

> Hume accepts what Kant, in the *Critique of Practical Reason*, calls a "universal empiricism of principles" (5: 13). This is a radical or unrestricted justification-empiricism that regards all truths, even the truths of mathematics, as *a posteriori* and therefore as contingent. "In this philosophic and critical age," Kant writes, such an "unlimited" skepticism "can scarely be taken seriously" (5: 13). That mathematical truths are necessary and universal, and therefore *a priori*, is something that Kant, in the *Critique*, simply takes for granted. The truths of metaphysics present a greater challenge. That they are synthetic – that it is not a contradiction to deny them – is hard to dispute. But whether they are true *a priori* can be doubted. In a striking passage in *On a discovery*, Kant advocates what he memorably calls "the doubt of deferment" – a "general mistrust" of the "synthetic propositions" of metaphysics "until a universal ground of their possibility has been discerned in the essential conditions of our cognitive faculty" (8: 227). Discovering those "essential conditions" is a main task of the *Critique*.

If one were to ask the cool-headed David Hume, especially constituted for equilibrium of judgment, "What moved you to undermine, by means of reservations brooded on with so much effort, the persuasion, so comforting and useful to humans, that the insight of their reason is adequate for the assertion and determinate concept of a highest being?," he would answer: "Nothing but the intention of bringing reason further in its self-knowledge [*Selbsterkenntnis*], and at the same time a certain aversion to the coercion which one would exercise against reason by treating it as great and at the same time preventing a free confession of its weaknesses, which becomes obvious to it in the examination of itself." (A 745/B 773)

Kant goes on to say that it would be wrong to decry the "well-intentioned Hume, unblemished in his moral character" (A 746/B 774), and the speech he gives to Hume is, perhaps, part of what Kant himself would say if the same question were asked of him. But the passage nonetheless points to a danger: that in our desire for self-knowledge, we will come to regard the self as just another object of inquiry – an unusually intricate object, to be sure, but one that we can investigate with the same scientific neutrality, or speculative ambition, that serves us so well elsewhere. We may find ourselves seeking theoretical knowledge of the self for its own sake alone, forgetting that we have a practical interest in our conclusions. In an unpublished note, Kant describes himself as having once fallen victim to something like this danger:

I am myself by inclination an investigator. I feel a complete thirst for knowledge and an eager unrest to go further in it as well as a satisfaction at every acquisition. There was a time when I believed that this alone could constitute the honor of mankind, and I had contempt for the rabble who know nothing. *Rousseau* brought me around. This blinding superiority disappeared, I learned to honor human beings, and I would find myself far more useless than the common laborer if I did not believe that this consideration could impart to all others a value in establishing the rights of humanity. (Notes on the *Observations on the Feeling of the Beautiful and the Sublime*, 2: 216–17; *Notes and Fragments*, p. 7.)

Like the essays of his empiricist predecessors, the *Critique* is an essay in self-examination, but Kant's essay is, he believes, more ethically directed. Its discoveries, particularly its discoveries of reason's limits, are of more than theoretical value. Reason's refusal to answer some of the "curious questions" of metaphysics is, Kant writes, a hint "that we should turn our self-knowledge [*Selbsterkenntnis*] away from fruitless and extravagant speculation toward fruitful practical uses, which, even if it is always directed only to objects of experience, takes its principles from somewhere higher, and so determines our behavior, as if our vocation extended infinitely far above experience, and hence above this life" (B 421).

Part II   The Arguments of the *Critique*

3   The Introduction to the *Critique*
Framing the Question

I. INTRODUCTION

Many philosophical advances provide solutions to well-known difficulties. Others arrive instead in the shape of new problems. In the *Critique of Pure Reason*, Kant adopts the second approach – framing a new question. The *Critique* aims to revolutionize metaphysics, so demonstrating the salience of a previously overlooked problem was a natural first step. It allowed Kant to present his novel ideas for the system of philosophy as the answer to a compelling challenge: "**How are synthetic judgments *a priori* possible?**" (B 19). The job of the "Introduction" to the *Critique* is to frame this question properly, to articulate the distinctions needed to understand it, and to show its relevance to Kant's larger aims. My exegesis will focus on the second (B) edition version of the "Introduction." Kant made substantial additions to this chapter in the second edition, but in my view, these alterations mainly aim to bring greater explicitness to points that were already present in the first,[1] so I will trace the argumentative structure in its more fully articulated form.

Kant's problem about synthetic *a priori* judgment must be understood in light of dominant currents in eighteenth-century philosophy, especially the extensive claims on behalf of conceptual truth made by G. W. Leibniz, Christian Wolff, and their followers. The Wolffians promised a metaphysics founded on the principle of contradiction alone

My first thanks go to my Kant teachers, Paul Guyer and Gary Hatfield, and co-teachers, Allen Wood and Ken Taylor, whose insights about the *Critique*'s general shape and aims have informed my views deeply. My ideas about concept containment have benefitted from many conversations with colleagues over the years, but Daniel Sutherland, Michael Friedman, Béatrice Longuenesse, John MacFarlane, and John Perry were influential for certain aspects discussed here. Katherine Preston made valuable suggestions on earlier drafts of this chapter.

[1] Consider as an example the replacement of the short full paragraph on A 10 by the entirety of section VI (about the "real problem of pure reason") in B (B 19–24).

and articulated through purely logical "containment" relations among concepts. This is the central conception that Kant means to overthrow in the *Critique*. His broadest argument against it is shaped by his discovery of a distinction between analytic and synthetic judgments. Analyticities are the conceptual truths used to formulate Wolffian metaphysics, so if there is an analytic/synthetic *distinction*, then any such system faces principled limits on its expressive power. A purely conceptual metaphysics can express only the analytic truths, besides which, Kant insists, there is a vast domain of essentially synthetic judgments that are indispensable for any adequate system of science. The German rationalist metaphysical program is therefore doomed from the start by the expressive poverty of conceptual truth. This basic insight guides many of Kant's more specific arguments for limiting the claims of traditional metaphysics – particularly those of the "Paralogisms" and "Ideal" (see Chapters 9 and 11 of this volume). The proper answer to his fundamental question also determines conditions of adequacy that have to be met by his own positive proposals for new metaphysical principles (see Chapters 5 and 6 of this volume).

But as Kant was aware, the larger import, and even the bare meaning of his new question, were far from obvious. If the "real problem of pure reason" is "**How are synthetic judgments *a priori* possible?**" (B 19), then from the outset we need to understand what makes a judgment "*a priori*" and what it is to be "synthetic." Each notion operates as one term in a distinction classifying judgments into two types: *a priori versus a posteriori* and analytic *versus* synthetic. Most of the "Introduction" aims simply to make these two distinctions clear. As we will see, however, even Kant's best efforts did not eliminate controversy.

2. *A PRIORI* VERSUS *A POSTERIORI*

The claim to provide purely rational insights that do not rely on sense perceptions (and potentially outstrip the sensible world altogether) is perhaps the most distinctive characteristic of metaphysics, so it is natural for Kant to begin with apriority. He makes three main points, each in a separate section: he clarifies the difference between *a priori* and empirical knowledge (sec. I); he then establishes criteria for recognizing *a priori* claims, and gives examples showing that we have such knowledge (sec. II); finally, he emphasizes that metaphysics would have to be *a priori*, and raises initial doubts about its claims (sec. III).

In the first instance, "*a priori*" is an epistemological term with adverbial usage; it qualifies verbs of cognition (e.g., "know," "judge"), thereby indicating a *way* we can form cognitive claims, which produces knowledge that is "independent of all experience, and even of all impressions of the senses" (B 2).[2] Kant writes, "One calls such **cognitions** *a priori*, and distinguishes them from **empirical** ones, which have their sources *a posteriori*, namely, in experience" (B 2). The main question arising from this definition is what constitutes "independence" from experience. Kant intends a relatively strong notion. As he notes, we might say that a person could have known in advance without waiting for the event (and thus known *a priori* in a sense) that her house would collapse when she undermined the foundations, but cases of this sort are not *a priori* in the intended sense because the principle from which we infer the consequence ("that bodies are heavy and fall if their support is taken away") is itself known only from experience (B 2). Thus, independence from some particular experience – even an experience of special relevance (e.g., one referred to in the content of the proposition being assessed, as in Kant's example) – is not sufficient for apriority. Instead, "we will understand by *a priori* cognitions not those that occur independently of this or that experience, but rather those that occur *absolutely* independently of all experience" (B 2–3).

Despite such pronouncements, Kant is forced to acknowledge some ways that *a priori* cognition might nevertheless rely on experience. For example, he claims that we have cognitive faculties capable of *a priori* knowledge, which he admits must be "awakened into exercise" (B 1) by *some* experience (of any old sort) before they can produce *a priori* knowledge. Such indirect dependence on experience does not compromise the knowledge's *a priori* status because we can "separate" the *a priori* use of the faculty from its empirical use (B 1–2). Even more clearly, Kant concedes that judgments can be known *a priori* even when we need experience to acquire the concepts necessary to understand them – consider: "Every alteration has a cause" (B 3); "The quantity of matter is conserved" (B 21n); "Bachelors are unmarried."[3]

Is there a principled way, then, to separate the kind of involvement with experience that does compromise the "independence" required

---

[2] See James Van Cleve, *Problems from Kant* (Oxford: Oxford University Press, 1999), pp. 15–16. A similar emphasis on the manner of knowing is salient in Philip Kitcher, "A Priori Knowledge," *The Philosophical Review* 89 (1980): 3–23.

[3] At B 3, Kant endorses the possibility of *a priori* cognitions involving empirical concepts, like <alteration>, <matter>, or <bachelor>. Indeed, he introduces the term "pure" precisely to accommodate them; pure judgments are *a priori* claims that include only *a priori* concepts, while *a priori* judgments with empirical concepts are impure. (Angle brackets ('< >') indicate the mention of a concept.)

for apriority from the kind that does not? Philip Kitcher considers the plausible suggestion that a proposition is suitably independent if a person could come to know it *whatever* course of experience she had, as long as that experience was sufficient to form the belief at all.[4] This proposal accommodates the general roles for experience that Kant reasonably conceded (e.g., experience needed to acquire the relevant concepts, or to activate the faculties used to know the proposition), while still providing a robust sense in which *a priori* knowledge is independent from the content of any particular course of experience. But as Kitcher notes, the suggestion still faces a fatal class of counterexamples: the standard propositions it classifies as *a priori* (because they *could* be known whatever one's experience) might also, in particular cases, be known in an empirical way. For example, I might know the Pythagorean theorem based on testimony rather than by following the proof.

There is also a broader puzzle about what kind of thing the qualifier "*a priori*" is supposed to modify. I noted that *in the first instance* it operates adverbially to capture a *way* of knowing things. But Kant also uses the term in an extended sense to describe the propositional contents known in that way, and even to describe *concepts* whose content is not drawn from experience.[5] The present issue arises from the gap between the initial and extended senses: a *proposition* that is *a priori* in the extended sense (i.e., it *can* be known *a priori*) could also be known empirically in some cases, and thus in an *a posteriori way* (initial sense). Something of a consensus has emerged in the literature that the initial, distinctively epistemic, sense of apriority is basic, and that therefore the fundamental bearers of the term "*a priori*" are not propositions or concepts, but the *warrants* that justify our knowledge or use of those judgments and concepts.[6] If my warrant for believing the Pythagorean theorem is one that I could have whatever my (sufficiently rich) experience, then

---

[4] Kitcher, "A Priori Knowledge," p. 5.

[5] The same basic distinction – concerning whether the notion of apriority is applied to the proposition, to the act of knowing or its epistemic features (e.g., its "warrant" or justification), or to the source of the proposition's or concept's *content* – seems to me to be the underlying fact captured by Patricia Kitcher's distinction among three different senses of "*a priori*" in Kant. See Patricia Kitcher, *Kant's Transcendental Psychology* (Oxford: Oxford University Press, 1990), pp. 15–19.

[6] For different lines of reasoning leading to this conclusion, see Kitcher, "A Priori Knowledge," pp. 6–10, *et passim*; Van Cleve, *Problems*, pp. 16–17; and John Divers, "Kant's Criteria of the A Priori," *Pacific Philosophical Quarterly* 80 (1999): 17–45, esp. pp. 23–34. More recently,

I know it *a priori*; otherwise, I lack *a priori* knowledge. We can then call concepts and judgments *a priori* derivatively, whenever they *can* be formed or known *a priori*, as long as we bear in mind that we cannot reliably infer from a proposition's being *a priori* in this extended sense that it is known *a priori* in a particular case.

Kant's second task is to establish criteria for identifying *a priori* cognitions and deploy them to show that we have *a priori* knowledge. He begins from the contrast with empirical knowledge:

> Experience teaches us, to be sure, that something is constituted thus and so, but not that it could not be otherwise. **First**, then, if a proposition is thought along with its **necessity**, it is an *a priori* judgment; ... **Second**: Experience never gives its judgments true or strict but only assumed and comparative **universality** (through induction), so properly it must be said: as far as we have yet perceived, there is no exception ... Necessity and strict universality are therefore secure indications of an *a priori* cognition. ... (B 3–4)

While this account of criteria for the *a priori* was largely accepted by Kant's contemporaries, it faced criticism in the twentieth century. It is now widely thought that necessity cannot be a "secure indication" of apriority, because of examples due to Saul Kripke exhibiting both necessary *a posteriori* and contingent *a priori* propositions.[7] But as John Divers observes, the counterexamples to the universality criterion are even more obvious: some universal generalizations are clearly *a posteriori* ('All ravens are black'); and some *a priori* truths are not universal ("That man is not my wife," "There is a natural number less than 2," or arguably, "7 + 5 = 12").[8] I see no way to save Kant's criteria if they are intended to be necessary and sufficient conditions of apriority that apply to propositions. Divers, however, provides a convincing defense of a weaker thesis: he focuses on apriority as applied to warrants rather than propositions, and limits himself to a sufficient condition only. Universality and explicit necessity turn out to be

---

Kitcher has proposed a more complicated and less sanguine view of the matter; see Philip Kitcher, "'A Priori,'" in Paul Guyer, ed., *The Cambridge Companion to Kant and Modern Philosophy* (Cambridge: Cambridge University Press, 2006), pp. 28–60.

[7] See Saul Kripke, *Naming and Necessity* (Oxford: Blackwell, 1980). Kripke argues that propositions like "Gold has atomic number 79," while known empirically, are necessary, since any substance with a different microstructure would not count as gold. The proposition "The meter stick in Paris is one meter long," by contrast, is *a priori*, since the length of the stick *defines* the meter in this world, but it is contingent because in other possible worlds that stick might be different, or be damaged in a way that affects its length, and so on.

[8] See Divers, "Kant's Criteria," pp. 18, 22–3.

criteria for apriority in the sense of providing sufficient condition for there being at least some important *a priori element* in the best kinds of warrant for the claim.[9] This reinforces the conclusion that warrants rather than propositions are the primary locus of apriority, and Divers' weaker claim does capture at least a key part of Kant's insight. At any rate, it is enough for the immediate purposes of the "Introduction," which aims only to show that there are clear cases of *a priori* knowledge, and so can make do with a sufficient condition. Kant offers the examples of mathematical cognition (which is necessary, and sometimes universal), and the proposition that every event has a cause (since "the very concept of a cause so obviously contains the concept of a necessity of connection with an effect and a strict universality of rule that it would be entirely lost if one sought, as Hume did, to derive it from [experience]" (B 5)). (For a discussion of the causal principle, see Chapter 6 of this book.)

While many claims to *a priori* knowledge are relatively uncontroversial in Kant's eyes, there can be serious doubt about the core cognitive claims of traditional metaphysics, which do not obviously enjoy the necessity plausibly attributed to mathematics. Kant complains that no general account of our title to such knowledge has been provided. Metaphysicians have not seen the need for such an account, he suggests, largely because many of their claims are just "analyses of [their] concepts," which offer "nothing more than illuminations or clarifications of that which is already thought" (A 5/B 9). Kant concedes the *a priori* status of those judgments, but worries that mere analyses are insufficient to the expansive ambitions of metaphysics. This doubt brings us to Kant's second distinction.

3. ANALYTIC VERSUS SYNTHETIC

Unlike the *a priori/a posteriori* distinction, Kant's analytic/synthetic distinction was an innovation of the *Critique*, and it has always been controversial. Kant strenuously complained about an early review that ignored his problem about synthetic *a priori* cognition (*Prolegomena,*

---

[9] Divers, "Kant's Criteria," pp. 23–37. Divers calls the privileged warrants "canonical" (p. 25). In Kitcher, "'A Priori,'" pp. 37–54, Philip Kitcher similarly observes that Kant needs some notion like an *a priori* "element" or "ingredient" in the warrant for an *a priori* claim. He then argues that the proper account of being an "ingredient" involves appealing to tacit knowledge in a way that reveals deep and unbridgeable tensions within Kant's notion of apriority. But I am not (yet?) convinced that the tensions are as deep as Kitcher now seems to think.

4: 377), and ever since, his distinction has attracted fire, sometimes from critics insisting that the idea was long well known and can easily be accommodated within traditional metaphysics,[10] but more often from skeptics, who doubt that there is any such distinction, or at least that it can be given any suitably clear logical basis. Kant, however, always insisted that the distinction "is indispensable" and indeed, "deserves to be *classical*" (*Prolegomena*, §3, 4: 270). His first statement of the idea raises deep issues about the logical nature of judgment and about the proper methods and first principles of metaphysics:

In all judgments in which the relation of a subject to the predicate is thought ... this relation is possible in two different ways. Either the predicate *B* belongs to the subject *A* as something that is (covertly) contained in this concept *A*; or *B* lies entirely outside the concept *A*, though to be sure it stands in connection with it. In the first case I call the judgment **analytic**, in the second **synthetic**. Analytic judgments are thus those in which the connection of the predicate is thought through identity, but those in which this connection is thought without identity are to be called synthetic judgments. One could also call the former **judgments of clarification**, and the latter **judgments of amplification**, since through the predicate the former do not add anything to the concept of the subject, but only break it up by means of analysis into its component concepts, which were already thought in it (though confusedly); while the latter on the contrary add to the concept of the subject a predicate that was not thought in it at all, and could not have been extracted from it through any analysis. (A 6–7/B 10)

Kant goes on to give examples: "All bodies are extended" is analytic since <extension> is already contained in the concept <body>, but "All bodies are heavy" is synthetic, for "then the predicate is something entirely different from that which I think in the mere concept of a body" (A 7/B 11).

This account raises four key issues. First, Kant introduces the idea as though he is simply stipulating meanings for the technical terms "analytic" and "synthetic," but that stands in tension with suggestions elsewhere that it is a controversial innovation. Second, the quoted passage appears to offer not just a single definition of analyticity, but *three*. There has been controversy over whether the three ideas are importantly different, and if so, which is fundamental. Third, Kant's appeal to "containment" has provoked particularly fierce criticism, beginning already with the complaints of J. G. Maaß in 1789,[11] which

[10] See J. A. Eberhard, "Ueber die Unterscheidung der Urtheile in analytische und synthetische," *Philosophische Magazin* I (1789): 307–32. Hrsg. J. A. Eberhard. Halle: J. J. Gebauer.
[11] J. G. Maaß, "Ueber den höchsten Grundsatz der synthetischen Urtheile; in Beziehung auf die Theorie von der mathematischen Gewissheit,"

were widely echoed in the twentieth century, following Quine's skeptical attack on analyticity.[12] I will defend the clarity and logical character of Kant's conception of containment. Finally, I will briefly explore Kant's conclusion that mathematical judgments are synthetic, a claim crucial to his case that there are important synthetic *a priori* judgments whose possibility must be explained in any credible philosophical system.

i. A Stipulative Definition?

The long quoted passage does *sound* like a stipulative definition of the terms "analytic" and "synthetic" (as applied to judgments).[13] But in the eighteenth-century context, Kant's remarks must have carried the force of substantive claims, not mere stipulation. Consider the seemingly innocuous first sentence, which asserts that the relation between concepts in a judgment is "possible in two different ways" – containment (analytic) and connection without containment (synthetic). Talk of the subject's containing the predicate would have been perfectly familiar to Kant's readers – but *not* as the characterization of some *special subclass* of judgments. Rather, it pretended to be a general definition of true judgment as such, due to Leibniz: "The predicate or consequent therefore *always* inheres in the subject or antecedent. And … the nature of truth in general or the connection between the terms of a proposition consists in this fact" (my ital.).[14] Here Leibniz insists that all judgments rest on containment based simply on the

Philosophisches Magazin II, 2 (1789–90): 186–231. Hrsg. J. A. Eberhard. Halle: J. J. Gebauer.

[12] W. V. O. Quine, "Two Dogmas of Empiricism," in *From a Logical Point of View* (Cambridge, MA: Harvard University Press, 1961), pp. 20–46.

[13] Kant uses "analytic" and "synthetic" to mark two distinctions, one applied to arguments, or proof methods, the other to judgments. The Introduction focuses on Kant's new distinction for *judgments*. It is related to the older distinction: analytic argument proves a proposition by showing that all its consequences are true (thus, from the bottom up), whereas synthetic argument proceeds from simpler, more general premises (from the top down). Kant's new distinction extends the older usage in that analysis reveals what is "contained in" a concept by discovering the more general concepts of which it is a special instance. In a sense, then, analytic judgments begin from a subject term at the "bottom," and reveal the higher, more general concepts that compose it, just as analytic proofs begin from consequences, and show how they depend on some higher principle.

[14] G. W. Leibniz, "First Truths," in *Philosophical Essays*, trans. Roger Ariew and Daniel Garber (Indianapolis: Hackett, 1989), p. 31. This is only one of many places where Leibniz advocated this "predicate in subject" definition of judgment.

logical nature of the proposition as a "connection between terms." In fact, this view was widespread among Kant's predecessors.[15] For that very reason, Wolffians found it plausible that the principle of contradiction alone was an adequate first principle for the entire system of philosophy[16]: after all, if every true proposition rests on containment, then denying a truth should result in a contradiction among its terms. Based on the same assumptions, Leibniz and Wolff also made the method of analysis central to metaphysics.

Thus, Kant's claim that the subject/predicate relation "is possible in *two different* ways" (A 6/B 10; my ital.) was no mere stipulation, but a controversial thesis. With it, Kant already introduces his critical rejection of traditional metaphysical theorizing, and particularly of Wolffian claims about the power of the principle of contradiction. Kant's quarry becomes increasingly apparent as the Introduction proceeds. After sketching his distinction, he organizes the next seven pages, leading up to his new framing question, around a series of emphasized topic sentences, the force of which is to suggest that essentially all important cognition falls on the synthetic side. They claim, in turn, that (1) All empirical judgments are synthetic (A 7/B 11); (2) Mathematics is synthetic (B 14); (3) The *a priori* parts of natural science are synthetic (B 17); and finally, (4) Metaphysical claims, if sustained, must likewise count as synthetic (B 18). That is, while the Leibnizian predicate-in-subject principle is not completely false, it *is* false for almost all knowledge of philosophical interest. We therefore need a fundamentally different view of cognitive judgment– one able to address the suddenly pressing question of how our copious synthetic judgments are possible at all.

ii. The Three Definitions

So Kant's agenda was not *merely* definitional, but still, what *is* his intended account of the analytic/synthetic distinction? Initial

---

[15] In R. Lanier Anderson, "The Wolffian Paradigm and its Discontents: Kant's Containment Definition of Analyticity in Historical Context," *Archiv für Geschichte der Philosophie* 87 (2005): 22–74, I present evidence of the containment theory in Antoine Arnaud (author of the influential Port Royal *Logic*), as well as Kant's predecessors (and targets) Wolff, Baumgarten, and Meier. Kant was well aware of these commitments (see *Prolegomena* §3, 4: 270), and shared them himself in his pre-critical period.

[16] See Christian Wolff, *Vernünftige Gedanken von Gott, der Welt, und der Seele des Menschens, auch allen Dinge überhaupt* (the "*Deutsche Metaphysik*"), new edition (Halle: Rengerische Buchhandlung, 1751), §10, p. 6, and §391, p. 239.

appearances suggest that Kant defines analyticity simply as concept containment: "Either the predicate *B* belongs to the subject *A* as something ... contained in this concept *A*; or *B* lies entirely outside the concept *A* ..." (A 6–7/B 10). But readers have complained about the containment definition since the earliest reception of the *Critique*. Some, like Maaß, or Quine and his followers, insist that the very idea is unclear. Others worry that the containment definition is too narrow, restricted to judgments in subject-predicate form.[17] But beyond these specific criticisms, Kant's account is puzzling because the very passage introducing the containment definition also offers two other criteria separating analytic from synthetic judgments: analyticities are "thought through identity" (or contradiction), and they are "merely explicative," rather than "ampliative" (A 7/B 10–11). How do these three ideas fit together?

Many scholars prefer the definition in terms of identity and contradiction,[18] either because it avoids the problematic idea of containment, or because it covers a broader class of judgments, or because the principle of contradiction seems a reasonable Kantian proxy for the present-day notion of logical truth, which is widely acknowledged as analytic.[19] Kant himself often relies on this second definition (see, e.g., *Prolegomena*, §3, 4: 270). Still, it is not free of difficulties, stemming precisely from its close tie to logical truth. After all, the notion of analyticity pretends to capture not just formal logical truths, but also conceptual truths resting on features of the *implicit content* of the concepts. Current philosophers tend to accommodate these further propositions by allowing as analytic any judgment that can be transformed into a logical truth by substitution of synonyms, or more generally by substitutions licensed under definitions.[20] From Kant's own standpoint, however, this move is not especially helpful. Officially, Kant insists that *only* mathematical concepts have strictly

---

[17] For this criticism, see Van Cleve, *Problems*, pp. 19–20, and Sun Joo Shin, "Kant's Syntheticity Revisited by Peirce," *Synthese* 113 (1997): pp. 1–41. Earlier versions can be found in Louis Couturat, "La Philosophie des Mathématiques de Kant," *Revue de Métaphysique et de Morale* 12 (1904): 321–83, and Quine, "Two Dogmas," p. 21.

[18] The inclusion of the principle of contradiction, in addition to identity, is justified by Kant's appeal to the former as the "supreme principle of all analytic judgments" (A 150/B 189).

[19] In addition to the sources mentioned in note 18, Van Cleve (*Problems*, p. 21) approvingly cites materially similar definitions of analyticity by Frege, Carnap, C. I. Lewis, and Quine.

[20] See Van Cleve, *Problems*, pp. 15–21, who proposes a version of the patch at pp. 20–1.

proper definitions (A 727–32/B 755–60), and truth by synonymy would surely look to him like the less adequate (because less general) cousin of truth by containment of concepts. Indeed, insofar as Kant countenances any substitute for definitions of non-mathematical concepts, such quasi-definitions rest squarely on the *analyses* of the concepts, which reveal what marks they contain. Extending the second definition to cover all the conceptual truths thus tends to throw one back onto the notion of containment after all.

The third idea was that analyticities are only "**judgments of clarification,**" whereas synthetic claims are "**judgments of amplification**" (A 7/B 11). That is, analyticities do not carry new information but simply clarify what was already implicit in the concepts.[21] Kant makes use of this definition when, for example, he claims that any metaphysics worthy of the title would have to be synthetic, since we want it "to amplify our cognition *a priori*" (B 18). But the appeal to clarifying and amplifying judgments makes little improvement over the containment definition. Consider, Kant acknowledges that the deliverances of conceptual analysis are often illuminating (*Prolegomena* §3, 4: 273–4). Thus the analytic part of metaphysics is not trivial or tautologous. But if Kant admits that analyticities can teach us something new in this sense, then applying the third criterion requires us to separate the analytic-clarifying kind of illumination from the synthetic, ampliative kind. The only obvious way to do this appeals to whether the truth can be had by *analyzing* the relevant concepts, so in practice, applying the third definition is *no different* from determining whether one concept is contained in another.

Plainly, Kant himself thought his three criteria – containment, the principle of contradiction (or identity), and the ampliative or explicative character of judgment – were equivalent. He is willing to use any of the three as a defining mark of analytic judgment. Unfortunately, he does not say which is fundamental. There are strong reasons, however, to rely on the containment definition. It has a *prima facie* claim to be basic; it is announced first, and looks to be the official definition. The principle of contradiction initially seemed more promising on philosophical grounds, and the explicative/ampliative definition highlights the epistemological force of Kant's distinction. Nevertheless, we saw that under pressure, both of these alternatives tend to collapse back

---

[21] This definition is preferred by Henry Allison because it emphasizes the epistemological consequences of Kant's distinction. See Henry Allison, *Kant's Transcendental Idealism*, rev. ed. (New Haven: Yale University Press, 2004), pp. 89–93, and Henry Allison, *The Kant-Eberhard Controversy* (Baltimore: Johns Hopkins University Press, 1973), pp. 53–6, *et passim*.

onto the containment idea. Elsewhere, I have argued that a careful assessment of textual evidence shows that for Kant, the containment definition always remained fundamental.[22] I will therefore assume that making sense of the analytic/synthetic distinction requires making sense of concept containment.

iii. What is Concept Containment?

So far we have seen that Kant's official containment definition is a good match to the logico-metaphysical views of his Leibnizian and Wolffian targets, and that his other definitions covertly rely on the containment idea. Still, the notion of concept containment has been the target of sustained attack. Critics complain that the very idea is fundamentally unclear[23]; or that, however intuitive it is, it remains merely metaphorical, or at best, dependent on idiosyncratic, variable psychological facts about what individuals happen to "think in," or associate with, a concept.[24] Either way, it would fail to carve out a natural and defensible logical distinction. Since Kant clearly intended a distinction with stability and objective logical standing, his position can only be saved if containment can be interpreted as a logical relation.

Fortunately, recent scholars have shown that concept containment can be given clear sense in the traditional logic, which recognized two standard, reciprocal notions of containment.[25] A higher genus was said to be "contained in" its lower species concepts, and they were "contained under" it. In this context, a concept's *content* is the group of more general concepts ("marks") contained in it, and reciprocally, its *logical extension* comprises the more specific concepts under it. This entire account – including logical *extensions* – is understood

[22] R. Lanier Anderson, "Containment Analyticity and Kant's Problem of Synthetic Judgment," *Graduate Faculty Philosophy Journal* 25 (2004): 161–204, especially pp. 172–6.

[23] See Peter Strawson, *The Bounds of Sense* (London: Methuen & Co., 1966), p. 43.

[24] See Maaß, "Ueber synthetischen Urtheile"; Quine, "Two Dogmas"; Jonathan Bennett, *Kant's Analytic* (Cambridge: Cambridge University Press, 1966), pp. 7–8, 10; and Kitcher, *Kant's Transcendental Psychology*, p. 27.

[25] See Willem de Jong, "Kant's Analytic Judgments and the Traditional Theory of Concepts," *Journal of the History of Philosophy* 37 (1995): 613–41; R. Lanier Anderson, "It Adds Up After All: Kant's Philosophy of Arithmetic in Light of the Traditional Logic," *Philosophy and Phenomenological Research* 69 (2004): 501–40; and Anderson, "Wolffian Paradigm."

intensionally (in the modern sense). That is, a concept's logical extension is made up of more specific *concepts*, rather than the objects to which it applies, as modern logic has it. For example, the logical extension of <metal> would comprise the concepts <gold>, <iron>, <mercury>, and so on, not the individual bits of gold, iron, mercury, and so on.

The containment relation can be given logical shape by appeal to the *logical division* of concepts. Logical division separates a concept's extension into sub-classes, each corresponding to a specific way of having that predicate; for example, the genus <number> may be divided into <even> and <odd>. The procedure clarifies containment because division was subject to definite logical rules– in the simplest case, two standard rules: (1) a division must be complete, so that the species taken together exhaust the genus, and (2) the members of the division must be exclusive, so no species can be predicated of any other (cf. *Logic*, §§110–13, 9: 146–8). That is, divisions are exclusive and exhaustive disjunctions. Since species concepts cover proper parts of the generic extension, we can see the content of a species like <even> as composed out of, and therefore defined by, the genus itself (<number>), plus some differentia marking off its particular way of having the genus concept (<divisible by two>). The composition of concepts can thus be reconstructed through division, which makes explicit what marks they contain and therefore their proper Aristotelian (genus/differentia) definitions.

On this picture, analytic containment relations can then be explicitly represented in a genus/species concept hierarchy. Moreover, the division rules guarantee that conceptual contents and extensions are *strongly reciprocal*. That is, everything in the extension of some concept, A, contains A as part of its content, and conversely, every mark in the content of A includes A within its extension. Further, a lower concept includes whatever is included by the higher concepts it contains and contradictorily excludes whatever they exclude, and reciprocally, a higher concept includes and excludes whatever all its lower concepts do (*Logic*, §14: 9: 98). These conditions effectively define equivalence conditions for concepts through their contents and extensions. Concepts with the same extension must also have the same content, and vice versa, since they include and exclude the same marks. So, under strong reciprocity, conceptual content and logical extension *cannot come apart*: any difference in content entails a difference in logical extension, and conversely.

The appeal to division-based concept hierarchies substantially clarifies containment. Crucially, the division rules insure that every relation between concepts in the hierarchy is one of complete inclusion or else total exclusion. Partial overlaps are forbidden by the exclusion rule. As a result, only two sorts of relations between concepts can give rise to a decidably true or false judgment: either they are directly above and below one another and can be connected in an (analytic) containment truth, or they are separated by an exclusive division of some concept so they exclude one another and any affirmative judgment connecting them is (analytically) false.[26] Otherwise, no connection between the concepts is represented within the hierarchy. This is quite a significant restriction on its expressive power, but any connection between concepts that *is* represented is guaranteed to be true (or false) by virtue of what the concepts contain, so we have a clear, logical account of containment analyticity. We can also understand the method of analysis as a matter of locating concepts within such a hierarchy. When we seek the marks contained in a concept, we need not rely on the unconstrained and potentially idiosyncratic intuitions of individuals. Instead, the conceptual content can be understood as having been reconstructed through a division constrained by explicit rules insuring that its component marks stand in containment relations.

iv. The Syntheticity of Arithmetic

Of course, it would not advance Kant's agenda to have a clear analytic/synthetic distinction if it entailed there being no significant synthetic *a priori* knowledge. As we saw, as soon as Kant draws his distinction, he is keen to emphasize how much of our knowledge is synthetic, including empirical knowledge (A 7/B 11), all of mathematics (B 14), *a priori* principles of natural science (B 17), and any important claims of metaphysics (B 18). Given the above conception of concept containment, are these claims justified?

It is natural to focus on mathematics, since it is uncontroversially *a priori*. If it turns out to be synthetic, then Kant's question about the possibility of synthetic *a priori* knowledge is definitely a live issue, and it is plausible to accept his suggestion that understanding the case of mathematics will help us see what would have to obtain for the more controversial claims of metaphysics to amount to genuine science (B 20–22; B xv–xvi). Sensing the need to make a stand in just this trench, Kant devotes a four-page stretch of the "Introduction" (B 14–17) to defending the syntheticity of mathematics, with special focus on propositions of elementary arithmetic, like "$7 + 5 = 12$."

---

[26] The denial of such a judgment, of course, is analytically true.

Unfortunately, Kant's remarks can seem frustratingly puzzling. Consider:

> One might initially think that ... "7 + 5 = 12" is a merely analytic proposition ... Yet if one considers it more closely, one finds that the concept of the sum of 7 and 5 contains nothing more than the unification of both numbers in a single one, through which it is not at all thought what this single number is ... The concept of twelve is by no means already thought merely by my thinking that unification of seven and five, and no matter how long I analyze my concept of such a possible sum, I will still not find twelve in it. (B 15; cf. A 164/B 205)

Apparently, Kant does not so much *argue* here as *pound the table*. Instead of explaining exactly what is revealed when "one considers it more closely," he simply restates his point in more emphatic form: Analyze all you want; you'll never find the predicate in the subject! Meanwhile, the *Critique* is silent on the pressing question: How can we know that a purported analysis of a concept is complete, or correct? Kant therefore remains open to the rejoinder that mathematics only seems synthetic because of his shallow analyses. Deeper analysis might reveal containment relations.

Kant's positive account of how mathematical cognition works is complicated, and its details exceed my scope.[27] But the account here of containment does help clarify Kant's answer to the preliminary question of why arithmetic is supposed to be synthetic. We saw that analyticity was quite a restrictive notion, and precisely that limitation suggests an approach to the question: elementary arithmetic turns out to be synthetic because a system of containment analyticities is so expressively weak that it cannot capture the arithmetic relations among numbers.

---

[27] For further discussion and references, see Chapter 4 of this volume. On the issues about the philosophy of arithmetic broached here, I have benefited from a number of recent papers, especially the important treatments in Charles Parsons, "Kant's Philosophy of Arithmetic," in *Mathematics and Philosophy* (Ithaca, NY: Cornell University Press, 1983), pp. 110–49, and Michael Friedman, *Kant and the Exact Sciences* (Cambridge, MA: Harvard University Press, 1992), ch. 2. More recent work of interest includes Anderson, "It Adds Up"; Emily Carson, "Kant on Arithmetic and the Conditions of Experience," unpublished ms., McGill University; Lisa Shabel, "Kant on the 'Symbolic Construction' of Mathematical Concepts," *Studies in History and Philosophy of Science* 29 (1998): 589–621; Daniel Sutherland, "Kant's Philosophy of Mathematics and the Greek Mathematical Tradition," *Philosophical Review* 113 (2004): 157–201; and Daniel Sutherland, "Kant on Arithmetic, Algebra, and the Theory of Proportions," *Journal of the History of Philosophy* 44 (2006): 533–58.

The strong reciprocity of conceptual contents and logical extensions does key work here. It effectively restricts containment relations to those of complete inclusion or contradictory exclusion of one concept by another, so analyticity affords only one type of affirmative connection between concepts. Moreover, that connection is constrained by reciprocity; if B is contained in A, then A must fall under B, and further, it must contain whatever B contains and exclude whatever B excludes, lest their contents and extensions come apart. But even elementary arithmetic truth requires contents and extensions to part company in just this way. Consider Kant's example, "$7 + 5 = 12$": if <12> is supposed to be contained in the sum concept, <7 + 5>, then <7 + 5> must exclude whatever <12> does, including, presumably, <5> and <7> (since $12 \neq 5$ and $12 \neq 7$). But now, since it permits only the one type of affirmative connection, containment analyticity affords no way of explaining the relation <7 + 5> bears to <7> and <5>, and thus it fails to express the relation *among the three numbers* that is essential to the content of the arithmetic proposition. Kant makes a related point in a letter explaining his position to his disciple Johann Schultz, where he considers propositions like "$3 + 5 = 2 \times 4$" (*Correspondence*, 10: 554–8). Here the failure of reciprocity is fully transparent, since it is obviously wrong to attribute the same content to the concepts, which involve different operations on different numbers, but the judgment is nevertheless true because the terms on each side "determine the same object" falling under them – that is, the magnitude to which they apply (*Correspondence*, 10: 555). That magnitude cannot be part of the terms' *logical* extensions since they have different contents and so cannot share any part of their logical extensions on pain of content and logical extension coming apart. Instead, to explain such truths we must postulate overlapping *non*-logical extensions, which, unlike logical extensions, need not be strictly reciprocal with conceptual content and can therefore be used to express *synthetic* truth.[28]

Thus, the conception of containment analyticity discussed offers good reason to believe that even the simplest truths of elementary arithmetic are not analytic for Kant, because their very expression would require violation of the rules governing logical division and concept containment. Those rules turn out to be surprisingly restrictive – so restrictive, in fact, that the project of capturing all the truths of metaphysics in such terms seems highly dubious. It was just that point, of course, that Kant's new framing question was designed to bring out.

---

[28] I expound the arguments sketched in this paragraph in much greater detail and explore their implications in Anderson, "It Adds Up," pp. 517–34, and Anderson, "Wolffian Paradigm," pp. 52–62.

4. FRAMING THE QUESTION

With the two crucial distinctions now in place, Kant is in a position to articulate the new question guiding his inquiry, and he does it in a dramatic tone:

> The real problem of pure reason is now contained in the question: **How are synthetic judgments *a priori* possible?**
>
> That metaphysics has until now remained in such a vacillating state of uncertainty and contradictions is to be ascribed solely to the cause that no one has previously thought of this problem and perhaps even of the distinction between **analytic** and **synthetic** judgments. On the solution of this problem, or on a satisfactory proof that the possibility that it demands to have explained does not in fact exist at all, metaphysics now stands or falls. (B 19)

Kant's question is fundamental for metaphysics because of the way his two distinctions classify its important cognitive claims. Many standard claims of metaphysics concern objects and properties that cannot be experienced at all, and almost all of them aspire to necessity and/or make universal claims; thus, metaphysics purports to be *a priori*. In addition, any substantive metaphysics would have to be synthetic: it clearly *aims* to expand our cognition beyond what is already assumed in our concepts, and the *Critique* will argue that its distinctive specific theses are all synthetic, just as mathematics is. So any science of metaphysics would be synthetic *a priori*, but there is a *prima facie* puzzle about how such knowledge is even possible. By hypothesis, it does not rest on containment relations among terms, so we must look beyond the contents of the concepts. But the obvious source of further information – experience – is ruled out if our knowledge is to be *a priori* (A 9/B 13). Kant is confident that there is a satisfactory answer to his problem in general; after all, mathematics and pure natural science contain "actually given" (B 20) synthetic *a priori* knowledge, so such knowledge *is* in fact possible, and there must be some explanation for it. But the needed explanation, and even any recognition of the problem, has been notably absent from previous metaphysics.

A satisfactory response to this question, moreover, would seem to be a *prior requirement* on any would-be metaphysical theorizing. Unlike mathematics and natural science, metaphysics cannot point to any solidly established paradigm achievements with the epistemic credentials of Euclid's or Newton's; on the contrary, the field is riven by disagreement and contradiction. So metaphysics cannot reasonably afford to ignore Kant's problem about the conditions for its possibility.

But refocusing metaphysical inquiry around this new framing question requires a fundamental, even revolutionary, transformation.

Rather than proceeding directly to develop and systematize substantive claims, metaphysics must first address the metatheoretical question about how its type of knowledge is possible. In Kant's terms, it must begin with a *critique* of reason, instead of proceeding "**dogmatically**," i.e., by addressing its questions – about the existence of God, the simplicity and immortality of the soul, the beginning of the world, and so on – without prior investigation into the basis of reason's entitlement to any such insights (see B 23–4). Thus, Kant proposes to replace traditional metaphysics with a new science of "**transcendental philosophy**" (A 12/ B 25). This inquiry begins "not so much with objects but rather with our mode of cognition of objects insofar as this is to be possible *a priori*" (A 11–12/B 25). That is, it begins by addressing Kant's new framing question, and then sketching, only on the basis of the resulting answer, a new system of principles for metaphysics.

In the event, Kant's transcendental critique does establish the possibility of synthetic *a priori* metaphysical knowledge, but only within very restricted limits. In its most famous arguments, the *Critique* claims that the synthetic principles of metaphysics can be justified only insofar as they are conditions for the possibility of experience (see Chapters 4–5 and 9–11 of this volume). Such principles (e.g., "Every event has a cause"; "Substance persists and is always preserved through change") are supposed to explain and guarantee the possibility of experience in general, so they precede it and can be known *a priori*. But at the same time, the appeal to possible experience is a source of information that provides a "third thing" in terms of which we can justifiably (synthetically) predicate one concept of a second, even when they lack any containment relation (A 155/B 194). As a result, though, the legitimate domain of metaphysics is sharply limited; its principles have no validity beyond the bounds of possible experience.

Thus the system of transcendental philosophy marks a dramatic departure from all previous metaphysics. It rules out traditionally central claims about the supersensible, and it dethrones the method of analysis favored by Kant's rationalist predecessors in favor of transcendental arguments about the preconditions for experience. Indeed, Kant wholly overturns the basic logical shape his contemporaries expected metaphysics to have, since he shows that their systems of conceptual truths resting on the principle of contradiction simply lack the power even to *express* our most important knowledge, which is *synthetic*. Such were the results of Kant's revolutionary insistence that we call a halt to all metaphysical theorizing until we have first answered his new critical question: How, and on what terms, is such knowledge possible in the first place?

4   The Transcendental Aesthetic

I. INTRODUCTION

Kant's *Critique of Pure Reason* is divided into two sections, the "Transcendental Doctrine of Elements" and the "Transcendental Doctrine of Method", the former of which is further divided into two parts, the "Transcendental Aesthetic" and the "Transcendental Logic."[1] Although it is comparatively very short, the Transcendental Aesthetic is a crucially important component of Kant's work, its stated aim being to present a "science of all principles of *a priori* sensibility" (A 21/B 35). Here, Kant articulates a theory of pure sensible intuition, and deploys arguments in support of the transcendental ideality of space and time. Taken together, the Transcendental Aesthetic and the Transcendental Logic ("which contains the principles of pure thinking")[2] are meant to provide an account of human cognition and judgment according to which sensibility and understanding – our capacities for being affected by and for thinking about objects, respectively – each play ineliminable roles.

In what follows, I will identify and explain the terminology that Kant introduces in the Aesthetic; present and discuss the arguments Kant offers in the Metaphysical and Transcendental Expositions of Space and Time; and show how (and why) Kant concludes from these "expositions" that space and time are transcendentally ideal.[3]

For helpful discussion and feedback on this chapter, I am grateful to Emily Carson, Brie Gertler, Paul Guyer, Dai Heide, Conrad Robinson, and William Taschek.

[1] The "Transcendental Logic" is further divided between the "Transcendental Analytic" and the "Transcendental Dialectic." These account for approximately three-quarters of the entire *Critique.*

[2] Elsewhere, Kant contrasts the "science of the rules of sensibility in general, i.e., aesthetic" with "the science of the rules of understanding in general, i.e., logic" (A 52/B 76).

[3] Despite important differences between Kant's treatment of space and time, I will focus on the case of space, as is customary. (As an explanation of this custom, Paul Guyer writes that although Kant was not "any less

2. TERMINOLOGY; MOTIVATION

One of Kant's overarching goals in the *Critique of Pure Reason* is to explain how it is that we come to represent objects, and to make objectively valid judgments.[4] He begins the Aesthetic by identifying sensibility as that faculty or capacity of mind by which we passively receive representations from things that affect us. When one is affected by something – when, for example, an item comes within one's visual purview – one represents that thing by means of the particular sensible characteristics it conveys. Via sensation, one forms empirical representations of such particular characteristics: I see the redness and smell the fragrance of the item before me, and I thereby form mental representations of these features and of the thing that bears them. Kant calls the representations so formed *empirical intuitions*. That which an empirical intuition represents, the object of the intuition, he calls *appearance*, but without the addition of concepts, the object so represented is, strictly speaking, undetermined.

As a species of representation,[5] intuition is described as a singular representation that is immediately and directly related to its object. In addition to the empirical intuitions formed via sensation, Kant identifies intuitions that are strictly *a priori*, in which "nothing is to be encountered that belongs to sensation" (A 20/B 34). Pure intuition,[6] or what Kant alternately calls the *pure form of sensible intuition*, is the subject matter of the Aesthetic: as noted earlier, Kant aims to discover

committed to the transcendental ideality of time than to that of space", and in the case of the theory of judgment "it is time rather than space which is foremost in Kant's thought," nevertheless, the theory of time as presented in the Transcendental Aesthetic was "derivative" on a more fundamental theory of space (Paul Guyer, *Kant and the Claims of Knowledge* [Cambridge: Cambridge University Press, 1987], p. 345). Also, I will focus on the B-edition of the Aesthetic over the A-edition, despite similarly important differences. All translations are from the Cambridge Edition of the Works of Kant.

[4] See Kant's letter to Marcus Herz, dated February 21, 1772, for a discussion of Kant's motivation to investigate the "ground of the relation of that in us which we call 'representation' to the object" (*Correspondence*, 10: 130).

[5] Kant identifies the "progression" of representations in the so-called "Stufenleiter" passage at A 320/B 376.

[6] Kant fails clearly to disambiguate between his multiple uses of "pure intuition": the term can signify the capacity or faculty for forming singular and immediate *a priori* representations, a representation so formed, or an object represented thereby. In certain contexts, he also tends to treat as synonymous the phrases "pure form of sensible intuitions", "pure form of sensibility," and "pure intuition." See A 20/B 34.

the rules that govern our sensible capacities, and it is the *a priori* component of such a science that interests him as a transcendental philosopher. So, he is interested in determining the sense in which we can stand in immediate and direct relation to a single object and thereby form *a priori*, and not merely empirical, representations. In order to motivate this study of pure intuition, and to make plausible the subject matter of a science of *a priori* sensibility, Kant offers two short arguments.

First, he endorses a hylomorphic conception of appearances, claiming that the matter of an appearance corresponds to what is given empirically in sensation, and is "manifold" or varied, and also that the form of an appearance is that set of relations that serves to order such a multitude of given sensations. He then offers a single premise: "that within which the sensations can alone be ordered and placed in a certain form cannot itself be in turn sensation ..." (A 20/B 34). On the basis of this claim, Kant concludes that the form of all appearance is available to the mind, *a priori*, and can therefore be studied *a priori*, apart from sensation. The strength of Kant's argument clearly depends on his denial of an empiricist's counter-claim that the impressions we receive via sensation might be thought to be delivered in well-ordered packages.[7]

Second, Kant offers a thought experiment that is meant to lend further support to the idea that the form of appearances can be investigated independently of their matter, and thus that the pursuit of a science of *a priori* sensibility is legitimate. Consider one's representation of a body. Kant suggests first that one can remove from one's representation that which the understanding thinks about the body – namely, that it falls under various conceptual categories "such as

---

[7] I take it that Kant here means simply to motivate an anti-empiricist methodology, and argue for the relatively weak claim that the "[form of appearance] can therefore be *considered* separately from all sensation" (A 20/B 34, emphasis added). Others read this and related passages with a different emphasis. Paul Guyer says Kant "simply assumes" here at the outset of the Aesthetic that "*if* something could be shown to be a 'form of appearance' – that is, something that allows a multiplicity of data to be 'ordered in certain relations' – then it would follow immediately that 'it must lie ready *a priori* in the mind.'" According to Guyer, Kant makes an argument for such a claim explicit only much later (Guyer, *Kant and the Claims*, p. 351). Henry Allison connects Kant's claim about the "original orderability" of what is sensibly received with the discursivity of cognition (Henry Allison, *Kant's Transcendental Idealism* (New Haven: Yale University Press, 2004, Chapter 1). Karl Ameriks discusses the possibility that such a claim could constitute a "short argument" to idealism (Karl Ameriks, *Interpreting Kant's Critiques* (Oxford: Clarendon Press, 2003), Chapter 5).

substance, force, divisibility, etc." (A 20/B 35). One can further remove from one's representation the features of the body that are received via sensation "such as impenetrability, hardness, color, etc." At this stage, one represents only those non-conceptual features of the body that cannot be acquired empirically, which Kant identifies as "extension and form." He concludes that one can represent the extension and form of things a priori.[8]

Having motivated his project – namely, an investigation into that which "sensibility can make available a priori" – Kant states the major conclusion at which his subsequent arguments will be directed: "In this investigation it will be found that there are two pure forms of sensible intuition as principles of a priori cognition, namely space and time ..." (A 22/B 36). That is, reflection on what is contained in one's representation of the sensible forms of things – the form or structure to which all sensible things conform – will turn out to reveal space and time, and nothing more.

3. THE METAPHYSICAL EXPOSITION OF SPACE

Kant provides two sets of "expositions" of space and time: one he considers metaphysical, and the other transcendental. A metaphysical exposition of space aims to expose the origin and content of our representation of space, while a transcendental exposition aims to explain whether and how our representation of space can serve as a principle or ground for cognition. The arguments offered in the Metaphysical Exposition are meant to show that our representation of space is a pure intuition: its source is non-empirical, and its content is singular and immediately given. It will follow from this that the object of our representation of space is an individual whose features are knowable a priori. Kant will proceed to show in the Transcendental Exposition that the representation so described is a subjective element of cognition that provides the ground for a body of synthetic a priori cognition – namely, geometry, the science of space. Given its subjective source, such cognition is ultimately taken to codify and describe facts about the *form* of all sensible intuition, and thus to reveal only the *formal* characteristics of appearances.

---

[8] He also claims at this point that one can thus represent the extension and form of things even in the absence of an actual object of sensation. But this inference does not seem to follow from what he has said thus far, and will require a further argument that what we represent at the end of the thought experiment is nothing more than the "mere form of sensibility" and, moreover, that the form of sensibility applies to all (and only) those things that come before us as appearances.

Kant introduces the Metaphysical Exposition of Space by describing features of our sensible experience that he takes to be evident upon simple inspection: we represent things "outside us" as spatially determinate, and we represent things internal to our conscious experience as temporally determinate. For example, an item in my visual field that I might reach out and touch can be represented as having a determinate shape, size, and position in space; a mental state can be represented as having a determinate location and duration in time.[9] Prompted by these observations about outer and inner sense, Kant poses the question, "Now what are space and time?" (A 23/B 38). He answers with a series of rhetorical questions meant to outline three possible accounts of space and time, each of which ought to provide some explanation of what it means to ascribe spatiality and temporality to the objects that we experience. First, he mentions the view held by Newton and those figures whom he will later identify as the "mathematical investigators of nature": space and time are themselves actual, subsistent entities. On this view, presumably, one represents things as spatio-temporal by situating them with respect to space and time themselves. Second, he mentions the view held by Leibniz and those figures whom he will later identify as the "metaphysicians of nature": space and time are relations among actual entities that are themselves non-spatio-temporal. On this view, one represents things as spatio-temporal by situating them with respect to each other.[10] And, finally, he mentions the view he seeks himself to defend: space and time are features of the subjective constitution of our minds, independent of which they do not apply as determinations of or relations among actual entities. On Kant's own view, one represents things as spatio-temporal by situating them with respect to oneself.

---

[9] Note that the relation between outer and inner objects is not symmetrical with respect to space and time: outer objects can be temporally located, but inner objects cannot be spatially located. This asymmetry, and the temporality of outer objects, plays an important role in Kant's "Refutation of Idealism" (B 274).

[10] According to Gary Hatfield, Kant here also identifies Crusian and Cartesian views of space as "mere determinations" of God and matter, respectively. Such views, in addition to those held by Newton and Leibniz, are cited in order to characterize Kant's transcendental realist opponents. See Gary Hatfield, "Kant on the Perception of Space (and Time)" in Paul Guyer, ed., The Cambridge Companion to Kant and Modern Philosophy (Cambridge: Cambridge University Press, 2006), pp. 77–78. See also Lorne Falkenstein, Kant's Intuitionism (Toronto: University of Toronto Press, 1995), p. 147.

Kant's view involves the strong claim that the objects of our representations of space and time, space and time "themselves," do not exist independently of our capacity to represent them; rather, space and time are the transcendentally ideal forms of our intuitions of empirically real things, *and nothing more*. In order to defend this claim (which he will do in the section entitled "Conclusions from the above concepts"), Kant must first defend a weaker claim about the character of our representations of space and time – namely, that these representations are non-empirical and non-conceptual, and as such constitute the pure form of sensibility. This is his task in the four[11] numbered arguments, which complete the Metaphysical Exposition of Space.

The first two numbered arguments aim together to show that space is represented *a priori*, and not *a posteriori* – that is, that space is not an empirical representation.[12] In the first argument, Kant begins by stating his conclusion – that "Space is not an empirical concept that has been drawn from outer experiences" (A 23/B 38). He proceeds to argue as follows: Certain of my sensations are related to things "outside of me" – that is, to things in "another place in space from that in which I find myself." This relation – between my sensations and things that occupy distinct spatial locations from myself – requires that I be able to represent sets of things, including myself, *as* spatially distinct from one another ("not merely as different but as in different places").[13] That is, I must be able to represent one thing as outside of

---

[11] There are five arguments in the case of time, since Kant did not separate out the third as a distinct "Transcendental Exposition" in the B-edition.

[12] Throughout the numbered arguments, Kant tends to characterize his conclusions in terms of what "space" is or is not – for example, "Space is not an empirical concept"; "Space is a necessary representation." He thereby elides a distinction between our representation of space and that which we represent when we represent space. In the end, of course, this elision is one of his philosophical aims: ultimately he means to claim that space is not itself something over and above the representation of spatial form (which is what it means to say that space *is* the pure form of sensibility). But at this point in his argument, when he is clearly describing the features of our *representation* of space (viz., apriority and intuitivity), he should consistently employ locutions such as "Space is represented as ... " and "the original representation of space is ...," which are also present in the numbered arguments.

[13] This seems to commit Kant to a theory of non-conceptual content. For a discussion, see Robert Hanna, *Kant, Science and Human Nature* (Oxford: Clarendon Press, 2006), Chapter 2; and Lucy Allais, "Kant, Non-Conceptual Content and the Representation of Space," *Journal of the History of Philosophy* 47:3 (2009): 383–413.

another, such that the two things do not share any space, and one thing as next to another, such that the two things are adjacent, and all things with which I come into sensible contact as outside of myself. But these representations of spatial differences, Kant claims, are "grounded" by the representation of space. That is, in order to be able to represent spatial differences in the way that is necessary to account for the relation between my sensations and things that are spatially distinct from myself, I must situate myself and such things *in space*, and organize my representations of spatial things with respect to my representation of the space that they occupy. Kant claims that it follows from this line of reasoning that the representation of space precedes[14] and makes possible the empirical representation of spatial relations among outer objects, and thus that the representation of space is *a priori*.[15]

The first argument might be thought to leave open the possibility that the representation of space and the representations of distinct spatial things are mutually determining: perhaps the empirical representation of spatial relations among outer objects is likewise some kind of condition on the representation of space.[16] The second argument rules this out. Kant again begins by stating his conclusion, this time in a slightly different way: "Space is a necessary representation, *a priori*, that is the ground of all outer intuitions." He argues via an evident asymmetry between the representation of space and the representation of distinct spatial things: while it is *impossible* to represent the absence of space, and so *impossible* to represent distinct spatial things without representing space, it is nevertheless *possible* to represent space empty of objects. This possibility is meant to secure the conclusion that the representation of space is not itself derived from the things that appear to us as spatial; rather, the representation of space is "to be regarded as the condition of the possibility of appearances" (A 24/B 38).

[14] This "precedence" might plausibly be construed as a logical, metaphysical or epistemic precedence, but not as a temporal precedence. (This is connected to Kant's claim in the Introduction that "As far as time is concerned, then, no cognition in us precedes experience, and with experience every cognition begins. But although all our cognition commences with experience, yet it does not on that account all arise from experience" (B 1).)

[15] By interpreting the argument this way, I mean to deny the "proves too much" objection. See Allison, *Kant's Transcendental Idealism*, pp. 103–104; and Daniel Warren, "Kant and the Apriority of Space," *The Philosophical Review* 107:2 (1998): 179–224.

[16] This sort of objection is offered by J. G. Maaß as early as 1789. See Henry Allison, *The Kant–Eberhard Controversy* (Baltimore: Johns Hopkins University Press, 1973), pp. 35–36.

With these two arguments, Kant takes himself to have shown that the representation of space is *a priori*, and moreover that it is a condition on the representation of any spatial relations between empirically given things. As such, the representation of space provides us with a "form of intuition": any intuition received via the outer sensible faculties is structured by space, which is represented *a priori*.[17] Thus, the "manifold of appearances" is necessarily "intuited in certain relations" that are "encountered in the mind *a priori*" (A 20/B 34); these relations have now been shown to be the spatial (and temporal) relations that obtain among the objects of possible experience.

In the third and fourth arguments, Kant's task is to show that the *a priori* representation of space is an intuition, and not a concept. He formulates his conclusion negatively at the start of the third argument, stating that space is not a "discursive" or "general concept of relations of things" (A 24/B 39). His argument proceeds on the basis of a single consideration, which he explains in some detail: it is possible to represent only one single and unique space. From this, Kant claims, it follows that all concepts of space are "grounded" by an *a priori* intuition, implying that the *original* representation of space is not itself a concept but rather an intuition. To elucidate his premise, Kant explains that when one refers to multiple spaces, one really refers to parts of a single whole space that contains them. Moreover, the parts of space are such that they do not together compose the whole; rather, the "essentially single" whole succumbs to limitations or divisions that determine its parts. Kant does not provide further support for these claims; he seems to think that the uniqueness of the whole of space, and the connectedness and homogeneity of all of its determinable parts, is phenomenologically evident.[18] His argument moves from the singularity of the represented space to the intuitivity of our representation thereof: only an intuition is suited to represent such a singularity. It follows further that any concept of space, say the concept of a particular

---

[17] Time is, of course, the other form of intuition. Kant also refers to space and time as the "pure forms of sensible intuition" and the "mere form[s] of appearances" (A 22/B 36).

[18] I do not believe that Kant means to invoke mathematical properties of space at this point in the argument, especially since his discussion of the singularity of space cites its being "all-encompassing," which strikes me as perceptually, but not mathematically, suggestive. For discussion, see Charles Parsons, "Infinity and Kant's Conception of the 'Possibility of Experience'," *The Philosophical Review* 73:2 (1964): 182–197; and Charles Parsons, "The Transcendental Aesthetic" in Paul Guyer, ed., *The Cambridge Companion to Kant* (Cambridge: Cambridge University Press, 1992), pp. 62–100.

finite region of space, "rests merely on limitations" of the original whole that is given in intuition.[19]

Kant's fourth and final argument begins with the premise that "Space is represented as an infinite given magnitude" (which Kant evidently accepts on the basis of the phenomenological evidence of its unboundedness)[20] and proceeds by *reductio*, showing that such a representation cannot be captured by a concept, at least as traditionally understood. According to the traditional logic with which Kant was familiar, a concept is a general representation of the mark(s) common to a potentially infinite number of possible representations. These representations (also concepts) are said to be "contained under" such a general representation, and the general representation is said to be "contained in" each of these lower concepts. The logical hierarchy is such that "no concept, as such, can be thought as if it contained an infinite set of representations within itself" (A 25/B 40). That is, while the analysis of that which is contained under a concept may yield an infinite set of differentiating marks (lower concepts), no concept contains within itself infinitely many defining marks (higher concepts).[21] Kant invokes this aspect of the traditional logic of concepts in order to make the point, by contrast, that our representation of space *does* "contain an infinite set of representations within itself" and so cannot be a concept. That is, the magnitude that is given in our

---

[19] Such "concepts of space" belong to mathematics, and specifically to geometry. These concepts are constructed and defined via the presentation of a corresponding intuition, which itself exhibits the part of space that is meant to be captured conceptually – for example, a triangular part of space is presented in order to exhibit the concept *triangle*. Kant's point is, in part, that such concepts and definitions do not provide the foundation for mathematics inasmuch as they are themselves "grounded" on the original representation of space, a pure intuition. I read the last sentence of the third argument (where Kant states that "Thus also all geometrical principles ... are never derived from general concepts of line and triangle, but rather are derived from intuition" (A 25/B 39)) as an addendum to the argument's main conclusion, and an illustration of this particular point about the dependence of geometrical reasoning on an original intuition of space.

[20] See note 18.

[21] For example, the concept *human being* contains within itself the concepts *rational* and *animal* and contains under itself the concepts *male human being* and *female human being*. See Kant's *Logic*, Part IIA, 24:910–912. For discussion of the traditional logic and Kant's notion of concept containment, see Lanier Anderson, "The Wolffian Paradigm and its Discontents: Kant's Containment Definition of Analyticity in Historical Context," *Archiv für Geschichte der Philosophie*, 87:1 (2005), and Chapter 3 in this volume.

representation of space contains infinitely many "simultaneous" parts, representations of which are "contained within" the original representation of space. Assuming that intuitions and concepts exhaust the possible mental tools with which to represent space, it follows that "the original representation of space is an *a priori* intuition, not a concept" (A 25/B 40).[22]

Taken as a group, the four arguments are meant to show that our representation of space is a non-empirical and non-conceptual representation of a unique individual that forms or structures all empirical intuition. At this point, Kant has not yet defended the full thesis of the transcendental ideality of space: Kant's isolation of the pure form of sensibility, even if convincing, does not preclude the possibility that the world as it is in itself is spatial in precisely the way that we perceive it to be via pure intuition, and so does not yet establish the claim that "Space is *nothing other than merely* the form of all appearances of outer sense" (A 26/B 42, emphasis added). So, Kant will need additional arguments in order to conclude that the pure intuition of space as described by the Metaphysical Exposition represents the properties of the appearances, and *nothing more*. In order to launch these arguments, he must first consider whether and how the pure intuition of space so described can serve as a principle or ground for cognition, and thus provide a foundation for a systematic body of knowledge. This is his task in the "Transcendental Exposition of the Concept of Space."

4. THE TRANSCENDENTAL EXPOSITION OF SPACE

A "transcendental exposition" of space would, according to Kant, explain the sense in which the representation of space is a "principle from which insight into the possibility of other synthetic *a priori* cognitions can be gained." Kant's use of the term "principle" to describe the representation of space here suggests the idea of an origin, or a fundamental source, from which something else is derived; indeed, the requirements[23] that he places on the sort of explanation that the

---

[22] For discussion of the argument at (B 40), see Michael Friedman, *Kant and the Exact Sciences* (Cambridge: Harvard University Press, 1992), Chapter 1, part II; Emily Carson, "Kant on Intuition in Geometry," *Canadian Journal of Philosophy* 27:4 (1997); and, Michael Friedman, "Geometry, Construction and Intuition in Kant and His Successors," in Gila Sher and Richard Tieszen, eds., *Between Logic and Intuition: Essays in Honor of Charles Parsons* (Cambridge: Cambridge University Press, 2000).

[23] Namely, "1) that such cognitions actually flow from the given concept, and 2) that these cognitions are only possible under the presupposition of a given way of explaining this concept" (B 40).

Transcendental Exposition is meant to provide call for an account of how synthetic *a priori* cognitions "actually flow from" and "presuppose" the representation of space. On this reading, the representation of space is the fundamental source of some set of synthetic and *a priori* cognitions. But it is more common, even for Kant, to use "principle" to describe a certain sort of fundamental judgment, and space has as yet been described only as the object of an intuition, and the form of sensibility. So it is also charitable, and not inconsistent with the reading just offered, to interpret the relevant "principle" to be the conclusion of the Metaphysical Exposition: from the presumably synthetic and *a priori* principle that "the original representation of space is an *a priori* intuition" and as such is "the condition of the possibility of appearances"[24] one gains insight into the possibility of other synthetic and *a priori* cognitions – namely, mathematical cognition (as well as the cognition mathematics will turn out to provide the spatial and temporal features of appearances). On this reading, Kant means to relate the claim that space is given in pure intuition, and is the form of sensibility, to a body of cognition – namely, mathematics – in a particular way: conceiving space as given in pure intuition accounts for the synthetic and *a priori* nature of mathematics.[25] More precisely, mathematical judgments derive directly from (they "flow from") and only from (they "presuppose") space as given in pure intuition[26] and they are not "possible" in any other way.

This way of thinking about the relation between Kant's claim that space is given in pure intuition and the synthetic and *a priori* status of mathematical cognition corresponds to Kant's argumentative strategy in the Transcendental Analytic. There, Kant argues that "all laws of nature stand under higher principles of the understanding" and "these higher principles alone provide the concept, which contains the condition and as it were the exponents[27] for a rule in general ... " (A 159/ B 198). The corresponding claim in the Aesthetic would be that all mathematical truths stand under higher principles of sensibility, and

---

[24] Kant refers to the claims about space and time as the "principles of the transcendental aesthetic" at A 149/B 188.

[25] I have explored the "grounding" relation between the pure intuition of space and the science of geometry in Lisa Shabel, "Kant's 'Argument from Geometry,'" *Journal of the History of Philosophy* 42:2 (2004): 195–215.

[26] Kant says explicitly that mathematical principles are "derived from" pure intuitions at A 159/B 199.

[27] I take it that Kant uses "exponent" in the sense of "that which sets forth, explains or interprets": a particular category – for example, cause – is that which explains the possibility of and is the condition for a corresponding rule – for example, the law of causality.

these higher principles, in particular that space is given in pure intuition, alone provide the representation – namely, space – that explains
the possibility of and provides the condition for the derivation of
mathematical truths.

The particular argument that Kant launches in the Transcendental
Exposition aims to explain the "possibility of geometry as a synthetic
a priori cognition" and thereby to establish a link between the claim
that space is given in pure intuition (established in the Metaphysical
Exposition) and the claim that space is not itself something over and
above the form of intuition (to be established in the Conclusions).
That is, once the synthetic and *a priori* status of the science of space
has been explained, Kant can invoke that explanation to draw conclusions about the ultimate nature of the objects to which the science
of space applies. Kant is not attempting here to show *that* geometry
actually contains synthetic and *a priori* judgments;[28] here Kant aims
to show rather that the special status of geometry – its syntheticity
and apriority – derives from the special status of our representation of
space, as described in the Metaphysical Exposition. Thus Kant begins
by stating that "Geometry is a science that determines the properties
of space synthetically and yet *a priori*" (B 40) and then proceeds to
identify the original representation of space, given as it is in pure
intuition, as the source of geometry's success. This is the relation he
needs – between space as described by the Metaphysical Exposition
and space as described by the science of geometry – in order to
establish later that all and only the appearances are spatial objects of
experience.

Kant argues first that the intuitivity of space explains the fact that
the geometer can derive[29] propositions the predicates of which "go
beyond the [subject] concept." For example, by invoking the *intuition*
of a triangular region of space, the geometer can derive propositions
about triangles that "go beyond" what is contained merely by the

---

[28] Kant explains this claim in the B-Introduction, at B 14–17 and in
the Transcendental Doctrine of Method, at A 716/B 744. See Lisa Shabel,
"Kant's Philosophy of Mathematics," in Paul Guyer, ed., *The Cambridge
Companion to Kant and Modern Philosophy* (Cambridge: Cambridge
University Press, 2006), 94–128. I do not think that invoking this understanding of mathematical practice in the Transcendental Exposition
is sufficient to warrant characterizing the argument that follows a
"regressive" or "analytic" argument. See my "Kant's 'Argument from
Geometry'" for discussion.

[29] Kant actually says here that the propositions of geometry are "drawn
from" in the sense of "extracted from" the intuition of space (B 41). This
seems to be a metaphor for "derivation."

concept of triangularity and prove that the interior angle sum of a triangle is equal to two right angles.[30] Kant's point here is that cognition of a synthetic proposition such as a theorem of geometry depends directly on the geometer's intuitive representation of spatial regions, which in turn depends directly on an original representation of the single and infinite space of which such regions are parts.[31] He argues next that the apriority of space explains the fact that the synthetic propositions so derived are apodictic, "i.e., combined with consciousness of their necessity" (B 41). Because the intuitions on which the propositions of geometry depend are themselves pure, cognition of such propositions does not depend on any empirical intuition, and so the propositions are necessary truths that are knowable *a priori*.

Kant offers an example of a geometric proposition that is related to the original representation of space in the relevant way: "space has only three dimensions" (B 41). This is a proposition that Kant thinks of as axiomatic for a science of space,[32] and it is immediately evident

---

[30] Kant here cites the B-Introduction; the example he offers there is of the intuitive synthesis required to establish that the straight line between two points is the shortest line between two points (B 16).

[31] Kant returns to this point much later when he writes that "[space] originally makes possible all forms which are merely limitations of it, even though it is only a principle of sensibility ..." (A 619/B 647). (Norman Kemp Smith translates the same passage as "Space is only a principle of sensibility, [but] is the primary source and condition of all shapes, which are only so many limitations of itself ...") The idea is that the original representation of space is the source for the representations of spatial regions that are indispensable in geometric reasoning: such regions constitute the pure objects of geometry without which geometric reasoning could not proceed. Elsewhere, I have characterized the dependence of geometry on the original representation of space as epistemic: the propositions of geometry are not knowable without the original representation of space, and the representation of space thus provides an epistemic foundation for such propositions (see my "Kant's 'Argument from Geometry'"). The dependence might also be characterized as ontological since geometry acquires its objects from the original representation of space.

[32] This is not a proposition that Euclid included in the front matter to his *Elements*; nevertheless, it is the sort of proposition that might have been included as an axiom in early modern geometry textbooks. See Lisa Shabel, *Mathematics in Kant's Critical Philosophy: Reflections on Mathematical Practice* (New York: Routledge, 2003), §2.1. It is clear that Kant thinks of it as an axiom given that he cites it alongside other axiomatic propositions – for example, "between two points there can be only one straight line" (A 239/B 299) – but does not cite it when he is discussing geometric theorems.

upon "placing three lines perpendicular to each other at the same point" (B 154), an *a priori* mental act that Kant further describes as the "description of a space, a pure act of the successive synthesis of the manifold in outer intuition in general through productive imagination, [which] belongs not only to geometry but even to transcendental philosophy" (B 155n). Although he does not make it explicit here, Kant evidently takes the original *a priori* representation of the single and infinite space to be the fundamental source of and condition on *all* mathematical cognition, including cognition of the objects, definitions, and axioms that are the basis of the science. That is, Kant conceives the original representation of space that is described in the Metaphysical Exposition both to warrant and constrain the production of the elemental geometric objects that the axioms of geometry codify and describe.[33] So cognition that "space has only three dimensions" requires situating the intuitive representations of lines and points in a particular way; the very possibility of such a "situation" is granted by the original representation of space, the pure form of sensibility.

Kant concludes the Transcendental Exposition by showing that outer sense can be the source of synthetic and *a priori* cognition about spatial objects *only* upon presupposing the conclusion of the Metaphysical Exposition, and also accepting that space is the *subjectively* supplied pure form of sensibility. Kant thus means to rule out any other explanation of the source of such cognition. He supposes, first, that to have a synthetic and *a priori* cognition about spatial objects is to have an "outer intuition ... that precedes the objects themselves, and in which the concept of the [objects themselves] can be determined *a priori*" (B 41). That is, to have a cognition of, say, the three-dimensionality of space, is to represent the three-dimensionality

---

[33] The production of such objects requires a move from space as "form of intuition" to space as "formal intuition," as described at B160n: "Space, represented as object (as is really required in geometry), contains more than the mere form of intuition, namely the comprehension of the manifold given in accordance with the form of sensibility in an intuitive representation, so that the form of intuition merely gives the manifold but the formal intuition gives unity of the representation." Presumably space as a form of outer sensible intuition provides a framework in which to delimit and determine the infinite given whole, and thereby to construct and exhibit distinct spatial parts, production of which combines and therefore unifies the manifold of intuition. He goes on to say that "the unity of this *a priori* intuition *belongs to* space and time" (B 160n, emphasis added) suggesting again that the source of and condition on the unity of the spatial objects of geometry is to be found in the original representation of space.

of spatial objects prior to a representation of any particular spatial thing.[34] This supposition is warranted since mathematics in general, and geometry in particular, is taken to be both *a priori* and applicable: mathematical claims are justified independent of experience, yet are thought to apply to empirically given objects.[35] So cognition that space is three-dimensional provides a representation of a feature or determination of objects prior to a representation of the objects themselves: outer intuition of the three-dimensionality of objects that appear to us precedes[36] the intuition of particular three-dimensional appearances. Kant's key claim is that the only way to explain this precedence is if outer intuition "has its seat merely in the subject, as [the subject's] formal constitution for being affected by objects and thereby acquiring immediate representation of them, i.e., intuition, of them, thus only as the form of outer sense in general" (B 41). That is, our particular receptivity to objects – our ability immediately and intuitively to represent objects as taking spatio-temporal form – is not only a condition on all perception of spatial relations but is also a condition that depends directly on our own subjective and "formal constitution", and in particular on our original representation of space. Thus, only upon supposing that the representation of space as given in pure intuition is the subjectively supplied form of all outer sensibility – only upon supposing that our representation of, for example, the three-dimensionality of space is the subjective source of and condition on the three-dimensionality of spatial things – can we explain both the apriority and the applicability of our mathematical claims.[37] With this, Kant takes himself to have shown that the synthetic and *a priori* cognitions of geometry both "flow from" and

---

[34] Admittedly, to have cognition of the three-dimensionality of space requires the representation of lines in the situation described earlier. But this does not count as the representation of a spatial object *per se*, since such representations will turn out to count as the spatial *forms* of objects of possible experience.

[35] Kant and his contemporaries would have agreed about this characterization of mathematical cognition, but they had very different ways of accounting for its apriority and applicability. See Lisa Shabel, "Apriority and Application: Philosophy of Mathematics in the Modern Period," in Stewart Shapiro, ed., *The Oxford Handbook of Philosophy of Mathematics and Logic* (New York: Oxford University Press, 2005), pp. 29–50.

[36] As before, the "precedence" involved in the apriority of such outer intuitions is not a temporal relation. See note 14.

[37] Kant will explain in greater detail the distinctive ways in which his opponents fail to account for such cognition. See my "Apriority and Application," and Section 5 of this chapter.

"presuppose" the sensible "principle" that "the original representation of space is an *a priori* intuition," and that space together with time provide the *subjective* form of all sensible intuition.[38]

5. THE TRANSCENDENTAL IDEALITY OF SPACE, TIME, AND SPATIO-TEMPORAL OBJECTS

Having demonstrated that the original representation of space is a pure intuition that serves as the subjectively supplied form of all sensible intuition, and also that the science of geometry is derived directly from such a representation of space, and thus codifies and describes the given content of that subjectively supplied form, Kant now takes himself to be warranted in inferring that space is not itself something over and above what is given in pure intuition, and so is neither a wholly mind-independent self-subsistent entity, nor a determination thereof. Rather, "space is *nothing other than merely* the form of all appearances of outer sense, i.e., the subjective condition of sensibility, under which alone outer intuition is possible for us" (A 26/B 42, emphasis added). This is Kant's thesis of the transcendental ideality of space (which holds also for time), which he states immediately upon concluding the Metaphysical and Transcendental Expositions, in a section entitled "Conclusions from the above concepts."

He demonstrates this thesis in two steps, first showing that space is not an objective property of things in themselves, and then concluding from this that space is "nothing other than merely" the subjective condition of sensibility. In order to draw his negative conclusion, he claims that we cannot have *a priori* cognition of the wholly mind-independent features of existents: "neither absolute nor relative determinations can be intuited prior to the existence of the things to which they pertain, thus be intuited *a priori*" (A 26/B 42). Here he means to recall the positions of his philosophical opponents, with which he introduced the arguments of the Transcendental Aesthetic.[39] On one such view, space is conceived to be an absolute determination of things in themselves; on another, space is conceived to be a relative

---

[38] At A 41/B 58, after the arguments about time that parallel those about space, Kant claims that "the transcendental aesthetic cannot contain more than these two elements – namely, space and time ... " His argument is that all other sensible concepts, even the concepts of motion and alteration, "presuppose something empirical." Thus, space and time, which presuppose nothing empirical, are the only *pure*, that is absolutely *a priori*, sensible representations.

[39] See note 10.

determination of things in themselves. So, "absolute and relative determinations" include properties of and relations among things that attach "to the objects themselves and that would remain even if one were to abstract from all subjective conditions of intuition" (A 26/B 42). If Kant's claim that such real determinations cannot be intuited prior to the existence of that to which they pertain is warranted, then on neither of these views can space be intuited prior to the representation of spatial things. But Kant takes himself to have shown that the intuition of space *does* precede the representation of things as spatial, and so that our cognition of space is *a priori*. It follows that space cannot be as a transcendental realist would have it, and so space can be neither an absolute nor a relative determination of things in themselves. Therefore, "Space represents no property at all of any things in themselves nor any relation of them to each other ... " (A 26/B 42)

This is to say that the representation of space is not a representation of an objective feature of things in themselves, and it is here that Kant means to forestall the objection to his view that later became known as the "Neglected Alternative."[40] According to this objection, Kant's claim that space is a subjective form of intuition is not sufficient to preclude the possibility that space is also an objective feature of things in themselves. On the alternative view, which Kant allegedly neglects, space could be a subjective form of intuition that conditions all empirical intuition while also representing the really spatial features of wholly mind-independent objects. On this view, the subjectively supplied spatial structure of perceivable objects corresponds to the formal structure of things as they are in themselves, independent of any perceiving subject.

But if Kant's argument goes through, space is a subjective form of intuition, but is *not* also an objective feature or determination of things "that attaches to objects themselves and that would remain even if one were to abstract from all subjective conditions of intuition" (A 26/B 42). The question that remains is whether or not Kant has a further argument to support the claim on which the foregoing argument depends – namely, that transcendentally real determinations

[40] According to Brigitte Sassen, H. A. Pistorius was the first to raise this objection. See Brigitte Sassen, *Kant's Early Critics: The Empiricist Critique of the Theoretical Philosophy* (New York: Cambridge University Press, 2000), p. 5. There is a recently renewed interest in this objection. For discussion, see Desmond Hogan, "Three Kinds of Rationalism and the Non-Spatiality of Things in Themselves," *Journal of the History of Philosophy* 47:3 (2009): 355–382; and, Dai Heide, "Kant's 'Rejected Alternative'," unpublished manuscript.

cannot be intuited prior to the existence of that to which they pertain.[41] Indeed, in the final "General remarks" section of the
Transcendental Aesthetic, Kant offers an argument that is meant to
secure the certainty and indubitability of the theory of transcendental
idealism, and that will also "serve to make that which has been
adduced in §3 even more clear" (A 46/B 64). Since the claim under
discussion is first advanced in §3, it is natural to look to this later
argument for its support.

Here, Kant proposes to investigate geometry further as an example
of a "large number of a priori apodictic and synthetic propositions,"
about which the following question must be answered: "Whence do
you take such propositions, and on what does our understanding rely
in attaining to such absolutely necessary and universally valid
truths?" (A 46/B 64). On Kant's view, all understanding relies on the
combination of concepts and intuitions, which are given either
a priori or a posteriori. On the basis of this background assumption,
Kant uses an argument from elimination to determine on what we
must rely in order to cognize the truths of geometry. First, he elimi-
nates empirical concepts and empirical intuitions, since such a posteriori representations cannot afford necessary and absolutely universal
a priori cognition. Second, and somewhat redundantly, he rules out
all concepts, both pure and empirical, since such general representations cannot afford synthetic cognition. Finally, he claims that in
order to cognize the truth of a geometric proposition, such as that
"with two straight lines no space at all can be enclosed," or that
"a figure is possible with three straight lines," one must therefore "give your object a priori in intuition, and ground your synthetic
proposition on this" (A 48/B 65). This suggests that, on Kant's view,
an adequate account of geometric cognition presupposes the a priori
production of the objects of geometry, the shapes or figures that delimit
spatial things. For instance, in order to cognize truths about triangles,
one must produce for oneself a figure enclosed by three straight
lines.[42] But Kant's claim is that the conceptual and/or empirical

---

[41] One might think that this claim is easily dismissed: it seems easy enough
to represent things or features of things that come into existence only
after being so represented. But Kant's claim is made with respect not to
the general category of "representation" but with respect to the species of
representation he describes as "intuition." His argument in support of the
claim that real determinations cannot be *intuited* prior to the existence of
that to which they pertain will, accordingly, turn on this distinction.

[42] On Kant's theory of mathematical construction, see my "Kant's
Philosophy of Mathematics," and the many sources cited there, including
Friedman, *Kant and the Exact Sciences*. See also Daniel Sutherland,

production of such "figures" is insufficient to the task: one must "add to [one's] concept (of three lines) something new (the figure) that must thereby necessarily be encountered in the object ... " (A 48/B 65).

Now, Kant has the tools to defend the claim that transcendentally real determinations cannot be intuited prior to the existence of that to which they pertain. Consider the possibility of a determination such that it is both intuited *a priori*, prior to the existence of those things to which it pertains, and also such that it attaches to things in themselves, independent of all subjective conditions of intuition. Consider further that triangularity could be such a determination, and suppose that triangularity is represented prior to the existence of triangular things and is also a feature of triangular-things-in-themselves. Notice first that Kant would grant the claim that such a determination can be represented conceptually: whatever the status of such a figure, one can form the concept of three lines enclosing a space simply by combining the relevant constituent concepts (i.e., 'three'; 'line'; 'closed' ...). One can even form the concept of two lines enclosing a space. But to represent such a determination in intuition, and to do so *a priori* in precisely the way that geometric reasoning demands, one must exhibit an individual and yet non-empirical figure that corresponds to the concept.[43] Such an exhibition involves the act of delimiting a finite spatial region, and so presupposes the *a priori* and intuitive representation of the whole space of which the resulting triangular figure is a part. Moreover, such acts are conditioned by the features of such a space, in accordance with which a three-sided figure can be exhibited, but a two-sided figure cannot. Thus, to *intuit* the determination of triangularity *a priori* is to produce a singular and immediate representation of a shape or spatial form of something prior to the existence of a thing that actually takes such a shape or form. Now, if the things that took such shape were things in themselves – if triangularity could be thought also to be a real feature of things independent of all subjective conditions of intuition – then Kant claims that one could never make the connection between "what necessarily lies in your subjective conditions for constructing a triangle" and what "necessarily pertain[s] to the triangle in itself."[44] The cost of such a failure to connect spatial determinations with the objects they determine is the necessary truth of geometry: if

"Kant on Fundamental Geometrical Relations," *Archiv für Geschichte der Philosophie* 87:2 (2005): 117–158.

[43] Kant explains this in a section of the Doctrine of Method entitled "The discipline of pure reason in dogmatic use." See A 713–714/B741–742.

[44] This way of arguing requires that spatially determined objects be *necessarily* spatial in the strongest possible sense, a claim to which Kant is

spatial determinations of things in themselves were independent of the conditions in accordance with which one *intuits* spatial determinations, then one "could make out absolutely nothing synthetic and *a priori* about outer objects"[45] (A 48/B 66). Kant here takes this consideration to entail the conclusion that space (and time) are "nothing in themselves" without the subjective conditions "under which alone things could be outer objects …"[46]

Kant holds that from the negative conclusion that "Space represents no property at all of any things in themselves nor any relation of them to each other," the positive conclusion, and the full doctrine of the transcendental ideality of space according to which space is *merely* the subjective condition of sensibility *and nothing more*, follows directly: space cannot be other than as subjectively given in pure intuition, and so as "a necessary condition of all the relations within which objects can be intuited as outside us" (A 26/B 42) is a condition on all but only things insofar as they appear to us.[47] With this caveat – that the "objects" that can be intuited as outside us, and so as spatially determinate, are objects of our possible experience but not things in

unentitled, according to Paul Guyer. See Guyer, *Kant and the Claims*, pp. 354–369.

[45] One might think that the way to make the required connection is via preestablished harmony, in which case it would be possible that things in themselves were spatial even though not *intuited* as such. But Kant denies this explanation. See especially B 166–168.

[46] Here Kant appears to have offered what has traditionally been construed as an "argument from geometry" in support of the strongest possible formulation of the thesis of transcendental idealism – namely, that "It is therefore indubitably certain and not merely possible or even probable that space and time, as the necessary conditions of all (outer and inner) experience, are merely subjective conditions of all our intuition, in relation to which therefore all objects are mere appearances and not things given for themselves" (A 49/B 66). This concluding statement makes clear that he is not here arguing for the claim that space and time are the necessary conditions of all experience, nor even for the claim that they are subjective conditions of all our intuition; these claims have been established earlier with distinct arguments, in the Metaphysical and Transcendental Expositions. Here he argues for the claim that space and time are *merely* as described in the Expositions, and so offers support for his ultimate conclusion that space and time are *not* determinations of things in themselves. (This reading is consistent with my position argued elsewhere – that Kant does not offer a traditional "argument from geometry" in the Transcendental Exposition in order to buttress claims already defended in the Metaphysical Exposition. See my "Kant's 'Argument from Geometry'.")

[47] For a subtle analysis of this argument based on the referential limits of spatial representation, see Heide's "Kant's 'Rejected Alternative'."

themselves – Kant is able to claim that he is both a realist *and* an idealist about space and spatially determinate objects. His position is idealistic in the transcendental sense that space "is nothing as soon as we leave aside the condition of the possibility of all experience, and take it as something that grounds the things in themselves" (A 28/B 44). That is, space is a feature of things only insofar as such things are conceived relative to the subjective conditions of cognition. But his position is realistic in the empirical sense that we can demonstrate the universal and unconditional validity of spatial claims about empirical objects "under the limitation that these things be taken as objects of our sensible intuition" (A 27/B 43). That is, space is a real feature of "everything that can come before us externally as an object" (A 28/B 44).[48] Thus, in being merely subjective conditions of sensibility and nothing more, space and time acquire objective validity with respect to the domain of appearances, but cannot be conceived to describe or determine anything conceived as lying beyond the bounds of that domain.[49]

At this point, Kant has the tools to draw a more precise contrast between his view and those held by his philosophical opponents, which he does in the "Elucidation" section of the Transcendental Aesthetic. Taking himself to have shown that the limits or boundaries of space, time and sensible cognition extend to include all but only the appearances, Kant is here concerned to show that his predecessors understand space and time in such a way as to cause representations thereof illegitimately to exceed their own sensible limits. He summarizes his own view as follows:

Time and space are accordingly two sources of cognition, from which different synthetic cognitions can be drawn *a priori*, of which especially pure mathematics in regard to the cognitions of space and its relations provides a splendid example. Both taken together are, namely, the pure forms of all sensible intuition, and thereby make possible synthetic *a priori* propositions. But

---

[48] Kant follows these passages with a discussion of why there are no other subjective representations (for example, subjective representations of the so-called secondary qualities of objects) that yield *a priori* and objective cognition. Here he introduces a distinction between appearances and things in themselves conceived in an empirical sense: the redness of the rose can be distinguished from the rose itself. This distinction should not be confused with the transcendental sense of the distinction. See A 28–30/B 44–46 and A 45–6/B 62–3.

[49] At this point in the text, Kant proceeds to develop parallel arguments with respect to time. Because time is the form of inner sense, there are various ways in which Kant's discussion differs from his discussion of space, the form of outer sense. He defends against objections particular to the transcendental ideality of time at A 37–9/B 54–6.

these *a priori* sources of cognition determine their own boundaries by that very fact (that they are merely conditions of sensibility), namely that they apply to objects only so far as they are considered as appearances, but do not present things in themselves. Those alone are the field of their validity, beyond which no further objective use of them takes place. (A 38–39/B 55–56)

As before, he wishes to contrast three sorts of positions: his own as just described; that advanced by Newton and other such figures[50] whom he here labels "mathematical investigators of nature"; and that advanced by Leibniz and other "metaphysicians of nature." Kant's strategy is to argue that any proponent of the transcendental reality (as opposed to the empirical reality and transcendental ideality) of space and time comes "into conflict with the principles of experience" (A 39/B 56). Of course, he takes both Newton and Leibniz to be such proponents: Newton assumes that space and time "subsist," while Leibniz assumes that space and time "inhere," but both suppose that space and time have objective reality independent of any transcendental cognitive conditions. As such, both of their accounts, according to Kant, face an irresolvable conflict.

One way to capture the conflict that Kant takes his predecessors to face is in terms of the apriority and applicability of mathematics, mentioned earlier in the context of the Transcendental Exposition. Kant takes the apriority and the applicability of mathematics to be necessary conditions on experience: any possible experience of an object as spatial presupposes both that the space in which the object is situated is cognizable *a priori* (and thus that the science of space is *a priori*) and that the spatial features of the object so situated are determined by space (i.e., that the science of space is applicable). This is, for Kant, a necessary principle of experience and one that determines the very limits thereof: mathematics applies to and is *a priori* true of all and only the appearances. According to Kant, neither the "mathematicians" nor the "metaphysicians" have the resources to account for *both* the applicability and the apriority of mathematics: although their accounts fail in different ways, neither can accommodate a principle that Kant, at least, takes to be necessary. Moreover, the particular way in which each account fails guarantees, according to Kant, that the limits of sensibility are traversed.

The details of Kant's critique of his predecessors cannot be explored fully here.[51] Briefly, Kant claims that the "metaphysicians" take space

---

[50] Descartes might be thought to be a better example than Newton of a "mathematical investigator of nature," at least for Kant's purposes here. See my "Apriority and Application," 35–40.
[51] See my "Apriority and Application," 44–49.

and time to be "relations of appearances ... that are abstracted from experience though confusedly represented in this abstraction" (A 39/ B 56). On this view, space and time are "only inhering" because they are relations among objects and not themselves self-subsisting entities; nevertheless, space and time are "absolutely real" since their relata are conceived to be "restricted by nature" independent of all human cognition. Such an account can explain the applicability of mathematics but not its apriority: because the original source of a science of space is experiential, mathematics is about the objects we experience, and so is applicable thereto, but all such cognition thereof must then be *a posteriori*.[52] Further, Kant claims that the "mathematicians" take space and time to be "two eternal and infinite self-subsisting non-entities ... which exist ... only in order to comprehend everything real within themselves" (A 39/B 56). On this view, we can have *a priori* cognition of the spatial features of objects that are so "comprehended" and so have *a priori* cognition of that which is contained within the domain of our possible experience. But such *a priori* cognition is unrestricted: it is applicable to all – but not only – the appearances. Mathematics, although *a priori*, is applicable to space itself, conceived as subsisting over and above both the objects it contains and all human cognition.

Kant thus charges that both of his opponents "come into conflict with the principles of experience," and thereby contradict one of its necessary conditions, albeit in two distinctly different ways. Since both opponents are, by Kant's lights, originally committed to the transcendental reality of space and time, Kant takes himself here to have argued indirectly for the opposing thesis, which does not face similar conflicts. He thus concludes that "On our theory of the true constitution of these two original forms of sensibility both difficulties are remedied" (A 41/B 58).

6. FINAL ARGUMENTS AND CONCLUDING CLAIMS

The final section of the Transcendental Aesthetic is where Kant offers his "General remarks" on the theory of sensibility he has just advanced. His first task is to highlight the fact that his transcendental distinction between sensibility and understanding cannot be construed as a logical distinction marking varying degrees of the clarity and distinctness of our cognition, but is rather meant to distinguish the

---

[52] Technically, the metaphysician does not exceed the limits of possible experience so much as fall short of them. See my "Apriority and Application," 46.

origins and contents of the representations delivered by the two faculties. Such a transcendental distinction thus serves to differentiate Kant's critical philosophy from his pre-critical philosophy, the latter of which was strongly influenced by the Leibnizian–Wolffian tradition. Whereas, on that tradition, sensible and intellectual objects are distinguished by virtue of the degree to which our cognition thereof is clear and distinct, it is Kant's mature view that "through sensibility we do not cognize the constitution of things in themselves merely indistinctly, bur rather not at all, and, as soon as we take away our subjective constitution, the represented object ... is nowhere to be encountered, nor can it be encountered ... " (A 44/B 62). Moreover, "what the objects may be in themselves would still never be known through the most enlightened cognition of their appearance, which alone is given to us" (A 43/B 60).

His second task is to establish that the theory of sensibility and transcendental idealism advanced in the Transcendental Aesthetic "not merely earn some favor as a plausible hypothesis, but that it be as certain and indubitable as can ever be demanded of a theory that is to serve as an organon" (A 46/B 63). Thus he supplements his earlier arguments with four additional considerations. First, he offers the argument that it is a contradiction to suppose that the subjective conditions for constructing and thereby determining spatial figures could also describe objective determinations of things in themselves. He takes this to support the conclusion that "much may be said *a priori* that concerns [the form of appearances] but nothing whatsoever about the things in themselves that may ground them" (A 49/B 66).[53] This argument, as we have seen, plays a crucial role in supporting Kant's theory of transcendental idealism. The other three arguments are best construed as supplementary: they provide further evidence in favor of transcendental idealism, but should not be read as comprising Kant's principal arguments in its support. One, outer sense represents "nothing but mere relations," but only relations of objects to a subject and never relations among things in themselves, since "through mere relations no thing in itself is

---

[53] Kant's commitment to the possibility that things in themselves might be the "ground" of appearances has been read to support both one-world and two-world interpretations of transcendental idealism. One finds at A 38/B 55 a passage that seems to support a one-world interpretation ("appearance, which always has two sides ... "), and at A 30/B 45 a passage that seems to support a two-world interpretation ("outer objects ... whose true correlate ... ").

cognized" (B 67).[54] Two, transcendental realism entails empirical idealism; on the assumption that one wishes to avoid the Berkeleyan "doctrine of illusion," one must also avoid transcendental realism. And,
three, if space and time were the objective forms of all things in themselves, then "as conditions of all existence in general they would also
have to be conditions of the existence of God." Presumably, God's
existence cannot be thought to succumb to such conditions.

With this, Kant concludes that he has identified "one of the
required pieces for the solution of the general problem of transcendental philosophy": the pure intuitions of space and time ground the
possible (and explain the actual) cognition of synthetic and a priori
judgments, judgments that can therefore "hold only for objects of
possible experience" (B 73).

---

[54] On the failure of this more general "no real relations" argument, see
Guyer's Kant and the Claims," pp. 350–352. For discussion, see Rae
Langton, Kantian Humility (Oxford: Clarendon Press, 1998).

5 The Deduction of the Categories
The Metaphysical and Transcendental Deductions

I. WHAT IS THE TRANSCENDENTAL DEDUCTION SUPPOSED TO PROVE?

In the Preface to the first edition of *Critique of Pure Reason*[1] in 1781, Kant wrote that he was "acquainted with no other investigations more important for getting to the bottom of that faculty we call the understanding, and at the same time for the determination of the rules and boundaries of its use, than those I have undertaken in the second chapter of the Transcendental Analytic, under the title **Deduction of the Pure Concepts of the Understanding**; they are also the investigations that have cost me the most, but I hope not unrewarded, effort" (A xvi). In 1786, in the Preface to the *Metaphysical Foundations of Natural Science*, Kant lamented that this deduction, "the very part of the *Critique* that ought to be precisely the most clear," had instead been found "rather the most obscure," even circular (*MANW*, 4:476),[2] and for the second edition of the *Critique*, a year later, Kant rewrote this chapter completely, hoping to remove its "obscurity" while maintaining that he had "found nothing to alter either in the propositions" of the whole work "or in their grounds of proof" (B xxxvii–xxxviii). The debate about both what Kant intended to prove in his Deduction and how he intended to prove it that began with Kant's earliest critics has continued unabated,[3] so it seems safe to say

[1] All translations are from Immanuel Kant, *Critique of Pure Reason*, translated and edited by Paul Guyer and Allen W. Wood (Cambridge: Cambridge University Press, 1998).

[2] Translation by Michael Friedman from Kant, *Theoretical Philosophy after 1781*, edited by Henry Allison and Peter Heath, trans. Gary Hatfield, Michael Friedman, Henry Allison, and Peter Heath (Cambridge: Cambridge University Press, 2002), pp. 188–9.

[3] The charge that the deduction is obscure even though it is the "part of the *Critique* that should be the clearest, if the Kantian system is to afford complete conviction," was made by Johann Schultz in a review of J. A. H. Ulrich's *Institutiones Logicae et Metaphysicae* (1785) in *Allgemeine Literatur-Zeitung* (13 December 1785): 297–9, translated in Brigitte Sassen, ed., *Kant's Earliest Critics* (Cambridge: Cambridge University Press, 2000),

that Kant's attempt in the second edition to remove the obscurity that had shrouded the Deduction in the first did not succeed. The present chapter aims to clarify what Kant was trying to prove in the Transcendental Deduction, explain why his two main attempts to reach his goal remained obscure, and yet suggest how the larger argument of the Transcendental Analytic can nevertheless be seen as a promising strategy for accomplishing the goal of the Transcendental Deduction.

Kant's own programmatic statements about the aims of the Deduction are not always very helpful. In the Preface to the first edition, Kant says that the inquiry has two sides, one that "refers to the objects of the pure understanding, and is supposed to demonstrate and make comprehensible the objective validity of its concepts a priori," which is thus called the "objective deduction," and which Kant says "belongs essentially to [his] ends," and another side that "deals with the pure understanding itself, concerning its possibility and the powers of cognition on which it itself rests"; the latter thus considers the understanding "in a subjective relation," and "is of great importance in respect of [Kant's] chief end" but "does not belong essentially to it" (A xvi–xvii). There are several problems with this statement: Kant does not define what he means by the central concept of the objective validity of the a priori concepts of the understanding; when he comes to the exposition of the deduction itself, he does not mention the contrast between the objective and subjective deduction nor explicitly associate specific parts of his text with either of these labels; and in any case it looks as if the greater part of his discussion concerns the various faculties of the mind on which certain key cognitive accomplishments are supposed to depend, thus that he has paid more attention to the less essential subjective deduction rather than to the more essential objective deduction. In the first section of the Deduction itself, identical in both editions, Kant introduces the Deduction with his famous distinction between the *quid juris* and the *quid facti*, the latter referring to empirical evidence for the legitimate employment or "objective reality" of merely empirical concepts, while the former refers to a deduction of the entitlement to use a priori concepts that must proceed "completely independently of all experience"; Kant then says that he calls "the explanation [*Erklärung*] of the way in which concepts can relate to objects a priori their **transcendental deduction**, and distinguish[es] this from the **empirical deduction**, which shows how a concept is acquired through experience and reflection on it, and therefore concerns not the lawfulness but the fact from which the possession has arisen" (A 84–5/B 116–17).[4] Kant's claim here that

pp. 210–14, at p. 213. Kant's echo of these words in the Preface to the *Metaphysical Foundations* is unmistakable.

4 What exactly Kant means by an "explanation" here is, however, necessarily unclear, because as Kant himself later points out, the German word *Erklärung* has to stand duty for at least four different concepts expressible

empirical concepts can readily demonstrate their "objective reality" through experience, which can directly or indirectly supply an instance of such concepts, but that *a priori* concepts cannot prove their reality so simply yet still must be determined not to be usurpatory, as for example the concepts of "**fortune** and **fate**" are, might suggest that the task of the deduction is to show that some concepts that do not arise *from* experience nevertheless have *some* legitimate application *to* experience.[5] This interpretation of Kant's goal might also be suggested by his original formulation of the task of the eventual critique in his famous letter to his protégé Marcus Herz of February 21, 1772, in which Kant says that the issue for his new work in progress, then provisionally entitled *The Bounds of Sensibility and Reason*, is to explain how "pure concepts of the understanding" that are neither "abstracted from sense perceptions" and "caused by the object nor do they bring the object itself into being" nevertheless can apply to the objects presented by the senses.[6] This too could suggest that the goal of a transcendental deduction is to prove that a pure concept has *some* empirical application.

The problem with such an interpretation is that it would make the argument of the transcendental deduction too easy, and undercut the distinction that Kant makes between the separate aims of the first *two* chapters of the Transcendental Analytic, the first of which is "On the Clue to the Discovery of all Pure Concepts of the Understanding" (A 66/ B 91), while only the second contains "the Deduction of the Pure Concepts of the Understanding" proper (A 84/B 116). In the first of these chapters, which he retroactively entitled the "Metaphysical Deduction" (B 159), Kant argues that cognition always takes the form of judgment, that judgments can only be made in a fixed variety of logical forms that arise from the permissible permutations of certain logical functions of quantity, quality, and relation (every judgment must be either singular or plural, affirmative or negative, categorical or hypothetical, and so on),[7] and that

in Latin – namely, "**exposition, explication, declaration**, and **definition**" (A 730/B 758). In particular, it can therefore always be unclear whether an *Erklärung* is a statement of meaning or a factual explanation of the real possibility of something.

[5] Konstantin Pollok's characterization of the "main task of the deduction" as simply to show that the categories "'can relate to objects'" is open to this interpretation; see his "'An Almost Single Inference' - Kant's Deduction of the Categories Reconsidered," *Archiv für Geschichte der Philosophie* 90 (2009): 323–45, at p. 326.

[6] Letter to Marcus Herz, 21 February 1772, 10:129–35, at 10:130–1, translation from Immanuel Kant, *Correspondence*, translated and edited by Arnulf Zweig (Cambridge: Cambridge University Press, 1999), pp. 132–7, at pp. 133–4.

[7] I leave out for the moment certain of the complexities of Kant's account, above all his special treatment of the modality of judgments.

judgments with such structures can only be made about objects if the concepts of objects are themselves structured in certain ways – judgments with subject-predicate structure, for example, can only be made about objects if objects are conceived of as substances with accidents. The general ways in which the particular concepts of objects must be structured if those objects are to be objects of judgments are nothing other than the "pure concepts of the understanding" or the categories, and then all that would have to be argued to demonstrate that the pure concepts of the understanding have *some* actual application would be that we have *some* cognition of objects, surely not something that should be very difficult to prove. If that were all that Kant wanted to prove, however, it would be hard to see why he would have followed the straightforward argument of the "Clue to the Discovery" of the categories with a further "Transcendental Deduction" so obscure that it has troubled interpreters for more than two centuries.

But Kant's language throughout the Transcendental Deduction, even if not in these initial programmatic statements, makes it clear that the goal of the argument is to establish more than that the pure concepts of the understanding that are discovered through reflection on the logical structure of judgments have "objective reality" in the sense of having *some* legitimate application, which could easily be demonstrated by showing that we have at least some knowledge of objects somewhere in our experience; in fact, what Kant wants to demonstrate is that these concepts necessarily apply to *any and all* experience that we might have, which is what he actually means by saying that he wants to demonstrate the "objective validity" or "lawfulness" of these concepts. While the Metaphysical Deduction's argument that all cognition of objects takes the form of judgment and thus requires the employment of the pure concepts of the understanding might be enough to establish the *conditional* that whenever we have knowledge of objects we must employ the categories, and could thus suffice to prove that "all empirical cognition of objects is necessarily in accord with such concepts, since without their presupposition nothing is possible as **object of experience**" (A 93/B 125–6) *as a conditional*, thereby rendering the Transcendental Deduction redundant if that is all that it too is supposed to show, in fact the Transcendental Deduction is supposed to show more. The Transcendental Deduction is supposed to show that "all experience contains in addition to the intuition of the senses, through which something is given, a **concept** of an object that is given in intuition, or appears, hence concepts of objects in general lie at the ground of all experiential cognition as *a priori* conditions" (A 93/B 126). The categories are supposed to be shown to be the formal conceptual conditions of all experience, just as space and time are supposed to be the formal conditions of all the intuitions that are the matter of experience.

Now, it could be argued that Kant's use of the term "experience" (*Erfahrung*) is ambiguous, meaning either whatever comes before our senses at all or else cognition of objects; if Kant meant "experience" in the latter sense in this passage, that would still leave open the possibility that the Transcendental Deduction is supposed to prove only the conditional that the categories must be used *if* and *when* we have knowledge of objects. However, Kant clearly excludes this interpretation in the second-edition revision of the Deduction when he says that it is supposed to show that "everything that may ever come before our senses must stand under the laws that arise *a priori* from the understanding alone" (B 160), that "all synthesis, through which even perception itself becomes possible, stands under the categories" (B 162), that "all possible perceptions, hence everything that can ever reach empirical consciousness, i.e., all appearances of nature ... stand under the categories" (B 164–5). Here Kant says that the goal of the Deduction is to prove that the categories necessarily apply to *all* our intuitions.

The argument of the Transcendental Analytic begins with two separate chapters, and the Transcendental Deduction is not a redundant repetition of the Metaphysical Deduction, because Kant's argument as a whole has to proceed in two steps:[8] first he wants to show that any cognition of objects involves the categories, but then he wants to show that the categories apply to *all* of our experience, experience in the broad sense of everything of which we are conscious at all. This means that the necessary conditions for cognition of objects apply to *all* of our conscious experience, indeed if the categories are also, along with any sort of input from intuition, sufficient conditions for cognition of objects, then there is some sense in which all of our experience is in fact experience of objects. Even experience that seems to be subjective, such as our experience of dreams and illusions, must in a sense be objective: even if what an illusion seems to represent is false, it must be possible to judge objectively that one *had* an illusion with a certain content at a certain place and time, thus to subsume the illusion itself under the categories.[9]

[8] These two steps of the first two chapters of the Transcendental Analytic as a whole are to be distinguished from the two steps *within* the second-edition version of the Transcendental Deduction alone that will be discussed in Section 5 of this chapter.

[9] That Kant wants to prove that the categories apply to *all* of our experience is why one must be cautious about Karl Ameriks's interpretation of the Deduction as a "regressive" argument, intended only to show that empirical cognition has *a priori* conceptual conditions, originally expounded in his "Kant's Transcendental Deduction as a Regressive Argument," *Kant-Studien* 69 (1978): 273–85, reprinted in his *Interpreting Kant's Critiques* (Oxford: Clarendon Press, 2003), pp. 51–66; proving that empirical cognition has *a priori* conceptual conditions is the task of the Metaphysical

In the hope of proving this second, unconditional claim, the Transcendental Deduction makes central a concept that is not mentioned in the Metaphysical Deduction at all – namely, the concept designated by the various expressions "**transcendental apperception** "(A 107), "the original and necessary consciousness of the identity of oneself" (A 108), "**pure apperception**," "**original apperception**," the "**transcendental** unity of self-consciousness" (B 132), or the "**transcendental unity** of apperception" (B 139). What Kant means by this concept is that any of one's experiences or representations, insofar as one is conscious of it at all, can be attributed to the same self as all of the other representations of which one is conscious: "Now no cognitions can occur in us, no connection and unity among them, without that unity of consciousness that precedes all data of intuitions, and in relation to which all representation of objects is alone possible" (A 107); "The **I think** must **be able** to accompany all my representations; for otherwise something would be represented in me that could not be thought at all" (B 131–2). The strategy of the Transcendental Deduction is then to demonstrate that the use of the categories is the necessary condition of transcendental apperception, of the ascription of any of one's representations to the one and the same self that is the subject of all of one's representations. The obscurity of both of Kant's versions of the Deduction, however, arises from the fact that in neither version does Kant execute this strategy very clearly: he does not succesfully exploit the "clue" to the discovery of the categories by clearly expounding the connection between apperception and *judgment*. More precisely, in the first-edition version of the Deduction, Kant omits any explicit account of the connection between apperception and judgment, while in the second edition, clearly having become aware of this problem in the interval, Kant burdens his argument with a problematic conception of judgment itself and an account of the connection between apperception and judgment that undercuts the original premise of the ubiquity of apperception itself.

Deduction, while the task of the Transcendental Deduction is to prove that all of our experience *is* or involves empirical cognition. The same reservation applies to the "semantic" approach to the Deduction of Robert Hanna, in *Kant and the Foundations of Analytic Philosophy* (Oxford: Clarendon Press, 2001), chs. 1–2, and A. B. Dickerson, *Kant on Representation and Objectivity* (Cambridge: Cambridge University Press, 2004); the semantic approach argues that the categories are the conditions of reference to objects, but that is what Kant establishes in the Metaphysical Deduction alone. The issue of the sense in which the categories apply even to subjective states like illusions was discussed by Lewis White Beck in "Did the Sage of Königsberg Have No Dreams?" in his *Essays on Kant and Hume* (New Haven: Yale University Press, 1978), pp. 38–60.

The heart of the present chapter will recount how Kant failed to make an explicit connection between apperception and judgment in the first edition of the Deduction, how he tried to avoid confronting this problem in the years between the two editions of the *Critique* by attempting to derive the objective validity of the categories from the concept of judgment alone without connecting it to apperception at all, and then how in the second edition of the Deduction he overcompensated for this failure by connecting apperception to an excessively strong conception of judgment.

However, I do not want to leave the impression that the Transcendental Deduction is an utter failure. On the contrary, I want to suggest that there is a straightforward connection between apperception and judgment, insofar as the self-ascription of representations or experiences in the broadest sense *is* itself a form of judgment and must therefore, by the argument of the "clue," involve the use of at least *some* categories as conditions of the possibility of judgment in general. That apperception actually involves the use of *all* the pure concepts of understanding that Kant enumerates is not something that can be proven within the confines of the Transcendental Deduction, and can be proven only in the subsequent sections of the Transcendental Analytic, the "System of the Principles of the Pure Understanding," including the "Refutation of Idealism" that Kant added to this system in the second edition of the *Critique*.[10] But Kant prepares the way for this eventual proof in the second half of the second-edition version of the Deduction, in which he emphasizes the spatio-temporal character of our specifically human experience, and thus the spatio-temporal character of the experiences out of which we have to constitute apperception or our consciousness of a unitary self. The mere fact that apperception is a form of self-ascription would suffice to imply that it must make use of *some* of the categories as conditions for the possibility of judgment, but the specifically spatio-temporal character of the representations to be taken up into the transcendental unity of apperception is what ultimately implies that the possibility of the kind of apperception that we actually have requires and thus entails the use of *all* of the pure concepts of the understanding. Kant does not complete this argument within the text of the Transcendental Deduction, but he does suggest and begin it there.[11]

---

[10] Eric Watkins discusses the "System of Principles" in Chapter 6 and Dina Emundts interprets the "Refutation of Idealism" in Chapter 7 of this volume.

[11] I have also discussed the relation between the Transcendental Deduction and the System of Principles in "Space, Time, and the Categories: The Project of the Transcendental Deduction," in Ralph Schumacher, ed., *Idealismus als Theorie der Repräsentation?* (Paderborn: Mentis, 2001), pp. 313–38. In their discussions of the first- and second-edition versions of the Transcendental Deduction respectively in *Immanuel Kant: Kritik der*

2. THE METAPHYSICAL DEDUCTION

We must begin with a brief account of the Metaphysical Deduction or the
"clue" to the discovery of the categories.[12] As already suggested, the gist
of this argument is that cognition of objects takes the form of judgments
about them; judgments, as ordinary or "general" logic makes evident,
have certain characteristic structures, and concepts of objects must
therefore be formed in certain characteristic ways, as expressed by the
pure concepts of the understanding or categories, in order to be employed
in such judgments – this is the heart of "transcendental" logic. In slightly
more detail, Kant begins with the assumption that intuitions, which have
already been defined as our immediate representations of objects (A 19/
B 33) and which, because they are immediate, are also singular (A 320/
B 377), must be subsumed under higher-order representations or "functions" in order to yield any cognition, and these higher-order functions
are concepts. But "the understanding," Kant continues, "can make no
other use of these concepts than that of judging by means of them," and
"Judgment is therefore the mediate cognition of an object, hence the

reinen Vernunft, edited by Georg Mohr and Marcus Willaschek (Berlin:
Akademie Verlag, 1998), Hansgeorg Hoppe (pp. 159–88) and Wolfgang Carl
(189–217) both argue against interpreting transcendental apperception
solely as the self-ascription of experiences, the approach championed by
Peter Strawson in The Bounds of Sense: An Essay on Kant's Critique of
Pure Reason (London: Methuen, 1966). Hoppe thinks that Kant's concept
of apperception within the Deduction is that of an ongoing process of the
incorporation of representations into a single body of knowledge, while
Carl holds that apperception should be understood more simply as self-
ascription, but that the account of self-ascription contained within the
text of the Deduction will not yield the application of all of the categories
to all of our experiences, which can only be proven later in the Critique.
My approach is closer to Carl's, although I think he does not recognize
Kant's failure to establish a connection between apperception and judgment in the Deduction that does not actually undermine his efforts to
establish the universal validity of the categories.

[12] The Metaphysical Deduction has been extensively discussed, especially its
claim to have provided a complete list of the categories. In the extensive
literature on the Metaphysical Deduction, see especially Klaus Reich, The
Completeness of Kant's Table of Categories, trans. Jane Kneller and
Michael Losonsky (Stanford: Stanford University Press, 1992); Reinhard
Brandt, The Table of Judgments: Critique of Pure Reason A 67–76; B 92–
101, trans. Eric Watkins, North American Kant Society Studies in
Philosophy, 4 (Atascadero: Ridgeview Publishing Co., 1995), and Michael
Wolff, Die Vollständigkeit der kantischen Urteilstafel, Philosophische
Abhandlungen, 63 (Frankfurt am Main: Vittorio Klostermann, 1995); a
concise and incisive discussion can be found in Michael N. Forster, Kant
and Skepticism (Princeton: Princeton University Press, 2008), pp. 70–5.

representation of a representation of it" (A 68/B 93). Kant illustrates his thought with the example of the judgment "All bodies are divisible": the mere intuition of a particular body, a particular representation of a particular object, does not amount to cognition of anything, and even the thought of a group of bodies or "all bodies" does not amount to cognition of anything; only when a property such as divisibility is linked to the thought of a body do we have even a possible cognition, and an actual cognition in case this linkage is both asserted and true, as in this case it is.[13] Kant infers from this that the faculty of **understanding in general can be represented as a faculty for judging**" (A 69/B 94), which will be a crucial although not always explicitly asserted premise in the ensuing Transcendental Deduction. His immediate concern, however, is to establish that judgments necessarily have certain forms, and that the concepts of objects of judgments must likewise necessarily have certain forms. The forms of judgments arise from the "logical functions" of judgments. These fall under the general headings of quantity, quality, relation, and modality, each of which may in turn be instantiated in several different ways. Thus, a judgment may concern one object in a group, some of them, or all of them, and thus be singular, particular, or universal in quantity; it may assert a predicate of its object or objects, deny a predicate of it or of them, or exclude one predicate of its object or objects while leaving open an indefinite range of predicates that may be asserted, and thus be affirmative, negative, or infinite in quality; it may simply relate one predicate to its subject in any of the previous ways, or link two judgments, each of which itself is structured by the various logical functions of judgment, asserting that one follows from the other or one excludes the other, and thus it may be categorical (a simple predication or its denial), hypothetical (expressing the entailment of one judgment by another), or disjunctive (expressing the exclusion of one judgment by another). Further, any of these varieties of connection may be thought of as possible, actual, or necessary – that is, judgments may be problematic, assertoric, or

---

[13] Of course, the concept of body is itself complex, being composed, let's suppose, of the predicates "extended" and "has mass," and might itself already imply or give rise to some judgment, such as "everything that has mass is extended." Judgments that follow directly from unpacking the contents of a concept are what Kant calls "analytic" judgments, while judgments that add a further predicate to those already contained in a concept – through pure or empirical intuition of its object – are what Kant calls "synthetic" judgments, *a priori* or *a posteriori*, respectively. See A 6–9/ B 10–14, and various of the notes in the so-called *Duisburg Nachlaß*, especially R 4674, 17:643–7, *Notes and Fragments* pp. 157–61; R 4676, 17:653–6, *Notes and Fragments* pp. 165–7; R 4678, 17:660–2, *Notes and Fragments* pp. 168–70, and R 4684, 17:670–2, *Notes and Fragments* pp. 176–7.

apodictic (all at A 70/B 95) – although Kant makes it clear that modality "contributes nothing to the content of the judgment (for besides quantity, quality, and relation there is nothing more that constitutes the content of a judgment), but rather concerns only the value of the copula in relation to thinking in general" (A 74/B 100) – that is, whether the judgment is merely entertained or is asserted, and, if asserted, with what force it is asserted. (For Kant, modality is subjective or epistemic.)[14] Any particular judgment then has a form that arises from its particular combination of these aspects: a particular judgment may be a singular affirmative categorical judgment held to be merely possible, a universal negative categorical judgment that is actually asserted, and so on.

The next step of Kant's argument is that the concepts of objects must be structured in certain ways in order for judgments that have these forms to be able to be about them. Since our immediate representations of objects are given by intuitions, Kant puts this point by saying that the combination or "synthesis" of particular intuitions must be structured into representations of objects in certain ways in order to yield objects of judgments structured in their various possible ways; as he says:

> The same function that gives unity to the different representations **in a judgment** also gives unity to the mere synthesis of different representations **in an intuition**, which [function], expressed generally, is called the pure concept of the understanding. The same understanding, therefore, and indeed by means of the very same actions through which it brings the logical forms of a judgment into a concept ... also brings a transcendental content into its representations by means of the synthetic unity of the manifold of intuition in general, on account of which they are called pure concepts of the understanding that pertain to objects *a priori*. (A 79/B 104–5)

That is, the general ways in which the understanding has to conceive of its intuitions as objects for its judgments are determined by the ways in which the understanding structures its judgments themselves; thus "transcendental logic" arises from "general logic" by adding the thought that the forms of general logic will be used to think about objects, and that the concepts of objects must be structured accordingly.

Kant's "Table of Categories" thus follows from his earlier table of the logical functions of judgments: just as judgments must be either singular, plural, or universal, their objects must be conceived of as unities, pluralities, or totalities; just as judgments must be either affirmative, singular, or infinite, their objects must be conceived of as realities, negations, or

---

[14] This is in contrast to contemporary approaches to modality inspired by the work of Saul Kripke, which turn modality into an extensional concept (truth in no, some, or all possible worlds) either formally or, in the case of "modal realists" such as David Lewis, substantively.

limitations; just as judgments must be either categorical, hypothetical, or disjunctive, their objects must be conceived of as relations of inherence and subsistence (*substantia et accidens*), of causality and dependence or cause and effect, and of "community" or "reciprocity between agent and patience"; and finally, just as judgments may be either problematic, assertoric, or apodictic, their objects must be conceived of as possibilities, existences, or necessities, although again these are to be understood epistemically rather than ontologically. All of these ways of conceiving of objects are, of course, highly general – in practice, we do not conceive of something before us abstractly, just as a substance with an accident, but concretely, for example as a computer encased in black plastic, nor do we conceive of it abstractly simply as the effect of a cause, but concretely, for example as a specific brand of computer assembled in a factory in China. This abstractness is why the ways of structuring our concepts of intuitions so that they can be objects of judgments are properly called "categories" rather than mere "concepts"– they are the forms of ordinary concepts of objects.

There are particular problems both with Kant's list of the logical functions of judgment and with his correlated list of categories – for one example, relations other than causal relations can be the proper objects of hypothetical judgments, such as the non-causal geometrical relation that is the object of such a judgment as "If this is a triangle, then the sum of its interior angles is 180 degrees"; for another, the difference between Kant's distinction between negative and infinite judgments as well as the connection between infinite judgment and the category of limitation have proven difficult to make out.[15] The most general problem, however, is that it is not obvious that just because we might be *able* to make judgments using *any* of the logical functions that we *must* make judgments using *all* of them, and thus it is not obvious that we must conceive of objects in terms of all of the categories even if they are all properly derivable from the logical functions of judgment. However, later sections of the *Critique*, above all the "System of the Principles of Pure Understanding," will offer individual arguments attempting to show why each of the categories must in fact be employed in human experience; the "Table of Categories" in the Metaphysical Deduction can be thought of as merely enumerating the possible ways of conceiving of the objects of human thought that will subsequently all be shown to be necessary ways of conceiving of those objects.

[15] For further discussion, see especially Jonathan Bennett, *Kant's Analytic* (Cambridge: Cambridge University Press, 1966), §23, pp. 79–83, and §26, 92–5.

In any case, the problems with Kant's Transcendental Deduction do not stem from any difficulties in the details of the Metaphysical Deduction. The more immediate problem with the Transcendental Deduction is that it does not follow the path that might naturally be expected from the Metaphysical Deduction. The "clue" offered by the latter might be summed up by the conditional proposition that *if* we are to conceive of objects at all, then we must employ (at least some of) the categories that have just been identified, and it might naturally be expected that Kant's next step would simply be to show that the antecedent of this conditional is in fact satisfied in our experience, that is, to argue – if the point of the Transcendental Deduction is to prove the "objective reality" of the categories – that is, that they have *some* legitimate application – that we do have *some* experience of objects, or – if the point of the Deduction is to prove the "objective validity" of the categories – that is, that they do necessarily apply to *all* of our experience – that *all* of our experience is experience of objects. But Kant's Transcendental Deduction does not take that straightforward form. Rather, as we will next see, Kant first bases the Transcendental Deduction on the concept of the transcendental unity of apperception without clear reference to the fact that any cognition must take the form of judgment at all, and then, after a period in which he entertains the possibility of building the Transcendental Deduction on his account of judgment without reference to apperception at all, attempts to base it on a connection between the idea of apperception and a conception of judgment that is actually too restrictive for his purposes. So let us now turn from the Metaphysical Deduction to Kant's several attempts to construct his Transcendental Deduction of the categories.

3. THE TRANSCENDENTAL DEDUCTION IN THE FIRST EDITION OF THE *CRITIQUE*

We might have expected the Transcendental Deduction to begin by reiterating the "clue" that cognition of objects must always take the form of judgment and then to proceed by trying to show that all our experience includes cognition of objects, *a fortiori* requires the use of the categories. Instead, in the second section of the first-edition version of the Deduction, after Kant has stated the goal of the argument, he begins with a preliminary exposition[16] of the conditions of the cognition of

---

[16] I am using the vague term "exposition" here in order to evade the question of whether Kant's procedure is an analysis of concepts that could yield only analytic truths or some sort of description of incontrovertible facts that could yield synthetic *a priori* results; see especially Jonathan Bennett, "Analytic

objects in time that is independent of this clue. This exposition reaches the conclusion that all cognition of objects involves concepts, but instead of then invoking the premise from the clue that concepts must be used in judgments and therefore their forms must complement the functions of judgment, Kant claims that concepts involve a kind of necessity that can only be grounded in the transcendental unity of apperception. He then attributes the unity of apperception to the faculty of judgment and infers that apperception must involve the *a priori* rules of that faculty, which are nothing other than the categories, but he does this without explicitly showing that apperception itself is or involves judgment, which makes the proof less than compelling. The same gap remains in his further attempts to accomplish the Deduction in the first edition by beginning directly from the transcendental unity of apperception without the preliminary exposition of the conditions for the cognition of objects in time.

Kant begins what he calls a preparation for the actual Deduction with the observation that whatever else may be true of our representations, however they may arise and whatever they might ultimately represent, "as modifications of the mind they nevertheless belong to inner sense," thus "all of our cognitions are in the end subjected to the formal condition of inner sense – namely, time – as that in which they must all be ordered, connected, and brought into relations" (A 98–9). In the second-edition-version of the Deduction, as we will see in Section 5, Kant initially abstracts from the temporality of the data for any kind of experience, but here it forms the basis for his exposition of the "threefold synthesis" that leads to the assertion of the unity of apperception as the condition of the possibility of any experience of objects. Specifically, Kant argues that since the data for any cognition of an object are given over a period of time, the data must be severally and serially apprehended ("the synthesis of apprehension in the intuition," A 98), earlier data in such a series of apprehensions must be able to be recalled when later data are experienced ("the synthesis of reproduction in the imagination," A 100), and finally a connection among the data that constitutes them into representations of a single object must be recognized by means of a concept that links them as representations of states or properties of such an object ("the synthesis of recognition in the concept," A 103). Here is the point where Kant might have been expected to remind us that such concepts will be used in judgments, in fact that to recognize the unity of several representations of an

Transcendental Arguments," in Peter Bieri, Rolf-Peter Horstmann, and Lorenz Krüger, eds., *Transcendental Arguments and Science: Essays in Epistemology* (Dordrecht: Reidel, 1979), pp. 45–64, and my discussion in *Kant and the Claims of Knowledge* (Cambridge: Cambridge University Press, 1987), Afterword, especially pp. 419–23. Since the argument as I will describe it does not reach Kant's goals, we need not discuss this question here.

object under a concept is nothing other than to judge that the various predicates subtended by the concept are conjointly instantiated by the intuitions apprehended and reproduced, and that such concepts must therefore be formed in a manner complementary to the functions of the judgment – that is, in accordance with the categories. But instead of thus taking up the clue from the Metaphysical Deduction, Kant here asserts that to relate several representations to each other under a concept as representations of a single object "carries something of necessity with it, since namely the latter is regarded as that which is opposed to our cognitions being determined at pleasure or arbitrarily rather than being determined *a priori* ... insofar as they are to relate to an object our cognitions must also necessarily agree with each other in relation to it" (A 104–5). He then maintains that such necessity requires "a transcendental condition as its ground," and that "this original and transcendental condition is nothing other than the **transcendental apperception**," "that unity of consciousness that precedes all data of the intuitions, and in relation to which all representations of objects is alone possible" (A 106–7). The idea here seems to be that whatever else I (any I) might come to know about the significance of my representations and prior to whatever else I might come to know about them, I necessarily know that they are one and all my representations, thus that *this* connection among them necessarily obtains and can be known *a priori*, independently of any particular empirical investigation of the significance of these representations, to obtain. Kant's claim is next that this connection must itself be produced by an activity of the mind which, since it is not contained in mere intuition, can only be assigned to the faculty of understanding, and must employ the rules of that faculty – namely, the categories. Actually, in his initial presentation of the argument, Kant does not even make explicit that the source of the connection that constitutes the unity of apperception must be the understanding, let alone make explicit that this connection must be expressed by some kind of judgment; he simply says that "the original and necessary consciousness of the identity of oneself is at the same time a consciousness of an equally necessary unity of the synthesis of all appearances in accordance with concepts" that "thereby determine an object for their intuition, i.e., the concept of something in which they are necessarily connected" (A 108).

In what is intended to be the conclusive rather than preparatory presentation of the argument of the Deduction, in the third section of the first-edition version, Kant does make explicit that the synthetic unity of apperception can only be produced by the faculty of understanding and that it must depend on the application of the categories to all the representations comprised in this unity for that reason, but he still does not make explicit that this is because apperception involves judgment, and thus still makes no direct use of his clue. In this presentation, Kant reduces the previous discussion of the threefold synthesis to the brief but illuminating remark that "The possibility of an experience in general and cognition of its objects rests on three subjective sources of cognition: **sense, imagination**, and **apperception**": sense for the original presentation of spatio-temporal data, of course; imagination for what was previously described as the syntheses of apprehension and reproduction; and apperception for the representation of "the thoroughgoing identity of oneself in all possible representations" (A 115–16). He then argues that because we must be conscious of any intuition as our own before we can have any further cognition by means of it – "All intuitions are nothing for us and do not in the least concern us if they cannot be taken up into consciousness" – our consciousness of the identity of ourselves in all of our representations must precede or underlie all our other knowledge by means of these representations, or "We are conscious *a priori* of the thoroughgoing identity of ourselves with regard to all representations that can ever belong to our cognition, as a necessary condition of the possibility of all representations" (A 116). Kant interprets this knowledge of our possession of all of our representations as knowledge of a connection or unity among them, indeed a synthetic connection because he takes them not just to share a name or a property but to be connected to one another (otherwise unrelated red things, such as different fire engines, have "analytic unity" insofar as they separately instantiate the same property; the parts of one red fire engine form a "synthetic unity" because they are not only severally red but also collectively constitute a single machine; see B 133–4); and because we know of our possession of our representations prior to knowing anything else about their significance, Kant takes this synthetic unity to be *a priori*, or, as he should say, known *a priori*. He then assumes that such a synthetic unity must be the product of an act of combination or synthesis, and because it is *a priori*, the product of an act of *a priori* synthesis: "This synthetic unity, however, presupposes a synthesis, or includes it, and if the former is to be necessary *a priori* then the latter must also be a synthesis *a priori*" (A 118). This synthesis can be considered a "**productive synthesis of the imagination**" insofar as it involves the apprehension and reproduction of data over time, a typical function of the imagination, but insofar as it results in apperception and involves a concept – the concept of the numerically identical self – it must ultimately be attributed to the faculty of understanding. Thus, speaking in terms of identity when perhaps he should speak in terms of production, Kant states that "The **unity of apperception in relation to the synthesis of the imagination** is the **understanding**, and this very same unity, in relation to the **transcendental synthesis** of the imagination, is the **pure understanding**" (A 119). Having in this somewhat clumsy way attributed the synthesis supposedly contained in apperception, itself the condition of the possibility of any experience whatsoever, to the understanding, Kant then immediately draws the inference that apperception and thus any experience whatsoever involve the application of the categories, as the rules inherent in the faculty of understanding, to intuition: "In the understanding there are therefore pure *a priori* cognitions that contain the necessary unity of the pure synthesis of the imagination in regard to all possible appearances. These, however, are the **categories**" (A 119). All of any subject's experience is part of a single apperception; this apperception is produced by the faculty of understanding; the categories are the house rules of this faculty; thus all of anyone's experience is subject to the categories – *quod erat demonstrandum*.

There are a number of problems with this argument. One question is whether Kant is really entitled to the claim that we have *a priori, de re* knowledge of a *synthetic* unity among all of our representations, or whether he is only entitled to the conditional, analytic, and *de dicto* claim that *if* I really do know that several different representations all belong to myself, then there must be some connection among them, but since I could not know this *a priori* of any particular representations, there would not need to be any *a priori* synthesis of them.[17] A second question is whether we could really derive the *objective* validity of the categories – that is, their necessary application to *objects* distinct from our mere representations – by this route: the argument might seem to establish at best that the categories are *necessary* conditions for knowledge of objects because they are conditions for apperception itself, but not to establish that they are *sufficient* conditions for cognition of objects, or that we have any cognition of objects at all – which was, one might have thought, the chief thing that needed to be established after the Metaphysical Deduction. A third question is whether anything in this argument could possibly establish that *all* of the categories must be used in order to achieve transcendental apperception and with that cognition of objects, or only *some*; in other words, the question is whether this argument could ever establish the objective validity of all of the categories. But the most serious question about this argument is simply whether it can prove any connection between apperception and the categories at all. Because Kant has not explicitly shown that apperception

17 For this criticism, see my early article "Kant on Apperception and *A Priori* Synthesis," *American Philosophical Quarterly* **17** (1980): 205–12. For a defense of Kant from this criticism, see Henry E. Allison, "Apperception and Analyticity in the B-Deduction," in his *Idealism and Freedom: Essays on Kant's Theoretical and Practical Philosophy* (Cambridge: Cambridge University Press, 1996), pp. 41–52.

consists in or involves judgments, he has not shown directly that it must involve the categories; his argument rests solely on the assertion that the unity of apperception is produced by the faculty of understanding, and that it must therefore in some unspecified way involve the categories because they are, so to speak, part of the package of the understanding. Perhaps Kant thinks it is self-evident that all combination or synthesis must be produced by the understanding, because it is not produced by sensibility, but the Deduction would surely be more compelling if Kant could show directly that apperception involves judgment, and for that reason must involve the understanding.

This is what Kant ultimately attempts to do in the second-edition version of the Deduction, with what success we shall subsequently consider. But the gap in his argument must have quickly become sufficiently glaring to Kant and the difficulty of filling it so considerable that in the first few years after the publication of the first edition of the *Critique*, he seems to have been tempted to accomplish the goal of the Deduction by appealing solely to a suitably enriched conception of judgment, thus obviating the need for constructing a convincing connection between apperception and judgment at all.

4. THE TRANSCENDENTAL DEDUCTION BETWEEN THE TWO EDITIONS OF THE *CRITIQUE*

Kant's primary strategy for the Deduction in the years between the two editions of the *Critique* seems to have been to transform the claim of A 104–6 that a *concept of an object* always asserts a necessary connection that had led him to the introduction of the unity of apperception into the claim that a *judgment* is an assertion of a necessary connection that must be grounded in an *a priori* concept, the only candidate for which is the pure concepts of the understanding (*en bloc*). We find this strategy in a number of texts from 1783 to 1786. One text is a sketch entitled "Deduction of pure cognitions *a priori*" that the editor of Kant's *Handschriftliche Nachlaß*, Erich Adickes, dated to 1783 or 1784, thus leaving it undecided whether Kant composed this note before publishing the *Prolegomena to Any Future Metaphysics* that was published in 1783, or afterward. Either way, the note seems to have been an attempt to simplify the repetitious exposition of the Deduction in the first edition of the *Critique*. Kant begins by stating that all experience must begin with "representation of the senses" and "empirical consciousness" thereof, which yields "perception." Then he says that "cognition of any things" or cognition of an object will also require a concept, but now immediately adds that in order to "think something about the object that is designated through a given concept" we must "connect ([or] separate) one concept with another in a judgment ... i.e., we cognize it by judging it. All cognition, hence also that of experience, accordingly consists of judgments." At this point, we might expect Kant then to invoke his clue and remind us that judgments necessarily have certain forms to which the concepts of objects must conform. Instead, he states that "The form of every judgment consists in the objective unity of the consciousness of the given concepts, i.e., in the consciousness that these **must** belong to one another" – that is, that a judgment expresses that in the "(complete) representation" of an object certain properties "are always to be found together," and then infers that since such "necessity of connection is not a representation of empirical origin," it rather "presupposes a rule that must be given *a priori*." He then concludes, without further explanation, that "This unity of consciousness is contained in the moment of the understanding in judging, and only that is an object in relation to which unity of consciousness of the manifold representations is thought *a priori*" (R 5923, 18:285–6; *Notes and Fragments*, pp. 305–6). The "moments of the understanding in judging" are clearly the categories, so these are supposed to ground the necessity of the connection among its terms that is asserted by a judgment of an object.

This sketch exemplifies the strategy that Kant attempts to employ in both the *Prolegomena* of 1783 and the *Metaphysical Foundations of Natural Science* of 1786. The *Prolegomena*, written in the hope of simplifying and popularizing the *Critique* and also of rebutting the first objections to it, does not contain a section explicitly labeled as a transcendental deduction of the categories. Instead, Kant attempts to demonstrate the necessity of pure concepts of the understanding for knowledge of objects by introducing a distinction between "judgments of perception" and "judgments of experience." Judgments of perception are *"only subjectively valid"* and "do not require a pure concept of the understanding, but only the logical connection of perceptions in a thinking subject." They merely use the logical form of judgment to report an apparently contingent connection of representations in the subject, not to say anything about an object. Judgments of experience, however, claim to *"have objective validity,"* to refer to an object in a way that "should also be valid at all times for us and for everyone else; for if a judgment agrees with an object, then all judgments of the same object must also agree with one another, and hence the objective validity of a judgment of experience signifies nothing other than its necessary unity" (*Prolegomena*, §18, 4:298). As in R 5923, a judgment that is genuinely about an object asserts a necessary connection among its terms. Kant illustrates his contrast by stating that mere judgments of perception like "the room is warm, the sugar sweet, the wormwood repugnant, are merely subjective valid judgments," by means of which I do not even "require that I should find it so at every time," let alone "that everyone else should find it just as I do; they express only a relation of two sensations to the same subject, namely myself, and this only in my present state of perception," whereas judgments of experience like "the air is elastic" are intended to be universally valid, to "teach me at every time and teach everyone else as well" (*Prolegomena*, §19, 4:299). Kant's claim is then, as in R 5923, that such an assertion of necessity requires an *a priori* ground, which can only be supplied by "special *special concepts originally generated in the understanding*" (*Prolegomena*, §18, 4:298). More specifically, he now claims that in a judgment of experience about an object,

The given intuition must be subsumed under a concept that determines the form of judging in general with respect to the intuition, connects the empirical consciousness of the latter in a consciousness in general, and thereby furnishes empirical judgments with universal validity; a concept of this kind is a pure *a priori* concept of the understanding, which does nothing but simply determine for an intuition the mode in general in which it can serve for judging.

Kant illustrates this with the concept of cause, which "determines the intuition which is subsumed under it, e.g., that of air, with respect to judging in general – namely, so that the concept of air, serves, with respect to expansion, in the relation of the antecedent to the consequent in a hypothetical judgment. The concept of cause is therefore a pure concept of the understanding" which serves "to determine the representation which is contained under it and so to make possible a universally valid judgment" (*Prolegomena*, §20, 4:300). Kant's thought seems to be that while a judgment of perception merely reports the subjective association of two intuitions – that of air and that of elasticity – a judgment of experience says that these two intuitions must be linked in a necessary and universally valid way, in this case that for anyone who considers the matter air must be considered as the ground of the consequence of elasticity, which is to say, since both air and elasticity are spatio-temporal phenomena, air must be considered as the cause of elasticity as its effect. Only the use of a logical concept such as that of the relation between ground and consequence and of a correlative spatio-temporal but pure concept – what Kant will later call a "transcendental schema" (A 138/B 177) – allows us to transform an arbitrary conjunction of intuitions into a universally and necessarily valid assertion about an object.

   Kant seems to have the same sort of argument in mind when he returns to the issue of the Deduction in the Preface to the *Metaphysical Foundations of Natural Science*. Here, after conceding, as we saw, that critics found obscure the part of the *Critique* that ought to have been clearest, he first claims that this is not really damaging to the "principle end" of the work, for as long as it is conceded that *if* the categories can ever yield cognition of objects at all, they can do so only when applied to intuitions, thus that they cannot be used to provide knowledge from pure reason alone, then the "determination of the limits of pure reason" will have been achieved – and this requires showing only "that categories of thought are nothing but mere forms of judgment insofar as they are applied to intuitions (which for us are always sensible)," not proving that any or all of our experience must be cognition of objects involving the categories (*MANW*, 4:474). In spite of this restriction of his own burden of proof, however, Kant goes on to sketch the "fundamental basis" of the deduction of the categories in three steps. The first step does not use the *Prolegomena*'s distinction between judgments of perception and of experience, but makes a different point about the necessity of judgment: it might seem to make no difference whether one uses a merely "logical function of judgment" to say that something hard is a stone or a stone is something hard, "but if I represent to myself as *determined in the object* that the stone must be thought only as subject, but hardness only as predicate, in any possible determination of an object (not of the mere concept), then the very same logical functions now become *pure concepts of the understanding* of objects, namely, as *substance* and *accident*." Categories, in other words, are supposed to tell us how we must apply the logical functions of judgment, although Kant does not in fact tell us how they do so.[18] Kant then just adds that in addition to the "synthetic *a priori* principles" contained in the understanding, "through which it subjects all objects that may be given to it to these categories," cognition of objects also requires spatio-temporal intuitions, and since these are never more than appearances, cognition of objects by means of the categories is never *more* than cognition of "*objects of possible experience* alone" (*MANW*, 4:475). The key claim in all of this is that a judgment about an object is the assertion of a necessary connection among its terms, just as Kant says in the case of judgment in general in R 5923 and of judgments of experience in the *Prolegomena*.

There are numerous problems with this style of argument. First, it seems clear that the categories can at most be necessary conditions of the

---

[18] Kant adds the idea that the categories make the use of the logical functions of judgment determinate to the second edition of the Deduction (B 128–9), suggesting there that the category of substance makes our use of the logical concept of the subject of a judgment determinate, but not explaining how it does so. Only in the First Analogy of Experience does Kant illustrate how this might work by suggesting that we must always make what endures the subject of a judgment and anything that is only a changing state of what endures a predicate of a judgment about an enduring substance. See A 186–7/B 230–1.

necessity asserted by judgments: that we must use the categories of substance and accident, for example, does not by itself seem sufficient to tell us that the stone should be the subject of our judgment and hardness the predicate, rather than the other way around.[19] Second, and more importantly, instead of exploiting the clue of the Metaphysical Deduction by arguing that concepts of objects must be formed in accordance with the categories so that judgments using the logical functions of judgments can be made about them, this style of argument breaks the connection between the logical functions of judgment and the categories: the application of the categories cannot be inferred merely from the use of the logical functions of judgments; instead, the categories appear to be something different from and additional to the logical functions of judgment, which constrain the use of those functions. But if this is so, then it threatens to become unclear how the categories are to be discovered from the logical functions of the judgment. Third, and perhaps most importantly, the present style of argument seems to undermine the kind of argument that Kant had attempted in the first edition of the *Critique* rather than filling in its gap: according to the present argument, the categories are used to *distinguish* judgments about objects from mere reports of the contents of one's own consciousness, but Kant's concept of apperception seemed intended to subtend *every* experience that one might attribute to oneself and to prove the application of the categories to *every* such experience. The present style of argument seems to *limit* the application of the categories to a domain of judgments that falls well short of everything that can be included in the unity of apperception. Even if this style of argument were successful in its own terms, it would thus seem to undermine rather than complete Kant's original Deduction of the categories.

In the second-edition version of the Deduction, presumably drafted not much later than the composition of the Preface to the *Metaphysical Foundations*, Kant seems bent on reestablishing the connection between the concepts of apperception and judgment so that the original clue to the Deduction, that the categories are necessary for judgment, can in fact be shown to entail that they must apply to any representation of which we can be conscious at all. Our question will now be whether Kant does this without importing a conception of judgment that is incompatible with this goal.

---

[19] To amplify upon the previous note: only once categories have been schematized, or associated with particular temporal properties or relations such as endurance or transitoriness, can we see why one thing must be the subject of a judgment and another only a predicate.

5. THE DEDUCTION IN THE SECOND EDITION
OF THE *CRITIQUE*

Our initial impression of Kant's latest and final version of the Deduction[20] can only be that Kant attempts to remedy the defects of both the original version and the style of argument that he employed from 1783 to 1786 by identifying the unity of apperception with a conception of judgment that is incompatible with the ubiquity of apperception. In this version, Kant expounds the Deduction in two phases. First, rather than beginning from the temporality of inner sense and thus of the materials for all cognition, Kant abstracts from the temporal character of our experience and attempts to establish a direct connection between the unity of apperception and judgment, and thus the categories. In the second phase of the argument, Kant reintroduces the specifically temporal character of all of our intuition (and the spatial character of some of it, our intuitions of outer sense), and then makes two chief points: first, the negative or critical point that the application of the categories to such data means that the categories yield cognition of appearances only, even in the case of self-knowledge; and second, the positive point that the categories are necessary conditions not only for the unity of apperception in the abstract but for the unity of space and time in the concrete. The first phase of the argument suffers from connecting apperception to a conception of judgment that is both implausible in its own right and that undermines the unity or perhaps better universality of apperception itself. The second phase of the argument, however, by intimating that the unity of apperception is a knowledge of the identity of the self through its various representations *in time*, also suggests the particular kind of judgments to which apperception must be connected – namely, judgments about the *temporal order* or *time-determination* of experience – and thereby prepares the way for the arguments of the subsequent section on the principles of judgment, in which Kant will demonstrate that *all* of the categories that *can* be derived from the logical functions of judgment according to the Metaphysical Deduction in fact *must* apply to *all* of our experience.

Kant begins the first phase of the Deduction with the general claim that since sensibility and its pure forms do not present their materials in combination, all combination or synthesis must be "an act of the spontaneity of

---

[20] Kant would revisit other parts of the *Critique of Pure Reason* after 1787, thus writing a dozen more versions of its new "Refutation of Idealism" after 1787 and of course expanding its treatment of the freedom of the will and moral belief into an entire second *Critique*. But he does not appear to have revisited the Deduction after publishing the revised version in 1787.

the power of representation," or an "action of the understanding," which carries with it "the concept of the unity of the manifold" (§15, B 129–31). He then argues that the "I **think**" of pure apperception "must be **able** to accompany all my representations," and that it too must be the product of an "act of **spontaneity**," or more specifically express not merely an analytic unity among my representations – that is, that they each severally belong to me – but a synthetic unity among them, that they each belong to me because of some substantive connection among all of them, which is itself the product of an act of synthesis on the part of my understanding (§16, B 131–3). At this point, one might expect that Kant would immediately invoke the clue of the Metaphysical Deduction – that is, that he would point out that any act of the understanding must take the form of making a judgment and therefore employ the logical functions of judgment as well as concepts of objects formed to complement those logical functions, thus the categories. What such an argument would have added to the conditional conclusion of the Metaphysical Deduction would be the fact of the ubiquity of apperception – that is, the premise for the conclusion that we do in fact make judgments and indeed make one judgment or system of judgments that comprises all of our possible experience, thereby proving the objective validity of the categories. However, instead of immediately reaching such a conclusion, Kant instead tries to link the concept of the unity of apperception to the particular conception of judgment as the assertion of necessary connection that he had tried to use in the period between the two editions of the *Critique*. Thus, after an intervening section in which he makes explicit that the necessary conditions for the possibility of apperception will also be conditions "under which every intuition must stand **in order to become an object for me**" (§17, B 138),[21] Kant then tries to link the concept of apperception directly to his strong conception of judgment as the assertion of a necessity rather than just asserting that apperception must be the product of the faculty of understanding. He does this by contrasting the "**transcendental unity** of apperception" as "that unity through which all of the manifold given in an intuition is united in a concept of the object" to the "**subjective unity** of consciousness," which is a mere "**determination of inner sense**, through which that manifold of intuition is empirically given for such a combination" (§18, B 139), and then asserting that a judgment

---

[21] This comes after a paragraph in which Kant misleadingly suggests that the necessary conditions of apperception are *sufficient* conditions for cognition of objects – "the unity of consciousness is that which alone constitutes the relation of representations" (B 137). The ensuing argument only needs the assumption that the conditions of the possibility of apperception are also the necessary conditions for the cognition of objects, however, so this unsubstantiated claim can safely be ignored.

about an object is an assertion of **"necessary unity** ... in accordance with principles of the objective determination of all representations insofar as cognition can come from them," which are obviously supposed to be the categories. Kant does not use the *Prolegomena*'s distinction between judgments of perception and judgments of experience here, but he uses the same kind of examples, thus distinguishing a relation of representations with merely "subjective validity" like "If I carry a body, I feel a pressure of weight" from a genuine judgment with objective validity like "It, the body, **is** heavy" (§19, B 142).[22] What Kant has now done is to identify apperception as the **"objective"** unity of consciousness (§18, B 139) with **"objectively valid"** judgments (§19, B 142), thereby making the *a priori* concepts of the understanding that are supposed to be the necessary conditions of the latter into the conditions of the possibility of the former as well, in turn securing the application of the categories to all the experience that is included in the unity of apperception – namely, all of our experience that is anything to us at all. The problem, however, is that by identifying the unity of apperception with objectively valid judgment in this way, Kant has now managed to *exclude* from the embrace of apperception mere reports about one's own experience, such as "If I carry a body, I feel a pressure of weight," which seem like perfectly good expressions of the self-ascription of experiences that should therefore be included within the scope of the complete unity of apperception whether they can be immediately transformed into judgments about objects or not, and has thereby potentially left a vast number of our properly self-ascribed experiences outside of the domain of the categories altogether. While it would be perfectly sound for Kant to distinguish between the manifold of intuitions of inner sense that is the data for the unity of apperception and the unity of apperception itself as a structured synthesis of such data, his equation of the distinction between the subjective unity of consciousness and the objective unity of apperception with the distinction between objectively valid judgments about objects and mere reports about subjective impressions means that he has ended up excluding many self-ascriptions of experience from the unity of apperception. He has

---

[22] Pollok argues that criticism of the *Prolegomena* by Johann Schultz led Kant to rethink the distinction between judgments of perception and judgments of experience and to organize the second-edition deduction around the premise "that we cannot imagine any synthesis of apprehension at all without a unifying concept" ("'Almost a Single Inference,'" p. 337). I believe that Kant's use of the same sort of examples to illustrate the second-edition Deduction's contrast between the transcendental and the subjective unity of consciousness that he previously used to illustrate the contrast between judgments of experience and of perceptions shows that Kant did not seriously rethink this distinction, but instead tried to base the second-edition Deduction on what is essentially the same distinction.

established a connection between apperception and judgment, and thereby between apperception and the categories, only by restricting the domain of apperception and undermining his initial claim that I must be able to attach the "I think" – and thereby the categories – to all of my representations. The key lemma that Kant has chosen for his proof undermines the conclusion it was meant to reach.[23]

After having summarized the argument thus far described, Kant says in the "Remark" offered in §21 that only "the beginning of a **deduction** of the pure concepts of the understanding has been made," so that the "aim of the deduction" – namely, the "*a priori* validity" of the unity that "the category prescribes to the manifold of a given intuition in general" – cannot "be explained" (*erklärt wird*) "until the sequel (§26)" (B 144). Of course, Kant does not mean by this to admit that he has recognized any flaw in the preceding argument that will not be remedied by starting over from some new basis. So what does he mean? In a famous article, Dieter Henrich argued that in the first half of the second-edition deduction, Kant had only established that the categories are involved whenever the subject has *some* or *one* unified intuition, but had not established that the categories must apply to *all* of a subject's intuitions, and that it is the latter that remains to be proved in the second half of the deduction in order to fulfill the promise of demonstrating the objective validity of the categories.[24] But since Kant began the first half of the deduction with the claim that it must be possible for the "I think" to accompany *all* of my intuitions (§16), and then attempted to show that the categories are necessary for this transcendental unity of apperception (§§17–20), such a move from *one* or *some* to *all* cannot be that what Kant means to say in §21 still needs to be made. Instead, Kant clearly means that the *abstraction* from the specific character of our sensibility – above all from the temporality of our experience, which had characterized the first part of

---

[23]   Wolfgang Carl holds that the argument of §§18–19 "does not suffice to convince" us of the necessity of the categories for apperception ("Die B-Deduktion," in Mohr and Willaschek, p. 201), but does not argue that the identification of apperception with judgment on which that argument turns actually undercuts Kant's claim in §16 of the applicability of apperception to any representation that may come before us at all.

[24]   Dieter Henrich, "The Proof-Structure of the Transcendental Deduction," *Review of Metaphysics* 22 (1969): 640–59. This article generated a large literature, some of the important contributions to which can be found in Burkhard Tuschling, *Probleme der "Kritik der reinen Vernunft"* (Berlin: Walter de Gruyter, 1984), especially the discussion between Henrich and Hans Wagner there (pp. 34–96), and Manfred Baum, *Deduktion und Beweis in Kants Transzendentalphilosophie: Untersuchungen zur "Kritik der reinen Vernunft"* (Königstein: Hain Verlag, 1986), Part II.

the exposition in the second edition (although in the first edition, as we saw, Kant had emphasized the temporality of our experience from the outset of the deduction) – will now be removed, and the consequences of the fact that the transcendental unity of apperception is *for us human beings* a unity of spatio-temporal experience will now be explored. This is what Kant says in the first paragraph of §21. He sums up the argument of §§15–20 thus:

A manifold that is contained in an intuition that I call mine is represented as belonging to the **necessary** unity of self-consciousness through the synthesis of the understanding, and this takes place by means of the category. This indicates, therefore, that the empirical consciousness of a given manifold of an intuition stands under a pure *a priori* self-consciousness, just as empirical intuitions stand under a pure sensible one, which likewise holds *a priori*.

Henrich interpreted the capitalization of the article (*Einer*) in the phrase "a given manifold of an intuition" to mean that Kant was referring to a single unified intuition, and that he now meant to extend the application of the categories demonstrated to be the necessary condition of the unification of any such intuition to all of our intuition, but there was no well-established orthographical or typographical convention for the use of capitalization in Kant's time to allow such an inference.[25] Rather, Kant makes it perfectly clear in what follows that what he has in mind is not a move from some to all but a move from abstract to concrete. Thus he continues:

– In the above proposition, therefore, the beginning of a **deduction** of the pure concepts of the understanding has been made, in which, since the categories arise **independently from sensibility** merely in the understanding, I must abstract from the way in which the manifold for an empirical intuition is given, in order to attend only to the unity that is added to the intuition through the understanding by means of the category. In the sequel (§26) it will be shown *from the way in which the empirical intuition is given in sensibility* that its unity can be *none other than the one the category prescribes to the manifold of a given intuition in general* according to the preceding §20; thus by the explanation of its *a priori* validity in regard to all objects of our senses the aim of the deduction will first be fully attained. (B 144, italics added)

This makes it clear that Kant now intends to move from an abstract account of the objective validity of the categories as the necessary condition of the transcendental unity of apperception regardless of the specific character of our sensibility to the objective validity of the categories

---

[25] Indeed, in the absence of any manuscript for either edition of the *Critique*, we cannot be entirely certain that this capitalization was intended by Kant himself.

as the necessary condition for our apperception of our specifically spatio-temporal empirical intuition.

The same move from abstract to concrete is also clear in §24, where Kant argues that the synthesis by means of the categories of a "manifold of an intuition in general," which could only be called "combination of the understanding (synthesis intellectualis)," must be called in *our* case, as the "**synthesis** of the manifold of sensible intuition," a "**figurative**" synthesis, "(synthesis speciosa)." That this synthesis that can in general be ascribed only to the understanding must in *our* case be applied to sensibility by calling it "the **transcendental synthesis of the imagination**." This is because since *our* manifold of intuition is temporally extended and thus consciousness of its unity at any one time requires reproduction of previously given intuitions, *which is what imagination does*, our synthesis of intuitions in accordance with the categories, even though in abstraction from the specific character of our sensibility it could be ascribed to the understanding alone, must be ascribed to the imagination as well as to the understanding: "insofar as its synthesis is still an exercise of spontaneity, which is determining and not, like sense, merely determinable, can thus determine the form of sense a priori in accordance with the unity of apperception, the imagination is to this extent a faculty for determining the sensibility a priori, and its synthesis of intuitions, **in accordance with the categories**, must be the transcendental synthesis of the **imagination**, which is an effect of the understanding on sensibility" (B 151–2). The move from understanding to imagination is not so much a move from one faculty to another as it is a move from an abstract description to a concrete description of our ability to synthesize our intuitions in accordance with the categories in order to yield the transcendental unity of apperception.

Kant makes this move from abstract to concrete in the second half of the deduction for two reasons.[26] First, by emphasizing the spatio-temporal

---

[26] Here, my interpretation of the second half of the second-edition deduction is similar but not identical to that of Frederick Rauscher in "A Second Look at the Second Step of the B-Deduction" (forthcoming). Rauscher argues that the difference between the two halves of the Deduction is that "Kant devotes the first half of the deduction to showing the necessity of the categories, and the second half to showing their universality." He bases this approach on Kant's remark, also added to the second edition, that it is sometimes easier to show the necessity of judgments, sometimes their universality (B 4). But in Kant's view, necessity and universality still mutually imply each other, so if the first half of the deduction successfully proved the necessity of the categories for any representation of which we have apperception, that would already entail that the categories apply to all of our representations, and the second half of the deduction could only

character of the empirical intuitions to which we must apply the categories in combining them all into the synthetic unity of apperception, he can make clear that in this synthesis, the categories are applied to *appearances*, and thus emphasize that even by means of the categories we obtain knowledge of things as they appear, not as they are in themselves (§§22–23). He emphasizes that this restriction holds even in the case of self-knowledge – that is, that by means of the categories we can obtain cognition even of our own selves as we appear to ourselves, not as we are in ourselves (§§24–25): "I therefore have no **cognition** of myself **as I am**, but only as I **appear** to myself" (B 158). This point is crucial to Kant's critical assessment of the metaphysical claims of "rational psychology" as well as of "rational cosmology" and "rational theology" that Kant details in the "Transcendental Dialectic," although in the second edition of the *Critique*, in which Kant emphasizes that he has "had to deny **knowledge** in order to make room for **faith**" (B xxx) and is preparing the way for the defense on *practical* grounds of the freedom of the will and for the cosmo-theological idea of a realm of nature authored by God in accordance with mutually consistent laws of nature and of morality, the conclusion that although we cannot *know* ourselves, nature, and God by means of the categories alone, we can nonetheless coherently *think* them by means of the categories assumes equal importance with the critical implications of the deduction.[27]

make explicit that for us these are always spatio-temporal. But I do agree with Rauscher that Kant is stressing the spatio-temporality of our experience in the second half of the Deduction, from which he had abstracted in the first, for two reasons, on the one hand to show that the categories necessarily apply *only* to the spatio-temporal appearances of things to us, not to those things in themselves, and on the other hand to suggest that the categories are implicated in making the spatio-temporal appearances of things determinate, which is the thesis Kant will develop in the following sections of the Transcendental Analytic. Wolfgang Carl also stresses that Kant's aims in the second half of the second-edition deduction are twofold – to demonstrate the necessary application of the categories to spatio-temporal intuition on the one hand, but the limits on metaphysical claims inherent in that fact on the other; see "Die B-Deduktion," in Mohr and Willaschek, p. 204.

[27] Kant's increasing emphasis upon the positive although practical role rather than on the theoretical role of the categories is evident in a comparison of the Preface to the 1786 *Metaphysical Foundations of Natural Science* and the Preface to the 1787 second edition of the *Critique*: the former states that the foundation of the *Critique* is the "proposition *that the entire speculative use of our reason never reaches further than to objects of possible experience*" (4:474n.) while the latter, as we have seen, includes Kant's statement that he has so limited the speculative use of reason in order to prepare the way for its positive use for "faith" – that is, its practical use.

The second, and for the purposes of this chapter[28] more important, reason why Kant makes the move from abstract to concrete in the second half of the deduction is to establish that the role of the categories as the necessary conditions for the unity of apperception is identical with their role as the necessary conditions for the unification of the spatio-temporal intuitions that we are actually given in sensibility – this is what he attempts to demonstrate, as promised, in §26. Here "the possibility of recognizing *a priori* **through categories** whatever objects **may come before our senses**, not as far as the form of their intuition but rather as far as the laws of their combination are concerned, thus the possibility of, as it were, prescribing the law to nature and even making the latter possible, is to be explained" (B 159–60). Following this statement, the premise that Kant explicitly adds to reach the conclusion of the deduction is that space and time are not merely forms for other intuitions but are "represented *a priori* ... as **intuitions** themselves" – that is, they are not just forms for the representation of other particulars but are themselves represented as particulars, as unities,[29] and that this unity too is a synthetic unity. Thus the unity of space and time themselves can be nothing other than the unity of apperception: "this synthetic unity can be none other than that of the combination of the manifold of a given **intuition in general** in an original consciousness, in agreement with the categories, only applied to our **sensible intuition**" (B 161). Here Kant's claim has become even more concrete than his previous claim that the unity of apperception in general is in our case a unity of apperception with regard to spatio-temporal intuitions; even more specifically, the unity of apperception or "original consciousness" and with it the use of the categories are asserted to be the condition of the possibility of the unity of space and time themselves.

But there are two problems with this argument, apart from the general problem that the connection of the categories with apperception itself remains dependent upon the unsatisfactory argumentation of §§17–20. First, Kant offers no illustration or explanation of how the specific categories enumerated in the Metaphysical Deduction are in fact involved in, let alone responsible for the unity of space and time as unified wholes – indeed, since he had earlier rejected the view that space and time are themselves to be conceived under the category of substance (A 23/B 37–8), what application of the categories to space and time he has in mind here is necessarily obscure. Second, it is hard to see how the unity of space and time could be identical to the unity of apperception: surely my representation of the scope of space and time extends far beyond what I take to be the scope of

[28] For more on Kant's positive, practical use of the categories see Chapter 12 of this volume by Frederick Rauscher.
[29] Recall the definition of intuition as not only immediate but also singular at A 320/B 376–7.

my own unified consciousness – even if I am lucky and the latter lasts for, say, ninety years, the former, Kant himself supposes, can only be represented as infinite.[30] At the very least, some additional explanation of the relation between the unity of individual consciousness and the unity of space and time is needed here to convince us that apperception, as the former, has anything to do with the latter.

However, in a second part of §26, Kant suggests an alternative account, that the categories are necessary not for the representation of the unity of space and time as such but rather for the representation, or judgment, of determinate objects of any kind *in* space and time. Thus, Kant argues, to represent an enduring object in space and time, such as a house, my representation of the object must be constructed not only in accordance with the formal structure of space (perhaps its three-dimensionality) and of time (perhaps its one-dimensionality), but also in accordance with the formal structure of conceptual thought, which is expressed by the categories: I do not just *picture* a house as taking up a stretch of space and time, but I *conceive* of it and *judge* it as occupying a determinate *quantity* of space and time, or use the category of quantity. And when I represent an event in space and time, such as the freezing of a particular volume of water, perhaps the water in the glass I left outside last night, I do not just *picture* a succession of states of affairs in some type of container, a glassful of liquid followed by a slightly domed glassful of ice, but I *conceive* of and *judge* a determinate sequence of states in that place, water *caused* to freeze by the overnight drop in temperature (B 162–3). Here what Kant suggests, in other words, is that it is not the unity of space and time themselves but the unity of objects in space and time that requires the categories. And indeed, in the ensuing section on the Principles of Pure Understanding, Kant will attempt to show that not just the categories of quantity (actually a general heading for the categories of unity, plurality, and totality) and causality (actually one of the three specific categories of relation), but *all* the categories are in fact necessary for the representation of the unity of objects in space and time:[31]

---

[30] See Kant's commentary on the First Antinomy of Pure Reason, A 430–3/B 458–61.

[31] Thus I agree with Pollok's remark that "we can mark the division of labor in terms of the lawfulness of our cognition by saying that the deduction demonstrates that (even) the synthesis of apprehension is governed by the laws of the understanding, whereas the Analytic of Principles substantiates these laws by showing the *particular* ways of subsuming any intuition under concepts a priori" ("'An Almost Single Inference'," p. 342). Of course, the project of showing that *any* intuition, including intuitions of inner sense, can and must be subsumed under the categories, is incompatible with Kant's assumption in the first half of the second-edition Deduction that there is a subjective unity of consciousness that does not involve the categories at all.

the "Axioms of Intuition" are supposed to demonstrate the necessity of using all the categories of quantity for empirical judgment of objects; the "Anticipations of Perception," the necessity of using all the categories of quality; the "Analogies of Experience" (most importantly), the necessity of using all the categories of relation for determining the temporal relations of objects in the empirical world; and the "Postulates of Empirical Thinking" show how the categories of modality are used to frame empirical judgments of possibility, actuality, and necessity.[32]

Such a method of argument would remedy one deficiency of the first part of §26, in which Kant did not succeed in making clear just how the categories are involved in the unity of space and time themselves. But once again, the connection to apperception seems obscure, and indeed in this case, the suggested method of argument seems to suffer from the opposite version of the other problem with the first part of the section, that space and time seemed much larger unities than (anyone's) unity of apperception: that is, it might seem that many of the representations that cognitive subjects ascribe to their unified self-consciousness do not constitute part of the representation of unified *objects* like houses and freezing glasses of water; in other words that the scope of apperception is *larger* than that of the domain of unified objects in anyone's experience even though it is also smaller than the unity of the whole of space and time. Is there any solution to these problems?

In this chapter, I can only suggest that the solution to these problems lies in another addition to the second edition of the *Critique* – namely, the "Refutation of Idealism" that Kant inserted into the section on the "Postulates of Empirical Thinking" in the Principles of Pure Understanding. For here Kant attempts to argue that determinate *self-consciousness* is possible only through cognition of objects, thus that there is a direct connection between the realization of the unity of apperception in empirical consciousness and the unity of empirical objects in space and time. An explanation of how this connection is supposed to be established will have to be reserved for Chapter 7 in this volume and for the large literature on the Refutation elsewhere,[33] but we can say here that if this connection can be established, then Kant may

---

[32] See Chapter 6 of this book by Eric Watkins.

[33] For my own account of the Refutation, see *Kant and the Claims of Knowledge*, Part IV, pp. 279–329, and "The Postulates of Empirical Thinking in General and the Refutation of Idealism," in Georg Mohr and Marcus Willaschek, eds., *Immanuel Kant: Kritik der reinen Vernunft* (Berlin: Akademie Verlag, 1998), pp 297–324. For alternative accounts, see Jonathan Vogel, "The Problem of Self-Knowledge in Kant's 'Refutation of Idealism'," *Philosophy and Phenomenological Research* 53 (1993): 875–87, and Chapter 7 of this volume by Dina Emundts.

finally succeed in following up the original "clue" to the Transcendental Deduction. Whatever the details, the Refutation is clearly supposed to work by showing that empirical self-consciousness actually *consists* in judgments about the relations of one's own experiences in time that in turn depend upon judgments about the temporal relations of external objects distinct from one's own representations of them, and if – following the clue suggested by the relation of the two halves of the second-edition Transcendental Deduction – the empirical self-consciousness of the Refutation is taken to be the *empirical realization* of the abstract concept of transcendental apperception, then the result of the Refutation would be to demonstrate that apperception ultimately consists in judgments about the self that use the categories and that in turn depend upon judgments about objects outside the self that use the categories. On this account, the difference between transcendental and empirical apperception would not be a distinction between two numerically distinct forms of self-consciousness, but rather the difference between an abstract characterization of the unity of self-consciousness and its concrete realization.[34]

Such an argument would not only overcome the inadequacy of the connection between apperception and judgment that plagued Kant's previous expositions of the Transcendental Deduction and undermined his attempts to exploit the clue afforded by the Metaphysical Deduction. It would also solve the problem about the disparity of scope recently mentioned, for the domain of objects conceptualized in accordance with the categories would not be narrower than the domain of apperception; rather, apperception on the one hand and cognition of objects on the other hand would both turn out to be comprised of judgments employing the categories, and the difference between them would not be that the latter employs the categories while the former does not, but only that the latter applies the categories to intuitions of outer sense – to representations of what is external to the self – while the former applies the

---

[34] Of course, to say that one representation and another both belong to me is not the same as to say that one stands in a determinate temporal relation to the other, and thus there seems to be a difference of meaning between a mere self-ascription of representations and a statement of their determinate temporal relation. The point would rather be that the possibility of the former depends upon the possibility of the latter, that self-ascription is an expression of self-consciousness that depends upon the possibility of determinate empirical consciousness. I believe that this is what Wolfgang Carl is driving at when he somewhat confusingly first accepts the characterization of apperception as self-ascription ("Die B-Deduktion," in Mohr and Willaschek, p. 192), but then argues that self-ascription is only a necessary but not a sufficient condition for the unity of self-consciousness (pp. 214–15).

categories to representations of inner sense – to representations of what is internal to the self.[35] The explication of such an argument in convincing detail, however, goes well beyond the hints afforded in the second half of the second-edition Transcendental Deduction, and therefore beyond the limits of this chapter. In the end, the Transcendental Deduction amounts to a promissory note for an argument to be completed later in the *Critique* rather than a self-contained argument upon which the rest of the *Critique* can build.

If the suggested argument works, however, it will work by showing that for us human beings, with our spatio-temporal experience, the transcendental unity of experience is *comprised* of judgments about the temporal relation of our experiences, which as judgments must clearly use at least *some* of the categories of the understanding in application to *all* of the experiences of which we can be conscious at all, and by showing further that these judgments about the temporal structure of our own experience can be made determinate only by being correlated to judgments about a domain of external objects, judgments that must in fact employ *all* of the categories. Only when transcendental apperception is itself understood as comprised by judgments can the "clue" of the Metaphysical Deduction be fully exploited and the "objective validity" of the categories that is the goal of the Transcendental Deduction be fully demonstrated.

---

[35] See Lewis White Beck, "Did the Sage of Königsberg Have No Dreams?" in his *Essays on Kant and Hume* (New Haven and London: Yale University Press, 1978), pp. 38–60.

6   The System of Principles

I. INTRODUCTION

The "System of all principles of pure understanding" is the second of three chapters in the Analytic of Principles. It is preceded by the Schematism chapter, in which Kant provides schemata, or time-determinations (in effect, spatio-temporal meanings), for the pure concepts of the understanding such that they can then be applied to objects given in sensible intuition. It is followed by the Phenomena/Noumena chapter, which summarizes the restrictions on cognition that Kant has established so far, and draws out some consequences thereof, especially insofar as they make clear the mistakes of earlier philosophers such as Leibniz and Locke. Despite the clear significance of these chapters, however, it is the System that forms the core of Kant's Analytic of Principles. For it contains his most detailed and specific positive account of how the categories – whose existence and legitimacy were established in a merely global way in the Metaphysical and Transcendental Deductions – are to be applied to appearances – that is, to objects given to us in sensible intuition. It does so not only by arguing for particular conditions under which each category must be applied, but also by providing insight into what Kant thinks any spatio-temporally unified world of experience must be for us – namely, a plurality of substances that stand in causal relations of mutual interaction, a view that is radically different from Hume's empiricism, though it has important parallels with the views of several of his predecessors, such as Wolff, Crusius, and Tetens.[1]

The System contains three sections. The first two sections succinctly state the supreme principles of all analytic and synthetic judgments, a topic directly relevant to the central critical question of how synthetic *a priori* cognition is possible. The long third section, the "Systematic representation of all synthetic principles of pure understanding,"

I thank Paul Guyer and Clinton Tolley for comments on an earlier version of this chapter.
[1] For translations of selected texts of Kant's most important immediate predecessors, see my *Kant's Critique of Pure Reason: Background Source Materials* (Cambridge: Cambridge University Press, 2009).

contains four subsections that argue for particular synthetic *a priori* principles stating "rules of the objective use of the categories" (A 161/B 200). Accordingly, the Axioms of Intuition explain how the quantitative categories are to be applied to intuition, the Anticipations of Perception establish the use of the categories of quality, the Analogies of Experience prove the employment of each of the relational categories, and the Postulates of Empirical Thought explicate the meaning of the modal categories. In the second edition, Kant adds the Refutation of Idealism.[2]

After briefly presenting the supreme principles of analytic and synthetic judgments (Section 2), I explain the principles of the Axioms of Intuitions and Anticipations of Perception and briefly state the main arguments Kant develops for them (Section 3). I then describe the general principle of the Analogies of Experience (Section 4), focusing on the problem of time-determination, which forms a basic framework for all three Analogies. The second half of the chapter is then devoted to explaining the main positions, arguments, and consequences of the First, Second, and Third Analogies (Sections 5, 6, and 7). Reference to Kant's broadly Newtonian account of physics provides guidance on several difficult issues of interpretation along the way.

2. THE SUPREME PRINCIPLES OF ANALYTIC AND SYNTHETIC JUDGMENTS

Kant states that the principle of contradiction can be used as a *negative* criterion (or necessary condition) of *all* truth insofar as any judgment that contradicts itself cannot be true, given that such a judgment annihilates itself (A 151/B 191) and is thus "nothing" (A 150/B 189). It can also be put to *positive* use insofar as it is sufficient to establish the truth of all *analytic* judgments. It is not, however, a *sufficient* criterion (or condition) of truth *simpliciter*, since it is not a determining ground of *synthetic* judgments.

Synthetic cognition requires, in addition to subject and predicate concepts, some "third thing" to justify their combination. Kant claims that the third thing is the possibility of experience, which consists of three elements: inner sense (along with its *a priori* form, time), the imagination's synthesis of representations (in inner sense), and the unity of apperception's synthetic unity (in concepts and judgment). Synthetic *a priori* judgment is possible, therefore, insofar as it can be supported by *a priori* intuition, *a priori* synthesis of the imagination, or the transcendental unity of apperception with its use of *a priori* concepts. Kant

---

[2] The Refutation of Idealism and the Postulates of Empirical Thinking will be discussed in Chapter 7 of this book.

summarizes his discussion with a rhetorically catchy, but potentially misleading conclusion: "the conditions of the **possibility of experience in general** are at the same time conditions of the **possibility of the objects of experience**" (A 158/B 197). While some think that it sets aside onto-logical conditions in favor of purely epistemological conditions (by focusing exclusively on conditions of experience instead of on conditions of objects), it can be understood simply as asserting that epistemological conditions can be, or at least involve, ontological conditions for a certain class of objects.

3. AXIOMS OF INTUITION AND ANTICIPATIONS OF PERCEPTION

The principle of the Axioms of Intuition, which is supposed to state a synthetic *a priori* principle for the applicability of the categories of quantity – unity, plurality, and totality – asserts: "**All intuitions are extensive magnitudes**" (B 201). The import of this principle is that when we represent any "formal" feature of an appearance as having a determinate magnitude, we must represent it as having an extensive magnitude. An extensive magnitude is one where "the representation of the parts makes possible the representation of the whole" (A 162/ B 203), which occurs when the parts of a homogeneous manifold are successively synthesized, or added, to form an aggregate. For example, if I represent nine one-foot-long squares placed next to each other so as to form a large square, the area of the large square is an extensive magnitude, since it depends on the successive addition of the areas of its parts.

The Axioms involves the quantitative categories because a *plurality* of homogeneous parts are represented in terms of a particular unit of mag-nitude, or *unity*, and the successive synthesis of these parts is responsible for the formation of a whole, or a *totality*. It is a *synthetic* principle because one can imagine magnitudes that do not aggregate in this way, such as colors, sounds, and tastes. Insofar as the definition of an intuition – a representation that refers immediately to a singular object – does not immediately entail that the magnitude of its object must be extensive, this feature must derive from some specific aspect of our partic-ular forms of intuition, such as their passivity or spatio-temporality.

Kant's argument for the principle of the Axioms, added in the second edition, is not stated particularly clearly, but seems to consist of two parts. The first part begins by recalling from the Transcendental Aesthetic that all empirical intuitions of appearances presuppose *a priori* intuitions of space and time. It then notes, as the Transcendental Deduction showed, that *a priori* intuitions of space and time are possible only through a synthesis of a (homogeneous) manifold, the consciousness of which involves the concept of a magnitude. Given these two points, Kant can argue that the formal features of empirical intuitions of appearances that presuppose *a priori* intuitions of space and time are similarly possible only through such a synthesis and the concept of a magnitude. The second part argues that because the magnitude of the *a priori* intuitions of space and time in general that make empirical intuitions of appearances possible is extensive, the magnitude of the formal features of empirical intuitions of appearances must be extensive as well.[3] The rest of the text of the Axioms of Intuition explains the significance of this principle for mathematics and its applicability to objects of experience.

The principle of the Anticipations of Perception, which is a synthetic *a priori* principle for the objective use of the categories of quality – reality, negation, and limitation – is: "**In all appearances the real, which is an object of the sensation, has intensive magnitude**, i.e., a degree" (B 207). This principle claims that any "material" feature of appearances – any feature that concerns not the mere form of intuition, but rather its "matter," or the object of sensation – must have an intensive magnitude. An intensive magnitude is one that "can be apprehended only as a unity and in which multiplicity can be represented only through approximation to negation = 0" (A 168/B 210), thus one that is not formed through the successive addition of equal homogeneous parts, as extensive magnitudes are. The magnitude of the motion of a body, for example, is not represented as the summation of several smaller motions. (An object does not travel at sixty miles per hour by traveling twenty miles an hour three times in succession.) Instead, the magnitude of the motion of a body, whatever it is, must be grasped immediately. Another example of an intensive magnitude might be a raw feel, such as the qualia of a color experience. Accordingly, the general idea underlying this principle is that whatever in appearance is due not to the forms of space and time but rather to sensation is to be represented as having a certain degree of reality that could, in principle, be greater or lesser (e.g., if one had different sensations).

Kant's most explicit proof of the principle of the Anticipations of Perception, added in the second edition, runs as follows. First, he notes that perception is an empirical consciousness and thus involves not only pure intuitions of space and time, but also sensation, which is a subjective representation by which the subject can be conscious of being affected. He then analyzes sensation, noting that it is present to different degrees in the empirical consciousness of perception. (In the first edition,

[3] For further discussion of this argument, see Paul Guyer, *Kant and the Claims of Knowledge* (ch. 7) and Béatrice Longuenesse, *Kant and the Capacity to Judge* (ch. 9).

he argues this point by noting that sensation fills only an instant and is therefore not apprehended through a successive synthesis of parts.) On the basis of this analysis, he contends that sensation cannot have an extensive magnitude, because it is distinct from the extensive magnitudes of space and time, which are present independent of sensation.[4] However, because sensation does still have a magnitude – it can vary from the limiting case of o in formal consciousness to any arbitrary magnitude in perception – its magnitude must be intensive (a conclusion that follows either immediately, if an intensive magnitude is defined negatively as a magnitude that is not extensive, or less directly, if Kant, relying on sensations being raw, feels that it can be grasped only as a unity). Now Kant is clear that a sensation is not an objective representation, so establishing that sensation has an intensive magnitude does not immediately entail that every object of perception must have an intensive magnitude. However, he asserts that since sensation is supposed to correspond to what is (empirically) real in such an object, it follows that if sensation has an intensive magnitude, then so too must whatever (empirically) real element is ascribed to the object on the basis of that sensation.

  Though Kant does not offer explicit statements as to how the principle of the Anticipations involves the categories of quality, he seems to think of a determinate intensive magnitude of an object as a limited degree of reality, with the *limitation* arising through a *negation* of a *reality*. In the Dynamics chapter of the *Metaphysical Foundations of Natural Science* (1786), Kant is somewhat more explicit about how the three qualitative categories apply to matter (4:523). He says that what is real in space – namely, solid matter – fills space as a result of its repulsive force, while its attractive force is what is negative insofar as, if taken by itself, it would penetrate all space and destroy solidity. If taken together, however, the second force limits the first such that matter fills a determinate region of space. As a result, the degree to which matter fills a determinate region of space depends on the limitation of reality, where the limitation is a kind of negation.

  The rest of the text of the Anticipations covers a range of topics that are more or less closely related to intensive magnitudes. For example, it clarifies that although one cannot anticipate the content or quality of sensations, since they are given only *a posteriori*, one can still cognize their continuity *a priori*. Kant also discusses the law of continuity of change at length, explaining that the dependence of change on empirical causes precludes any *a priori* proof. Further, he warns that one should not mistakenly assume (e.g., on metaphysical grounds) that the real in space *must be* the same everywhere such that one must accept a void to explain

---

[4] This step is particularly difficult, both exegetically and philosophically.

differences in the quantity of matter at equal volumes. For as the Anticipations has shown, it is at least possible that what is real in space has different intensive magnitudes. He also suggests that no perception, whether direct or indirect, could prove the entire absence of everything real in experience (e.g., a void).

4. THE ANALOGIES OF EXPERIENCE

The Analogies of Experience are those principles that state the conditions under which the relational categories – substance-accident, cause-effect, and community or mutual interaction – must be applied. Unlike the Axioms and Anticipations, in the Analogies of Experience Kant devotes a separate principle to each category.[5] However, he prefaces these three Analogies of Experience with a single principle, which, in the first edition, reads: "As regards their existence, all appearances stand *a priori* under rules of the determination of their relation to each other in **one time**" (A 176). In the second, it states: "**Experience is possible only through the representation of a necessary connection of perceptions**" (B 218). Although these statements provide only a glimpse of what is crucial to all three Analogies, the general idea is that each of the three relational categories represents a necessary connection that is required for experience of a single time and of objects existing and being temporally related to each other within a single time to be possible.

Time itself has, Kant argues, three modes: persistence, succession, and simultaneity. By this, Kant seems to mean that time persists (or at least does not change) and all of its moments are either successive or simultaneous (though Kant also denies simultaneity this status at A 183/B 226). Moreover, if appearances are supposed to be in one time and temporally related to each other in that time, then every state of every appearance must be before, after, or at the same time as every other. As a result, if our experience is to be of objects and their states existing in this one time, we must be able to represent objects as expressing these three modes of time and their states as related to each other in these ways. In light of this, Kant structures his argument as follows. Each of the three Analogies states that one of the relational categories is necessary for experience of one of the modes of time. Thus, the First Analogy states that the category of substance is required for experience of persistence (which is in turn required for experience of succession), the Second Analogy asserts that the category of causality is required for experience of succession, while

---

[5] Kant also distinguishes between the "mathematical" and the "dynamical" principles (A 160–2/B 199–201) such that the Axioms and Anticipations belong to the former and the Analogies and Postulates to the latter class.

the Third Analogy maintains that the category of mutual interaction is required for experience of simultaneity.

Before turning to these more specific, though still highly abstract claims, it is important to consider at a very general level why there should be any substantive requirements at all on experiencing objects in a single time. Why is it not trivial to determine, say, the simultaneity of the book in front of me and the table on which it rests – for example, simply by looking at both? One main task of Kant's general discussion of the Analogies is to address this issue. Two points are particularly central. First, we do not, he says, perceive "time itself" (B 219) or objective time. That is, we do not immediately cognize any timeline or any spatial *x-y-z* coordinates that would allow us to know when and where objects exist. Second, there is a distinction between what one might call objective time and subjective time, which is nicely illustrated by one of Kant's most famous examples, that of the ship and the house in the Second Analogy (A 192/B 237). Although our apprehension of an object is always successive, the various states of the apprehended object may not be, since for example, the parts of a house, although apprehended successively, nonetheless coexist. Once one has distinguished in this way between the temporal relations of the states of objects and the temporal relations of the representations by means of which these states are apprehended, it is clear that substantive questions can be raised about how to justify our judgments about objective temporal relations.

These points can be illustrated by Newton's project in the *Principia*. What we are given in observation are the "apparent" motions of the heavenly bodies (or the motions of bodies relative to us) and the non-trivial task is to determine what the "true and objective" (non-relative) motions are. Newton argues that we must make substantive determinations about the masses of objects and the gravitational relations that they have with each other to be able to determine these motions. While Kant's argument here has important parallels with Newton's, it is both more general (by focusing on generic causal relations between substances instead of specifically gravitational attraction between bodies endowed with mass) and more explicitly epistemological (by focusing on the particular kind of epistemic representations necessary for cognition of objective temporal relations). This latter difference illustrates the point of Kant's analysis of the conditions of the possibility of experience and of the contrast he draws between what is subjective and contingent and what is objective and necessary in our perceptions. For at this level, Kant wants to argue that the cognition of objective temporal relations cannot be based on purely contingent, subjective empirical representations alone, but rather requires necessary, objective, *a priori* representations in the form of the relational categories.

Another important question that arises regarding the problem of time-determination is whether it assumes Transcendental Idealism. That is, does the problem of time-determination concern merely how we *perceive* the temporal relations that already exist between objects, or does it also involve the question of how such temporal relations could *exist* in the first place? Given that Kant's arguments in each of the Analogies (as we shall see shortly) involve both epistemological and broadly ontological commitments – for example, to real and not merely ideal causal relations – and that the Transcendental Aesthetic has already established that temporal relations do not exist independently of us, it is clear that Kant thinks that he is warranted in interpreting the problem of time-determination based on the prior acceptance of Transcendental Idealism. A proper evaluation of Kant's arguments would need to keep this dimension of his thought firmly in mind.[6]

5. THE FIRST ANALOGY OF EXPERIENCE

Kant's statement of the principle of the First Analogy in the first edition is: "All appearances contain that which persists (**substance**) as the object itself, and that which can change as its mere determination, i.e., the way in which the object exists" (A 182). That is, Kant is committed to a permanent substance as an object in which any changing determinations inhere as accidents. In the second edition, Kant adds the further thought that the quantity of this permanent substance is neither increased nor diminished, despite whatever changes occur in nature.

Kant's primary argument for the principle of the First Analogy, added in the second edition, proceeds in the following steps. First, he notes that time is a permanently persisting substratum in which the other modes of time – succession and simultaneity – as well as all appearances must be represented. Second, we do not perceive time itself. Therefore, to have cognition of (or even represent) appearances as temporal (e.g., as successive), one must identify a permanent substratum that can represent time in appearances (in the objects of perception). The appearances that we immediately apprehend are always changing, whereas substance alone, as "the substratum of everything real" (B 225), is permanent and thus the only object of perception that can represent time. Therefore, if we are to have cognition of appearances as successive, these appearances must be represented as the successive states of a permanent substance.

It is crucial to note here the difference between a permanent perception and a perception of something permanent (as Kant does in a footnote at B xli). His argument attempts to establish not that we have a

---

[6] See, for example, Guyer, *Kant and the Claims of Knowledge*, pp. 371–383.

permanent perception – that is, a perception that remains the same while all of our other perceptions change – but rather that what we perceive is permanent, whether or not we are constantly perceiving it. In fact, Kant draws a further distinction between the states of a substance, which may change with some frequency, and the substance whose states are changing, and claims that only the former can be given to us immediately in intuition, but that we can still perceive the latter insofar as we apply concepts to what is given to us such that sensible qualities are perceived as states *of* permanent substances. This allows Kant to avoid one objection that empiricists sometimes raise against substance – namely, that we can perceive only sensory qualities and not, as Locke says, "a supposed I know not what, to support those *ideas* we call accidents." For Kant can concede that substance is not given to us immediately in intuition, while still maintaining that a permanent substance can be perceived by way of its changing states.

Even with these points duly noted, however, Kant's argument faces several serious questions. First, even if one grants that there must be something permanent in perception to represent time, why must it be substance as it is traditionally understood – namely, as the bearer of properties?[7] Two lines of response can be briefly noted. First, Kant can be plausibly interpreted as starting with the traditional notion of substance in the Metaphysical Deduction, and then as simply adding permanence in the Schematism chapter. Therefore, it would not be right to object to the First Analogy that it does not present an argument for understanding substance as the bearer of properties. This is not to say that no objection can be raised, but only that it would need to be aimed at a different target (such as the Schematism chapter). Second, and now facing the objection head on, substance must not only express time by being permanent, but also stand in a relation to the changing states we apprehend in direct perception that time itself does not stand in to them, and it is for that reason that substance must be the bearer of properties. For only the inherence relation that obtains between a single permanent substance and its various accidents or states can guarantee that its states are really temporally related – that is, related in empirically determinable ways. Otherwise, we would have no reason to think that the states exist within one and the same time rather than as temporally unrelated to each other.[8]

---

[7] Guyer, *Kant and the Claims of Knowledge*, pp. 220–221.
[8] A further possibility here is that what is permanent must be a substratum, or bearer, of properties, because time itself is a kind of substratum for the moments of time. Accordingly, if what is permanent were not the bearer of properties, it would not express this feature of time, even if it would express time's permanence.

Second, commentators have questioned whether Kant's argument establishes the *absolute* rather than the *merely relative* permanence of substance.[9] That is, even if one grants that there must be a substance underlying two changing states at t_1 and t_2, it does not follow that the same substance that underlies these states must also underlie two other changing states at t_3 and t_4 and so on, and therefore be absolutely permanent. What is ruled out, it might be argued, is only that there be *no* substance underlying any two changing states. However, several points are relevant here. For one thing, if one granted only relatively permanent substances, no single thing would represent time itself, but that time itself must be represented is a basic presupposition of Kant's argument. (For textual support, see A 188–9/B 231–2.) For another, insofar as substances are perceived only through the states that are their determinations, it is unclear on what grounds one could assert a plurality of relatively permanent substances rather than one absolutely permanent substance. For there is no way of determining when one substance perishes and another arises, as opposed to a single substance persisting permanently throughout all change. With no possible evidence supporting the proliferation of merely relatively permanent substances, it would be more economical to posit absolutely permanent substances.

If substances are absolutely permanent, however, one must be curious as to what kinds of things they are supposed to be according to Kant. Garden-variety objects (houses, ships, books, etc.) will obviously not qualify as substances, since they are not absolutely permanent. Nor, for that matter, will the sun and the planets, as is clear from Kant's account of their origin in the *Universal Natural History and Theory of the Heavens*. However, recalling Kant's commitment to Newtonian science is helpful, because Newtonian mass would seem to fit the bill insofar as even when the sun passes out of existence, its mass does not.[10] Moreover, thinking of substance along these lines helps one to understand Kant's claim that the quantity of substance remains unchanged in nature, because the quantity of mass remains the same according to Newtonian principles. This is not to say that Kant can appeal to the identification of the quantity of substance with mass in his argument for the conservation of the quantity of substance, since the concept of mass is more specific and more empirical than can be used in the *Critique* (as opposed to the *Metaphysical Foundations of Natural Science*). At the

[9] See, for example, Henry Allison's discussion of this objection in *Kant's Transcendental Idealism: An Interpretation and Defense*, pp. 207–209.
[10] In post-Newtonian physics, mass is treated as equivalent to energy (according to $E = mc^2$), such that this kind of identification can be retained even with the rejection of Newtonian physics.

same time, it can be helpful to have an appropriate concrete model of what Kant is describing only very abstractly in the First Analogy.[11]

6. THE SECOND ANALOGY OF EXPERIENCE

Kant's statement of the Second Analogy in the second edition is: "All alterations occur in accordance with the law of the connection of cause and effect" (B 232). An alteration is a *change* of state of a substance, which Kant calls an "event" in a technical sense that is unlike contemporary Humean notions, and he often refers to the law of the connection of cause and effect simply as a causal rule, so the content of the principle of the Second Analogy is that every event occurs according to a causal rule. This much is clear and uncontroversial. There is, however, an important ambiguity in what the causal rule amounts to. Some read Kant as asserting simply that every event has a cause, while others read him as being committed to causal *laws* such that the same type of event must always have the same type of cause.[12] Some textual evidence supports the latter, stronger reading: For every event, or occurrence, there must be a causal rule "in accordance with which this occurrence *always* and necessarily follows" (A 193/B 238, emphasis added, cf. A 198/B 243 and A 200/B 245). And one might suppose, on strictly philosophical grounds, that the very notion of a rule entails some kind of law-like regularity. Whether this or some other kind of argument can be identified in Kant's texts that is also philosophically plausible has been a matter of considerable debate.[13]

Kant's text in the Second Analogy is not clearly structured. As a result, there has been significant disagreement about how many arguments he is offering for its principle.[14] I find it most helpful to understand the text in terms of two kinds of arguments.[15] The first kind, which is expressed most clearly in text added in the second edition (B 232–234), relies on Kant's analysis of the kinds of representations and faculties that we have. Its main thrust is that the succession of two states of an object cannot be

---

[11] Unfortunately, this model does not clarify whether substance is for Kant a count noun or a mass noun. This question turns on issues discussed in the Third Analogy of Experience, the Second Antinomy, and Proposition 4 of the Dynamics chapter of the *Metaphysical Foundations of Natural Science*.

[12] See Friedman, "Causal Laws and the Foundations of Natural Science" for a discussion of both interpretations and an argument in favor of the latter.

[13] See, for example, Lewis White Beck, *Selected Essays on Kant* (esp. "Once More Unto the Breach: Kant's Answer to Hume, Again").

[14] See, for example, Norman Kemp Smith, *Commentary*, p. 363.

[15] For more detailed discussion of the Second Analogy, see Watkins, *Kant and the Metaphysics of Causality* (ch. 3).

represented either in sensibility's intuition or in the imagination's synthesis, because neither can represent the kind of objective connection that is contained in the change of its states. For if an object changes from state A to state B, in order to have cognition of this event we must represent A first and B second and not the reverse. However, our intuitions of A and B are isolated from each other and thus do not represent their temporal relations, and our imagination is free to represent either A before B or B before A. Instead, only the understanding's category of causality is able to represent the proper kind of connection. Therefore, to have cognition of objective succession, we must apply the category of causality. This argument obviously depends heavily on Kant's account of our cognitive psychology, specifically on his taxonomy of the kinds of representations we have being not only correct, but exhaustive. That is, this argument requires that Kant's characterizations of our faculties of sensibility, imagination, and understanding and of the representations that each such faculty can have be fully supported. In the absence of such support, this first argument is vulnerable.

The second kind of argument, which is scattered throughout this section of the text in various guises, does not rely as directly on the contrasts between sensibility, imagination, and the understanding, and can be reconstructed as follows:

P1 Apprehension of objects (the subjective order of perceptions) is always successive.

P2 There is a distinction between the subjective order of perceptions and the successive states of an object such that no immediate inference from the former to the latter is possible.

C1 One cannot immediately infer objective succession from the successive order of perceptions.

P3 To have knowledge of objective succession, the object's states must be subject to a rule that determines them as successive.

P4 Any rule that determines objective succession must include a relation of condition to conditioned – that is, that of the causal dependence of successive states upon a cause.

C2 To have knowledge of the successive states of an object, the object's successive states must be dependent upon a cause – that is, must stand under a causal rule.[16]

P1, P2, and C1 express the problem of time-determination discussed earlier and are supported by ample textual evidence (e.g., at A 189/B 234). They also show that one *prima facie* tempting reading of the Second Analogy cannot be correct. One might think that the way to know whether a cause is present is to note that the order of our representations of the different

---

[16] See Watkins, *Kant and the Metaphysics of Causality*, pp. 209–210.

states of the object in apprehension is irreversible. That is, the irreversibility of the order of our representations in apprehension might be taken as a criterion that indicates the presence of a cause. However, in addition to the fact that such an argument commits, as Peter Strawson famously put it, "a non-sequitur of numbing grossness" by confusing conceptual with causal necessity, P1, P2, and C1 show that Kant does not (and cannot) accept irreversibility as an *assumption* of his argument.[17] Instead, as Paul Guyer has noted, Kant brings up irreversibility as a *consequence* of our knowledge of causality, a point Kant makes clearly when he notes: "I must therefore derive the **subjective sequence** of apprehension from the **objective sequence** of appearances" (A 193/B 238).[18]

P1, P2, and C1 also clarify Kant's strategy in the Second Analogy. Not only is he not trying to derive causality from the irreversibility of the order of our subjective representations, but his project is also not one of trying to find a sufficient condition for causality in what is given to us immediately in intuition. Accordingly, he is not trying to uncover an "impression" of causality that would allow us to distinguish accidental regularities from genuine causal bonds, as Hume is, and, more generally, he is not trying to refute a skeptic about the external world (by appealing only to what is immediately evident in our impressions). The only kind of skeptic whom he is addressing here is one who denies that we must have cognition of causal relations (or laws). However, even in that case, his argument presupposes a substantive premise that a hardcore skeptic would reject – namely, knowledge of objective succession, whose requirements are discussed further in P3 and P4.

P3 introduces the idea that a *rule* is supposed to make knowledge (or "experience") of objective succession possible. Kant seems to be expressing this point when he argues that only by assuming that a change of state proceeds according to a rule "can I be justified in saying of the appearance itself, and not merely of my apprehension, that a sequence is to be encountered in it" (A 193/B 238). That is, the difference between representations that are merely apprehensions and those that are knowledge of objective succession presupposes the notion of a rule according to which the second state must follow the first state. P4 then characterizes this rule as a *causal* rule:

In accordance with such a rule there must therefore lie in that which in general precedes an occurrence the condition for a rule, in accordance with which this occurrence always and necessarily follows. ... I must necessarily relate it [i.e., the succession] to something else in general that precedes, and on which it follows in

[17] Strawson, *The Bounds of Sense*, p. 137.
[18] Guyer, *Kant and the Claims of Knowledge*, p. 247.

accordance with a rule, i.e., necessarily, so that the occurrence, as the conditioned, yields a secure indication of some condition. (A 193–194/B 238–239)

Kant seems to be arguing here that the rule that is required for knowledge
of objective succession must (i) be such that given a preceding condition,
necessarily the later state follows the earlier state, and (ii) entail knowledge that the condition has been satisfied when one knows that the
change of state occurs. As a result, the rule that Kant is arguing for is
both causal – it necessitates the change of state – and epistemic – it allows
one to know that the cause necessitates the succession. This two-fold
claim is evident in Kant's summary statement: "the occurrence, as the
conditioned, yields a secure *indication* of some condition, but it is the
latter that *determines* the occurrence" (A 194/B 239, emphases added).

In the rest of the text of the Second Analogy, Kant repeats this basic
argument in different formulations, but along the way he also discusses a
number of closely related issues. For example, he describes how the
category of causality contains an element of necessity that Hume's
empirically derived concept cannot (A 195/B 240ff.), and he provides
illustrations of why objectivity requires rule-governedness (A196/B
243). He also explains that the rule in question must be causal because
only a causal relation with respect to appearances is consistent with time
itself, which sensibility represents in *a priori* fashion such that one
moment in time determines the next (A 199/B 244). In addition, Kant
considers a reservation that arises regarding simultaneity, and invokes
for its clarification traditional metaphysical notions such as action, force,
activity, and substance (A 202/B 247), concluding with an intriguing and
lengthy discussion of the law of the continuity of change (A 206/B 252),
which stands in a complicated relation to the discussion of this law in the
Anticipations.[19]

7. THE THIRD ANALOGY OF EXPERIENCE

The principle of the Third Analogy of Experience in the first edition is:
"All substances, insofar as they are **simultaneous**, stand in thoroughgoing community (i.e., interaction with one another" (A 211). The
similarities with the Second Analogy are, at a certain level of generality,
obvious and pervasive. For just as the Second Analogy asserts the necessity of causality for cognition of objective succession, so the Third
Analogy maintains the necessity of mutual interaction for cognition of
simultaneity. Kant's arguments for this principle can also be viewed as

---

[19] For detailed discussion of this issue, see Watkins, "Kant on Rational
Cosmology."

roughly analogous to those of the Second Analogy. The first of his arguments, added in the second edition (B 256–58), proceeds by eliminating sensibility and the imagination as faculties that could represent an objective temporal relation, thereby leaving only the understanding and its category of community, while the second (A 211–13/B 258–60) pushes the idea that only a certain kind of causal relation can be responsible for simultaneity. Specifically, the first step of this second argument proceeds from the problem of time-determination, asserting that one cannot immediately perceive the objective simultaneity of two states nor can one immediately infer the objective simultaneity of two states from the order of apprehension (A 212/B 258–59). The second step then asserts that only a rule could warrant an inference to objective simultaneity and, in fact only a special kind of causal rule, called community or mutual interaction (A 212–13/B 259–60). (The last two paragraphs of the text of the Third Analogy then attempt to clarify the notion of community, distinguishing causal community from spatial community and noting that it can be either direct or indirect, if it involves more than two substances.)

However, despite these extensive similarities, there are fundamental differences between the Second and Third Analogies, differences that derive from genuine philosophical features.[20] One important difference concerns the symmetrical nature of the temporal relation of simultaneity and the reciprocal kind of causality that it requires in the form of mutual interaction (rather than a "simple" cause-effect relation). For the Third Analogy requires not only that the place in time of the states of (at least) *two* substances be determined (as opposed to the change of states of only one), but also that the states of these two substances be determined as simultaneous. If one grants that a substance cannot determine its own place in time (A 212/B 258–9), then it follows that, in the simplest case involving only two substances, S_1 must determine, or cause, the state of S_2, and S_2 must determine, or cause, the state of S_1. However, S_1 causing the state of S_2 cannot be completely independent of S_2 causing the state of S_1. For if they were independent, simultaneity would not be established given that the state of S_1 that S_2 caused could be later than the state of S_2 caused by S_1. So what is in fact required to account for simultaneity is that these two causal bonds must be understood *jointly*. (It would not help to say that the two causal bonds must obtain *at the same time*, since that would be viciously circular.) While such a causal notion might sound strange to contemporary ears, it is instantiated in Newtonian physics in

[20] For detailed discussion of the complexities that derive from the Third Analogy's notion of mutual interaction, see Watkins, *Kant and the Metaphysics of Causality* (ch. 4).

the mutual attraction of two bodies in virtue of their gravitational forces or, in fact, in any case of the communication of motion, which is governed, Kant maintains, by the law of the equality of action and reaction. Viewed in its fuller context, mutual interaction turns out to be ubiquitous.

Another important difference between the Second and Third Analogies is that the Third Analogy makes clear how Kant's general model of causality must be understood. It is quite common, starting with the Second Analogy, to understand Kant's model of causality as similar to Hume's, with one state causing another – with the difference, of course, that Hume rejects, whereas Kant accepts, an element of necessity in the causal relation. In that case, the question is simply what Kant's argument is for necessity and whether Hume is really forced to accept it. However, the Third Analogy's notion of mutual interaction is inconsistent with such a model. In mutual interaction, one state cannot cause a second state if the second state causes the first.[21] While some have held on to their Humean interpretation of Kant's model of causality and rejected the Third Analogy as a philosophical lost cause, this is a high exegetical price to pay, all the more so if rejecting the Humean assumption makes possible an interpretation that renders mutual interaction and the principle of the Third Analogy intelligible. Fortunately, it is possible to read Kant as committed not only to events as determinate changes of state but also to substances endowed with causal powers that are exercised according to their circumstances and natures such that these determinate changes of state necessarily occur. Thus, as one can see by appealing to a Newtonian example, when two bodies accelerate toward each other as a result of their mutual gravitational attraction, the change in motion in the one body is caused by the exercise of the attractive force of the other in accordance with the distance between the two bodies and the mass of the latter (just as the change in motion of the second body is caused by the exercise of the attractive force of the first in accordance with their distance and the mass of the second body, such that this is indeed a case of mutual interaction).

On this interpretation, Kant's model is different from the Humean one in a number of ways. In terms of basic ontological frameworks, Kant's model involves substances and their natures, whereas Humean models do not. Further, when it comes to causation specifically, the exercise of causal powers are clearly fundamentally different from Humean events. To stay with the example of gravitation, there are important differences, both epistemologically and metaphysically, between the accelerations of

---

[21] For extended argument, see Watkins, *Kant and the Metaphysics of Causality* (ch. 4).

bodies toward each other and the exercise of their attractive forces. Epistemologically, the exercises of the attractive forces are not observable, as the accelerations of the bodies are (which Newton assumed with his bucket experiment). Metaphysically, Kant (now perhaps unlike Newton) insists on fundamental asymmetries between the cause and the effect. For (1) the cause is active insofar as it determines the (change of) state of the effect (29:807–808), while the effect is passively determined by it, and (2) the cause is temporally indeterminate insofar as its activity is continuous (A 208/B 254), whereas the effect is temporally determinate insofar as it has temporally determinate initial and terminal states (29:863).[22]

Given these fundamental points of contrast, the question of how Kant is replying to Hume is not as straightforward as is often assumed. While it would be natural to expect Kant's arguments in the Analogies to make use only of those assumptions that a Humean ought to grant, Kant appeals to a series of views that are, as we have seen here, rather foreign to Hume's empiricist picture: Transcendental Idealism, a distinction between our apprehension of objects and the objects themselves (though still as appearances), and a different model of causality (invoking substances, natures, causal powers, and changes of state rather than Humean events). It is also the case that Kant's overall project, including his ambitions in practical philosophy and the unity that he hopes to establish between his theoretical and practical philosophy, brings with it yet further contrasts between his and Hume's positions. In light of these radical differences, a proper evaluation of Kant's response cannot be carried out by focusing simply on one or two narrowly specified issues, but rather involves basic issues that depend on one's entire philosophical outlook.

---

[22] See pp. 252–297, esp. pp. 255–282, of *Kant and the Metaphysics of Causality* for clarification and detailed argumentation.

7 The Refutation of Idealism and the Distinction between Phenomena and Noumena

In the "Refutation of Idealism" that he added to the second edition of the *Critique of Pure Reason*, Kant claims to refute what he calls problematic idealism. According to Kant, problematic idealism is a position, traceable to Descartes, which "declares the existence of objects in space outside us to be [...] doubtful and indemonstrable" (B 274). Against this position, Kant wants to prove "that even our inner experience, undoubted by Descartes, is possible only on the presupposition of outer experience" (B 275). Kant presents the following argument for this thesis:

(1) "I am conscious of my existence as determined in time" (B 275).

(2) "All time-determination presupposes something persistent in perception" (B 275).

(3) "This persisting thing,[1] however, cannot be something in me, since my own existence in time can first be determined only through this persisting thing" (B 275).

(4) "Thus the perception of this persistent thing is possible only through a thing outside me" (B 275).

(5) "Consequently, the determination of my existence in time is possible only by means of the existence of actual things that I perceive outside me" (B 275).

Each of these claims needs interpretation. Concerning premise (1), it is not clear what "determination" or "determined" means. With respect to claims (4) and (5), it is not clear what Kant means by "a thing outside me". His explanation of the "thing outside me" as something that is not "a mere representation of a thing outside me" does not help at all to clarify what is meant. The explanation suggests that a thing outside me is something ontologically distinct from the self. However, Kant's theory

There are many people with whom I discussed this chapter intensively, and I would like to thank all of them very much. I can mention some of them – Paul Guyer, Rolf-Peter Horstmann, James Messina, Bernhard Thöle, and Jonathan Vogel.
[1] It should be noted that Kant's expression for "something persistent" and "persisting thing" is uniformly "das Beharrliche".

168

of space and time leads to an understanding of outer objects that excludes their ontological distinctness, insofar as space is only a subjective form of intuition. Finally, it is not at all evident that and how the conclusion is to be obtained. Claim (4) is obviously meant to follow from (3) as the specification of the persistent thing. Claim (5) is the conclusion of the whole argument – that is, given that the premises are right, then this conclusion is also supposed to be right. Claim (2) goes back to the first "Analogy of Experience," but one must ask whether this Analogy really justifies making such a general claim about time-determination. With respect to the third claim – that the persistent thing cannot be something in me – it is not obvious how this claim is to be justified. Kant must be able to exclude all other possible candidates for the persistent thing; in particular, he must exclude the empirical self as a possible candidate – and it is not clear that and how he can do this. Kant himself obviously doubted that claim (3) was convincing. In the preface to the second edition, he says that it should be replaced with the following:

(3') "But this persisting element cannot be an intuition in me. For all the determining grounds of my existence that can be encountered in me are representations; and as such they themselves need something persisting distinct from them, in relation to which their change, and thus my existence in the time in which they change, can be determined" (B xxxix).

But even with this version of the claim, one can question whether Kant is entitled to exclude all candidates for the persistent thing other than the outer object in space. Also, it must still be asked what sense it makes to call something "distinct" from representation within the framework of Transcendental Idealism.

In order to understand the refutation, we need to take into account the fact that the "Refutation of Idealism" only occurs in the second edition of the first *Critique*, though we also find a refutation of problematic idealism in the first edition. The discussion in the second edition is not only remarkably changed. It is also located in another part of the *Critique of Pure Reason*. In the first edition Kant discusses the problematic idealist in the context of the Paralogisms – that is, in the Dialectic – but in the second edition he presents the refutation in the Postulates of Empirical Thinking – that is, in the Analytic. Different reasons for the changes in content and location can be given, and some of them will be discussed later. But apart from the details, it can be said generally that the changes were motivated by Kant's desire to distance his Transcendental Idealism more visibly from other forms of idealism. Historically, the reason for this is that in the reviews of the first *Critique*, Kant's transcendental idealism was accused of being a form of subjective idealism like Berkeley's.[2]

The argumentation in the Refutation has – at least in the version that Kant presented in the *Critique of Pure Reason* – most often been seen as a failure. A commonly given reason for the argument's failure is that Kant cannot exclude other candidates for the role of the persistent thing.[3] In what follows, I will try to defend the argument. I will argue that the Refutation is based on the Analogies, which already claim that all time-determination needs something that can be determined as being in time and space. My defense of the argument will start with an examination of the second and third premise. Concerning the first premise, I will at first simply presuppose that it means: I am able to order everything (or almost everything) that I have experienced in time.[4] The expression "thing outside me" in the conclusions (4 and 5) will initially be understood in the following way: there are objects in space to which I can relate as objects distinct from my subjective representations of them. A more detailed discussion of the meaning of the conclusions (4 and 5) and of the first premise will be presented after the examination of the second and third premise. Because the discussion of the Refutation leads to some considerations about things in themselves, I will end with some remarks on Kant's distinction between phenomena and noumena.

I. THE "REFUTATION OF IDEALISM"

In the second premise of the argument, Kant claims that all time-determination needs something persistent in perception. He then adds a third premise to the argument stating that the requisite persistent thing

---

[2] In particular, this was claimed in the review by Garve and Feder in *Göttingische Gelehrte Anzeigen*, 19 January 1782. For a presentation of the whole development of Kant's attitude toward idealism from the pre-critical period up to the later writings, see Luigi Caranti, *Kant and the Scandal of Philosophy: The Kantian Critique of Cartesian Scepticism* (Toronto: University of Toronto Press, 2007).

[3] See Moltke Gram, "What Kant Really Did to Idealism," in *Essays on Kant's Critique of Pure Reason*, edited by J.N. Mohanty and R.W. Shahan (Norman: University of Oklahoma Press, 1982), pp. 127–156. For a discussion of two influential views, see Jonathan Vogel, "The Problem of Self-Knowledge in Kant's Refutation of Idealism. Two Recent Views," in *Philosophy and Phenomenological Research*, vol. LIII, no. 4 (1993): 875–887.

[4] Like most commentators, I also think that this premise must be understood as including a kind of knowledge about inner states. See especially Myron Gochnauer, "Kant's Refutation of Idealism," in *Journal of the History of Philosophy* 12 (1974): 195–206.

cannot be anything other than an outer object. In the version of premise (3) that Kant gives first in the second edition, he argues that the empirical self is the product of time-determination and therefore cannot be presupposed for such determination. By this Kant wants to exclude the empirical self as a candidate for the persistent thing. But this is only a good argument if one has a particular theory about the empirical self. In such a theory, one could, for instance, claim that the self is nothing other than the product of synthesized states. Under this condition, it would be clear that the empirical self could not be the persistent thing that is presupposed for syntheses in time. Though Kant may indeed hold this claim, it is not something that he could just assume without argument in the Refutation of Idealism. The premise requires some theoretical support to be made plausible. One way to make Kant's argument more convincing consists in exploring Kant's theory of the empirical self. Henry Allison, among others, has taken this route.[5] Another possibility is to look more specifically at why we need something persistent for time-determination. The required condition for determining something in time could be such that the empirical self would obviously be no candidate for it. This seems to be the strategy that Kant himself preferred. In the version of the third premise that Kant inserted in the Preface to replace the former claim (3), he argues (3') that the necessary conditions for time-determination are not given by something purely inner. Representations can only be determined in time if there is something distinct from the representation with which the succession of the states can be compared. Why should this be so?

It seems as though Kant has to claim something like the following: Whenever someone wants to judge in which order her inner states really occurred, she can only do so if she relates her inner states to facts that take place in the outer world and that stand is in a causal connection to one another. Only then does she have a criterion for the correctness of the right order of her inner states. In other words: That there are outer objects is the condition for judgments about the order of inner states, because only outer objects give a criterion for the objective time order of inner states. Such a reconstruction of the Refutation is, for instance, defended by Paul Guyer.[6] Following this line of thought leads in the end to a quite sophisticated theory of ordering inner states. In this context, one has to be aware of the following: If we really want to identify outer objects as the

---

[5] See Henry Allison, *Transcendental Idealism: An Interpretation and Defense*, revised edition (New Haven: Yale University Press, 2004), pp. 275 ff.

[6] See Paul Guyer, *Kant and the Claims of Knowledge* (New York: Cambridge University Press, 1987), pp. 305 ff.

basis for ordering all (or most) inner experiences, it is not enough to correlate inner experiences with outer objects that are causally connected to one another. Rather, there must also be a causal connection between outer objects and inner states. Only then can we, on the basis of causally related outer objects, judge that one inner state preceded another.[7] However, in the Critique of Pure Reason there is no such theory of how outer objects are either correlated with, or cause, inner states. Therefore the Refutation can only be completed by a theory that, according to Guyer, Kant elaborates in his later writings. Thus, the refutation of the problematic idealist in the first Critique is incomplete, though it may be completed by later writings.

In what follows, I will give another answer to the question of why we need something persistent for ordering (inner) representations. According to this answer, the argument in the Critique of Pure Reason is complete. I will begin with a closer look at the Analogies because there we find the reason why we need something persistent for time-determination. In fact, I will argue that we find there already the thesis that we need something spatial for time-determination.[8] According to the Analogies, the unity of experience presupposes the definite determination of experiences in time. Therefore, an absolute persistent or, more precisely, an absolutely persistent substance must be presupposed. It is especially important to comprehend why it must be an absolute persistent. Kant offers a complex answer to this question that can be roughly summarized as follows: To determine something in time must mean to determine something as something that can change. Suppose that you want to determine two different experiences in time – for instance, two perceptions of a ship. To claim that the two perceptions are to be understood as perceptions of a ship crossing the river in a stretch of time – and thereby to order the two perceptions of the ship in time – presupposes that the ship is treated as something persistent over time. It is not that we just assume that the ship persists because we want to say that we perceive it as crossing the river. To determine the ship as something occurring in time and thereby to determine our perceptions of it in time presupposes that the ship can be taken to be something that can

---

[7] For this argument about causal relations, see also Georges Dicker, "Kant's Refutation of Idealism," in Nous 42:1 (2008): 80–108, especially pp. 93 ff.

[8] That the Analogies already prove that we need something outer is doubted by most Kant scholars. See, for example, Guyer, Claims of Knowledge, p. 283 and p. 308, and Christian Klotz, Kants Widerlegung des problematischen Idealismus (Göttingen:Vandenhoeck & Ruprecht, 1993), p. 100. I have discussed this in more detail in Dina Emundts, "Kant über die innere Erfahrung," in Was ist und was sein soll: Natur und Freiheit bei Immanuel Kant, edited by U. Kern (Berlin: Walter de Gruyter, 2007) pp. 189–205.

last and that can change in time.[9] All determination of what we perceive as being simultaneous or successive presupposes something persistent. This consideration does not yet, however, lead to the claim that there must be something that is absolutely persistent. So far, it only shows that one must presuppose something relatively persistent. To complete the argument for the claim that there must be something absolutely persistent, one must say the following: It must be possible to determine all experiences in only one time. Therefore all experiences must be linked to one another according to the laws of causality and interaction, because these are the laws that determine something objectively in time. Whenever we want to determine something according to these laws, we must presuppose that there is something that persists. The crucial point is that this has to be something that persists through all changes we want to determine. If, for example, we want to determine the relation of two balls in time, it is not enough to think of the balls as persistent substances. Rather, we have to presuppose something that lasts while the interaction between the balls take place. One might object that we need no other persistent substance besides the two balls to think of causal relations between them. But the causal relations between the balls are more precisely to be understood as exchanges of forces, and in order to determine these exchanges we must presuppose something that persists through the alterations of the balls. Now, in addition to this idea, the following can also be said: If all experiences are to be ordered in one time, there must be something that is persistent through all changes. Otherwise there would be experiences that could not be linked to each other according to laws. As a consequence, we must think of all changes as alterations of something that persists. As Kant says: "If you assume that something simply began to be, then you would have to have a point of time in which it did not exist [...] but if you connect this origination to things that existed antecedently and which endure until that which arises, then the latter would be only a determination of the former, as that which persists" (A 188/B 231). In other words: We can only determine all experiences in one time if we determine the manifold as standing in a thoroughgoing causal connection, and for this all changes must be determined as alterations of one absolutely persistent substance.

Now we can say the following: If we need something absolutely persistent for the unity of experience, and if the determination of inner states is possible only within the unity of experience, then the

---

[9] If, to take another example, we came to the conclusion that the two perceptions were perceptions of two different ships existing simultaneously with each other, then this result, too, would presuppose that the ships are persistent. This is already necessary because they must last while we are perceiving either one of them.

first Analogy states that we need something absolutely persistent for time-determination. Since neither the inner representation nor the empirical self can be thought of as absolutely persistent, they are excluded by the Analogies as possible candidates for the persistent thing.

However, one can still doubt that this is enough for the refutation of idealism. One could, on the one hand, be skeptical that the first Analogy really shows that the absolute persistent is something outer. On the other hand, one could doubt whether Kant really wants to claim that we need an absolute persistent for all possible time-determinations. The second doubt is possible because the reconstruction of the first Analogy given here is not without alternatives. In Kant's own presentation of the argument of the first Analogy, the claim that we cannot perceive time itself plays a remarkably important role. Because we cannot perceive time itself, something must represent time, and only something absolutely persistent can represent the one time-line with respect to which all different experiences can be ordered. The problem with this argument is that it is not easy to see why it should lead to something absolutely persistent. Why cannot several relatively persistent substances represent the one time?[10] Following my reading, the answer to this question would go roughly like this: Suppose that you perceive two relatively persistent substances and you want to determine them in time. Then you have to connect them by causal relations. This is the only way to give them an objective order in time. For the determination of these causal relations, you must presuppose that there is something persistent that underlies both substances. Only if we determine all changing perceptions as perceptions of only one substance can we determine all experiences in one time. This argument is meant to exclude the possibility that there is any objective time-determination without an absolute persistent. It may look as if it is enough to think, in the example of the ship, of the ship itself as persistent for determining the perceptions of the ship in time. But, indeed, according to Kant, this is not the case. An objective determination of the ship in time is not possible as long as the ship is not also determined as causally linked to what has happened before. Otherwise, there would be no objective order at all, because the objective order is

---

[10] One might simply respond that we would have several time-lines rather than one time-line if we had several substances instead of one. See Jay Rosenberg, *Accessing Kant. A Relaxed Introduction to the Critique of Pure Reason.* (Oxford: Clarendon, 2005), pp. 199–214. However, this response does not explicitly exclude the possibility that several overlapping substances represent the one time-line. This is only excluded by Kant's further claims that only causally related substances can represent one time-line, and that for the causal relations we must presuppose something that persists.

nothing other than the succession of thoroughgoing causally linked states of affairs. Unless the ship is causally related to all other things (which presupposes something persistent underlying all different things), it is not possible to determine the two perceptions of the ship objectively in time. If one were to claim, contrary to this proposal, that something relatively persistent can function as a basis for objective time order,[11] then, but only then, according to the first Analogy, would the empirical self as something relatively persistent be an option. But with my reading, this option is excluded.

In the face of this result, we should address the other doubt that I mentioned earlier: Does the first Analogy prove that the absolute persistent must be something outside me? Can the empirical self or even the transcendental self serve as the absolute persistent? These questions lead to Kant's theory of the self. More precisely, they lead to the question of what we can claim to know about the self. Kant gives the answer to this question in the section of the *Critique of Pure Reason* called the "Paralogisms of Pure Reason." But is it really necessary to follow this line of thought and to go into the details of Kant's conception of the self? One should here take into account the fact that the Refutation of Idealism has been shifted in the second edition to the section after the Analogies and hence in front of the Paralogisms. Whereas in the first edition of the *Critique of Pure Reason*, the discussion of Descartes's idealism really took place in the context of the Paralogisms, Kant changed this in the second edition. It is not very likely that he would have done this if he had thought that we need the Paralogisms for excluding the self as a basis for the refutation. Indeed, we do not need to elaborate the theory of the self. The first Analogy of Experience not only claims that we need an absolute persistent; it also claims that we need something spatial for time-determination. This is because, for Kant, the absolute persistent must be something that can be understood as lasting even though it is changing. It is, as we have seen, a

---

[11] Some Kant scholars think that it is enough to conceive of substances as relatively persistent. See Jonathan Bennett, *Kant's Analytic* (Cambridge: Cambridge University Press, 1966), p. 198. This is obviously not what Kant thinks. But there is a further possible interpretation that does not deny that Kant wants to argue for an absolute persistent, but that does not (as I do) take the absolute persistent as a necessary condition for all time-determination. One could, for instance, claim that the reason that we must conceive all substances as one absolute persistent substance is that we cannot determine a substance as beginning or ending in time. Thus, though we can determine relatively persistent substances in time, we must in the end think of all substances as one substance. For such an interpretation, see Guyer, *Claims of Knowledge*, p. 233.

substance that alters. A condition for the determination of something as lasting though it is changing is that it is in time and space. The first Analogy says: "In all change of appearances substance persists, and its quantum is neither increased nor diminished in nature" (B 224). We can determine something as lasting though the appearances change by thinking of it as having one magnitude that stays the same while it changes with respect to all its other determinations. This is only possible with respect to something that has not only an extension in time but also in space.[12] Thus, objective time-determination presupposes something that is in time *and* space, and therefore objects of outer sense are the condition for time-determination. What is claimed by the second and third premise of the argument in the Refutation of Idealism is already claimed by the Analogies.[13] To determine something in time presupposes something persistent. More precisely, it presupposes a thoroughgoing causally linked chain of affairs, and this is only possible under the presupposition of something absolutely persistent that is spatial.[14] If this is so, we do not need to elaborate on the theory of the self to identify unambiguously the outer object as the only candidate for the persistent. Kant is justified in just presenting it without further explanation right after the Analogies of Experience.

[12] One might claim that this condition is not necessary but a contingent fact about our psychology. However, according to Kant, it is not a contingent fact that time has only one dimension, nor is it contingent that we can only realize an objective sequence by determining the manifold as standing in a thoroughgoing causal relation of outer objects.

[13] In the second edition of the *Critique of Pure Reason*, Kant makes it in general much more explicit that the Analogies refer to outer objects. Thus in the general remark to the principles he inserted a passage in which he declares that it is most remarkable "that in order to understand the possibility of things in accordance with the categories, and thus to establish the objective reality of the latter, we do not merely need intuition, but always outer intuition [. . .]" (B 291). I think that this thesis is also implicit in the first edition, but it seems that Kant realizes its great importance only in the second edition. The new location and content of the Refutation is obviously also a product or even a motivation for this new view.

[14] One could object here that the Analogies only treat the conditions for the determination of objective affairs but not of perceptions of outer things. However, what I am claiming here is that the Analogies give the necessary conditions for all sorts of determination in time. Thus, even though we should be able to distinguish the determination in time of perceptions of things from those of the perceived things, it is for both cases that we must refer to outer objects. I will come back to the distinction between perceptions and things at the end of the chapter.

However, there are still reasons not to be satisfied with this result. Although neither the second nor the third premise of the Refutation really contains any problem for Kant, the interpretation of the Refutation given so far is not yet convincing. The reason for this is that it is not yet clear what is meant by the first premise and the conclusions (4) and (5). The first conclusion that Kant draws says (4): "Thus the perception of this persistent thing is possible only through a thing outside me" (B 275). This follows, as I showed, from the Analogies. But the meaning of "a thing outside me" in this context is ambiguous. It could simply mean that something is in space. In what I have said so far, there is – at least explicitly – nothing that would contradict simply identifying "outside" with "in space". But the question arises: Could not something spatial still be a purely inner representation? In this case, it would not be enough to justify the spatiality of things to refute the problematic idealist completely: The problematic idealist could still claim that all representations, spatial or not, are purely inner representations. To completely refute the problematic idealist we obviously need to justify an understanding of "outer object" that includes not only the meaning of "spatial object" but also the meaning of "real object".

According to the problematic idealist, the representation of something outer is a representation of something real if it is caused by something that is ontologically distinct from us. Reality thus consists in things that cause inner representations and that we only know by their effects. Their existence can therefore always be doubted. Kant has to provide an alternative to this view. The position of the problematic idealist can be refuted by removing the idea that the experience of outer objects is mediated. If we refer immediately to something outer and not via an inner representation, then the basis for the doubt of the problematic idealist is taken away. Following the version of the discussion of Descartes's idealism in the first edition of the first Critique, it seems to be enough to show that there is no justified doubt that things can be outside me in the sense that they are in space.[15] But this does not rule out the possibility that all representations are figments of the imagination and in this sense, inner. Kant must prove the existence of outer objects. Otherwise the problematic idealist could claim that all sorts of representations – including the spatial ones – are imagined. It is this doubt concerning imagination that Kant brings up several times in the Refutation in the second edition.[16] He says,

---

[15] "Thus external things exist as well as my self, and indeed both exist in the immediate testimony of my self-consciousness" (A 371).

[16] In the fourth Paralogism of the first edition, Kant also discusses the difference between imagination and real things (A 374). But he then identifies what is real with what is in space (A 375), and this does not help much.

for instance, that the aim of the proof must be to "establish that we have experience and not merely imagination of outer things" (B 275). In addition, in the first note to the Refutation, he adds a footnote to explain why not all outer objects can be imagined (B 277), and in the third note he states that his proof of the existence of outer objects does not mean "that every intuitive representation of outer things includes at the same time their existence" (B 278). Thus, the situation turns out to be the following: Even if it is, as I have argued so far, proven by the first Analogy that we need something in space in order to account for time-determination, it is, at least as it looks so far, not yet proven that this something outside is real – that is, not imagined.

Facing this situation, we should be aware of the following: In the first edition (A 373), Kant himself states that the expression "outside us" is ambiguous. He distinguishes two senses of "outside us." It can mean that something is in space. A thing that is outside in this sense is an empirical external object – an object that stands under the subjective conditions of space and time. But the expression can also have a transcendental sense and mean a thing that is distinct from us as a thing in itself. This is, however, not the ambiguity that I am stressing here. I am talking about something that seems to be outside us in the first sense but that is really not an object outside us but rather only something imagined to be outside us. I think we must take this further complication concerning the meaning of "outside us" into account. Nevertheless, we cannot just leave the ambiguity of "outside us" that Kant himself mentions behind us. Obviously we find a similar ambiguity with respect to the meaning of "real" and "independent of us". To say that something is real – that is, independent of us – can mean that it is ontologically distinct, a thing outside us in the transcendental sense. But it can also mean that it is objective – that is, it is something about which we can judge objectively and that is in this sense not dependent on our subjective perspective. If we now want to provide what has turned out to be necessary for a complete refutation – namely, a proof of the *reality* of things outside us – then we must determine in what sense one has to understand "real" or "independent of us" here.

Most contemporary Kant scholars hold that, in this context, Kant means by real things things in themselves in the sense of things that are ontologically distinct from us.[17] As far as I can see, there are mainly

---

[17] See Guyer, *Claims of Knowledge*, especially p. 282 and 290–292. Compare also Paul Guyer, "The Postulates of Empirical Thinking in General and the Refutation of Idealism," in *Immanuel Kant: Kritik der reinen Vernunft*, edited by Georg Mohr and Marcus Willaschek (Berlin: Akademie Verlag, 1998) pp. 297–324, especially p. 311. See Béatrice

two motives for this thesis. One is Kant's idea of something real in general. According to Kant, a perception is of a real thing if there is a given sensation: "Thus sensation is that which designates a reality in space and time" (A 374). This idea has suggested to many commentators that the difference between representations of imaginary things and representations of real things hangs together with the cause of the sensation. Thus, a representation of something real must be caused. And this cause cannot be anything other than the thing in itself, because it is only sensation that is given as material for the determination of an object of experience. Accordingly, the sensation cannot be produced by the object of experience. If Kant intended to show more convincingly than in the first edition that there must be something real, then he must, according to this consideration, argue for a cause of our representations as something ontologically independent of us. The second reason to hold this thesis is given by the Refutation itself. More precisely, the way the first premise is stated suggests that Kant has an understanding of inner experience that he shares with the problematic idealist.[18] If this were true – if Kant thought of inner experience as a complete history of inner states, including perceptions of outer objects as inner states – then it would indeed be natural to think of outer objects as an ontologically independent source of inner representations. We do not need to elaborate this point here. But I will pick it up later on because we must take it into account for a closer understanding of the first premise.

Affirming the thesis that Kant must refer to things in themselves is, according to this line of thought, to understand the Refutation as claiming that for inner experience we need existing outer things that cause at least some of our inner states and that are ontologically distinct from us. Note that Kant does not have to show which representation is caused and which one is only imagined. But he has to show that at least some of our representations of something outer must be caused.[19] This can be done roughly in the way I presented earlier by following an idea by Paul Guyer

Longuenesse, "Kant's I Think versus Descartes' I Am a Thing That Thinks," in *Kant and the Early Moderns*, edited by D. Garber and B. Longuenesse (Princeton: Princeton University Press, 2008), pp. 9–31, especially p. 29, and Christian Klotz, *Kants Widerlegung*, pp. 50 and 67.

[18] That Kant has problems developing his own position because he relies on the premise of the problematic idealist is also claimed by Longuenesse, "Kant's I Think," p. 31

[19] At least it seems to me that as a criterion to know which representation is real, one could still have the one that I will mention later on – namely, the lawful connection with other things that we perceive. But I will not discuss this here.

and others – that Kant could argue that we need causal relations for the definite time order.[20]

As I have also said before, in the "Refutation of Idealism" Kant does not say anything about causal effects. Though we can find remarks on inner states as causal effects in Kant's later reflections, the refutation in the *Critique of Pure Reason* would obviously fail if it were to argue for ontologically distinct things. But this is not the only problem for this reading. If Kant were to go this way, this would lead to deep philosophical problems within his philosophy. If he were talking about the thing in itself as that whose affection causes a representation, then he would have to claim that the thing in itself has to be conceived as persistent. He thereby would give up the difference between appearances and things in themselves, he would deny that space and time are only subjective forms of intuition (because the real persistent thing must be spatial), and he would contradict the claim that "it will not occur to us to seek information about what the objects of our senses may be in themselves" (A 380).[21] It could, of course, be the case that Kant transformed his theory of things in themselves in the second edition of the first *Critique*.[22] But any reference to things in themselves as ontologically distinct things

---

[20] That the necessity of causal relations is enough to claim that outer objects are really distinct from representations is doubted by Jonathan Vogel, "The Problem", 885. There are other possibilities to argue for the existence of ontologically independent things. For example Andrew Chignell, "Causal Refutations of Idealism", in *Philosophical Quarterly* (forthcoming 2010) defends a strategy that makes use of conceptual implications. But the problems I will discuss here are not restricted to the causal claim but concern the very idea of a proof of ontologically distinct things within a Kantian framework.

[21] Guyer thinks that the difficulties that are brought up here are not really substantial. See *Claims of Knowledge*, especially p. 344. Although he sees a tension between this sort of realistic claims and transcendental idealism, he thinks that we should give up transcendental idealism anyway. This cannot be discussed here. Although Dicker follows Guyer and defends the argument found in Kant's later writings that refer to causal relations, he thinks that these considerations do not lead to problems with transcendental idealism. This is because, according to him, transcendental idealism has to be understood in the weakest possible way – that is, as saying that we do not know how things are independent of our understanding of them. See Dicker, "Kant's Refutation," pp. 100f. For a discussion of this difference between Guyer and Dicker, see also Chignell, "Causal Refutations".

[22] As far as I can see, most Kant scholars who hold the thesis that Kant refers to things in themselves also maintain that Kant modified his whole theory. See, for example, Guyer, *Claims of Knowledge*, p. 282. Klotz, *Kants Widerlegung*, p. 50.

that takes these things to be a source of affection that we can or even must know something about would contradict at least some of Kant's claims about things in themselves. Note that this is true independently of which interpretation of the thing in itself one maintains. It is hard to believe that Kant broke with such deep convictions of his philosophy. This is not very likely, at least insofar as there is another route that he could have taken to reach his aim in the Refutation. And as I will argue in what follows, there is indeed another, and in my eyes, even more convincing route.

We are thus again looking for an interpretation of the Refutation according to which Kant can not only show that we need something spatial to determine inner states but also that we need something that is real. However, we should be aware that, in the Refutation of Idealism as well as in the Analogies, Kant seems to presuppose that the spatial outer things are real. He talks, for instance, about the persistent in perception in the argumentation given at the beginning of this chapter.[23] A perception of a persisting thing has a sensational component. If sensation designates reality, there is no question that the second premise of the refutation is talking about something real. This is important to recognize because it helps to clarify what we are really looking for. We are not looking for a more realistic picture of things – a demand with respect to which the reference to the thing in itself might be a solution. Rather we are looking for something that we can distinguish from our inner states in such a way that we can take it to be independent of them. For if we can argue for something that is independent from inner states, it is not possible that this is a mere figment of the imagination. Whereas merely proving that we need to represent something spatial would leave room for the problematic idealist, the proof of the existence of independent objects would be a complete refutation. What has to be proven is that for inner experience we need spatial objects – objects that are in space and about which we know that they cannot be imagined. For that, we do not need to refer to ontologically distinct things. Instead, we must consider the ground for the objectivity of representations. Not surprisingly, this ground is found in the Analogies. Representations are objective if and only if they are determined in the way the Analogies declare. Thus we can say: If we follow the arguments given by the Analogies, we not only know that we need something absolutely persistent that is spatial for all time-determinations, but we also know that whenever we refer to an absolute persistent that is spatial and that is determined by thoroughgoing causal

---

[23] In addition, in the discussion of Descartes in the first edition (A 373 f), he explicitly says that something is real in time or space if there is given sensation.

laws, we have something that is independent of our subjective inner states. Thus it cannot be merely imagined. There is no room left for a position that claims that our representations are all imagined. Assuming that the Analogies are true, the problematic idealist is refuted.[24] Hence, we can say that the Refutation uses the results given by the Analogies to explicitly refute the problematic idealist.

Following this line of thought, Kant does not need to elaborate a more realistic picture of things for refuting the problematic idealist.[25]

[24] Here I follow Abela, who claims that the "refutation offers no argument not already implicitly contained in the Analogies." See Paul Abela, *Kant's Empirical Realism* (Oxford: Oxford University Press, 2002), 186.

[25] Kant himself seems to have contradicted this thesis in the so-called reflections – notes that he had written soon after the second edition of the *Critique of Pure Reason*. Compare especially Reflections 5653–5654 (probably dating to 1788–89) and 6312–6316 (probably dating to 1790), 18: 306–313 and 610–623. In these reflections, Kant obviously tries to argue against idealism by introducing the thing in itself. He does so by claiming that in all spontaneous thinking, there lies some sort of "original passivity" (307) that we are aware of and that we can explain only if we accept something like things in themselves that affect us. In comparison with the Refutation, this idea gives a new argument in content and structure. However, this does not mean that Kant gave up his argument of the refutation. First, it is not clear whether Kant is really dealing here with Descartes and not with Berkeley. That Kant wants to hold the claim that we somehow know from our receptivity that there are things in themselves does not contradict my interpretation of the Refutation. Second, in these reflections, there is also some continuity with what Kant says in the Refutation, at least if one follows my interpretation of it. There are many passages in which Kant says that the outer object cannot be a mere representation that is related only to the subject but must be a real outer object (see 309f). According to my interpretation, this is already claimed in the refutation in the *Critique of Pure Reason*. It should be mentioned that Paul Guyer's interpretation of Kant's completing of the Refutation is based on these reflections; see Guyer, *Claims of Knowledge*, 305ff. However, it is not the idea of passivity that Guyer wants to elaborate. (For this, see Eckart Förster, "Kant's Refutation of Idealism," in *Philosophy, Its History and Historiography*, edited by A. J. Holland (Dordrecht: D. Reidel Publishing Company, 1985), pp. 295–311, at pp. 296 ff.) Guyer, instead, argues that Kant in the end came to a new understanding of an outer object (because representations cannot function as objects with respect to which we can determine inner states), and this partly because Kant learned to give up the alternative that the presupposition that there are external objects would be either immediate or inferential (327). I cannot deal with these theses here. I only want to claim that these reflections do not make it necessary for Kant to give up his strategy of the Refutation itself.

Rather, it is enough to trust his theory, already stated in the first edition, that a real thing can be sufficiently distinguished from a product of the imagination by the criterion that it stands in a thoroughgoing lawful connection with all other things of perception. This reading provides, by the way, a perfectly good explanation for the location of the Refutation in the second edition – namely, at the end of the section on the postulate of actuality. The postulate of actuality is part of the "Postulates of Empirical Thinking in General," the final section of the "System of all Principles of Pure Understanding," in which Kant provides the "definition of the concepts of possibility, actuality and necessity in their empirical use" (A 219/B 266).[26] According to the postulate of actuality, that which is lawfully "connected with the material conditions of experience (of sensation) is actual" (A 218/B 266). One might think that this is not enough to distinguish imagined things from real things. But it is Kant's thesis that we have no other meaningful sense of the existence of an object than that of a given sensation that is related to spatial intuition and that stands in a thoroughgoing connection to other things of perception so that we can take it to be objective and independent of our subjective inner states. The criterion of standing in a thoroughgoing connection must be applied in each single special case to decide if a representation can be taken to be a real object. But the thoroughgoing connection is not only a criterion for the evaluation of single cases. That we determine objects as standing in a thoroughgoing lawful connection is a condition for experience in general. It is a condition

---

[26] According to Kant, the categories of modality do not give conditions of the possibility of experience, but they have the peculiarity that they "only express the relation to the faculty of cognition" (A 219/B 266). In the Postulates, Kant thus explains mainly how we use the concepts of possibility, actuality and necessity. According to the Postulates, "possibility" means that something "agrees with the formal conditions of experience" (A 218/ B 265). Thus it is not sufficient for something's being possible that its concept includes no contradiction. Rather it also must be something that could be an occurence in our world (for example, a miracle might be logically possible but it has no "real" possibility because it is not in agreement with the Principle of Causality). The postulate of actuality claims, as I said earlier, that something that we call real must be given by a perception or standing in a lawful connection with something that we can perceive. Kant explains necessity further by pointing out that something exists necessarily if its "connection with the actual is in accordance with general conditions of experience" (A 218/ B 266). This means that whatever is actual and what is lawfully determined can be said to exist necessarily. For a further discussion of the relation between the actual and the necessary, see also Paul Guyer, "The Postulates." At the end of the section on the Postulates, Kant tries to make clear that further questions with respect to modalities tend to go beyond the limits of what we can know.

for the time-determination of inner states that is undoubted by Descartes. This is made explicit by the Refutation.

What I have said so far can be summarized in the following way: The aim of the Refutation of Idealism is to prove the existence of outer objects in the sense of objects of experience. The premises about time-determination (2, 3) are justified by the Analogies. We would not have any experience at all – neither outer nor inner – if we did not determine our representations according to the Analogies. But if we determine our representations according to the Analogies, there can be no doubt that there are real outer objects. The reason for this is that the conditions for time-determination are such that we must refer to an absolute persistent that is spatial. This is what was shown in the first part of this chapter. Furthermore, to determine something in time is only possible in a way that includes the objective status of at least some of our representations. Thus the determination makes it possible to conceive of something as independent of our inner states. If time-determination is only possible in this way, all experience – that is, all inner experience – presupposes the existence of outer objects.

I have not yet discussed the meaning of the first premise in the argument. However, the last discussion has some implications for the understanding of what can be meant by it. At least at first glance, these implications seem to raise problems for the whole argument. If one follows the line of thought I have outlined here, one comes to the result that for Kant there is no purely inner experience. Whenever we determine something in time, we thereby determine (at least some) things we represent as things outside of us. Therefore we must deny the very idea of purely inner experience.[27] Instead we should say that the consciousness of my own being in time is a process in which I determine myself and other things as being real things in time and space. Although this idea may be convincing in itself, it leads to a problem in the argument of the Refutation. After all, one could make the following objection: If Kant had held this theory, he was not right to present the Refutation as an argument in the form he did. This argument is only valid if Kant and the problematic idealist share the first premise and understand it in the same way. But, as it looks now, Kant's understanding of "inner experience" or of "consciousness of my own existence as determined in time" is remarkably different from the problematic idealist's understanding of inner experience. If this is true, the argument is a failure. This does not mean that Kant cannot show that the position of the problematic idealist is

---

[27] I do not want to deny that there can be purely inner states – like feelings – but these states do not build an "inner experience" and they are in themselves very elusive.

untenable. He can show this by demonstrating that inner experience in the real sense presupposes the existence of outer objects. This actually looks more like the discovery of a paralogism than an argument against the problematic idealist. We could say something like this: The expression "my own existence as determined in time" is indeed empty as long as we abstract from the conditions of experience that include the existence of outer objects. Was Kant in the end wrong to shift the Refutation to the Analytic and present it not as a paralogism but as an argument with which he could refute the problematic idealist? Or, contrary to what I have said so far, in the second edition did he in principle follow the theory of inner sense of the problematic idealist? Then indeed he would have to think of real things as things in themselves and try to prove their existence. However, there is also a third possibility. Although Kant and the problematic idealist have very different ideas of inner experience, there is something that they nevertheless share. Both of them want to claim that we can order our representations in time in such a manner that this order can be judged to be wrong or right. If we understand the premise of the argument in exactly this way, then the argument is valid. The ordering of my representations presupposes, according to Kant, that we can refer to (at least to some) of them as objective, whereas the problematic idealist thinks that we can order them and treat them at the same time as imagined or purely inner. Since Kant claims that "even our inner experience, undoubted by Descartes, is possible only under the presupposition of outer experience," it sounds as if we could also separate, in the framework of Kant's own philosophy, inner experience from outer. But this is not the case. In this Kantian framework, we can have representations that are not objectively determined, and in this sense there are representations in inner sense that can be called purely inner. But as far as we determine them – that is, as far as we have indeed inner *experience* – the inner experience is not separable from the outer one. Suppose that Kant and the problematic idealist are both asked to describe the situation of determining inner states. As the problematic idealist sees it, we would have an inner representation of coming home and another one of sitting at the desk. Ordering them in time must mean to correlate them with real things. Most Kant scholars just transfer this picture to Kant. The result is that we are looking for a real outer source of affection. But the transfer is not justified. At least according to my interpretation, Kant's description would sound very different; it would be something like this: Ordering the representations of coming home and sitting at the desk means to determine coming home and sitting at the desk as outer facts. This is done by a causal history. However, with this the very idea of an inner experience in opposition to an outer one is denied.

One could object to my reading that the manner in which I describe the determination of representations is not well suited to explain the order of *perceptions* of things in opposition to the order of things as objects in time and space. More precisely, one could say the following: Whereas according to the common reading the perceptions of things can be taken to be inner representations in opposition to outer objects, there is no possibility of making the distinction between the order of things and the order of perceptions if one follows my reading. But this objection is not justified. It must indeed be taken into account that the perceptions of things can stand in a different sequence in time from the objects that are perceived. We can, for instance, perceive parts of a house that are objectively at the same time in a sequence of time. Nevertheless, it is not right that I cannot make sense of this difference within my interpretation. According to it, perceptions of things are dependent on the causal relation between the object and the embodied human being. In order to determine the perceptions in time, we must first determine the objects that we perceive and then we must determine ourselves and the objects as standing in a relation in time and space. This determination provides sufficient grounds for objective judgments about the order of our perceptions. Without doubt, this theory needs more elaboration.[28] However, this is not necessary for the refutation of the problematic idealist. In order to refute the problematic idealist, it is sufficient if it is true that the determination of outer objects is a necessary condition for all time-determination. This is, as I argued, shown by the Analogies.

What I have said so far can be summarized in the following way: Kant shares with the problematic idealist the assumption that we can order our representations in time. As already shown in the Analogies, this ordering is possible only under the presupposition of the existence of outer objects. Thus, if the problematic idealist wants to maintain that we can order our representations in time, she must give up the thesis that we can doubt the existence of outer objects.

Although I have brought up several times the question of why Kant shifted the discussion of the problematic idealism in the second edition of the *Critique of Pure Reason*, there is one aspect of this question that I have not yet mentioned. The Analytic, within which the Refutation occurs, does not end with the Postulates. Rather, the last considerations of the Analytic begin the endeavor of the Dialectic – to provide a fundamental critique of traditional metaphysics. These considerations must contain

---

[28] This, in my eyes, is what Kant tries to elaborate in his later reflections, especially in his so called "Selbstsetzungslehre." See Eckart Förster, "Kant's Refutation of Idealism," pp. 287–303.

Kant's view on things in themselves. Since one result of my interpretation is that Kant need not to refer to things in themselves to refute the problematic idealist, we should take a look at these considerations.

2. "PHENOMENA AND NOUMENA"

At the end of the Analytic, in the section "On the ground of the distinction of all objects in general into phenomena and noumena," Kant reminds us of the lesson we have learned so far: We can use concepts meaningfully only if we use them with respect to something that stands under the conditions of time and space. Even the categories as forms of thinking only tell us something about objects if we use them in the schematized form – that is, if we treat them as concepts to determine something in time and space. "The Transcendental Analytic accordingly has this important result: That the understanding [. . .] can never overstep the limits of sensibility" (A 246/B 303). In this context, Kant interprets this result in the following way: "the proud name of an ontology, which presumes to offer synthetic a priori cognitions of things in general in a systematic doctrine (e.g., the principle of causality), must give way to the modest one of a mere analytic of the pure understanding" (A 247/ B 303). It is natural to understand this statement as saying that all the proofs in the Analytic concern nothing but our conditions of knowledge, not ontologically distinct things. If this is the right interpretation – which I do not want to discuss here – then it supports the thesis of my interpretation that the only sense Kant can attach to the concept of reality is that of something given in sensation that we determine according to the categories as an object of experience.

Following Kant's line of thought, we should thus be aware of the limits of our meaningful use of the categories. Limiting our use of the categories is, in Kant's eyes, not without difficulties. Since we also have the categories in the form of pure concepts, we tend to think that there is something to think with them independently of time and space – that is, "I suppose there to be things that are merely objects of the understanding" (A 249). In opposition to phenomena, these objects would be called noumena. But, as Kant points out, it not only seems to be the case that the categories are applicable independently of our sensible constitution. The idea that there is a possible cognition of things other than the objects in space and time is also suggested by the Transcendental Aesthetic – namely, that the conditions of sensibility spelled out in the Transcendental Aesthetic seem to imply that there are objects beyond the field of our possible knowledge. For if we state that we only cognize objects as they appear to us, this seems to imply the possibility that another intelligence can also cognize them as they are. Thus the concept of a noumenon arises not only from the Analytic but also from the Aesthetic (A 249 ff; compare B 305 ff). What is important here is that Kant sees the possibility that one could draw on the Aesthetic to argue that we can cognize non-empirical objects by the categories. This is because of the following: The meaningful use of the categories beyond our sensibility presupposes that there are things that can be given for another form of intuition than ours to which we could refer with the categories. If the Aesthetic could be understood as saying that there are things that can be cognized as they are, then there seem to be real objects to which we can apply our categories independently of the conditions of our sensibility. An example of these objects would be the soul, as well as monads, understood as the real essence of matter. The Aesthetic then would support another use of the categories than the empirical one.

It goes without saying that Kant wants to deny this possibility. However, it is not so clear on what ground he wants to deny it. More precisely, it is clear that Kant indeed thinks that our categories reach farther than the realm of our sensibility, but he wants to deny that we can cognize objects by categories that are not schematized. What is less clear is his position with respect to the thing in itself. In the section on phenomena and noumena, Kant argues in the following way: It is one thing to claim with regard to the objects of experience that they entail something given that we did not produce.[29] But it is another thing to claim that there is indeed an object that is in principle cognizable as it is and that causes the given sensation. Only the second claim implies that there are things of an intuition different from ours. Thus only the second claim supports the idea of the meaningful use of the categories beyond our sensibility. The first one, on the contrary, does not make any positive statement. It does not say that there are objects that can be given to any intuition at all. The Aesthetic yields, according to what Kant is saying here, only the first claim. Thus, if one were to ask whether there are things independently of our cognition, the answer has to be that a positive answer to this question lies beyond our possible knowledge, because it presupposes too much knowledge about how things could be independently of us. Thus the Aesthetic provides no basis for a non-empirical use of the categories. Especially in the second edition, Kant tries to fix the

---

[29] I think that, for Kant, it follows from the receptivity of our sensibility that there is something we can call thing in itself. But we have no idea what this is and, more importantly, there is no need to say what it is as far as we can determine given sensations as objects of experience. For this interpretation, see Dina Emundts, "Kant's Critique of Berkeley's Concept of Objectivity," in *Kant and the Early Moderns*, edited by D. Garber and B. Longuenesse (Princeton: Princeton University Press, 2008) pp. 117–141.

difference between these two claims by distinguishing between a noumenon in a positive and a negative sense. A noumenon in a positive sense
would be an object of an intuition other than our sensible one. The
answer to the question if there is such an intuition lies outside our
possible cognition (B 309). A noumenon in a negative sense is something
that is not an object of our sensible intuition (B 307). This only means,
according to Kant, that we know that the way we cognize things is
dependent on our form of intuition.

It has to be taken into account that these statements do not cover the
whole story about things in themselves.[30] But as far as we follow them,
the theory of things in themselves does support my interpretation of the
Refutation of Idealism. First, it has to be mentioned that Kant changed
some passages in the second edition of the section on phenomena and
noumena. Obviously he tried especially to clarify the terminology.[31] If
Kant had had a new stance toward things in themselves, he would very
likely have made this clear in the changed passages in this chapter. But
this sort of change cannot be found there. Second, by following the
discussion in the section on phenomena and noumena, we can learn the
following: What Kant seems to find worth discussing is the question of
whether we can know that there is another form of intuition or, in other
words, whether there is a possible knowledge of things in themselves.
This suggests that it did not occur to him to question that there is something given to us. It is indeed not the case that he denies that the concept
of appearances presupposes that there is something that we can think of
as a thing in itself. This already follows from the Aesthetic, or more
precisely from the receptivity of our intuition. But what Kant denies in
the section on phenomena and noumena is that there is any chance of
referring to this something as a thing independently of time and space. If
this is true, then it is to be expected that all he thought one could do to
make the refutation of problematic idealism more convincing lies in his
concept of objectivity: We cannot think of something as being an independent object of our representations if we cannot determine it lawfully,
since objectivity means lawful determination.

---

[30] It can be doubted that the theory which Kant develops here is compatible
with all other parts of the *Critique of Pure Reason*. Compare Guyer,
Claims of Knowledge, pp. 344 and 402, and Kenneth Westphal, *Kant's
Transcendental Proof of Realism* (Cambridge: Cambridge University
Press, 2004), pp. 38 ff.
[31] Kant deleted, for example, the expression "transcendental object" in the
second edition.

8   The Ideas of Pure Reason

The beginning of the Transcendental Dialectic marks an important transition in the *Critique of Pure Reason* and in Kant's philosophical system as a whole. In approximately the first half of the *Critique*, Kant argues that we can have immanent metaphysical knowledge of synthetic *a priori* principles that structure all possible human experience, because they are grounded in our pure forms of intuition (space and time) and the pure concepts of our understanding (the categories). But Kant's argument for this immanent metaphysics rests on his claim that human knowledge can result only from applying concepts to intuitions, or more precisely to schemata mediating the application of concepts to appearances. This key claim implies that transcendent metaphysical knowledge – knowledge of objects that transcend the boundaries of possible human experience – is impossible for us, since it would involve deploying concepts independently of intuitions or schemata.

If Kant had ended the *Critique* at this point, then his positive argument for an immanent metaphysics in the first half of the book would be wide open to attack from those unwilling to accept its strong negative implication that transcendent metaphysics is impossible. But as Kant was well aware, the Leibniz–Wolffian tradition that dominated German philosophy in the eighteenth century held that transcendent metaphysics is not only possible but actual. Its proponents used a battery of arguments to show that we can have *a priori* knowledge about three transcendent objects in particular: the human soul, the world-whole, and God. For this reason, at least, Kant's work in the *Critique* is not finished. In order to defend the territory staked out in the Analytic, he needs to fight a rearguard action against at least the strongest Leibniz–Wolffian arguments. This is one of Kant's main goals in the Dialectic, which he pursues mainly in Book Two: to refute specific German rationalist arguments for transcendent metaphysical claims.

But Kant also has another, more ambitious goal in the Dialectic. In the Introduction and Book One, he develops an account of the faculty of reason according to which the errors of Leibniz–Wolffian metaphysics are not arbitrary but due to a natural illusion that has its seat in reason itself. On Kant's view, human reason necessarily produces ideas of the soul, the world-whole, and God; yet these ideas are illusory, because they unavoidably seem to give us a priori knowledge of transcendent objects, though in fact they are only subjective ideas. The point of developing this account of reason is not only to explain why smart people (including the young Kant) are deceived into believing the fallacious arguments of Leibniz–Wolffian metaphysics. Kant's ultimate goal in developing his account of reason in these sections is to reframe the part of metaphysics that deals with ideas of the soul, the world-whole, and God as a practical science. That is, he will eventually argue – by the end of the Dialectic, in the Canon of Pure Reason, and in later works – that we misunderstand the ideas of pure reason if we treat them as objects of speculative knowledge, but that they nevertheless have a positive use as regulative principles in the practice of empirical science and morality.

2. TRANSCENDENTAL ILLUSION

The place to begin considering how the subject matter of the Dialectic differs from that of the Analytic is with Kant's distinction between the "transcendental use" of a concept or principle, and "transcendent" principles (A 296/B 352–3). In the Analytic, Kant frequently warns against the transcendental use of concepts, which he characterizes as the (futile) attempt to use a pure concept of the understanding independently of the sensible conditions of its application (schemata) in order to think "things in general and in themselves" (A 238/B 298).[1] Kant insists that the "transcendental use of the categories is thus in fact no use at all, and has no determinate or even ... determinable object" (A 247–8/B 304). Instead, it is "a mere mistake of the faculty of judgment when it is not properly checked by criticism, and thus does not attend enough to the boundaries of the territory in which alone the pure understanding is allowed its play" (A 296/B 352). Kant accuses Leibniz of this mistake in the Amphiboly chapter on the grounds that he "intellectualized the appearances" (A 271/B 327). According to Kant, Leibniz mistook appearances for things in themselves, which he would not have done had he correctly assigned appearances to sensibility through transcendental reflection.

There are two important points to note in this context. First, Kant is criticizing Leibniz here on the subject of general metaphysics, the

---

[1] See also A 139/B 178, A 180–1/B 223, A 219/B 266–7, A 238–48/B 297–305, A 257/B 313, and A 289/B 345.

Aristotelian science of being *qua* being.[2] He is claiming that Leibniz misclassifies appearances as "things in general and in themselves" because he attributes them to the wrong cognitive faculty. So Leibniz's mistaken ontology results from his mistaken view of our cognitive powers, according to Kant. Second, Kant believes that this error can be fully remedied once and for all by a thorough critique. If we take Kant's advice in the Analytic, engage carefully in transcendental reflection, and embrace transcendental idealism, then we can avoid even the temptation to make a transcendental use of concepts. Kant claims that the Analytic therefore undermines the grounds for this type of error in ontology or general metaphysics entirely.

Kant's project in the Dialectic differs from that of the Analytic on both counts. First, the subject matter of the Dialectic is not general metaphysics, which deals with being as such, but the traditional sciences of special metaphysics, which deal with particular kinds of being. In the Leibniz–Wolffian tradition, the central topics of special metaphysics are the soul (rational psychology), the world-whole (rational cosmology), and God (rational theology).[3] Kant classifies these as branches of transcendent metaphysics because they purport to deal with (*a priori* knowledge about) objects that transcend the boundaries of possible experience. So while the transcendent use of the categories of which Kant accused Leibniz in the Analytic involved mischaracterizing objects of experience as things in themselves, Kant in the Dialectic shifts his attention to *a priori* knowledge claims about three specific things that are not possible objects of experience because they transcend its boundaries. The Dialectic therefore deals with a different kind of judgmental error than the Analytic: error in judgments whose putative objects transcend the boundaries of experience, rather than judgments about objects of experience.

Second, Kant claims that the errors of Leibniz–Wolffian philosophers in special metaphysics have a unique motivation that is unlike anything encountered so far in the *Critique*. The transcendental use of categories has no special motivation and can be eliminated through criticism. But

---

[2] This point and the following distinction between general and special metaphysics are emphasized by Henry E. Allison, *Kant's Transcendental Idealism: An Interpretation and Defense*. Revised and enlarged edition. New Haven and London: Yale University Press, 2004, pp. 326–7.

[3] See, for example, Christian Wolff (1719). *Vernünftige Gedanken von Gott, der Welt, der Seele des Menschen auch allen Dingen überhaupt* [*Rational Thoughts on God, the World, the Soul of Human Beings, and All Things in General*]. Hildesheim and New York: G. Olms Verlag, 1983. For discussion, see Lewis White Beck, *Early German Philosophy: Kant and His Predecessors*. Cambridge, MA: Harvard University Press, 1969.

erroneous judgments about the soul, the world-whole, and God are motivated by special principles that are natural to human reason and can
never be uprooted. Kant distinguishes here between the faculties of
understanding and reason. The concepts and principles of the understanding do not inevitably bid us to make a transcendental use of them:
the cause of this mistake is not the understanding's principles themselves but our optional misuse of them, which is caused in turn by our
avoidable failure to engage in criticism.[4] Kant calls the understanding's
principles "immanent" because their proper "application stays wholly
and completely within the limits of possible experience" (A 295–6/B 352).
But in the Dialectic, he introduces reason as a distinct cognitive faculty
whose principles he calls "transcendent" because they "actually incite us
to tear down all those boundary posts and to lay claim to a wholly new
territory" beyond the limits of possible experience (A 296/B 352). In other
words, merely possessing reason itself motivates us to make judgments
about transcendent objects.

Why? Kant explains:

The cause of this is that in our reason (considered subjectively as a human faculty
of cognition) there lie fundamental rules and maxims of its use, which look
entirely like objective principles, and through them it comes about that the
subjective necessity of a certain connection of our concepts on behalf of the
understanding is taken for an objective necessity, the determination of things in
themselves. [This is] an **illusion** that cannot be avoided at all, just as little as we
can avoid it that the sea appears higher in the middle than at the shores, since we
see the former through higher rays of light than the latter, or even better, just as
little as the astronomer can prevent the rising moon from appearing larger to him,
even when he is not deceived by this illusion. (A 297/B 353–4)

Kant draws an analogy here between empirical (optical) illusion and
the illusion that he claims is caused by reason itself. This analogy
holds, Kant believes, because both kinds of illusion consist in "the taking
of a **subjective** condition of thinking for the cognition of an **object**"
(A 396). In optical illusion, the relevant subjective conditions are rules
used by our perceptual faculties to interpret visual cues. Relying on the
same visual cues that normally enable us to perceive objects accurately
can, in exceptional circumstances, distort the way objects appear to us.
Yet even if we understand, for example, why the moon appears larger
and thus closer to us than it really is when it is near the horizon, this does
not change the fact that it continues to appear that way to us. We cannot
avoid this optical illusion (except by looking away), although we can

---

[4] At A 248/B 305, Kant says that we are prone to this mistake because the
categories are *a priori*, which makes them seem to have an application that
extends beyond sensibility. See also A 289/B 345–6.

avoid allowing it to deceive us into judging erroneously that the moon actually is larger and closer to us when it is near the horizon.

Analogously, Kant claims that reason also contains subjective principles that unavoidably "look" objective, and that this causes a special kind of illusion that he calls transcendental illusion.[5] What distinguishes these two kinds of illusion is that empirical illusion is caused by rules for interpreting perceptual cues, while transcendental illusion is caused by rules of reason "whose use is not ever meant for experience" (A 295/ B 352). So empirical illusion concerns objects of experience, such as the moon and the sea, while transcendental illusion concerns objects that transcend experience: specifically, the soul, the world-whole, and God. More importantly, in the moon illusion we know that we are perceiving the moon, an (empirical) object distinct from us. The optical illusion is only that it sometimes appears larger and closer than it is. But in transcendental illusion, we do not actually know whether there are objects corresponding to our ideas of the soul, the world-whole, or God. The transcendental illusion is precisely that our ideas appear to give us knowledge of such transcendent objects, when in fact they do not: these are only subjective ideas in us that project the illusion of transcendent objects to which we seem to have non-sensory access. In calling this an illusion, Kant is certainly not denying that transcendent objects exist that correspond to our ideas of the soul, the world-whole, and God. To deny (or affirm) this would overstep the boundaries of possible human knowledge that Kant draws so carefully in the Analytic. His claim is rather that we could not have knowledge about such transcendent objects even if they exist, and that our reason nevertheless inevitably produces the illusion that we can and do have such knowledge.

It is important to be clear about exactly what Kant is claiming to be inevitable. As with empirical illusion, Kant's view is that transcendental illusion itself is inevitable; but it is not inevitable that this illusion deceive us into making erroneous judgments about the soul, the world-whole, or God.[6] According to Kant, we naturally and unavoidably seem to have *a priori* knowledge about these transcendent objects, and this illusion persists even if we recognize it as an illusion, just as the moon

---

[5] It is unclear why Kant does not call this transcendent illusion. Presumably he calls it transcendent*al* because, as he argues in the Appendix to the Dialectic, he holds that our illusory ideas make possible an extended and corrected experience when we use them as regulative principles in empirical science.

[6] This point is emphasized by Michelle Grier, *Kant's Doctrine of Transcendental Illusion*. Cambridge: Cambridge University Press, 2001, pp. 9–10, 128–9.

illusion does. But just as we can still avoid judging that the moon is larger and closer to us when it is near the horizon, we can also avoid claiming to have *a priori* knowledge about the soul, the world-whole, and God; likewise, we can avoid trying to justify such knowledge claims by appealing to Leibniz–Wolffian arguments. Kant thinks that revealing the fallacies in these arguments and uncovering the origin of transcendental illusion in our reason can protect us from being deceived by them. But since even this will not eliminate the illusion itself, Kant eventually wants to identify a positive (practical) use for reason's inherently illusory ideas.

3. REASON

The subjective principles of reason that Kant thinks inevitably produce transcendental illusion because they look like objective principles are what he calls transcendental ideas of the soul, the world-whole, and God. Kant devotes a chapter to each of these ideas in Book Two of the Dialectic. (These will be discussed in the next three chapters of this volume.) But first he develops an account of the faculty of reason that is supposed to explain why all human beings are naturally subject to illusions about these ideas.

Kant's use of the term "reason" (*Vernunft*) is not univocal throughout the *Critique*. Especially before the Dialectic, he sometimes uses it in a wide sense that is interchangeable with "understanding" (*Verstand*); and sometimes he uses it in an even wider sense that refers to all *a priori* elements of cognition, including those of sensibility.[7] But the Dialectic introduces reason in a narrow sense as a faculty distinct from the understanding (A 299/B 356). Reason in this narrow sense is the source of transcendental ideas and illusion. This is the sense in which I use the term in the remainder of this chapter.

Briefly setting aside Kant's terminology, what is unique to reason on Kant's view is that it demands a complete explanation for given facts. The function of reason is not to generate experience in the first place, which is the task of the understanding working together with sensibility (A 307/B 363–4). Instead, already given experience or more precisely judgments about experience are the starting points or input for reason. Reason's basic function is to ask about any given empirical judgment: *why?* Moreover, once reason finds an answer to this question, it subjects that answer in turn to the same question: *why?* This process goes on

---

[7] See B ix-x for examples of both. On the distinction between narrow and wider senses of "reason," see Norman Kemp Smith, *Commentary to Kant's 'Critique of Pure Reason.'* Second edition. Atlantic Highlands, NJ: Humanities Press International, Inc., 1923, p. 2.

indefinitely: "the questions never cease" (A viii). Reason is never satisfied with the understanding it currently has, but always demands a more
complete explanation. Reason's restless search for explanations is
driven by its assumption that a complete explanation for each and
every given fact is out there to be found, and reason demands to know
what that explanation is.

Kant's term for a complete explanation is "the unconditioned." So the
essence of reason, in Kant's terminology, is the demand for the unconditioned. This term originates in early modern logic, and Kant explicitly
associates his view of reason with the traditional early modern view that
reason is a faculty for drawing syllogistic inferences (A 299/B 355).[8] In
fact, Kant absorbs this traditional view within his own highly original
view of reason, since he both modifies the traditional view of reason as a
logical faculty and claims that reason also has a "real use" in which it
generates its own concepts or ideas (discussed later).

To illustrate Kant's use of the term "unconditioned," consider the
following syllogism:

(1) All humans are mortal. (rule or major premise)
(2) Caius is human. (minor premise)
(3) Therefore, Caius is mortal. (conclusion)[9]

Kant holds that in any syllogism, one judgment (the conclusion) is
derived from another (the major premise) by means of an intermediate
judgment (the minor premise).[10] The minor premise is key because it
supplies the "condition" for subsuming the conclusion under the major

---

[8] Early modern logic books such as the *Doctrine of Reason* by George
Friedrich Meier (1752), which Kant used in his logic courses, or the *Port
Royal Logic* by Antoine Arnauld and Pierre Nicole (1662), traditionally
divided intellectual operations into the formation of concepts, the combination of concepts in judgments, and combining judgments through chains
of inferences or reasoning. (Arnauld and Nicole added a fourth operation of
ordering or method.) Meier's text is printed in Volume 16 of the Academy
edition of Kant's works. See Antoine Arnauld and Pierre Nicole, *Logic or
the Art of Thinking*. Edited by Jill Vance Buroker. Cambridge: Cambridge
University Press, 1996. W. H. Walsh traces Kant's reference to traditional
logicians back to Peter Ramus. See W. H. Walsh, *Kant's Criticism of
Metaphysics*. Edinburgh: Edinburgh University Press, 1975, p. 172.
[9] Kant uses this example at A 322/B 378.
[10] The German word for "syllogism" (*Vernunftschluß*) literally means
"inference of reason." Kant contrasts inferences of reason with inferences
of understanding (*Verstandesschlüsse*), as mediate and immediate inferences, respectively: "An **immediate** inference (*consequentia immediata*)
is the derivation (*deductio*) of one judgment from the other without a
mediating judgment (*judicium intermedium*). An inference is **mediate** if,

premise. In this example, the condition is the concept "human," which the minor premise predicates of Caius, therefore providing the link between (1) and (3).

On the traditional early modern view, reason mainly descends from the major premise to the conclusion: from (1) to (3). But on Kant's view, the opposite is true: reason is concerned mainly with *ascending* from (3) to (1), because reason begins from given facts and seeks to explain them by deriving them from general rules or principles.[11] Kant expresses this by saying that reason searches for "conditions" that enable it to explain given facts by subsuming judgments about them under general rules. In this example, the fact that Caius is mortal is "conditioned" by his humanity, which enables reason to explain it from the rule that all humans are mortal.

But this explanation is not complete. So it cannot satisfy reason, because reason demands a complete explanation. On Kant's view, then, such an inference only begins reason's ascent to a higher principle via some more universal condition. For example:

(1′) All animals are mortal.
(2′) All humans are animals.
(3′) Therefore, all humans are mortal.
(4′) Caius is human.
(5′) Therefore, Caius is mortal.

Here the original syllogism is extended upwards by a "prosyllogism" (A 331/B 388) that treats the original major premise (3′) as a conclusion to be derived from a higher rule (1′) via the concept "animals," which is a more universal condition that enables reason to find a more (but still not entirely) complete explanation for why Caius is mortal. Any such explanation remains incomplete, from reason's point of view, as long as it lacks absolute universality, which is to say as long as it can be subsumed under a still higher principle via some more universal condition.

To say that reason demands the unconditioned is therefore to say that reason presupposes the existence of an explanatory principle that, because it is absolutely universal, does not admit or stand in need of further explanation. Reason seeks this unconditioned principle through a series of syllogisms ascending from experience because it demands to

besides the concept that a judgment contains in itself, one needs still others in order to derive a cognition from it" (*Logic*, §42, 9:114; see also A 303/B 360). If an inference can be reduced to two judgments through formal analysis with no loss of content, then it is an inference of understanding. If it irreducibly requires at least three judgments, then it is an inference of reason or a syllogism. See *Logic*, §44, 9:115.

11 "Because to explain means to derive from a principle" (*Judgment*, §78, 5:412). See A 331–2/B 388–9 and A 336–7/B 393–4.

know what (the content of) this principle is. It wants to put an end to its restless search for explanations by arriving at something that fully explains given facts and that requires no further explanation itself, so that no further questions remain to be asked.

In seeking to explain given facts from absolutely universal or unconditioned principles, reason also seeks to unify our cognition, according to Kant. Returning to the example, the general rule that all humans are mortal provides a single explanation for the mortality not only of Caius but also of Socrates and every other human being; and reason's search for a still more universal condition (such as "animals") aims at finding a higher explanatory principle (such as that all animals are mortal) that would unify an even larger body of cognition. Kant says:

[I]f I find such a condition and if the object of the conclusion can be subsumed under the given condition, then this conclusion is derived from the rule that is **also valid for other objects of cognition.** From this we see that reason, in inferring, seeks to bring the greatest manifold of cognition of the understanding to the smallest number of principles (universal conditions), and thereby to effect the highest unity of that manifold. (A 304–5/B 361)

In this respect, Kant claims, the function of reason is similar to that of the understanding, since both faculties aim to unify our cognition, though in different senses. He writes:

If the understanding may be a faculty of unity of appearances by means of rules, then reason is the faculty of the unity of the rules of understanding under principles. Thus it never applies directly to experience or to any object, but instead applies to the understanding, in order to give unity *a priori* through concepts to the understanding's manifold cognitions, which may be called "the unity of reason," and is of an altogether different kind than any unity that can be achieved by the understanding. (A 302/B 359)

In other words, the understanding aims to produce the unity of self-conscious experience, which it accomplishes by combining intuitions and concepts in accordance with *a priori* rules based on the categories and forms of intuition. Reason is then a higher-order faculty that aims to unify judgments of the understanding under more universal principles.

Now some scholars interpret passages like these to mean that the difference between the faculties of understanding and reason is only a matter of degree, not a difference in kind. Some claim that Kant himself regards understanding and reason as fundamentally a single faculty whose lower- and higher-order uses go by different names.[12] Others recognize that

---

[12] See, for example, Ralph C. S. Walker, *Kant.* London: Routledge & Kegan Paul, 1978, p. 141; and T. E. Wilkerson, *Kant's Critique of Pure Reason.* Oxford: Clarendon Press, 1976, p. 102.

Kant in fact regards understanding and reason (in the narrow sense) as distinct faculties, but claim that he is unjustified in drawing a distinction in kind between them. Jonathan Bennett, for example, claims that "there is no determinate border between understanding and reason," and that Kant should base "the understanding/reason line on a difference of degree rather than a sharp difference of kind" by regarding reason as "the faculty for theorizing which is *at least fairly-high level.*"[13]

But this criticism is based on a misunderstanding of Kant's view. In fact, there is a difference in kind between understanding and reason: as we have seen, the essence of reason is its demand for the unconditioned, but the understanding has no concept of the unconditioned, as Kant repeatedly says. For example:

Thus reason relates itself only to the use of the understanding, not indeed insofar as the latter contains the ground of possible experience (for the absolute totality of conditions is not a concept that is usable in an experience, because no experience is unconditioned), but rather in order to prescribe the direction toward a certain unity of which the understanding has no concept, proceeding to comprehend all the actions of the understanding in respect of every object into an **absolute whole**. (A 326–7/B 383)[14]

Kant also expresses this point by distinguishing what he calls comparatively universal rules of the understanding from absolutely universal principles of reason (A 299–301/B 356–8). The law of causality is Kant's favorite example of a rule of the understanding. This law is comparatively universal because it is more general than any rule that we could arrive at by valid induction from experience. Because of its comparative universality, it can function as a principle or major premise in a syllogism (for which Kant uses *Grundsatz*). But the law of causality is not absolutely universal, Kant says, because our knowledge of this law derives from reflection on the conditions of possible human experience, which is limited by our forms of intuition. As a result, we know only that the law of causality is universally true of human experience, but not whether it applies more universally to things in themselves beyond the limits of possible human experience. Reason, however, seeks a principle that is not limited to possible human experience but that applies with absolute universality even to things in themselves. Only such an absolutely universal principle (for which Kant uses *Princip*) would put an end to reason's questions and satisfy its demand for the unconditioned. The

---

[13] Jonathan Bennett, *Kant's Dialectic*. Cambridge: Cambridge University Press, 1974, pp. 262–3. Bennett calls this the "demarcation problem" (263).

[14] See also A 333/B 390, A 416–17/B 443–5, A 482–83/B 510–12; and Allison, *Kant's Transcendental Idealism*, pp. 317–18.

understanding does not even have a concept of the kind of absolutely universal principle that reason seeks, because the understanding is limited to possible experience. But reason's demand for the unconditioned leads it beyond possible experience in search of an explanatory (synthetic) principle that it can cognize directly from concepts, without being limited by specifically human forms of intuition.

Since the principles that reason seeks have a different kind of universality than rules of the understanding, and since reason is guided by an idea of the unconditioned of which the understanding has no concept, the unity that reason seeks is also different in kind from the unity produced by the understanding, as Kant indicates in the previous two quoted passages.[15] Kant identifies the faculty of understanding and its rules by reference to the unity of self-conscious experience, which is the understanding's distinctive product. But he individuates the faculty of reason by reference to the transcendental ideas and illusion that he associates with reason's unique demand for the unconditioned.[16] Eventually Kant will argue that reason can use these illusory ideas to progress toward three special "unities of reason": a completed natural science in the theoretical domain, a realm of ends in the moral domain, and finally a world that harmonizes all of our theoretical and moral interests (the highest good).[17] Each of these unities of reason is different in kind from the unity of self-conscious experience produced by the understanding.

4. TRANSCENDENTAL IDEAS

It should now be clear why Kant says that there is something "very paradoxical" in what reason demands (A 302/B 358). Reason demands the unconditioned, but the Analytic rules out the only kind of knowledge that could satisfy this demand: we cannot achieve knowledge about things in themselves that transcend possible experience. But Kant holds that human reason nevertheless generates *ideas* of such transcendent objects. Moreover, some of these ideas – the transcendental ideas of the soul, the world-whole, and God – inevitably produce the illusion that we have *a priori* knowledge about objects corresponding to them. This putative knowledge seems to satisfy reason's demand for the unconditioned, though in fact these **"are only ideas"** that do not give us

---

[15] See also A 306–7/B 363–4.

[16] On the origin of this distinction, see H. J. de Vleeschauwer, *The Development of Kantian Thought*. Translated by A. R. C. Duncan. London: Thomas and Nelson Sons, 1962, pp. 82–88.

[17] See John Rawls, *Lectures on the History of Moral Philosophy*. Edited by Barbara Herman. Cambridge, MA: Harvard University Press, 2000, p. 309.

knowledge about transcendent objects but only produce the illusion of doing so (A 329/B 385).

In Kant's terminology, generating ideas is the task of the real or transcendental use of reason (A 299/B 355) or simply of pure reason (A 305/B 362), which he distinguishes from the logical use of reason in which it draws syllogistic inferences while abstracting from the content of its ideas. Kant draws a similar distinction between logical and real uses of the understanding. In its logical use, the understanding combines concepts in accordance with the logical forms of judgments while abstracting from all cognitive content. But the understanding also has a real use in which, as pure understanding, it generates categories by applying the logical forms of judgments to the forms of intuition. In both uses, the understanding performs the same function of judging (A 80–1/B 106), either in abstraction from or applied to sensible intuition. Likewise, reason has a single function in both its logical and real uses, which is to explain given facts through syllogisms ascending toward the unconditioned. The principle of reason's logical use, Kant says, is "to find the unconditioned for conditioned cognitions of the understanding" (A 307/B 364). But the principle of its real use is:

[To] assume that when the conditioned is given, then so is the whole series of conditions subordinated one to the other, which is itself unconditioned, also given ... Such a principle of pure reason, however, is obviously **synthetic**; for the conditioned is analytically related to some condition, but not to the unconditioned. (A 307–8/B 364–5)

So only the real use of reason assumes that an unconditioned explanation for every given fact is there to be found, while the logical use of reason abstracts from this assumption. The logical use of reason draws ascending series of syllogisms, and its real use generates ideas of absolutely universal principles that would terminate these series of syllogisms.

In Book One, Kant claims to find inspiration for his conception of ideas in Plato. This is somewhat surprising because Plato conceives of ideas (or forms) as extra-mental entities that exist in a separate intelligible realm and govern the structure of the visible world. For Plato, ideas are intelligible archetypes of things in the visible world: they play the metaphysical role of causing sensible things to exist and to have whatever properties they have, and the epistemological role of enabling us to acquire knowledge of sensible things through our grasp of ideas.[18] Plato uses the term "dialectic" (another term Kant adopts from him) for the most direct and reliable method of obtaining knowledge about ideas. For Plato, dialectic is the highest level of philosophy, the only method of inquiry that yields

---

[18] Plato, *Republic*, Books V–VII, esp. 474b–480a.

knowledge by directly grasping and reasoning systematically about ideas themselves. The analogy of the line in the *Republic* represents dialectic as a step above other so-called sciences that never directly grasp ideas but instead begin with sense perception and ascend only to hypotheses about ideas.[19] But Kant has a different view of both ideas and dialectic. He calls dialectic "a logic of illusion" and emphatically contrasts it with "the logic of truth, i.e., the analytic" (A 131/B 170).[20] Moreover, at least after Kant surrenders his short-lived Platonism from the *Inaugural Dissertation* of 1770, he denies that the human intellect can grasp extra-mental entities in a separate intelligible realm. So ideas for Kant in the *Critique* are subjective: they are concepts in the human mind, not extra-mental entities as they were for Plato. Kant also denies that our ideas govern the structure of the sensible world, as Platonic ideas were supposed to do and as Kant holds that our categories and forms of intuition do. Kant's ideas produce the illusion of insight into objects that transcend the sensible world. They do not give us genuine knowledge of the kind that Plato sought.

Nevertheless, there is a limited but important sense in which Kant shares Plato's view of ideas. Both Plato and Kant regard ideas as normative standards against which the sensible world is to be measured, and they agree that ideas are not drawn from experience, because nothing in experience can ever fully measure up to the standard of ideas (A 313/B 370, A 327/B 383–4). In this sense, Kant regards ideas as useful – indeed "indispensable" in the case of moral ideas (A 328/B 385) – for representing ends or goals that we strive to achieve, although he rejects Plato's view that our grasp of ideas constitutes knowledge of an intelligible realm that the visible world itself somehow strives to imitate. Besides the three special transcendental ideas, Kant holds that there are many ideas of reason that function as goals or standards in this way: he also mentions,

[19] Plato, *Republic*, 509d-511e. See also 532a-535a. Plato's science of dialectic resembles what Kant calls "the 'apodictic' use of reason" in the Appendix to the Dialectic, and Plato's method of hypothesis is similar to Kant's "hypothetical use of reason" (A 646–7/B 674–5). Although the method of hypothesis is a distant second best for Plato, Kant believes that the only legitimate theoretical use of reason's ideas is their hypothetical use.

[20] "Dialectic" takes on a two-fold meaning for Kant. On the one hand, it refers to these illusions themselves that Kant claims have their seat in the nature of human reason, and to any sophistical reasoning based on these illusions. In this sense, human reason itself is dialectical (i.e., illusory), as are the rationalist arguments that purport to justify the claims of transcendent metaphysics. On the other hand, Kant also uses the term to refer to his own "critique of dialectical illusion" in both of these senses (A 61–2/B 86).

for example, the practical idea of a just constitution (A 316–17/B 372–4) and "the idea of a necessary unity of all possible ends" (A 328/B 385); and later the theoretical ideas of "pure earth, pure water, pure air," and "a fundamental power" of the mind (A 646/B 674, A 649/B 677). The practical ideas represent states of affairs that do not exist but ought to exist, and which we aim to realize through our actions.[21] Theoretical ideas represent imaginary focal points (A 644/B 672) that guide our study of nature and help us to achieve a more extensive and interconnected system of scientific knowledge.[22]

But although Kant under Plato's influence recognizes many ideas of reason, he privileges the transcendental ideas of the soul, the world-whole, and God that correspond to the central topics of Leibniz–Wolffian special metaphysics. Kant holds that only these three ideas produce transcendental illusion, and he gives a special account of how reason's demand for the unconditioned necessarily generates these ideas. According to this account, since the nature of reason is to draw ascending inferences or syllogisms from judgments of experience to absolutely unconditioned principles, transcendental ideas are "inferred concepts" (A 310/B 366) of the unconditioned (A 322/B 379). But there are three logical forms of syllogisms: categorical, hypothetical, and disjunctive. The logical form of syllogisms, in turn, derives from the categories of relation, since it is determined by the logical relation between the judgments in the syllogism, which is itself the same as the relation between the subject and predicate in the major premise (A 304/B 361).[23] So the categories of relation fix three paths or "exponents" that reason follows in its ascent to the unconditioned (A 331/B 387). From this Kant concludes:

> There will be as many concepts of reason as there are species of relation represented by the understanding by means of the categories; and so we must seek an **unconditioned, first,** for the **categorical** synthesis in a **subject, second** for the **hypothetical** synthesis of the members of a **series,** and **third** for the **disjunctive** synthesis of the parts in a **system.** (A 323/B 379)

This is the first stage of an argument that Kant explicitly models on the metaphysical deduction of the categories, which derives the categories from the logical forms of judgments on the basis of the principle that judging is the function of the understanding. Analogously, since the function of reason is to explain given facts through ascending series of

---

[21] For Kant's distinction between theoretical and practical cognition, see A 633/B 661.

[22] See A 329/B 385 and the Appendix to the Dialectic. In the Third Critique, Kant introduces a third class of aesthetic ideas. See *Judgment*, §49, 5:313–17.

[23] See *Logic*, §61, 9:122.

syllogisms toward unconditioned principles, this provides a clue to the discovery of all transcendental ideas of reason: they must correspond to the logical forms of syllogisms, and thus to the categories of relation (A 321/B 378, A 333/B 390).

The second stage of Kant's argument specifies the content of the transcendental ideas corresponding to these forms of syllogisms. At this stage, Kant introduces a new trichotomy:

> Now what is universal in every relation that our representations can have is (1) the relation to the subject, (2) the relation to objects, and indeed either as appearances or as objects of thinking in general. If we combine this subdivision with the above division, then all the relation of representations of which we can make either a concept or an idea are of three sorts: (1) the relation to the subject, (2) to the manifold of the object in appearance, and (3) to all things in general. (A 333–4/B 390–1)

Kant overlays this trichotomy onto the previous one to specify the three transcendental ideas:

> Consequently, all transcendental ideas will be brought under **three classes**, of which the **first** contains the absolute (unconditioned) **unity** of the **thinking subject**, the **second** the absolute **unity** of the **series** of **conditions of appearance**, the **third** the absolute **unity** of the **condition of all objects of thought** in general.
>
> The thinking subject is the object of **psychology**, the sum total of appearances (the world) is the object of **cosmology**, and the thing that contains the supreme condition of the possibility of everything that can be thought (the being of all beings) is the object of **theology**. (A 334/B 391)

Many scholars are unimpressed by this argument. The principal complaint is that Kant seems to make an arbitrary and artificial connection between the forms of syllogisms or the categories of relation and the ideas of the soul, the world-whole, and God.[24] Some interpreters point out that Kant's motive in giving this argument is to develop a complete and final list of the problems of pure reason, as part of his project of setting metaphysics on the secure path of a science.[25] But many dismiss Kant's architectonic as inadequate to this task, either on the grounds that it relies on outdated scholastic logic, or especially on the grounds that there

[24] See, for example, Kemp Smith, *Commentary*, p. 439; Karl Ameriks, "The Critique of Metaphysics: The structure and fate of Kant's dialectic." In *The Cambridge Companion to Kant and Modern Philosophy*. Edited by Paul Guyer. Cambridge: Cambridge University Press, 2006, p. 277; and Graham Bird, *The Revolutionary Kant: A Commentary on the* Critique of Pure Reason. Chicago and La Salle, IL: Open Court, 2006, pp. 602–3.

[25] Walsh, *Kant's Criticism*, p. 175; and Allen W. Wood, *Kant*. Malden, MA: Blackwell, 2005, p. 79.

is a tenuous connection between this logic and the traditional topics of Leibniz–Wolffian special metaphysics.[26]

Paul Guyer, though sympathetic to these criticisms, argues that they undermine only one of two different strategies for deriving the transcendental ideas that Kant develops in notes from the 1770's, which surface in the *Critique* as the two stages distingushed earlier.[27] One strategy is to derive the transcendental ideas from the categories of relation or forms of syllogisms. But a second, independent strategy derives them from "the three basic constituents of knowledge in general – namely, the subject, appearance, and the object."[28] Guyer explains this second strategy as follows:

> The main point is that reason simply seeks completeness in its thought of the thinking subject, its thought of the series of appearances, and in the thought of the connections among objects in general; but in so doing it gives rise to purely dialectical inferences to a unitary self, a completed series of appearances, or an *ens entium* or *realissimum*. This explanation of the origin of transcendental illusion does not ... begin with any exploitation of the three specifically relational categories.[29]

This second strategy has the merit of circumventing the criticisms mentioned earlier. But the problem is that the first strategy is not only present but prominent in the *Critique* as well, and that Kant seems to claim that the two strategies are somehow related.

I suggest that these two strategies are related in the following way. Kant may hold that reason generates the content of the ideas of the soul, the world-whole, and God according to the second strategy: as Guyer says, reason simply demands completeness in its thought of the three basic constituents of knowledge. This would explain why these ideas have a special status: because reason derives them from the basic constituents of knowledge, they are the best candidates for the absolutely universal principles that reason demands. But this by itself would not explain why these ideas produce transcendental illusion, while the ideas of pure earth, pure water, and pure air, for example, do not. I suggest that Kant gives prominence to the first strategy because he holds that what makes only these ideas unavoidably seem objective is that reason associates only them with the three forms of syllogisms. Recall Kant's

---

[26] Bennett, *Kant's Dialectic*, chapter 12, levels both criticisms.

[27] Paul Guyer, "The Unity of Reason: Pure Reason as Practical Reason in Kant's Early Conception of the Transcendental Dialectic." In Paul Guyer, *Kant on Freedom, Law, and Happiness*. Cambridge: Cambridge University Press, 2000, pp. 80–84. The principal *Reflexion* Guyer discusses in this connection is R 5553.

[28] Guyer, "The Unity of Reason," p. 80.   [29] Ibid., 83.

analogy with optical illusion: what makes the moon seem larger and closer than it actually is when near the horizon is that this interpretation of our perceptual data is forced by rules that normally enable us to perceive objects accurately. Analogously, the forms of syllogisms normally enable us to reason correctly. So perhaps Kant holds that associating ideas of the soul, the world-whole, and God with the forms of syllogisms unavoidably causes it to seem as if there must be some inferential route or other – a sound argument – leading from non-controversial premises about experience to conclusions about transcendent objects corresponding to these ideas.[30]

This interpretation not only fits the text, which specifies the content of these ideas only at the second stage of Kant's argument, but which appeals to the forms of syllogisms (or categories of relation) to explain what makes them transcendental ideas – that is, why they cause transcendental illusion. It also implies a distinction between the process that generates the transcendental ideas and the rationalist arguments that Kant criticizes in Book Two. On this interpretation, these ideas pre-exist and motivate the search for arguments that attempt to justify knowledge claims about transcendent objects corresponding to them. So the ideas must be generated not by the inferences represented in those arguments themselves, but by a separate inferential process. But Kant does not yet explain why he correlates specific ideas with specific forms of inference in the way he does, and this may leave an impression of artificiality or arbitrariness. Only in Book Two does Kant explain why he associates the idea of the soul with categorical syllogisms, the world-whole with hypothetical, and God with disjunctive.

5. ASSESSING KANT'S ACCOUNT

There are two types of questions to distinguish when assessing Kant's account. First, on what grounds does Kant claim that transcendental illusions of the soul, the world-whole, and God are inevitable, and does he have a convincing argument for this claim? Second, how does Kant

---

[30] Note that Kant distinguishes transcendental illusion from logical illusion: "Logical illusion, which consists in the mere imitation of the form of reason (the illusion of fallacious inferences) arises solely from a failure of attentiveness to the logical rule. Hence as soon as this attentiveness is focused on the case before us, logical illusion entirely disappears" (A 296–7/B 353). So Kant's criticisms in Book Two should undermine the logical illusion that particular rationalist arguments are sound, but they cannot undermine the transcendental illusion that there must be some sound argument or other (perhaps undiscovered) that justifies these transcendent knowledge claims.

defend his general view that the nature of reason is to demand the unconditioned? The second question is important because, even if we answer "no" to the first question, there is more to Kant's account of reason than his claim that these transcendental illusions are inevitable.

On the first question, Henry Allison seems to hold that transcendental illusion has a kind of logical necessity, since he claims that the principle of reason's logical use implies that of its real use, which causes transcendental illusion.[31] The principle of reason's logical use tells us to seek conditions for anything given as conditioned, and Allison points out that it is incoherent to seek conditions for something *given as conditioned* without assuming that its conditions exist (though we may not find them). But Allison claims that it is also incoherent to seek conditions for something given as conditioned unless we assume that something unconditioned exists – that is, unless we accept the principle of reason's real use to assume the existence of something unconditioned. Now this cannot be Kant's view because Kant emphasizes that "the conditioned is analytically related to some condition, but not to the unconditioned" (A 308/B 364–5). In other words, the fact that something is given as conditioned does not logically imply or assume that anything unconditioned exists: it implies only the existence of conditions. If *we* need to assume the existence of some complete explanation in order to seek explanations for given facts, then it is not because seeking explanations logically implies or presupposes that a complete explanation exists.[32]

It is more plausible to interpret Kant's argument for the inevitability of transcendental illusion as epistemological.[33] This interpretation is suggested by the fact that Kant models his derivation of the transcendental ideas on the metaphysical deduction of the categories, which provisionally identifies a table of categories on the assumption that the pure understanding has a real use in which it generates concepts for thinking about objects a priori (A 57/B 81). The transcendental deduction then attempts to justify this assumption by showing that the categories are conditions of experience (A 93–4/B 126). This suggests that at the beginning of the Dialectic, Kant may identify the transcendental ideas only on the provisional assumption that reason has a real use, and that later he

---

[31] Allison, *Kant's Transcendental Idealism*, pp. 330–2.
[32] Ameriks also claims, mistakenly in my view, that it follows analytically from Kant's claim that everything in experience is conditioned that something unconditioned exists. See Ameriks, "The Critique of Metaphysics," p. 287.
[33] Allison holds that transcendental illusion is also epistemologically necessary. See *Kant's Transcendental Idealism*, chapter 15. Grier, *Transcendental Illusion*, chapter 8, also emphasizes the epistemological role of ideas.

may give an argument analogous to the transcendental deduction that attempts to justify this assumption. To be sure, Kant denies that it is possible to give the same kind of transcendental deduction of ideas that he gave for the categories, on the grounds that nothing in experience is congruent to ideas, while everything in experience conforms to the categories (A 336/B 393, A 663–4/B 691–2). But in the Appendix to the Dialectic, he does give a "transcendental deduction of all the ideas of speculative reason," which argues that although the ideas of the soul, the world-whole, and God do not give us knowledge of objects that transcend possible experience, it is always beneficial and never harmful for us to use them as regulative principles for extending our knowledge of experience itself, especially in empirical science (A 671/B 699, A 687/B 715). Kant seems ambivalent, however, about whether this argument can show that transcendental illusions caused by these ideas are epistemologically necessary for the practice of empirical science, or whether it shows only that, *if* we have these illusory ideas, *then* we can put them to a positive use as regulative principles in the practice of science.[34]

In any case, Kant certainly holds that transcendental illusions about these three ideas are at least psychologically unavoidable.[35] Many critics dismiss his account for making unwarranted and false generalizations about human psychology, and these objections are serious even if Kant has other arguments in support of his account. Bennett, for example, thinks that Kant's account reflects "not the structure of reason but the preoccupations of German academic philosophers at the time when Kant was writing."[36] Likewise, W. H. Walsh writes that "[t]he illusion of which he speaks was perhaps 'natural and inevitable' to a thinker with Kant's background in rationalist metaphysics, but would be less dangerous for, say, a scientifically minded positivist."[37] Kant is surely right that the *tendency* to speculate about God, the soul, and the cosmos is not peculiar to eighteenth-century German rationalists, and this tendency may reflect something more universal and even unchanging about the structure of human reason itself. But evidently he exaggerates its power to ceaselessly tease and mock all human beings (A 339/B 397), perhaps because he underestimates the role of cultural factors in shaping both our ideas and the influence they have on us.

However, the plausibility and explanatory power of Kant's overall account of reason does not depend on transcendental illusion being necessary in any of these senses. The immediate goal of Kant's account

---

[34] For criticism of the epistemological argument for the unavoidability of transcendental illusion, see Walsh, *Kant's Criticism*, pp. 248–9.

[35] This is denied by Grier in *Transcendental Illusion*, pp. 111–12.

[36] Bennett, *Kant's Dialectic*, p. 258.   [37] Walsh, *Kant's Criticism*, p. 173.

is to explain the errors of Leibniz–Wolffian special metaphysics as resulting from a natural illusion that is grounded in reason itself, and he can
achieve this goal even if transcendental illusion is avoidable. More
importantly, Kant's further goal of reframing special metaphysics as a
practical science does not require transcendental illusion to be unavoidable either. To achieve this goal, Kant must show that we *cannot* satisfy
reason's demand for the unconditioned with speculative knowledge
about the soul, the world-whole, or God because such knowledge is
beyond our reach; and that we *can* hope to satisfy this demand by putting
these ideas to a practical use aimed at realizing the three unities of reason:
a completed natural science, a realm of ends, and the highest good.

But achieving both of these goals does require Kant to have a unified
and defensible account of reason, which he first develops in the opening
sections of the Dialectic. The test of whether this account accurately
captures the nature of human reason must ultimately lie in its explanatory power: can different manifestations of human reasoning plausibly
and helpfully be explained in terms of a demand for the unconditioned?
These opening sections of the Dialectic begin an extended argument,
running through the rest of the *Critique* and later works, in which Kant
continues to develop and defend this account of reason by showing how,
in his view, all of its applications – not only in syllogistic logic and
special metaphysics, but also in scientific and especially moral reasoning – crucially involve a demand for the unconditioned.[38] So the account
of reason first developed here both requires confirmation from and
provides a blueprint – or, as Kant says, "the idea of the whole" – for
his entire philosophical system.[39]

---

[38] For example, Kant's three main formulations of the categorical imperative
in the *Groundwork* progressively articulate different senses in which,
on Kant's view, the moral law is an unconditioned principle of practical
reason.

[39] "When it is a matter of determining a particular faculty of the human soul
as to its sources, its contents, and its limits, then, from the nature of
human cognition, one can begin only with the *parts*, with an accurate
and complete presentation of them … But there is a second thing to be
attended to, which is more philosophic and *architectonic*: namely, to
grasp correctly the *idea of the whole* and from this idea to see all those
parts in their mutual relation by means of their derivation from the
concept of that whole in a pure rational faculty" (*Practical Reason*, 5:10).

9   The Paralogisms of Pure Reason

I. INTRODUCTION

After analyzing our cognitive powers of sensibility and understanding in the first *Critique's* Transcendental Aesthetic and Transcendental Analytic and arguing that these powers can together yield synthetic *a priori* knowledge, albeit knowledge limited to objects of appearance, Kant turns to an analysis of the power of reason in the Transcendental Dialectic. Here the outcome is far more negative. Kant identifies many ways in which reason oversteps its bounds, and repeatedly charges the rationalists with such errors. At the same time, he is empathetic toward the rationalists, underscoring that their errors are not obvious or even disingenuous, as the overly simplistic empiricists hold, but instead deep and inevitable, grounded in transcendental confusions that only Kant's transcendental researches can identify if not eradicate.

In the first of the Dialectic's three chapters, the "Paralogisms of Reason," Kant's focus is the rationalists' errors in the field of psychology. The sole purpose for the rationalists' ventures in psychology, Kant repeatedly tells us, is to establish the immortality of the soul. Toward this end, he believes, they need to establish three things about the soul: its permanence, incorruptibility, and personality. So how do they argue for these conclusions? They don't. Instead, Kant thinks they argue for the conclusions of the soul's *substantiality*, *simplicity*, and *identity*. They then simply assume that these conclusions entail permanence, incorruptibility, and personality.

Kant clearly rejects the rationalists' conclusions. On this basis, commentators commonly take Kant to reject these conclusions in *any* ontologically significant sense. What I will argue, by contrast, is that Kant's criticism is more focused than that and more closely tied to the particular teachings of his transcendental philosophy. If we consider the remainder of Kant's recorded thought from across his career – the *Critique*, Kant's other published works, his personal notes, and the notes on his lectures – it is plainly clear that Kant himself believes that the soul is a simple, identical substance in an ontologically significant sense. Moreover, he maintains this while denying all theoretical arguments for the immortality of the soul and while simultaneously advancing his critical epistemological tenets. This presses us to find the more precise source of his disagreement with the rationalists.

The source of disagreement, it turns out, concerns the *determinacy* and with it the *usefulness* of these ontologically significant conclusions of the soul's substantiality, simplicity, and identity. Against the rationalists, Kant sees the objects of sensibility, including phenomenal substance, as mere appearances, distinct in kind from things in themselves. In application to these objects of appearance, the concepts of substantiality, simplicity, and identity have a determinate meaning, specifying something about these objects in terms of their phenomenal properties, and here this meaning includes permanence, incorruptibility, and personality. The rationalists, for lack of recognition of the distinction in kind between sensibility and understanding, apply these phenomenal, determinate sensible concepts indiscriminately to the soul as a thing in itself in pure apperception. As Kant makes clear, however, the soul as a thing in itself in pure apperception is without phenomenal properties, and so only pure, indeterminate concepts apply to it. We are aware, through pure self-consciousness, that we are a something in general, that as such we have powers through which we can bring about accidents (thoughts, in our case), but that we are distinct from and so empty of all accidents and so all predicates. This awareness is therefore sufficient negatively to make clear that we are not anything in space or time, but the pure concepts add nothing to this, only specifying logical characteristics of this subject and telling us nothing positive, determinate, or useful about ourselves.

Because most previous treatments of the Paralogisms have done little with the very revealing broader context of Kant's recorded thought in which this chapter is situated, I think that this chapter on the Paralogisms can best add to our understanding of the Paralogisms by focusing on this context. I first consider the immediate context of the Paralogisms in the *Critique* before turning to the Paralogisms' broader context outside the *Critique*, first in Kant's other published work and then in Kant's other unpublished recorded thought; here, nearly all the materials considered will be from Kant's post-*Critique* period. I then turn to the Paralogisms chapter itself.

2. THE CONTEXT FOR THE PARALOGISMS WITHIN THE *CRITIQUE OF PURE REASON*

Determinate empirical apperception versus indeterminate pure apperception. In the *Critique*'s "Deduction of the Pure Concepts of the Understanding," Kant draws a distinction between what he takes to be the two types of self-consciousness: (1) "empirical apperception," or "inner sense," and (2) "pure apperception," "original apperception," or "transcendental apperception." "Empirical apperception" is nothing more than the consciousness of our particular, constantly changing, temporally located mental states, or the "consciousness of oneself in accordance with the determinations of our state in internal perception [which] is merely empirical, forever variable" (A 207).[1] We can have knowledge of ourselves through empirical apperception, or inner sense, but because the states of inner sense are all located in time and are thus merely phenomenal, as Kant argues in the Aesthetic, inner sense provides us with knowledge of ourselves merely as we exist as phenomena.

By contrast, "pure apperception" is a bare consciousness of one's own existence as a thinking thing distinct from its particular mental states, a consciousness that "produces the representation I think" (B 132). Because this consciousness of existence is distinct from a consciousness of any particular mental states in inner sense (and so, in turn, in outer sense, which forms part of inner sense), it is not an *intuition*, and indeed "does not have the least predicate of intuition" (B 278). This consciousness is instead *mere consciousness*, so that Kant says we have no

---

[1] For an explanation of the method of citation used in this chapter, see the "Method of Citation" section at the start of this book, which lists many of the abbreviations used for Kant sources in this text. A supplemental list of abbreviations is included here. Sources cited infrequently are listed by full title in the text. Translations from the German are my own, unless a translation of the source is listed here, in which case I often follow the translation. All translations by Karl Ameriks and Steve Naragon are found in *The Cambridge Edition of the Works of Immanuel Kant, Lectures on Metaphysics* (Cambridge: Cambridge University Press, 1997). Translations of the *Critique of Pure Reason* are from *The Cambridge Edition of the Works of Immanuel Kant, Critique of Pure Reason*, eds. and trans. Paul Guyer and Allen Wood (Cambridge: Cambridge University Press, 1997). Translations of *Kant's Metaphysical Foundations of Natural Science* are from *Philosophy of Material Nature*, ed. and trans. James W. Ellington (Indianapolis: Hackett Publishing Company, 1985). Translations of *What Real Progress Has Metaphysics Made in Germany since the Time of Leibniz and Wolff?* are by Ted Humphrey (New York: Abaris Books, 1983).

MD   *Metaphysik Dohna* (1792–3), trans. Ameriks and Naragon.
MK2   *Metaphysik K2* (early 1790s), trans. Ameriks and Naragon.
ML1   *Metaphysik L1* (1777–80), trans. Ameriks and Naragon, 28:195–301.
ML2   *Metaphysik L2* (1790–1), trans. Ameriks and Naragon.
MMr   *Metaphysik Mrongovius* (1782–3), trans. Ameriks and Naragon.
MVi   *Metaphysik Vigilantius* (1794–5), trans. Ameriks and Naragon.
MVo   *Metaphysik Volckmann* (1784–5), trans. Ameriks and Naragon.
MvS   *Metaphysik von Schön* (1780s).

"intellectual *intuition*" of it, but instead a mere "intellectual *consciousness*" (B xl n, emphasis added).

This is significant on Kant's account because it is only in conjunction with an intuition, given in inner sense, and so in sensibility, that a concept can become "determinate." To have a determinate concept of something is to have a concept of it such that, of at least one pair of opposed predicates, one of the predicates in the pair is included in the concept to the exclusion of the other. A thoroughly determinate concept would include one predicate from each of all possible pairs of opposed predicates (A 573/B 601). Because we do not have a creative, or intellectual intuition, whereby our thoughts match their objects by virtue of creating them, but instead must turn to experience to perceive inner or outer objects, all of which in Kant's view fall under the forms of space and time, determination for us assumes the form of selection of predicates from opposed pairs of *empirical* predicates; accordingly, "[w]ith us understanding and sensibility can determine an object only in combination" (A 358/B 314).

This epistemology applies to our epistemic contact to ourselves, as an existing thing, too: "the inner intuition, in which alone my existence can be determined, is sensible" (B xl n). It is this determinacy that is required for cognition, so that "for the cognition of myself I also need in addition to the consciousness, or in addition to that which I think myself, an intuition of the manifold in me, through which I determine this thought" (B 158). Our pure apperception therefore avoids the fate of empirical apperception, of providing knowledge of ourselves merely as phenomena, because it avoids the phenomenal states of inner sense, but it does so at the cost of complete indeterminacy, so that "the consciousness of oneself is therefore far from being a cognition of oneself" (B 158).

What pure consciousness of ourselves is a pure consciousness of: an indeterminate thing in itself. But while Kant clearly holds that pure apperception does not yield *determinate* insights into ourselves as things in themselves, this still leaves the question of what our pure, indeterminate consciousness is a consciousness of. What we will see in the Paralogisms is that Kant unequivocally rejects the rationalists' answers to this question. As repeatedly characterized by Kant, their sole quest in psychology is to establish the soul's immortality, and toward that end they conclude the soul's permanence, incorruptibility, and personality, seeing these conclusions as entailed in their conclusions that the soul in pure apperception is a substance, simple, and identical. If we assume that, by rejecting the *rationalists'* richly endowed conclusions of our substantiality and simplicity, Kant rejects *any* ontologically significant version of these conclusions, however, we encounter a problem. For what many interpreters have overlooked is that Kant tells us in the *Critique* (as well as elsewhere) that we are warranted in concluding that the soul is a simple, identical, substance in some sense. We will review these conclusions briefly before turning to the *Critique*'s account of the distinction between the pure concepts of understanding and the empirical concepts of understanding, especially that of substance.

First, Kant tells us that pure apperception precedes and is independent of the states of inner sense. In his words, pure apperception "precedes all data of the intuitions" (A 107), "preced[es] all particular experience" (A 117n), "precedes *a priori* all my determinate thinking" (B 134), and "does to be sure precede ... consciousness of a relation to something outside me" (B xl), and that "only by means of [outer experience] is possible not, to be sure, consciousness of our own existence, but its determination in time, i.e., inner experience" (B 277).

After the last quote, in which Kant again distinguishes the subject of consciousness from any empirical predicates in inner sense, he segues to another common refrain, telling us that this subject, of which we have a *consciousness*, though not a *cognition*, is a "thing in itself": "Of course, the representation **I am**, which expresses the consciousness that can accompany all thinking, is that which immediately includes the existence of a *subject in itself*, but not yet any **cognition** of it, thus not empirical cognition, i.e., experience" (B 277, emphasis added). In the Deduction, he likewise holds that "I therefore have **no cognition** of myself **as I am**, but only as I **appear** to myself. The consciousness of oneself is therefore far from being a cognition of oneself" (B 158), where this is obviously a consciousness of oneself as a thing in itself because we *do* have a cognition of ourselves as appearance; and that "in the synthetic original unity of apperception, I am conscious of myself not as I appear to myself, nor **the way** in which I am in myself, but only **that** I am" (B 157). In the Paralogisms, Kant tells us that "in the consciousness of myself in mere thinking I am the being itself, about which, however, nothing yet is thereby given to me for thinking" (B 429). And in the "Antinomy of Pure Reason," Kant explains that "Yet the human being, who is otherwise acquainted with the whole of nature solely through sense, is acquainted with himself also through pure apperception, and indeed in actions and inner determinations which cannot be accounted at all among impressions of sense; he obviously is in one part phenomenon, but in another part, namely in regard to certain faculties, he is a merely intelligible object" (A 546/B 574).

If we are conscious of ourselves as things in themselves through pure apperception, does this mean that we are conscious of ourselves as substances, or for that matter as simple, identical substances? While Kant certainly rejects the rationalists' heavily freighted versions of these conclusions, he accepts other versions. In his lengthy concluding section of the Paralogisms in the first edition of the *Critique*, the "Observation on the sum of the pure doctrine of the soul, following these paralogisms," which is seldomly considered in the commentary, Kant explains his view:

Now mere apperception ('I') is substance in concept, simple in concept, etc., and thus all these psychological theorems are indisputably correct. Nevertheless, one by no means thereby cognizes anything about the soul that one really wants to know, for all these predicates are not valid of intuition at all, and therefore cannot have any consequences that could be applied to objects of experience; hence they are completely empty. For that concept of substance does not teach me that the soul endures for itself, that it is not a part of outer intuitions that cannot be further divided and hence could not arise or perish through any natural alterations ....
Now if I say through mere category: 'The soul is a simple substance,' then it is clear that since the understanding's naked concept of substance contains nothing beyond the fact that the thing is to be represented as a subject in itself without in turn being the predicate of another subject, nothing about its persistence follows, and the attribute of simplicity certainly cannot be added to this persistence; hence one is not in the least instructed about what the soul can encounter in the alterations in the world. (A 400–1)

Kant often repeats this point that the conclusions of the soul's substantiality, simplicity, and identity hold, but do nothing to advance the conclusion of our immortality because of their emptiness of all empirical predicates. The First Paralogism thus tells us that "one can quite well allow the proposition **The soul is substance** to be valid, if only one admits that this concept of ours leads no further, that it cannot teach us any of the usual conclusions of the rationalistic doctrine of the soul, such as the everlasting duration of the soul through all alterations, even the human being's death" (A 350–1). And in his "Appendix to the Transcendental Dialectic," Kant discusses the question of how far we can consolidate seemingly disparate powers of a substance, and here the example of a substance with powers that he uses is that of the human mind. His example makes clear what he reinforces often elsewhere, that this substance has powers by means of which it relates to its accidents, or mental states in our case: "Among the different kinds of unity according to concepts of the understanding belongs the causality of a *substance*, which is called 'power.' At first glance the various appearances of one and the same *substance* show such diversity that one must assume almost as many powers as there are effects, *as in the human mind* there are sensation, consciousness, imagination, memory, wit, the power to distinguish, pleasure, desire, etc." (A 648/B 676; A 649/B 677, emphasis added).

In sum, then, Kant distinguished two sorts of apperception in the *Critique*, empirical apperception and pure apperception. While empirical apperception is the sum total of our mental states and provides us with knowledge of ourselves as appearance, pure apperception is a mere awareness of ourselves as a thinking subject, devoid of all empirical predicates, completely indeterminate, and thus inadequate for knowledge. Moreover, Kant regularly refers to the subject of this empty apperception as a thing in itself. Here, however, he rejects the thick conclusions of the rationalists that imply immortality, while accepting a thinner set of identical-sounding conclusions, of the soul's substantiality, simplicity, and identity, which do not imply immortality.

Sensibility and understanding, empirical concepts and pure concepts, and the transcendental distinction between useful and useless concepts of substance. We need to take a closer look now at the nature of the distinction between these thinner and thicker versions of the concepts of the soul's substantiality, simplicity, and identity, which demands consideration of another important piece of context for the Paralogisms within the *Critique*. This is Kant's transcendental distinction between sensibility and understanding and his resulting transcendental distinction between empirical and pure concepts. In particular, we will follow this distinction as it applies to the concept of substance. This review will help to reveal the depth and complexity of the rationalists' mistakes that Kant identifies in the Paralogisms.

Long before the *Critique*, Kant sets the stage for a sharp distinction in kind, not degree, between our lower and higher cognitive faculties with his rejection of the rationalist view on substance and power. He argues that the rationalists mistakenly equate substance with power and therefore mistakenly assume that the soul, as simple substance, must have only one basic power, of representation. By contrast, both before and after the *Critique*, Kant consistently holds that a substance is not the same thing as a power; a substance instead is that which possesses powers by means of which it can ground accidents. Kant can accordingly recognize our possession of powers different from one another not merely in *degree* – as the rationalists were forced to conclude on the basis of their definition of substance and power – but also in *kind*. A substance can possess as many distinct kinds of powers as there are irreducibly distinct types of accidents that it grounds, allowing Kant to recognize a distinction in kind between sensibility and understanding. And in Kant's view, the rationalists' murky distinction in degree between sensibility and the understanding carries over to a murky distinction in degree between phenomena and noumena. On their account, the phenomena of sense are actually noumena, albeit confusedly understood, and so, in theory, clarification of the logical nature of these phenomena will reveal noumena.

In the *Critique*, in what precedes the Paralogisms, Kant draws this sharp contrast between our cognitive powers of sensibility and understanding and confronts Hume's challenge to synthetic *a priori* knowledge (among other challenges) by arguing for a technically defined series of concepts and principles that we necessarily employ in application specifically to the phenomenal, spatiotemporal world. Understanding and reason, examined in the "Transcendental Analytic" and the "Transcendental Dialectic," respectively, are both "higher" faculties and distinct in kind from sensibility because they presuppose self-consciousness, reflection, and spontaneity, and are in this sense active. Sensibility, studied in the "Transcendental Aesthetic," is for Kant a "lower" faculty of cognition because it does not presuppose self-consciousness, reflection, and spontaneity, and so is, in this sense, passive. In another sense, though, sensibility *is* active in its passivity, registering the action of things in themselves (even ourselves as things in themselves) on us, but necessarily *contributing* something to the resulting representations in the process, thereby coloring them, as well. The Aesthetic does not merely assert this point about activity in passivity generally, but instead argues that space and time are the pure forms of intuition, in particular, that issue from our exercise of our power of sensibility, framing all sensible input in temporal terms and some in spatial terms as well. According to this account of our *contribution* of the pure forms of intuition of space and time, the objects of sensibility are not phenomenal for *lack* of an appropriate synthesis of some sort (and for lack of a resulting logical clarity) but for the *presence* of contributed and ineliminable pure forms of intuition, and the objects of sensibility are accordingly not noumenal objects merely confusedly understood but instead merely phenomenal objects, even when clearly understood. It is because these objects of sensibility are merely phenomenal and framed by sensibility in *a priori* forms of intuition that our *a priori* concepts of the understanding can manage to apply to, or reach, these objects of sensibility, so that synthetic *a priori* knowledge is possible. In Kant's view, then, as he states it here in the Aesthetic, the rationalists, for lack of recognition of the transcendental distinction between sensibility and understanding, cannot recognize the irreducibly phenomenal status of objects of sensibility: "The Leibniz–Wolffian philosophy has therefore directed all investigations of the nature and origin of our cognitions to an entirely unjust point of view in considering the distinction between sensibility and the intellectual as merely logical, since it is obviously transcendental, and does not concern merely the form of distinctness or indistinctness, but its origin and content, so that through sensibility we do not cognize the constitution of things in themselves merely indistinctly, but rather not at all" (A 44/B 61–2).

Because Kant recognizes a deep transcendental rift in kind between sensibility and understanding, he can recognize parallel yet distinct ways in which the language of "things in themselves" can be used to refer to objects of sensibility and understanding. For Kant, there is no thing in itself to be found among sensibility's offerings in time and space where this thing in itself is understood in a *transcendental* sense, as a thing in itself outside of space and time. But Kant recognizes an additional sense in which we can speak of a thing in itself: an everyday, merely *empirical, not transcendental* sense of a "thing in itself" *within* sensibility, limited to the phenomenal, spatiotemporal realm. This merely *empirical* thing in itself, he tells us in the "Transcendental Aesthetic," is that in appearance that "is valid for every human sense in general" (A 45/B 62), by which it is contrasted with what pertains to us only contingently and in a "particular situation" (A 45/B 62). Kant's example of what we might call a thing in itself in this everyday, empirical sense would be a raindrop, while a rainbow would be the contrasting mere appearance in the same empirical sense. But Kant makes clear that understood *transcendentally, both* the raindrop and the rainbow are mere appearance, as is the very space in which the raindrop is located (B 63/A 46).

This distinction between a thing in itself in a merely phenomenal sense and a thing in itself in a transcendental sense will undergird Kant's response to Hume's challenge to universally valid and necessary laws regarding objects, as presented in the Transcendental Analytic. There, in the first chapter of the "Analytic of Principles," "On the Schematism of Pure Concepts of the Understanding," Kant moves away from the pure categories understood indeterminately in the Analytic of Concepts to "schematized" categories, which are pure categories rendered temporally. Their new temporal meaning for the first time gives these categories meaning in relation to temporal objects – that is, gives them what Kant terms "significance" (A 146/B 185). Thus, whereas the pure category of substance refers to a "something in general" in which accidents inhere and which is, as such, always a subject and never a predicate, the temporally situated category of substance, or the "schema of substance," "is the persistence of the real in time, i.e., the representation of the real as a substratum of empirical time-determination in general, which therefore endures while everything else changes" (A 144/ B 183). In the phenomenal, temporal realm, then, "there corresponds in appearance that which is unchangeable in existence, i.e., substance" (A 144/B 183).

This account carries over to Kant's argument in the First Analogy for the permanence of *phenomenal* substance, in particular. The concept of "substance" as applied to objects in the phenomenal realm must refer to something that we assume to be permanent, for without this assumption of the permanence of substances in the phenomenal realm there would be no unity of time and hence no experience. Kant explains that "time cannot be perceived in itself; thus this persisting thing in the appearances is the substratum of all time-determination, consequently also the condition of the possibility of all ... experience ... " (B 226). But this meaning of "substance" as something that is permanent is a *special* meaning that applies only to the "thing in itself" as understood in the *empirical* sense, in appearance, not in the transcendental sense, as outside of space and time. Kant therefore follows the preceding passage with the following one: "Therefore in all appearances that which persists is the object itself, i.e., the substance (*phaenomenon*)" (B 227).

At the close of the Analytic, Kant describes the sort of deep confusion into which rationalism lapses because it fails to recognize the transcendental distinctions we have just reviewed. He does this in the "Appendix on the amphiboly of the concepts of reflection through the confusion of the empirical use of the understanding with the transcendental," which, while still technically in the Analytic, begins the critique of metaphysics that is the goal of the Dialectic, by criticizing Leibniz's rationalism. Because the rationalists see the distinction between sensibility and understanding as logical and as in degree only, they do not recognize that the objects of sensibility and understanding are distinct in kind, that the things in themselves, or substances, within each realm are distinct in kind, and therefore that the concepts that apply to them have meanings that are, accordingly, distinct in kind also. Kant thus observes that "if it is not the *logical form* [as the rationalists suppose] but the *content* of concepts that is concerned ... the things can have a twofold relation to our power of cognition, namely to sensibility and to understanding... " (A 262/B 318, emphasis added). Any attempt at a comparison of these concepts first requires reflection on their transcendental status and whether they are concepts of understanding or of sensibility and so whether they are of pure or of empirical use (A 264/B 320). One example that Kant here returns to is that of the distinction between the pure and empirical use of the concept of substance: "As the object of the pure understanding ... every substance must have inner determinations and forces that pertain to its inner reality"; by contrast, "the inner determinations of a *substantia phaenomenon* in space ... are nothing but relations, and it is itself entirely a sum total of mere relations. We know substance in space only through forces that are efficacious in it" (A 265/B 321), and so when we speak of substance in the empirical sense we are speaking of a substratum within appearance distinguished from other appearances by being that which is extended, impenetrable, and permanent – that is, "a persistent appearance in space (impenetrable extension)" (A 284/B 340).

We saw earlier that Kant rejects the rationalists' thicker conclusions of our substantiality, simplicity, and identity in favor of a thinner version of the same, and that Kant understands these thinner conclusions in a pure sense that applies to the soul as thing in itself. We have now reviewed a transcendental basis for such a distinction between thinner and thicker concepts. Kant recognizes a merely comparative, empirical and so phenomenal concept of a thing in itself, which is a substratum *within appearance*, or a *comparative* substance. And Kant's argument in the First Analogy only gives us grounds to draw the "useful" conclusion of permanence of *this* comparative, phenomenal substance. Accordingly, we can anticipate that, insofar as Kant believes that the rationalists are prone to amphibolies whereby they fail to recognize the transcendental status of the concepts with which they are dealing, they will mix and match their meanings. They will ascribe permanence – a property for Kant entailed only by the concept of phenomenal substance – indiscriminately to noumenal substance as well, including the soul as a noumenal substance. We can therefore imagine that Kant will reject the rationalists' thick conclusions as ones that rightfully pertain only to empirical objects, not to the subject as a thing in itself outside of space and time.

Kant's rejection, specifically, of the application of the empirical, useful conclusion of substance to the soul as thing in itself. And indeed this is what we will find in the *Critique*, the *Prolegomena*, and elsewhere. For example, in the first edition of the First Paralogism, Kant identifies permanence as the single possible *use* that we might have for the concept of substance in application to the soul, and it is this meaning specifically that he rejects. First he asks: "But now what sort of use am I to make of this concept of a substance?" (A 349), and next he answers "That I, as a thinking being, **endure** for myself, that naturally I **neither arise** nor **perish** – this I can by no means infer, and yet it is for that alone that the concept of the substantiality of my thinking substance can be useful to me; without that I could very well dispense with it altogether" (A 349). Kant thus specifically rejects the application of the useful, *empirical* concept of substance to the soul, while granting that the *pure category* of substance can be applied. The Second Paralogism accordingly summarizes the First Paralogism in observing that "the proposition 'I am substance' signifies nothing but the pure category, of which I can make no (empirical) use *in concreto*" (A 356). The 1783 *Prolegomena*, written during the period between the two editions of the first *Critique*, likewise characterizes the soul as substance while highlighting the uselessness of this conclusion insofar as it does not imply permanence: "though we may call this thinking self (the soul) substance, as being the ultimate subject of thinking which cannot be further represented as the predicate of another thing, *it remains quite empty and inconsequential if permanence* – the quality which renders the concept of substances in experience *fruitful* – *cannot be proved of it*" (*Prolegomena*, 4:334, italics added). And the First Paralogism itself echoes this view, asserting that "one can quite well allow the proposition **The soul is substance** to be valid if only one admits that this concept of ours leads no further, that it cannot teach us any of the usual conclusions of the rationalistic doctrine of the soul, such as, for example, the everlasting duration of the soul through all alterations, even the human being's death" (A 350–1).

3. THE BROADER CONTEXT FOR THE PARALOGISMS IN KANT'S RECORDED THOUGHT OUTSIDE THE *CRITIQUE*

Kant's pre-1781 views on the permanence of substance. Kant regularly rejects the assumption of the permanence of substance during the two decades preceding the *Critique*. From the 1760s onward, he argues that accidents are mere modes of a substance and so cannot migrate between substances; that thoughts accordingly cannot be placed into us by another substance, even by God, but must arise from our own activity; that we accordingly cannot inhere in an intramundane God; and that we accordingly cannot assume our permanence as part of a necessarily existing being.[2] In Kant's view, nothing we know rules out the destruction of substances despite God's continued existence: *"Because all accidents are variable and the* substantiale *is not at all known, thus is the permanence of the* substantialis *precariously assumed … Especially when everything is sustained only through the divine power"* (R 4054, 17:399 (1769), italics added; see also *Dissertation,* 2:410 (1770); R 4060, 17:401).

But while Kant believes that the permanence of substance has not been established, he thinks that we assume it nonetheless, and here, in 1769, he ventures an explanation for *why* we do this. We assume the permanence of substance because it serves as a necessary prerequisite for something quite elemental, not yet experience itself, as he later argues, but instead for "the method of philosophizing": *"The always lasting duration of substances, i.e., the same age of each with the whole world, cannot as much be proved, as that it must lie at the base of the method of philosophizing"* (R 4105, 17:416, italics added). In the 1770 *Inaugural Dissertation,* Kant again offers an assessment of the assumption of the permanence of substance (which he here refers to as one example of a "principle of harmony"), again holding not that it is a prerequisite for *experience,* but instead a prerequisite for *advancing understanding:* "This postulate [that nothing material at all comes into

---

[2] *Negative Quantities,* 2:202 [1763]; *MH,* 28:52 [1762–3]; *Dreams of a Spirit Seer,* 2:321n [1766]; R 4137, 17:430 [1769]; *ML1,* 28:343 [1777–80]; 28:1052 [1782–3]; *ML2,* 28:563 [1792/1]; *MD,* 28:638, 699 [1792/3]; R 6405, 18:706 [1790–5]; *Danziger Rationaltheologie,* 28:1298 [1784].

being or passes away] is, at the urging of the common understanding, spread abroad through all the schools of the philosophers, not because it has been taken as discovered or demonstrated by *a priori* arguments. It is spread because, *if you concede that matter itself is in flux and transitory, there would be nothing left at all which was stable and enduring, which would further advance the explanation of phenomena in accordance with universal and constant laws, and which would, therefore, further advance the use of the understanding"* (*Dissertation,* 2:418–19, italics added).

The *Inaugural Dissertation* also introduces the reviewed distinction in kind between sensibility and understanding, and, as we saw, this will allow Kant to draw a distinction in kind between phenomenal and noumenal substance. This allows Kant to subsequently argue for the permanence of *phenomenal* substance, in particular, providing Kant with an instance of a synthetic a *priori* truth against Hume. All the while, however, Kant rejects the conclusion of the permanence of noumenal substance, including the soul, telling us the following in *Reflexion* 5454, from 1776–8: "*Metaphysical predicates: 1. The soul is substance; 2. a substance distinguished from material, no object of outer sense; 3. Simple, therefore immaterial; 4. but, if it is permanent, does not follow"* (*R* 5454, 18:186, italics added).

Kant's post-1781 published work (outside the Critique), *personal notes, drafts, and lecture notes describing the soul as a noumenal substance in an indeterminate sense that does not include permanence.* We now turn to passages from throughout Kant's post-*Critique* recorded thought outside the *Critique* that concern the nature of the self as substance. What we find is a consistent pattern. In our relation to all other things, Kant tells us, we deal only with the *effects* of the things on us, which as such are colored by our manner of actively receiving these effects – in our case, by imposing the pure forms of intuition on them. In only one case, that of our relation to ourselves, do we stand in the relation to an existing thing in itself of *being* the thing in itself. In this one case, we are immediately aware of being a something that has powers – including those cognitive powers that Kant ascribes to us in the first *Critique*, of sensibility, imagination, judgment, understanding, and reason – by means of which we relate to our accidents – that is, our mental states – that inhere in us. This is what it is to be a substance in the most basic ontological sense of a *substantiale*, a something in general, that is distinct from all of its accidents. But precisely because this underlying *substantiale* is distinct from all of its accidents, or predicates, it is completely empty and therefore *indeterminate*. All of the *determinate* versions of the concepts of substantiality, simplicity, and identity must refer to determinate phenomena, and accordingly have no application to the indeterminate soul. Although we can say nothing determinate about this something in general, we can characterize it in strictly logical terms. We can say that this *substantiale*, or something in general, stands in the relation to its accidents of always being the subject and never these accidents, or predicates; that it is simple in the sense of being a single subject of inherence for these accidents and so never anything complex *per se*; and that it is identical in the sense of being numerically identical in relation to its temporally distributed accidents. We can also characterize our empty *substantiale* of immediate apperception in negative terms. Our self-consciousness of ourselves as distinct from and so devoid of all predicates reveals that we are *not* anything phenomenal, defined in terms of these phenomenal predicates. So the self is not permanent, is not extended in time and space, and is not identical in time and space. Kant therefore defends a weak immaterialism, arguing that we are not matter *per se*. But because matter is a mere *appearance*, it remains possible that we, as things in themselves, might still *appear* as matter, or, conversely, that what underlies matter is a *thinking thing*. And while we could be corruptible *per se* as matter, we might appear as (corruptible) matter and suffer from a corruptibility of a parallel sort – namely, through the gradual loss of our powers. Thus Kant consistently underscores the fact that our substantial, simple, immaterial nature does not amount to a *pneumatology* – that is, does not establish our existence as a spirit, which as such can live without a body. Our conclusions are therefore useless insofar as they do not confirm our permanence, incorruptibility, identity in time and space, or immortality.

I will first review what Kant himself wrote, both in published and unpublished works, mainly from the period after the first edition of the first *Critique*. In Kant's 1783 *Prolegomena*, Kant boils down the *Critique's* discussion of the four paralogisms to a discussion of two paralogisms: the first, concerning the substantiality of the soul; and the fourth, concerning the existence of objects in space – the discussion that, in the second edition of the *Critique*, Kant moves from the Paralogisms to a new chapter, the Refutation of Idealism, neither of which I will discuss here because they are treated elsewhere in the present book. Kant not only limits his discussion of the first three paralogisms, which are the only three discussed in the second edition *Critique*, to the first paralogism but also, in turn, essentially reduces his treatment of the first paralogism to a discussion of the question of the permanence of the soul as substance. Kant reminds us that our understanding is discursive, providing us with determinate knowledge only when intuition provides us with predicates (4:333). This is crucial in relation to the question of knowledge of a *substantiale*, he tells us, because this is distinguished from all of its accidents, so that here the means for a determinate concept is missing, making it unreasonable to demand determinate knowledge of this *substantiale*. Kant's discussion of the paralogisms begins with this charge: "People have long since observed that in all substances the subject proper, that which remains after all the accidents (as predicates) are abstracted, hence the *substantiale* itself, remains unknown, and various complaints have been made concerning these limits to our insight. But it will be well to consider that the human understanding is not to be blamed for its inability to know the *substantiale* of things, i.e., to determine it by itself, but rather for demanding to cognize it determinately as though it were a given object" (4:333). Precisely that which makes something always a subject and never a predicate rules out a determinate conception of it: "Consequently, it cannot be itself a predicate of any other thing; but just as little can it be a determinate concept of an absolute subject" (4:334).

This is relevant because, while Kant says we can indeed conclude that the soul is a *substantiale*, this rules out any determinate conception of the soul, and this in turn rules out the possibility of concluding the soul's permanence, which is a determinate concept that applies only to objects of experience. Kant begins with an open-ended observation: "But though we may call this thinking self (the soul) substance, as being the ultimate subject of thinking which cannot be further represented as the predicate of another thing, it remains quite empty and inconsequential if permanence – the quality which renders the concept of substances in experience fruitful – cannot be proved of it" (4:334). But *can* permanence be proved of the soul as substance? Kant's answer is clear, that the concept of permanence applies only to phenomena, as established in the First Analogy: "But permanence can never be proved of the concept of a substance as a thing in itself, but only for the purposes of experience. This is sufficiently shown by the first Analogy of Experience" (4:335). In a footnote on the same page, Kant explains how the rationalists, for lack of the deep, transcendental researches needed to understand the nature and origin of the assumption of the permanence of substance – that is, for lack of the researches Kant has just mentioned, from the first Analogy – failed to notice these distinctions in their account of the soul and so mistakenly applied the empirical concept of substance, which entails permanence, to the substantial soul:

It is indeed very remarkable how carelessly metaphysicians have always passed over the principle of the permanence of substances without ever attempting a proof of it ... People then boldly applied this postulate [of the permanence of substance] to the concept of soul as a *substance*, and concluded a necessary continuance of the soul after the death of man (especially as the simplicity of this substance, which is inferred from the indivisibility of consciousness, secured it from destruction by dissolution). Had they found the genuine source of this principle – a discovery which requires deeper researches than they were ever inclined to make – they would have seen that the law of the permanence of substances finds a place for the purposes of experience only, and hence can hold good of things so far as they are to be cognized and conjoined with others in experience, but never independently of all possible experience, and consequently cannot hold good of the soul after death.

We next turn to Kant's *Metaphysical Foundation of Natural Science,* from 1786, after the first edition of the *Critique* and the *Prolegomena* and just before the publication of the second edition of the *Critique.* Here he presents the point that the second edition *Critique* raises against Mendelssohn's improved version of the rationalists' argument for immortality – namely, that we could cease to exist by virtue of the elanguescence of the powers of our soul, making clear that these powers inhere in a soul that is substantial, that this soul is indeterminate, and that it would accordingly not be permanent in the manner of phenomenal substances:

To wit, consciousness has a degree that may be greater or smaller without any substance needing to arise or perish. And hence the clarity of the representations of my soul has such a degree, and in consequence of this fact the faculty of consciousness, namely, apperception – and along with this faculty even the substance of the soul – has also such a degree. But inasmuch as a total disappearance of this faculty of apperception must finally ensue upon the gradual dimunition of the same, even the substance of the soul would be subjected to a gradual perishing, even though the soul were of a simple nature, because this disappearance of its fundamental force could not ensue through division (separation of substance from a composite) but, as it were, by expiration, and even this not in a moment, but by gradual remission of its degree, from whatever cause. The 'I,' the universal correlate of apperception and itself merely a thought, designates as a mere prefix a thing of indeterminate signification, namely, the subject of all predicates without any condition to distinguish this representation of the subject from that of a something in general, namely, substance; by the expression 'substance,' one has no concept as to what this substance is. On the other hand, the concept of matter as substance is the concept of the movable in space. Hence it is no wonder if permanence of substance can be proved of matter but not of the soul. This is because in the case of matter there follows from its concept, namely, that it is the movable, which is only possible in space, the fact that what has quantity in matter contains a plurality of real parts external to one another, and hence contains a plurality of substances. Consequently, the quantity of matter can be diminished only by division, which is no disappearance; such disappearance would, according to the law of permanence, be impossible in the case of matter. The thought 'I' is, on the other hand, no concept at all but only an internal perception. Therefore, from this thought, nothing at all can be concluded (except the complete distinction of an object of the internal sense from what is thought merely as object of the external senses); consequently, the permanence of the soul as substance cannot be concluded from the thought 'I.' (4:542–3)

In *Reflexion* CV, written in Kant's personal copy of the first edition of the *Critique*, Kant plainly asserts the noumenal status of the I: "The I is noumenon; I as intelligence" (23:34). *Reflexion* 6000, from 1780–9, takes for granted that the soul is a substance, asking only whether it is a *special* substance: "Whether the soul is a special substance?" As noted earlier, *Reflexion* 6001, from 1780–9, adds that the soul is a noumenal substance, that it is the soul of transcendental apperception, and that there is no permanence for this sort of substance, as for empirical substance: "The soul in transcendental apperception is noumenal substance; therefore no permanence of the same in time; and this can hold only for objects in space."

In the drafts of his *Schrift gegen Eberhard* from 1790, Kant adds that this thinking subject of consciousness is simple, and that, because it is not *intuited* as simple, it cannot be *known* as simple: "the simple is not given in outer intuition. In the inner there is the simple but only in the subject of consciousness ... in so far as it thinks not insofar as it has an intuition of itself through the inner sense therefore it is also not given for knowledge" (20:359). In his loose notes for the 1793 *What Real Progress*, Kant emphasizes the immediacy of self-consciousness, and that while empirical apperception is limited to the mere appearance of ourselves, pure apperception is of ourselves as a thing in itself: "How is it possible that a subject becomes immediately conscious of himself as mere appearance and at the same time as thing in itself? The former through empirical, the latter through pure apperception" (20:340).

Reflexion 6334, from 1795, also focuses on the fact that the soul is a substance in the ontologically significant sense of being something in which accidents inhere, and that this is a "bare category of the subject" precisely because it is distinct from its accidents and so lacks all determinate properties and so cannot be intuited as permanent, as are the heaviness and impenetrability of bodies: "It appears that, if one admits that the soul is substance, that one also needs to admit permanence as with bodies. But we can recognize absolutely nothing permanent in the soul, as, e.g., heaviness or impenetrability with bodies. – Thus is the concept of the soul as substance only a concept of a bare category of the subject to distinguish it from its inhering accidents."

Finally, in 1795, Samuel Sömmerring sent Kant a work "On the Organ of the Soul" about the anatomy of the brain and the functions of nerves, which he informed Kant he would dedicate to Kant. In response, Kant sent Sömmerring a four-page commentary on the work, with permission to publish it. This commentary spoke approvingly of Sömmerring's empirical research and addressed the question of the relation between empirical research on empirical matters concerning the brain versus philosophical reflection on the metaphysics of the soul, and here Kant addresses (a few years before his 1798 *Conflict of the Faculties*) the rightful intellectual domains of the medical and philosophical faculties, respectively. Sömmerring published his essay in 1796 along with Kant's commentary. In addition to the published version, found in the *Akademie* edition volume 12 on Kant's correspondence and in the *Cambridge Edition of the Works of Immanuel Kant* volume on anthropology, history, and education, there are three drafts of this letter included in volume 13 of the *Akademie* edition. Here is a passage from one of the drafts in which Kant not only underscores the possibility that the noumenal soul appears as matter, but also reveals his own opinion that the soul indeed does appear as such: "We pursue not the immediate effect and action of the soul but instead only the appearances of the same. The former would concern the nonsensible substrate of material as the soul itself is" (13:407).

We turn last to the notes on Kant's lectures on metaphysics from after 1781, proceeding chronologically. What we find here, as with much of what we find in Kant's lectures leading up to the *Critique*, is that Kant presents his critical philosophy while contrasting it with the rationalists' views – not only in psychology but also in cosmology and ontology. We begin with the *Metaphysik Mrongovius* notes on rational psychology, from soon after the 1781 first *Critique*, in 1782–3. Here, as in all of Kant's lectures on rational psychology, Kant divides his analysis into three parts, and we will later see that he does the same thing in the very long concluding section of the first edition version of the Paralogisms, the "Observation on the sum of the pure doctrine of the soul, following these paralogisms." The first part considers only the "transcendental" (*MMr*, 29:903) or "sheer" (*MMr*, 29:905) predicates of the soul, where the soul is considered "in and for itself" (*ML1*, 28:263), using *pure* categories of ontology. The second section addresses "the soul in comparison with other beings" (*MMr*, 29:904), asking whether the soul is material or immaterial. The third section is the first in which Kant addresses the usefulness of these conclusions: he considers the connection of soul to body, and so addresses whether the soul could or must live without our bodies before or after death – that is, he addresses the question of immortality. It is important to keep this tripartite division of Kant's discussion of the soul in mind, because it tells us that we have to look to these later sections to understand how these transcendental conclusions relate to the question of immortality that Kant thinks is the sole purpose for rational psychology, and to understand how they relate to the closely related question of whether the soul is material or immaterial. That is, we ought not to move too fast and assume that the first section already commits Kant on these questions and puts him in agreement with the rationalists without considering the later sections.

As in the evidence we have already surveyed, the notes on Kant's lectures on metaphysics from the 1780s through 1795 all specify that the soul is a substance in the most basic ontological sense of a something in general, a *substantiale*, and that we have an immediate, pure apperception of it as such. But the notes also make clear that, precisely because this substance is completely distinct from and so devoid of all accidents, and because we can know things only through predicates, we can have no determinate knowledge of this subject. Here is Kant, in the ontology section of *Metaphysik Mrongovius*, from 1782–3. He is discussing the category of substance after having earlier presented it along with the other eleven categories, making a point we saw him making, referred to earlier, in the *Critique* (A 648/B 676; A 649/B 677), that the soul is a substance and that we cannot assume that the powers of a substance will reduce to one fundamental power: "But we cannot reduce all powers to one, because the accidents are so different that we cannot take them as the same. If we leave aside all accidents, then substance remains; this is the pure subject in which everything inheres or the substantial, e.g., I" (*MMr*, 29:770–1). Next, after rejecting the rationalists' conflation of the concepts of power and substance, Kant explains that this I is indeterminate because it is distinct from all its accidents: "if I leave aside the accidents, the substantial remains. Of that we cannot make the least concept, i.e., we cognize nothing but accidents. For our understanding cognizes everything through predicates" (*MMr*, 29:770–1). Next, in the section on rational psychology, Kant again talks about the soul as a substance, but as one about which we can know nothing because it is distinct from its accidents: "The soul is substance, and not only that, but rather I am also conscious of the substantial of the soul. For of matter only the accidents are known to me, but not the *substantiale*. I am the ultimate subject and am aware of myself without accidents. But of the substantial, in body as well as in me, I have no proper concept; I know nothing of it but that it is a something. Now it all comes down to deriving the properties of the soul from this sterile concept of a something" (29:904). In other words, the soul's substantiality does not necessarily entail its permanence, and so Kant tells us further along that rational psychology needs to establish "the perdurability of the soul" and that "one believes to be done with [this] since substance is perdurable. But since the soul is cognized as substance only through the I, we do not at all know whether it is substance in the sense that as such it could not perish" (29:912).

Kant makes a similar observation in *Metaphysik v. Schön*, after rejecting Spinoza's account of substance, according to which all accidents inhere in an intramundane God: "If in thinking we sunder all accidents from a substance; in whom do these accidents inhere? In the subject, which serves as their ground and that it called *substantiale*. The *substantiale* is an important concept of reason, but what is it actually? One demands often to know of the soul, what it actually is, not content with its inhering accidents, one demands also to know the subject of the same. In this the demand is unjust; for if I would name this then I would have to determine it and these are just what are taken away. The *substantiale* is simply the concept of something, in which the accidents inhere. That I am, expresses the *substantiale* in me, but the I cannot be determined, that cannot be done other than through accidents" (*MvS*, 28:511).

In *Metaphysik L2*, from around 1790–1, Kant again discusses the category of substance in his account of ontology and distinguishes his account from Descartes' and Spinoza's insofar as they believe that a substance needs to be responsible for its own existence. He repeats that "Substance is that which exists in itself only as subject; accident, what exists only as a predicate or determination of a thing, or whose existence is inherence" and he repeats the by-now familiar point about the unknowability of the substance as divorced from its accidents, or the *substantiale*, because the *substantiale* "is the subject that exists after the separation of all accidents," which therefore "is unknown to us, for we know the substances only through the accidents. This *substantiale* is the something in general" (28:563; see also *MVi*, 29:1005).

What we therefore see here and elsewhere is that the I is a substance in an ontologically significant sense, while at the same time we can say nothing determinate about it. Instead, the category of substance specifies only the spare logical relation that we are conscious of – namely, that of the *substantiale* to its accidents, whereby this *substantiale* must always be the subject of inherence, never the mere accidents that inhere. This logical characterization is not to the exclusion of ontological significance but instead to the exclusion of *determinate* and *phenomenal* significance. And, as we will soon see, because it is at the level of determinate, phenomenal significance that the conclusions exist that the rationalists seek toward the end of establishing our immortality, this indeterminacy is all-important to Kant's rejection of their conclusions. In the section on rational psychology in *Metaphysik L2*, Kant therefore begins by rejecting Descartes' claim that "I think, therefore I am" on the same grounds that he rejects this claim much earlier in his writings (in his 1772/3 *Anthropology Collins*, 25:10, 14, as well as in the *Critique* A 355) – namely, that we do not *infer* our existence. Our consciousness of our existence is instead the "first original experience" (28:590). And just as he argued against the rationalists in his pre-*Critique* writings that the standard conclusions of the soul's substantiality, simplicity, and identity are not inferred but instead immediately apperceived, so too here he makes clear that the conclusion of substantiality is not inferred: "But

Descartes still speaks incorrectly when he says: I think therefore I am, just as if it were an inference. In the concept of I lies substance, it expresses the subject in which all accidents inhere. Substance is a subject that cannot inhere in other things as accident. The *substantiale* is the proper subject ... The soul is a substance, this is a category. The category is a mere concept of the understanding, of logical form. The pure concepts of understanding, if they are merely thought, give no stuff for thinking" (*ML2*, 28:590).

The broader post-1781 context and Kant's views on the soul as simple and identical. Kant's discussions of the soul across his recorded thought focuses largely on the question addressed in the First Paralogism, of the soul's nature as substance, and so we have focused on these discussions. But the question of the Second Paralogism, of the simplicity of the soul, is also very important, and we will now turn to Kant's discussions of this question, as well as the question of identity addressed in the Third Paralogism, which introduces little new material. Because Kant's criticisms of these rationalist arguments follow the same pattern as his criticism of their conclusion of the soul's substantiality, we will cover them quickly. In the most general terms, Kant again argues that it is the rationalists' inattention to the transcendental status of these conclusions that leaves them with flawed, inflated, determinate versions of these conclusions.

In our review of Kant's conclusions of the soul's noumenal substantiality, earlier, we also saw Kant repeatedly asserting the soul's simplicity. The basis for this conclusion throughout Kant's writings is nothing more or less than the simple nature of the thinking subject in immediate apperception; as with Kant's conclusion of the soul's substantiality, his own indeterminate conclusion of the soul's simplicity is not *inferred* but instead grounded in our pure apperception of ourselves. As we have seen, in this immediate, pure consciousness of ourselves, we are conscious of being something that has powers by means of which we can effect accidents – that is, we are conscious of being a *substantiale*, or a something in general, and not of being accidents. Distinct from all of our accidents, we are empty of all determinate predicates, and we are therefore simple in the *negative* sense of not being anything complex (*MVi*; 29:1025); as such, we cannot be anything in space. In *Reflexion* 5650 from 1785–8, Kant therefore says that "'The soul is simple' means that it does not consist of many subjects in space" (18:299), and nothing is as certain across Kant's recorded thought as that he rejects the possibility that the soul is matter *per se*, because we are not aware of the soul through outer sense (*MH*, 28:44; *DS*, 2:328n; R 4230, 17:467–9; R 4234, 17:470–1; *AC*, 25:10–13; *APa*, 25:244–5; *AF*, 25:473; *MLI*, 28:225–8, 266–7, 273; *MMr*, 29:876–9; *Vorarbeiten zur Schrift gegen Eberhard*, 20:359; *ML2*,

28:590–2; *MD*, 28:681–6; *MK2*, 28:754–6, 759; *MVi*, 29:1025–7; *R 5453*, *R 5454*, *R 54–60*, 18:186–9; *R 5984*, 18:415–6; *R 6005*, 18:421; *What Real Progress*, 20:308–9).

Further, we are conscious of the need to have our disparate representations unified in one simple subject, and anything in space would be, *per se*, complex, so its representations would be distributed across subjects. In the pre- and post-1781 decades, Kant presents an argument of sorts, which I term his "Virgil Argument," to do nothing more than highlight features of our immediate consciousness of being a thinking thing. This argument asks us to imagine what would happen if individual words of a verse, say by Virgil, were distributed across different people. Would the whole verse be thought together? Kant's answer is no, that this unity of words requires a common, simple subject, and that, likewise, distinct parts of matter would be unable to together unify a thought. Here Kant presents this argument in *Metaphysik Mrongovius*:

> Should the soul be composite, then its representations would have to be so divided that in every part of the soul there would be a representations which, taken together, would constitute the entire representation (With every single thought there is a unity of consciousness, always the same I, which therefore also presupposes a unity of the subject.) That would be as if in a society of my thoughts each member of the society would say one word. But it is impossible that the entire thought could arise in this way and I be conscious of it, rather there then must again be a subject that puts together all the parts of the thought and thus constructs the entire thought. (29:905)

But, as noted, Kant does not take this or any of the other indeterminate conclusions regarding the noumenal soul to be grounded in inferences, and so this argument of sorts yields nothing beyond what immediate consciousness alone offers us, which is the "sterile concept of a something" (*MMr*, 29:904). As Kant tells us in *Metaphysik L2*, "A composite substance is an aggregate of many substances. Unity of consciousness is not an aggregate. Simple is that which is not divisible. Consciousness already allows us to cognize that the soul is simple" (28:590).

So if the rationalists run together the phenomenal and noumenal concepts of substance, applying the useful and determinate implications of phenomenal substantiality to the noumenal soul, and they make the same form of error in the case of simplicity, how does this work, in Kant's view? The concept of simplicity would be *useful* in application to the soul, Kant argues, only insofar as this would imply that our soul is incorruptible. This would imply our inability to lose our powers in the afterlife, a loss of powers that would threaten our ability to think or even threaten the permanence of our substance, insofar as powers might be lost to the point where there are none and the substance ceases to exist.

So how would simplicity imply incorruptibility? It would, according to Kant, if these two assertions were true: (1) our simplicity as soul means that we are not spatially extended, and (2) corruptibility is possible only by means of spatial division. According to Kant, however, neither assertion is warranted. While Kant thinks the rationalists believe both assertions, the former is possibly false in one sense, while the latter is completely unwarranted. In Kant's view, they first assume that all composites presuppose simples and that the composites in space – that is, bodies, when properly understood – are recognized to be composed of non-extended simples – namely, physical points, or monads. They next assume that corruptibility comes only with extension, with the result that they think that these monads escape the only sort of corruptibility possible, spatial corruptibility.

Kant argues against them that sensibly intuited bodies are in space, which is infinitely divisible, and that no matter how clearly we come to understand these sensibly intuited bodies, none of their parts could be simple, but would instead always be infinitely complex (MMr, 29:930; Vorarbeiten zur Schrift gegen Eberhard, 20:365). In Kant's view, simplicity only comes at the nonsensible, nonspatial, intelligible level, of noumena. And this brings Kant to the next point: if the soul is simple at the noumenal level, this leaves entirely open how it might appear. Indeed, Kant repeatedly emphasizes that it is possible that while, as things in themselves, we are not matter per se, we might well appear as spatially extended matter (Progress, 20:308–9). What is always clear here is that, if there is a relationship of something noumenal to something phenomenal in the case of the relationship of the soul to matter, it will be a relationship between the soul as noumenon to body as phenomenon and not the opposite. In Metaphysik K2, after telling us that the soul is not matter, he tells us that "If the soul is not matter, and cannot think as such, then it is perhaps a substrate of matter, i.e., the noumenon, of which matter is merely the phenomenon" (MK2, 28:759 [early 1790s]). Likewise in Reflexion 6002, Kant observes that "The first substances, that lie at the ground of matter, must also be simple, but they give no appearances other than composite ones. Thus perhaps also the soul" (6002, 1780–9). And while Kant repeatedly refers to his unequivocal conclusion that the soul is not matter as a conclusion of immaterialism, he is happy to specify next that, if it turns out that the noumenal soul has matter as its mere appearance, a "virtual materialism arises" (MK2, 28:759 [early 1790s]; see also MMr, 29:904–7; MD, 28:682; MVo, 441–2; and MVi, 29:1029). Indeed, it is because of this sort of possibility that Kant dismisses the traditional understanding of the mind-body problem: insofar as our mental states and physical states are both mere appearances, one in time only, the other both in space and time, it is possible that their respective underlying noumena are of the same sort, eliminating the incommensurability problem that obtains at the level of appearance.

So where does this leave the question of the corruptibility of the soul? We cannot rest assured, Kant makes clear, that the soul is some simple part of body that is, as such, indivisible and impervious to the body's corruptibility. It now turns out that a complex body may have a simple soul underlying it, raising the possibility of a nonspatial corruptibility at the noumenal level to parallel the body's corruptibility at the phenomenal level. And this is precisely the possibility that Kant acknowledges in the form of his response to Mendelssohn's argument for incorruptibility. In his pre-1782 recorded thought, Kant often made clear his view that, because we have multiple powers – despite the rationalists' view that there is just one fundamental power – we could lose these powers, such as our higher ones, and thus lose our rational abilities and identity, effectively ending our lives (*MLI*, 28:295 [1777–80]; *R* 4239, 17:473 [1769–71]; *R* 4556, 17:592–3 [1772–6]; *R* 4561, 17:594 [1772–8]). But starting in 1782, Kant begins presenting his argument against Mendelssohn, that we could lose our intensive powers by means of a process of elanguescence, to the point even where our substance would cease to exist (*MMr*, 29:905–6, 912–3; B 413–16 [1787]; *MK2*, 28:764 [early 1790s]; *MVi*, 29:1037 [1794–5]). So our simplicity as a noumenal substance does nothing to insure our incorruptibility, even though it would provide this assurance if we assumed that we were a simple part of matter and that corruptibility could only take place by means of spatial division.

We now come to Kant's views on the question of the third paralogism as Kant addresses this question outside of the Paralogisms – that is, the question of whether the identity of our personality, or self-consciousness, in all of our thinking, implies our permanence as an identical soul even after death and the destruction of our bodies. Kant's treatment of this question overlaps with his treatment of the question of the soul's status as a simple substance, and he accordingly tends to devote less attention to it than to the other questions. But this question nonetheless adds something of importance, because he recognizes repeatedly that establishing the immortality of the soul requires that we establish the following three conditions regarding the soul, not just the first two, which we have already seen addressed: "(1) [the soul's] perdurability, i.e., the survival of the substance, (2) its survival as intelligence, i.e., of a being whose faculty of reason and its acts also survive, [and] (3) the actual survival of the personality of the human soul, that after death it be conscious of itself that it was the same soul, for otherwise I could not say that it itself exists in the future world, but rather that there would be another rational being there" (*MVo*, 28:440–1; *MD*, 28:688; *MMr*, 29:911, 913).

As Kant sees it, the argument for our continued, identical personality is simple: in all of the time in which we have thought, we have been alive, and therefore, because our self-consciousness, or personality, is in all time, it is permanent and so will continue to exist even when our body has decomposed. The holes in this argument are exposed by the reviewed Virgil argument. This argument, we saw, rests on a simple fact of self-consciousness: what it means to me to have a conscious thought, as I know from my own first-person experience of having thought and not from some definition of thought, is that it is something accessible to me within my simple, unified self-consciousness. It is not the case, Kant makes clear, that we believe a thought to be ours for some other reason – for example, that someone has it who is in the same building as us, or that it stands in the appropriate functional or causal relation to thoughts I am aware of having had such that this thought could not have existed but for these thoughts, as in the case of the thought someone is having while reading the thoughts expressed in my writing. Accordingly, it follows from Kant's account that we cannot identify something as our thought without committing on the question of our capacity for consciousness of ourselves at that time: if we say a thought was ours, then we say that our personality, or self-consciousness, was present at that time, so that at that time we had the capacity for self-consciousness (which is why, in Kant's view, our self-consciousness does not extend back to before our second year, when self-consciousness begins, in his estimation), as opposed to the definition of "our representations" that would allow the thoughts, say, of other people reading my work and functionally or causally affected by it to be thoughts that are "mine" even though my personality is not present.

But while this rules out our remembrance of representations from a time during which we did not exist as a self-conscious being, it by no means rules out a time in the past or present in which we had or will have no representations and did not or will not exist. To assume the opposite is to assume that what we have established on the basis of our constant presence in all of our thoughts is that we are permanent, and not merely permanent as a substance but as a rational, self-conscious, identical substance. So this takes us back to Kant's views on permanence. As we saw, Kant argues that it is only with regard to substance *in sensibility* – that is, with regard to that which is extended, impenetrable, and persists – that we need to assume permanence for the sake of the possibility of experience. Kant thus explains in *Metaphysik K2* that his argument against Mendelssohn that our powers could elanguesce to the point where our substantial soul wholly disappears "seems contradictory to [the] representation that in all alterations in nature the substance perdures and only the accidents change. But here the talk is merely of bodily substances, which we cognize" (28:764).

4. THE PARALOGISMS OF PURE REASON

"Observation on the sum of the pure doctrine of the soul, following these paralogisms." We now turn to the *Critique's* Paralogisms, where we find more of the same. We begin with the concluding section of the first edition Paralogisms, the "Observation on the sum of the pure doctrine of the soul, following these paralogisms." Kant turns to this section after having summarized succinctly the rationalists' individual fallacious inferences to their inflated conclusions of the soul's substantiality, simplicity, and identity in the First Paralogism, Second Paralogism, and Third Paralogism, respectively.

Kant's aim in this section is to take stock of what remains of a pure doctrine of the soul once we have purged it of the rationalists' excesses, and here it quickly becomes clear that Kant's account of what remains is nothing other than the account of the soul that we have seen him presenting in his many treatments of the soul from 1781 onward. Having reviewed Kant's accounts as presented in his lectures on rational psychology, we quickly see that the Paralogisms account bears an especially striking resemblance to these treatments, even unfolding according to their usual tripartite division. At A 383, he addresses the traditional section (2) of his discussion of rational psychology (for example, MMr, 29:903–4), regarding the soul in *comparison* with other beings, chiefly in comparison with matter. As in his lectures, Kant concludes that we are not matter *per se* and so succeeds in "securing our thinking Self from the danger of materialism." But also as in his lectures, Kant adds that this gives us no insight into whether the soul might not be the same sort of noumenal substance as that which *underlies* (merely phenomenal) matter, and that it gives us no insight into the *permanence* of the soul.

Kant next (A 384) presents what is the traditional section (3) of his lectures on rational psychology (for example, MMr, 29:904). And, just as in his lectures, he breaks this section down into three subsections. These concern (a) the community of the soul with an organic body, (b) the possibility of life prior to our connection to our bodies, and (c) the possibility of life after this connection – that is, after death. He discusses (a) from A 384 through A 393, blaming our tendency to see a deep dualism between mind and body on our misguided tendency to view matter as a thing in itself in the transcendental sense and hence as necessarily distinct, at bottom, from the soul. He then discusses (b) and (c) together from A 393 through A 396, dismissing as groundless all theoretical claims about life before or after our community with our organic body.

And finally, in the last pages of the "Observation on the sum of the pure doctrine of the soul, following these paralogisms," Kant turns to the traditional section (1) of his lectures on rational psychology (for example,

MMr, 29:903), offering his usual, pared down, indeterminate versions of the conclusions regarding the soul as in the other sources we have reviewed, in a manner consistent with his views in sections (2) and (3). Kant notes that, in considering the relation of our thoughts to ourselves as a subject, we generally fail to do what we earlier saw the Amphiboly demands we do – namely, engage in "transcendental reflection" about "the distinction of the cognitive power to which the given concepts belong ... [i.e.] as belonging to the pure understanding or to pure intuition" (B 317). He then distinguishes between the pure categories and the schematized, empirical categories, says that only the former apply to the I of apperception, and then makes clear that these do not provide us with anything that we really want to know for the purposes of establishing our immortality, such as our permanence or incorruptibility, and that only the empirical analogues of the pure categories supply this. Here is the remarkable, and quite long, passage:

They are nothing more than pure categories, through which I never think a determinate object ... If I declare a thing to be a *substance in appearance*, predicates of its intuition must be given to me previously, in which I distinguish the persistent from the changeable and the substratum (thing itself) from that which merely depends on it. When I call a thing **simple in appearance**, then by that I understand that its intuition is of course a part of the appearance, but cannot itself be further divided, etc. But if something is cognized as simple only in concept and not in appearance, then I really have no cognition of the object, but only of my concept, which I make of something in general that is not susceptible of any real intuition. I say only that I think something entirely simple, because I really do not know anything further to say about it than merely that it is something.

Now mere apperception ('I') is substance in concept, simple in concept, etc., and thus all these psychological theorems are indisputably correct. Nevertheless, one by no means thereby cognizes anything about the soul that one really wants to know, for all these predicates are not valid of intuition at all, and therefore cannot have any consequences that could be applied to objects of experience; hence they are completely empty. For that concept of substance does not teach me that the soul endures for itself, that it is not a part of outer intuitions that cannot be further divided and hence could not arise or perish through any natural alterations – pure properties that could provide acquaintance with the soul in the connection of the experience, and disclosure concerning its origin and future state. Now if I say through mere category: 'The soul is a simple substance,' then it is clear that since the understanding's naked concept of substance contains nothing beyond the fact that the thing is to be represented as a subject in itself without in turn being the predicate of another subject, nothing about its persistence follows, and the attribute of simplicity certainly cannot be added to this persistence; hence one is not in the least instructed about what the soul can encounter in the alterations in the world. If one would tell us that it is a **simple part of matter**, then from what experience teaches us about this, we could derive its persistence and, together with its simple nature, its immortality. But the concept of the I, in the psychological principle ('I think'), tells us not one word about this. (A 399–401)

The Paralogisms. We now turn to the individual paralogisms. In the Critique, Kant explains that "[a] logical paralogism consists in the falsity of a syllogism due to its form, whatever its content may otherwise be. A transcendental paralogism has a transcendental ground for inferring falsely due to its form. Thus a fallacy of this kind will have its ground in the nature of human reason, and will bring with it an unavoidable, although not insoluble, illusion" (A 341). Because of the natural, transcendental form of error it involves, a paralogism is accordingly not presented disingenuously: in his lectures on logic, Kant tells us that a fallacious inference is "a paralogism insofar as one deceives oneself through it, a sophism insofar as one intentionally seeks to deceive others through it" (Jäsche Logic, 9:134–5; A 298/B 354). Moreover, in these paralogisms "the conclusion is drawn per Sophisma figurae dictionis" (B 411), or by a sophism of a figure of speech, or fallacy of equivocation. This equivocation concerns the "middle term" in a syllogism, Kant explaining in his logic lectures that in "the sophisma figurae dictionis ... the medius terminus is taken in different meanings" (Jäsche Logic, 9:135). Specifically, this is a "fallacia a dicto secundum quid ad dictum simpliciter, sophisma heterozeteseos, elenchi ignorationis, etc.," or, "a fallacy [of inferring] from what is said with qualification to what is said simpliciter, the sophism of misdirection, the ignoratio elenchis, etc." (trans. Michael Young).

And what is a middle term? All of the paralogisms concern a categorical inference, Kant tells us, and in a categorical inference there is always a major premise that states "a categorical proposition" (Jäsche Logic, 9:122; A 330/ B386–7), also called a "universal rule" (Jäsche Logic, 9:120), and in this universal rule, a condition is set out under which we can apply a certain predicate. This condition is also referred to by Kant as the "middle term," "mediating mark," "mediating concept," or "terminus medius" (Jäsche Logic, 9:122–125). After the major premise sets out the condition, or middle term, that needs to obtain in order for a certain predicate to follow, the minor premise introduces a subject and asserts that it satisfies the condition of the major premise. The conclusion then follows, linking the predicate of the major premise to the subject of the minor premise. Thus, in Kant's shorthand, the categorical syllogism follows the pattern (1) MP, (2) SM, therefore (3) SP, where "M" is the mediating concept, "P" the predicate, and "S" the subject (Jäsche Logic, 9:126). Connecting this to Kant's explanation of a paralogism as a fallacy in which there is an equivocation in the middle term, we see that Kant is arguing that the condition, or middle term, of the major premise is ambiguous and that only understood in one way, *simpliciter*, does the predicate follow as understood in a particular way. We then believe that a subject satisfies this condition, or middle term, although it only satisfies it understood in another, *qualified* sense. But because we do not recognize the different senses of the middle term – for a transcendental reason – we attach the predicate that holds only for the middle term *simpliciter* to the subject, to which the middle term does not apply *simpliciter*.

This account of the structure of a paralogism, together with Kant's reviewed account of the self and its departure from rational psychology, provides us with a key to understanding Kant's accounts of the individual paralogisms. Consider, first, substantiality. We saw that Kant recognizes *two ways* in which we can understand *the concept of a subject that is never a predicate*: one in the empirical sense, which is determinate; the other in the transcendental sense, which is indeterminate. The former sense implies that the subject is a *substance in the empirical sense*, which implies permanence; the latter sense implies that the subject is a *substance in the transcendental sense*, which does not imply permanence. We also saw that Kant said that the rationalists are not willing to restrict themselves to the indeterminate offerings of our *immediate apperception* of ourselves as things in themselves, but instead arrive at their conclusions by means of an *inference*. So Kant would seem to have the rationalists slipping between the two concepts of substance by means of an ambiguous middle term – namely, that of a subject that is never a predicate – in the course of their inference.

And, turning to the First Paralogism – and later to the Second Paralogism and Third Paralogism – this is precisely what we find. Here is his presentation of the first paralogism in the second edition of the *Critique*:

What cannot be thought otherwise than as subject does not exist otherwise than as subject, and is therefore substance.

Now a thinking being, considered merely as such, cannot be thought otherwise than as subject.

Therefore it also exists only as such a thing, i.e., as substance. (B 410–11)

And here is Kant's anticipated explanation of this paralogism:

The major premise talks about a being that can be thought of in every respect, and consequently even as it might be given in intuition. But the minor premise talks about this being only insofar as it is considered as subject, relative only to thinking and the unity of consciousness, but not at the same time in relation to the intuition through which it is given as an object for thinking. Thus the conclusion is drawn *per Sophisma figurae dictionis*, hence by means of a deceptive inference. (B 411)

Kant next adds further detail about the precise sense in which the rationalists have fallen short in their attempt to establish their conclusion of the soul's substantiality. Again, this is just more of the same of what we saw elsewhere, with Kant arguing that the rationalists failed to established the soul's substantiality in the sense that entails permanence:

But now what sort of use am I to make of this concept of a substance? That I, as a thinking being, **endure** for myself, that naturally I **neither arise** nor **perish** – this I can by no means infer, and yet it is for that alone that the concept of the substantiality of my thinking subject can be useful to me; without that I could very well dispense with it altogether.

So much is lacking for us to be able to infer these properties solely from the pure category of substance, that we must rather ground the persistence of a given object on experience if we would apply to that object the empirically usable concept of a subject. But now we have not grounded the present proposition on any experience, but have merely inferred [it] from the concept of the relation that all thought has to the I as the common subject in which it inheres. (A 349–50)

It is easy to follow the Second Paralogism, as well, as it proceeds along the same well-worn path that Kant travels in the material that we have reviewed, rejecting the rationalists' inflated version of the conclusion of the soul's simplicity that entails the soul's incorruptibility. Here is Kant's formal statement of the paralogism:

The thing whose action can never be regarded as the concurrence of many acting things, is **simple**.
    Now the soul, or the thinking I, is such a thing.
    Thus etc.

Kant's analysis of this paralogism begins with a discussion of what we earlier termed the Virgil argument and how the rationalists misunderstand this argument. As we saw, Kant argued that the conclusion that our thoughts need to be united in a simple subject is not something *inferred* and *conceptual*, nor could we ever *intuit* this, as we could not intuit something simple, much less intuit the necessity of something's being simple. In Kant's view, the force of the Virgil argument rests solely in our first-person, immediate awareness of what it is like to be a thinking thing, an awareness that is, once again, completely indeterminate, negative, and useless with regard to the question of incorruptibility.

Kant first identifies the key insight in the Virgil argument: "[t]he so-called *nervus probandi* (the nub (literally, 'nerve') of what is to be proved) of this argument lies in the proposition that many representations have to be contained in the absolute unity of the thinking subject in order to constitute one thought" (A 352). He then, predictably, targets the rationalists' claims about *how* it is that we arrive at this insight. First he asserts that "But no one can prove this proposition from **concepts** ... [it] cannot be treated as analytic" (A 352). One paragraph later he turns to the next option, claiming that "But now it is also impossible to derive this necessary unity of the subject, as a condition of the possibility of every thought, from experience" (A 353). He then presents his alternative explanation of the source of this insight, as he has repeatedly done elsewhere, saying that here we rely on nothing more or less than our unique, first-person self-awareness, as in no other investigation: "It is obvious that if one wants to represent a thinking being, one must put oneself in its place, and thus substitute one's own subject for the object one wants to consider (which is not the case in any other species of investigation); and it is obvious that we demand absolute unity or the subject of thought only because otherwise it could not be said: 'I think'" (A 354). Kant thus turns away, as usual, suggestions that the source of our insight is anything other than our immediate self-consciousness, not to mention suggestions that this other means of epistemic access somehow reveals more than does our immediate self-consciousness.

Kant then ties this *methodological* point to the question of the *nature* of the conclusion of simplicity, telling us that our simplicity is not inferred but is instead the product of immediate apperception and that it is simple only in the sense of being empty of predicates:

But the simplicity of my self (as soul) is not really **inferred** from the proposition 'I think' but rather the former lies already in every thought itself. The proposition **I am simple** must be regarded as an immediate expression of apperception, just as the supposed Cartesian inference *cogito, ergo sum* is in fact tautological, since the *cogito (sum cogitans)* immediately asserts the reality. But **I am simple** signifies no more than that this representation I encompasses not the least manifoldness within itself, and that it is an absolute (though merely logical) unity. (A 354–5)

Kant then offers the by-now familiar claim that, for lack of predicates, the subject is an indeterminate transcendental subject about which we have no *cognition*, and that it is a mere "Something in general": "it is obvious that the subject of inherence is designated only transcendentally through the I that is appended to thoughts, without noting the least property of it, or cognizing or knowing anything at all about it. It signifies only a Something in general (a transcendental subject), the representation of which must of course be simple, just because one determines nothing at all about it" (A 355). Kant accordingly explains that "I do not cognize the real simplicity of my subject. Just as the proposition 'I am substance' signifies nothing but the pure category, of which I can make no (empirical) use *in concreto*, so it is permitted to me to say, 'I am a simple substance,' that is, a substance the representation of which never contains a synthesis of the manifold; but this concept, or even this proposition, teaches us not the least bit in regard to myself as an object of experience" (A 356). Taken out of context, the claim that I do not cognize the "real simplicity" of my subject could mean any number of things;

here it means what Kant makes clear immediately thereafter – namely, that this subject is not simple in the *empirical* sense of "simple," or the meaning of "simple" *in concreto*, Kant telling us that this conclusion lacks "the reality of an objective use" (A 357), just as he emphasizes that the default meaning of "reality" in play in this discussion is the empirical one when he tells us later in the Paralogisms that "Every outer perception therefore immediately proves something real in space, or rather is itself the real" (A 375) and in the Ideal, when he speaks of "that which constitutes the thing itself (in appearance), namely the real" (A 581 /B 609).

Kant next relates this discussion of the indeterminate versus determinate meaning of simplicity to the only question that matters in the discussion of our simplicity – namely, whether we are incorporeal in the sense of being incorruptible. Kant claims that "[e]veryone must admit that the assertion of the simple nature of the soul is of unique value only insofar as through it I distinguish this subject from all matter, and consequently except it from the perishability to which matter is always subjected. It is really only to this use that the above proposition is applied, hence it is often expressed thus: the soul is not corporeal" (A 356). Kant then explains that he will show the worthlessness of the conclusion of our simplicity by showing that this conclusion applies "in its pure significance as a merely rational judgment (from pure categories), [so that] not the least use of this proposition can be made in respect of its dissimilarity to or affinity with matter" (A 357). He does this in the manner in which we have seen him do it many times elsewhere. He is firm in his conviction that the soul as simple substance is distinct from matter *per se*, once again noting that obviously "thinking beings, **as such,** can never come before us among outer appearances" (A 357); in this sense, Kant rejects a crude materialism that would equate us with matter as such. But as we have seen him do so many other times, Kant recognizes that matter as such is mere appearance, that we "know nothing at all" about "the intelligible that grounds the outer appearance we call matter" (A 360), and that, while we cannot assume that what underlies it is a thinking thing (B 330), this cannot be ruled out. Accordingly, we cannot rule out the possibility that we, as simple noumenal thinking subjects, could be what appears as matter, even if we are not matter *per se*. Thus Kant notes that, despite our distinctness from matter *per se*, transcendental idealism allows that "that same Something that grounds outer appearances and affects our sense so that it receives the representations of space, matter, shape, etc. – this Something, considered as noumenon (or better, as transcendental object) could also at the same time be the subject of thoughts" (A 358). While our simplicity as noumenal beings therefore rules out that we are matter *per se*, this does not rule out the possibility of our *connection* to matter, because we could be the sort of thing that underlies matter, and therefore we could be the sort of thing that is not simple in appearance and thus indivisible in the way that matter is not, but instead would be that in appearance that is still corruptible matter.

This is how Kant ends the first edition of the Second Paralogism, but his argument is obviously incomplete. He has shown that we may appear as something extended and corruptible, and so he denies the rationalists the conclusion that we are simple in appearance and in turn their conclusion that we are therefore incorruptible. At the same time, however, Kant's transcendental idealism has deepened the rift between appearances and things in themselves, making them distinct in kind. The result of this is that the question of our simplicity as appearance is now mute: appearance is mere phenomena, whereas what we want to know about is the future state of ourselves as a thing in itself. While Kant has shown that we as appearance may be corruptible, he has insulated the thing in itself from this scene, and because he still concludes the simplicity of this thing in itself, he still needs to show how simplicity at this level does not guarantee our incorruptibility. In other words, Kant needs to finish what he has started and explain how simplicity in the sense given is compatible with corruptibility – that is, he needs to render coherent a scenario in which our possible corruptibility *as mere appearance* is also paralleled by our corruptibility *as noumena*.

And this is exactly what Kant offers in the form of his rejection of Mendelssohn's argument to immortality from simplicity, which he added to the 1787 second edition of the Paralogisms but which we also saw Kant offer in his earlier, 1782–3 lectures on ethics, his 1786 *Metaphysical Foundations of Natural Science*, and his 1783 *Prolegomena*. This argument is that while our simplicity as noumena rules out our extensive magnitude *per se* and so rules out the possibility that we, as noumena, are as such divisible in space, not only is it possible that we might appear as something in space, which, as such, is something that has extensive magnitude and is corruptible, but it is also possible that we are corruptible as noumena insofar as we can have *intensive* magnitude as noumena.

Finally, we turn to Kant's Third Paralogism. Here he presents the paralogism:

What is conscious of the numerical identity of its Self in different times, is to that extent a **person**.
  Now the soul is etc.
  Thus it is a person.

The big question with the first paralogism was whether we are a substance in intuition and so in the empirical sense that implies permanence; with the second paralogism, it was whether we are simple in intuition and so in the empirical sense that implies incorruptibility; and here, with the third paralogism, it is whether we are identical in intuition, as an object, and so in the empirical sense that implies substantiality, thus permanence, and, as a self-conscious substance, permanence as a self-conscious being. Thus the question here is whether our numerical identity, as we are aware of it in all of our thoughts (and, once again, "not as inferred" (A 362)), is the basis for concluding our numerical identity as an external object. The numerical identity of an external object is something that we must conclude on the basis of what is "persisting in its appearance" (A 362), however, so the question is whether our identity in our own thought implies our persistence in our appearance as an external object. In other words, does our identity in our own thought imply our identity as an object "if I consider myself from the standpoint of another (as an object of his outer intuition)," which would mean that now we are being seen in time rather than seeing time in us, so that we would now see the "objective persistence of my Self"? (A 362–3). This would obviously be a coup, for if we could infer to our identity as an object of outer sense from our identity in all of our own time, then we would be inferring to our empirical substantiality and thus our permanence. But why would we assume that our identity in our own time implies that we are identical as an object in space and time? It is *possible* that we appear as matter, Kant acknowledges in the Second Paralogism and many other places, but it is not *necessarily* the case that we do. And if we are not even sure *whether* we appear as anything in space and time at all, we can hardly assume that we appear as an *identical* object in space and time. For all we know, our appearance in space and time could be as a successive series of different objects, with our consciousness moving "across" them in a virtual sense, in a manner analogous to motion moving across successive elastic balls, so that we would not be wed to an object and its permanence, just as motion is not (see A 363n).

5. CONCLUSION

Our examination of Kant's account of the soul in the *Critique* and many other sources from 1781 onward has revealed Kant's considered view that our soul as thing in itself is a simple, identical substance. Our examination of these same sources also reveals that Kant's transcendental researches identify the rich, determinate, and useful implications of these conclusions as obtaining only for phenomena. Because the rationalists do not recognize the deep divide in kind and not merely degree between phenomena and noumena, and because they accordingly cannot recognize the proper and restricted domains of application of these concepts, they run them together in their inferences to the nature of the soul, applying the determinate and useful versions where only the indeterminate and useless versions are warranted. Of course, that Kant should accept any ontologically significant conclusion in application to the soul may strike us as odd. But far from reflecting awareness of the rationalists' errors, this response may instead reflect the deeply engrained tendency that Kant recognized in the rationalists and empathized with, to conflate ontologically significant but determinate conclusions with determinate ones.

10   The Antinomies of Pure Reason

I. INTRODUCTION

The Second Chapter of Book Two of the Transcendental Dialectic, which deals with the pretensions of rational cosmology, contains one of the most ambitious discussions in the *Critique of Pure Reason*. Its argument is as far-ranging and complex as any in the entire *Critique* (even that of the Transcendental Deduction of the Categories). One aim is to show that any pure rational doctrine of the world's constitution is led inevitably, through a system of cosmological ideas or pure concepts of reason, into contradictions, based not on the contingent errors of any individual metaphysician but on reason's own necessary principles and procedures. A second aim is to discredit, more specifically, the pseudo-science of rational cosmology that was part of Wolffian metaphysics, by showing that if its claims to cognition were valid, they would drive reason into contradiction with itself. A third aim is to establish the central claims of the critical philosophy, especially transcendental idealism, as essential to the resolution of the antinomies.

Yet a fourth aim is to understand each of the issues that give rise to the antinomies individually, resolving the problem from which it arose. Finally, Kant claims that the antinomies concern not only theoretical philosophy but also the *practical* interests of reason. He sees the two sides as representing (respectively) "dogmatism" (or "Platonism") and "empiricism" (or "Epicureanism") (A 466–72/B 494–500).[1] His view that morality and religion are on the side of the thesis of each antinomy may be what provoked Schopenhauer's insistence that only the antitheses are rationally defensible.[2] Specifically, Kant argues that a proper

---

[1] The *Critique of Pure Reason* will be cited according to standard A/B pagination. Other writings of Kant will be cited by volume and page number in *Kants Schriften*, Berlin Akademie Ausgabe (Berlin: W. De Gruyter, 1900-).

[2] Arthur Schopenhauer, *The World as Will and Representation*, tr. E. J. F. Payne (New York: Dover, 1958), Volume I, pp. 488–507. Schopenhauer does seem to be right, at least to this extent: Kant's own resolution of the antinomies appears to hold that there is no beginning of the world, no limit of it space, no simple substance, and neither a free causality nor a necessary

resolution to the Third Antinomy will include a solution to the metaphysical problem of freedom of the will, on which depends the validity of moral laws.

Kant's argument for many of these ambitious claims – especially the claim that the antinomies provide an "indirect proof" of transcendental idealism – depends on the success both of the positive arguments for both sides of the antinomies and of the Kantian strategy for resolving the contradictions, as well as the affirmative claim that the Kantian solution, including transcendental idealism and the regulative status of rational principles, is indispensable to their resolution. The second chapter of Book Two also involves a complex interplay between a general theory about the antinomies – how they arise and what is at stake in them – and detailed discussions of metaphysical issues about the age and spatial extent of the world, the composition of matter, the structure of causal connectedness in nature, and the ground of the existence of natural beings. If Kant's arguments for the most far-reaching conclusions are to work, the project must succeed on all fronts. Given the complexity of the issues, that is probably asking too much.

Like the Dialectic as a whole, the Antinomies have been relatively neglected in comparison to the Aesthetic and Analytic. But the history of scholarship on them both acknowledges, in one way or another, their ambitious aims, and also tends to take a position, one way or the other, on these aims. For Fichte and Hegel, Kant's Antinomies provided a model for a new kind of constructive transcendental philosophy – the "synthetic method" (Fichte) or "dialectic" (Hegel).[3] For most neo-Kantians, the

being *as part of the natural world itself.* But this is perhaps not so much an agreement with the antithesis as such, as only with its *arguments* against the thesis. If the claim, however, is (what Schopenhauer wants to accept as positive doctrine) that the world in time or space, the divisibility of matter, the series of causally dependent powers or contingent beings is *infinite,* then Kant does not agree with that either. He thinks the series of conditions in the mathematical antinomies is neither finite nor infinite, and that the series in the dynamical antinomies *may* be finite, but only if its first member is beyond nature.

[3] "If the I reflects upon itself and thereby determines itself, the not-I is infinite and unbounded. If, on the other hand, the I reflects upon the not-I in general (upon the universe), and thereby determines it, it is itself infinite. In representation, therefore, I and not-I are reciprocally related; if the one is finite, the other is infinite, and vice-versa; but one of the two is always infinite. – (Here lies the ground of the antinomies expounded by Kant.)" *Foundations of the Entire Wissenschaftslehre, Sämtliche Werke* (ed. I. H. Fichte). Berlin: de Gruyter, 1971) 1:246. Fichte's "synthetic method," modeled on the Antinomies, is present throughout his works. For a few prominent examples, see *Foundations of the Entire Wissenschaftslehre* 1:113–115, 123–127, 211–217; *Foundations of*

primary function of the Antinomies, as of the Transcendental Dialectic as a whole, was purely negative: a rejection of transcendent metaphysics. In the earlier analytic tradition (Strawson and Bennett), there was interest in the problems of the antinomies, but little sympathy with Kant's theory of reason.[4] By contrast, more recent Kant scholarship (such as that of Allison and Grier) has become quite sympathetic to his larger theoretical aims.[5]

2. THE GENERAL PROBLEM OF THE ANTINOMIES

The cosmological ideas arise from the fact that in the world there are relations of dependency, in which one part of the world is *conditioned* by another. The fundamental idea here is that of a *world* or world-whole, which is internally complete in itself regarding the various dependency-relations that hold between its parts. These dependencies give rise in each case to a *series* of conditioned-condition relations – the series of events going back in time, the series of enclosing parts of the world in

Natural Right, Sämtliche Werke 3:30–41; *System of Ethics, Sämtliche Werke* 4:102–105. "It may also be remarked that, as a result of his failure to study the antinomy in more depth, Kant brings forward only *four* antinomies .... The main point that has to be made is that antinomy is found not only in the four particular objects taken from cosmology, but rather in *all* objects of all kinds, in *all* representations, concepts and ideas. To know this, and to be cognizant of this property of objects, belongs to what is essential in philosophical study; this is the property that constitutes what will determine itself in due course as the dialectical moment of logical thinking"; Hegel, *Encyclopedia Logic* §48R, tr. Geraets, Suchting, and Harris (Indianapolis: Hackett, 1991), pp. 92–93.

4   "Kant's theory of reason, as well as being false, has little bearing on the real contents of Book II and is often positively inconsistent with them; and so it cannot help to solve the problems in Book II. Nor does it explain why there are just such and such metaphysical problems: that is just Kant's undignified attempt to derive his choice of topics from the structure of human reason rather than the philosophical preoccupations then current in German Universities ... The troubles which Kant treats in the Dialectic do indeed arise partly from a failure to root one's thoughts in one's experience; but this has nothing to do with reason, and so I cannot take seriously the title of Kant's great masterpiece. Considered as a critique of pure reason, the *Critique of Pure Reason* is negligible." Jonathan Bennett, *Kant's Dialectic* (Cambridge: Cambridge University Press, 1974), p. 3. See Strawson's discussion of the Antinomies in *The Bounds of Sense* (London: Methuen, 1966), Part Three, III, pp. 176–221.

5   Henry Allison in *Kant's Transcendental Idealism*, revised edition (New Haven: Yale University Press, 2004). Michelle Grier, *Kant's Doctrine of Transcendental Illusion* (Cambridge: Cambridge University Press, 2001).

space, the series of parts of parts of composites, the series of causes, the series of dependent beings.

Kant holds that these various series of dependencies or conditionings are generated by transcendental conditions of the possibility of experience, which require a condition for each existence that is conditioned in any of these ways. Regarding each series, the question arises: Does the series of conditioned conditions terminate in a first member of the series that is utterly unlike the other members in needing no further condition, or does the series go on to infinity, with every member presupposing further conditioned conditions without end? The former answer generates the cosmological ideas of a first event in time (a beginning of the world in past time) and a limit to the world in space, of a simple substance (or atom), of a first (or transcendentally free) cause, and of a necessary being (which exists by its own nature), and also prompts an argument that the object of such an idea must actually exist if the conditioned members of the series are to be possible. The latter answer denies the existence of such a first member, arguing that it is excluded by the very principles that give rise to the cosmological series in the first place.

Each of these two competing answers gives us a different interpretation of the more basic rational idea of a *world-whole*, and thus two incompatible interpretations of the constitution of a world (or nature) as a whole, between which we apparently have to choose. The choice, moreover, seems an impossible one, since whichever way we respond to each of the cosmological questions, our answer seems open to insuperable objections. If we say that the regressive series of conditions goes on infinitely, then we seem to be saying that at whatever point we consider it, it is bound to be still incomplete, in which case the conditioned entity has not been supplied with what is presupposed by, hence required for, its existence. On the other hand, if we say that the series comes to an end in an object corresponding to one of the cosmological ideas, then we seem to be committed to the existence of a being that violates a necessary law of experience – the law requiring that each entity of that kind must be conditioned in the way that generates the series. The impossibility of each alternative can be represented by an argument for and against the existence of an object corresponding to each cosmological idea. This threatens us with a set of contradictions: There *must* be, yet there also *cannot* be, a first event in time, a largest quantity of the world in space, a simple substance, a first or free cause, a necessary being.

Formal structure of the antinomies. The four antinomies (or five, since the first antinomy has both a temporal and a spatial part), may accordingly be summarized as follows:

x *conditions* y =df· y so depends on x that had x not been, y could not have been.[6]

x *R-conditions* y = df· There is an irreflexive and transitive relation R such that for all x and for all y, if xRy, then x conditions y in virtue of the fact that xRy. (We can also call x the 'R-condition' of y, and say that y is 'R-conditioned' by x.)

Now suppose there are entities called 'φs' given in our experience, that the *a priori* laws of experience are such that every φ is R-conditioned, and that the *a priori* laws of experience are also such that we cannot encounter in experience any R-condition of a φ that is not also a φ.

The *thesis* of each antinomy then asserts that:

Something that is not R-conditioned must exist as the first member of the R-conditions of any given φ.

The *antithesis* of each antinomy asserts that:

All the R-conditions of any given φ are themselves φs, hence R-conditioned by further φs to infinity.

We may represent the four (or five) antinomies using the following scheme of values for φ and R:

Antinomy	φ	R
First (time)	state of the world	precedes
First (space)	spatial world region	properly encloses
Second	composite body	is a (proper) part of
Third	alteration	grounds the causal power producing
Fourth	alteration	grounds the (contingent) existence of

The pull of both sides of the antinomies. There is some reason to doubt that the arguments on either side of the antinomies should convince us of anything. Regarding the general argument against the thesis of each antinomy, why must we suppose that the "conditions" relation is transitive? Perhaps every φ is conditioned by another φ, and this other by

---

[6] Desmond Hogan points out to me that this formulation of the general "conditions" relation, when applied to causation (as in the dynamical antinomies) is similar to David Lewis's account, which seems more Humean than Kantian, and is subject to notorious objections: The death of a prisoner before a firing squad is caused by one guard's bullet, but the prisoner would have died even if the bullet had not hit him because ten others who fired would have done the job just the same. I agree that this formulation would be inadequate to capture what Kant means by causality, but it seems to me to suffice as an account of the conditions relation involved in the general problem of the antinomies, even if it would be inadequate as an analysis of causality (and especially of Kant's account of causality).

yet a third φ, but why should this third φ be regarded as a condition of the first one? Then, too, perhaps each conditioned item is conditioned by its own condition, and it is an altogether separate question as to what conditions that condition in turn, or whether anything must condition it. The argument for the antithesis of the antinomies, leading to an infinite regressive series, thus may not seem very compelling.

There is also something suspicious about the general argument against the antithesis, and thus for the thesis. If a conditioned existence requires an infinite series of conditions, why should we see any problem with this, or worry that it threatens us with an insufficiency of conditions? After all, the actual existence of the conditioned object is pretty clear evidence that all its conditions have been fulfilled, whether there are finitely or infinitely many of them.

A series can be *infinite* in any of three ways: by having a beginning and no end, or an end and no beginning, or neither an end nor a beginning. Why should we worry about the infinity of an "ascending" or "regressive" series – in the direction of the condition – any more than we worry about the infinity of a "descending" or "progressive" series – from each condition to what it conditions? What gives the antinomies their grip on us, however, is the deeper worry that without an unconditioned condition, either residing mysteriously in the entire infinite series as a whole or else concentrated in some exceptional first member of it, we have not yet specified the *kind* of condition that could truly *satisfy the conditions required* for the existence of the conditioned thing. Thus a series of conditioned conditions, even an infinite one, still does not yield anything that truly satisfies the conditions for the conditioned thing, which would mean satisfying them *unconditionally*. The antinomies work on us because there is a philosophical inclination, having a profound grip on us, that some things depend on other things in a systematic series, and that the connectedness among things that makes them constitute a single world, or a whole of nature, involves the transitivity of these essentially *asymmetrical* relations of conditioning or dependency.

Kant even agrees with this philosophical inclination, formulating it as a fundamental principle of reason: "**If the conditioned is given, then the whole sum of conditions, and hence the absolutely unconditioned, is also given**" (A409/B436). The problem is that this unconditioned might be "given" in either of two ways: as a first member exempt from the conditioning relation or as an infinite series of members, none of which is exempt from it. To both answers there seem to be decisive objections, leaving us dissatisfied whichever answer we might favor. Or as Kant also puts it: When we try to form a concept of these cosmological series, one alternative seems to present us with a concept that is *too small*, while the other presents us with one that is *too large* (A 485–490/B 513–518). (It is as if Goldilocks had found the Bear family unhappily childless.) Kant does not expect that we can ever finally rid ourselves entirely of the sense of puzzlement and dissatisfaction occasioned by these abysmal problems. But he hopes to settle them before the bar of reason, so that we can free ourselves from *error*, from *judgments* on one side or the other whose rational grounds are illusory rather than genuine – even if we can never entirely escape the sense of metaphysical torment they occasion.

3. THE FOUR ANTINOMIES (ONE AT A TIME)

The four antinomies (or five, since the First Antinomy has two parts) are all traditional philosophical problems that go back at least to Aristotle, if not further. Kant was not a very knowledgeable historian of philosophy, but he is at least aware of this history in general terms; he clearly intends the chapter to resolve a set of traditional (and vexed) metaphysical problems.[7] He also intends this resolution to confirm his own transcendental idealist metaphysics and his theory of reason, as well as the critical view of space, time, matter, causality, modality, and freedom of the will. His formulation of the particular problems, however, may not always perfectly match the general theory, partly because of their independent historical origins, and partly because of the philosophical uses to which Kant wants to put them.

Bennett, as we saw earlier, denies that there is any general problem at all lying behind the antinomies. I hope the discussion of the previous section has allowed us to see that this is an error. But there is something right about it, too, insofar as Kant's treatment of each individual antinomy also always reveals features peculiar to it, arising from its history as a philosophical problem, or from the philosophical uses Kant wants to make of it. A full discussion of any of the antinomies would therefore have to take up much more space than we have here. But it may help if we briefly note some of the features of each antinomy that might not be suspected merely from the general problem they are supposed to illustrate.

---

[7] See Sadik Al-Azm, *The Origins of Kant's Arguments in the Antinomies* (Oxford: Clarendon Press, 1972). For a discussion of the relation of the Dialectic as a whole to the older metaphysics, see Karl Ameriks, "The Critique of Metaphysics: The Structure and Fate of Kant's Dialectic," in Paul Guyer, ed., *The Cambridge Companion to Kant and Modern Philosophy* (Cambridge: Cambridge University Press, 2006), pp. 269–302.

First Antinomy: Does the world have a beginning in time?
A limit in space?

This antinomy concerns the mathematical limits of the world, both temporal and spatial. Kant holds that space and time themselves are given in pure intuition as infinite magnitudes (A 25/B 39–40, A 32/ B 47–48), but it is a separate question as to whether the *world* (matter and its alterations) had a beginning in time or has a greatest outer limit in space. The issue about the finitude or infinitude of the world in space goes back at least to Anaximander's conception of the *apeiron* and its rejection by Aristotle (*Physics* 3.5, *On the Heavens* 3.5).[8] But it is the temporal half of the first antinomy that has the more interesting history, so it is that to which I will devote the present discussion.

The beginninglessness of the world, or at any rate of motion (*kinesis*), was defended by Aristotle (*Physics* 8.1, 250b10–15, 251a17–26, b12–27, 252b5–7), as well as in commentaries on him by Averroes (Ibn Rushd). Contrary arguments that the world must have had a first beginning very much like Kant's argument for the Thesis of the First Antinomy were first presented by John Philoponus in *On the Eternity of the World Against Proclus* (529). Like Kant's argument (A 426/B 454), it begins with the premise that the past is that which has been traversed or completed, and makes use of Aristotle's own definition of infinity as that which cannot be traversed or completed, concluding that the past cannot be infinite. Philoponus's argument seems not to have been known to Richard Rufus of Cornwall, who apparently reinvented the same argument in the first extant Western scholastic commentary on the *Physics* about 1238.[9] (The same argument was later used by St. Bonaventure and others.) Kant too was apparently ignorant of earlier (scholastic) versions of the argument, though it is possible that he may have known them indirectly from the presentation of the argument by the Newtonian theologian Richard Bentley in 1690.

Kant's own argument for the antithesis is based on the idea that a beginning of the world in time must have been preceded by an empty time. Kant then argues, as he had in the First Analogy, that an empty time would be indeterminable, hence that no coming to be out of such a time is thinkable (A 427/B 455). It is sometimes thought that there is something illegitimate, because viciously circular, about Kant's appealing to this argument as a strategy for indirectly proving transcendental idealism, since the indeterminability of empty time seems to belong to his arguments for the Analogies and the Refutation of Idealism (in B) that

---

[8] Aristotle's works will be cited by title, book chapter, or Becker number.
[9] Richard Rufus, *In Physicam. Aristotelicum.* 8.1.8 (ed. Rega Wood) (Oxford: Oxford University Press, 2003), p. 211.

presuppose that doctrine (B xxxix–xl, A 166/B 218–19, B 275–9). But it would not be circular for Kant to appeal to the same *arguments* for the Antithesis that seem to him also to support principles advanced within a transcendental idealist framework; and it would not even be viciously circular for him to appeal to them even if he had directly used them in support of transcendental idealism itself.

In the scholastic discussions, however, there was a third position besides that of Aristotle–Averroes and Philoponus–Rufus–Bonaventure – namely, that of Aquinas and Ockham – who held that neither the beginninglessness of the world nor its beginning in time can be proved. Ockham argues that although an infinity cannot *be traversed*, there is no contradiction in supposing an infinity that *has been* traversed, since on that supposition there was never any determinate past time, infinitely removed from the present, which *was to be* traversed in order to arrive at the present.[10] Aquinas and Ockham regard the beginning of the world as something that cannot be demonstrated by philosophical argument, but may be known from the authority of scripture (*Genesis* 1:1). Their view is therefore the one most of us accept today – that whether the world had a beginning is knowable, if at all, only empirically (though we would be more likely to rest our empirical arguments for the Big Bang on radio-astronomy than on Holy Scripture).

Second Antinomy: Is matter composed of simple substances or divisible to infinity?

If the First Antinomy is based on the categories of quantity (totality as extensive magnitude in space and time), the Second is based on the

---

[10] "For it is generally true that an infinite which was to be traversed at some time can never actually be traversed. Nor can there ever be a last [revolution], and this is because its infinity must always be accepted. But an infinite that at no time was to be traversed, but always had been traversed can be traversed, notwithstanding its infinity. Hence because something was traversed that at some time was to be traversed, it is infinite. But if something is traversed that never was to be traversed, it need not be finite but can be infinite. Moreover, if the world were now from eternity, all past revolutions would never have been to be traversed, since in no instant of the duration was this proposition true: 'all these revolutions – pointing to all the past [revolutions] – are to be traversed'. Therefore the conclusion does not follow." William of Ockham, *Disputed Questions, Opera Theologica* 8: 64, 81–82. Similar criticisms of Kant's argument for the Thesis of the First Antinomy have been presented by Bertrand Russell, *Our Knowledge of the External World* (London: George Allen & Unwin, 1914), pp. 160–161, and Strawson, *The Bounds of Sense*, pp. 176–185.

categories of quality (reality as intensive magnitude). It concerns the composition of substance in appearance, or matter. This too is traceable back to the Greek atomism of Democritus and Leucippus, and their rejection by Aristotle (*On Generation and Corruption* 1.2), as well as the medieval indivisibilist controversy,[11] the revival of atomism in early modern science, and Leibniz's monadism. In another way, however, the Second Antinomy brings into conflict a conception of material substance based (as in the Leibnizian concept of substance, or even Kant's own conception of matter in the Metaphysical Foundations of Natural Science, as a construction out of two forces) on intensive magnitude, and one focused on the *spatiality* of matter, hence on extensive magnitude. The Thesis of the Second Antinomy, namely, focuses on material substance as intensive magnitude, while the Antithesis appeals to the idea of material substances as extensive magnitude in space. A "dogmatic" idealist, such as Berkeley or Leibniz, might have used this conflict to show the untenability of the whole idea of a material substance. Kant, who accepts the concept of material substance in the world of appearance, must draw a different conclusion.

The Thesis of the Second Antinomy argues that composite matter must be composed of simple substances, since if all composition, hence all composite parts, are removed in thought, then either there would be simple parts remaining or there would be no parts at all and hence nothing. Further, since substance is what persists by itself and independently, and whatever is composite is dependent on its parts, if matter is composed of nothing but composite parts, then no part of matter can exist independently, and material substance is impossible (A 434/B 462). The Antithesis, on the other hand, begins from the premise that any material substance must fill space. But space is continuous, infinitely divisible, having no smallest parts, so the same must be true of any part of matter that fills space. Therefore, matter as well as space must be divisible to infinity.

---

[11] This was a controversy that occupied many of the major figures of the thirteenth and fourteenth centuries, including Henry of Harclay, Robert Grosseteste, Walter Chatton, and William Crathorn (on the side of the indivisibilists) and John Duns Scotus, William of Alnwick, Walter Burley, and William of Ockham (on the opposite side). A sophisticated and late contribution to this is controversy is provided by the Ockhamist opponent of indivisibilism, Adam of Wodeham, *Treatise on Indivisibles*, ed. and tr. Rega Wood (Dordrecht: Kluwer, 1988).

*Third Antinomy: Does the causality producing any event
in nature depend on a spontaneous cause beyond nature?*

The Third and Fourth Antinomies are called "dynamical" (in contrast to
"mathematical") antinomies because they concern causal dependencies
in the world. Both also have something to do with arguments for a "first
cause" of some sort, relating them in some way or other to Aristotle's
'first mover' arguments of *Physics* 8.4–10. But the issues involved in
them must not be confused. The Third Antinomy arises from the categories of relation – specifically, the category of causality. It is about the
causes of *events* or *alterations* in nature, and it is concerned with the
necessary conditions for or source of the causal power itself of any natural
cause.

The Third Antinomy starts from the position, resulting from all three
Analogies, if they are understood together, that causal connections are
more than mere empirical regularities. The cause of any change in a
natural substance must be a causal power residing in a natural substance,
whose presence in the substance itself has a natural cause, in such a way
that this causal power itself is dependent on the causal power of its cause,
and also on the causal powers from which that cause in turn derived its
causal power. More specifically, for Kant a cause must be a causal power
of an agent substance acting at a time on a patient substance.

The question posed by the Antinomy is whether this regressive series
of derived or dependent causal powers belonging to natural causes must
be regarded as infinite, as the Antithesis maintains (A 445–8/B 473–6), or
(as the Thesis claims) it must be thought of as derived from a cause that is
spontaneous or *free*, hence distinct from every causality belonging to
nature and falling under natural laws (A 444–6/B 472–4).

Since the question begins with any particular causal power belonging
to the particular natural cause of some particular event, it is not a question about how a world in general came to be, or even about a possible
cause of all change or a possible unitary source of all causal power.
Therefore it does not raise the question of the existence of anything like
a God, or a "first cause" of the world, or of change or of motion. Instead, it
raises the question as to whether natural causal powers, arising from the
exercise of other natural causal powers, can be regarded as self-contained
orders, or whether they must instead be thought of as dependent on a
causal power that transcends nature. Hence the Third Antinomy is the
only one of the antinomies that – in the claims of its Thesis – proposes
that events in the natural world must be conditioned by something
(a causal power) not belonging to nature or subject to its laws. It is the
only one purporting to show (in the Thesis) that nature depends on something outside nature. This power, however, is not necessarily located in a

supernatural being, but is claimed to attach, as their condition, to the series of natural powers that produce any natural event or alteration. One might say that it argues for a supernatural power residing in a natural being.

The Third Antinomy, therefore, is carefully crafted by Kant to raise a question that might be seen as the problem of freedom of the will, or the possibility (perhaps even the necessity) of conceiving, at the origin of any natural causal series, of a kind of cause that owes its causal efficacy entirely to itself, as a free agent might be thought to do if it is to be held unqualifiedly and unconditionally responsible for its actions and the series of their effects.

Fourth Antinomy: Is nature (or any part of it) necessarily existent?

The series of causal dependencies at issue in the Fourth Antinomy is therefore very different from that at stake in the Third. The idea of a necessary being might make us think of theistic arguments for necessary existence, such as the Third Way of Aquinas, or the cosmological arguments of John Locke, or Samuel Clarke, or Christian Wolff. But this kind of argument, and its critique, is considered, and criticized by Kant, later in the third chapter of the Dialectic (A 603–14/B 631–42; the critique of the inference from contingent to necessary being is presented at A 609–10/B 637–8). The thesis of the Fourth Antinomy clearly allows that the necessary being whose existence is at stake there is a necessary being that might belong to the world (or be identical to the world itself). With this possibility in mind, we might sooner think of Spinoza or (still better) of eighteenth-century materialists such as the Baron d'Holbach, who argued that material nature exists necessarily.[12] Further, although both the Third and Fourth Antinomies talk about the causes of *alterations* in the world, the focus of the Third is on whether causal power must ultimately be grounded in a being (not subject to natural necessity) that has such *power* spontaneously or from itself, whereas the issue in the Fourth Antinomy is whether the dependency of one contingent cause on others must terminate in a *cause* that *exists necessarily*. The Thesis of the Third Antinomy argues for a being whose existence might be contingent but whose causal power might be exercised freely, hence

---

[12] "Nature is the cause of everything. It exists by itself. It will always exist. It is its own cause. Its movement is a necessary consequence of its necessary existence." Baron d'Holbach, *Système de la nature* (1770) (Paris, 1821) 2:155. Compare David Hume, *Dialogues Concerning Natural Religion*, ed. R. Popkin (Indianapolis: Hackett, 1983), p. 56.

contingently and outside the necessity of natural mechanism, whereas the Thesis of the Fourth argues for a being falling within the causal necessity of nature whose existence is also necessary.

The Fourth Antinomy also has one peculiarity that sets it apart from the other three. Kant thinks that in the first three antinomies, the Thesis offers us an unconditioned that is "too small" for its concept, while the Antithesis offers us one that is "too large." In the Fourth Antinomy, however, he thinks it is the idea of a necessary being that is "too large" while it is the endless series of contingently existing causes that is "too small" (A 486–90/B 514–18).

4. RESOLVING THE ANTINOMIES

We saw earlier that there are reasons to doubt that the general argument behind the antinomies is going to be sound for each thesis and each antithesis. Are each of the conditioning relations transitive, as these arguments require? Is there a ground to doubt that the *givenness* of the unconditioned (whether as a first member of the series or as the infinite series itself) is a necessary condition for each member of the series? Once we begin to appreciate that the four antinomies are not simply applications of the general argument but each involve special issues of their own, we will find other reasons to doubt that all the arguments on both sides could ever be considered sound, quite apart from any critique of them that Kant may offer based on transcendental idealism or his theory of the regulativity of reason.

If Ockham is right, for instance, then the argument for the Thesis of the temporal half of the First Antinomy is unsound (since if an infinite series is one that *cannot* be completed, it need not follow that there could not be an infinite series that *has been* completed); and the argument for the Antithesis might be unsound as well, if Kant is wrong in thinking that nothing could arise immediately out of an empty time (either because such a time is after all somehow determinable or because the determinability of empty time is not a necessary condition for something to arise immediately out of it). So perhaps the arguments on both sides of the First Antinomy collapse of themselves. Similar worries may beset the other antinomies as well. But these matters cannot be finally decided here (or perhaps anywhere else either). So let us put these qualms aside, and look at Kant's general attempt to resolve the antinomies on the assumption that there is nothing fatally wrong with any of the eight (or ten) arguments on which the specific antinomies depend.

Kant's solution to the antinomies depends on drawing a distinction between things of nature as appearances and a realm of things in themselves (A 490–7/B 518–25). Because he regards this distinction as necessary for their solution, he considers the solution to be an indirect proof of transcendental idealism, which insists on the distinction (B xv–xxi). Paul Guyer has argued that this was a relatively late development in Kant's thinking about the Antinomies.[13] Michelle Grier has pointed out that it is only the Antinomies, and in fact only in the mathematical antinomies, that Kant could hope to provide an indirect proof of transcendental idealism.[14] For it is only in the case of the *world* (not the soul-substance or the *ens realissimum*) that we have before us the idea of an appearance, and it is only in the case of the mathematical antinomies that we are considering the rational *idea* corresponding to an appearance, which therefore compels us to distinguish it *as appearance* from the same object *as it is in itself.*

Transcendental idealism as the key. The mathematical antinomies are generated by mathematical principles that apply to things only insofar as they are given in sensible intuition. As so given, however, they constitute a regressive series of conditions that is indefinitely long – but neither finitely nor infinitely long. For each event in time, it must be conditioned by an earlier one; for each extensive portion of the world in space, it must be conditioned by a larger one; and for each part of a substance having spatial extension, it must be a composite conditioned by its proper parts. But these series of conditions are never given to intuition as a whole. Kant thinks that to assume they must exist either as infinite wholes or finite wholes is to assume that they are not merely appearances but things in themselves, whose determinations must exist independently of the manner in which they can be given to our intuition. But if transcendental idealism is true, this assumption is false. It follows that both the thesis and the antithesis of the mathematical antinomies are *false.* The theses are false because the principles of possible experience make it impossible for objects corresponding to the cosmological ideas of a first event, a largest extent of the world or a simple substance, ever to be given to intuition. The antithesis is false because there is *no fact of the matter* about the age of the world in time, its extent in space, or about whether the divisibility of composites given in experience is finite or infinite. Consequently, there can be no fact that these are infinite. The arguments for both sides of these antinomies, Kant maintains, rest on a fallacy of ambiguity similar to the one found in the paralogisms. They draw on principles that apply to conditioned existences considered as

[13] Paul Guyer, *Kant and the Claims of Knowledge* (Cambridge: Cambridge University Press, 1987), pp. 385–415. This claim conflicts with the view of others, such as Benno Erdmann, who see evidence of interest in the antinomies even before 1770.

[14] Grier, *Kant's Doctrine of Transcendental Illusion*, pp. 172–182.

appearances given to our intuition, but they try to reach conclusions that would have to be true of these things only if they were considered as existing in themselves apart from the way they are given (A 517–27/ B 545–56).

Regarding the dynamical antinomies, Kant's solution again makes use of the distinction between things as appearances and things considered in themselves. But this time, he concludes not that both sides are false but that both the thesis and antithesis are (or might be) true. The thesis is false when it is applied to appearances. For no state or alteration uncaused by another, and no being whose existence is independent of other beings, can ever be given in appearance. But if we consider the cosmological ideas of a first or free cause and of a necessary being as referring to things in themselves (that cannot be given in experience), then there is no contradiction in supposing the existence of such things. But since they cannot be given in intuition, we could have no cognition of them and so their existence must forever remain an unsettled question, at least from the standpoint of theoretical reason (A 532–7/B 560–5; A 559–65/B 587–93). Again, the arguments for both sides depend on a fallacy of ambiguity in failing to distinguish the supposed objects of the cosmological ideas as appearances and as things in themselves.

Doubts about Kant's solution. There is good reason to be skeptical of Kant's solution to the antinomies, and especially of his thesis that the antinomies provide an "indirect proof" of transcendental idealism. Kant's solution depends on the claim that both sides of the antinomies err in supposing that if the conditioned is given, then the totality of its conditions, hence the unconditioned, must also be given. He seems to concede that if the totality of conditions is given, then that totality would have to be either finite or infinite in extent – thus leading to an equally valid argument on each side, and thus to an irresolvable opposition between equally demonstrable contradictories. Kant's way out is to deny that the conditions (and the world, regarded as the series of conditions) can be given as a totality. This would be plausible if the claim is only that under the laws of experience established in the Transcendental Analytic, we can have no direct experience either of a first event in time or of an endless past series of events, of an indivisible part of a composite or of its infinite division, and so on. If we understand "given" in this sense, then Kant's arguments would seem to be question-begging, since they would appear to assume transcendental idealism, and hence could not be used to "prove it indirectly."[15] But a more natural sense of "given" in this context is not "directly experienceable" but rather "existent" or

---

[15] This is a point made by Paul Guyer in *Kant and the Claims of Knowledge,* Chapter 18, pp. 404–415.

"actual" in the sense of the Postulates of Empirical Thought – namely, that something exists or is actual if it is *connected to* some intuition by (either transcendental or empirical) laws of experience (A 217/B 266, cf. A 376). This postulate of actuality is needed if Kant is to admit the actual existence of corpuscles too small to be visible or tangible by us, or celestial objects too distant ever to be visited by us, or even of most of the past, which we cannot now actually perceive or even directly remember, but must infer from its connection with directly perceivable evidence (archives, written memoirs, fossils, Carbon-14 decay, and so forth). But if "given" means "existent" in that sense, then surely "the world" (the various series of conditions of any given conditioned) is also "given." The only question is whether "the world" is really an 'object' at all – that is, whether the category of totality (a pure concept of the understanding, hence a necessary concept of an object in general) is applicable to "the world." If it is, then it would seem that there is necessarily a world-whole (the unconditioned totality of the series of conditions), and then it is either finite or infinite. So the arguments of the antinomies threaten us with the conclusion that it must be both (hence with a contradiction).

Kant's way of avoiding the contradiction, then, comes down to the claim that the category of totality cannot be legitimately applied to "the world" (to the various series of conditions that generate the antinomies). But it is not clear how he can avoid applying the category of *totality* to the series, any more than he could avoid applying the categories of *unity* or *plurality* to it. For surely each series is *one* series that has *many* members – and if so, why is it not a *whole* series – whose magnitude, therefore, must be either finite or infinite?

It is also unclear how transcendental idealism is supposed to help out here. For why should the category of totality be less applicable to appearances than it is to things in themselves? It might be thought less applicable to appearances if we are using the notion of "given" – as applied to appearances – to mean "directly presentable in present (or future) experience." But we have seen that Kant cannot consistently apply the notion of the "given" in this restrictive way to the world of appearance as long as he wants to count imperceptible corpuscles, or distant bodies, or even the prehistoric past as belonging to the world of appearance.

The one device still left open to Kant by his official doctrines is to distinguish between two sorts of "laws" by means of which a putative "given" might be connected with actual perception. One sort includes both the transcendental laws spelled out in the Principles chapter of the Analytic and the empirical laws grounded on them. The other sort includes principles not of the understanding but of reason – in particular, the principle that if the conditioned is given, then the whole (unconditioned) series of its conditions is given. This principle, as Kant rightly points out, is synthetic: "for the conditioned is analytically related to some condition, but not to the unconditioned" (A 308/B 365). Kant's official position is that such synthetic principles of reason are only regulative and not constitutive – they instruct us how to inquire, and what assumptions to use as the basis of our inquiries, but they do not guarantee the truth of these assumptions or guarantee that the world in its real constitution corresponds to them. This distinction would permit Kant to say that the totality of each series of conditions is not "given" relative to constitutive principles, but only assumed by regulative principles, and that this blocks the inference that the whole series of conditions must be an actually given finite or infinite whole.

Yet it seems that one of the aims of the Dialectic is to *establish* that principles of reason are merely regulative, not constitutive. Perhaps we should see the Antinomies as Kant's indirect proof of *this* claim, if its acceptance is our only way of avoiding the contradictions. On this showing, however, the role of transcendental idealism in resolving the Antinomies would seem to have vanished entirely. If principles of reason are regulative, not constitutive, it would seem that they must be equally so when applied to appearances and when applied to things in themselves. In other words, Kant has given us no reason to think that the antinomies would be any more irresolvable if we take the world-whole to exist in itself than if we take it to consist of appearances. For there are many philosophers, including robust realists scorning the very idea of a noumenal world, who recognize the merely heuristic (or "regulative") status of various principles yet without thinking that this commits them to anything like Kant's distinction between appearances and things in themselves. They could apparently accept the Kantian solution to the Antinomies without accepting anything like transcendental idealism. Or if the regulative status of principles of reason does commit us to transcendental idealism, then *that* claim seems to be the crucial one; and it seems quite independent of the Antinomies or their resolution.[16]

5. THE PROBLEM OF FREEDOM

The antinomies have special interest for Kant insofar as the Third Antinomy in particular relates to the problem of freedom of the will, which he regards as profoundly important for the possibility of practical

---

[16] Here I am disagreeing with the defense of Kant's "indirect argument" presented by Allison, *Kant's Transcendental Idealism*, revised edition, pp. 384–395. For an airing of this dispute, see our respective articles in *Kantian Review* 12 (2007).

(or moral) reason. Kant returned repeatedly to this topic, not only adding two extraordinary sections to the first *Critique* in order to deal with it, but also devoting to it the Third Section of the *Groundwork for the Metaphysics of Morals* (1785) and large portions of the *Critique of Practical Reason* (1788), as well as revisiting it in the First Book of *Religion Within the Boundaries of Mere Reason* (1793–1794). I doubt that any of these accounts of freedom are in all respects mutually consistent, or that there is any single defensible account of freedom present anywhere in Kant's writings. Kant's greatest (and only consistent) insight on this topic, in fact, seems to be his repeated admission that freedom, though it must be assumed both for theoretical and practical purposes, is nevertheless inexplicable and even incomprehensible (A 557/B 585; *Groundwork* 4:459, *Practical Reason* 5:5, 28–30, 93–98, *Religion* 6:117–118, 144, 221). The present discussion is confined to the account given in the first *Critique*.[17]

Kant holds that the validity of the moral law depends on our having "practical freedom" – the capacity to act on principles we give ourselves through reason, and to resist the pull of the desires arising from our natural needs as living beings. In the first *Critique*, at least, Kant seems to think that in order to regard ourselves as acting from principles of reason rather than merely responding mechanically to sensible impulses, we must regard ourselves as transcendentally free – independent of all natural causality, as represented in the cosmological idea that is the focus of the Third Antinomy. There is nothing in Kantian ethics itself – in its conception of acting according to rational principles or from the motive provided by the objective ground of rational nature as an end in itself – requiring such a strong metaphysical presupposition, or at least nothing that would not also be present in other ethical theories involving the common sense notion that human beings are able to act from reasons and on principles rather than immediately responding to impulses. Even Kant himself thinks that practical freedom can be "proven" empirically simply by the way we do act on principles and the differences between this and the action of non-rational animals or other natural beings (A 801–4/B 829–32). So the metaphysical problem, requiring transcendental freedom in the strong sense, is not one that Kant thinks will affect our practical affairs or even our empirical understanding of ourselves as natural yet free beings. Either Kant is mistaken in thinking that acting rationally requires this metaphysics, in which case his own ethics is not hostage to it, or he is

---

[17] For more detailed discussions of this topic, see "Kant's Compatibilism," in Allen Wood (ed.), *Self and Nature in Kant's Philosophy* (Ithaca: Cornell University Press, 1984), pp. 57–72, and Allen Wood, *Kantian Ethics* (Cambridge: Cambridge University Press, 2008), Chapter 7.

correct in this argument, in which case virtually all ethical theories would be in the same unenviable metaphysical predicament.

If Kant is right on the metaphysical point, there is a problem even in trying to think of ourselves as practically free without falling into a theoretical self-contradiction. For all our actions, as events in the world of appearance, fall under laws of natural causality, and are thus causally determined by natural events preceding them in time. Yet Kant sees no way in which we can be practically free unless we are able to begin a series of events in the natural world independently of any natural causes that might determine us. Consequently, he holds that we cannot regard moral laws as valid for us – we cannot regard ourselves as morally responsible beings, or even as rational theoretical judges – unless we ascribe to ourselves the capacity to be the kind of cause we conceive under the cosmological idea of a first or free cause – the very idea that is at issue in the Third Antinomy. But it is not clear how we can avoid an outright self-contradiction if we apply that idea to ourselves while also acknowledging that our actions are natural events causally determined by natural laws.

Kant's solution to this problem is once again to appeal to transcendental idealism's distinction between appearances and things in themselves. Determination by natural causality applies to our actions as parts of the world of appearance, but Kant holds that it is consistent with this to regard ourselves as free when we are considered as things in themselves. Since space and even time are features of things only as appearances, our actions as events in time may fall under causal regularities governing such events, yet at the same time they may fall under an intelligible causality proceeding from a timeless choice we make as members of a noumenal world. Kant's metaphysical story thus attributes to us both an *empirical character* (an observable regularity of our actions, and also occasional variations from it, that belong to the natural causality of those actions as events in the world of appearance) and also an *intelligible character* (belonging to us as noumenal beings, and grounding our empirical character in a transcendentally free cause of the kind asserted by the Thesis of the Third Antinomy) (A 538–41/B 566–9).

It is important, however, not to exaggerate the metaphysical claims Kant must make here, misunderstanding this solution by mistaking its purpose and status. Kant does not think that we can ever *prove theoretically* that we are free, or achieve any actual cognition of our free actions.[18] Since he thinks knowledge of what goes on in a noumenal or intelligible world of things in themselves is entirely impossible for us, it

---

[18] Karl Ameriks has argued that in 1781, Kant believed he could theoretically prove transcendental freedom. See *Kant's Theory of Mind: An Analysis of*

264   ALLEN W. WOOD

would be self-contradictory for him to claim that we *know* that we are free agents in the intelligible world, or indeed to make any positive claims whatever about how such a free causality might operate. His legitimate aim can be only to show that there is *nothing self-contradictory* in regarding our actions as events falling within the causal mechanism of nature and also asserting that they are effects of the free causality of our reason. All he needs in order to do this is to establish that there is no self-contradiction in supposing that we exercise free causality as noumenal beings. He says as much himself in his concluding remarks to the discussion of freedom in the Third Antinomy:

The problem which we had to solve ... was only this: Do freedom and natural necessity in one and the same action contradict each other? ... [To show] that the antinomy rests on a mere illusion, and that nature at least **does not conflict with** causality through freedom – that was the one single thing we could accomplish, and it alone was our concern. (A 557–8/B 585–6)

Once Kant has established the self-consistency of asserting we are free while also viewing our actions as events in nature, he can (and indeed *must*) disavow any positive account of how freedom and natural causality actually relate to one another. It is sadly true, however, that Kant seems to have thought it appropriate that in thinking of ourselves as free, we should also think of ourselves as members of an invisible world (a kingdom of God or realm of grace) hovering luminously (but to us invisibly) somewhere beyond the realm of nature. This wretched crotchet leads him at times to attribute a sort of positive reality to the theory of free action as noumenal causality. The point to insist on, however, is that his actual doctrines do not require this indulgence of metaphysical bad taste – indeed, they even strictly *forbid* it. These doctrines allow us – indeed, constrain us – to say that we can without inconsistency regard ourselves as free and also as parts of the natural world. Beyond that, they require us to be austere metaphysical skeptics about what freedom of the will is, in what world it is located, or even how it is possible. Kantian principles, consistently applied, discredit equally the facile attempts of naturalists to fit human freedom comfortably into the causal order of nature and also the wishful religious (or religious-like) faith that we are beings with supernatural powers or a supernatural destiny. It should be sad, disillusioning, and more than a little shameful to Kantians that Kant

the Paralogisms of Pure Reason (Oxford: Clarendon Press, 1982), pp. 193–203. I am not convinced of this, but whatever Kant may have believed at this time, he does not seem to have stayed with it, and the claim to be able to prove transcendental freedom (to prove the existence of an object of an idea of pure reason) seems inconsistent with Kant's general epistemological strictures in the *Critique*.

himself sometimes succumbed to the latter deplorable impulse, which represents a serious and unforgivable violation of his own critical principles. Kant's final word on freedom ought always to have been simply the comfortless doctrine that "freedom can never be comprehended, nor even can insight into it be gained" (*Groundwork*, 4:459).

11   The Ideal of Pure Reason

I. INTRODUCTION

Discussions of the "Ideal of Pure Reason" in the Transcendental Dialectic often focus on Kant's rejection of the three types of argument traditionally offered in support of the existence of God (the so-called "ontological," "cosmological" and "physico-theological proofs).[1] Kant's critique of these arguments, however, is prefaced by two very dense preliminary sections, the purpose of which is evidently to illuminate the "grounds of proof of speculative reason for inferring the existence of a highest being" (A 584/B 612). I am referring here to Sections 2 and 3 in the Ideal (A 572/B 600-A 590/B 618). Kant's prefatory discussions in these two sections appear to be designed to accomplish two distinct things. First, in Section 2, Kant wants to demonstrate the rational necessity of the idea of the *ens realissimum*. This idea, as we shall see, is said to be philosophically necessitated by our need to represent the "necessary thoroughgoing determination of things" (A 578/B 606). Second, Kant wants to account for what he takes to be an inevitable confluence of the idea of the *ens realissimum* with that of a **necessary being.**

Because Sections 2 and 3 seem to be offering two distinct accounts of the origin of the idea of God, some have suggested that Kant was simply confused or uncertain about the basis for the idea of rational theology.[2] Against this view, I have argued that Sections 2 and 3 of the Ideal are both essential to Kant's attempt to "justify" the rational necessity of the idea of God.[3] In what follows, I will develop the way in which the rational ideas of both the *ens realissimum* and the necessary being lead, on Kant's view, to the postulation of God's existence. Here it is essential to keep in mind that Kant's considered view is that the proofs for God's existence are based solely on the "coincidence [*Reziprokabilität*] of the concepts of

[1] Citations from the *Critique* in English are all from the *Cambridge Edition of the Critique of Pure Reason*, edited and translated by Paul Guyer and Allen W. Wood (Cambridge: Cambridge University Press, 1998).
[2] P. F. Strawson, *The Bounds of Sense* (London: Methuen, 1966) p. 221.
[3] See my *Kant's Doctrine of Transcendental Illusion* (Cambridge: Cambridge University Press, 2001), Chapter 7.

the most real being and necessary being" (A 789/B 817). I shall discuss these in turn.

2. THE *ENS REALISSIMUM*

Kant's attempt to provide some rational justification for the idea of the supremely real being is provided in a twisting, dense argument that extends from A 572/B 600 to A 583/B 661. The general claim is that the idea of the *ens realissimum* is philosophically necessitated in our speculative attempts to account for the pure possibility of particular things.[4] Kant begins his discussion by citing the principle of complete determination ("Every **thing** as regards its possibility, stands under the principle of **thoroughgoing determination**; according to which, among **all possible predicates** of **things**, insofar as they are compared with their opposites, one must apply to it"; A 572/B 600). The essential point here is that the real possibility of a particular thing is grounded in its complete determination (specification) with respect to all possible pairs of contradictory predicates. To thoroughly determine our concept of an individual thing, in other words, we must either affirm or deny of it each positive predicate (each individual thing is either A or not A, B or not B, and so on). In Kantian terms, the principle of complete determination considers things in their relation to the whole of possibility, the sum total of all predicates of things in general (A 572/B 600).[5]

It is from this principle of the complete determination of things that Kant proceeds to argue that the process of determining our concepts of things ultimately leads us to the idea of the *ens realissimum*. The movement from the principle of complete determination to the idea of the *ens realissimum* allegedly succeeds by means of an intermediate step that consists in showing that the principle of complete determination presupposes the idea of a "totality of all reality" (the *omnitudo realitatis*). Despite its scholastic overtones, Kant's claim is rather straightforward.

---

[4] For very helpful discussions of Section 2, see Allen Wood, *Kant's Rational Theology* (Ithaca: Cornell University Press, 1978), especially pp. 25–64, and Béatrice Longuenesse, "The Transcendental Ideal and the Unity of the Critical System" in *Proceedings of the Eighth International Kant Congress*, ed. Hoke Robinson, Vol. 1, part 2 (Milwaukee: Marquette University Press, 1995).

[5] There are a number of very good discussions of this. See Allen Wood, (op. cit), pp. 42–59; Longuenesse (op. cit). See also Henry E. Allison, *Kant's Transcendental Idealism*, revised edition (New Haven: Yale University Press, 2004), pp. 396–402. I discuss this in *Kant's Doctrine of Transcendental Illusion*, pp. 234–252. See also Allison, *Kant's Transcendental Idealism*), pp. 397–399.

If the process of specifying or completely determining a thing requires that every positive predicate be either affirmed or denied of the thing, then we must presuppose that the entire storehouse of all possible predicates is given. Indeed, it is precisely this presupposition that distinguishes Kant's principle of the determination of things from the merely logical principles of contradiction and excluded middle. Thus, Kant tells us that through the principle of complete determination "predicates are not merely compared logically with one another, but the thing itself is compared transcendentally with the sum total of *all possible* predicates" (A 573/B 601).[6] Given its reference to *all possible* predicates, it seems clear that the idea of the *omnitudo realitatis* is deployed in conjunction with a pure (*a priori*) rational procedure of attempting to determine each thing thoroughly. It is important to note in this regard that the idea of the totality of all reality (or of the sum of all possible predicates), as it plays out in the Ideal, is one issuing from pure reason. Here Kant is speaking about the principle of complete determination for "things in general," not merely for empirical objects. Even though, as we shall see, Kant does not think this principle yields knowledge of any actual object, he does suggest that reason necessarily postulates this idea of the complete determinability of things in general, and that this idea has an important regulative use in guiding empirical investigations.[7] This motivates many of Kant's claims in Section 2 of the Ideal. In examining the "progress of reason" in this effort, Kant undertakes to do two things. On the one hand, he wants (ultimately) to account for the rational (subjective) *necessity* of this idea, to show that the idea of the *omnitudo realitatis* (and as we shall see, its transformation into the idea of an *ens realissimum*) is *inevitable*. On the other, he wants to distance himself from the errors that flow from taking this idea to yield metaphysical conclusions. The latter effort is tantamount to an implicit argument against the rationalist metaphysicians.[8]

One way of addressing these competing interests in Kant's account might be to note that the principle of complete determination may be construed in one of two ways – one that reflects the pre-critical rationalist understanding, and another that reveals Kant's critical interpretation of the same principle.[9] With respect to the former, it is clear that Kant inherited this principle from the Leibniz–Wolffian school, which held

---

[6] See Longuenesse, *op. cit*, p. 217.
[7] See my *Kant's Doctrine of Transcendental Illusion*, esp. pp. 234–253.
[8] Wood, *Kant* (Oxford: Blackwell Publishing, 2005), p. 101.
[9] In what follows, I am drawing on the discussion by Béatrice Longueness in her *Kant on the Human Standpoint* (Cambridge: Cambridge University Press), Chapter 8.

the principle of complete determination (and its attendant presupposition of the totality of all reality) to be a metaphysical principle that accounts for individuation of objects. The problem, from a Kantian standpoint, is that the procedure of complete determination had been thought by the rationalist metaphysicians to be one undertaken *a priori*, simply through conceptual specification, independently of sensibility and its *a priori* forms. From the vantage point of the critical philosophy, such a procedure seems to be blatantly illegitimate; objects are always given to us under the formal conditions of sensibility and individuated as sensible objects.[10] It can thus be argued that in Section 2 of the Ideal, Kant is not actually endorsing the principle at face value so much as he is illuminating problems with it in order to demonstrate the basis for reason's error and in order to distance himself from the rationalist tradition.[11] In this connection, Béatrice Longuenesse has suggested that Kant can, and does, endorse a principle of thorough determination (and therefore the presupposed ideas of a totality of all possibility and all reality), albeit one substantially limited in comparison to the rationalist version, and one that can be defended by appeal to the transcendental epistemology articulated in the Transcendental Analytic. The upshot is that Kant accepts the principle so long as it is properly restricted to phenomena. More specifically, Kant can, and does, accept that the complete determination of objects of the senses presupposes the idea of the "whole of reality," but this whole of reality is reality understood as given in space and time. The restriction of the totality of all reality (positive predicates) to those given in space and time allows Kant to defend a critical reinterpretation or version of the principle of determination, and to suggest a legitimate use of it in the context of the transcendental epistemology outlined in the Analytic. Even so, this experientially thought whole is not actually given (in, say the mind of God, as for the rationalists), but only given as an idea, as a goal to which the understanding aspires. Thus, reading forward from the Transcendental Analytic, Section 2 can be viewed as a consequence of Kant's view that the "conditions for the possibility of experience are the conditions for the possibility of the objects of experience" (A 158/B 197).[12]

[10] Longuenesse, *ibid.*
[11] Longuenesse, *ibid.* See also Graham Bird, *The Revolutionary Kant*, (Chicago and La Salle: Open Court, 2006), pp. 724–727.
[12] In my book, I had criticized Longuenesse for failing to appreciate what I take to be Kant's insistence that the principle in its more abstract, general form is at issue in the Ideal (*Kant's Doctrine of Transcendental Illusion*), pp. 237–243. For her response, see *Kant on the Human Standpoint*, Chapter 8.

Such a view makes sense, for although there are resources in the Analytic for appealing to some version of the principle of complete determination, Kant is equally concerned to highlight the problems associated with the conclusions drawn by the rationalists. This becomes clear when we look to Kant's account of the errors involved in the movement from the principle of complete determination to the ideas of the *omnitudo realitatis* and the *ens realissimum*. What Kant tells us, in a notoriously tortured passage, is that the rationalists have dialectically substituted the "collective unity of experience as a whole for the distributive unity of the empirical employment of the understanding" (A 583/ B 610). Consider the following:

No other objects besides those of sense can be given to us, and they in fact can be given nowhere except in the context of a possible experience; and consequently, nothing is an object **for us**, unless it presupposes the sum total [*Inbegriff*] of all empirical reality as condition of its possibility. In accordance with a natural illusion, we regard as a principle that must hold of all things in general that which properly holds only of those which are given as objects of our senses. Consequently, ... we will take the empirical principle of our concepts of the possibility ... of appearances, to be a transcendental principle of the possibility of things in general. (A 582/B 610)[13]

Given that Kant had already undermined the more general rationalist understanding of the totality of all reality by appealing to the resources of the Transcendental Analytic, why should he spend so much time in the Ideal going back over the bases for the necessity of this very same idea? The answer is that the Dialectic introduces another element into Kant's criticism of rationalist metaphysics. That element is the influence and interests of the third and presumably distinct "faculty of knowledge," reason. In connection with this, Kant can argue that even though his critical philosophy has demonstrated the error of extending the principle beyond the limits of sensibility and its *a priori* forms, we are naturally compelled to do so by certain interests of reason that quite independently foist themselves upon us. More specifically, Kant believes that

---

[13] In Longuenesse's words, "By defining complete determination in terms of concepts alone, rationalist metaphysicians have run away with an illusory version of a perfectly sound principle of cognition" (p. 219). The Kantian passage is part of a much more extended discussion of the errors involved in rational theology. Indeed, Kant argues that by a certain subreption, an empirical principle is subject to a transcendental use. This subreption grounds the subsequent hypostatization of the idea of the *omnitudo realitatis*, and leads to the alleged personification of the *ens realissimum*. I discuss this issue at length in *Kant's Doctrine of Transcendental Illusion*, Chapter 7.

reason is compelled by a certain inherent "transcendental illusion" to expect and demand complete explanations. This rational demand, according to Kant, is grounded in the so-called "supreme principle of pure reason" – that "If the conditioned is given, the unconditioned is also given" (A 308/B 364). On the basis of this assumption, reason is enjoined to "Find for the conditioned knowledge given through the understanding the unconditioned whereby its unity is brought to completion" (cf. A 308/B 363). The problem is that the "unconditioned" is never actually *given*, and the assumption that it is instantiates the transcendental illusion that motivates transcendent metaphysics. Moreover, rather than being an avoidable or merely logical error, transcendental illusion lies in the very nature of reason. It is, indeed, Kant's efforts to link up traditional rationalist metaphysics with this unavoidable demand of reason that characterizes not only the critique of the Ideal, but all of Kant's criticisms throughout the Dialectic. With respect to the Ideal, as we shall see, the *ens realissimum* is an idea to which theoretical reason is inevitably led by this illusion, for reason demands not just the idea of the totality of all *empirical* reality, but indeed the idea of all reality *in general*. It is in conjunction with this claim that Kant can maintain that the idea of the *ens realissimum* is, as are other ideas in the Dialectic, "subjectively necessary."[14] Indeed, in his *Lectures on Philosophical Theology*, Kant insists that "we are justified in assuming and presupposing an *ens realissimum* as a necessary transcendental hypothesis."[15] Presumably, the idea is justified insofar as it provides "the supreme and material condition of the possibility of all that exists, the condition to which all thought of objects, so far as their content is concerned, has to be traced back" (A 577/B 605). To this extent, Kant appears to want to defend the necessity of the idea for *speculative* reason, to justify it as essential to reason's theoretical use.

Despite his efforts, in Section 2, to demonstrate the subjective necessity of the idea of the supremely real being, Kant admits that such an idea lacks objective reality. What we are not entitled to do, he claims, is to "presuppose the existence of a being that corresponds to this ideal; we can presuppose only the idea of such a being, and this only for the purpose of deriving from an unconditioned totality of complete determination the conditioned totality, i.e., the totality of the limited" (A 578/B 606). What this means is that this thoroughly philosophical conception of a supremely real being is recognizably insufficient to motivate the

---

[14] I argue at length for the subjectively necessary status of the idea of the *ens realissimum* in *Kant's Doctrine of Transcendental Illusion*, Chapter 7.

[15] *Lectures on Philosophical Theology*, translated by Allen W. Wood and Gertrude M. Clark (Ithaca: Cornell University Press, 1978), p. 68.

postulation of God's existence. Kant notes this insufficiency in the following passage:

In spite of its urgent need to presuppose something that the understanding could take as the complete ground for the thoroughgoing determination of its concepts, reason notices the ideal and merely fictive character of such a presupposition much too easily to allow itself to be persuaded by this alone straightaway to assume a mere creature of its own thinking to be an actual being, were it not urged from another source to seek somewhere for a resting place in the regress from the conditioned, which is given, to the unconditioned, which in itself and as regards its mere concept is not indeed actually given, but which alone can complete series of conditions carried out to their grounds. (A 584/B 612)

As we shall see presently, the "other source" that leads us to posit the existence of God is the demand for a necessary being, an idea to which we are also inevitably led in accordance with our rational interests (both speculative and practical), and which is also motivated by "transcendental illusion."

3. THE NECESSARY BEING

Before the Ideal, Kant had already contended with the presumably natural assumption that there exists some necessary being. More specifically, the claim that we must posit some necessary being was allegedly defended in the thesis argument of the Fourth Antinomy (see Chapter 10 of this volume). The thesis argument is difficult to follow, and there has thus arisen a number of different interpretations of what it is supposed to demonstrate.[16] Be this as it may, it is safe to say that the argument is designed to show that there must exist some necessary being (some being whose non-existence is impossible), and that the urgency of this requirement flows from our rational need to account for the world of appearances, understood as a series of alterations, or contingent beings. It is well known that the antithesis argument counters that the postulation of any necessary being violates the conditions of possible experience.

It is this impasse that leads to Kant's critical solution – that is, the claim that both the demand for a necessary being and the denial that there could be any such being in the world (or even outside it, but in causal connection with it) could be legitimate. Kant's solution is to suggest that reason's demand for a necessary being might well be allowed to stand, but only if the necessary being is construed to be a non-empirically conditioned

---

[16] For an extended discussion of the thesis argument, and the various interpretations of the argument, see my *Kant's Doctrine of Transcendental Illusion*, pp. 218–227.

condition of the entirely conditioned series of appearances.[17] Consider the following:

Therefore there remains only one way out of the apparent antinomy lying before us: since, namely, both the conflicting propositions can be true at the same time in a different relation in such a way that all things in the world of sense are completely contingent, hence having always only an empirically conditioned existence, there nevertheless occurs a non-empirical condition of the entire series, i.e., an unconditionally necessary being. (A 561/B 589)

Kant of course notes that the idea of an unconditionally necessary being, as a merely intelligible condition of existence in the world of sense, goes well beyond the cosmological debate that characterizes the antinomial conflicts concerning the world. As such, the idea of the necessary being is not just transcendental, but is a concept that is altogether "transcendent" (A 566/B 594). In connection with this, Kant tells us that the transcendent idea has a merely intelligible object about which we can "know nothing." Indeed, according to Kant, the idea is a mere "thought entity" (ibid). Nevertheless, we are told that "among the cosmological ideas, the one occasioning the Fourth Antinomy presses us so far as to take this step" (ibid).

Herein lies one of the most perplexing aspects of Kant's account of the basis for proofs for the existence of God. As before, he is committed to the claim that such proofs stem from our apparently unavoidable need to take our independently grounded idea of the *ens realissimum* and, as it were, "insert it" so as to fill in the space of what such a necessary being might be.

Thus among all the concepts of possible things the concept of a being having the highest reality would be best suited to the concept of an unconditionally necessary being, and even if it does not fully satisfy this concept, we still have no other choice, but see ourselves compelled to hold to it, because we must not just throw the existence of a necessary being to the winds; yet if we concede this existence, then in the entire field of possibility we cannot find anything that would make a more well-grounded claim to such a privilege in existence. (A 586/B 614)

---

[17] I am glossing over an admittedly difficult issue here. Strictly speaking, the thesis argument of the Fourth Antinomy states that "There belongs to the world, either as its part or its cause, a being that is absolutely necessary." As Paul Guyer notes, this is not the thesis that Kant subsequently defends in his critical solution. Rather, Kant suggests that we might allow a necessary being, but certainly not as part of or cause of the world. Kant thus undermines the cosmological terms of the dispute. See Guyer, *Kant and the Claims of Knowledge* (Cambridge: Cambridge University Press, 1987), p. 412.

Embedded in this passage is a number of claims. First, Kant takes the idea of a necessary being to be unavoidable. In Kant's words, "if something, no matter what, exists, then it must be conceded that something exists **necessarily**" (A 585/B 613). As we saw in the Fourth Antinomy, the idea of a necessary being is one we are compelled to adopt in order to account for contingency. The problem is that despite our adherence to the idea, there is no object that is or could be given that could not consistently be thought not to exist, no object whose non-existence is impossible. The "necessary being" is thus an idea that enjoys an ambiguous position in Kant's philosophy. It is simultaneously "indispensably necessary" as a final ground of all things, and the "true abyss," an "insoluble problem for human reason."[18] It is thus that Kant claims that we must answer our demand for a necessary being by seeking to identify the concept of a being that most closely "squares" with it. As we have seen, the *ens realissimum* is precisely such a concept, for it alone is a concept which has nothing "within itself conflicting with absolute necessity" (A 585/B 613).

Kant does not, however, simply take this linkage of the *ens realissimum* and the necessary being to be "convenient." On the contrary, he claims that there are a number of considerations that make the postulation of some necessary being urgent. Perhaps the most dominant rational interest in this regard, and certainly the one most often cited, is a practical interest: according to Kant the idea of a necessary being, from which we might derive and account for the unity and purposiveness in the world of appearances, provides a cornerstone "of morality and religion" (A 466/B 494).[19] For our present purposes, what is most interesting about this coupling of the ideas of the *ens realissimum* and necessary being is that it displays all the elements of the traditional conception of God, as an object of rational theology – that is, a supremely real being containing all perfections (positive predicates) that exists necessarily.

The fact that Kant cites our practical, moral interests as providing a motivation for the movement to the postulation of the supremely real being as the "necessary Being" is understandably emphasized by many commentators.[20] Less often emphasized is Kant's further claim, to wit, that reason has specific *speculative* interests in positing a necessary being. Thus, in articulating the interests of reason in promoting the thesis arguments of the antinomial conflicts (the so-called "Platonist" interests), Kant emphasizes that the idea of the necessary being is indispensably necessary in order to secure the "greatest possible unity of

---

[18] See *Lectures on Philosophical Theology*, pp. 64–65.
[19] See also R 5109 (18: 90–2).
[20] See Longuenesse, *Kant on the Human Standpoint*, p. 233.

appearances" (A 617–18/B 645–6). In accordance with this, Kant tells us that when assuming and employing those ideas of reason motivating the thesis arguments one "can grasp the whole chain of conditions fully *a priori* and comprehend the derivation of the conditioned, starting with the unconditioned, which the antithesis cannot do ... " (A 467/B 495).[21]

Here again, Kant refers to the fundamental or "supreme" principle of pure reason from the Introduction to the Transcendental Dialectic as the ground of this inference: ("If the conditioned is given the unconditioned is also given" (A 308/B 364)). According to Kant, all of the dialectical metaphysical conclusions of rationalist metaphysics (including those relating to the existence of God) are grounded in and motivated by the rational assumption that the absolutely "unconditioned" is already given.[22] As we have seen, however, this assumption is both necessary for the use of reason and *illusory*; the unconditioned we presuppose is never actually given to us. For our present purposes, the point is that Kant thinks that he has successfully explicated rational sources, or the "grounds," for the specific arguments for the existence of God. This allows him to defend the subjective necessity of the philosophical idea of God. Although he champions reason as the highest faculty character-ized by the ongoing demand for absolute explanations, he nevertheless wishes to denounce the proofs for God's existence. Thus, while the ideas of the supremely real being and the necessary being are necessary and unavoidable, the proofs for the existence of any being matching those ideas are bound to fail.

4. THE ONTOLOGICAL ARGUMENT

It is well known that Kant identifies three different kinds of proof for God's existence (ontological, cosmological, and physico-theological). The ontological argument clearly takes center stage for Kant, not only because it enjoyed a prominent status in the rationalist tradition, but also because, according to Kant, each of the other two kinds of argument (the cosmological and the physico-theological) ultimately succeed only because they implicitly rely on it. In this, the demand for a necessary being plays a particularly important role in motivating the ontological proof. Thus, for example, Kant begins his discussion by repeating his

---

[21] It should be noted that Kant also thinks that there are certain "popular" interests compelling the thesis argument for a necessary being; cf. A 467/ B 495.

[22] I have argued extensively for this claim, that the assumption that the unconditioned is given grounds the dialectical illusions of rationalist metaphysics, in my *Kant's Doctrine of Transcendental Illusion*.

earlier claim that the idea of a necessary being is "imperative," "legitimate," and "required by reason." But he also again asseverates that this
idea of pure reason is deeply problematic:

> But here we find something strange and paradoxical, namely, that the inference
> from a given existence in general to some absolutely necessary being seems to be
> both urgent and correct, and yet nevertheless in framing a concept of such
> necessity, we have all the conditions of the understanding entirely against us.
> (A 592–3/B 620–21)

Despite its problematic status, Kant notes that the ontological argument
is alleged to provide one instance in which determinate knowledge of the
existence of a necessary being is proven. Simply stated, the ontological
argument seeks to demonstrate that there is one being, and one being
only, that can be known to exist necessarily. That being, of course, is
alleged to be the supremely perfect being, the *ens realissimum*:

> ... you challenge me with one case that you set up as a proof through the fact that
> there is one and indeed only this one concept where the non-being or the canceling
> of its object is contradictory within itself, and this is the concept of a most real
> being. (A 597/B 625)

The ontological argument is thus characterized by the attempt to deduce
the necessary existence of the supremely real being simply from an
analysis of its concept. Kant summarizes the argument as follows:

> It is declared that it [the *ens realissimum*] possess all reality, and that we are
> justified in assuming that such a being is possible .... Now [the argument
> proceeds] all reality includes existence; existence is therefore contained in the
> concept of a thing that is possible. If, then, this thing is rejected, the internal
> possibility of the thing is rejected, which is self-contradictory. (A 597/B 625)

The first thing to note is that Kant is criticizing two different arguments,
one that might be called a Leibnizian argument seeking to establish the
real *possibility* of the *ens realissimum*, and the other a Cartesian argument designed to prove its real (necessary) existence. According to
Leibniz, the ontological argument proper (that offered by Descartes, as
we shall see) can only get off the ground if it is antecedently shown that
such a being is really possible, and to show this one needs to demonstrate
that there is no contradiction in supposing that all realities can be combined in the same subject.[23] Not only does Leibniz claim to establish the
real possibility of such a being by showing that there is nothing internally
incoherent (inconsistent) in the concept of such a being, he goes on to

---

[23] Leibniz, *Philosophical Papers and Letters*, ed. L. E. Loemker (Dordrecht:
D. Reidel, 1969), p. 167.

suggest that the mere possibility of the necessary being is "sufficient to produce actuality."[24] Consider the following:

God alone (or the Necessary Being) has this prerogative that if he be possible he must necessarily exist, and, as nothing is able to prevent the possibility of that which involves no bounds, no negation, and consequently no contradiction, this alone is sufficient to establish a priori his existence."[25]

Kant presumably agrees with Leibniz that the ontological argument presupposes the assumption of the real possibility of the *ens realissimum*. However, Kant disagrees that Leibniz has demonstrated this. From a Kantian point of view, Leibniz seeks to establish the real possibility of a thing from the non-contradictoriness of its concept. For Kant, this is tantamount to conflating the conditions for *conceivability*, or mere *logical* possibility, with *real* possibility:

A concept is always possible if it is not self-contradictory. This is the logical mark of possibility, and thereby the object of the concept is distinguished from the *nihil negativum*. Yet it can nonetheless be an empty concept, if the objective reality of the synthesis through which the concept is generated has not been established in particular; but as was shown above, this always rests on principles of possible experience and not on the principles of analysis (on the principle of contradiction). This is a warning not to infer immediately from the possibility fo the concept (logical possibility) to the possibility of the thing (real possibility). (A 597/B 625n)

It is in this context that Kant claims that Leibniz failed to achieve "gaining insight *a priori* into the possibility of such a sublime ideal being" (A 602/B 630).

Having dispensed with the Leibnizian preliminaries, Kant moves on to examine the ontological argument offered by Descartes, which may be summarized in the following way: God, or the *ens realissimum*, is a being that possesses all realities or perfections (all perfections must be predicated of God); (necessary) existence is a perfection; therefore God must exist. As Allen Wood notes, this argument is grounded in a specific ontology according to which entities or things are thought to consist of specific combinations of realities or perfections (positive predicates) and negations.[26] And it is in this context, too, that the concept of a supremely real being (a being containing all realities or perfections) so naturally links up with (or as Kant had said, "best squares with") the idea of a necessary being. For if existence or necessary existence is a reality or perfection, it could only be contained in the concept of a being in which there is nothing contradicting absolute necessity. And as we have seen,

---

[24] *Monadology*, section 44, p. 260.   [25] Ibid, section 45, pp. 260–261.
[26] Wood, *Kant*, p. 103.

the concept of a being that has absolutely all predicates or realities answers this rational demand.

Kant has a number of distinct criticisms of this argument. The first charge, which could just as easily be directed against Leibniz, is that there is a contradiction "in introducing the concept of existence – no matter under what title it may be disguised – into the concept of a thing which we profess to be thinking solely in reference to its possibility" (A 597/ B 625). The suggestion here seems to be that the ontological argument begs the question; if "existence" (or necessary existence) is already "contained" in the concept of the subject, then the judgment "God exists" (or "God necessarily exists") is tautologically true. In other words it is an analytic judgment. Kant's response is to deny that any propositions of the form "X exists" are analytic:

> ... if you concede ..., as in all fairness you must, that every existential judgment is synthetic, then how would you assert that the predicate of existence may not be cancelled without contradiction? – since this privilege pertains only in the analytic propositions, as resting on its very character. (A 598/B 626)

Clearly Kant finds there to be something deeply problematic in defining a concept in such a way that it already presupposes the conclusion one wishes to draw. Presumably, the proponent of the ontological argument could agree with the claim that existential judgments are for the most part synthetic. However, the point of the ontological argument is precisely that the concept of the *ens realissimum* provides a (*the only*) exception to this rule. What Kant must show, then, is that the concept of the supremely real being does *not* provide an exception, that the judgment "God exists" is also synthetic. The problem is that Kant, following Leibniz, takes a synthetic judgment to be a judgment in which the concept of the predicate is not already "contained" in the concept of the subject. It is for this reason that Kant takes synthetic judgments to extend our knowledge materially. They assert of the subject-concept (in this case "God") something not already thought in it. Herein lies the problem, for the concept of a supremely real being (a being that contains all realities or positive predicates) is precisely a concept that contains *all* predicates.

Kant's most celebrated response to this amounts, of course, to a denial that "existence" is a real (determining) predicate. Before discussing this claim, it might be noted that there seems to be something odd about denying that existence "really determines" a concept. Indeed, it has been suggested that Kant cannot simultaneously argue that "existence" is not a real determining predicate on the one hand, and, on the other, that propositions of the form "X exists" are always synthetic. Since a synthetic judgment adds to or enlarges (further determines) our concepts, it would seem that the claim that "X exists" involves a further determination of the subject-concept. If it does not then the judgment would by default be analytic, which is precisely what Kant denies![27]

This problem can be resolved by noting that there are two sorts of synthetic judgments, or two ways of "extending" our knowledge beyond the subject concept. The first involves determining the concept of the subject by adding to it some reality or negation not already part of it. But there is another way in which we might "extend" our knowledge, and that is to "posit" the concept and the determinations it contains. In other words, to say that "X exists" is not to add a new "reality" or predicate to the concept of X; it is merely to assert that "X," with its determinations, is instantiated.[28] This gets us to the crux of the Kantian complaint. Although "existence" may be used as a *logical* predicate (as in "The cat exists") it is not a "real" predicate that succeeds in further determining the subject concept (cf. A 598/B 626). At the heart of this objection lies another, that the *ens realissimum* is not an object that could ever be given to us in any possible experience. It is merely a rational idea, one to which we are necessarily and inevitably led by reason, to be sure, but not one that has any possible object corresponding to it. Because Kant thinks we are merely dealing with a product of pure reason, he takes any attempt to draw substantive conclusions about the "existence" of the supremely real being to involve what he calls a "transcendental misapplication" of the categories. In particular, he objects to applying the category of existence to an object in general.

It is well known that in the Transcendental Deduction, and throughout the Analytic, Kant denies that the categories yield knowledge independently of their application to objects of sensibility. In effect, Kant argues that the ontological argument seeks to deduce materially substantive conclusions merely by applying the pure (unschematized) category of existence to an idea of reason that lacks any "objective reality." The idea of the *ens realissimum*, according to Kant, is merely a concept of a "being in general that possesses all realities." To say of such a being that it possesses all realities is simply to say that in its concept "nothing is missing in my concept of the possible real content of a thing in general" (A 600–1/B 628–9). But concepts of "objects in general" do not, by themselves, yield knowledge of any real objects because they abstract from any

[27] This criticism was advanced by Jerome Shaffer ("Existence, Predication, and the Ontological Argument," p. 126), and is discussed in detail by Allen W. Wood, *Kant's Rational Theology* (Ithaca: Cornell University Press, 1978), pp. 104–110.

[28] Wood makes this distinction between different kinds of syntheticity in *Kant's Rational Theology*, p. 106–107. The distinction is later appealed to by Allison in *Kant's Transcendental Idealism*, p. 415.

necessary relation to sensibility and its *a priori* forms. Clearly, the proponent of the ontological argument wishes to go beyond an analysis of the concept of God; she wants, indeed, to establish the real existence (actuality) of God, something only attempted because the being in question is taken to be a real object that "possesses all realities" not simply by the connection of logical predicates to a subject-concept, but rather because it is represented as a real object to which determining predicates could be synthetically attached. In Kantian terms, a mere idea of reason has been "hypostatized," assumed to have a real existence independently of the idea. It is only on this assumption that the rationalist metaphysician even *tries* to acquire knowledge of its real existence. Although the propensity to such metaphysical flights is unavoidable, and endemic to the very nature of reason, it is also grounded in the transcendental illusion that Kant aims to disclose.[29]

5. THE COSMOLOGICAL AND PHYSICO-THEOLOGICAL PROOFS

The cosmological argument for the existence of God attempts to argue from the claim that there must exist some necessary being to the claim that this being is the *ens realissimum*. Thus the argument deploys a different "directional" strategy from the ontological proof, which seeks to argue from the concept of the *ens realissimum to* its necessary existence. Nevertheless, the cosmological argument, like all the arguments for God's existence, is based on what Kant calls the "coincidence" of the supremely real being with necessary existence. Kant takes the proof to proceed in two parts, one that concludes that some necessary being must exist, and the other that attempts to show that this necessary being is none other than the supremely real being, the *ens realissimum*. Kant presents the first part as follows: "If anything exists, an absolutely necessary being must also exist. Now I, at least, exist. Therefore an absolutely necessary being exists" (A 605/B 633). The argument here reiterates many of Kant's earlier claims in Section 3 of the Ideal, where he argues that the postulation of a necessary being is foisted upon us in our efforts to account for contingent being. There, recall, we were told that "if something, no matter what, exists, then it must be conceded that something exists **necessarily** (A 585/B 613). The argument thus expresses what Leibniz had called an *a posteriori* proof for God's existence. We have already seen that Leibniz thought the necessary existence of God followed straightforwardly (and *a priori*) merely from His (God's) possibility.

---

[29] I discuss this topic in more detail in *Kant's Doctrine of Transcendental Illusion*, pp. 256–260.

But Leibniz also believed that an *a posteriori* proof could be provided, one motivated by the principle of sufficient reason, for, he contended, there must be a sufficient reason for all contingent truths, or "truths of fact," and this sufficient reason must exist outside the series of contingent particulars.[30] Moreover, he held that only a necessary being could provide such a sufficient reason for contingent existence or the series of contingent particulars, for otherwise the series would lack completeness. Indeed, according to Kant, the inference to the necessary being "depends on the supposedly transcendental law of natural causality: that everything contingent has a cause, which, if itself contingent, must have a cause ... till the series ends with an absolutely necessary cause, without which it would have no completeness" (A 605/B 633n). Kant presents this line of reasoning, but he modifies it slightly. Whereas Leibniz had argued by means of a fairly abstract or intellectual argument about contingency, Kant here has the argument proceed (as Locke had done) from a subjective experience of our own existence.[31] According to Kant, "The minor premise contains an experience, the major premise from experience in general to the existence of something necessary" (A 605/B 633).

The second step of this argument, where the necessary being is allegedly demonstrated to be the *ens realissimum*, is presented by Kant in the following way:

> The necessary being can be determined only in one single way, i.e., in regard to all possible predicates, it can be determined by only one of them, so consequently it must be **thoroughly** determined through its concept. Now only one single concept of a thing is possible that thoroughly determines the thing *a priori*, namely that of an *ens realissimum*. Thus the concept of the most real being is the only single one through which a necessary being can be thought, i.e., there necessarily exists a highest being. (A 606/B 634)

Kant tells us that the argument is so riddled with dialectical principles that in this case, "speculative reason seems to have summoned up all its dialectical art so as to produce the greatest possible transcendental illusion" (A 607/B 635). Kant enumerates a number of dialectical assumptions that he thinks are involved in the argument (A 610/B 638).[32] One problem is that the argument assumes that we can infer from a merely intellectual concept of the contingent to a real cause, and even more

---

[30] *Monadology*, section 36.
[31] This marks a shift from the thesis argument of the Fourth Antinomy, where Kant has the proponent move from general and intellectual considerations about the contingent in general to the necessary being. The shift is not significant, but it is interesting.
[32] For a very clear summary of these dialectical errors, see Graham Bird, *The Revolutionary Kant*, p. 725.

precisely, it assumes that we can infer that the principle of causality might apply to something outside the series of contingent particulars. This complaint reiterates the arguments presented in the Fourth Antinomy. There, the thesis argument was originally designed to prove that there must exist some necessary being as either part of the world or as its cause. And the problem, as noted by the antithesis, is that (1) any postulation of a necessary being at the beginning of, but still a part of, the series of particulars conflicts with the fact that in possible experience we could never come across something whose non-existence is impossible, and (2) we cannot argue for any causal connection between empirical or temporal conditions and a non-empirical condition, for this would be to apply the causal principle beyond the conditions of sensibility.[33] As we have seen, this is precisely why Kant "resolved" the antinomy by suggesting that *if there is any* necessary being, it cannot exist as part or as cause of the empirical series, but would have to be construed as a non-empirically conditioned condition of the entirely conditioned series of appearances. In other words, the allegedly "cosmological proof" for necessary being must give way to the Ideal of pure reason. So too, Kant suggests, the cosmological proof for God's existence carries with it the dialectical errors of that earlier antinomial argument.

Related to this is the fact that despite the argument's appearing to proceed from experience, it actually abandons any appeal to experience in the second part – that is, the subsequent attempt to infer that the necessary being is the supremely real being. Thus experience, which is allegedly the basis for the conclusion, becomes superfluous in the last portion of the proof. While reason may very well be led by experience to the concept of *absolute necessity*, no experience of any kind is sufficient to present us with an object that matches this description (we can find in experience no object whose non-existence is impossible). Indeed, as we have seen, this is why Kant takes the idea of necessary being to be the "true abyss of pure reason."[34]

In fact, what is interesting about this argument is that, as we have seen, Kant does not really reject the inference to a necessary being in the first part of the proof. In the cosmological argument, what he objects to is the marriage of this idea with that of the highest reality. The argument seems to be that if the concept of the *ens realissimum* is in fact the *only* concept that "squares with" the concept of a necessary being, if it is the

[33] Cf. the antithesis argument for the Fourth Antinomy, A 453–5/B 481–3.
[34] I agree with Wood that the problem is not *that* the appeal to experience is entirely superfluous, for it does play a role in the first part of the argument in which Kant discusses the inference to necessary being. See Wood, *Kant's Rational Theology*, p. 126.

only concept that answers the demand for absolute necessity, then, since *ex hypothesi* the concept of the *ens realissimum* is the concept of an individual thing, we would be justified in assuming that every *ens realissimum* necessarily exists.[35] We would be justified in assuming this because necessary existence would be contained in the completely determined concept of the *ens realissimum*.

Many take Kant's complaint here to be that at this point, the cosmological argument tacitly relies on the ontological argument, which had sought to show that necessary existence *is* part of the concept of the most real being. And, so the story goes, since the ontological argument fails, so does the cosmological argument. Kant does indeed suggest that the cosmological argument gets its momentum from the assumption that the ontological argument succeeds. But it is somewhat simplistic to say that the entire problem with the cosmological proof is its reliance on that previous argument. Notwithstanding Kant's repeated assertions that the two arguments coincide, it is worth noting that early on in the discussion of the cosmological argument, Kant appears to argue for the opposite claim. That is, he seems to suggest that the problem is that the *ontological* argument presupposes the *cosmological* one. Although I have not seen it emphasized in connection with the cosmological argument, what Kant tells us is that reason requires us to assume as a basis of existence in general something necessary. As he had argued in Section 3, reason is thus forced to seek a concept adequate to this demand, one that would allow us "to know an existence in a completely *a priori* manner." (A 603/B 631):

It was believed that this was to be found in the idea of a most real being, and this was used only therefore to provide more determinate acquaintance with something of which one was already convinced or persuaded on other grounds that it must exist, namely, the necessary being. Meanwhile this natural course of reason was concealed, and instead of ending with this concept (necessary being), one sought to begin with it in order to derive the necessity of the existence from it, which, however, this concept was fit only to augment. From this arose the unfortunate ontological proof, which brings no satisfaction either to the natural and healthy understanding, nor to scholastically correct examination. (A 604/B 632)

The clear suggestion here is that if the ontological argument seems so persuasive, it is because it is motivated by the natural course of reason,

[35] For a discussion of the claim that the *ens realissimum* is necessarily the concept of an individual thing, see my *Kant's Doctrine of Transcendental Illusion*, pp 243–251. For a discussion of this issue as it relates to the critique of the cosmological argument, see Wood, *Kant's Rational Theology*, p. 125–130.

with its demand for the unconditioned, which in turn leads us inextricably to the idea of a necessary being. In admitting the real basis for the ontological proof, the cosmological argument (however dialectical) at least has the advantage of being "natural," and more convincing, both for common sense, and for the speculative understanding (A 604/B 632). I take it, then, that the problem with the cosmological argument is not in the final analysis that it is entirely (logically) dependent on the conclusion of the ontological argument (that the supremely real being exists necessarily). Rather the problem is with the assumption that *whatever exists necessarily* must be the *ens realissimum*. Whereas the cosmological argument presumes this, it is equally clear that the ontological argument presumes the opposite – to wit, that whatever is a supremely real being must exist necessarily. Each of these inferences is problematic:

The whole problem of the transcendental ideal amounts to this: either to find a concept for the absolute necessity or to find the absolute necessity for the concept of some thing. If one can do the first, then one must be able to do the other too; for reason cognizes as absolutely necessary only what is necessary from its concept. But both entirely transcend all the utmost efforts to **satisfy** our understanding on this point, but also all attempts to make it **content** with its incapacity. (A 613/B 641)

As Wood notes, then, the problem is not precisely that the cosmological argument appeals to the ontological one as an implicit premise. The problem is that one cannot accept one of them without being committed to the other. In Wood's words "if we suppose that the cosmological argument is sound, we must also suppose that the ontological argument is sound too."[36]

Looking back over these allegedly distinct proofs for the existence of God, it becomes clear that, from a Kantian point of view, they are bound to one another by their shared commitment to the "coincidence" of necessary being and the highest reality. Indeed, it seems that disclosing the grounds of this shared commitment is at least as (if not more) important as undermining the cogency of each of the arguments in its own right. Consider the following:

Now what in these transcendental proofs is the cause of the dialectical but natural illusion that connects the concepts of necessary and highest reality and that realizes and hypostatizes that which can be only an idea? (A 615/B 643)

It is in the section entitled "Discovery and explanation of the dialectical illusion in all transcendental proofs of the existence of a necessary being" that Kant addresses this question. What becomes clear in this section is again the contention that it is ultimately the demand for the

---

[36] *Kant's Philosophical Theology*, p. 127.

necessary being that underlies the endeavors of rational theology. For, as Kant continues:

What causes it to be unavoidable to assume something among existing things to be in itself necessary, and yet at the same time to shrink back from the existence of such a being as an abyss? And how is one to bring reason to an understanding of itself over this matter, so that from a vacillating state of different approval it may achieve one of calm insight? (A 615/B 643)

At first it seems that Kant's attempt to disclose the grounds of this illusion merely reiterates what he has said many times before. That is, Kant seems to be appealing to reason's demand for the unconditioned and its need for complete explanation. We are once again told that we cannot but conclude, from the fact of anything's existing, that there must be something that exists necessarily. The perplexity (or abyss) into which reason falls as a result of this unavoidable inference stems from the fact that we seem to be incapable of finding anything that either corresponds to this idea or would allow us to think it in anything like a determinate manner:

There is something ... remarkable in the fact that when one presupposes something existing, one can find no way around the conclusion that something also exists necessarily. It is on this ... inference that the cosmological argument rested. ... although for the existing in general I must assume something necessary, I cannot think any single thing itself as necessary in itself. That means: in going back to the conditions of existing I can never **complete** the existing without assuming a necessary being, but I can never **begin** with this being. (A 616/B 644)

In effect, it seems to me, what Kant is doing is going all the way back to the Fourth Antinomy – that is, the conflict between the thesis contention that there must exist something necessary in order to account for contingency, and the antithesis retort that nothing satisfying the conditions of experience and knowledge meets this demand. The difference in this case is that Kant is already conceding that the "necessary being" would have to exist outside the temporal series altogether. And it is only because the rational idea of the *ens realissimum* seems the best suited to this that we assume this "coincidence." Thus, what we find in the Ideal is a modified version of the fourth antinomial conflict. However, whereas in the Fourth Antinomy, Kant claimed *to have resolved the conflict* by allowing the thesis argument to stand with the stipulation that the necessary being be construed as the unconditioned condition *outside* the empirical series, he now notes that even *this* resolution leads to what we might call its own, as it were, higher-order antinomial confrontation:

... namely, on the one side, for everything given as existing to seek something that is necessary, i.e., never to stop anywhere except with *an a priori* complete explanation, but on the other side also never to hope for this completion, i.e., never to assume anything as unconditioned, thereby exempting oneself from its further derivation. (A 617/B 645)

As with the antinomies, Kant is determined to disclose the underlying grounds of the dispute and to negotiate between the competing claims. His resolution consists in relying on a familiar strategy, suggesting that both positions can coexist. Whereas the "thesis" proof proceeds from purely rational requirements relating to the existence of "things in general," the "antithesis" proof clings to the claim that no *thing in itself* can be found to be necessary. From a Kantian perspective, both sides to the dispute can equally be allowed to stand on their own terms, each expressing an essential interest of reason. This suggests a shift from the earlier resolution to the cosmological conflict.

Earlier, in the antinomies, the so-called "thesis" arguments, representing the interests of reason, were said to be admissible as merely "subjectively necessary" principles having no objective status. Thus, whereas the antithesis positions were grounded in the empirical employment of the understanding (limited to sensibility and its *a priori forms*), and enjoyed an "objective" status, they nevertheless could not be viewed as usurping reason's subjectively necessary interests in guiding empirical investigations. Although this might suggest that Kant is wrong to say that there is (or ever was) a real, "genuine" conflict between these arguments, it seems that implicit in this "resolution" is the view that the distinction between things in general (and in themselves) on the one hand, and appearances on the other, allows him to pursue this reconciliation.[37] There is, in other words, an unavoidable conflict only if one has already "conflated" appearances with things in general and in themselves. This conflation is the hallmark of the transcendental realist. The transcendental distinction between these,

---

[37] This is one of the most interesting aspects, to my mind, of the antinomies. For while Kant talks about an unavoidable "conflict of reason with itself," the resolutions to the antinomies actually amount to showing that there really is no conflict precisely because the opposing claims are competing in different domains. This kind of strategy is reflected in Kant's early arguments (*Inaugural Dissertation* and many of his notes). On this, see the discussion by Guyer in *Kant and the Claims of Knowledge*, pp. 387–401. As Guyer notes, Kant in these earlier writings is concerned merely to avoid confusing the principles of reason with those of sensibility. He is concerned to avoid subreptive forms of thinking rather than arguing that there is a genuine conflict. I have tried to make sense of this by suggesting that the early strategy prevails in the *Critique* and that there *is* a genuine conflict on the transcendentally realistic assumption that appearances are things in themselves. *Kant's Doctrine of Transcendental Illusion*, pp. 191–194.

issuing from Kant's transcendental idealism, is supposed to provide us with the resources for extricating ourselves from a conflict that would otherwise entrap us.[38]

In the Ideal, however, Kant shifts his position. Because, in the Ideal, both sides to the dispute are presumably thinking things absolutely *a priori*, utterly independent of all empirical conditions (both sides are committed to *transcendent* applications of reason), the possibility of resolving the conflict by relegating each position to a different "epistemological domain" is undermined. In this case, reason truly does seem to be in conflict with itself. Kant's solution here, then, involves arguing that both the demand for necessary being and the opposing, overarching, commitment to the view that everything is contingent are merely subjective:

> If I must think something necessary for existing things in general but am not warranted in thinking any thing in itself as necessary, then it follows unavoidably from this that necessity and contingency do not pertain to or concern the things themselves .... hence neither of these two principles is objective, but they can in any case be only subjective principles of reason ... In such a significance, both principles can coexist with one another, as merely heuristic and regulative, taking care of nothing but the formal interest of reason. (A 617/B 645)

Thus the hybrid idea of a "necessary all-sufficient original being" (the "highest being") is to be viewed as merely a regulative idea, or what Kant later calls a *"focus imaginarious"* which serves to guide our theoretical inquiries into nature. We are enjoined to philosophize about nature "as if" there were already given a necessary ground for everything existing, and to do so in order to systematically unify our knowledge. On the other hand, we are simultaneously required to refuse to allow any resting place for thought, to strive indefinitely for further conditions. Whereas the first requirement demands our assumption that there is an unconditionally necessary being, the second warns us that we shall never be justified in claiming to have located it.[39]

---

[38] Henry Allison continues with this line of argument and applies it to the claims in the Ideal in his *Kant's Transcendental Idealism*, pp. 419–422. I am not convinced that it applies here, for in the Ideal, where both parties are arguing in accordance with transcendent ideas, the resolution involves showing that *both* are merely subjectively necessary and regulative.

[39] These two rational requirements are expressed in two formal principles of reason introduced in the Dialectic – namely, (1) "If the conditioned is given, the unconditioned is also given," and yet (2) forever seek to "Find for the conditioned knowledge given through the understanding the unconditioned whereby its unity is brought to completion."

It is precisely because the concept of the highest being (construed as both a *necessary* being and a *being containing all reality* or perfection) is merely a regulative idea of reason that the last proof, the physico-theological one, cannot succeed. Unlike the previous two proofs, which were "transcendental," (ultimately operated independently of empirical principles), this last argument for God's existence allegedly succeeds by appeal to determinate experience, to "things in the present world, their constitution and order" (A 621/B 649). But the project fails from the beginning:

For how can any experience be given that is supposed to be adequate to an idea? For what is special about an idea is just that no experience can ever be congruent with it. The transcendental idea of a necessary all-sufficient original being is so overwhelmingly great, so sublimely high above everything empirical, which is at all times conditioned, that partly one can never even procure enough material in experience to fill such a concept, and partly if one searches for the unconditioned among conditioned things, then one will seek forever and always in vain, since no law of any empirical synthesis will ever give an example of such a thing, or even the least guidance in looking for it. (A 621/B 649)

The problem, in brief, is that the physico-theological proof moves quite naturally from our (justified) astonishment over the purposiveness, beauty, order, and magnitude of the world to a metaphysical claim about the nature and constitution (and existence) of the necessary cause of all of this. In so doing, it relies (according to Kant) on the cosmological proof – that is, irresistibly assuming that there must be a necessary being that accounts for the features of the world, it then infers that such a being must be the *ens realissimum*. In this, the physico-theological argument throws us right back into the thicket of dialectical principles that together motivate the first two proofs.

The physico-theological proof is often (as it has been here) marginalized in discussions of the Ideal, treated as subordinate to the other two "transcendental" proofs for God's existence.[40] It has often been so marginalized because Kant himself seems to dispense easily with the argument merely by claiming to show that it presupposes the cosmological, and therefore the ontological, proofs. These are theoretical criticisms, stemming from Kant's critique of speculative reason. However, the real problem with the physico-theological proof, it seems to me, is not that it is the least persuasive. Indeed, according to Kant, it is in some sense the argument most commended to us by our feelings of sublimity in apprehending nature. Perhaps the more apposite, the deeper, problem with the argument from design is not simply that its premises fail to support its

[40] Allen Wood provides an exception. See *Kant's Rational Theology*, 130–145.

conclusion, but rather that the sublimity that we feel is not in nature as it is in itself, but rather that it is in us:

> The present world discloses to us such an immeasurable showplace of manifold-ness, order, purposiveness, and beauty, whether one pursues these in the infinity of space or in the unlimited division of it, that in accordance with even the knowledge about it that our weak understanding can acquire, all speech concerning so many and such unfathomable wonders must lose its power to express, all numbers their power to measure, and even our thoughts lack boundaries, so that our judgment upon the whole must resolve itself into a speechless, but nonetheless eloquent, astonishment. (A 623/B 651)

Of course, in the *Critique of the Power of Judgment*, published nine years after the first edition of the *Critique of Pure Reason*, Kant would argue that the aesthetic experience of sublimity and the teleological judgment of the purposiveness of the grand system of nature do reflect the character of our own minds and cannot be used to ground metaphysical claims about nature itself.

12 The Appendix to the Dialectic and the Canon of Pure Reason

The Positive Role of Reason

I. INTRODUCTION

"There must somewhere be a source of positive cognitions that belong in the domain of pure reason, and that perhaps give occasion for errors only through misunderstanding, but that in fact constitute the goal of the strenuous effort of reason" (A 795–6/B 823–4). After 800 pages of a book officially dedicated to critiquing reason, and one that seems up to this point to have disparaged reason to the point that its proper role in knowledge appears to be simply to avoid any involvement, Kant seems finally to begin to speak of reason in encouraging terms. In the first page of the Canon of Pure Reason, Kant holds out the hope that the practical use of reason can succeed where the theoretical use of reason has failed – namely, to satisfy "the unquenchable desire to find a firm footing beyond all bounds of experience" (A 796/B 824). The highest aim of reason concerns "what is to be done", and the ideas of soul, world, and God have their true value in defending the related morally important claims of immortality of the soul, freedom of the will from natural causality, and the existence of God (A 797/B 825f). The practical use of reason, it seems, is the only legitimate use of reason at all.

Despite this language, Kant had in fact already provided a legitimate *theoretical* use of reason 100 pages earlier in the Appendix to the Transcendental Dialectic. The three main ideas of reason – soul, world, and God – cannot refer to any object beyond experience but must be used within experience to order cognitions of the understanding.

And this is the transcendental deduction of all the ideas of speculative reason, not as **constitutive** principles for the extension of our cognition to more objects than experience can give, but as **regulative** principles for the systematic unity of the manifold of empirical cognition in general, through which this cognition, within its proper boundaries, is cultivated and corrected more than could happen without such ideas, through the mere use of the principles of understanding. (A 671/B 699)

Theoretical reason does have a legitimate use, not as constitutive of the transcendent objects it purports to present but only as regulative in relation to the cognitions of the understanding. In fact, Kant holds this theoretical use of reason to be an essential element of knowledge when, at the end of the Appendix, he boldly states "Thus *all human cognition begins with intuitions, goes from there to concepts, and ends with ideas*" (A 702/B 730, my emphasis). There must then be a positive role for the theoretical use of reason, not merely the practical use.

Or perhaps there are *two* legitimate theoretical uses of reason. Kant's Appendix comes in two parts. The second part, entitled "On the Final Aim of the Natural Dialectic of Human Reason," contains the passages just quoted in the previous paragraph and includes lengthy discussions of how the ideas of soul, world, and God can function regulatively to give coherence to the particular cognitions of the understanding, as, for example, when various mental states are assumed to have unity as if they were states of a persistent soul. The first part, entitled "On the Regulative Use of the Ideas of Pure Reason," does not even mention the triad soul-world-God in its explanation of the positive theoretical use of reason. Instead, it presents an analysis of the systematization of particular concepts of the understanding using principles of reason for similarity among concepts (homogeneity), variety among concepts (specification), and affinity of concepts (continuity) (A 657–8/B 685–6). These principles are not directly tied to the ideas of soul, world, and God, but they are tied to various other ideas of reason such as species and genera, pure earth and pure water, and fundamental powers of the mind. Nowhere does Kant explain how these ideas relate to the transcendent ideas of soul, world, and God, nor precisely how the principles for homogeneity, specification, and continuity relate to any or all of these ideas.[1]

The positive role of reason in the *Critique* will be shown to have more coherence than is suggested earlier. The section following will explain how the regulative use of the ideas of reason presents one fundamental use of theoretical reason in relation to empirical cognition, the main topic common to both parts of the Appendix to the Dialectic. The second section will examine the arguments of the Canon regarding the practical use of reason, highlighting the similarities between the practical and theoretical uses of these transcendent ideas of reason. In the end, there is one reason that has one kind of positive use in two different arenas, the practical and theoretical.

---

[1] A further complication that will pass without detailed discussion is that Kant revised his conception of regulative principles and systematicity by the time of the *Critique of the Power of Judgment*. In that work, he seldom or never uses the same terms as he did in the *Critique of Pure Reason*. The terms Kant uses for the first of the two sets of ideas of reason seldom or never appear in the *Critique of the Power of Judgment*. "*Gleichartigkeit*", "*Varietät*", "*Affinität*", "*Homogenität*", and "*Kontinuität*" do not appear at all in the third *Critique*. "*Spezifikation*" appears twice in the published "Introduction" (5:186, 5:188) and once in §75 (5:400).

2. THE LEGITIMATE USE OF THEORETICAL REASON
IN THE APPENDIX TO THE DIALECTIC

The key to comprehending the regulative use of reason is in this passage: "[I]n regard to the whole of possible experience, it is not the idea itself but only its use that can be either **extravagant** (transcendent) or **indigenous** (immanent) according to whether one directs them straightway to a supposed object corresponding to them, or only to the use of the understanding in general regarding the objects with which it has to do" (A 643/ B 671). Kant is here contrasting an idea (a "concept of pure reason"; A311/ B 368) with its use. Concepts themselves are neither transcendent nor immanent – that is, neither extending beyond experience nor remaining within experience. Concepts themselves have no intrinsic relation to experience. Only an act of judgment applying the concept to some content is transcendent or immanent. As Kant argues throughout the *Critique*, the only possible content for concepts is sensible intuition (see especially A 50–1/B 74–5). But the concepts of reason cannot be directly applied to sensible intuition – for example, no collection of sensible intuitions ordered in space and time can correspond to the soul. Any act of judgment that applies an idea of reason directly to an object, then, is transcendent and illegitimate. (Since empirical concepts of the understanding can be applied directly to sensible intuition, their use is always immanent, not transcendent.) All immanent use remains within the boundaries of experience. Now, earlier in the Dialectic, the triad of ideas soul, world, and God had been painstakingly shown to have no reference within the boundaries of experience. So how can they have any immanent use at all?

The key passage here also suggests that the proper way to use an idea of reason immanently is not to apply it directly to any objects, whether empirical or transcendent, but to employ it indirectly by means of the understanding in its cognitions of empirical objects. So the legitimate theoretical use of reason is to aid the understanding in systematizing the concepts and laws of understanding.[2] It will turn out that the process of systematization of these concepts also involves application of ideas of

---

[2] I say here "concepts and laws of understanding" in order to include both under Kant's term "cognition of empirical objects". The Appendix can be taken to discuss empirical laws as well as empirical concepts. In many ways, these two are linked in Kant, since concepts are "functions" of ordering various representations under a common one (A 68/B 93). Concepts and laws can both be arranged hierarchically, although concepts' hierarchical relation is easier to picture. I use the term "concept" throughout this chapter rather than "concept or law" or "empirical cognition". For a discussion of the Appendix that discusses laws more than concepts, see

reason such as the soul, and even results in the introduction of some other ideas of reason such as species.

First, to understand the nature of systematization, it helps to turn to the Architectonic of Pure Reason chapter in which Kant insists that science (*Wissenschaft*) is a system rather than simply a collection of cognitions. A system is the unity of a manifold of cognitions under a single idea. The idea in turn provides "the domain of the manifold as well as the position of the parts with respect to each other" (A 832/B 860). The domain of a science can be understood as its external relations, its topic as delimiting the subset of all possible cognitions to be included and its relationship to other sciences and their own domains. The position of the parts of a science (which Kant calls a "schema" at A 833/B 861) can be understood as its internal relations, the arrangements of particular cognitions within the science vis-à-vis one another. Kant further classifies sciences as possessing either "technical" unity if the domain is determined by an empirical concept, or "architectonic" unity if the domain is determined by an idea of reason (A 833/B 861). This distinction will turn out later to be problematic. Since all sciences, whether technically or architectonically unified, are to have systematicity, I suggest that the immanent role of reason presented in the Appendix to the Dialectic is to perform this systematization. This requires an approach that identifies both domains and schema for organizing cognitions within each domain.

Such a two-fold approach is precisely what Kant provides in the first part of the Appendix. Kant provides a set of principles – homogeneity, specification, and continuity – that can be used both to specify domains for particular sciences and to organize particular concepts within those domains in a schema. The three principles work together to systematize particular cognitions or concepts of the understanding into a hierarchical ordering that can serve the architectonic interests of reason in ordering our empirical cognitions.[3]

Kant lays out these three principles for the use of reason as three complementary parts of one whole:

Reason thus prepares the field for the understanding: 1. by a principle of **sameness of kind** in the manifold under higher genera, 2. by a principle of the **variety**

Paul Guyer, "Kant's Conception of Empirical Law" in his *Kant's System of Nature and Freedom* (Oxford: Clarendon Press, 2005).

[3] Commentators often stress the principle of homogeneity because it functions specifically to unify various empirical concepts. The other ideas are equally important for the full systematization of empirical cognition. Kenneth Westphal argues for the importance of affinity (that is, continuity) in his *Kant's Transcendental Proof of Realism* (Cambridge: Cambridge University Press, 2004), where he argues that affinity cannot have merely a regulative but must have a constitutive function.

of what is same in kind under lower species, and in order to complete the systematic unity it adds 3. still another law of the **affinity** of all concepts, which offers a continuous transition from every species to every other through a graduated increase of varieties. We can call these the principles of the **homogeneity**, **specification** and **continuity** of forms. The last arises by uniting the first two, according as one has completed the systematic connection in the idea by ascending to higher genera, as well as descending to lower species; for then all manifolds are akin one to another, because they are all collectively descended, through every degree of extended determination, from a single highest genus. (A 657–8/B 685–6)

The three principles complement one another. Homogeneity is when reason seeks unity among particular cognitions under a common, higher, concept. Specification in contrast is when reason recognizes that particular concepts are themselves, qua concepts, intrinsically general and can contain multiple different particulars under them. Finally, continuity stresses that particular varieties that are contained under a particular concept are themselves capable of relating one to another along a continuum of gradual change.

Kant offers a helpful way to picture this set of relationships among concepts (A 658–9/B 686–7) that can be presented roughly as follows. Consider a concept as a single point in a two-dimensional vertical plane. The principle of continuity holds that there are other points lying horizontally, stretching indefinitely[4] into the distance, each point representing a concept that is only slightly different from the adjacent points. The principle of homogeneity holds that sets of these horizontally situated points can be grouped in accordance with their similarities, allowing the positing of a more general concept that includes them as a point higher on the plane vertically. Since all of the points in the first horizontal line can be so grouped, there would be many such higher-level concepts forming a second horizontal line above the first. These concepts could in turn be grouped in order to posit still more general concepts on an even higher third line, until the highest concept comprehending every particular is reached. Finally, the principle of specification holds that starting from the first line, every point can be understood as itself a general concept that can have multiple narrower concepts falling vertically under it, thus forming another line below the first line, and the points on this new line in turn can be understood as allowing for still narrower concepts on a yet lower line, and so on to infinity.

---

[4] I say "indefinitely" while Kant says "be able to be given to infinity." Kant clearly does not intend any actual infinity in this passage, and so the term "indefinitely" stretching provides his meaning of an advance that is always able to provide more.

This plane has several important features. First, each point, Kant stresses, must be understood as a general concept and never as an individual. The subsumption of individuals under concepts is the role of the understanding, not reason. If by using the principle of specification, reason did reach individuals, the downward progression of specification would have to stop. Second, since the plane stretches indefinitely in all directions (up, down, across, corresponding to the three principles), there is no privileged point, with the single exception of a possible highest universal concept at the top. The result is that there is no specific level at which concepts impinge on intuitions; rather, judgment can subsume some particular intuition under a variety of concepts at different levels (Rex is a dog, a mammal, an animal). Concepts are comprehended by reason in relation to other concepts, not in relation to intuitions. The systematic structure of the sciences is not built up from sense data, nor does it impinge on sense data only at the edges; all concepts in the system are capable of referring to intuitions.

The work of reason then, is at least to arrange concepts in this hierarchical system. But it is more than just that. The entire set of possible concepts is not provided to reason *a priori* for it to arrange into a system; rather, reason *obtains* concepts that it is to systematize from the empirical concepts of the understanding and *creates* new concepts to fill in blank spaces in the arrangement. (How empirical concepts are created or obtained by the understanding is another issue entirely.) The set of empirical concepts provided by the understanding must be finite. Reason would then seek to arrange these concepts into hierarchical order. In the process of creating this order, reason would presumably find gaps both horizontally and vertically. What fills in these gaps are then products of reason. Kant denies that reason can create concepts of objects, but allows that reason can create concepts that can unite (or otherwise relate) the empirical concepts of the understanding (A 643/B 671). Kant stresses in his examples of reason's creation of ideas the upward vertical move of uniting particular concepts under more general concepts. For example, powers of the mind such as memory, wit, understanding, and so on are postulated to be united by a more fundamental power of the mind (A 649/B 677). In other cases, the activity of reason does not provide a specific idea, but prompts the understanding to discover a new empirical concept to fill the gap. This is exhibited when Kant looks at the creation of concepts in the opposite direction, through the downward vertical move of specification, in discussing different kinds of absorbent earths as a task for the understanding given by reason (A 657/B 685). There appears to be no reason, however, to claim that the discovery of higher concepts is solely through ideas of reason and lower concepts solely through the empirical work of the understanding, provided that existence claims are reserved for the understandings synthesizing particulars under concepts. Reason can think of new ideas through specification: we can conceive of different breeds or sub-breeds of dog that do not now and may not ever exist. Physicists conceived of subatomic particles before any empirical determination of their precise characteristics was made. Similarly, the understanding is needed to confirm any higher, more general concepts in experience before they can be said to constitute experience: the unity of the electrical and magnetic forces was postulated by reason but only confirmed through empirical experiment.

Reason's work in applying the methodological principles is certainly an example of what Kant had called "schema" in the architectonic, or a plan for systematizing internally the various cognitions contained in a particular science. It can also be seen as the way in which reason determines the domain of particular sciences – that is, the topic of each science that will dictate which particular cognitions to include and which to exclude from that science. When reason creates ideas, especially but not exclusively by applying the principle of homogeneity, those ideas may be used to specify domains of particular sciences. Primatology, for example, is centered on the idea "primate." Kant is somewhat ambiguous regarding the terminology to be applied to ideas such as "primate." In the *Critique of Pure Reason*, he refers to such products of reason as ideas, while in the *Metaphysical Foundations of Natural Science*, he refers to very similar domain-determining concepts, "matter" and "thinking nature," the bases of physics and psychology respectively, as two "empirical concepts" (4:470). I believe that beneath this terminological inconsistency lies a philosophical consistency. The concepts created by reason in its application of the three methodological principles are not themselves borrowed from the understanding, but are clearly products of reason and hence deserve the name ideas. But these ideas are taken to have reference to experience, albeit not directly through reason but indirectly through the activity of judgment in subsuming a particular object under that concept, and to that extent deserve to be labeled empirical. It is not contradictory to call a product of reason "empirical" when, as in this case, it is not a product of *pure* reason but only of reason applied to a set of concepts provided by the understanding. I will refer to these "empirical" concepts of reason as "mundane" concepts or ideas, in contrast to pure concepts or ideas of reason, which are the product of pure reason alone.[5] This result casts some doubt on Kant's classification, described earlier, of sciences as possessing either "technical" unity if

---

[5] Thomas Wartenberg calls them "theoretical ideas" in "Reason and the Practice of Science" in Guyer, ed., *Cambridge Companion to Kant* (Cambridge: Cambridge University Press, 1992) pp. 228–248. He argues

the domain is determined by an empirical concept or "architectonic" unity if the domain is determined by an idea of reason (A 833/B 861). In practice, it appears that many "empirical" concepts are the result of mundane ideas of reason affirmed by the understanding in practice.

While the first part of the Appendix emphasizes mundane ideas of reason, the second part centers on the pure ideas of the soul, world, and God, which are not dependent upon any particular empirical information.[6] These do not arise from the activity of reason in its attempt to systematize cognitions obtained from the understanding, but are transcendental ideas of reason that arise from any possible use of reason in regard to any set of empirical concepts. These three pure ideas of reason correspond to the three possible relations involving a concept: first to the thinking subject (soul), second to the unity of the series in appearance (world), and third to the condition of all possible objects in general (God) (A 334/B 391). I will not deal with precisely how these ideas are derived by pure reason *a priori*.[7] The question here is how these pure ideas of reason are used regulatively and how this use compares with that of the mundane ideas.

Just as Kant began his first section by pointing to the immanent as opposed to the transcendent use of reason, he begins this section by

   that these theoretical ideas are incapable of any empirical instantiation (pp. 229–230). Certainly some of the mundane ideas Kant suggests, such as pure earth, are incapable of instantiation; however, other mundane ideas that Kant suggests stem from reason, such as particular species and genera, are capable of empirical instantiation. Just as with any empirical concept, the instantiation of a mundane concept does not require that the particular embody *only* marks contained in that concept. The difference between Wartenberg's use of the term "theoretical ideas" and my use of the term "mundane ideas" lies in my claim that the understanding may appropriate mundane ideas through empirical confirmation, thus transforming them into empirical concepts with empirical instantiation.

6   Michelle Grier attempts to link the two parts of the appendix to the dialectic, but not the two sets of ideas themselves. She argues instead that the ideas of soul, world, and God are supposed to be the basis of the unity of our knowledge in general, in very broad areas (mental, physical, and the totality, respectively). She then relates these three ideas to particular ideas of reason such as pure earth, pure water, pure air, which Kant offers as examples of ideas of reason in the first half of the Appendix, by claiming that these latter, more specific ideas function in the same way as the former, broader ideas "to unify a rather particular branch of knowledge (or, correlated with this, a very particular set of phenomena) into a whole" (Grier, *Kant's Doctrine of Transcendental Illusion* (Cambridge: Cambridge University Press, 2001), p. 297.

7   For a discussion of precisely how Kant derives these ideas *a priori*, see Chapter 8 in this volume, "The Ideas of Reason" by Michael Rohlf.

contrasting "an object absolutely" and "an object in the idea" (A 670/ B 698). Each of the pure ideas of soul, world, and God is not to be taken as referring to particular objects but only taken as a "schema for which no object is given, not even hypothetically, but which serves only to represent other objects to us, in accordance with their systematic unity, by means of the relation to this idea." He further explains that the "objective reality" of these ideas is not any relation to an object, "for in such a signification we would not be able to justify its objective validity," but only "a schema, ordered in accordance with the conditions of the greatest unity of reason, for the concept of a thing in general, which serves only to preserve the greatest systematic unity in the empirical use of our reason." Kant clearly intends these pure ideas to have only immanent, not transcendent, use. Unlike the mundane ideas discussed earlier, these pure ideas could not even possibly be employed in a synthetic judgment of existence in which some particular intuition is subsumed under the concept. While reason employs both kinds of ideas in systematization of cognitions of the understanding, reason can provide the understanding with only mundane ideas for possible constitutive confirmation.

The three pure ideas of reason hold a distinct place in reason's systematic work. One would assume that, since they are derived a priori, they play a role in the chart of concepts that is determined a priori. That is, the pure ideas would be posited a priori as the highest possible concepts to be reached via the methodological principle of homogeneity. They would presumably be a priori ideas dictating the domain of sciences at the highest level: soul for psychology, world for physics, and God for some science that ranges over everything. Reason would then be providing the a priori structure of the sciences at the broadest level.

Of the three ideas, that of the soul fits this use the best. The idea of the soul is used to connect all appearances of mental activity to a single inner experience as if the mind were a simple substance – that is, like an immaterial soul (A 672/B 700). One might consider this then to be an idea that determines the domain of psychology as the study of all mental activity unified by a soul. This is as close as Kant comes to the ideal structure of reason in its regulative role. The idea of the soul is not taken to correspond to any reality in itself, but is used only functionally to unite various cognitions of the understanding together to form an empirical science. Like any idea of reason qua idea (that is, prior to any possible appropriation by the understanding for constitutive use as described above), the idea is taken only to be a placeholder in the system for organizing cognitions. The entire content of the idea is merely its relation to the particular cognitions below it: "reason has nothing before its eyes except principles of the systematic unity in explaining the appearances of the soul – namely, by considering all determinations as in one subject, all powers, as far as possible, as derived from one unique fundamental power, all change as belonging to the states of one and the same persisting being, and by representing all **appearances** in space as entirely distinct from the actions of **thinking**" (A 682–3/B 710–11). The entire content of the idea of the soul is its functional relation as unifying mental and excluding non-mental particulars (which may themselves be general ideas – for example, the powers of the mind).

The idea of the world is less apt for this use. One might in fact be suspicious that there can be no idea "the world" because Kant had argued at length in the Antinomy of Pure Reason that any such concept leads unavoidably to a contradiction. While Kant acknowledges this problem (A 673/B 701), he attempts to diffuse it by essentially invoking two different concepts of the world in general, both derived from the Antinomy (A 684–5/B 712–13).[8] One takes the world to consist of an infinite series, and is applied in the physical sciences; the other takes the world to consist of a finite series that has a beginning in an intelligible absolute, and is applied to give unity to practical principles. In the former case, Kant actually adopts his solution to the first and second Antinomies by saying that the physical sciences ought to proceed as if the series of regresses or ascents (conditions) were infinite – namely, by proceeding indefinitely but presumably not claiming that the physical world is a given infinite. This use of the idea fits the model well, with "the physical world" serving as a pure idea atop the hierarchical structure, playing the same role in unifying concepts of the physical that the idea "the soul" played for concepts of the mental. In the practical case in which the finite series is invoked, on the other hand, reason does not seem to use the idea of a finite limit to the world so much to unify particular cognitions but to justify an attribution of independence for reason itself in the practical realm as an absolute cause, making his claim similar to the practical ideas of reason that will be discussed in the Canon (and later).

The idea of God fits the model to some extent. Its most appropriate use would be to serve as the single highest concept uniting all lower concepts. Kant suggests this function when he says that in using the idea of God, "we have to consider everything that might ever belong to the context of possible experience **as if** this experience constituted an absolute unity" (A 672–3/B 700–1). However, unlike the ideas of soul and world, which purport to represent actual entities in which the objects corresponding to lower concepts – that is, mental and physical entities – could subsist,

---

[8] Kant moves from a singular "second regulative idea" to a plural "the cosmological ideas" in the course of this paragraph, finally directing the inquisitive reader to look in the Antinomy chapter for "the rest" of the explanation.

Kant suggests that this overarching unity can be done only by considering possible experience "as if the sum total of all appearances (the world of sense itself) had a single supreme and all-sufficient ground *outside its range*" (italics added).

This unity is supplemented by a further, and broader, function of the idea of God that specifies the particular kind of unity of all possible experience: "we direct every empirical use of our reason in its greatest extension as if the objects themselves had arisen from that original image of all reason" (A 672–3/B 700–1). This role is to employ teleological laws invoking purpose to generate the greatest possible unity of things (A 676/B 714). Kant hints that the use of teleological reasoning can forge connections among concepts that escape mechanical or physical sciences (A 687–8/B 715–16). He does not deny that there can be mechanical connections and does not adequately show that mechanical unity is impossible (and given his agreement with Newtonian physics, he certainly agrees that physical causal unity in nature is necessary). The highest kind of unity that can be reached would unify mental and physical phenomena as well as practical principles, but Kant does not pursue that unity here but only in the Canon.[9] These topics receive much more attention in the *Critique of the Power of Judgment*, where unity is attributed not to reason but to the reflecting power of judgment, teleology is connected with the apparent systematic unity of nature, and theoretical and practical principles are unified in one teleological system (see in particular 5:180 and 5:425ff).

These three pure ideas of reason are integrated into the methodological procedures explained in the first section of the Appendix differently from the way that mundane ideas are. Since the pure ideas of reason are *a priori*, they do not have as their source the activity of reason in systematizing cognitions given by the understanding. Since they are to provide this highest unity, they would be placed, as it were, at the top of the hierarchy. These two considerations show that there would be no direct relation between the pure ideas at the top of the hierarchy and the nexus of mundane ideas and empirical concepts that form the remainder of the hierarchy. The pure ideas function only as a *"focus imaginarius"* for the main systematizing work of reason, a point that itself lies outside the system of ideas that can have empirical reference (see A 644/B 672).

---

[9] Using the idea of God as the unifying idea for everything should be contrasted with Kant's discussion in the Architectonic, where he identifies the highest unity of philosophy as "the relation of all cognition to the essential ends of human reason," which is itself divided into philosophy of nature and philosophy of freedom that is, theoretical and practical philosophy (A 839–40/B 867–8).

An illustration of this point would be that various particular ideas of powers of the mind that reason creates would be unified by attribution to one single enduring mental substance without any of the particular ideas of these powers being taken to actually describe the soul itself. One could say that the pure ideas of reason make possible the broad extent of the unifying work of reason without providing it any particular unifying system.

Does the role of reason in creating our scientific theories make Kant a scientific anti-realist? At A 664–5, Kant provides an analogy between the understanding and its objects and reason and its objects. The understanding has only pure schema as a formal framework that provides for objectivity. Particular intuitions in the manifold of appearance will be brought under those objective schema to create empirical laws. The precise empirical laws depend upon the manifold provided by intuition. (Even pure physics as discussed in the *Metaphysical Foundations* requires the empirical concept of matter.) Analogously, pure reason has only its methodological principles (homogeneity, specification, and continuity) and the pure ideas of reason (soul, world, and God) as a formal framework to provide for objectivity. Particular cognitions (empirical laws and empirical concepts) collected by the understanding will be brought under these objective principles and ideas to create a system of sciences. The precise sciences depend upon the cognitions provided by the understanding. In this way, the principles of pure reason "will also have objective reality in regard to this object [of experience], yet not so as to **determine** something in it, but only … [by] bringing it **as far as possible** into connection with the principle of thoroughgoing unity" (A 665–6/B 693–4). Reason is not constitutive of experience because reason does not determine particular objects in experience. Rather, reason obtains cognitions from the understanding, which are themselves constitutive of experience, and orders them objectively through its own principles, providing a regulative systematicity to them. In the process, reason creates mundane ideas that are not as such constitutive of experience and which the understanding may then employ and possibly synthesize with particular intuitions to make them constitutive. Thus, in the words of Philip Kitcher, reason is "projecting the unity of nature" – that is, neither determining any specific unity nor operating without any connection to the actual order of nature. He should be seen as offering a middle ground between scientific realists and anti-realists.[10]

---

[10] See Philip Kitcher, "Projecting the Order of Nature," in Robert Butts, ed., *Kant's Philosophy of Science* (Dordrecht: D. Reidel, 1986) pp. 201–35.

3. THE LEGITIMATE USE OF PRACTICAL REASON IN THE CANON OF PURE REASON

Broadly speaking, in the Canon of Pure Reason, Kant offers a counterpart for practical reason of the regulative use of theoretical reason described earlier. Kant does not offer his detailed moral theory here but only its critical framework. The Canon also offers a more detailed explanation of the status of beliefs stemming from reason in relation to cognitions of the understanding. These topics will further illuminate the coherence of the positive role of reason.

Kant defines a "canon" as "the sum total of the *a priori* principles of the correct use of certain cognitive faculties in general" (A 796/B 824). The canon of the understanding, he says, was given in the Analytic. Speculative reason in its "synthetic cognition," however, is not susceptible to a canon but only a discipline, which Kant defines in negative terms as the compulsion that limits the tendency to stray from certain rules (A 709/B 737). Is Kant overlooking the indispensable use of reason described in the Appendix? Perhaps not. Perhaps he intends the canon of reason to be limited to "synthetic cognition," in contrast to the regulative principles of the Appendix that only support the understanding's synthetic cognitions. We shall see, however, that the results of the Canon do not bear out this suggestion, since practical reason will not provide any synthetic cognition either. The epistemic status of the topics in the Canon will be nearly identical to that of the ideas of reason in the Appendix.

The Canon's three sections build upon each other as follows. The first section, "On the Ultimate End of the Pure Use of Our Reason," concludes that *there is* a practical canon. The second section, "On the Ideal of the Highest Good, as a Determining Ground of the Ultimate End of Pure Reason," determines the *content* of that practical canon. The third section, "On Having an Opinion, Knowing, and Believing," describes the *epistemological status* of that content of the practical canon.

The first section answers the question regarding whether there is a canon of pure reason affirmatively. The first topics of reason that Kant discusses are three "objects" (*Gegenstände*) of pure reason: the freedom of the will, the immortality of the soul, and the existence of God (A 798/B 826). Kant immediately acknowledges that, as no direct theoretical employment of them is possible, they can have a legitimate use only through the practical. The practical, in turn, is defined as "everything ... that is possible through freedom" (A 799–800/B 827–8). And what is possible through freedom? Whatever is done by the free power of choice. This free power of choice can operate on a variety of ends. When the power of choice is directed toward empirical ends (those related to happiness), reason can operate only pragmatically in uniting these various ends into a harmonious whole; the particular rules of conduct reason thereby creates would not be purely *a priori* but would depend on our inclinations and particular nature, and not being pure, could not constitute a canon. But when the power of choice is directed only by an "end given by reason completely *a priori*" it is directed by a law that is a product of pure reason. "Of this sort, however, are the moral laws; thus these alone belong to the practical use of reason, and permit a canon." Recall that a canon is "the sum total of the a priori principles of the correct use of certain cognitive faculties in general" (A 796/B 824). Kant is claiming that the "objects" that constitute the Canon are themselves are *a priori* principles of the correct – that is the moral – use of reason. They can be understood only in relation to the final end of pure reason – namely, the moral law itself:

> Thus the entire armament of reason, in the undertaking that one can call pure philosophy, is in fact directed only at the three problems that have been mentioned. These themselves, however, have in turn their more remote aim, namely, what is to be done if the will is free, if there is a God, and if there is a future world. Now since these concern our conduct in relation to the highest end, the ultimate aim of nature which provides for us wisely in the disposition of reason is properly directed only to what is moral. (A 800–01/B 828–29)

Although Kant expressly declines to get into detail about the nature of the moral law in order to remain within the framework of the first *Critique*'s focus on representation and cognition (see his footnote at A 801/B 829), it is important not to lose sight of this part of the Canon as attention turns to immortality, freedom, and God. The moral law will form the basis of Kant's argument for the specific content of the Canon.

Before turning to the task of describing the connection between these ideas and the moral law, Kant narrows his discussion to two of the three ideas. The idea of freedom, he now claims, need not be made part of the canon. The free choices one makes in following the moral law can be understood simply as choices that are not determined through sensible impulses but by motives represented by reason in experience, and this practical freedom can be proved through experience (A 801–2/B 829–30). Practical freedom, in turn, can be subject to a transcendental investigation in which the "independence of this reason itself" is questioned, but such a transcendental investigation is not necessary for practical purposes (A 803/B 831). Whatever the status and validity of these controversial claims,[11] it is clear that freedom of the will is not to be part of the Canon

---

[11] Dieter Schönecker has devoted an entire book to this passage. His *Kants Begriff transczendentaler und praktischer Freiheit* (Berlin: de Gruyter, 2005) puts this claim regarding practical freedom in the context of every other reference to the relation between transcendental and practical freedom. In the end, Schönecker concludes that Kant is not consistent.

of Pure Reason because Kant thinks that action on the basis of the moral law requires only a practical, experiential concept of freedom, not one to be guaranteed by any labor of pure reason in justifying ideas. The canon will include only the ideas of immortality and God.

Section Two of the Canon provides the arguments that the two ideas of God and immortality constitute the Canon because they are necessary for action on the basis of the moral law. Kant takes this opportunity to situate these ideas in philosophy in a way he had not raised up to this point in the text. The interests of reason are summarized in three core questions (A 804–05/B 832–3).[12] "What can I know?" is a theoretical question that has formed the subject for the bulk of the *Critique*. "What should I do?" is a purely practical question that lies outside the subject of the *Critique*, and accordingly Kant invokes the existence of pure moral law as an assumption, not as a conclusion to any argument (A 807/B 835). Finally "What may I hope?" is both practical and theoretical in that it asks theoretical questions on the basis of the practical moral law. This question "comes down to the inference that something is … **because something ought to happen**" – that is, the theoretical concerns about God and immortality are a conclusion based upon the practical demands of the moral law.

Kant will link them by means of the ideal of the highest good. (The argument that Kant offers here should be compared with his later arguments in the *Critique of Practical Reason* (5:122f) and *Critique of the Power of Judgment* (5:469f).)[13] Starting with the assumption that there are moral laws that command certain actions, Kant claims that pure reason insists that there must be some systematic unity in nature that would allow for these actions to occur in nature even though human beings have control only of their own free actions rather than the whole of nature (A 807/B 835). A world that does conform to morality in its entirety is thus the first idea of reason: "The idea of a moral world" (A 808/B 836). Such a world as one in which "free choice under moral laws has thoroughgoing systematic unity in itself as well as with the freedom of everyone else" is set as a model for behavior as human beings are commanded to make the actual world conform to this model as much as possible. This idea of reason, it must be noted, is not itself the conception of the highest good, because this conception of the moral world does not yet involve any assessment of the happiness of agents. Human

---

[12] Kant offers a fourth fundamental question for philosophy in his *Logic*, "What is the human being?" (9:25).

[13] The transformation of Kant's conception of the highest good is discussed in Andrews Reath, "Two Conceptions of the Highest Good in Kant," *Journal of the History of Philosophy* 26 (1988): 593–619.

beings must also reflect upon the consequences of their actions in relation to their own expectation for happiness in life; it is rational to hope that if one acts so as to be worthy of happiness (that is, morally), one will in fact receive the happiness one deserves. Nature itself seems indifferent to human happiness, and there is no guarantee that any individual acting morally will through her own actions bring about the happiness she deserves because part of her happiness depends on the actions of others that are beyond her control.[14] A human being can hope for happiness while still pursuing morality only if some other cause of the distribution of happiness is assumed, and since nature does not appear to us to be such an ideal world, human beings must assume God and a future life as the cause and as the occasion for the rightful distribution of happiness. Kant summarizes:

> Thus without a God and a world that is now not visible to us but is hoped for, the majestic ideas of morality are, to be sure, objects of approbation and admiration but not incentives for resolve and realization, because they would not fulfill the whole end that is natural for every rational being and determined a priori and necessarily through the very same pure reason. (A 813/B 841)

The idea of God here operates in a similar manner to the pure ideas of reason in the Appendix by providing the ultimate basis for systematizing and unifying the moral elements of our experience. We must interpret the sensible world as if it were organized in a way that facilitated the realization in it of a moral world. That is, human beings must view nature as if it were the result of a purposive organization and unity aimed at the possibility of human morality. "All research into nature is thereby directed toward the form of a system of ends, and becomes, in its fullest extension, physico-theology" (A 816/B 844). Presumably this system of ends functions like the hierarchy of concepts in the Appendix. The idea of God as guarantor of morality and happiness might ground a hierarchy of

---

[14] Kant actually states that if there were no hindrances to morality such as inclinations and the weakness of human nature, and the idea of the moral world were actually to be realized in the world, this system "would itself be the cause of the general happiness, and rational beings, under the guidance of such principles, would themselves be the authors of their own enduring welfare and at the same time that of others" (A 809/ B 837). He is not considering the effect that natural causes independent of human beings might have on happiness. Despite the best efforts of human beings, for example, there may still be disease, famine, and other natural events whose negative effect on happiness can be neither prevented nor overcome simply by virtuous actions. Further, his specification of the "general happiness" instead of the particular happiness of each makes it likely that Kant does not mean to imply that human beings could bring about the highest good through their own efforts alone.

subordinate ends in nature. Kant does not enter into detail about the kind of system of ends he has in mind here; this topic will be given much more attention in the *Critique of the Power of Judgment* (5:176f). Nor does Kant explain the relation between this system of ends and the aforementioned systematic unity of free choice under moral laws that forms part of the idea of the moral world; this topic will receive more attention in the *Groundwork of the Metaphysics of Morals* (4:433f).

The third section of the Canon on "having an opinion, knowing, and believing" explains the epistemological status of the ideas of reason. In the second section, Kant had hinted that these ideas have immanent use – for example, when he said that the idea of the moral world "has objective reality, not as if it pertained to an object of an intelligible intuition (for we cannot even think of such a thing) but as pertaining to the sensible world" (A 808/B 836). He ended the second section by insisting that the idea of God as source of the teleological unity of the world and as lawgiver must be understood only as derivative of the moral law itself and as thus having "only immanent use, namely for fulfilling our vocation here in the world"(A 818–19/B 846–7). But the full explanation of the status of ideas of reason that confirms their immanent rather than transcendent use comes only in the third section.

Kant presents a schematic of ways in which human beings can take something to be true, which can been read independently as an analysis of justification of belief.[15] The three stages culminate in objective validity (A 822//B 850). The first stage, having an opinion, occurs when someone takes something to be true, conscious that the grounds for it are insufficient both subjectively and objectively. The second stage, believing, occurs when the grounds are subjectively sufficient but objectively insufficient. The third stage, knowing, occurs when the grounds are sufficient both subjectively and objectively. To understand these stages, one needs to understand what Kant means by objective and subjective sufficiency.

Unfortunately Kant is not precise in his definitions of the terms "objective" and "subjective."[16] At the very least, objective grounds are those valid for everyone. But Kant is not clear about whether the validity for everyone rests on a shared cognitive framework, invoked when Kant identifies an objectively sufficient ground as one valid "as long as he has

---

[15] Andrew Chignell, "Belief in Kant," *Philosophical Review* 116 (2007): 323–360, offers the most extensive reading of this sort.

[16] An excellent discussion of the many nuances in Kant's various formulations is Leslie Stevenson's "Opinion, Belief or Faith, and Knowledge" (*Kantian Review* 7 (2003): 72–101). Stevenson, in contrast to Chignell, stresses the practical, immanent nature of belief.

reason" as the basis of "conviction" (A 820/B 848), or on the object itself, invoked as the basis for the possibility of communicating and finding agreement among individuals, which is said to be the "touchstone" of conviction (A 820–1/B 848–9). The difference between these two is important when dealing with ideas of reason that are precisely products of a shared faculty that do not have empirically accessible objects to serve as the basis for agreement. This problem is brought into sharp focus in a subsequent paragraph in which Kant discusses an illusion that might be grounded in human nature:

If, moreover, one can unfold the subjective causes of the judgment, which we take to be objective grounds for it, and thus explain taking something to be true deceptively as an occurrence in our mind, without having any need for the constitution of the object, then we expose the illusion and are no longer taken in by it, although we are always tempted to a certain degree if the subjective cause of the illusion depends upon our nature. (A 821/B 849)

This paragraph might be a reference to optical illusions. But Kant might also have in mind transcendent ideas of reason created by reason, which can be understood as deceptive transcendental illusions that depend upon our nature and not upon the constitution of any object, and which can be exposed as illusions but not eliminated from our set of beliefs. Since these ideas do not have any direct relation to an object, they are not objective in the sense of being mediated by an object. But since they do stem from the faculty of reason, they are objective in the sense of stemming from a shared faculty.

I take Kant's use of "objectively sufficient" to mean a claim that has some direct reference to publicly available empirical objects. "Subjectively sufficient" means a claim that stems from or is in accord with shared faculties of the mind.[17] Using these definitions, Kant's three stages can be understood as follows. Having an opinion is taking something to be true that has no justification either with reference to the object or with reference to the nature of the cognitive faculties. Believing has reference to the cognitive faculties but not any object. Knowing has reference to an object and accords with the cognitive faculties. The difference between these believing and knowing would be that knowing but not believing includes grounds related to empirical objects. Clearly, for Kant, the entire *Critique* can be understood as an argument that knowledge requires both reference to the object (intuition) and reference to the cognitive faculties (concepts), so his conception of knowing is not controversial. Believing would have to be a taking to be true

---

[17] Stevenson makes much the same suggestion.

that has reference to the cognitive faculties but not to intuitions. Only pure products of reason fit this bill.[18]

The difference between believing and knowing can therefore be corre-lated with the difference between the pure use of reason and the use of the understanding.[19] As Kant notes: "In the transcendental use of reason, on the contrary, to have an opinion is of course too little, but to know is also too much" (A 823/B 851). This conclusion is consistent with the imma-nent use of ideas of reason in the Appendix. They do not themselves refer directly to any empirical objects, but they are inescapable products of pure reason. One would assume that Kant would consider them as prime examples of belief. Alas, he offers contradictory explanations. On the one hand, he claims that "subjective grounds for taking something to be true, such as those that produce belief, deserve no approval in speculative questions," and asserts that belief is appropriate only in a "practical relation" (A 823/B 851). He specifies the practical ends of skill and morality as the basis for belief. On the other hand, he admits the theo-retical use of the idea of God in teleology as "an **analogue** of practical judgments, where taking them to be true is aptly described by the word **belief**," which he names "**doctrinal beliefs**" (A 825/B 853).[20] This appa-rent inconsistency can be resolved if Kant can be understood to be using the term "practical relation" in a broad sense that includes the practice of science.[21] In this way, the theoretical, immanent use of the ideas of reason is practical as opposed to theoretical because the idea is used immanently to organize other concepts into a system rather than spec-ulatively or transcendently to make an existence claim about the object

---

[18] This conclusion has an obvious objection: Kant discusses "pragmatic beliefs" that do relate to particular empirical events (A 824/B 852). But at the very least, pragmatic beliefs have no firm basis in empirical objects – that is, they do not rise to the level of cognition and thus remain objectively insufficient because their grounds are not firmly in empirical objects. They might just have a basis in reason's deductive powers.

[19] Stevenson thinks the difference is practical/theoretical. But see the rest of my paragraph.

[20] Kant also very briefly offers a teleological justification for the idea of immortality: "In regard to this same [divine] wisdom, in respect of the magnificent equipment of human nature and the shortness of life which is so ill suited to it, there is likewise to be found sufficient ground for a doctrinal belief in the future life of the human soul" (A 827/B 855). As far as I have been able to discover, this justification is not repeated anywhere in his corpus.

[21] This relates to the Introduction to the *Critique of the Power of Judgment* where Kant distinguishes "technically practical" from "morally practi-cal" (5:172).

of the idea. At least Kant is clear that the ideas do not refer to objects but only provide the function of stimulating empirical action:

> The expression of belief is in such cases an expression of modesty from an objective point of view, but at the same time of the firmness of confidence in a subjective one. ... The word "belief", however, concerns only the direction that an idea gives me and the subjective influence on the advancement of my actions of reason that holds me fast to it, even though I am not in a position to give an account of it from a speculative point of view. (A 827/B 855)

In the case of the doctrinal beliefs, this action is scientific investigation. In moral cases, it is moral action. In both cases, belief is immanent, not transcendent. It is used only to stimulate certain actions in nature.

The third section of the Canon of Pure Reason has clarified the status of the ideas of reason. The canon itself is based upon the moral law and includes only two practical ideas, God and immortality, that are necessary for systematizing the demands of morality with the remainder of human existence. They are immanent rather than transcendent in their use because they serve to further the work of reason in guiding moral action.

These pure, practical ideas of God and immortality, like the pure, theoretical ideas of soul, world, and God, serve not as presentations of extra-mundane objects but only as rules for unity and systematicity that function with reference to human life in nature. The positive role of reason in both theoretical and practical matters is to use the principles and ideas of reason within the natural and moral experiences of human life, not to transcend them.

13 The Transcendental Doctrine of Method

I. INTRODUCTION

The "Transcendental Doctrine of Method" is the second of the two main parts into which Kant's *Critique of Pure Reason* divides after its introduction. This means that, *prima facie*, I have an unfair assignment! For my brief is to cover all but one of its four chapters in this chapter,[1] while coverage of the rest of the *Critique* is accorded ten chapters altogether.

In fact, however, this is a misleading way to put it, as anyone remotely familiar with the *Critique* will know. There is a reason of pure size as to why it is misleading: the second part of the *Critique* is only one sixth of the length of the whole. But even in a metaphorical sense of magnitude, the second part brooks no real comparison with all that has gone before. It is very common for commentators on the *Critique* not to pay it any attention at all. Even Norman Kemp Smith, whose 650-page commentary comes as close as any to being a section-by-section companion to the *Critique*, relegates discussion of this part to a twenty-page appendix and remarks: "[Its] entire teaching ... has already been more or less exhaustively expounded in the earlier divisions of the *Critique*."[2]

I should like to thank Paul Guyer for his very helpful comments on an earlier version of this chapter.

[1] The exception is Chapter II, which is covered by Frederick Rauscher in Chapter 12 of this volume.

[2] Norman Kemp Smith, *A Commentary on Kant's 'Critique of Pure Reason'* (Atlantic Highlands, N.J.: Humanities Press International, Inc., revised ed., 1992), p. 563: cf. also note 1 on that page. Graham Bird's commentary comes second closest to being a section-by-section companion, and he provides even less – namely, an 18-page chapter in a book of more than 850 pages: see Graham Bird, *The Revolutionary Kant: A Commentary on the* Critique of Pure Reason (Chicago and la Salle, IL: Open Court, 2006), Ch. 29. (Nevertheless, it is an extremely interesting chapter, with a very different focus from my essay, and well worth consulting.) The comparative dearth of material on the second part of the *Critique* actually exemplifies a more general rough-and-ready rule: that the amount of attention paid to any given section of the *Critique* is inversely proportional to its distance from the beginning of the book.

It would be grotesque, however, to conclude that there is nothing worth discussing in the Transcendental Doctrine of Method. In due course, I shall outline what I take to be its important contribution to the overall architectonic of the *Critique*. But first I want to mention some of its incidental delights, of which it contains as many as any other comparably sized portion of the *Critique*. I have two favorites. One is a remarkable anticipation of contemporary views about the functioning of natural kind terms. At A 728/B 756, Kant writes:

[What] would be the point of defining [an empirical concept such as that of *water*]? – since when … water and its properties are under discussion, one will not stop at what is intended by the word "water" but rather advance to experiments, and the word, with the few marks that are attached to it, is to constitute only a *designation* and not a concept of the thing …[3]

My other favorite, to which I shall return, is a wonderful analogy that Kant uses when discussing the importance of pushing enquiry beyond where it is without trying to push it beyond where it can be, of eradicating ignorance without striving to know what is unknowable. A careful balance needs to be struck, and Kant's analogy, which occurs at A 759 – 762/ B 787 – 790, is designed to illustrate his own way of trying to strike it – namely, by setting precise bounds. He likens what is knowable to a surface, which, like the surface of the earth, appears flat, so that, given our limited acquaintance with it, we cannot know how far it extends, although we can know that it extends farther than we have managed to travel: however, like the surface of the earth, it is in fact round, and once we have discovered this we can, even from our limited acquaintance with it, determine both its extent and its bounds.[4]

There is much else in this vein to savour in the Transcendental Doctrine of Method. But the really significant contribution made by the

---

[3] The emphasis is Kant's. See Essays 9–11, by Hilary Putnam, Saul Kripke, and David Wiggins, respectively, in A. W. Moore (ed.), *Meaning and Reference* (Oxford: Oxford University Press, 1993), for an indication of the contemporary views to which I refer.

[4] I have borrowed material here from my *Points of View* (Oxford: Oxford University Press, 1997), pp. 250 – 251. (A third incidental delight, or rather a curio of sorts, occurs at A 757/B 785. It is well known that in the preface to *Prolegomena*, Kant describes his memory of Hume as having interrupted his dogmatic slumber (4: 260). And it is only a little less well known that in §50 of *Prolegomena*, and in a letter to Christian Garve, Kant describes the antinomy of pure reason in much the same way (respectively, *Prolegomena*, 4: 338, and letter to Christian Garve, 21 September 1798, in *Correspondence*, 12: 258). But it is not at all well known that there is a fourth use of the metaphor – historically the first – at this point in the *Critique*.)

second part of the *Critique* is this.[5] It contains Kant's most sustained and most reflective account of what is generally regarded as *the* distinctive style of argument that he initiates in the *Critique*: transcendental argument (or, as Kant himself usually calls it, transcendental proof).[6] This is of patent interest, not only in relation to the rest of the *Critique* but also in its own right. However little attention may be paid to this part of the *Critique*, the literature on the nature, scope, and limitations of transcendental arguments is vast.

But why is so much written about Kant's distinctive style of argument with so little reference to his own explicit views about it? This anomaly is explained, in part, by the fact that people have found his practice a clearer guide to his conception of such arguments than his own reflections on that practice. Graham Bird is representative. In an essay entitled "Kant's Transcendental Arguments" he writes:

[Kant's account of the peculiarities of transcendental arguments], though clear and uncontroversial in some respects, is also puzzling and obscure in others ... For the most part I shall consider Kant's *practice* of arguing transcendentally rather than his *theory* about the special features of such arguments.[7]

The fact remains that no one grappling with Kant's project in the *Critique* can reasonably ignore what he himself has to say about its principal methodological tool. This tool – transcendental argument – is a style of argument which proceeds from a premise of the form

(P) We enjoy experience of kind *K*

to a conclusion of the form

(C) Condition *c* obtains,

where: condition *c* is a necessary condition for the possibility of our enjoying experience of kind *K*; the necessity in question is non-empirical; and experience is defined as "a cognition that determines an object through perceptions" or in other words "an empirical cognition"

---

[5] I should again except Chapter II (see note 1), which contains very important material of a different kind.

[6] See, for example, A 786/B 814 ff. (Kant himself almost never uses the expression "transcendental argument." Its sole occurrence in the *Critique* is at A 627/B 655 (though see also A 589/B 617). Moreover, Kant is here arguably referring to something rather different.)

[7] Graham Bird, "Kant's Transcendental Arguments," in Eva Schaper and Wilhelm Vossenkul (eds.), *Reading Kant: New Perspectives on Transcendental Arguments and Critical Philosophy* (Oxford: Basil Blackwell, 1989), p. 21, his emphasis.

(A 176/B 218).[8] In the contemporary literature on transcendental arguments, their scope is allowed to extend further than in Kant. More
particularly, the premise is not always of form (P). Sometimes it is of a
less demanding form: for instance, experience is understood in a more
attenuated sense that involves no reference to any object determined by
the experience. Sometimes it is of a more demanding form: for instance,
there is some reference to our having a certain kind of belief about what
we experience or to our using language (of a certain kind) to characterize
it. The necessity, however, is always understood to be a non-empirical
necessity – not, say, physiological or psychological necessity. (To be sure,
there is a real question about how clearly any such distinction between
the non-empirical and the empirical can be drawn. But both Kant himself
and those following him take transcendental argument to be a paradigmatically *a priori* exercise: any objection to the very idea that there *is* a
clearly defined non-empirical necessity is an objection to the possibility
of arguing transcendentally.)[9] As for the nature of condition *c*, in a transcendental argument of a more ambitious kind it is a condition that is in
some sense independent of us, while in a transcendental argument of a
less ambitious kind it is a condition concerning what we must think or
concepts we must possess.[10]

Much of the controversy surrounding transcendental arguments concerns what is required to turn a transcendental argument of the less
ambitious kind into a transcendental argument of the more ambitious
kind; in other words, what has to be added to a conclusion about what we
must think or about concepts we must possess to yield a conclusion
about that which is independent of us. In particular, there is an issue
about whether only idealism of the sort that Kant himself advocates fits

---

[8] Note: the kind *K* of experience is often the broadest kind for which (P) is
true and is left implicit. Note also: in the expression "necessary conditions
for the possibility of," if the possibility in question is of a piece with the
necessity in question, then "the possibility of" is effectively redundant –
though this formulation is both standard and Kantian.

[9] There is a further issue about whether the necessity is to be construed
as analytic or as synthetic: Ralph C. S. Walker, in his *Kant* (London:
Routledge & Kegan Paul, 1978), pp. 18 – 23, argues for the former; Robert
Stern, in his *Transcendental Arguments and Scepticism: Answering the
Question of Justification* (Oxford: Oxford University Press, 2000), pp. 6–
11, argues for the latter. Others, of course, are suspicious of this distinction
too. The *locus classicus* for all such suspicion is W. V. Quine, "Two
Dogmas of Empiricism," reprinted in his *From a Logical Point of View:
Logico-Philosophical Essays* (New York: Harper & Row, 1961).

[10] From the extensive literature on the nature of transcendental arguments, I
single out Robert Stern's *Transcendental Arguments and Scepticism* as
providing an excellent overview.

this bill.[11] There are two ways in which such idealism might itself be said to fit the bill. First, it might be said to close the gap between how we must think of that which is independent of us and how it actually is, the point being that the independence in question is of a merely empirical kind: it is not independence at the level of things in themselves (where the character of empirical reality is constitutively linked to how we must think of it). The second way is less direct but very closely related. On the assumption that the gap in question can be closed anyway, say by appeal to some principle of charity, such idealism might be said to explain what would otherwise be a mystery – namely, why there is ever anything of any substance that we *must* think about that which is independent of us. The idea would be that it is only about that which is independent of us merely in an empirical sense, not at the level of things in themselves, that there *is* anything of any substance that we must think.[12] However that may be, we have here a glimpse of why so many people have taken the fate of transcendental arguments to be bound up with the fate of transcendental idealism. Kant himself certainly takes their fates to be bound up with each other, as we shall see.

2. ANALYSIS OF THE TEXT

i. Overview

The "Transcendental Doctrine of Method" is concerned, quite generally, with the philosophical use of pure reason, which has been explored and exemplified in the first part of the *Critique*, and with how this relates to other uses of pure reason. It is divided into four chapters. Each of these, as if in some evocation of Zeno, is roughly half the length of its predecessor. Chapter I is entitled "The Discipline of Pure Reason." Among other things, it compares and contrasts transcendental argument, the kind of argument that Kant takes to be characteristic of philosophy, with the kind of argument that is characteristic of that other paradigm of a purely rational discipline, mathematics. It is in this chapter that we find Kant's own most explicit account of the nature, scope, and limitations of transcendental arguments. Chapter II is entitled "The Canon of Pure Reason" and anticipates Kant's later work on pure reason's practical use.

---

[11] See, for example, Barry Stroud, "Transcendental Arguments," reprinted in Ralph C. S. Walker (ed.), *Kant on Pure Reason* (Oxford: Oxford University Press, 1982).

[12] Cf. Bernard Williams, "Knowledge and Meaning in the Philosophy of Mind," reprinted in his *Problems of the Self: Philosophical Papers 1956–1972* (Cambridge: Cambridge University Press, 1973), p. 128.

I shall not discuss this chapter any further here.[13] Chapter III, "The Architectonic of Pure Reason," provides a definition of metaphysics and thereby further situates the philosophical use of pure reason with respect to its non-philosophical use. And finally, Chapter IV, "The History of Pure Reason," situates the philosophical use of pure reason with respect to its philosophical *misuse* – as exemplified in what Kant takes to be the various most significant false starts in the history of philosophy preceding his own discovery of its correct method.

ii. Chapter I, Section I, "The Discipline of Pure Reason in Dogmatic Use"

Kant's starting point is the main lesson of the Dialectic. This lesson is that when pure reason is allowed free rein and put to "dogmatic" use – that is to say, non-analytic use without reference to intuition – it leads to confusion and incoherence. It follows that one of pure reason's most important philosophical uses is to keep itself in check and to guard against just such extravagance. I say one of its most important philosophical uses: pure reason has an equally important *positive* philosophical use, exemplified in the Analytic. Both uses are captured in Kant's delightfully memorable *aperçu* that "philosophy consists precisely in knowing its bounds" (A 727/B 755). The negative use enables philosophy to know not to reach beyond these bounds; the positive use enables it to know how to reach as far as them.

Kant compares and contrasts this positive use with pure reason's most prominent positive use, its use in mathematics, the subject matter of the Transcendental Aesthetic. Kant holds that, in philosophy no less than in mathematics, the positive use of pure reason extends farther than the mere analysis of concepts and issues in knowledge that is synthetic. This means that, in accord with the dictates of its negative use, it must make suitable reference to what is given to us in intuition. In the case of mathematics, we refer to what is given to us in intuition by actually exhibiting it – that is to say, by actually exhibiting particular objects of intuition, a process that Kant calls, a little misleadingly, "the construction of concepts" (A 713/B 741).[14] A prime example is the exhibition of a triangle to initiate a geometrical proof, though Kant also cites, intriguingly, the exhibition of symbols in the course of an algebraic proof, thereby perhaps doing as much to anticipate Hilbert's formalism as to

---

[13] See note 1.
[14] As Kant explains, to "construct" a concept is to exhibit, *a priori*, its corresponding intuition.

anticipate Brouwer's intuitionism.[15] But such construction, however vital the role played in practice by paper and ink, is made possible by the fact that the intuition in question is *a priori*. In philosophy, where the focus is on *experience* – in other words, on *empirical* cognition – and where the intuition in question must therefore likewise be, at least in part, empirical, no such construction is possible, for philosophy is an *a priori* exercise. The positive use of pure reason in philosophy thus proceeds directly from concepts, not from the exhibition of any corresponding objects of intuition. (This indeed is what Kant takes to be the most fundamental difference between mathematics and philosophy – rather than, as he once thought, a difference of subject matter; see A 714/B 742.)[16] The fact remains that the positive use of pure reason in philosophy does not consist in the mere analysis of concepts. So it needs *some* suitable (non-empirical) grounding in what is given to us in (empirical) intuition. What, then, is this grounding? It is the sheer *possibility* of our being given objects in empirical intuition in the various ways that we are. And this is precisely what grounds the use of transcendental arguments too, which in turn is why transcendental arguments are philosophy's most characteristic methodological tool. A paradigm is Kant's argument that every occurrence has a cause (Second Analogy, A 189 – 211/B 232 – 256), whose conclusion, as he puts it, "makes possible its ground of proof" (A 737/B 765).

iii. Chapter I, Section II, "The Discipline of Pure Reason With Regard to is Polemical Use"

This section develops the idea that philosophy consists in knowing its own bounds. The section is divided into two parts. In the first part, Kant focuses on the negative aspect of the idea, the aspect associated with the Dialectic. He is keen to distinguish between those cases where pure reason, in reaching beyond its bounds, broaches questions that are in some sense illegitimate (such as whether the physical world as an unconditioned whole is finite or infinite – there being, in Kant's view, no such thing as the physical world as an unconditioned whole), and those cases where pure reason, in reaching beyond its bounds, broaches questions that are perfectly legitimate but whose answers it is in principle incapable of settling (such as whether there is a God). In cases of the latter kind, Kant allows us scope of a sort to believe as we will, a vindication of his famous declaration, in the preface to the second edition of the *Critique*,

---

[15] See A. W. Moore, *The Infinite* (London: Routledge, 2nd ed. 2001), Chapter 9, §§ 2 and 1, respectively.
[16] See Kemp Smith's *Commentary*, p. 564, for further references.

that he had to deny knowledge in order to make room for faith (B xxx). It is in this connection that he urges the importance, if not of open debate (for debate is fruitless where there is no settling a question one way or the other), at least of that free, attentive, open-minded, and honest exchange of ideas that will bring us to a clearer understanding of the issues and of what would be involved in having particular beliefs about them.

In the second part,[17] Kant focuses on the positive aspect of the idea that philosophy consists in knowing its own bounds, the aspect associated with the Transcendental Analytic. Here the lesson is that, just as it is a mistake to put pure reason to dogmatic use beyond its bounds, so too it is a mistake, at the opposite extreme – the mistake of Humean scepticism – to deny pure reason its proper philosophical use within its bounds. It is in this connection that Kant uses the analogy of the globe to which I referred in Section 1. And again he urges that this proper use of pure reason involves the investigation not just of how concepts relate to one another but of how they relate "to a third thing – namely, *possible* experience" (A 766/B 794) – where the emphasis on 'possible' indicates how the investigation manages to be *a priori*.

iv. *Chapter I, Section III, "The Discipline of Pure Reason With Regard to Hypotheses"*

In this section, Kant further considers the questions that pure reason broaches when reaching beyond its bounds. In particular, he considers those that are perfectly legitimate. Because these questions *are* perfectly legitimate, there can be no objection to our speculating about their answers. Of course, we must not allow such speculation to tempt pure reason back beyond its bounds in an effort to settle the questions. Nor must we think that a hypothetical answer to one of these questions could ever serve as a good explanation in natural science. It would be "no explanation at all, since that which one does not adequately understand on the basis of known empirical principles would be explained by means of something about which one understands nothing at all," (A 772/B 800). But if we avoid such errors, then speculating about the answers to these questions can be positively beneficial, not only when it comes to framing what Kant calls in the Dialectic "regulative principles" (A 508 – 515/B 536 – 543, A 568 – 569/B 596 – 597, and A 669/B 697 ff.), but also as a way of reminding those who dogmatically claim to have an answer to one of these questions that there is just as much to be said for the opposite answer.

---

[17] Kant entitles this part "On the Impossibility of a Skeptical Satisfaction of Pure Reason that is Divided Against Itself."

v. Chapter I, Section IV, "The Discipline of Pure Reason With Regard to its Proofs"

It is in this section that Kant gives his most explicit account of transcendental arguments. Emphasizing once again that it is the possibility of experience that grounds such arguments, he likewise emphasizes, once again, what he takes to be a corollary of this – namely, that the conclusion of any such argument must similarly concern possible objects of experience. He then makes two further claims about transcendental arguments, both of which mark a contrast with mathematical proofs.

The first of these claims is that the conclusion of a sound transcendental argument can never be established by any other means. (A mathematical theorem, by contrast, often admits of several quite different proofs.) Kant's reason for this claim is that the conclusion of a sound transcendental argument is established directly from concepts, without immediate appeal to intuition (see, Section 2.ii); and only where there *is* immediate appeal to intuition is there "a manifold of material for synthetic propositions that [can be connected] in more than one way" (A 787/ B 815). Kant says less than we might have hoped, however, either about why concepts do not afford their own analogous manifoldness or about why that which can be established directly from concepts cannot *also* be established by immediate appeal to intuition. (Consider: I might observe that the cat is on the mat and conclude from this that something is such that, unless *it* is on the mat, nothing is; yet the latter is a logical truth that can also be established by purely logical means.)

The second of Kant's claims is that a sound transcendental argument can never take the form of a *reductio ad absurdum*. (A mathematical proof, by contrast, may well take this form.) It follows that we can never tell whether or not something is a necessary condition for the possibility of experience of a given kind by assuming otherwise and considering the consequences. For if the thing in question is *not* a necessary condition for the possibility of experience of that kind, then this method will succeed only if we can know independently that all of these consequences are true, but "to have insight into all possible consequences of any proposition that is assumed exceeds our powers" (A 790/B 818). If, on the other hand, the thing in question *is* a necessary condition for the possibility of experience of the given kind, then this method will succeed only if we can know independently that at least one of the consequences of the assumption is false, hence only if we can construct a sound transcendental argument that takes the form of a *reductio ad absurdum*, which is precisely what is precluded.

But why this surprising hostility to the idea that a sound transcendental argument can ever take the form of a *reductio ad absurdum*, a form that we might indeed have thought was peculiarly suited to such arguments? Kant remarks that this form of argument can at most establish *that* something is so, not *why* it is so. But that is not enough, even in Kant's view, to make the form invalid.[18] The real problem with a transcendental argument's taking the form of a *reductio ad absurdum*, in Kant's view, is rather as follows. In order for such an argument to succeed, we need to be able to recognize absurdity in an assumption of the following form:

(A) We can enjoy experience of kind *K* in the absence of condition *c*.

But now suppose that we *think* we have recognized absurdity in an assumption of that form. We cannot rule out the possibility that we are victims of a simple failure of imagination preventing us from seeing that there are quite different conditions in which we can enjoy experience of kind *K*.[19] Nor, Kant urges, can we rule out the possibility that what we have really done is to recognize absurdity in some presupposition that the assumption shares with what we are trying to establish – for instance, a presupposition without which the question whether condition *c* obtains does not so much as arise. Kant is particularly alive to this sort of problem because, as he reminds us, it is precisely the sort of problem that afflicts our reasoning in the Antinomies.

<hr>

[18] It is nevertheless interesting to note that Brouwerian scruples about this form of argument are a variation on this theme. See again the material cited in note 15; and see also ibid., Chapter 14, §5.

[19] Stephan Körner's highly influential repudiation of transcendental arguments is based on the conviction that they are *always* vulnerable to this objection, whether or not they take the form of a *reductio ad absurdum*: see his "The Impossibility of Transcendental Deductions," reprinted in Lewis White Beck (ed.), *Kant Studies Today* (La Salle, IL.: Open Court, 1969); and, for a rejoinder, see Paul Guyer, *Kant and the Claims of Knowledge* (Cambridge: Cambridge University Press, 1987), pp. 422–424. Cf. also the worry about Kant's own transcendental arguments voiced by his contemporary G. E. Schulze, who wrote, "Because the human understanding, at the present level of its culture, can represent to itself the possibility of something in just one way, it does not follow in principle, nor with any certitude whatever, that it will be able to think it in only that way at all times." This is from his *Aenesidemus*, trans. Georg di Giovanni in George di Giovanni and H. S. Harris (eds.), *Between Kant and Hegel: Texts in the Development of Post-Kantian Idealism* (Albany, N.Y.: State University of New York Press, 1985), p. 117. I am grateful to Paul Franks for this reference: see his "Transcendental Arguments, Reason, and Scepticism: Contemporary Debates and the Origins of Post-Kantianism," in Robert Stern (ed.), *Transcendental Arguments: Problems and Prospects* (Oxford: Oxford University Press, 1999), of which §III is especially pertinent to our current discussion.

vi. Chapter III, "The Architectonic of Pure Reason"

Kant is now in a position to define metaphysics – construed as a proper unified systematic science, not as that pseudo-science exemplified in the Dialectic. Again he develops the idea that philosophy consists in knowing its own bounds. What he does, in effect, is to define metaphysics as that part of philosophy that investigates philosophy's own scope and limitations; that part, in other words, that maps the round surface of philosophical knowledge, and thereby indicates not only what lies on the surface but also, through the determination of the curvature of the surface, *how much* lies on it and what sort of thing lies *beyond* it. In Kant's own words, metaphysics is "the investigation of everything that can ever be cognized *a priori* as well as the presentation of that which constitutes a system of pure philosophical cognition of this kind" (A 841/ B 869). This definition, Kant insists, is to be preferred to the Aristotelian definition, whereby metaphysics is "the science of the first principles of human cognition" (A 843/B 871).[20] For the Aristotelian definition invokes a difference of degree (at what point does a principle cease to be a "first" principle and become a "secondary" one?), whereas the difference between metaphysics and any other science is, in Kant's view, a difference of kind. This means that the Aristotelian definition is at best a nominal definition, not a real definition, and an imprecise one at that.

Finally in this chapter, Kant reflects on how noble and exalted a science metaphysics is, as against the impression that we might have formed in the Dialectic after our encounter with its impostor. "We will always return to metaphysics," he observes, "as to a beloved from whom we have been estranged" (A 850/B 878).

vii. Chapter IV, "The History of Pure Reason"

Kant's final chapter is a potted survey of previous attempts to put pure reason to positive philosophical use. Although this chapter is only about a thousand words in length, it has had considerable influence on subsequent conceptions of the history of philosophy.[21] Kant classifies his philosophical predecessors in three ways: first, with regard to what they took their subject matter to be (objects of the senses or objects of the understanding); second, with regard to what they took the source of their knowledge to be (experience or pure reason); and third, with regard to what they took their methodology to be (an appeal to common sense or

[20] See Aristotle, *Metaphysics*, Book I, Chapter 1, 981b25 – 982a2.
[21] I am here partially quoting Paul Guyer and Allen W. Wood: see their introduction to the *Critique*, p. 19.

something more scientific and more systematic).[22] By this stage in the *Critique*, the reader needs no further guidance as to what Kant sees as the errors of his predecessors' various ways, nor as to what he thinks entitles him to affirm, "The critical path alone is still open" (A 855/B 883).

3. ASSESSMENT: THE BOUNDARIES OF KNOWLEDGE

One crucial recurring theme of the Transcendental Doctrine of Method, as of the *Critique* as a whole, is that philosophy has bounds whose very investigation is itself a primary task of philosophy. These bounds, which preclude philosophical knowledge of things in themselves, are one aspect of the transcendental idealism that Kant has defended in the preceding pages. And this in turn connects with transcendental arguments. For Kant is convinced that transcendental idealism is what explains the possibility of sound transcendental arguments. This is because he takes a sound transcendental argument to be, in effect, an exploration of those *a priori* conditions of experience that ensure that the objects of experience are not things in themselves. Indeed, the conclusion of a sound transcendental argument, such as that every occurrence has a cause, is in Kant's view an item of synthetic *a priori* knowledge, and thus a direct testament to the truth of transcendental idealism.

But should we agree with Kant about these connections? Much of the discussion of transcendental arguments, in the subsequent history of this subject, has started from the assumption that there might be non-idealist variations on this Kantian theme, say a style of argument which, by dint of nothing but the analysis of concepts, establishes what we have to think about the world if our experience is to have a certain conceptual structure, and which does nothing to suggest that our having to think what we do stands in any constitutive relation to its being true. The real debate then, as I indicated in Section I, is whether a *non*-idealist variation on the original Kantian theme can at the same time deliver conclusions about that which is in some sense independent of us.

It is a large debate, and I shall not try to contribute to it here. Instead, I shall use this last section of my chapter, which is itself the last of the chapters in this volume directly on the arguments of the *Critique*, as an opportunity for a retrospectus on transcendental idealism itself. Suppose that the price we have to pay for securing a conclusion about that which is independent of us, as opposed to a conclusion merely about our

---

[22] There is a faint echo, in the third of these, of P. F. Strawson's distinction between descriptive metaphysics and revisionary metaphysics: see his *Individuals: An Essay in Descriptive Metaphysics* (London: Methuen, 1959), pp. 9–11.

thinking (say), is to accept transcendental idealism. Is it too high a price? In particular, what are we to make of the idea, which is integral to transcendental idealism, that there are bounds to our philosophical knowledge; indeed, that there are bounds to *all* our knowledge?

This idea is obviously more than the platitude that there is knowledge we do not have. It is rather that there is knowledge we are in principle incapable of having – notably, of course, knowledge of things in themselves. The wonderful analogy of the globe is designed to illustrate the difference between these. Kant also sometimes expresses the difference in terms of a distinction that he draws between what he calls "limits" (*Schranken*) and what he calls "boundaries" (*Grenzen*). The territory covered by the knowledge we have, which is capable of extending over time into what it currently excludes, is marked by "limits"; the territory covered by the knowledge we are in principle capable of having, which is of an altogether different kind from what it excludes, is marked by "boundaries" (A 767/B 795; cf. also *Prolegomena*, § 57).²³ To say that the latter territory is of an altogether different kind from what it excludes is not to take a stance on the issue of whether, on Kant's conception, the knowledge we are in principle capable of having has an altogether different kind of *subject matter* from knowledge of things in themselves (as though the distinction between phenomena and things in themselves were like the distinction between items inside our light cone and items outside it, or like the distinction between physical objects and spirits).²⁴ It is merely to say, what is as close to being exegetically uncontentious as any claim about these matters can be, that, on Kant's conception, the knowledge we are in principle capable of having is *itself* of an altogether different kind from knowledge of things in themselves (see, for example, A 256/B 311 – 312). This leaves open the possibility that knowledge of things in themselves is a distinctive kind of knowledge concerning that which, in other ways, we know a great deal about (much as eye witness knowledge of events that occurred in the eighteenth century – knowledge

²³ Note: the word that Guyer and Wood translate as "bounds" in the quotation from A 727/B 755 on which I have laid so much emphasis – "philosophy consists precisely in knowing its bounds" – is *Grenzen*.
²⁴ See H. E. Matthews, "Strawson on Transcendental Idealism," reprinted in Walker (ed.), *Kant on Pure Reason*, and Henry E. Allison, *Kant's Transcendental Idealism: An Interpretation and Defense* (New Haven: Yale University Press, 1983), for two of the many notable attempts to urge a negative answer to this question, in apparent opposition to P. F. Strawson, *The Bounds of Sense: An Essay on Kant's 'Critique of Pure Reason'* (London: Methuen, 1966) – though let us not forget that they might be as guilty of misinterpreting Strawson as they take him to be of misinterpreting Kant.

that is of course no longer available to us – is a distinctive kind of knowledge concerning that which, by standard historical means, we know a great deal about).

But now: is there perhaps an incoherence in the very idea of drawing any such boundary (*Grenze*)? Wittgenstein, in the preface to his *Tractatus*, famously declares that "in order to be able to draw a [*Grenze*] to thought, we should have to be able to find both sides of the [*Grenze*] thinkable (i.e. we should have to be able to think what cannot be thought)."[25] Is there not an analogous predicament here?

Prima facie, no. For one thing, the very fact that the Kantian boundary may ultimately be a boundary between two kinds of knowledge, not between two kinds of subject matter – in contrast, perhaps, to the Wittgensteinian boundary – means that there cannot be any immediate self-stultification here; for why should we not have knowledge of one kind concerning the impossibility of our having knowledge of another kind? But also, even if both boundaries are somehow to be construed as boundaries between two kinds of subject matter, the shift from knowledge in Kant to thought in Wittgenstein is crucial. Little enough is required of thought for the very exercise of drawing a boundary between one territory and another to be a way of thinking about both territories. But it cannot similarly be claimed that the very exercise of drawing a boundary between one territory and another is a way of *knowing* about both territories – lest we create difficulties even for the more modest exercise of drawing a limit (*Schranke*) between our knowledge and our ignorance.[26] It is a vital part of Kant's overall conception that thought can extend further than knowledge, and, more specifically, that we can have thoughts, without intuitions, about things in themselves (B xxvi and A 253 – 254/B 309).[27]

[25] Ludwig Wittgenstein, *Tractatus Logico-Philosophicus*, trans. D. F. Pears and B. F. McGuiness (London: Routledge & Kegan Paul, 1961), p. 3. Note: Pears and McGuiness translate *Grenze* as "limit."

[26] It is worth noting in this connection that there is a famous argument purporting to show that, *unless* we can draw some such boundary between knowledge we are in principle capable of having and knowledge we are not, then neither can we draw the straightforward limit between knowledge we do have and knowledge we do not: see F. B. Fitch, "A Logical Analysis of Some Value Concepts," in *Journal of Symbolic Logic* **28** (1963). I believe that this argument has less impact than it appears to have, for reasons advanced by Joseph Melia in his "Anti-Realism Untouched," in *Mind* **100** (1991).

[27] *Pace* John McDowell, who, commenting on the most famous of the passages in which Kant alludes to the emptiness of thoughts without intuitions (A 51/B 75), writes, "For a thought to be empty ... would be for it not really to be a thought at all, and that is surely Kant's point; he is

To be sure, this whole discussion reminds us of just how delicate a matter it is to say what precisely the unknowability of things in themselves consists in; whether, for instance, it requires a distinction between positive knowledge and negative knowledge; and why it would not be compromised, as it had presumably better not be, either by our knowing of the *existence* of things in themselves (B xxvi–xxvii) or indeed by our knowing of their unknowability. Be that as it may, there is no obvious incoherence in the idea that our knowledge has boundaries that we can draw, and that these boundaries exclude knowledge of things in themselves.

There is no *obvious* incoherence in the idea. But there is still enough to give us pause. Kant's distinction between what we can know and what we can think comes under pressure from some especially radical versions of anti-realism, for which there exist powerful and well-known arguments. (I mean anti-realism in the sense made famous by Michael Dummett.[28] According to the more radical versions of this doctrine, unless we can know whether or not a given proposition is true, we cannot understand it and hence cannot so much as think that it is true.) Indeed, the distinction comes under pressure from within Kant's own system, where these radical versions of anti-realism have a clear precursor. For the emptiness of thoughts without intuitions, the thoughts that outstrip our knowledge, is, by Kant's own lights, a very radical emptiness indeed. Such thoughts, Kant insists, *make no sense to us.* They are, for us, a mere play of concepts (see, for example, A 139/B 178; A 239/B 298; B 308; A 679/B 707; A 696/ B724; and *Prolegomena*, § 30). And even if this does not give pause in its own right, it may well make trouble for Kant's overall conception. To see why, let us revert once more to the analogy of the globe. We can legitimately refer to the boundaries (*Grenzen*) of the surface of the globe, because we have access to a dimension other than the surface's own two. But if we ourselves were two-dimensional beings on the surface, and had no access to any third dimension, then, while we might still acknowledge the surface's curvature and indeed its finitude, we would have no reason to think of it as having any boundaries (*Grenzen*) at all.[29] It is therefore a real question whether, in these

not, absurdly, drawing our attention to a special kind of thoughts, the empty ones" (*Mind and World* (Cambridge, MA.: Harvard University Press, revised ed. 1996), pp. 3–4). The philosophical point that McDowell is making here may well be right. The exegetical point is precisely wrong.

[28] See, for example, his *The Logical Basis of Metaphysics* (London: Duckworth, 1991) and *Thought and Reality* (Oxford: Oxford University Press, 2006).

[29] It is in this sense that contemporary physics allows for the finitude but unboundedness of physical space: see Albert Einstein, *Relativity: The*

glimpses of ours beyond the boundaries of our own knowledge – in this play of concepts of ours in which we can find no sense – there is anything remotely like access to a third dimension of space. If not, then it is inappropriate to think of these "boundaries" *as* boundaries, which in turn means that it is inappropriate to think that there is any genuine contrast between our own knowledge and "knowledge of things in themselves."

There are also some very large questions, which I can do no more than raise in this context, about whether Kant's overall conception succumbs to an even more immediate self-stultification. Consider the very judgment that we have synthetic *a priori* knowledge. This must itself, presumably, count as an item of synthetic *a priori* knowledge. And yet, precisely in registering the non-analytic character of the knowledge in question, does it not also have some claim to being, at least to that extent, the very thing that an item of synthetic *a priori* knowledge supposedly cannot be – namely, a judgment about things in themselves? For, arguably, there is nothing *"from the human standpoint"* (A 26/B 42, my emphasis) to preclude our arriving at the knowledge in question by means of pure conceptual analysis. *From the human standpoint*, the various *a priori* conditions of our experience cannot be other than they are. Hence, from the human standpoint, these conditions cannot make a substantial contribution to any of our knowledge – that is to say, they cannot make the kind of contribution that they would not have made if they had been suitably other than they are. In acknowledging that these conditions do make such a contribution, which is what we are doing when we register the non-analytic character of the knowledge in question, must we not therefore already have taken a step back from the human standpoint?[30]

As I have said, I can do no more than raise these questions in this context. But I shall close by mentioning one respect in which their threat is exacerbated by what Kant has argued in the Transcendental Doctrine of Method. I have in mind his repeated insistence that, in philosophy, as opposed to mathematics, we arrive at synthetic *a priori* knowledge directly from our concepts, without having to exhibit any relevant objects of intuition. Admittedly, he also insists that the sheer possibility of our being given objects in (empirical) intuition grounds this process (see Section 2.ii). But, whatever obstacles there might be, from the human standpoint, to acknowledging more than conceptual analysis in cases of

Special and the General Theory, trans. Robert W. Lawson (London: Methuen, 1960), Chapter XXXI.

30 Cf. W. H. Walsh, *Kant's Criticism of Metaphysics* (Edinburgh: Edinburgh University Press, 1975), p. 253. For some very interesting material relating to this problem, see Bird, *op. cit.* in note 2 here, Ch. 29, §2.

reasoning where an object of intuition needs to be exhibited, how much greater will the obstacles be in cases where no such object needs to be exhibited? Again it looks as though a step back, of the very kind that Kant prohibits, is required for us to recognize the synthetic character of our philosophical knowledge.

However that may be, it is both highly significant and very fitting that such fundamental questions about Kant's project should be raised by these final, philosophically self-conscious sections of his book.

Part III The Impact of the *Critique*

14 The Reception of the *Critique of Pure Reason* in German Idealism

I. INTRODUCTION: REINHOLD, JACOBI, AND MAIMON

The reception of Kant's first *Critique*, the *Critique of Pure Reason*, by the main members of the German idealistic movement – that is, by Johann Gottlieb Fichte (1762–1814), Friedrich Wilhelm Joseph Schelling (1775–1854), and Georg Wilhelm Friedrich Hegel (1770–1831) – is a complex and complicated story that is intimately connected with the history of the controversies to which the first *Critique* gave rise.[1] Kant's *Critique of Pure Reason* was not an immediate philosophical success. On the contrary, in the first couple of years after its appearance in 1781, there was, much to Kant's disappointment, little public reaction, and most of it was rather hostile, like the notorious review by Garve and Feder. This led Kant then to publish, in 1783, the *Prolegomena*, most of which he had already written down before the publication of the *Critique of Pure Reason* (cf. 23:362ff.) with the explicit hope of making his teachings more accessible (4:261, 263f.). Then, four years later (1787), and again reacting to what he thought to be misunderstandings about the foundations of his theoretical philosophy (cf. footnote to the Preface of the *Metaphysical Foundations*, 4:447ff.), he published a second edition of the *Critique* in which considerable parts of the original work were rewritten. Within the small community of those who contributed to the early discussion of the significance and the consequences of Kant's critical philosophy, the most prominent became Friedrich Heinrich Jacobi (1743–1819), Karl Leonhard Reinhold (1758–1823), and Salomon Maimon (1752–1800), who were also the most influential figures in the

---

[1] There are numerous well-informed versions of this history from different perspectives. Among the most recent are Frederick Beiser: *German Idealism: The Struggle against Subjectivism*, 1781–1801. Cambridge, MA: Harvard University Press, 2002; William Bristow: *Hegel and the Transformation of Philosophical Critique*. Oxford: Oxford University Press, 2007; Eckart Förster: *The 25 Years of Philosophy*. Cambridge, MA: Harvard University Press, forthcoming; Dieter Henrich: *Between Kant and Hegel: Lectures on German Idealism*. Edited by David S. Pacini. Cambridge, MA: Harvard University Press, 2003.

reception of the *Critique of Pure Reason* by German idealist philosophers. Whereas Reinhold established himself early on as the leading defender of Kant's philosophical position, Jacobi was very soon recognized as its most outspoken critic. Maimon thought of himself as neither a Kantian nor a non-Kantian, but as a systematic philosopher in his own right who relied on elements of Kant's philosophy in order to set up his own version of what he called, like Kant, "transcendental philosophy." Because the German idealists read Kant's philosophy, and especially the first *Critique*, against the background of its initial controversial assessment by Reinhold, Jacobi, and Maimon, it is necessary to provide a short outline of these early debates in order to come to an understanding of the German idealist assessment of the merits and shortcomings of Kant's thought.

As early as 1786–7, Reinhold published a series of articles in a leading intellectual journal of the time, days, the *Teutsche Merkur*. He entitled the series the *Letters on Kantian Philosophy* (*Briefe über die Kantische Philosophie*). These letters, which were published in a modified form as a two-volume book in 1790 and 1792, were meant to demonstrate that the main doctrines of Kant's philosophy are not in conflict with fundamental moral and religious convictions, but that, on the contrary, they give a sound and rational basis for shared ethical principles and belief in God. Kant was so pleased with Reinhold's exposition of central elements of his teachings that at the end of his 1788 essay *On the Use of Teleological Principles in Philosophy* (*Über den Gebrauch teleologischer Prinzipien in der Philosophie*), he publicly praised the discerning understanding of his position by Reinhold (cf. 8:183). This recognition by Kant made Reinhold an authority on Kant's philosophy and led to the view that his reading of Kant's writings had to be taken very seriously. But hardly more than a year after Kant's public announcement, Reinhold gave up his role as interpreter of Kant's position and began to present himself as a thinker who improves Kant's theory, especially his theoretical philosophy. This was done in a book published in 1789 that Reinhold entitled *An Attempt at a New Theory of the Human Faculty of Representation* (*Versuch einer neuen Theorie des menschlichen Vorstellungsvermögens*) and that was dedicated to Kant among others. In the introductory essay to this book, entitled *On the Fate of Kantian Philosophy up Till Now* (*Über die bisherigen Schicksale der Kantischen Philosophie*), Reinhold claimed that although Kant had given a correct and exhaustive theory of the faculty of knowledge (*Erkenntnisvermögen*) in his first *Critique*, he had not given an account of the principles that lie at the basis of his theory as its premises. Without stating these premises explicitly and without demonstrating them independently from the results of the *Critique of Pure Reason*, Reinhold argued, there can be no really convincing foundation for Kant's endeavor. Thus, according to Reinhold, it is the task of philosophy after Kant to supply the premises for Kantian results (p. 67 f.). For methodological reasons, pursuing this task meant for Reinhold finding a first principle that is universally valid and self-evident from which to deduce Kantian epistemological claims. The principle he suggested, the so-called "principle of consciousness" (*Satz des Bewusstseins*), which relies on the concept of representation (*Vorstellung*), turned out to be rather controversial, and was considered to be untenable by influential critics such as G. E. Schulze, Maimon, and the young Fichte. Nevertheless, Reinhold's central idea that philosophy has to be founded on a first principle that expresses an indubitable fact of consciousness was successful insofar as it gave rise to the impression that Kant's theoretical philosophy was incomplete and thus in need of a new foundation.[2]

At almost the same time as the assumed Kantian Reinhold voiced suspicions about the lack of foundation in Kant's theory, the unadulterated anti-Kantian Jacobi launched an attack on a central distinction that Kant draws in the first *Critique*, the distinction between things in themselves and appearances. Jacobi had set off the so-called pantheism controversy in 1785 with his *On the Doctrine of Spinoza*. In this book, he claimed that it is a mistake to think of reason and rationality as understood by modern philosophy as privileged means for acquiring knowledge of the world and our situation in it. Instead, he claimed, one has to acknowledge that in the end, all knowledge rests on faith and revelation (cf. *Werke* II, p. 3, and II, p. 210 f., p. 249). For Jacobi, the most telling example of a philosophical project that claims to rely solely on reason and scientific rationality and that nevertheless fails badly in the attempt to gain knowledge is Kant's theoretical philosophy. This is so, according to Jacobi, because Kant starts from assumptions that make no sense at all. Jacobi's attack on Kant's theory of knowledge is documented impressively in his 1787 book *David Hume on Faith, or Idealism and Realism* (*David Hume über den Glauben, oder Idealismus und Realismus*), especially in the appendix to this book entitled *On Transcendental Idealism* (*Über den transzendentalen Idealismus*). Jacobi's main line of criticism here is roughly as follows. For Kant, knowledge is the joint product of the faculties of sensibility and understanding, where sensibility provides the data by being affected through something or other, and the understanding is in charge of the ordering of these data into the representation of an object by subjecting these data to conceptual

---

[2] A very informed analysis and assessment of Reinhold's position is to be found in Karl Ameriks, *Kant and the Fate of Autonomy. Problems in the Appropriation of the Critical Philosophy*. Cambridge: Cambridge University Press, 2000, pp. 81–160.

---

rules. Now, if with Kant we call the source of the affection of our sensibility "thing in itself," and if we name what can be known by us as an object an "appearance," then, according to Jacobi, Kant faces a dilemma: on the one hand, he has to claim that we cannot know anything about what affects our sensibility, – that is, about the thing in itself – because what can be known by us as an object has to be conceptually constituted; on the other hand, he has to acknowledge that we know at least something about the thing in itself – namely, that it is the source of affection. This knowledge seems to imply that the thing in itself somehow is an object of knowledge, which in turn seems to imply that it is an appearance. Thus the distinction between appearances and things in themselves either turns out to be no distinction at all or, if there is a distinction between them, then one cannot say anything about their relation to us, not even that things in themselves are the source of affection. Jacobi famously expresses this dilemma in the following words: "*without*" the presupposition of things in themselves "I could not enter into the system, but *with* it I could not stay within it" (*Werke* II, p. 304, *Writings*, p. 397). Whether this criticism of Kant's distinction between appearances and things in themselves is justified or not has itself become a topic of controversy that is still going on and that cannot be discussed here. For the assessment of the validity of Kant's philosophy by his contemporaries, this criticism had far-reaching consequences, giving rise to worries that at the very basis of Kant's doctrine there might be tensions between its central and constitutive elements, tensions that cannot be overcome by means of the resources from within the Kantian framework.[3] In the eyes of Kant's contemporaries, these worries, although initiated by the problems connected with the distinction between appearances and things in themselves raised by Jacobi, were not restricted to this distinction but were raised against other distinctions of Kant's philosophy as well – for example, against the distinction between concepts and intuitions and between a sensible world and an intelligible world. The aim of avoiding these so-called dualisms led most of the post-Kantian idealists to favor anti-dualistic or monistic models of reality.

Concerns from Reinhold about the absence of foundations and worries from Jacobi about irreconcilable dualisms were not the only motives that determined the reception of Kant's philosophy by the German idealists. A third important motive was provided by the suspicion articulated most forcefully by Maimon (and later in a different way

---

[3] For a more extensive treatment of Jacobi's role in German Idealism, see Rolf-Peter Horstmann, *Die Grenzen der Vernunft: Eine Untersuchung zu Zielen und Motiven des Deutschen Idealismus*, third edition (Frankfurt: Vittorio Klostermann Verlag, 2004).

by G. E. Schulze) that in the end, Kant's critical epistemology cannot refute skepticism with regard to the external world. Maimon made a lasting impression on some of his contemporaries with a book published in 1790 under the title *Essay in Transcendental Philosophy (Versuch über Transzendentalphilosophie)*. Even Kant, although he was ultimately somewhat ambivalent with respect to its merits – for rather opposite assessments by Kant one may compare his letter to Marcus Herz from May 26, 1789 (11:48ff.) and his letter to Reinhold from March 28, 1794 (11:475f.) – paid close attention to it. Among the many topics Maimon pursues in this book, his main point concerning Kant seems to be that although Kant succeeded in giving a convincing account of the conditions of the possibility of experience, he failed to show that there are experiences, or that experiences are real. This is so, according to Maimon, because by means of Kant's theory of space, time, and the categories, one is not in a position to determine an actual experience. For Maimon, this means that Kant just presupposes the fact of experience as organized according to the forms of sensibility and the categories (cf. *Versuch*, p. 70ff., p. 186ff.) and hence cannot refute the skeptic who doubts that there are any experiences. Although in his *Essay*, Maimon criticized Kant's theoretical philosophy with respect to quite a number of different points, it was mainly the charge that Kant was unable to refute the skeptic that became connected with Maimon's name.[4]

It is against this background of a growing awareness that there might be limitations and shortcomings in the way in which Kant realized his epistemological project that the German idealists started to read the first *Critique*. For them, the situation with respect to Kant's philosophy was further complicated by the fact that their doubts concerning the well-foundedness of Kant's doctrine induced by critics such as Reinhold, Jacobi, and Maimon were at odds with their belief in the overall superiority of Kant's teachings. This belief was rooted in their conviction that Kant's philosophy had been successful in overcoming the divide between rationalism and empiricism by insisting on *a priori* conditions of the empirical and on the fundamental role of self-consciousness in constituting the unity of experience in all its different forms as theoretical, practical, and aesthetic experience. This conflict between their doubts and their belief gave rise to an ambivalent attitude toward Kant's philosophy: on the one hand, they wanted to save what they called the "spirit" of Kant's philosophy, by which they meant those elements that in their eyes

---

[4] On Maimon, Kant, and skepticism see Paul Franks: *All or Nothing: Systematicity, Transcendental Arguments, and Skepticism in German Idealism* (Cambridge, MA: Harvard University Press, 2005).

made Kant superior over the modern philosophical tradition; on the other hand, they were forced to acknowledge that what they called the "letter" of Kant's philosophy, which meant the way in which he presented his teachings, was to some extent deficient.

2. FICHTE

This ambivalent attitude can be seen clearly in Fichte's assessment of Kant's first *Critique*.[5] Fichte became acquainted with Kant's philosophy early in his intellectual development, even before he started his academic career. As early as 1790, he made notes on the Transcendental Logic of the *Critique of Pure Reason* and prepared an excerpt with comments from the *Critique of the Power of Judgment* (*Versuch eines erklärenden Auszugs aus Kants Kritik der Urteilskraft*). However, what made him a devoted Kantian was neither the first nor the third *Critique* but the second *Critique*, the *Critique of Practical Reason*. He emphatically expressed the deep impression the second *Critique* made on him in a letter written in late summer of 1790 (*GA* III, 1, p. 193, No. 63). Thus, from the beginning, he became interested in Kant's theoretical philosophy, not for its own sake but because an assessment of its results was necessary in order to accept the practical side of Kant's philosophy. Because of the foundational role the first *Critique* played in Fichte's eyes for Kant's practical philosophy, he became – after he came to know of Jacobi's and Maimon's criticism of central elements of the first *Critique* – increasingly frustrated with what he took to be Kant's imperfect and confused presentation of his theoretical philosophy (cf. *GA* III, 2, p. 28, Nr. 171) and thought it his intellectual duty to find out how to improve it. Thus he was not primarily concerned with replacing Kant's doctrine by an alternative theory but with transforming it in such a way that it could properly function as the basis of practical philosophy.

The claim that he is pursuing Kantian ends by different means runs through all his published writing until 1800. As early as his review of Schulze's *Aenesidemus* (written 1793, published 1794), he professes that although the inner content of Kant's philosophy is, above all, criticism, it will need a lot of work to present it as a well-founded whole (cf. *GA* I, 2, p. 67). In the programmatic essay *On the Concept of the Doctrine of Science* (1794), especially in the preface to the second edition (1798), he again points out that Kant was on the right track but did not succeed in

---

[5] A complete overview of the relevant documents is given in Christoph Hanewald, *Apperzeption und Einbildungskraft: Die Auseinandersetzung mit der theoretischen Philosophie Kants in Fichtes früher Wissenschaftslehre* (Berlin: Walter de Gruyter Verlag, 2001).

realizing his insights in a convincing manner. We find the same assessments in the *Foundation of the Entire Doctrine of Science* (*Grundlage der gesamten Wissenschaftslehre*) from 1794/95, as well as in the two *Introductions* from 1797–8. However, Fichte's claim to have transformed Kant's critical principles into a coherent "system" of theoretical and practical philosophy by giving up the "letter" of Kant's theory for the sake of preserving its "spirit" is characteristic of Fichte's own philosophical work only until about 1800. In the years after 1800, he embarked on a new philosophical voyage and thought of his philosophical project then as so radically new that it could not fit at all into a Kantian framework, whether improved or not.

What exactly Fichte found defective in Kant's theoretical philosophy as presented in the first *Critique* is difficult to determine. This is because Fichte was very reluctant to criticize or even discuss Kant directly. The most extensive comments on Kant's philosophy can be found in Section 6 of the *Second Introduction to the Doctrine of Science*. Given the topics Fichte addresses there and alludes to in other places, the main critical points he seems to be concerned about can be summarized thus: (1) Kant's theory of space and time is unfounded; (2) the role of intellectual intuition in Kant's theory of apperception is not sufficiently clear; and (3) Kant's concept of the thing in itself is misleading.

Fichte's objections with respect to the first topic, Kant's theory of space and time (cf. *GA* I, 2, p. 61f., p. 350, and p. 335 note), are not meant to criticize Kant's major claim that space and time are subjective forms of sensibility or (what amounts to the same) ideal forms of intuition. On the contrary, Fichte unreservedly endorses this claim. What he found objectionable is the way Kant proves this claim in the Transcendental Aesthetic of the first *Critique*. According to Fichte, in order to prove such a claim, one has to deduce it from a fundamental principle that can be shown to be basic to all knowledge claims whatsoever. This fundamental principle is, as Fichte claims, the I understood as an original act (*ursprüngliche Handlung*). If Kant had grounded his account of the ideality of space and time in this principle, he would have realized, so thought Fichte, that it is not necessary to think of these forms of sensibility as only subjective, in opposition to real objectivity. Now, it is only to be expected that Kant would not have been convinced by this critical line of reasoning, and not only because it does not address his own arguments for the subjectivity or ideality of space and time as presented in the "Metaphysical Expositions" in the Transcendental Aesthetic of the first *Critique* directly. What one might find even less convincing is that Fichte's complaint seems to neglect Kant's claim of the irreducibility of the faculty of sensibility to any spontaneous activity, a claim that seems to exclude the possibility of grounding space and time in the original act.

The second complaint concerning the role of intellectual intuition in Kant's conception of apperception (cf. *GA* I, 4, p. 224ff.) seems also to be confusing because in Kant's first *Critique*, there is no place for a cognitive function of intellectual intuition at all. Yet, according to Fichte, the original act or the I is consciously present in each of us in intellectual intuition, and without intellectual intuition there is no I. Thus, at first sight, Fichte's conception of the I as an original act and Kant's view of apperception seem to be entirely incompatible. However, this complaint has also to be seen against the background of Fichte's own approach. Fichte is quite well aware that Kant has an aversion to intellectual intuition because he sees in it an epistemic mode that is not accessible to subjects like us. At the same time, he insists that Kant has to acknowledge intellectual intuition as a mode of awareness in order to account for our consciousness of the moral law, the categorical imperative. Fichte concludes that the intellectual intuition that Kant explicitly abolishes must be distinguished from what he, Fichte, calls intellectual intuition, and that Kant also has to subscribe to this Fichtean mode of awareness that is constitutive of the I if his philosophy is to be consistent. Kant just fails to have a name for it, and for that reason he does not succeed in making his conception of apperception sufficiently clear. Here again one may have doubts about whether this complaint has a basis in Kant's doctrine of apperception. Although it is true that Kant's remarks on this topic are rather obscure (a fact that is well documented by the history of their interpretation), it does not seem to be the case that their obscurity is intimately connected with his stance toward intellectual intuition. On the contrary: if Kant had allowed intellectual intuition to play a positive role in his theory of apperception, he would have faced enormous difficulties with the rest of his theoretical philosophy.

Fichte's third main objection deals with Kant's conception of the thing in itself (cf. *GA* I, 4, p. 232ff.). As will be remembered from what was said earlier, it was Jacobi who made this topic prominent. In direct reference to Jacobi, Fichte states the problem as follows: if Kant's notion of a thing in itself is meant to designate a real object that is totally independent of us and is at the same time the source of the affection of our sensibility, then indeed he would be guilty of making his whole position incomprehensible. But, as Fichte puts it in a rather polemical way: "To impute this absurdity to any man still in possession of his reason is, for me at least, impossible; how could I attribute it to Kant?" (*GA* I, 4, p. 239). Fichte then points out rightly that although there are indeed some passages in the text of the first *Critique* that burden Kant with such a notion, most of his remarks either explicitly or implicitly reject the idea of a subject-independent thing in itself as the source of affection. What Kant means with his notion of the thing in itself is the representation of *something in thought (etwas das nur gedacht wird, GA* I, 4, p. 241) that we interpret as the given source of affection. And because this thing in itself is an object in thought, it follows necessarily that it has to be taken as a product of thinking or as being posited (*gesetzt*) by a thinking subject. This indeed is, in Fichte's eyes, an understanding of the thing in itself that can claim to be truly idealistic and that is thoroughly in line with the spirit of Kant's philosophy. It has to be regretted – and thus be considered a criticism of Kant – that he misled his readers with respect to the meaning and the function of the thing in itself by giving rise to the impression that he was willing to accept the idea of an independently real given. That this Fichtean explanation of Kant's conception of the thing in itself would have found Kant's approval is not very likely. This is so because (1) like Fichte's first objection, it again ultimately blurs the opposition, fundamental to Kant's epistemology, between the receptivity of sensibility and the spontaneity of thinking, and because (2) it does not respect Kant's well-considered reluctance to give any indication as to the ontological status and the constitution of what he calls "the matter of sensation." In any case, there are strong grounds for suspecting that Kant would not have wanted to agree with the claim that in the end all matter is somehow mental.

Thus Fichte's attempt to engage critically with the first *Critique* proved not to be very fruitful from a Kantian point of view. Although Fichte might indeed have raised important questions, his very approach to Kant's philosophy is biased by his own un-Kantian presuppositions. That this is the case is confirmed by Kant's blunt refusal to acknowledge any connection between his philosophical aims and Fichte's system (cf. *Erklärung in Beziehung auf Fichtes Wissenschaftslehre* of August 7, 1799, 12:370 f.).

3. SCHELLING

At about the same time Fichte published his ambivalent assessment of Kant's first *Critique* to the public, Schelling published his early philosophical writings in which he not only admits his close relation to Fichte's philosophical approach, but also follows Fichte's strategy in criticizing Kant. Schelling too uses the distinction between the letter and the spirit as well as that between the premises and the results of Kant's philosophy, and claims to defend the latter in order to avoid the impression of a direct disagreement with Kant in his discussion of the merits and the limits of Kant's philosophy. He too is rather unspecific with respect to the question as to what exactly has to be taken as Kant's results or as the spirit of his philosophy. As with Fichte, Schelling's engagement with Kant becomes less dominant in his later

writings. His most explicit comments and allusions to Kant's philosophy
are to be found in his very early essay *On the Possibility of a Form
of Philosophy in General* (1794), in his writing *Of the I as Principle of
Philosophy* (1795), in his *Philosophical Letters on Dogmatism and
Criticism* (1795), and in the *Essays in Explanation of the Idealism of
the Doctrine of Science* (1797).

The *Letters* and the *Essays* essentially repeat Fichte's reservations
against the first *Critique* in that they take up the worries about the limits
of what Kant intended to achieve with his theoretical philosophy (for
example, *Letters*, Schröter I, p. 225 ff.) and rehearse Fichte's misgivings
about Kant's theory of space and time and of the thing in itself (for
example, *Essays*, Schröter I, p. 279 ff. and 328 ff.). It is in the essay on
the *Form of Philosophy in General* that Schelling becomes a bit more
specific as to what he takes to be problematical with the first *Critique*.
What he seems to be concerned about is "the lack of a founding principle
and of a solid connection of the Kantian deductions" (*Form*, Schröter I,
p. 47). The deductions to which he refers are the deductions of the forms of
judgment and of the categories. He complains that Kant did not succeed in
deducing both the forms of judgment and the categories from what he calls
"the fundamental form of all thought" (*die Urform alles Denkens*,
Schröter I, p. 63 ff.). Although worries about the well-foundedness of the
table of judgments and its connection with the table of categories go back
to Reinhold, Schelling's complaint is not just an echo of these earlier
worries, because he utters this complaint from a different perspective. It
has to be seen in relation to his own imaginative attempt to figure out a
deduction of the categories and the forms of judgment. This attempt was
influenced by the efforts – characteristic of for example, Dietrich
Tiedemann (1748–1803) and especially Wilhelm Gottlieb Tennemann
(1761–1819) – to interpret Plato's doctrines within a Kantian framework.[6]
The young Schelling joined their approach and was led to write a commentary on the *Timaeus* that was committed to this attitude. Now, in the

[6] Both Tiedemann and Tennemann were influential historians of philosophy
whose works were known to have been read by Schelling and Hegel. The
best-known work by Tiedemann is his *Geist der spekulativen Philosophie*,
6 vols. (Marburg, 1791–97). Tennemann's most remarkable achievement is
his incomplete *Geschichte der Philosophie*, 11 vols. (Leipzig, 1798–1819).
For Tiedemann's Kantian approach toward Plato, see his *Theaetet, oder
über das menschliche Wissen. Ein Beitrag zur Vernunftkritik* (Frankfurt,
1794). An informative discussion of Tennemann's interpretation of Plato
under the influence of Kant and Reinhold is to be found in Manfred Baum,
"The Beginnings of Schelling's Philosophy of Nature," in Sally Sedgwick
(ed.), *The Reception of Kant's Critical Philosophy: Fichte, Schelling, and
Hegel* (Cambridge: Cambridge University Press, 2000), pp. 199–215.

essay on the *Form of Philosophy in General*, Schelling in his so-called deduction of the categories and the forms of judgment uses this approach in the opposite direction: he relies heavily on Platonic conceptions in deriving forms of judgments and categories from a common source. Thus, what he found missing in Kant's deductions was not a Reinholdian first principle but rather an ontological underpinning for Kant's epistemology. However, it is hard to think of Schelling's deduction as an improvement on Kant's theory. It has to give up almost everything that is genuinely Kantian. Schelling's most obvious deviations from Kant consist in giving a completely new meaning to the Kantian analytic–synthetic distinction and in virtually identifying categories and forms of judgment.

In the text *Of the I*, which claims again "to reveal the results of the critical philosophy in tracing them back to the ultimate principles of all knowledge" (Schröter I, p. 76), it becomes quite clear that many of the critical objections Schelling raises against Kant's philosophy have their basis in a very un-Kantian assessment of what his project in theoretical philosophy is all about. For Schelling, Kant's three critiques are not primarily three investigations into the function and the achievements of the three irreducible faculties of the human mind that, taken together, give rise to a coherent view of the world as a unified totality. For him, the three critiques are the rather obscure expression of an undertaking that starts with the basic assumption of an underlying unity of being and thinking. This, from a Kantian point of view, rather strange characterization of Kant's critiques Schelling makes unambiguously explicit in a footnote toward the end of *Of the I*. He writes, "Kant was the first to establish the absolute I as the ultimate substratum of all being (though he established it nowhere directly but at least everywhere indirectly), and the first to fix the real problem of the possibility of a certain something determinable even beyond mere identity – in a manner that (how shall one describe it? Whoever has read his deduction of the categories and his critique of the teleological power of judgment in the spirit in which everything he ever wrote must be read, sees the depth of his meaning and insight, which seems almost unfathomable) – in a manner that appears possible only in a genius who, rushing ahead of himself, as it were, can *descend* the steps from the highest point, whereas others can *ascend* only step by step" (Schröter I, p. 156; Marti trans., p. 120). This view of the three critiques made it possible for Schelling on the one hand to uncover problems within the critiques that can only be found if one shares his perspective, and on the other hand to claim that he is pursuing the Kantian project. He is, however, honest enough to confess in the *Essays in Explanation of the Idealism of the Doctrine of Science* "that it never came into my mind to copy again what Kant has written or to know what ultimately Kant was after with his philosophy but only what *according to my understanding* he had to be after if his philosophy was to be coherent" (Schröter I, p. 299).

Although, in the end, Schelling's criticism of elements of Kant's first *Critique* does not really help to improve the Kantian doctrine understood in its own terms, he at least succeeded – contrary to Reinhold and Fichte – in putting forward a very imaginative hypothesis as to why Kant did not explain himself in accordance with the intentions that Schelling and the other critics who publicly declared themselves to be Kantians attributed to him. Whereas Reinhold and Fichte could not think of anything better than to claim that Kant did not want to make explicit his real intentions, Schelling blames Kant's "spiritless age" (*erschlaffte Zeitalter*) and his style. He writes: " ... the representatives of this age promptly tried to tone down the first great product of [Kant's] philosophy. They could do so without much difficulty, because its language seems to indulge the mood of the time. Consequently they saw nothing but the old established obsequiousness under the yoke of objective truth, and they tried at least to reduce its doctrine to the humiliating tenet that the limits of objective truth are not set by absolute freedom but are the mere consequence of the well-known weakness of man's mind and are due to the limitation of his power of perception" (Schröter I, p. 81 f.; Marti trans., p. 68). Thus, according to Schelling, it was partly Kant's own fault that he was misunderstood.

4. HEGEL

Hegel by and large followed the common critical stance of his fellow idealists. However, he differs from both Fichte and Schelling in that he is a much more careful reader of Kant's text. This is already documented by the extent of his interchange with Kant's philosophy in general, and especially with the first *Critique*. Hegel's published comments on elements of Kant's doctrine are to be found in almost all of his major writings and are distributed over his entire philosophical career. The most extensive discussions of topics from the first *Critique* are found in three texts. The first is one of the earliest texts Hegel published, the article *Faith and Knowledge* from 1802–3, which appeared in the *Critical Journal of Philosophy* that he and Schelling edited jointly. The second is his metaphysical *magnum opus*, the *Science of Logic*, published in three volumes between 1812 and 1816. The third is the second edition of his *Encyclopedia of the Philosophical Sciences in Outline* from 1827, his only published presentation of his entire system.

In *Faith and Knowledge*, Hegel gives what could be called a transformative reading of the main elements of the first *Critique*, which aims at presenting Kant's epistemological doctrines as an ontological theory in disguise.[7] According to Hegel, Kant's principle of the synthetic unity of apperception (which he identifies with productive power of imagination, cf. *Werkausgabe* vol. 2, p. 308; trans. Cerf, Harris, p. 73) is an ontological claim to the effect that reality has to be understood as a conceptually undifferentiated whole that bifurcates (*entzweit*) itself into subject and object by imposing a conceptual structure on itself. With this perspective on the first *Critique* in mind, Hegel's leading critical claim then is that although Kant indeed had this profound philosophical insight into the real constitution of reality, he lacked the proper understanding of this insight, which led him to an objectionable psychological or "Lockean" interpretation of what he recognized as a basic ontological fact: the unity of being and thinking or of object and subject (cf. *Werkausgabe* vol. 2, p. 304; trans. Cerf, Harris, p. 69). This mistake, according to Hegel, results from Kant's conviction that our ontology is founded on the mechanisms of our cognitive faculties. Kant therefore takes the objective world to be a product of a human activity: "... an objective determinateness that is man's own perspective and projection" (*eine objective Bestimmtheit, welche der Mensch hinsieht und hinauswirft*) (*Werkausgabe* vol. 2, p. 309; trans. Cerf, Harris, p. 74). This, however, is a clear case of privileging the subject over the object and thus of failing to do justice to the ontological equality of subject and object.

This general line of criticizing Kant by attributing to him an ontological project that it is rather doubtful that he ever wanted to pursue is accompanied by a long list of critical remarks concerning the details of the first *Critique*. They start with the already familiar allegation of "the shallowness of the deduction of the categories" (*Werkausgabe* vol. 2, p. 304; trans. Cerf, Harris, p. 69). They continue by ridiculing Kant's notion of the thing in itself underlying the distinction between appearances and things in themselves by comparing it to the ore-king (*eherne König*) in Goethe's fairy tale (*Märchen*), who is a formed object only as long as a human subject provides categories as blood vessels, and becomes a formless clod (*Klumpen*) after "the formal transcendental idealism sucks out" (*ausleckt*) (*Werkausgabe* vol. 2, p. 312 f.; trans. Cerf, Harris, p. 77) his conceptual veins. And they critically address the question of whether Kant's concept of objectivity as it emerges from his system of the principles of the understanding is not unsatisfactory because it ultimately makes it impossible to distinguish between

---

[7] Cf. the illuminating account of Hegel's appropriation and transformation of Kant's philosophy by Béatrice Longuenesse, *Hegel's Critique of Metaphysics* (Cambridge: Cambridge University Press, 2007), especially chapters 5 and 6.

representations and things since the principles of the understanding, according to Hegel, cannot provide a criterion that can function as a distinguishing mark between an existing thing and an ordered succession of representations (*Werkausgabe* vol. 2, p. 311 f.; trans. Cerf, Harris, p. 75 f.).

Of special critical interest for Hegel is Kant's distinction between understanding and reason and his repudiation of the idea of an intuitive understanding. In Hegel's eyes, these topics are intimately connected because it is an impoverished notion of reason that leads to this repudiation. Concerning the distinction between understanding and reason, Hegel points out that both are supposed to be unifying activities of the subject. But whereas the activity of the understanding has at least a genuine content on which it can operate (the sensibly given manifold), the activity of Kantian reason has no real content at all; it is in Hegel's words an "empty unity", a "dimensionless activity" (*Werkausgabe* vol. 2, p. 317 f.; trans. Cerf, Harris, p. 80 f.). The sole function of this activity without content is to regulate the product of the understanding, as Hegel remarks in allusion to Kant's notion of the regulative use of reason. Because of this lack of real content, reason in the first *Critique* can play only a negative role when it comes to those matters; the understanding is not in the position to apply its categories to them, such as the soul, the world, and God. Instead of recognizing them as real, although not within the limits of the understanding, Kantian reason elevates them into "intellectuality" (*Intellektualität*) (*Werkausgabe* vol. 2, p. 319).

Here is where Hegel's regret of Kant's rejection of an intuitive understanding comes into play via the following consideration: if Kant had not favored a conception of the understanding that is cut off from the sensible given (because of the alleged irreducible opposition between understanding and sensibility)[8] in such a way that the understanding cannot relate non-conceptually to the given in experience, but if he had allowed instead for an understanding that interacts in an individuating – that is, intuitive manner – with the empirical, then he could have avoided the purely negative claim that there is nothing to know with respect to the soul (understood as the I), the world (understood as an individual totality) and God, and could have closed the insurmountable gap between the contentless unifying activity of reason and the empirical manifold (*Werkausgabe* vol. 2, p. 322; trans. Cerf, Harris, p. 85) characteristic of his philosophy. According to Hegel, Kant's position with respect to the

---

[8]   A careful analysis of this charge is given by Paul Guyer, "Absolute Idealism and the Rejection of Kantian Dualism," in Karl Ameriks (ed.), *The Cambridge Companion to German Idealism* (Cambridge: Cambridge University Press, 2000), pp. 37–56.

concept of an intuitive understanding in the first *Critique* is even more puzzling if one takes into account Kant's assessment of the role of the intuitive understanding in the *Critique of the Power of Judgment*. In the context of his theory of the teleological power of judgment, according to Hegel, Kant recognizes the necessity of an intuitive understanding in order to account for the inner constitution and the form of organisms (*Werkausgabe* vol. 2, p. 324 ff.; trans. Cerf, Harris, p. 88 ff.). Thus Hegel concludes that ultimately Kant's position is not acceptable because his subjectivist and psychologistic approach, especially in the first *Critique*, fails to answer the question as to how to think of reality in a proper – that is, more balanced – or, for Hegel, "speculative" way.

In his *Science of Logic*, Hegel does not change his early assessment of the limitations of Kant's views in the first *Critique*, although he moves away from the polemical tone characteristic of *Faith and Knowledge*. He acknowledges explicitly the merits of Kant's philosophy by emphasizing that it has been "the foundation and the starting point of the newer German philosophy" (*Werkausgabe* vol. 5, p. 59 fn.) and gives this as the reason for referring that extensively to his work, which indeed he does. The overall message he wants to convey is again that Kant was on the right track when he made the synthetic unity of apperception the highest point from which every philosophy has to start, but that his notion of this synthetic unity made it a purely subjective unity that stands in opposition to an objective world (cf. *Werkausgabe* vol. 6, p. 260 f.). However, this moderately balanced general message is somewhat distorted by Hegel's attitude, especially toward the details of Kant's first *Critique*, which remains utterly critical. In particular, Kant's antinomies and his theory of matter are the targets of Hegel's extensive critical scrutiny.[9] His criticism with respect to the theory of matter is only indirectly concerned with the first *Critique* although it is meant to highlight a point that can be raised against the antinomies and thus against topics in the first *Critique* too – namely, that Kant's arguments are sometimes unsound and circular. With respect to matter, Hegel deals primarily with Kant's attempt in the *Metaphysical Foundations of Natural Sciences* to construct matter out of attractive and repulsive force (*Werkausgabe* vol. 5, p. 200ff.). Hegel claims that what Kant calls a "construction" is in fact no construction at all but just an analysis of what forces are necessarily presupposed if one starts with a specific conception of matter. In Hegel's eyes, this procedure amounts to giving a circular argument. His very comprehensive discussion of the antinomies, which is scattered all over the *Science of Logic* (first

[9] Cf. Sally Sedgwick, "Hegel on Kant's Antinomies and Distinction between General and Transcendental Logic," in *The Monist* 74 (1991): 403–20.

antinomy: *Werkausgabe* vol. 5, p. 109 f. and 271 ff., second antinomy: *Werkausgabe* vol. 5, p. 218 ff., third antinomy: *Werkausgabe* vol. 6, p. 441 ff.), yields a similar result: according to Hegel, each of them is on formal grounds unconvincing. This assessment is by no means unpersuasive and is based firmly in a very close reading of the Kantian text. Thus, in the *Science of Logic*, Hegel again comes to the conclusion that Kant's impressive and revolutionary philosophical program was badly executed by him and therefore had to be pursued by different and more adequate means.

Presumably Hegel's best known statement concerning Kant's philosophy is the discussion in the introductory parts to the very short version of the *Science of Logic* in his *Encyclopedia of the Philosophical Sciences*. The extended version of this discussion appeared in print for the first time in the second edition of this work in 1827. It deals with traditional metaphysics, empiricism, and Kantian critical philosophy, and what Hegel calls "immediate knowledge" as *Three Positions of Thought towards Objectivity* (*Werkausgabe* vol. 8, p. 93 ff.). These remarks represent Hegel's last published judgment on Kant's philosophy. This discussion adds nothing that could be considered new in comparison with his aforementioned views on the accomplishments and the insufficiencies of Kant's critical philosophy. It shows that from his Jena beginnings until his late Berlin years, Hegel never gave up the conviction that in order to establish the "right" philosophy, one first has to overcome Kant.

5. CONCLUSION

This short sketch of the reception of Kant's first *Critique* in the German idealistic period cannot claim to have dealt adequately with all the different aspects, and especially with all the details both historical and systematic, of the discussion of Kant's work. However, it should be sufficient to make three main points. The first is the enormous amount of attention Kant's transcendental idealism received within a relatively short period of time. Within less than twenty years from its first publication in 1781, the *Critique of Pure Reason*, together with the other two *Critiques*, changed the German philosophical landscape completely. Whether people reacted dismissively to the Kantian project or whether they endorsed it, no one felt able to disregard Kant's teachings in attempting to formulate a philosophical viewpoint of his own. This intense influence of Kant's philosophy from very early on was not restricted to philosophical contexts alone: it extended into many other disciplines, most notably to theology and legal studies, and even into political life. The second point that is noteworthy has to do with the specific manner in which Fichte, Schelling, and Hegel tried to accommodate Kant's theoretical philosophy as espoused in the first *Critique*. They all shared the sense that there was something essential missing in Kant's exposition of his doctrine that made it impossible to grasp the real intentions and the most significant consequences of his endeavor. This sense of dissatisfaction led each of them to his own very individual attempt to transform the principles of Kant's theoretical philosophy from epistemological principles to downright ontological principles, thus liberating them from what they thought were unreasonable and unjustified restrictions. The third and final point of interest concerns what could be called the dynamics of the attitude toward Kant's philosophy by the German idealists. Although all of them started their own philosophical projects with the objective of somehow staying within an appropriately modified Kantian "space of reasons," their transformational efforts led them to systematic realizations of their own philosophical conceptions that ultimately proved to be incompatible with Kant's position. The growing tension between their ways of transforming Kant's philosophy in order to "save" its true "spirit" and what Kant himself had been eager to defend as the roots and the boundaries of knowledge ultimately alienated them from Kant. This, however, does not mean that there is nothing to learn from their admiration and their criticism of Kant if one takes into account their own projects.

One last thing is worth mentioning. Looking at the criticism of Kant's theoretical philosophy by the German idealists from a contemporary perspective, one has to acknowledge that their attempt to avoid what they thought to be Kantian shortcomings by transforming Kant's philosophy into a monistic metaphysical system was not very successful. Only twenty-five years after the death of Hegel in 1831, with the emergence of what then became known as Neo-Kantianism, the conviction started to grow that one should "go back to Kant" and wrestle with the problems of theoretical philosophy within an untransformed, that is to say, broadly non-metaphysical Kantian framework. There is no doubt that much of contemporary theoretical philosophy, especially epistemology and philosophy of science, is deeply rooted in and indebted to such an untransformed Kantian approach toward issues in theoretical philosophy, an approach that relies heavily on privileging what can be called scientific rationality in contrast to metaphysical thinking. But even these contemporary endeavors in theoretical philosophy – nowadays most prominently exemplified by the work of Wilfrid Sellars and John McDowell – cannot get rid of the very problems the German idealists took to be the main obstacles for a successful realization of Kant's philosophical project by Kant himself. Thus these problems are still with us in one form or another.

15   The "Transcendental Method"

On the Reception of the *Critique of Pure Reason* in Neo-Kantianism

The term 'neo-Kantianism' must be determined
functionally rather than substantially [...]; it is
a matter of a direction taken in question-posing.[1]

I.   WHICH NEO-KANTIANISM?

In the history of philosophy, there have been several waves of Kantianism
since the first publication of the *Critique of Pure Reason*. They differ from
each other not only with respect to the textual basis available at a certain
point in time. They are also rooted in quite diverse motives of appropriation of Kant's philosophy and pursue different argumentative goals.

   The first wave appeared almost immediately after Kant had launched
his critical project: Johann Schultz wrote the first commentary on the
Critique of Pure Reason in 1784; Carl Christian Erhard Schmid published
the first Kant dictionary in 1786; and in 1796, Jacob Sigismund Beck
provided the rising German idealism with the *Only possible standpoint
from which the Critical Philosophy must be judged*. Some of these early
Kantians had an extensive correspondence with Kant, thereby supporting
the development of Kant's philosophy in the first place. In contrast to the
aims of Johann Gottlieb Fichte and other German idealists who no longer
were Kant scholars, the aim of those Kantians was confined to a better
understanding of Kant's critical works, starting with the *Dissertation*.

I would like to thank Michael Friedman for helpful comments on an earlier
version of this chapter. I am also grateful to Reinhard Brandt, who introduced
me to the Neo-Kantian reading of Plato and Kant while supervising my
dissertation on Kant's philosophy of science at Marburg University. Brandt
was a student at Marburg of Klaus Reich's who in turn was a student at
Freiburg of Julius Ebbinghaus's who in turn was a student of Windelband's at
Heidelberg.
[1]   Ernst Cassirer in his Davos disputation with Martin Heidegger; appendix to
   Heidegger, *Kant und das Problem der Metaphysik* (Frankfurt/Main:
   Klostermann, 1991), pp. 271–96, here p. 274; trans. Richard Taft, *Kant
   and the Problem of Metaphysics* (Bloomington: Indiana University Press,
   1997), p. 193.

At the other end of the time scale, the most recent and still continuing wave of Kantianism has its origins in Peter Strawson's *Bounds of Sense* (1966) as well as Jonathan Bennett's *Kant's Analytic* (1966) and *Kant's Dialectic* (1974). They brought Kant's transcendental philosophy to broader attention among English speaking philosophers and, together with Strawson's *Individuals* (1959), triggered the debate on "transcendental arguments."

The revival of Kant's philosophy, which is commonly referred to as Neo-Kantianism (*Neukantianismus*), began with Otto Liebmann's *Kant und die Epigonen* and Friedrich Albert Lange's *Geschichte des Materialismus und Kritik seiner Bedeutung in der Gegenwart* in the 1860s. It ended with the deaths of Alois Riehl and Paul Natorp and the declaration of the end of Neo-Kantianism as a "historical appearance"[2] by Heinrich Rickert in the 1920s. Depending on one's perspective, of course, any clear-cut definition of that period remains problematic. In point of fact, the movement to "return to Kant" was already an epiphenomenon of the predominance of the post-Kantians (first of all Hegel) in the first half of the nineteenth century.[3] But these essays neither reached the level of serious philosophical work nor did they share basic assumptions in their interpretation of Kant. In the following, I will therefore limit the usage of the term *Neo-Kantianism* and its cognates to the particular philosophical movement, approximately from 1870 to 1924.

But another, local qualification of the term Neo-Kantianism must also be made. Whereas the English-speaking reception of Kant in the nineteenth century never reached the level of a Neo-Kantianism but remained largely a Kant-oriented criticism of empiricism, there were Neo-Kantian approaches to metaphysics in France (for example, Charles Renouvier) and in Italy (for example, Carlo Cantoni).[4] But only in Germany did philosophers rely on Kant in order to repel post-Kantian idealism as well as certain forms of materialism and naturalism that had emerged as a response to Hegelian idealism. Only here do we find a

---

[2] Heinrich Rickert, "Alois Riehl", *Logos* 13 (1924/25), 164 ("geschichtliche Erscheinung").

[3] See, for example, Friedrich Eduard Beneke, *Kant und die philosophische Aufgabe unserer Zeit: Eine Jubeldenkschrift auf die Kritik der reinen Vernunft* (Berlin: Mittler, 1832), p. 89: "Only the true *Kantian* doctrine … is what brings us the future, purged of its cinders and freed of its distorting covers."

[4] See Charles Renouvier, *Essais de Critique Générale*, 3 vols. (Paris: Ladrange, 1854–1864), and Carlo Cantoni, *Emanuele Kant*, 3 vols. (Milano: Brigola, 1879–1884). See also Alice Bullard, "Kant in the Third Republic: Charles Renouvier and the Constructed Self", *Proceedings of the Western Society for French History* 25 (1998), 319–28.

Neo-Kantian movement institutionally differentiated into "schools," commonly referred to as the Marburg and the Southwest German or Baden schools.[5] The first included Hermann Cohen, Paul Natorp, and Ernst Cassirer, among others, the latter included Wilhelm Windelband and Heinrich Rickert, to mention only the most important.

What these philosophers shared with those of the first wave of Kantianism was a greater interest in the literal meaning of Kant's texts than the next generation, including Arthur Schopenhauer, Johann Friedrich Herbart, and Jakob Friedrich Fries, had shown. Some of the Neo-Kantians took great efforts in preparing new and critical editions of Kant's texts, among them the still incomplete *Akademie Ausgabe* (1900–). But at the same time, what the present wave of Kantianism inherited from the Neo-Kantians is a systematic interest in Kant's theoretical philosophy, with an emphasis on epistemology at the expense of ontology. This is not to say that Neo-Kantians or Kantians in the analytic tradition restrict themselves to theoretical or even epistemological issues, but the origins of both movements can be found in the preoccupation with Kant's first *Critique*. And both movements committed themselves to utilizing Kant's texts for a systematic elaboration of his thoughts rather than for a philological accounting. It was Wilhelm Windelband who provided the motto for the Neo-Kantians in his *Präludien*: "Understanding Kant means transcending Kant."[6]

There is no one Neo-Kantian manifesto. Hence it is quite difficult to determine what exactly these philosophers have in common. We can reasonably expect that the closer we look at their specific works, the more noticeable will their philosophical differences become, and what initially look like connecting elements will turn into more or less vague family resemblances. But there are a few principles to be found in Kant's *Critique of Pure Reason* that can structure at least a coarse-grained picture. This does not mean that Neo-Kantians completely subscribe to these principles, their premises, or their conclusions in Kant; as already mentioned, all of them saw themselves developing philosophically self-standing approaches in a Kantian "spirit." So although I cannot deal here with *the* Neo-Kantians but have to focus on some of the most significant

---

[5] See Klaus Christian Köhnke, *Entstehung und Aufstieg des Neukantianismus: Die deutsche Universitätsphilosophie zwischen Idealismus und Positivismus* (Frankfurt am Main: Suhrkamp, 1986), pp. 179, 478, 484–85. Köhnke traces the term *Neo-Kantianismus* back to 1859; as opposed to *Schopenhauerianismus* and *Hegelianismus*, the term *Neukantianismus* became popular in the 1870s.
[6] Wilhelm Windelband, *Präludien: Aufsätze und Reden zur Philosophie und ihrer Geschichte* (1884), 9th ed., vol. 1 (Tübingen: Mohr, 1924), p. iv.

figures, I think one can identify some central claims of the *Critique* that more or less implicitly served not so much as the common ground but rather as the starting-points of the Neo-Kantian project. These are:

i) *Metaphysics* – a wholly isolated speculative cognition of reason that elevates itself entirely above all instruction from experience, ... has up to now not been so favored by fate as to have been able to enter upon the secure course of a science ... (B xiv)

As Kant saw the model for a justified metaphysics in the sciences with respect to the apodictic certainty available in them, so did the Neo-Kantians base epistemology on the premise that knowledge in the strict sense necessarily includes claims of *universal validity*. Validity (*Gültigkeit, Geltung*) is one of the most central concepts for them. And as they also share with Kant the view of the systematicity of proper knowledge, the Neo-Kantian goal is to philosophically account for the principles of all kinds of cultural articulations, not only the natural sciences but also ethics, aesthetics, religion, and even pedagogy and political economy.

ii) The conditions of the *possibility of experience* in general are at the same time conditions of the *possibility of the objects of experience*, and on this account have objective validity in a synthetic judgment *a priori*. (A 158/B 197)

Unlike the speculative idealism of Schelling or, even more comprehensive, that of Hegel, Neo-Kantians do not directly attempt to explain those cultural articulations. They distinguish between the conditions of the being of particular cultural phenomena and the conditions of their validity, and argue – as did Kant – for the priority of the latter over the former. Or, to put it in scholastic terms: the analysis of the *ratio cognoscendi* obtains priority over the investigation of the *ratio essendi*, with the concept of cognition (*Erkenntnis*) not restricted to scientific knowledge but rather including all kinds of experience (*Erleben*) or worldviews. However, the fact that the Neo-Kantians emphasized the logical conditions of possible experience and often equated *Erkenntnistheorie* with *Erkenntnislogik* by no means entails that they intended a formal logic. Natorp writes paradigmatically: "There are, also according to Kant, no laws of a merely formal truth that would not have their roots in the laws of material truth [*gegenständlichen Wahrheit*]; consequently also no formal logic that would not have to be founded on a 'transcendental' logic."[7] As we shall see in the sequel, following the "*transcendental*

---

[7] Paul Natorp, "Über objective und subjective Begründung der Erkenntniss (Erster Aufsatz)", *Philosophische Monatshefte* 23 (1887), pp. 257–86, at p. 257.

method" would secure philosophy the status of a science, or so the Neo-Kantians hoped. Unlike philosophers from the Marburg school, some of their colleagues from the Southwest school sought to provide some kind of ultimate foundation (*Letztbegründung*).

iii) The *transcendental unity* of apperception is that unity through which all of the manifold given in an intuition is united in a concept of the object. It is called *objective* on that account, and must be distinguished from the *subjective unity* of consciousness, which is a *determination of inner sense*, through which that manifold of intuition is empirically given for such a combination. (B 139)

Although Cohen in the first edition of his *Kants Theorie der Erfahrung* gave an account of Kant's concept of synthesis in terms of psychic processes, and other Neo-Kantians later tried to account for that "subjective unity of consciousness" by providing the basic lines of an empirical psychology, their primary approach not only to an understanding of Kant's first *Critique* but also to epistemology in general was determined by the *quaestio juris*, or the question of the validity of our knowledge (see A 84/B 116). The main thrust of any Neo-Kantian theory of cognition (*Erkenntnistheorie*) was *anti-psychological*.[8] The concepts of fact (*Faktum*) and validity (*Geltung*) mark off the basic Neo-Kantian dualism. The concept of the subject of cognition is the logical subject, or better, the transcendental-logical subject, rather than an empirical subject, a human being, or a person. Whereas existence or non-existence can be predicated of subjects of the latter kind, it cannot be predicated of the former. It is the concept of a subject implied by the general concept of knowledge, and therefore treated as necessary for the establishment of the basic principles of the objective validity of any cognition.

As a transcendental investigation of the basic standards of validity of any cultural articulations, Neo-Kantianism sees itself as interpreting

---

[8] Even Rickert, who tries to incorporate a "transcendental psychology" into epistemology, calls the "'Critique of Reason' ... a science that asks not for the being but for the sense, not for the facticity but for the validity, not for the reality but for the values." ("Zwei Wege der Erkenntnistheorie: Transscendentalpsychologie und Transscendentallogik", *Kant-Studien* 14 (1909), 228.) For a profound discussion of the Neo-Kantian antipsychologism, see R. Lanier Anderson, "Neo-Kantianism and the Roots of Anti-Psychologism", *British Journal for the History of Philosophy* 13 (2005), 287–323. See also Martin Kusch, *Psychologism: A Case Study in the Sociology of Philosophical Knowledge* (London: Routledge, 1995), pp. 169–77, who primarily focuses on the anti-psychologism of Windelband and Rickert.

and at the same time broadening the scope that Kant had assigned to the *Critique*. Philosophy can attain the status of a science by providing the *transcendental analysis* – not a genealogical description – of cultural phenomena such as the sciences, religion, the arts, and so on. It was Ernst Cassirer who stated this most explicitly and related it to Kant's first *Critique* and its use of the word "understanding": "The 'understanding' here is not to be taken in the empirical sense, as the psychological power of human thought, but rather in the purely transcendental sense, as the whole of intellectual and spiritual culture."[9]

---

[9] Ernst Cassirer, *Kants Leben und Lehre* (1918), *Gesammelte Werke*, vol. 8, ed. B. Recki (Hamburg: Meiner, 2001), p. 150. In this context, it is remarkable that Cassirer's later view on culture is more akin to that of the Southwest Neo-Kantians, especially Windelband, than to that of Cohen or Natorp, whereas in his early writings, Cassirer followed more the scientific reading of Kant's transcendental philosophy. Concepts like 'object', 'reality', 'perception', or 'experience' essentially refer to scientific, law-oriented worldviews in his *Substanzbegriff und Funktionsbegriff: Untersuchungen über die Grundfragen der Erkenntniskritik* (1910), *Gesammelte Werke*, vol. 6, ed. B. Recki (Hamburg: Meiner, 2000). However, in his *Philosophie der symbolischen Formen* (1923, 1925, 1929), he acknowledges *autonomous* forms of a "primitive thinking" as related to our non-scientific "world of perception" (*Wahrnehmungswelt*); see, for example, *Philosophie der symbolischen Formen: Dritter Teil, Phänomenologie der Erkenntnis*, in *Gesammelte Werke*, vol. 13, ed. B. Recki (Hamburg: Meiner, 2002), pp. 13–18, 52–53. Retrospectively, Cassirer describes this shift in "Zur Theorie des Begriffs: Bemerkungen zu dem Aufsatz von G. Heymans" (1928): "What I now believe to see more clearly and sharply than in the discussion in my earlier work is this: that for such a 'theory of meaning' mathematics and the mathematical sciences will always be an important and indispensable *paradigm* but they do not constitute the whole sphere of meaning itself. The entire sphere of 'exact' concepts ..., in order to be correctly understood, grasped, and assessed as a particular kind of meaning, must be contrasted with other forms of giving meaning [*Sinngebung*]. ... For we can no longer attempt to infer the general form of the 'concept in general' [*Begriff überhaupt*] from the particular form of mathematical and mathematical-physical concepts" (*Gesammelte Werke*, vol. 17, ed. B. Recki, Hamburg: Meiner, 2004, p. 84). On Cassirer's development and his change in view around 1920 (the beginning of the Weimar Republic, 1919), Cassirer's *Zur Einsteinschen Relativitätstheorie. Erkenntnistheoretische Betrachtungen*, 1921), see also John Michael Krois, *Cassirer. Symbolic Forms and History* (New Haven: Yale University Press, 1987), and Michael Friedman, *A Parting of the Ways: Carnap, Cassirer, and Heidegger* (Chicago, IL: Open Court, 2000), chapter 6.

2. THE *CRITIQUE* AS A "TREATISE ON THE METHOD" (B XXII)

i. The precursors of Neo-Kantianism

In what follows, I will focus on those Neo-Kantians who on the one hand gave the most detailed account of Kant's first *Critique*, and on the other were most influential on subsequent Kant interpretations. Although there are authors who are sometimes, or even standardly, taken to be Neo-Kantians, such as Natorp, Vorländer, Paulsen, Riehl, Vaihinger, Windelband, Rickert, Bauch, or Lask, this chapter will not touch, or will only secondarily touch, on them because their interpretation of the *Critique* is either not very articulate, or is more of a self-standing theory than an interpretation, or is without any significant impact on other prominent interpretations.[10] The main focus will thus be Cohen's and Cassirer's account of the *Critique*. But in order to fully appreciate their achievements, it may be helpful to have an idea of the philosophical background for their interpretations.

Otto Liebmann and **Friedrich Albert Lange** are generally seen as significant pathfinders of Neo-Kantianism. It is always difficult to determine the beginning of a philosophical movement, and Klaus Köhnke has already shown that Liebmann was not one of the most powerful proponents of Neo-Kantianism.[11] But from early on, Liebmann's *Kant und die Epigonen* (1865) was taken to be one of the avatars of the movement.[12] This historical reconstruction was at least partly due to the stereotypical sentence with which Liebmann closed chapters 2–5 as well as the whole book: "we must return to Kant."[13]

---

[10] Following the terminology introduced by Anderson, the authors treated here count as orthodox Neo-Kantians who share the "commitment ... to the idea that every norm, or claim to 'validity', must have some a priori or non-contingent 'transcendental' basis" (Anderson, "Neo-Kantianism," 306). Since the works of Windelband or Rickert, who are "orthodox" Neo-Kantians in Anderson's sense, present self-standing theories rather than interpretations of the *Critique*, I will nevertheless not deal specifically with them here. For Windelband's and Rickert's anti-psychologisms, see Anderson, "Neo-Kantianism," 313–18.

[11] See Köhnke, *Entstehung*, p. 214.

[12] See Bruno Bauch's Preface to the 1912 reprint of Liebmann's *Epigonen*, as well as Wilhelm Windelband, "Otto Liebmanns Philosophie," *Kant-Studien* 15 (1910), III-X.

[13] Otto Liebmann, *Kant und die Epigonen: Eine kritische Abhandlung*, ed. B. Bauch (Berlin: Reuther & Reichard, 1912), p. 216 and passim ("Es muß auf Kant zurückgegangen werden").

However, it was not the historical Kant nor the *Critique of Pure Reason* in particular that these proto-Neo-Kantians found worth reconsidering. They recognized the criticisms put forward by Kant's "epigone" and tried to separate what they considered fruitful from what was owed to the German *Schulphilosophie* and therefore speculative and untenable. "It is our task", Liebmann starts his investigation, "to separate the real substance (*echten Gehalt*) of Kant's doctrine from the impure dross."[14] In order to get a clear view of the "real Kant," one has basically to free the *Critique* from its "medieval convolutions," and concentrate on "the quintessence of the Critique of Pure Reason",[15] the Transcendental Aesthetic. Whereas the Analytic and the table of the categories in particular "must and can significantly be simplified,"[16] according to Liebmann and other Neo-Kantians, the practical use of the ideas of reason (Dialectic) cannot be dealt with in critical philosophy at all. The ideas concern what cannot be said, and therefore belong to aesthetics and religion. This anti-metaphysical impetus, which was closely connected with their anti-idealistic or anti-Hegelian attitude, was later weakened and replaced with attempts of a critical approach to ethics, aesthetics, and religion.

It takes Liebmann only a few pages to tell the reader what the tenable part of the *Critique* – what the *echte Kant* – consists in. His main concern, however, is Kant's "so clear mistake": "How did Kant come to incorporate a 'thing in itself' into his philosophy which obviously leaves no room for it?"[17] Before he gives his own answer to this question, Liebmann defends Kant against his epigoni – for instance "Aenesidemus" (Schulze) – who "had no idea of the *transcendental* point of view" because he did not see that "'to be empirical' and 'to be a representation' is the same for Kant."[18]

Liebmann's own way leads back to Kant's epistemology, which no longer includes the thing in itself but is restricted to the world of appearances. As we shall see soon, it was especially his interpretation of those appearances constituting the scientific world of experience that was conducive to the rise of Marburg Neo-Kantianism. For Liebmann, no understanding, no reason can grasp what is beyond the phenomenal world. To talk about things in themselves or even noumena mistakenly

---

[14] Ibid., p. 18.   [15] Ibid., p. 20.   [16] Ibid., p. 21.   [17] Ibid., p. 28.
[18] Ibid., p. 45. In the subsequent chapters, Liebmann deals with other prominent epigoni, the idealistic (Fichte, Schelling, Hegel), the realistic (Herbart), the empirical (Fries), and the transcendent (Schopenhauer) tendencies. All of them tried but failed to improve on Kant's philosophy because they followed, or at least did not sufficiently modify, Kant's doctrine of the thing in itself.

suggests that reason has access to that "intelligible world." In lieu thereof, Liebmann recommends the "contemplation" of masterpieces of art – Beethoven's *Ninth Symphony*, Raphael's *Sistine Madonna*, Goethe's *Faust* – in order to find the "surrogate" for Kant's thing in itself, a "feeled answer", "nothing to be said or even thought."[19] Liebmann thus sees the true basis of philosophy in what he takes to be the phenomenalism of the Aesthetic, and with some qualification of the Analytic. He does not even mention the Doctrine of Method, and he completely disapproves of the Dialectic.

In returning to and renewing Kant's first *Critique*, Lange, like Liebmann, saw a chance to overcome the poor condition into which philosophy had been brought by the materialism that had been the response to Hegelian idealism. Both of them separated what could help in accomplishing this task from the parts of Kant's theoretical philosophy that they took to be radically flawed. According to Lange's *Geschichte des Materialismus* (1866), the problem that led Kant beyond his predecessors was that of the possibility of synthetic judgments *a priori*. It finally brought Kant to his famous insight that "the objects, or what is the same thing, the *experience* in which alone they can be cognized (as given objects) conforms to those concepts" (B xvii). But for Lange, these objects are "only *our* objects ..., the whole objective world is ... not absolute objectivity, but only objectivity for man and any similarly organized beings, while ... the absolute nature of things, the 'thing-in-itself,' is veiled in impenetrable darkness."[20] He completely discards Kant's thing in itself as the "supersensible"[21] and expels the concept of freedom from epistemological consideration.[22]

What became important for later Neo-Kantians was Lange's reassessment of sensibility as a source of knowledge on an equal footing with the understanding. But they did not follow his view of critical philosophy, which, for Lange, is mainly concerned with the apriority of space and time as "forms that, through organic conditions, which might be wanting in other beings, necessarily follow from our mechanism of sensation."[23] So in the end, Lange not only got rid of the thing in itself, as had Liebmann, but also modified the positive part of Kant's transcendental philosophy in such a way that it is difficult to see anything

---

[19] Ibid., pp. 65, 67.
[20] Lange, *Geschichte des Materialismus und Kritik seiner Bedeutung in der Gegenwart*, ed. A. Schmidt (Frankfurt am Main: Suhrkamp, 1974), p. 455.
[21] Ibid., p. 484.
[22] Influenced by Cohen, Lange accepts the thing in itself as a limiting concept in the second edition of his *Geschichte* from 1873–75; cf. Ibid., p. 498.
[23] Ibid., p. 485.

transcendental in it. His reconstruction of the Transcendental Aesthetic in terms of a "psychophysical arrangement, by virtue of which we are compelled to intuit things in space and time"[24] can hardly be brought into agreement with the *Critique*. Nevertheless, according to Karl Vorländer, one of the Marburg Neo-Kantians of the next generation, Lange's *Geschichte* "most effectively marked the victory of the neo-Kantian movement."[25] Although the Marburg Neo-Kantians soon dissociated themselves from Lange's psychophysicism, his *Geschichte* was among the mostly read works of the entire Neo-Kantian movement.[26] What "most effectively marked that victory" is on the one hand Lange's rejection of Kant's separation of sensibility and understanding at the outset of the *Critique*, and on the other his insistence on Kant's doctrine that objective knowledge is necessarily restricted to appearances. Lange was much more explicit in his criticism of the *Critique* than Liebmann was. But both of them shared the view that the *echte Kant* was an empirical realist without being a transcendental idealist. And both of them thought that what they subsumed under Kant's idealism would better be captured by aesthetic and religious contemplation.

It is by no means accidental, however, that they almost entirely restricted their interest in the *Critique* to the Aesthetic, and that Lange sought the solution of the *Critique's* problems in psycho-physics. For among their immediate predecessors and contemporaries were, on the one hand, Friedrich Adolf Trendelenburg and Kuno Fischer, who had an intense debate over Kant's theory of space and time,[27] and on the other hand, the likes of Johann Friedrich Herbart, who explicitly criticized Kant for the weak psychological basis of his (supposedly) faculty-oriented *Critique*, and Hermann Helmholtz, who denied *a priori* valid forms of intuition and argued instead for a physiological interpretation of Kant's theory of experience.[28]

---

[24] Ibid., p. 486; Lange acknowledges the influence of psycho-physiologists such as Herman Helmholtz, Wilhelm Max Wundt, and Gustav Theodor Fechner; see sect. III, chs. II-IV of his *Geschichte*, pp. 776–872.

[25] Vorländer, *Geschichte der Philosophie*, 2nd ed., vol. 2 (Leipzig: Dürr, 1908), p. 420.

[26] See Köhnke, *Entstehung*, p. 233.

[27] For a documentation of this controversy over our fundamental ignorance about spatio-temporal properties of things in themselves, and also for Cohen's philosophical dependency on his teacher Trendelenburg, see Köhnke, *Entstehung*, pp. 257–72.

[28] See Herbart, *Psychologie als Wissenschaft, neu gegründet auf Erfahrung, Metaphysik und Mathematik*, in *Sämtliche Werke*, vol. 5, eds. K. Kehrbach and O. Flügel (Langensalza: Beyer, 1890), pp. 426–34, and

The opening period of Neo-Kantianism came to an end when the Marburg Neo-Kantians first rejected the interpretation of the *Critique* as a mere theory of the psycho-physiological organization of our cognitive apparatus, and, second, widened the scope of Kant scholarship. They not only took the whole *Critique* into consideration but also tried to make sense of the rest of Kant's critical philosophy. Although the philosophical starting point of Cohen was prefigured by Lange, to whose advocacy Cohen owed his Marburg professorship, Cohen argued for a "resurrection of Kant's authority"[29] against those psycho-physiological distortions of central tenets of the *Critique*. It was Cohen who most extensively and explicitly dealt with Kant's first *Critique*, and it was Cohen's epistemological reading of the *Critique* in relation to which every subsequent Neo-Kantian positioned himself. Whether his *Kants Theorie der Erfahrung* was seen, depending on one's own perspective, as a close commentary of the *Critique* or as a systematic reconstruction, this work represents the *Critique*'s return to serious philosophical discussion in 1871.

ii. The Marburg school

The most distinctive feature of the Marburg account of the first *Critique* is its epistemological orientation as opposed to the prevailing

Helmholtz, *Die Thatsachen in der Wahrnehmung* (1878), repr. in *Vorträge und Reden*, 4th ed., vol. 2 (Braunschweig: Vieweg, 1896), pp. 213–47. It seems that despite his remoteness from the *Critique's* literal meaning, Helmholtz must nevertheless be seen as a Kantian of some sort and therefore one of the precursors of Neo-Kantianism. In his *"populärwissenschaftliche"* address given in Königsberg in 1855, he advertises Kant's philosophy as the only possible way to close the recently opened gap between philosophy and natural science (see Helmholtz, "Über das Sehen des Menschen" [1855], repr. in *Vorträge und Reden*, 4th ed., vol. 1, Braunschweig: Vieweg, 1896, pp. 85–117). But still, Helmholtz's Kantianism remains within the limits of what Kant called a "physiological derivation" (A 86/B 119) when he speaks of the "standpoint of a human being without any experience" as the starting point of the investigation of space and time as subjective and necessary forms of intuition that are "given ... insofar [their] perception is tied to the possibility of motoric impulses of the will for which the mental and bodily ability must be given to us by our organisation" (*Thatsachen in der Wahrnehmung*, p. 225). Instructive Neo-Kantian readings of Helmholtz can be found in Michael Friedman, *Dynamics of Reason: The 1999 Kant Lectures at Stanford University* (Stanford, CA: Center for the Study of Language and Information, 2001), pp. 108–110, and in David Hyder, *The Determinant World: Kant and Helmholtz on the Physical Meaning of Geometry* (Berlin: De Gruyter, 2009), p. 578a, fn 28, line 7.
[29] Cohen, *Kants Theorie der Erfahrung* (Berlin: Dümmler, 1871), p. vi.

psychologistic approaches of the time. According to the Marburg Neo-Kantians, the main merit of the *Critique* is its restriction to an investigation of the epistemological problem of the *objective validity* of judgments. But on his way to accomplishing this task, Kant stopped short right before the "true transcendental idealism." Therefore, against the historical Kant, the *Critique* must be freed from the dualistic remnants of the *Dissertation*. Since this means, in the Neo-Kantians' eyes, that intuition should be conceived as a kind of thinking, their interpretation in the end amounts to a significant modification of Kant's own views.

Following **Hermann Cohen**, the Marburg Neo-Kantians see "Kant's originality and mission,"[30] in analogy to Newton, who established a new (mathematical) method in physics, in the discovery of the *transcendental method*. This method reliably leads to the philosophical constitution of natural science by way of an analysis of the "elements of a cognizing consciousness which are sufficient and necessary for the foundation and the assurance of the fact of science."[31]

As we shall see shortly, however, when Cohen started his inquiry into Kant's philosophy, he still tried to incorporate some kind of psychologistic reading into his otherwise transcendental or anti-psychologistic account of the *Critique*. This led to substantial ambiguities and tensions that he later sought to overcome. But from the outset, Cohen was very clear on his stance toward the exactness of a historical reading of Kant on the one hand, and the fruitfulness of a systematic reconstruction on the other: most of those who tried to disprove Kant can easily be refuted by pointing at the "documentary existing Kant."[32] Thus there is no way around the

[30] Cohen, *Theorie*, 2nd. ed., 1885, p. 63.
[31] Ibid., p. 108. For an instructive discussion of Cohen's stance toward the relationship between transcendental logic and the exact sciences, see Alan Richardson, "'The Fact of Science' and Critique of Knowledge: Exact Science as Problem and Resource in Marburg Neo-Kantianism," *The Kantian Legacy in Nineteenth-Century Science*, eds. M. Friedman and A. Nordmann (Cambridge, MA: MIT Press, 2006), pp. 211–26. However, keeping in mind the Neo-Kantian goal of a philosophical account of the principles of all kinds of cultural articulations, not only the (natural) sciences but also ethics, aesthetics, religion, and even pedagogy and political economy (see section 1), Richardson's classification of scientific vs. more general notions of experience on the one hand, and epistemologist vs. psychologistic conceptions on the other, appears to be overgeneralized with respect to (at least) some of the Southwest Neo-Kantians (for example, Rickert), who take a more general but nevertheless epistemologist reading to be the appropriate way; see Richardson, "'The Fact of Science'" pp. 215–16.
[32] Cohen, *Theorie*, p. iv.

"daunting labor"[33] of making oneself familiar with all the relevant texts. Any kind of free-floating positive or negative talk about the *Critique* must be replaced with an accurate analysis. At the same time, this analysis should be critical – that is, pointing out where and in what respect Kant went wrong. Since this presupposes a specific angle from which one judges the text, any valuable Kant interpretation cannot avoid a "systematic partisanship": "It is impossible to make a judgment about Kant without revealing in every single line the world which oneself has in mind."[34]

According to the Marburg interpretation of the *Critique*, the given element of cognition cannot consist in brute sense data. Thus, in the wake of Cohen's *Theorie*, the Marburg Neo-Kantians minimize the Kantian sensible, push back the empirical beyond what Kant called perception, and thereby transform the *given* into facts of (natural) science. In a regressive investigation, we find that these empirical facts are the products of the subject's construction. The elements of this construction – forms of intuition and pure concepts of the understanding – are not to be found *a priori*; they must rather be grasped in a "psychological reflection," as Cohen points out against earlier interpretations in the first edition of his *Theorie*.[35] Marking the difference between this metaphysical deduction or exposition on the one hand and the transcendental deduction of those elements on the other, their validity as presuppositions of our experience must be seen as necessary, or *a priori*.

When Cohen comments on the title of his book in relation to the *Critique*, his point of view becomes evident: "*Kant discovered a new concept of experience*. The critique of pure reason is a critique of experience."[36] Or a "doctrine of the *a priori*,"[37] as he declares in the first sentence of the book. When he later deals with the chapter on the Principles of Pure Understanding, Cohen explains this basic concept of experience: "The goal is: the explanation of the possibility of synthetic propositions *a priori*. They make for the real and entire content of experience. And this content of experience, given in mathematics and pure natural science, which is demonstrated against *Hume* as an *a priori* possession, shall be explained from its possibility."[38] So it is not experience in general but scientific experience that this theory attempts to

---

[33] Ibid., p. iv.   [34] Ibid., p. v.

[35] Ibid., p. 105. Cohen follows Kuno Fischer here, who made this point against Jakob Friedrich Fries; see Fischer, *System der Logik und Metaphysik oder Wissenschaftslehre*, 2nd ed. (Heidelberg: Bassermann, 1865), § 55, pp. 111–13.

[36] Ibid., p. 3.   [37] Ibid., p. iii.

[38] Ibid., p. 206. See also ibid., p. 208: "Kant wanted to explain experience, which is given in mathematics and natural science with the character of necessity and universality, from its possibility."

provide with a philosophical foundation. For only the synthetic *a priori* propositions of mathematics and the mathematical sciences are capable of an *a priori* justification. Unlike analytic propositions, which exhibit only the relationships between concepts independently of experience, synthetic propositions contain the "manifold of the inner sense" unified under the "synthetic unity of apperception."[39] This unity is the function of the understanding that is to be specified in terms of categories. The latter in turn have only "the value of forms of cognition as *schematized* concepts," according to Cohen.[40]

Against those who think that the categories are imaginary concepts as well as against those who think that Kant's forms of intuition are empty non-entities (*leere Undinge*), Cohen aims to demonstrate that sensibility and understanding as the two stems of knowledge necessarily belong together.[41] So in order to show that with the *Critique* the disjunction of innate and acquired has been overcome with respect to basic representations such as space and time and the categories, Cohen argues that there are several levels (*Grade*) of the *a priori*.

There is on a first level – equivalent to Kant's metaphysical exposition – an *a priori* of space and time "in a psychological respect," where the "originality" (not "beginning") comes as a fact of consciousness (*Tatsache des Bewusstseins*) that all spatial sensations presuppose the intuition of space.[42] On the second level, according to Cohen, Kant excludes any "possibility of the physio-psychological explanation of the gradual emergence of spatial representations" in the transcendental exposition (cf. B 40–41).[43] He reaches this second apriority with the proof that space is a *form* of sensibility. But since this is only the *subjective* form of our intuition, we have at this point the necessity of space (and time) but no universality. The forms of intuitions could still be seen as "innate."[44] Therefore, only the third and decisive step enables us to leave

---

[39] Ibid., p. 197.   [40] Ibid., p. 190.

[41] See Ibid., p. 86; Schopenhauer, for instance, found in the chapter on the categories only "groundless assumptions" (*Die Welt als Wille und Vorstellung*, vol. 1, "Anhang: Kritik der Kantischen Philosophie", 3rd ed., Leipzig: Brockhaus, 1859, p. 536).

[42] See Cohen, *Theorie*, p. 88–89. For a sympathetic reading of Cohen's interpretation of the Aesthetic (though restricted to the second edition of Cohen's *Theorie*), see Rolf-Peter Horstmann, "Hermann Cohen on Kant's Transcendental Aesthetic", *Philosophical Forum* 39 (2008), 127–38.

[43] Cohen, *Theorie*, 1871, 90.

[44] In contrast to the second edition, here Cohen thinks that in some sense this second level is still within the psychological domain for which Herbart had justly demanded a real demonstration that Kant had failed to provide; see Cohen, *Theorie*, 1871, 38–39.

behind the dichotomies of innate/aquired or subjective/objective: "Space is a *constitutive condition of experience*."[45] According to Cohen, this is what Kant means by space (and time) as "formal conditions of sensibility" (B 122).

By making the best sense of the Transcendental Aesthetic, Cohen's reconstruction is also meant to be a solution to the already mentioned controversy between the Aristotelian Trendelenburg and the Kantian Fischer over the subjectivity of space and time: the constructive aspect of the transcendental *a priori* that becomes most obviously evident in §24 of the B-deduction excludes any further sense of objective space and time independent of that construction. So, in contrast to Liebmann and Lange, Cohen thinks that Kant was correct when he claimed the empirical reality of space and time *and* their transcendental ideality. There is not and cannot be any "higher, more secure objectivity"[46] because the *a priori* subjectivity of space and time is a condition of and thus logically prior to their objectivity.

For Cohen, there is a structural identity between the apriority of space and time and the apriority of the categories – or, more precisely, the category. He suggests a philosophical deviation from Kant's text here because the apriority of the categories, their "real *a priori*,"[47] is restricted to the synthetic unity of the manifold as such. The specific – categorial – unities cannot be demonstrated *a priori* in a strict sense.

As with the forms of intuition, we find the categories in a "psychological reflection,"[48] which is what Cohen sees in the Metaphysical Deduction of the Categories. The categories manifest themselves as original and unifying concepts of judgmental forms. Thus they are the subjective forms of the understanding. But the "real *a priori*" of the third level concerns their function as formal conditions of experience, and this is what prevents the *Critique* from dissolving into a "discipline of psychology":[49] "As space is the form of outer intuition, and time the form of inner intuition, so is the transcendental apperception *the form of the categories*. The self-consciousness is the transcendental condition under

---

[45] Ibid., p. 94.

[46] Ibid., p. 54. See also Cohen's contribution to this dispute in "Zur Controverse zwischen Trendelenburg und Kuno Fischer", *Zeitschrift für Völkerpsychologie und Sprachwissenschaft* 7, eds. M. Lazarus and H. Steinthal (Berlin: Dümmler, 1871), 249–96. See also Vasilis Politis, "Invoking the Greeks on the Relation between Thought and Reality: Trendelenburg's Aristotle – Natorp's Plato," *Philosophical Forum* 39 (2008), 191–222 (here pp. 195–98), as well as note 27, together with the paragraph to which it is appended.

[47] Cohen, *Theorie*, 1871, p. 119.   [48] Ibid., p. 105.   [49] Ibid., p. 123.

which we produce the pure concepts of the understanding."[50] According to Cohen, the transcendental deduction of the categories argues for these productive processes of the consciousness as the formal conditions of any objective or scientific experience rather than as contingent attempts to interpret the world.

Although Cohen sees a "systematic harmony between the first and the second edition of the *Critique*,"[51] he prefers the second edition for its clearer deduction of the categories (esp. §24) and a clearer exposition of the Analogies, including their close relationship with the principles of Newtonian mechanics. From the *Critique's* second edition as well as the *Prolegomena*, it becomes evident that these latter principles demand an *a priori* explanation, which leads to the pure principles of the understanding as "the basic forms of that thinking which connects the manifold of intuition through synthetic unities."[52]

The transcendental analysis of real scientific knowledge reveals space, time, and the category as the indispensable elements of the construction of experience.[53] It is not the case that they are innate, and in this sense *a priori*. Rather, conversely, they are the *a priori* elements of experience, and therefore seem to be innate. What lies beyond these elements is a "transcendent*al* x,"[54] the necessary concept of an object independent of our spatio-temporal and categorial cognition: "One sees that there is no other difference between the object in general and the thing in itself, which is the object as distinguished from its representation, than that

---

[50] Ibid., p. 144. As the latter part of this quote already indicates, Cohen finds in the transcendental deduction of the categories the "germs of a sound psychology" (ibid., 164). Cohen criticizes Kant for conceptualizing these syntheses and their forms in terms of "faculties of the soul" (ibid.). It is rather due to the "mechanical processes" of our consciousness that we produce the categories. – These passages are omitted in the second edition of the *Theorie*.

[51] Ibid., p. 250; see also pp. 139, 208, 211.

[52] Ibid., p. 209. With the dismissal of psychological questions in the second edition of Cohen's *Theorie* this emphasis on the Principles of the Understanding as the center of the theory of experience becomes even stronger. Here he puts more weight on the deduction of the categories (the Principles chapter) than on the deduction of the category as the synthetic unity of cognition (Kant's transcendental deduction of the categories); see Cohen, *Theorie*, 2nd. ed., 1885, pp. 267, 291, 406–413. For an instructive account of Cohen's respective development through the first three editions of the *Theorie*, see Geert Edel, "Transzendentale Deduktion bei Kant und Cohen," *Kant im Neukantianismus: Fortschritt oder Rückschritt?* eds. M. Heinz and Ch. Krijnen (Würzburg: Königshausen & Neumann, 2007), pp. 25–36, esp. 29–34.

[53] See Cohen, *Theorie*, 1871, p. 104.   [54] Ibid., p. 177.

between the transcendental *subject* and the transcendental *object*. Both are for Kant ... = x."[55] From the perspective of the Aesthetic, this "x" is a limiting concept (*Grenzbegriff*) or a "noumenon in the negative understanding"[56] because there is no way to form an intuition of this thing in itself. From the perspective of the Analytic, however, this "x" is a positive noumenon, or an "idea, an *extended* category".[57]

What Cohen finds worth dealing with in regard to this positive noumenon is only the cosmological idea of the unconditioned in relation to the world as a whole. The psychological idea must either be dealt with in psychology, where it ceases to be an idea, and is instead transformed into a determinable concept; otherwise it dissolves itself into the dust (*Dunst*) of a paralogism. The theological ideal has practical meaning as a regulative principle, but otherwise has no constitutive validity for the entire field of theoretical, or scientific cognition. Against the "almost unbelievable misunderstandings" of Schopenhauer and Trendelenburg,[58] Cohen defends the solution of the Antinomies as an essential element of Kant's transcendental idealism, which contains the methodological program for the sciences. First, in the series of appearances, there is no first and no final element, and second, the different appearances become united and re-divided all over again in order to find a purer unity in another idea: "The thoroughgoing task of the *Critique* is: the objects turn around the concepts, the reduction of absolute realities to objective validities, the dissolution of substances into ideas = extended categories, the construction of appearances out of forms which the transcendental investigation affirms as a priori = conditions for the possibility of experience."[59]

In the second edition of Cohen's *Theorie* (1885), we find extensions and revisions that are incisive enough to call it "not only considerably enlarged but in fact totally rewritten."[60] The main thrust of these revisions lies in an exclusive focus on the epistemological (at the expense of the psychological) aspect of our cognition. With Cohen's turn from mental description to propositional content, the mechanical or psychical processes of our consciousness as necessarily complementing the *quaestio iuris* no longer had any explanatory value. More generally, this move marks the watershed between the psychologistic and the more characteristic Neo-Kantian anti-psychologistic readings of the *Critique*.[61] Whereas in the first edition of the *Theorie*, Cohen thought that space, time, and the category were proven as *introspectively given* elements in the metaphysical deductions, he later came to see them as necessary

---

[55] Ibid., p. 179.   [56] Ibid., p. 253.   [57] Ibid., p. 256.   [58] See Ibid., p. 164.
[59] Ibid., p. 257. See also ibid., pp. 269–70.
[60] Horstmann, "Hermann Cohen", 128.
[61] See Cohen, *Theorie*, 2nd. ed., 1885, pp. 69–79.

conditions of any objective or scientific *judgments*, and this is what the metaphysical deduction reveals. Hence, according to the second edition of the *Theorie*, the "fact of science" is not so much the starting point of a regressive analysis that directs us to the discovery of a solipsistic "fact of consciousness." Rather the "fact of science" must itself be seen as the intersubjective fact of "scientific consciousness."[62] The transcendental method is, therefore, fundamentally different from the empirical method in psychology. It is supposed to reveal the necessary conditions of the *validity* of scientific propositions, and this in turn is the only concern of theoretical philosophy.

Cohen now speaks of a "collision with psychology"[63] since it may seem that psychology is required for the explanation of the first level (*Grad*) of the *a priori*. But in fact, the metaphysical deduction of time and space shows that the genetic account of psychology already presupposes the metaphysical difference between sense impressions on the one hand and the intuition of time and space on the other. The question of "*how* it can happen"[64] that we have representations, that we conceive of causality, and so on is irrelevant when we consistently follow the transcendental method. Explicitly dealing with Bernhard Riemann's and Helmholtz's writings on space and geometry,[65] Cohen now comes to the conclusion that the representations of space, time, and any other *a priori* element of experience must not be seen as unities of consciousness the *existence* of which were to be explained in a theory of cognition. Moreover, the *Critique* cannot and does not deal with an individual or personal consciousness at all. Transcendental apperception is "the transcendental condition, the highest principle of all synthetic *judgments*, rather than a transcendent state of a personal consciousness."[66] Cohen therefore corrects every passage of the first edition where the term "theory of cognition" (*Erkenntnistheorie*) appears and replaces it with the term "critique of cognition" (*Erkenntniskritik*). Not pretending that we must and can give an analysis of the psychological processes, as the term "theory" does, a "critique of cognition" rather can and must draw the line between psychological questions about the existence of representations and philosophical questions about their validity: insofar as we – along the lines of Kant's metaphysical deductions or expositions – discover and systematize the "fundamental tools of science" and subsequently give a deduction of their objective reality, we "confirm the transcendental value of validity (*Geltungswert*) of *a priori* conditions and do critical philosophy according to the transcendental method."[67]

[62] Ibid., p. 198.   [63] Ibid., p. 198.   [64] Ibid., p. 207.
[65] Ibid., chap. 5, esp. pp. 223–31.   [66] Ibid., p. 142, my emphasis.
[67] Ibid., pp. 217, 582.

Cohen now finds that Kant's forms of intuition must be taken as "sources of scientific methods" (*Verfahrungsweisen*) rather than as psychological processes; space and time are the "sources of the lawfulness of all spatiality and temporality" establishing the laws of geometry, arithmetic, and dynamics.[68] Along these lines, the dichotomy of intuition and thinking appears in a new light: the former designates the method of mathematics, the latter the method of mechanics. They are not "forms of the mind" but have transcendental significance only with regard to the "validity" of specific scientific cognitions.[69]

Cohen is well aware that mechanics or the exact sciences in general that find their foundation in Kant's Principles do not exhaust the concept of a science of nature. In an explicit departure from Kant's text, he therefore understands the positive concept of a thing in itself as the transcendental idea of all scientific knowledge, including the teleological science of organic bodies. As the Antinomies chapter of the *Critique* has demonstrated, the deductive method of the mathematical sciences presupposes the idea of the unconditioned. But, as Cohen now adds to the Kantian doctrine, the inductive method of descriptive sciences of nature, which, unlike the mathematical sciences, are not based on the concept of motion, also presupposes the transcendental idea of the unconditioned because it necessarily includes the regulative idea of purposiveness.[70] Only with this correction of Kant's theory can we see the ideal unity of all scientific experience. With regard to their transcendental validity as regulative principles, Cohen finally claims an "aequipollence" of the concepts of the thing in itself, the unconditioned, the idea, the limiting concept, and the systematic unity. They serve for the unification of the natural sciences to a systematic experience that also includes the description of nature. Hence, implicitly secularizing Paul's *Epistle to the Corinthians* (1:13), the Jewish philosopher Cohen summarizes: "The thing in itself is not so much an object as rather the task of limitation [*Begrenzungsaufgabe*]. ... we identify the big chain of questions contained in that 'scope and connection' [of our knowledge] as the thing in itself which is to be objectivized synthetically, as the problem [*Aufgabe*] to be solved. ... All our knowledge is piecemeal, only the thing in itself is complete; since the task [*Aufgabe*] of research is infinite."[71]

---

[68] Ibid., pp. 210–11.   [69] Ibid., p. 584.

[70] In the third edition of the *Theorie*, Cohen even calls the end or purpose (*Zweck*) a "category" (Cohen, *Theorie*, 1918, p. 795).

[71] Cohen, *Theorie*, 2nd. ed., 1885, p. 520. See also ibid., pp. 501–26, 556–74, as well as footnote 100, together with the paragraph to which it is appended. That limiting concept of an 'X' becomes systematically relevant in Cohen's book *Das Princip der Infinitesimal-Methode und seine*

In contrast to Kant, therefore, who had no idea of a second, or even a third *Critique* when he wrote the first *Critique*, Cohen's reconstruction of the first *Critique* already includes a smooth transition to the teleological investigations of the *Critique of the Power of Judgment*. Although some of the Southwest Neo-Kantians criticized Cohen for his focus on *scientific* experience and his underestimation of the teleological aspects in Kant, it was in point of fact Cohen's rapprochement of the first and the third *Critiques* that led the Southwest Neo-Kantians to their even stronger appreciation of the third *Critique*. Central concepts here are *telos* and system. I will come back to their approach briefly later.

Cohen's colleague at Marburg, **Paul Natorp**, definitely belongs among the Neo-Kantians. But unlike Cohen, he never published a book explicitly elaborating on Kant's first *Critique*. In his paper "Kant und die Marburger Schule," however, he gave a concise account of the Marburg interpretation of the *Critique* that was influential insofar as it pointed out some of Cohen's significant "corrections" of the historical Kant, or what Natorp took them to be. Apart from Cohen's interpretation of the thing in itself as a pure limiting concept that limits experience by nothing else than "its own creative law,"[72] Natorp sees the most important of these corrections in the mitigation of Kant's dichotomy of sensibility and understanding. Whereas Cohen tries to accommodate this change in view to the original Kant, saying essentially that Kant himself rescinded the strict separation in §26 of the second-edition deduction, Natorp intensifies this revision: "Intuition ... *is* thinking, not mere thinking of laws but complete thinking of objects."[73] However, Natorp does not

Geschichte: ein Kapitel zur Grundlegung der Erkenntnisskritik (Berlin: Dümmler, 1883); see Marco Giovanelli, "Kants Grundsatz der 'Antizipationen der Wahrnehmung' und seine Bedeutung für die theoretische Philosophie des Marburger Neukantianismus," *Kant im Neukantianismus: Fortschritt oder Rückschritt*? ed. M. Heinz and Ch. Krijnen (Würzburg: Königshausen & Neumann, 2007), pp. 37–55.

72 Natorp, "Kant und die Marburger Schule", *Kant-Studien* 17 (1912), 193–221; here 199. Equally programmatic, although different in scope, Rickert's *populärwissenschaftliche* address *Die Heidelberger Tradition in der Deutschen Philosophie* (Tübingen: Mohr, 1931) can be seen as a Southwest counterpart to Natorp's paper.

73 Natorp, "Kant und die Marburger Schule", 204; see also the third edition of Cohen's *Theorie*, 1918, pp. 275–76, 785–87, and his *Logik der reinen Erkenntnis*, 2nd ed., (Berlin: Cassirer, 1914), pp. 12, 150–51, 192–93. For differences between Cohen's and Natorp's views on logic and the *Critique of Pure Reason*, see Helmut Holzhey, "Zu Natorps Kantauffassung," *Materialien zur Neukantianismus-Diskussion*, ed. H.-L. Ollig (Darmstadt: Wissenschaftliche Buchgesellschaft, 1987), pp. 134–49, and Wolfgang Marx, "Die philosophische Entwicklung Paul Natorps im

want to do away with that conceptual distinction altogether. He rather sees intuition and thinking as two indispensable and inseparable aspects of experience in a different sense from Kant's. Experience is taken to be a form of determinacy, and determination always comes from thinking. So there is, first, a merely "abstract determinacy of thinking of general laws" and, second, the "full," or "real determination .... Both of them are 'spontaneity' but one of them as the law, the other as the real execution of the always spontaneous, never receptive determination according to the law."[74] More generally, for Natorp, sensibility does not contain the given matter of cognition. It rather represents the category of modality, the expression of the *problem* of the determinacy of experience. Therefore what is beyond the determination of thought, the "given," is in fact not given. It is a hypothesis postulated by the thinking.

Natorp's shift is remarkable insofar as he thinks that transcendental philosophy, especially the Transcendental Aesthetic, can no longer be called into question by non-Euclidean geometry or the theory of relativity because the universal validity of the (three-dimensional) determinacy of space is nothing that can or must be presupposed for transcendental philosophy: "In the light of the 'fact of science' as it developed since Kant, he himself would certainly have seen ... that in the basic determinations of time and space *thinking* typically expresses itself as '*function*' and not as 'intuition' which still had some character of receptivity."[75] Thus philosophy cannot be fixed by scientific data. It rather must follow the critical or "transcendental method ..., *progressive, developing* and also coping with an *infinite* development" of the sciences.[76] With this move, Natorp established Kant's methodology, not specific concepts and theorems, as that which rightly survived the "corrections" of the *Critique*. Thus, transcendental method essentially

Hinblick auf das System Hermann Cohens," *Materialien zur Neukantianismus-Diskussion,* ed. H.-L. Ollig (Darmstadt: Wissenschaftliche Buchgesellschaft, 1987), pp. 66–86.
[74] Natorp, "Kant und die Marburger Schule," 205.
[75] Natorp, "Kant und die Marburger Schule," 203–4. For Natorp's interpretation of the fact of science as a *fieri*, the never accomplished enterprise of systematic experience, see Holzhey, "Zu Natorps Kantauffassung," pp. 137–40. For Cohen's and Natorp's – and in greater detail – the Southwest Neo-Kantian views on the problems of the Transcendental Aesthetic, see Ch. Krijnen, "Das konstitutionstheoretische Problem der transzendentalen Ästhetik in Kants 'Kritik der reinen Vernunft' und seine Aufnahme im südwestdeutschen Neukantianismus," *Kant im Neukantianismus: Fortschritt oder Rückschritt?* eds. M. Heinz and Ch. Krijnen (Würzburg: Königshausen & Neumann, 2007), 109–34.
[76] Natorp, "Kant und die Marburger Schule," 199.

means two things: first, whatever philosophy deals with it must be related to the historical facts of science, ethics, art, or religion. Second, it has to show and elaborate the lawful ground (*Gesetzesgrund*) or *logos* of those creative acts of culture.[77] Since the *Critique* is restricted to the self-cognition of reason, it is able to account for any science, even those that have emerged since Kant, or will emerge in the future. But in fact it is really more the spirit than the letter that we should fall back upon, according to Natorp, and in this sense, his way of understanding Kant by transcending him is typical for the ensuing Neo-Kantian movement. Following what they take to be the transcendental method, the Neo-Kantians systematically investigate a variety of epistemological problems that can be related to the *Critique* only *as* problems, not with regard to Kant's solutions. Natorp acknowledges that "almost everything in Kant's explanations must be changed."[78] So, when he gives an outline of the logical structure of mathematics and the mathematical science of nature, it is only the conceptual framework that remains of the *Critique*.[79] In the synthetic part of his *Logik*, however, Natorp tries to specifically defend Euclidean geometry against non-Euclidean geometry, and Newton's mechanics against Minkowski's and Einstein's principle of relativity.[80] He later dismissed this intervention in the real sciences and instead recommended its better treatment in Cassirer's essay on Einstein's theory of relativity.[81]

[77] See Natorp, "Kant und die Marburger Schule," 196–97, 216–17. In this context, one should also consult Natorp's book on Plato because it includes an approximation of Plato's and Kant's idealisms, or more specifically of Plato's *logos* and Kant's transcendental method; see Natorp, *Platos Ideenlehre: Eine Einführung in den Idealismus* (Leipzig: Dürr, 1903), esp. pp. 159, 190–92, 300, 375, 382. For a sympathetic interpretation of Plato as a Neo-Kantian, see Politis, "Invoking the Greeks," 203–22.

[78] Natorp, "Kant und die Marburger Schule," 201.

[79] See Natorp, *Logik: Grundlegung und logischer Aufbau der Mathematik und mathematischen Naturwissenschaften in Leitsätzen zu akademischen Vorlesungen* (1904), 2nd. rev. ed. (Marburg: Elwert, 1910).

[80] Ibid., pp. 54–55, 68–70.

[81] See the Preface to the 2nd ed. of Natorp, *Die logischen Grundlagen der exakten Wissenschaften* (Leipzig: Teubner, 1921), p. vii, as well as Cassirer, *Zur Einstein'schen Relativitätstheorie* (1921), in *Gesammelte Werke*, vol. 10, ed. B. Recki (Hamburg: Meiner, 2001), 1–125. For Einstein's dependence on Neo-Kantian principles, see Massimo Ferrari, "Cassirer, Schlick und die Relativitätstheorie: Ein Beitrag zur Analyse des Verhältnisses von Neukantianismus und Neopositivismus," *Neukantianismus: Perspektiven und Probleme*, eds. Ernst Wolfgang Orth and Helmut Holzhey (Würzburg: Königshausen & Neumann, 1994), pp. 418–41, here 420–22.

Like Natorp and other Neo-Kantians, Ernst Cassirer shared his Marburg teacher's Cohen's concern about Kant's distinction between constitutive and regulative principles and tried to give it a new sense. But unlike the Southwest Neo-Kantians, his primary interpretative target, at least in his early writings, was still Kant's first – not the third – *Critique*. Following his predecessors, Cassirer sees the starting point of Kant's critical project and thus the transcendental method in the reconstruction of the constitutive elements of certain basic "facts" – the "form and structure of mathematics and mathematical physics," "the conduct of 'common human reason'," as well as "art" and "organisms."[82] But unlike the rest of the Neo-Kantians (Cohen excepted), Cassirer goes into a detailed (re-)interpretation of the first *Critique*, the central tenet of which he takes to be the proof of "the objective validity of our *a priori* cognitions."[83] The latter are, for Cassirer, the "ultimate logical invariants": "A cognition is called *a priori*, not as if it were in any sense *before* the experience; rather because and insofar as it is included in every valid judgment about facts as their necessary *premise*."[84]

With a specific interpretative tendency, Cassirer's main interests in the *Critique* concern the thing in itself, the concept of self-consciousness, space and time, and the problem of objectivity. The *Critique's* "primary concern is the lawfulness and the logical structure of experience."[85]

Since Cassirer locates Kant in the Platonic tradition of ideas, for Cassirer it is the meaning of concepts such as quantity or identity, the basic predicates of possible things that indicate their objectivity. Clearly emphasizing the epistemological perspective of the *Critique*, it is "not the things but the judgments about things" that is the "material" for the Kantian investigation.[86] As Cassirer reformulates Kant's Copernican turn, what up to Kant was seen as a "difference in being" must henceforth

---

[82] Cassirer, *Kants Leben*, pp. 264, 297, 323–24.

[83] Cassirer, *Das Erkenntnisproblem in der Philosophie und Wissenschaft der neueren Zeit* (vol. 2, 1907), *Gesammelte Werke*, vol. 3, ed. B. Recki (Hamburg: Meiner, 1999), p. 613. Apart from vol. 2, book 8, chap. 2 of his *Erkenntnisproblem*, his Kant biography *Kants Leben und Lehre* (1918) is also of particular interest here.

[84] Cassirer, *Substanzbegriff und Funktionsbegriff*, p. 290. For an instructive interpretation of Cassirer's view of the *a priori* and his relationship to Cohen and Natorp in this regard, see Massimo Ferrari, "Ist Cassirer methodisch gesehen ein Neukantianer?" *Der Neukantianismus und das Erbe des deutschen Idealismus: die philosophische Methode*, eds. D. Pätzold and Ch. Krijnen (Würzburg: Königshausen & Neumann, 2002), pp. 103–21.

[85] Cassirer, *Erkenntnisproblem*, p. 553.

[86] Ibid., p. 554; see also ibid., pp. 547–49, and Cassirer, *Kants Leben*, pp. 143–44.

be seen as a "difference in validity."[87] Consequently, when Kant introduces the concept of a "consciousness in general" (B 143), this must not
be seen as a psychological faculty. It rather refers to a purely logical
relationship of value (*reines logisches Wertverhältnis*), the judgmental
connection of concepts, considered not as taking place in an empirical
subject but as governed by universal principles. It is the determinacy of
the synthesis of the understanding guided by categories that is responsible for the transformation of mere perceptions into experience that
otherwise "would be incapable of any scientific fixation and hence any
universal communicability."[88]

Following Cohen and Natorp, who had prepared this interpretative
shift from ontology to epistemology, from facticity to normativity, from
the "given" to construction, Cassirer focuses on the Kantian insight
about the "critical objectivity of space and time."[89] Attributing the
architectonic status of the Aesthetic to Kant's ontologically dualistic
view in the *Inaugural Dissertation*, Cassirer sees the full realization of
Kant's theory of space and time in §§24–26 – especially the footnotes to
B 155 and 160 – where Kant points to the synthetic aspect of the forms of
intuition. It is this synthetic or constructive unity of space and time as
formal intutions that is responsible for the objectivity of scientific judgments. Space and time are not genus concepts that could only be identified as analytic unities, essentially unrelated to objects of possible
experience: rather, "Space and time are 'intuitions' because they are the
first and *fundamental* systems to which any empirical content must be
related; because only due to them the raw material of sensation first and
originally is elevated to a conscious 'representation'."[90] Calling them
"subjective" does not refer to us as individuals who have perceptions. It
rather means their ideality as a "*standard* for all our judgments about
'things' and 'facts'."[91] Indeed, this ideality or validity as a norm (*Geltung
als Norm*) is what makes them even "more objective than things" but,
again, only as synthesized unities, not as mere forms. Space and time as
specific and unique rules of synthesis have the objectivity of a condition
(*Bedingung*) but not the objectivity of a thing (*Ding*).[92] What is of the

---

87 Cassirer, *Erkenntnisproblem*, p. 555.
88 Ibid., p. 565. For Cassirer's criticism of Kant's adherence to the terminol-
    ogy of faculty psychology (*Vermögenspsychologie*) which gave rise to the
    interpretation of the understanding as a "form-giving manufactory," see
    his *Philosophie der symbolischen Formen: Dritter Teil, Phänomenologie
    der Erkenntnis*, 222.
89 Ibid., p. 574.   90 Ibid., p. 585.   91 Ibid., p. 590.
92 See Ibid., pp. 587, 584. Cassirer here clearly invokes the German etymo-
    logical proximity of *Ding* and *Bedingung*; the latter entered the German
    language via philosophical terminology only in the eighteenth century.

utmost importance for Cassirer is that one and the same synthesis is responsible for the unity in an intuition and in a judgment (cf. A 79/ B 104–105). Intuition and concept are merely two basic directions or "two separate sides of the basic act of synthesis in general."[93] Synthesis is for Cassirer an indivisible process of cognition, originating from the understanding and oriented toward the intuition, which consequently should not be seen as distinct faculties. Intuition and concept rather are two aspects – a "pure logical correlation"[94] – of one and the same cognition.

When it comes to the problem of self-consciousness, or subjectivity, Cassirer notices a delusive proclivity of our thinking to transform the pure means of cognition into an equal number of objects of cognition, or to transform conditions into things, and thus to treat the pure I as a "separate object" instead of a mere "vehicle" of concepts.[95] The empirical I of an individual is epistemologically as accessible as any other empirical object – through intuitional and conceptual determination. The synthetic unity of apperception, however, is nothing but the correlate of the transcendental object of any representation = X. Furthermore, since this concept of an object in general (*Gegenstand überhaupt*) signifies "that something, the concept of which expresses such a necessity of synthesis" (A 106), transcendental apperception is nothing substantial but one of the "general logical requirements" or "constitutive elements" of any cognition, to be detached only in a transcendental analysis of the real experience. Kant's idealism, Cassirer points out, was never about the existence of things, but about the validity of cognitions.[96]

According to Cassirer, when Kant freed the concept of appearance (*Erscheinung*) from its metaphysical remnants, he worked out what was already foreshadowed in Newton's physics. An appearance or phenomenon is not merely a partial expression of the true being.[97] Any attempt to find out the nature of things as they are in themselves is futile because as an objective cognition, such an investigation must be related to a subject of cognition and thus deprive that thing of its transcendent status. Objectivity (*Gegenständlichkeit*), therefore, can only be obtained "by the inclusion of a certain condition of cognition."[98] From the point of view of the Transcendental Logic, not that of the Transcendental Aesthetic, Cassirer determines the thing in itself as "the horizon that

---

[93] Ibid., p. 576. See also his *Kants Leben*, pp. 153–63, 167–68.
[94] Cassirer, *Erkenntnisproblem*, p. 583. See also ibid., pp. 626–27, and *Pure Reason*, A 250.
[95] See Cassirer, *Erkenntnisproblem*, p. 613.
[96] Ibid., p. 607. See also ibid., pp. 591, 601, 617–18.   [97] Ibid., p. 615.
[98] Ibid., p. 618.

encompasses the perimeter of our experience."[99] Building on Cohen's *Theorie*, and in contrast to those precursors of Neo-Kantianism who simply tried to rid the *Critique* of the thing in itself, Cassirer attempts to give a deduction the result of which is that the thing in itself – the unconditioned – must be conceived of as the limit (*Grenze*) of experience, the necessary idea of the absolute completeness of the series of conditions of experience. But since the concept of experience does not include anything fixed and unrevisable apart from the general rules on the basis of which empirical knowledge is obtained and justified, the thing in itself is a regulative idea for the "continuously evolving process of determination."[100]

Cassirer sees the idea of a thing in itself as the problem that led Kant through the first *Critique* and beyond. The thing in itself is rejected as a self-standing entity. But it must be retained as the necessary counterpart to the essentially relative experience, first as a correlate for the passivity of sensibility, then as a counterpart to the objectifying function of the category, and finally as a scheme of the regulative principle of reason. The positive idea of the unconditioned, however, is only revealed in ethics as the lawgiving authority, or the concept of personality.[101] Therefore, no thing or being but the "ought" is the "true 'unconditioned'."[102] According to Cassirer, epistemology and ethics are not to be distinguished with regard to their objects. It is only a matter of the "point of view of judgment," a unification of the manifold in terms of causality in the first case, and of freedom in the second. Hence, for Cassirer, "the dissolution of the 'given' into the pure functions of cognition is the ultimate goal and the result of the critical doctrine."[103]

In Cassirer, we find the clearest and most precise articulation of the Marburg Neo-Kantian, and perhaps any Neo-Kantian interpretation of Kant's first *Critique*. Based not only on Kant's published writings but also on many letters and *Reflexionen*, Cassirer's interpretation is inventive and at the same time true to Kant like no other Kant interpretation before

[99] Ibid., p. 621. For Cassirer's systematic elaboration of the relationship between "object" and "concept" referring to Kant, see *Philosophie der symbolischen Formen: Dritter Teil, Phänomenologie der Erkenntnis*, pp. 362–76.

[100] Cassirer, *Erkenntnisproblem*, p. 628. See also Cassirer, *Kants Leben*, pp. 195–96, as well as his *Substanzbegriff und Funktionsbegriff*, p. 290; see Friedman's critical treatment of this doctrine in his *Parting of the Ways*, chap. 6, as well as in his "Ernst Cassirer and the Philosophy of Science," *Continental Philosophy of Science*, ed. Gary Gutting (Malden, MA: Blackwell, 2005), pp. 71–83.

[101] See ibid., p. 635–66. [102] Cassirer, *Kants Leben*, p. 209.

[103] Ibid., p. 638.

his, carefully indicating where he departs from the authentic text in order to find a new sense in the general idea of Kant's transcendental method.

iii. The Southwest German school

The explicit defense of Kant's first *Critique* as an anti-psychological epistemology is not the central problem of the Southwest Neo-Kantians. They take for granted that transcendental philosophy must have its own distinctive status independent of psychology. Whether or not they see the *Critique* as having accomplished this task depends on the specific view of their members. The Marburg interpretative concern with the dividing line between psychology and philosophy is here replaced with the distinction between a logic of being and a logic of validity, or, put differently, between an ontology and a "doctrine of value (*Wertwissenschaft*)."[104] Kantianism – not Kant at any rate – must be defended as an axiological enterprise.

Furthermore, the Southwest school is not so much concerned with Kant's concept and theory of experience as the Marburgers were. Two of the basic concepts that help identify the Southwesterners' main interests are value (*Wert*) and world-view (*Weltanschauung*). For **Heinrich Rickert**, for instance, who together with **Wilhelm Windelband** was one of their most influential representatives, the doctrine of science (*Wissenschaftslehre*) or epistemology (*Erkenntnistheorie*) has significance only when systematically related to the "entire doctrine of world-view," or the "philosophy of modern culture."[105] Consequently, it is not the first *Critique* but Kant's ethics and teleology that most attracted the Southwest Neo-Kantians. Windelband claims in his *Präludien* that Kant's "world-view," which he takes not to be a "personal opinion" or "private metaphysics," is best articulated in "the most gigantic of his works, the *Critique of the Power of Judgment*."[106] Pointing to the achievements of his teacher Kuno Fischer, who drew his

---

[104] Rickert, *Der Gegenstand der Erkenntnis: Einführung in die Transzendentalphilosophie*, 6th ed. (Tübingen: Mohr, 1928), p. 268.

[105] Rickert, *Kant als Philosoph der modernen Kultur: Ein geschichtsphilosophischer Versuch* (Tübingen: Mohr, 1924), p. 151.

[106] Windelband, *Präludien*, pp. 150–51. See also Bruno Bauch, *Immanuel Kant*, 3rd, enlarged ed. (Berlin: De Gruyter, 1923), p. viii: "It was of utmost importance to me [...] to proceed from the *Critique of the Power of Judgment*." For the influence of the Southwest Neo-Kantianism on Frege, see, Gottfried Gabriel, "Windelband und die Diskussion um die Kantischen Urteilsformen," *Kant im Neukantianismus: Fortschritt oder Rückschritt?* eds. M. Heinz and Ch. Krijnen (Würzburg: Königshausen & Neumann, 2007), pp. 91–108.

attention from Kant the "all-crushing" philosopher to Kant's transcendental idealism in its "metaphysical meaning,"[107] Windelband emphasizes the primacy of practical reason together with a mutual dependence of all three *Critiques*.

Thus, where the Southwest Neo-Kantians take issue with the first *Critique* they focus on its metaphysical rather than its epistemological aspects: "the main problem of this work is not a theory of the sciences of experience but the old and constantly recurring *problems* of metaphysics. ... The basic question is: what can we know about the 'nature' of the *world* and of the *deity*?"[108] But unlike Cohen or Cassirer, the Southwest Neo-Kantians rarely go into the details of the first *Critique*'s arguments – "the proofs that Kant provides for his view are irrelevant here."[109]

What both the Marburg and the Southwest Neo-Kantians seem to have in common, at least at first glance, is that they take a "fact" as the starting point of their investigations. But on closer examination, this similarity is hardly substantial. As we saw in Cohen and Cassirer, it is the "fact of science" the objectivity of which must be explained by transcendental philosophy. For Rickert, on the other hand, transcendental logic (which in part takes on the form of a semantic analysis) begins with the "fact" of the "sphere of value" as the "transcendent 'something' in general," the "sense independent of the act of thinking."[110] This "transcendent sense" must be assumed if our thinking is to be "true thinking," or "cognition."[111] Transcendent here means that the validity of propositions is independent of the actual acts of thinking. Rickert's sphere of value is not a limiting concept (*Grenzbegriff*), as the Marburg school saw Kant's thing in itself. In fact, the thing in itself does not have any importance for him because the fundamental concept of a "transcen*dent* object"[112] is what *constitutes* the truth of any cognition.

Therefore, independent of the intrinsic cogency of the Southwest "logic, doctrine of truth, or theory of cognition,"[113] Kant's first *Critique* must obviously be transcended not only with respect to the "letter" but also with respect to its "spirit," as Rickert hesitantly observes. He discards Kant's distinction between theoretical and

---

[107] Windelband, "Kuno Fischer und sein Kant," *Kant-Studien* 2 (1897/98): 1–10, at p. 8.

[108] Rickert, *Kant als Philosoph der modernen Kultur*, p. 153.

[109] Rickert, *Kant als Philosoph der modernen Kultur*, p. 156.

[110] Rickert, "Zwei Wege der Erkenntnistheorie," pp. 193, 203, 171, 206.

[111] See Rickert, "Zwei Wege der Erkenntnistheorie," 209.

[112] Rickert, "Zwei Wege der Erkenntnistheorie," 174; my emphasis.

[113] Rickert, "Zwei Wege der Erkenntnistheorie," 170.

practical because the correct theory of cognition is a transcendental "science of value,"[114] whereas, for Rickert, Kant's first *Critique* essentially follows the "method of transcendental psychology."[115] His own science of value is a critique of reason, but it owes as much to Bolzano and Husserl as it does to Kant.[116] It results in a new conception of reality (*Wirklichkeit*). The form of the object of experience is described by the forms of judgments; the object itself, or as Rickert terminologically – not substantially – modifies this term, the objectivity (*Gegenständlichkeit*) is an "*ought*, recognized in the act of judging,"[117] a requirement to think in categories.

For Rickert, there are two kinds of categories or forms, constitutive and methodological categories. The former concern any cognition including the cognition of the individual case, while the latter only concern the cognition of the general, or the (scientific) laws. Thus Rickert sees his theory as transcending the Kantian (and Marburg Neo-Kantian) restriction of epistemology to the methodology of mathematical sciences.[118] Kant's distinction between judgments of perception and judgments of experience can only be understood in light of that Kantian restriction – and consequently must be dropped. For any cognition, not only scientific or general cognition, comes in a categorial form: "For us, there is no longer a *pure* a posteriori judging. 'Thinking' in the form of a judgment that acknowledges the ought and thus the category conceptually precedes any particular perception and experience."[119]

---

[114] See Rickert, *Kant als Philosoph der modernen Kultur*, pp. 165 and 215.

[115] Rickert, "Zwei Wege der Erkenntnistheorie", 227.

[116] See Rickert, *Gegenstand der Erkenntnis*, pp. 299–301.

[117] Rickert, *Gegenstand der Erkenntnis*, pp. 213, 222.

[118] See Rickert, *Gegenstand der Erkenntnis*, pp. 202–24, 405–32.

[119] See Rickert, *Gegenstand der Erkenntnis*, p. 379. In my paper, "'An almost single inference' – Kant's deduction of the categories reconsidered" (*Archiv für Geschichte der Philosophie* 90, 2008, pp. 323–45), I follow a systematically similar line; my central argument, however, entails that Kant himself overcame the distinction between pre-categorial judgments of perception and actual judgments of experience with the second proof step of the revised deduction of the categories in the *Critique*. See also Cassirer, *Substanzbegriff und Funktionsbegriff*, pp. 264–65, who is critical of the distinction between judgments of perception and judgments of experience but does not take into consideration the deduction of the categories that I think is essential for this purpose. For a Neo-Kantian view on this Kantian distinction, emphasizing the aspect of intersubjectivity, see also Alois Riehl, *Der philosophische Kriticismus und seine Bedeutung für die positive Wissenschaft*, vol. II/2, *Zur Wissenschaftstheorie und Metaphysik* (Leipzig: Engelmann, 1887),

Although reaching quite different results, **Emil Lask**, perhaps the most brillant student of Rickert's, elaborates on that doctrine of the categories.[120] According to his two-worlds theory (*Zweiweltentheorie*), there must be separate sets of categories to conceive of the world of being and the world of validity, respectively. Time, space, materiality (*Dinghaftigkeit*), causality, and so on, are categories or predicates of the former, whereas truth, identity, ground and consequence, and so on are categories or predicates of the latter. Thus, for Lask, transcending Kant really means modifying the fundamental direction of Kant's first *Critique*. He calls Kant's view of the impossibility of comprehending the non- or supersensible "Kant's dogma": "Kant believed that he had to confine himself to the pure reason that cognizes reality or nature. He assigned a place in the positive part of the Critique of Reason only to the cognition of the sensible hemisphere of being."[121] In explicit opposition to Kant, Lask demands a "logic of philosophy" investigating the world of non-being (*Nichtseiendes*) or the sphere of validity: "After Kant who preceded us with his Copernican deed (*Kopernikanische Tat*), this act must prove itself in its full range."[122] Since Kant's transcendental idealism is based on the restriction of our cognition to objects of possible experience, this second Copernican deed effectively means rejecting the

pp. 63–64. I did not discuss Riehl in this chapter because, in my view, his critical realism is more foreign to Kant's "spirit" than the critical idealisms of the Marburg or the Southwest schools. One could even say that he is closer to nineteenth-century positivist tendencies. For the relationship between Riehl and the neo-positivism of Moritz Schlick, see Michael Heidelberger, "Kantianism and Realism: Alois Riehl (and Moritz Schlick)," *The Kantian Legacy in Nineteenth-Century Science*, ed. M. Friedman and A. Nordmann (Cambridge, MA: MIT Press, 2006), pp. 227–47, esp. pp. 233–40.

120 For the (only at first glance implausible) claim that Lask replaces Rickert's concern with the "*quaestio juris*" with a new focus on the "*quaestio facti*," see Rudolf Malter, "Heinrich Rickert und Emil Lask," *Materialien zur Neukantianismus-Diskussion*, ed. H.-L. Ollig (Darmstadt: Wissenschaftliche Buchgesellschaft, 1987), pp. 87–104; see also Dina Emundts, "Emil Lask on Judgment and Truth," *Philosophical Forum* 39 (2008), 263–81, who sheds some interesting light on Lask's otherwise rather obscure doctrine of judgment. For a survey of Lask's personal and philosophical development away from Kant and Kantianism, including his early scepticism regarding Kant's theoretical philosophy, see Frederick Beiser, "Emil Lask and Kantianism," *Philosophical Forum* 39 (2008): 283–95.

121 Lask, *Die Logik der Philosophie und die Kategorienlehre: Eine Studie über den Herrschaftsbereich der logischen Form* (Tübingen: Mohr, 1911), p. 20; cf. also ibid., pp. 27, 89, 131–2.

122 Lask, *Logik der Philosophie*, p. 23.

Critique of Pure Reason. For Kant, the principle that "the conditions of the *possibility of experience* in general are at the same time conditions of the *possibility of the objects of experience*" (A 158/B 197) is intrinsically related to the principle that any objective experience comes in the form of judgments. Therefore, for Kant, the basic element of the transcendental logic is the judgment. Lask, by contrast, finds that judgments are unable to capture the real object: "The judgment must be expelled from the field of transcendental logic. It is separated from the latter by an abyss, and thus must be understood as something of merely formal-logical relevance."[123] For Lask, the essence of the judgment consists in a systematically distorted representation of the object itself.

One might think that **Bruno Bauch**'s interpretation of the thing in itself comes somewhat closer to the *Critique* than that of his teacher Rickert, for he relates his view to the authentic text as well as to the Marburg view. According to Bauch, Cohen was right that the first *Critique* was concerned with a mathematical-scientific concept of experience. But from this point of view, the thing in itself, as a mere task, appears to be a historical remnant of dogmatism: "Kant himself overcame realism and dogmatism in his critical philosophy, for the 'thing in itself', in its most important and real function, is logical: it is the transcendental, logical basis of the unity of a particular appearance."[124] Therefore, in order to fully understand Kant's real *telos*, we have to work out the concept of the "real lively experience of the eternally lively reason"[125] which reveals itself only from the standpoint of the third *Critique*. It is in the latter work that Bauch finds the suspension (Hegel's *Aufhebung*) of the concept of intuition in the concept of concept.

With this reading of Kant, it is not surprising that at the end of the Neo-Kantian movement, as opposed to its beginning, Hegel's system is sometimes seen as the ultimate *telos* of Kant: "One could show germs in Kant which reached such a flourishing in Hegel that those 'Kantians' who do not want to know anything of Hegel were pretty helpless with their Kant."[126] When Kant in the Doctrine of Method of the *Critique* states that the world must be represented as having originated from an idea (A 816/B 844), Bauch reads this passage as revealing that Kant himself

[123] Lask, *Die Lehre vom Urteil* (Tübingen: Mohr, 1912), p. 5.
[124] Bauch, *Immanuel Kant*, p. ix.   [125] Bauch, *Immanuel Kant*, p. ix.
[126] Bauch, *Immanuel Kant*, p. 471. See also Bauch, *Die Idee* (Leipzig: Reinicke, 1926), pp. 193–194: The "new systematic fecundity" of Kant's thing in itself can be found when we see in it the "essence" which "functionally lets emerge from itself the appearance," and thereby "reaches its reality in the existence of the appearance."

already acknowledges the idea as constitutive for the world in general (*überhaupt*), and regulative only for the cognizance of the world.[127]

3. NEO-KANTIANISM AFTER NEO-KANTIANISM

When the Neo-Kantianisms of the Marburg and the Southwest schools came to an end in the 1920's, it seemed as if there were no continuation or further reception of them elsewhere. Logical positivism, *Lebensphilosophie*, phenomenology, existentialism, and hermeneutics took over with quite different agendas.

But, first, some of the distinctive exponents of those disciplines, such as Edmund Husserl, Nicolai Hartmann, and Martin Heidegger, had close philosophical and personal relations to some of the Marburg Kantians as well as to Southwest Neo-Kantians. Although Heidegger later distanced himself from Neo-Kantianism, and in particular from his teacher Rickert, Heidegger's metaphysical Kant interpretation is in certain aspects akin to the Southwest reading of the first *Critique* and their emphasis on the third *Critique*. It sounds like an echo of Lask when Heidegger in his *Kant und das Problem der Metaphysik* (1929) claims that "the new interpretation of knowledge as judging (thinking) violates the decisive sense of the Kantian problem."[128] Furthermore, recent work has shown that there

---

[127] See Bauch, *Idee*, p. 94. For a sympathetic reading of Bauch's interpretation of the *Critique*, see Werner Flach, "Das Problem der transzendentalen Deduktion: seine Exposition in der Kritik der reinen Vernunft und seine Wiederaufnahme im Neukantianismus der Südwestdeutschen Schule," *Materialien zur Neukantianismus-Diskussion*, ed. H.-L. Ollig (Darmstadt: Wissenschaftliche Buchgesellschaft, 1987), pp. 150–62, at pp. 157–62.

[128] Heidegger, *Kant und das Problem der Metaphysik*, p. 22. See also his lecture from 1920: "Lask discovered in the ought and in the value, as an ultimate experience (*Erlebtheit*), the world which was [...] factic." (Heidegger, *Gesamtausgabe*, II. Abteilung: Vorlesungen, vol. 56/57, *Zur Bestimmung der Philosophie*, ed. B. Heimbüchel, Frankfurt/Main: Klostermann, 1999, p. 122). By outlining his own account of the *Critique* in the Davos disputation with Cassirer (1929), Heidegger made his critical stance on the Marburgers (who are *the* Neo-Kantians for him) apparent: "I understand by neo-Kantianism that conception of the *Critique of Pure Reason* which explains, with reference to natural science, the part of pure reason that leads up to the Transcendental Dialectic as theory of knowledge. For me, what matters is to show that what came to be extracted here as theory of science was nonessential for Kant. Kant did not want to give any sort of theory of natural science, but rather wanted to point out the problematic of metaphysics, which is to say,

is a Kantianism to be found in logical positivism that is immediately related to the works of some of the authors dealt with in this chapter.[129] Second, there are also Neo-Kantian traces to be found in the Kantianisms of the recent past and present, especially those of the analytic tradition. A prominent example here is the work of Wilfrid Sellars, whose rejection of the "myth of the given" can be traced back to Cassirer's conclusion to his interpretation of the *Critique*: "The dissolution of the 'given' into the pure functions of cognition is the final task and the result of the critical doctrine."[130] Sellars also wrote a critical review of Cassirer's *Sprache und Mythos*. (Sellars is discussed further in Chapter 16 of this volume.)

With more attention to the historical Kant and the Neo-Kantians, Michael Friedman sees Kant's first *Critique* as providing the *a priori* principles of Newton's mechanics, which can be understood as an elaboration on the Marburg Neo-Kantian view of the *Critique* represented, for instance, by Cohen who claimed: "Kant worked out Newton's Principles to his own synthetic Principles."[131] Moreover, the epistemological or anti-psychological interpretations of the *Critique* put forward

the problematic of ontology" (Heidegger, *Kant und das Problem der Metaphysik*, p. 275). Heidegger was habilitated by Rickert in 1915 and held a professorship at Marburg (1923–27) with Natorp and Nicolai Hartmann as his colleagues.

[129] Rudolf Carnap earned his Ph.D. at Jena University in 1921 under the direction of Bruno Bauch. On the respective historical and the philosophical dependencies, see Michael Friedman, *Reconsidering Logical Positivism* (Cambridge: Cambridge University Press, 1999), and also his *Parting of the Ways*.

[130] Cassirer, *Erkenntnisproblem*, p. 638. Sellars's review of the English translation of Cassirer's *Sprache und Mythos. Ein Beitrag zum Problem der Götternamen* (Leipzig/Berlin: Teubner, 1925; *Language and Myth*, trans. S. K. Langer, New York: Harper, 1946), appeared in *Philosophy and Phenomenological Research* 9 (1948/49), 326–29. See also Sellars, "Empiricism and the Philosophy of Mind," *Minnesota Studies in the Philosophy of Science*, vol. 1, eds. Herbert Feigl and Michael Scriven (Minneapolis: University of Minnesota Press, 1956), pp. 253–329, repr. with an introduction by Richard Rorty and a study guide by Robert Brandom (Cambridge, MA: Harvard University Press, 1997).

[131] Cohen, *Theorie*, 2nd. ed., 1885, p. 245. For Friedman's interpretation of the *Critique* from a Newtonian point of view see his *Kant and the Exact Sciences* (Cambridge, MA: Harvard University Press, 1992), esp. "Introduction" and Part I. This tendency of the *Critique's* interpretation, of course, represents the fundamental characteristic of Marburg Neo-Kantianism. See, for example, Cassirer, who in his article "Hermann Cohen und die Erneuerung der Kantischen Philosophie" (1912) states: "It is the *mathematical science of nature* to which the

by Henry Allison and Paul Guyer, among others, clearly mirror the debate on the *Critique*'s psychology that launched the Neo-Kantian movement in the first place.[132]

However, the philosophical conditions under which recent Kantianisms came to exist, as well as some of its consequences, are quite different from those of classical Neo-Kantianism. This means that the historical appropriation need not and should not have the form of a chronicle. Rather, understanding Kant – and Neo-Kantianism – still means transcending them.

transcendental question must be addressed primarily." (*Gesammelte Werke*, vol. 9, ed. B. Recki (Hamburg: Meiner, 2001), p. 122). This means that Friedman is not a specific adherent of Cohen's doctrine but rather stands in that Marburg Neo-Kantian tradition notwithstanding all the differences between them. Friedman, for instance, strongly disagrees with the Marburg view that Kant's sharp distinction between sensibility and understanding is a relic of the *Dissertation* and that this view is not really essential to Kant's view in the first *Critique*. Nevertheless, his emphasis on the importance of the "fact" of Newtonian science in his interpretation places him squarely in the tradition of the Marburg understanding of Kant's transcendental method; see his "Ernst Cassirer and Thomas Kuhn: The Neo-Kantian Tradition in History and Philosophy of Science," *Philosophical Forum* 39 (2008), 239–52, where he traces back his own approach to the Marburg Neo-Kantians, especially Cassirer, while also mentioning Kuhn's explicit acknowledgement of *his* Neo-Kantian roots (see pp. 243–44). On Friedman's Neo-Kantianism, see Andrew Chignell, "Neo-Kantian Philosophies of Science: Cassirer, Kuhn, and Friedman," *Philosophical Forum* 39 (2008), 253–62; Konstantin Pollok, "Sedimente des Wissens – Kants Theorie der Naturwissenschaft und ihre Dynamisierung bei Michael Friedman," *Oldenburger Jahrbuch für Philosophie* 1 (2007), 51–82; and the collection *Discourse on a New Method: Reinvigorating the Marriage of History and Philosophy of Science*, ed. M. Dickson and M. Domski (Chicago, Il: Open Court, 2009).

[132] See Henry Allison, *Kant's Transcendental Idealism. An Interpretation and Defense*, revised and enlarged ed. (New Haven: Yale University Press, 2004), and Paul Guyer, *Kant and the Claims of Knowledge* (Cambridge: Cambridge University Press, 1987). For a discussion of these historical relations, see Guenter Zoeller, "Review Essay: Main Developments in Recent Scholarship on the Critique of Pure Reason," *Philosophy and Phenomenological Research* 53 (1993), 445–66, here pp. 461–66, as well as Anderson, "Neo-Kantianism", 300.

16 The *Critique of Pure Reason* and Continental Philosophy
Heidegger's Interpretation of Transcendental Imagination

I. INTRODUCTION

The *Critique of Pure Reason* has been a constant source of inspiration for philosophers on the European continent for well over a century. In Germany, Kant's theoretical outlook had a noticeable impact even on thinkers struggling to distance themselves from Neo-Kantian thinking. Husserl's controversial recasting of his phenomenological project along transcendental lines inherited from Kant is still evident in Heidegger's early critical revisions of Husserl's method.[1] For Jaspers, "the fate of philosophy hinges on our attitude toward Kant," more precisely, on our capacity to differentiate the critical method from the uncritical elements of Kant's system.[2]

In France, the focus on Kant's theoretical philosophy is no less prevalent, if more critical. Sartre crafts his account of phenomenon, transcendence, selfhood, and others in direct confrontation with Kant's conceptions of them.[3] Similarly, by locating the transcendental

---

For careful and critical readings of an earlier version of this chapter, I am grateful to Alfredo Ferrarin and Manfred Kuehn.

[1] Though the influence of Kant's theoretical philosophy on Husserl's transcendental turn (circa 1907) is controversial, Husserl clearly extols its legacy in "Kant und die Idee der Transzendentalphilosophie" (1924); see Edmund Husserl, *Erste Philosophie (1923/24)*, ed. R. Boehm (The Hague: Martinus Nijhoff, 1956), 286; Iso Kern, *Husserl und Kant. Eine Untersuchung über Husserls Verhältnis zu Kant und zum Neukantianismus* (The Hague: Martinus Nijhoff, 1964), 28–31.

[2] Karl Jaspers, *The Great Philosophers*, tr. Ralph Manheim (New York: Harcourt, Brace & World, 1962), 380; *Philosophy*, tr. E. B. Ashton, Volume I (Chicago: University of Chicago Press, 1969) 2, 79–83; see Raymond Langley, "Kantian Continuations in Jaspers" in *Karl Jaspers*, eds. Joseph Koterski and Raymond Langley (Amherst, NY: Humanities, 2003), 193–204.

[3] Jean-Paul Sartre, *Being and Nothingness*, tr. Hazel Barnes (New York: Philosophical Library, 1956), xlviii–l, lix, 133, 148, 225–230; *The*

conditions of knowledge in the lived body's interaction with its environment, Merleau-Ponty conceives his work as a radical revision of Kant's
philosophy.[4] In *Kant's Critical Philosophy* ("a book about an enemy"),
Deleuze attempts to show how a different hierarchical order of faculties
dominates each *Critique*, but – to Kant's credit – without suppressing
their differences or neglecting human finitude.[5] Despite arguing for a
critical inversion of Kant's Enlightenment project, Foucault insists that
his own work is critical in a manner analogous to its Kantian sense and
framed by Kant's conception of the transcendental.[6] Derrida, in his
deconstructive efforts to show that anything like a transcendent legiti-
mation must always be "deferred," repeatedly notes analogies with
Kant's transcendental moves in the *Critique of Pure Reason*, while freely
availing himself of its terminology.[7]

Transcendence of the Ego, tr. Forrest Williams and Robert Kirkpatrick
(New York: Noonday, 1957), 32–35, 43f, 54.

4 Maurice Merleau-Ponty, *Phenomenology of Perception*, tr. Colin Smith
(London: Routledge,1962), ix–xviii, 6off, 218ff, 301–304; M. C. Dillon,
"Apriority In Kant and Merleau-Ponty," *Kant-Studien*, 78 (1987): 403–423.

5 Gilles Deleuze, *Negotiations, 1972–1990*, tr. Martin Joughin (New York:
Columbia University Press, 1990), 6; *Kant's Critical Philosophy*, tr. Hugh
Tomlinson and Barbara Habberjam (Minnneapolis: University of
Minnesota Press, 1993); Deleuze returns to the *Critique of Pure Reason*
in the 1978 Cours Vincennes "Synthesis and Time" (www.webdeleuze.
com).

6 Michel Foucault, *Essential Works*, tr. Robert Hurley and others, Volume
One (New York: New Press, 1997), 303–319; see Gary Gutting, *Michel
Foucault's Archaeology of Scientific Reason* (Cambridge: Cambridge
University Press, 1989), 2f, 182–185, 198–201, 262; Christina Hendricks,
"Foucault's Kantian critique: Philosophy and the Present," *Philosophy &
Social Criticism*, 34/4 (2008): 357–382, and Marc Djaballah, *Kant, Foucault,
and Forms of Experience* (London: Taylor & Francis Group, 2008).

7 Jacques Derrida, *Dissemination*, tr. Barbara Johnson (Chicago: University
of Chicago Press, 1981), 168: "*Difference*, the disappearance of any origi-
nary presence, is *at once* the condition of the possibility and the condition
of the impossibility of truth." See Stephen Watson, "Regulations: Kant and
Derrida at the End of Metaphysics," in *Deconstruction and Philosophy*, ed.
John Sallis (Chicago: University of Chicago Press, 1987), pp. 71–86, and
Daniel W. Smith, "Deleuze and Derrida, Immanence and Transcendence"
in *Between Deleuze and Derrida*, eds. Paul Patton and John Protevi
(London: Continuum, 2003), p. 65n18. Like many French thinkers,
Lyotard draws more inspiration from the *Critique of the Power of
Judgment* than from the *Critique of Pure Reason*, but construes Kant's
analysis of knowledge's *a priori* conditions as, ironically, a precursor to the
delegitimizing revelation of science's language games; *The Postmodern
Condition*, tr. Geoff Bennington and Brian Mssumi (Minneapolis:
University of Minnesota Press, 1984), 38ff.

Yet for all the attention paid to Kant's theoretical philosophy by prominent "Continental Philosophers," only Heidegger offers an interpretation of the entire *Critique of Pure Reason*. In *Kant and the Problem of Metaphysics* (1929; hereafter *KPM*) and five different lecture courses from 1926 to 1936 (across his self-proclaimed metaphysical and post-metaphysical phases), Heidegger pores over practically every passage in the *Critique*.[8] According to Heidegger, *KPM* arose as misinterpretations of *Being and Time* (1927) mounted, and he noticed in Kant's doctrine of schematism a connection between the traditional problem of being ("the problem of categories") and the phenomenon of time, leading him to interpret Kant as "an advocate for the question of being" that Heidegger was posing (XIV/xv–xvi).[9] Heidegger views his subsequent writings on the *Critique* – the 1935–36 lectures on the System of Principles and the 1961 essay "Kant's Thesis about Being" – as attempts to "take back" the "overinterpretation" in *KPM* (XIV/xvi).[10] Leaving behind the analyses of subjectivity in *KPM*, Heidegger is bent in these later works on demonstrating how Kant's allegedly meager and overly constrained conception of being as the objectivity of objects is central to the modern, metaphysical concept of being.[11]

[8] For a review of Heidegger's "commentary," encompassing articles, books, and posthumously published lectures, see my "Heidegger's Kantian Turn: Notes to his Commentary on the *Kritik der reinen Vernunft*," *Review of Metaphysics* 45/2 (1991): 329–361.

[9] Martin Heidegger, *Kant und das Problem der Metaphysik*, ed. Friedrich-Wilhelm von Herrmann, *Gesamtausgabe*, Band 3 (Frankfurt am Main: Klostermann, 1991). All numbers placed alone in parentheses in this chapter refer to this edition, followed by a slash and the corresponding page numbers of *Kant and the Problem of Metaphysics*, tr.Richard Taft (Bloomington: Indiana University Press, 1990). All translations, however, are my own.

[10] Martin Heidegger, *Die Frage nach dem Ding: Zu Kants Lehre von den transzendentalen Grundsätzen*, ed. Petra Jaeger, *Gesamtausgabe*, Band 41 (Frankfurt am Main: Klostermann, 1984; separately published in 1962); English translation: *What is a Thing?* tr. W. B. Barton, Jr. and Vera Deutsch (Chicago: Regnery, 1967); "Kants These über das Sein" (1961) in *Wegmarken*, *1919–1958*, ed. Friedrich-Wilhelm von Herrmann, *Gesamtausgabe*, Band 9 (Frankfurt am Main: Klostermann, 1996); "Kant's Thesis about Being," *Pathmarks*, ed. William McNeill (Cambridge: Cambridge University Press, 1998), 337–363.

[11] "Kants These über das Sein," 288f; see, too, Martin Heidegger, *Nietzsche* II (Pfullingen: Neske, 1961), 231f, and *Der Satz vom Grund* (Pfullingen: Neske, 1978), 115. Heidegger likely thought that the changed ("*seynsgeschichtliche*") focus of his subsequent readings sufficed to take back the *Being and Time*-dominated "*Überdeutung*" – though in these readings Kant comes out even worse, as the purveyor of a theoretical conception of

Nonetheless, of all Heidegger's studies of the *Critique of Pure Reason*, *KPM* remains arguably the most important, not only for its impact on others but also for its controversial interpretation of the Transcendental Analytic. Heidegger himself continued to recommend the book, despite its shortcomings, publishing a fourth edition as late as 1973. Yet, in contrast to their Continental European counterparts, Anglo-American scholars have paid far less attention to *KPM*.[12] This chapter contributes to making up this deficit by reviewing *KPM*'s central contention that the Transcendental Analytic succeeds only by according transcendental imagination the foundational role in all objective cognition. Heidegger's interpretation has, I will show, not only a strong textual basis but also a distinctively phenomenological and realist character that bears heavily on the question of its plausibility. In conclusion, I also flag a fundamental limitation of the interpretation as a reading of the Transcendental Analytic, even if that phenomenological realism is granted.

Before turning to Heidegger's interpretation itself, however, a word is in order about the expression "phenomenological realism," since the coherency of conjoining these notions may be less than obvious and since Heidegger rejects both realism and idealism as ways of characterizing his own philosophical endeavors, then and later. He regards talk of realism or idealism as an outgrowth of a misguided epistemology – misguided because it rests on an ontologically naïve presumption about the nature of the subject – object relation. In this connection, Heidegger singles out the all too precipitous inquiry by Kant and his latter day "epigones" (the Neo-Kantians) into the ground of the possibility of the relation of consciousness to its object.[13] By centering the analysis of human existence in being-in-the-world rather than in being conscious, Heidegger attempts in *Being and Time* to supply the requisite fundamental ontology and, in the process, to remove the motivation for realist or idealist theories of knowledge.

the being of beings as the objectivity of objects, leaving claims for practical reason in a state of bad faith.

[12] Notable exceptions: L. W. Beck's review of *Kant and the Problem of Metaphysics* in *Philosophical Review* 72/3 (1963): 396–398; Charles Sherover, *Heidegger, Kant and Time* (Bloomington: Indiana University Press, 1971); Wayne Waxman, *Kant's Model of the Mind* (New York: Oxford University Press, 1991); Béatrice Longuenesse, *Kant and the Capacity to Judge* (Princeton: Princeton University Press, 1998); Gary Banham, *Kant's Transcendental Imagination* (London: Palgrave, 2006).

[13] Martin Heidegger, *Metaphysische Anfangsgründe der Logik*, ed. Klaus Held, *Gesamtausgabe*, Band 26, second edition (Frankfurt am Main: Klostermann, 1990), 163f.

Yet while it is wrongheaded or, at least, misleading to characterize Heidegger's own philosophical standpoint as realist, his reading of the epistemology of the *Critique of Pure Reason* has unmistakable affinities with a self-styled realist interpretation that he commends to this students – that of Alois Riehl.[14] Riehl (in)famously contends that, for Kant, "the existence of things is given, independent of consciousness," that "perceptions are the appearances of things, existing in themselves," and that Kant's idealism applies solely to space and time, as a means of restricting "pure knowledge," but not to logical functions and the concepts of things in general, corresponding to those functions.[15] "The actuality of things intuited in these forms [i.e., space and time] remains unaffected in this doctrine; even more, it is placed beyond doubt by the latter. The ideality of space refutes the idealism of external things and proves 'dualism'."[16] At the same time, Riehl insists that the dualism here is not a "doubling of objects" but the two meanings of "the same object": as appearance in relation to sensory intuition and as thing in itself "apart from this relationship."[17] As will become evident later, Heidegger's interpretation echoes each of these contentions – even as he rejects the

[14] Martin Heidegger, *Phänomenologische Interpretationen von Kants Kritik der reinen Vernunft*, ed. Ingtraud Görland, *Gesamtausgabe*, Band 25, second edition (Frankfurt am Main: Klostermann, 1987), 8; Heidegger's criticisms of Riehl's proposed "corrections" of the wording in certain passages further underscores his attentiveness to Riehl's approach; KPM 84n118/57n118, 182n252/124n252.

[15] Alois Riehl, *Der Philosophische Kritizismus*, erster Band, zweite, neu verfasste Auflage (Leipzig: Engelmann, 1908), 395–398, 403–413, 561, 571f; zweiter Band, zweiter Theil (Leipzig: Engelmann, 1887), 171. See, too, Michael Heidelberger, "Kantianism and Realism: Alois Riehl (and Moritz Schlick)" in *The Kantian Legacy in Nineteenth Century Science*, ed. Michael Friedman and Alfred Neumann (Cambridge, MA: MIT Press, 2006), 227–248. It bears noting that Heidegger's enthusiasm for this realist but Kantian approach, critical of empiricism, is evident in his earliest academic publication, "*Das Problem der Realität in der neuzeitlichen Philosophie*," which extols the work of Oswald Külpe, the other major figure (besides Riehl) associated with the Neo-Kantian realism (though Heidegger adds that Eduard von Hartmann's transcendental idealism prepares the way for this development); see Martin Heidegger, *Frühe Schriften*, ed. Friedrich-Wilhelm von Herrmann, Gesamtausgabe, Band 1 (Frankfurt am Main: Klostermann, 1978), 1–15.

[16] *Der philosophische Kritizismus*, erster Band (1908), 404; see, too, Oswald Külpe, *Immanuel Kant*, dritte Auflage (Leipzig: Teubner, 1912), 75: "*Denn warum müßte die Subjektivität der Bestimmungsmittel eine Erkenntnis der Realitäten, wie sie an sich sind, unmöglich machen?*"

[17] *Der philosophische Kritizismus*, erster Band (1908), 406.

proposition that the primary project of the *Critique* is to provide an epistemology of science.[18]

Nor are the affinities of his approach with Riehl's realistic interpretation inconsistent with the investigations that Heidegger considers paradigmatic of Husserl's phenomenology – that is, the phenomenology of the *Logical Investigations*, prior to Husserl's infamous transcendental idealistic turn. For example, Heidegger interprets intentionality as the most decisive discovery of Husserl's phenomenology precisely because Husserl does not confuse the object of intentionality (consciousness) with a representation of its object, a confusion that is the first step on the slippery slope of idealism. Moreover, in the *Logical Investigations* and in stark contrast to Brentano, Heidegger submits, Husserl not only clearly distinguishes between the object and the content of intentionality (consciousness), but also – through his theory of the coincidence of what is meant and what is perceived – provides an account of how knowledge of the object itself (*die Sache selbst*) is possible. While phenomenology investigates the essential make-up of mental acts and contents – for example, perceiving, imagining, meaning – precisely with a view to their role in knowing, Heidegger in his commentary on the *Critique* examines through a phenomenological lens Kant's own analysis of them. But neither that investigation nor Heidegger's commentary entails that *objective reality* – to use a Kantian phrase favored by Riehl – is nothing more than an idea.[19]

2. THE TWO DIMENSIONS OF *KPM*

Heidegger's interpretation of the *Critique of Pure Reason* has metaphysical and cognitive dimensions. He contends that it lays the groundwork for metaphysics in some sense and thereby coincides at some level with fundamental ontology, Heidegger's own project at the time. This metaphysical dimension dominates the opening and closing sections of *KPM*.

---

[18] The mention of Riehl in this connection is telling, not only because he is arguably the Neo-Kantian most insistent on aligning Kant's philosophical approach with contemporary scientific developments (for example, non-Euclidean geometry), but also because Cassirer presents him, for that very reason, as the author of the sort of epistemological interpretation of the *Critique* that is the very antipode and, indeed, the target of *KPM*; Ernst Cassirer, "*Bemerkungen zu Martin Heideggers Kant-Interpretation,*" *Kant-Studien* XXXVI/1 (1931): 2f.

[19] For Heidegger's interpretation of the phenomenology of Husserl's *Logical Investigations* along these realist lines, see *Prolegomena zur Geschichte des Zeitbegriffs*, ed. Petra Jaeger, *Gesamtausgabe*, Band 20 (Frankfurt am Main: Klostermann, 1979), 54ff.

Within this framework, he also interprets key passages in the Transcendental Analytic, designed to demonstrate the possibility of cognition or experience of objects (A 158/B 197) – what Heidegger dubs "transcendence" (71/48) and "finite knowing" (119/81).[20] These metaphysical and cognitive dimensions ultimately converge since only an explanation of the possibility of transcendence (empirical knowledge of objects) can provide the grounds (the fundamental ontology) for any future metaphysics. But as a reading of the Transcendental Analytic, the cognitive dimension stands on its own and, indeed, the trenchancy of Heidegger's interpretation as a whole turns on that reading and its account of the basic synthesis that makes experience of objects possible. Heidegger contends that the most consistent and compelling interpretation of the Transcendental Analytic (in the first edition) points, on Kant's own terms, to the conclusion that what makes experience of objects possible can be nothing else than the transcendental imagination, rooted in a basic sort of temporality.[21]

Heidegger sets the stage for his argument by citing the opening sentence of the Transcendental Aesthetic:

(I) In whatever way and through whatever means a cognition may relate to objects, that through which it relates immediately to them, and at which all thought as a means is directed, is intuition. (A 19/B 33)

Heidegger glosses (I) in terms of the difference between human and divine knowing, both a kind of intuition, but differing because human beings do not create what they intuit in the process of doing so. Human knowing is finite by virtue of its dependency both upon something already there that it takes up (hinnimmt) and upon the need to relate what it takes up to other things in the course of doing so.[22] Unlike the divine mind, a human mind can know only objects – that is, entities that present themselves (appear) to it – and it can only know them in a round about way (umwegig), by "running through" (thinking) more than one thing. By virtue of this discursiveness, thinking determines what is intuited "as this and that" or in view of some generality, thereby rendering it accessible and communicable to others.[23] Human knowing is finite because it is at once receptive and discursive – that is, an intuiting that takes something up

[20] Because transcendence for Heidegger means more than cognitive experience of objects, he glosses it as "finite comportment towards entities" (71/48).
[21] Heidegger reconstructs Kant's argument in five stages. The body of this chapter reviews the second, third, and fourth stages; for the remaining stages, see notes 24 and 34.
[22] Here, the affinities with Riehl's and Külpe's "critical realism" are patent.
[23] The intuited, Heidegger adds, is determined with a "view" to the universal, though the latter remains unthematized; he interprets this process of

and can do so only by thinking it (*hinnehmende und deshalb denkende Anschauung*) (30/20). Citing Kant's *Opus postumum* (and echoing Riehl), Heidegger adds that the difference between things in themselves and appearances is "merely subjective," referring to different ways that infinite and finite knowing refer to "the same object," such that "what is 'behind the appearances' is the same entity as the appearance" (32ff/21ff).

This emphasis on human knowing's finitude, underscored by the primacy of an intuition at once receptive and requiring thought, introduces the central issue of the synthesis of intuiting and thinking. Merely juxtaposing them and acknowledging their interdependency hardly suffices to explain the possibility of knowing. Citing Kant's remark that "only from the fact that they combine can knowledge arise" (A 51/B 75f), Heidegger submits that "only in the joining of both, prefigured by their structure, can a finite knowledge be what its essence demands" (36/24). The task is to understand the synthesis of these elements, not as something after the fact, but as something that allows them "to emerge in the way that they belong together and in their unity" (36/24). Since it must constitute the essential unity of pure intuitions and pure concepts that enables empirical syntheses, this synthesis is necessarily *a priori* and pure, not contingent or empirical.[24] That Kant entertained a fundamental synthesis in this way is supported, Heidegger suggests, by his characterization of pure intuition and pure thinking respectively as "synthetic" (59f/40). The sense in which each is synthetic requires their synthesis with each other, and that synthesis, Heidegger attempts to show, is the work of the transcendental imagination, "necessarily forming them originally themselves in the process of unifying them" (61/41).[25]

3. INTRODUCING THE SYNTHETIC FUNCTION OF THE IMAGINATION

According to Heidegger, Kant introduces the first characterization of "the original essential unity of the pure elements" with the observation that the spontaneity of our thinking requires that the "manifold

thinking "unifying" with intuition as a veritative synthesis, the basis of predicative and apophantic syntheses (27ff/18ff).

24 The alleged "first stage" of Kant's argument is his introduction of pure intuitions and concepts separately, without reference to the requisite synthesis – for Heidegger an irreversible misstep borne out by the uneven lengths of the transcendental aesthetic and transcendental logic and by the placement of that synthesis within the latter (59/40; 66ff/44ff).

25 The synthesis is a constitutive condition, roughly like homeostasis in an organism, at once forming and synthesizing the elements.

[provided by the pure intuition of space and time] first be gone through in a certain way, taken up, and bound together in order to produce an instance of knowledge from it. I name this action 'synthesis' " (A 77/B 102). Thinking requires what pure intuition supplies ("without which it would be completely empty") but only if it is first "gone through and gathered up" – that is, only if there has been a synthesis of it (62/42). Indeed, all analysis, Kant contends, presupposes the synthesis of a given manifold. Since that synthesis is what combines elements into a content at all, "it [that synthesis] is therefore the first thing to which we have to pay attention if we want to judge the first origin of our knowledge" (A 77/B 103). After asserting this primacy of synthesis over analysis, Kant attributes synthesis in general to the imagination:

(II) Synthesis in general is ... the mere effect of the imagination, of a blind, though indispensable function of the soul, without which we would have no cognition at all, but of which we are seldom even conscious. (A 78/B 105)

From (II) and its context, Heidegger infers that the imagination "brings about" (erwirkt) every synthetic structure essential to knowing (63/42). It is thus the imagination that synthesizes the unified whole represented in a pure intuition, with a view to a guiding unity provided by a pure concept. In the process, it secures for pure concepts the necessary cognitive traction (63/42). Kant's expositions of pure intuitions and of pure concepts of the understanding reveal in each case a synthesis – ultimately their synthesis with each other – that depends upon the imagination. The imagination is accordingly indispensable and irreducible to the functions of intuition and thinking in knowing. To underscore the distinct role of the imagination, Heidegger cites Kant's identification of the three parts of "the complete essence of pure knowledge" (63/42): the manifold of pure intuition, its synthesis by the imagination, and the concept of the understanding that lends this pure synthesis unity (A 78f/B 104).

Cautioning against a wooden conception of the relations among these three parts, Heidegger emphasizes that the manifolds unified in pure intuition and accordingly conceived do not simply meet but fit together (sich fügen) in the synthesis produced by the imagination. Pure intuition and pure understanding alike have a synthetic character thanks to their fit in the imagination's mediating synthesis. For its part, the imagination is ubiquitous, indispensable, and irreducible to intuition or understanding because it synthesizes them.

Yet even if the passages cited corroborate Kant's acknowledgment of the features of the imagination mentioned, Heidegger recognizes that these initial characterizations of the fundamental, synthetic role of the imagination are merely the first step to establishing its nature. As one might expect, matters become clearer in the transcendental deduction, the demonstration that the pure concepts of the understanding make experience of objects possible.[26]

4. THE SYNTHETIC FUNCTION OF PURE IMAGINATION IN THE TRANSCENDENTAL DEDUCTION (A)

Reiterating his realist construal of human knowing's dependence upon something given, not created in intuition, Heidegger interprets objects as something "already on hand" (70/47). Explaining how knowledge of objects is possible ("the inner possibility of transcendence" in Heidegger's jargon) entails explaining how we are able to turn to the objects in such a way that they confront us at all – that is, how we are able to orient ourselves to them as objects. Herein lies the role of pure concepts. As original representations of unity that themselves unify, they represent the constraints – the rules – that enable something to present itself as an object.[27] The transcendental deduction's task is to demonstrate how they do so, how pure concepts dictate what can be experienced and thus serve as constitutive conditions of the objecthood of objects (the possibility of knowing them). Heidegger interprets the third section of the first-edition deduction to demonstrate "how pure understanding and pure intuition are dependent upon one another *a priori*" (77/52) and, more importantly, upon "the pure synthesis" that makes their connection possible (78/52f). Heidegger follows Kant's way of proceeding (a) from the understanding (A 116–120) and then (b) "from below" (A 119) – that is, from intuition (A 120–128).

(a) *From pure apperception to imagination.* The "first way" begins with Kant's remarks on the "necessity of consciousness of the identity of oneself" for the knowledge of a manifold synthesized by it and the equivalence of that identical self-consciousness to "a consciousness of the equally necessary unity of the synthesis of all appearances according to concepts" (A 108). As Heidegger puts it, in representing a unity, it is apparent to the representing itself that it is binding itself to the unity, maintaining itself as the same throughout the process of representing the unity (78f/53). Only in this tacit apparentness to itself that it is this self-sustaining process of representing unity ("pure apperception") can

---

[26] Equivalently, the deduction's task is to demonstrate the categories' "objective reality" – to be distinguished, Heidegger submits, from their "existence" or "objective validity" (*quid juris*) (85–88/57ff).

[27] "The understanding, as a whole, provides in advance what is at odds with the arbitrary. Representing unity originally and as unifying, it places before itself a constraint that regulates in advance every possible [gathering] together" (76/50).

something confront it. Pure self-consciousness as this oblique "turning toward itself" (*Selbstzuwendung*) is a necessary condition for the fact that something confronted, in Kant's words, "matters to us" (A 116). In this way, Heidegger interprets the sense in which "the pure concept, as consciousness of unity in general, is necessarily pure self-consciousness" and "pure understanding acts as transcendental apperception in originally holding a unity up to itself" (79/53).

Heidegger's interpretation, here as elsewhere, is unmistakably phenomenological. He labors to retrieve the lived but overlooked senses of Kant's nomenclature, insofar as they are essential to cognition. Hence he construes concepts generally as unities that we keep in view, for the most part implicitly, in the process of unifying some manifold. He similarly characterizes pure apperception as the tacit obviousness of this process that can always be made explicit (79f/53f).[28]

From this phenomenological perspective, Heidegger poses the question crucial for his interpretation of these passages: what is represented in the unity? Since the understanding cannot itself be the source of what is united, it must "await" the latter, albeit in a way enabling such an encounter. In other words, the pure concepts of the understanding are directed toward the unifying of what is not yet unified in itself (79/53f). For this reason, Heidegger submits, transcendental apperception "presupposes or includes a synthesis" (A 118).

While Kant supposedly often wavers in determining precisely the unity's relation to the unifying synthesis,[29] he attributes the relevant synthesis to the imagination:

(III) The principle of the necessary unity of the pure (productive) synthesis of imagination prior to apperception is thus the ground of the possibility of all cognition, especially that of experience. (A 118)

According to Heidegger, the term 'prior' in this passage – which he takes as following from (II) – does not signify a synthesis taking place before transcendental apperception or obtaining on its own somehow. Nor could it mean anything of the sort, given the transcendental character of the synthesis. Yet, insofar as a pure concept of the understanding is "a unifying unity, that is to say, the representing is in itself unifying," something must be given a priori for this unifying to take place (80f/54f).

---

[28] Similarly, Kant writes "synopsis" (A 94), Heidegger submits, to capture how pure intuition originally forms (*bildet*) a discernible unity while tacitly holding the manifold "together" in that (142/97f).

[29] Kant wavers between asserting that the unity "belongs together" with the synthesis and that the unity is presupposed by it; the first alternative is, Heidegger contends, the "essentially necessary" one, since "the unity is from the outset unifying" (80/54).

(b) *From intuition to imagination.* Because perceptions are "encountered in a dispersed way and individually" (A 120), they need to be bundled – that is, related to one another, and for them to be bundled, their relations must be represented from the outset. Insofar as the issue is the pure relations – that is, the sorts of relations formed by a finite knower – as conditions of the possibility of knowing any empirical relations, these relations are those afforded by the pure intuition of time (A 99). The power of initially forming such relations (*Verhältnisse bildend*) in the course of representing them is the power of pure imagination (*Einbildungskraft*) (82/56). In his way, Heidegger glosses Kant's own conclusion "that there is an active capacity for synthesis of this manifold, that we call 'imagination'" (A 120). The imagination bundles the manifold in a rule-governed rather than haphazard manner (83/56). The resulting horizon of constraints contains the pure affinity among appearances – thereby explaining Kant's remark "that even the affinity of appearances becomes possible only by means of the transcendental function of the imagination" (A 123). At the same time, insofar as the imagination's temporal synthesis of perceptions is *a priori*, it must involve a constant representing of unity in itself – namely, "the standing and persisting I (of pure apperception)" (A 123). Just as the first way demonstrates the dependency of transcendental apperception (pure understanding) on pure imagination, so the second way demonstrates the dependency of pure intuition in its transcendental function on pure imagination.

(IV) We therefore have a pure imagination, as a fundamental faculty of the human soul, that grounds all cognition *a priori*. . . . Both extremes, namely sensibility and understanding, must necessarily be connected by means of this transcendental function of the imagination, since otherwise the former would to be sure yield appearances but not objects of an empirical cognition, hence there would be no experience. (A 124)

Like (III), this passage affirms that the relevant synthesis by pure imagination makes experience – that is, empirical cognition of objects (for Heidegger, "transcendence") – possible at all.

5. SYNTHESIZING BY WAY OF SCHEMATIZING

Heidegger attempts to drive home his thesis about the unifying function of transcendental imagination by turning next to the Schematism chapter, the "core" of the *Critique* (89/60; 113/77). Kant makes it clear that the task of a transcendental schema, as a "mediating representation," is to provide a category with a sensory character (A 138/B 177). With this task in mind, Heidegger considers ordinary senses of accomplishing this by picturing or imagining what something falling under the concept looks like. Heidegger claims, albeit without documentation, that Kant uses the term *Bild* ("image" or "picture") in three senses of "look" (*Anblick*): the immediate look of some entity – for example, the New York skyline; a look in the sense of a copy – for example, a photo of that skyline; and the look of something in general – for example, that photo as a picture of an urban skyline.[30] A picture can be said to picture a concept in this third sense, showing "how something appears 'in general', in the one aspect that holds for many" (94/64). We are interested in the look of this skyline only as an instance of how skylines in general look – or, better, how they have to look according to our concept of skyline. What counts as a possible picture of a skyline serves as an "advance sketch" of how skylines look as a rule, not as a list of features but as a means of outlining and highlighting what is generally meant by "skyline" (95/65).

On this interpretation, a concept is the rule for a possible look; equivalently, it sketches in advance that aspect of any possible look that accords with the rule (95/65). To be a concept at all, it must be rendered sensory in this attenuated sense. A concept affords neither an immediate intuitive look nor any free-floating mental content as such. Far from being something grasped in itself, a conceptual unity serves as a preview (*Vorblick*) that rules or governs only as long as we do not look directly at it. "The representing of the process of the rule-governedness [*Regelung*] as such is the genuinely conceptual representing" (96//65). The specific way this takes place is the work of the imagination. A schema, produced by the imagination, represents how, as Heidegger puts it, the rule dictates itself onto the look that presents itself (*wie sie sich ... in den darstellenden Anblick hineindiktiert*). As Kant himself notes, the schema, though a product of the imagination, is not itself an image but instead represents how the imagination produces the relevant image.

(V) Now this representation of a general procedure of the imagination for providing a concept with its image is what I call the schema for this concept. (A 140/B 179f)

Cognition requires conception but concepts can only play a role in cognition thanks to their respective schemata, products of the imagination. The schema for an empirical concept (for example, a house) or a mathematical concept (for example, a triangle) is a rule for producing an image

---

[30] Heidegger also distinguishes a reproduction (*Nachbild*) – for example, a photograph – from a copy (*Abbild*) (93f/63f). He also makes the general observation that since an image of something can mean the look of it, the image can mean the look of something present, past, present, future, or non-existent (92f/63).

precisely as a possible instance – one of potentially many – of the relevant concept. To distinguish this sense of "image" from others, Heidegger designates it a "schema-image." A schema-image is necessarily different from any arbitrary empirical look (*Anblick*) of a house as well as from any image or copy (*Abbild*) of that look (and *mutatis mutandis* for the mathematical concept of triangle). Indeed, only a schema, Heidegger submits, produces the sort of prefigured, regulated look that makes it possible to identify that look of a house or that aspect of a triangle at all. Kant claims that a concept immediately refers to a schema and, on Heidegger's interpretation, it is apparent in what sense he does so.[31] A concept refers to its schema as the representation of how the rule – that is, the regulative unity represented by a concept – can be imagined or envisioned.[32]

Kant appears to contradict (V) when he claims that "the schema of a pure concept of the understanding can never be brought to any image at all" (A 142/B 181). In this claim, Heidegger submits, "image" refers to schema-images for empirical and mathematical concepts. He provides little defense of this interpretative move. To be sure, the assertion comes on the heels of glosses of schemata for empirical and mathematical concepts as Kant attempts to distinguish transcendental schemata from those other schemata. Still, Kant's assertion is unqualified: the transcendental schema can never be brought "to any image at all" (*in gar kein Bild*). Yet if forced in this respect, Heidegger's interpretation has the advantage of removing the apparent contradiction in Kant's account and preserving a clear connection among imagination, images, and schemata for pure concepts.

But then what sort of schema-image is produced by the imagination for pure concepts? Drawing on Kant's talk of a "pure image" and, in particular, of time as "the pure image of all objects of the senses in general" (A 142/B 182; A 320/B 377), Heidegger contends that time, as that pure image, is the schema-image. A schema of a pure concept of the understanding represents unities "as rules imposing themselves onto any possible look" (104/71). Given the transcendental deduction's conclusion that the categories refer necessarily to time, the look in question can only

---

[31] Here, Heidegger generalizes what Kant says of an empirical concept: "*dieser bezieht sich jederzeit unmittelbar auf das Schema der Einbildungskraft*" (A 141/B 180).

[32] In keeping with the necessity of the synthesis of a concept with intuition for cognition, Heidegger contends in effect that concepts without schemata are blind – that is, only schematized concepts function epistemically: "What logic calls a concept is grounded in the schema" (98/67) and "All conceptual representing is essentially schematism" (101/69).

be the look or image of time. Heidegger accordingly reasons that the schematism of pure concepts inserts into time the rules (*hineinregeln*) provided by them. Not only is time the pure schema-image corresponding to the schemata of pure concepts, but time as such (that is, the schema-image produced by the schematism) presents the only possible pure view of them (104/71). In this way, Heidegger explicates Kant's contention that the transcendental schemata are "nothing but *determinations of time* a priori according to rules" (A 145/B 184) and, as such, a "transcendental product of the imagination" (A 142/B 181).[33]

Heidegger's gloss on transcendental schemata, like his interpretation of the imagination in the Transcendental Analytic generally, proceeds from the realist standpoint that entities are already on hand. In order for those entities to be taken up, the subject must turn toward them in the appropriate way, making the encounter possible in advance. "The turning-toward must be, in itself, a way of holding up to oneself what might present itself at all, by pre-forming [or modeling: *vorbildendes*] it" (90/61). Playing on the word *"bilden"* (which can mean imagining, picturing, and/or forming), Heidegger construes the work of the transcendental imagination as that of forming the pure preview that makes the encounter possible (and, in that sense, may be called the "horizon" for the encounter). "The pure imagination, forming a schema, provides in advance a view ("picture") of the horizon of transcendence," a view that is initially formed in the process of perceiving something but is not itself the view of any particular object (91f/62; 105/71f).[34]

6. THE ROOT SYNTHESIS OF COGNITION

Heidegger cannot ignore the fact that Kant affirms that there are only two sources of cognition, to which the two parts of the Doctrine of Elements

[33] Heidegger attributes Kant's scanty elaboration of the schemata to his failure to understand time more fundamentally as a form of self-affection rather than as a mere succession of nows (201/137).

[34] Kant's identification of the supreme principle of synthetic judgments (A 158/B 197) figures as the fifth stage in Heidegger's reconstruction of the Transcendental Analytic's basic argument. Precisely by directing itself toward entities in the sense of letting them stand opposite it, the subject forms the horizon of objectivity (118/80). This gloss of the coincidence of enabling experience and enabling experience of objects (expressed by the principle) thereby resembles Heidegger's existential analysis of the ecstatic-horizon constitutive of being-here (*Da-sein*). In addition to supplying further crucial texts about the imagination (A 155/B 194), this fifth stage provides Heidegger with the opportunity to give interpretations of the transcendental object and transcendental truth.

correspond (A 50/B 74; A 294/B 350). But Kant also identifies the imagination as one of three distinct sources of cognition (A 94, A 115, A 155/ B 194) and repeatedly – as in (II)–(IV) – characterizes the transcendental imagination's fundamental role in cognition. Far from being an external source of coupling the other two basic capacities, the transcendental imagination is "a capacity of its own that forms the unity of the other two that themselves have an essential structural relation to it" (137/94).[35]

Heidegger is not content to demonstrate Kant's affirmation of the irreducible and indispensable synthesizing role of pure imagination. Pure imagination is foundational in an even more basic sense, to which Kant himself alludes, Heidegger contends, in the following passage:

(VI) We shall content ourselves here with the completion of our task, namely, merely outlining the *architectonic* of all cognition from pure reason, and begin only at the point where the general root of our cognitive power divides and branches out into two stems. ... (A 835/B 863)

Elsewhere, Kant mentions two stems of human cognition, "which may perhaps arise from a common but to us unknown root" (A 15/B 29). But in (VI), Heidegger submits, that root counts for something that exists, even if Kant is content merely to gesture toward it.[36]

Heidegger exploits this metaphor to argue that the transcendental imagination is that common root. The use of the metaphor is bound to appear murky, especially since the relation of root to stems in this case is neither causal nor inferential. But that original synthesis, it bears recalling, supposedly underlies causal and inferential claims. Moreover, far from pretending that Kant says as much, this interpretative move explicitly aims at what Kant's basic argument allegedly points toward (*Vorweisungen*) – where even characterizing the 'imagination' as the root proves inadequate (140f/96f).[37] Thus the attempt to show that the basic argument of the transcendental analytic entails the rootedness of

---

35 This fundamental role, Heidegger adds, did not escape the notice of the German idealists (137n198).

36 At the same time, by eschewing "the crystal clear absolute evidence of a first principle," Kant's reference to the unknown root exemplifies "a philosophizing way of laying the foundation for philosophy" (37/25).

37 Heidegger thus heralds the concluding, most speculative steps of his interpretation, glosses on both the imagination's unifying temporal character, encompassing syntheses of apprehension, recognition, and apperception (A 95–110) and its roots in time's original unfolding as sheer "self-affection" (B 67f) – the essential structure of subjectivity (176–197/120–135). A complete assessment of Heidegger's interpretation would have to weigh this thesis of the temporal roots of the

intuition and concepts in the imagination is an attempt to show what Kant was struggling to say.[38]

(a) *The rootedness of pure intuition in transcendental imagination.* An intuition affords a view of something, a pure intuition a view of a whole, the parts of which are nothing but limitations of it. What distinguishes a pure intuition from an empirical intuition is the fact that the content of the pure intuition originates with the corresponding activity of intuiting without any (relevant) input of the senses. Yet the process of holding the parts together, however tacit, is a synthesis and, as established in (II), every synthesis is the work of the imagination.[39] Hence, Heidegger concludes, "pure intuiting is, in the ground of its essence, pure imagination" (143/99). As Kant himself observes, pure space and pure time are not objects to be intuited but are nonetheless something to be intuited and, indeed, as forms; what is intuited in a pure intuition is an *ens imaginarium* (A 291/B 347). These pure intuitions are not grasped thematically – that is, as objects – in the course of experience. Instead, "they form [*bilden*] from the outset the pure look that serves as the horizon of empirical objects" (143/98). Interpreting pure intuitions as forming in advance this unthematic look explains, Heidegger suggests, how we empirically intuit spatio-temporal things without having first to grasp spatial and temporal manifolds as such (145/99).[40]

(b) *The rootedness of pure understanding in transcendental imagination.* Perhaps the biggest hurdle to demonstrating the rootedness of pure understanding in the transcendental imagination is the apparent difference of thinking from intuiting and imagining. As a prelude to his argument for this rootedness, Heidegger offers several textual reasons for doubting that Kant conceives thinking as utterly cut off from intuition. He iterates the point made in (I) that the understanding is essentially "referred to" intuition, and notes Kant's identification of thinking and intuiting as species of the same genus (A 320/B 376f). Nor does logic's *a priori* status entail thinking's autonomy, since Kant himself claims that "every use of the understanding, indeed, the entire logic

imagination – not, to be sure, as something that Kant intends, but as something that his basic argument calls for.

[38] The differences introduced in the second edition supposedly confirm that Kant "shrunk back" from these implications (160f/110).

[39] While locating the difference between form(s) of intuition and formal intuition in the difference between intuition's synopsis and the understanding's synthesis (146n203/100n203), Heidegger contends that the imaginative synthesis encompasses both (142/97f).

[40] Thus, while agreeing with the Marburg Neo-Kantians that the transcendental aesthetic is incomplete, Heidegger contends that the proper response is not to reduce intuitions to concepts but to grasp their synthesis by the imagination.

must fix on the transcendental unity of apperception" (B 133n) and we know from (IV) that the unity of apperception and understanding depend, for any *a priori* cognitive function, on the imagination. Given these considerations, Heidegger infers that "preconceptions about thinking's self-standing character," as suggested by the existence of logic as a discipline, "ought not be the standard for a decision about the possibility of an origin of pure thinking from the transcendental imagination" (149/102).

Heidegger's main argument for this origin begins with a phenomenological consideration of what the depiction of the understanding as a faculty of rules entails. "To have this capacity of rules means from the outset, in the process of representing, to hold up to oneself unities that provide the lead for every possible representative unifying" (150/103). The unities in question are the categories as *a priori* conditions of the possibility of anything that is unified in our consciousness. The categories work together (holistically) and accordingly have a distinctive affinity for one another (hence, the quantity, quality, relation, and modality expressed in any empirical judgment). "But it is necessary for them as ruling, represented unities (notions or categories) not only to be brought into play on the basis of their own affinity, but also that this affinity is grasped from the outset in a persisting unity through an even more anticipatory re-presenting of this unity" (150/103). Only in the affinity of the categories with one another as a complex of rules are they enabling unities, and this affinity must be grasped and represented from the outset as the abiding sameness of that complex. Heidegger designates the representing of this abiding sameness as the basic feature of the process of letting something stand opposite the I, a process that is equivalent to representing it in the course of turning or orienting oneself toward it. Heidegger not only equates the I here with the reflexive in the phrase "turning oneself towards," but contends that this tacit reflexiveness underlies Kant's remark that the "I think" must be able to accompany all clear representations.

Heidegger is making two notable points here, albeit with insufficient argumentation. The I only is what it is in the "I think," interpreted as a tacit reflexiveness. The essence of the I, like that of pure thinking, lies in this pure – unthematic – consciousness-of-oneself that in turn can be illuminated only on the basis of the way the self is – i.e., behaving in this way or that (including cognitively) toward something. In other words, self-consciousness presupposes a self, and not vice versa. By the same token, (and this is the second, equally phenomenological point), there is never simply an "I think" but rather an "I think something" or, more precisely in the Kantian context, an "I think substance" and "I think causality." "The I brings them [the categories] in its foregoing orienting-of-itself-towards ... to the point where they can unify as represented, ruling unities" (150/103).⁴¹

The next step in Heidegger's argument is fragmentary to a fault, but the basic import is clear. The process of turning toward something (having an experience at all) presupposes, as a constitutive condition, representing or holding up to oneself in an abiding and holistic, typically tacit manner, the unities supplied by the categories. The process of pure understanding, of holding up those categorical unities as rules, is spontaneous and *a priori*, relative to actual experience, pre-determining what counts as an object of experience. But if pure understanding is this spontaneous pre-forming of the unity in which something can be encountered, then it is fundamentally the work of the transcendental imagination.⁴² Pure concepts of the understanding serve as rules only insofar as they are schematized. As Heidegger is quick to point out, Kant characterizes a transcendental schema as both a schema of the understanding (A 149f/B 179f) and a product of the imagination (A 142/B 181). The dual characterization is understandable, Heidegger adds, since the pure understanding, far from occasionally activating transcendental schemata, is what it is – representing categories as unities that enable empirical unities – only insofar as it "works with the schemata" produced by the imagination (A 140/ B 179). Hence, Heidegger infers: "The accomplishment of the pure understanding, seemingly on its own, in the thinking of the unities is, as spontaneous formative representing, a pure, basic act of the transcendental imagination" (151/104).⁴³

---

⁴¹ Again, the realism informing Heidegger's interpretation is patent. Orienting oneself toward such and such brings the categories to the point "from where, as represented, regulating unities, they can unify" – but what is unified is otherwise already on hand (150/103), even self-sufficient (122/83).

⁴² In other words, the rules must be held together in an anticipatory representation of an abiding sameness. Representation of that abiding sameness incorporates the "I think substance," "I think unity," and so on in a foregoing, unthematic orientation toward objects that allows them to stand opposite the subject accordingly. So interpreted, pure understanding is a spontaneous modeling or pre-forming (*Vorbilden*) of the unified horizon that enables cognition of objects (transcendence). But this spontaneous modeling is the transcendental schematism. Since the transcendental schematism is a product of the transcendental imagination, so is pure understanding.

⁴³ Based largely upon a phenomenological analysis of understanding and imagination, Heidegger rejects the objection that the understanding's spontaneity excludes the imagination's receptivity (qua sensory) and vice versa (153f/105).

7. "OVERINTERPRETING": CONCLUDING REMARKS

Insofar as the Transcendental Analytic sets out to explain transcendental conditions of the possibility of empirical knowledge, Heidegger's interpretation makes a powerful case that it succeeds – by Kant's own lights, at least in the *Critique*'s first edition – only by according pure imagination a foundational role. The imagination is the source of every synthesis (II) and without the pure imagination's synthesis described in (III)–(V), neither pure intuition nor pure understanding can function as epistemic conditions at all. Yet Heidegger's aim is not simply to capture in other terms what Kant says, but to give the most plausible interpretation of what Kant is mightily trying to say or should say (201f/137f). Accordingly, when Heidegger claims (VI) that pure intuition and pure understanding are themselves rooted in pure imagination, he exercises a certain "violence," as he puts it (XVII/xviii), moving beyond Kant's own self-imposed constraints and, in the process, exposing the fruitlessness of attempting to explain the possibility of knowledge through analysis of imagination (or other faculties, for that matter).

Heidegger reads the epistemology of the *Critique of Pure Reason* from a realist point of view, but it is a phenomenological realism rather than the critical realism popular in his day. The object, on this reading, is the thing in itself as it appears against a horizon (world) co-constituted by the subject's activity of turning toward entities on hand in a way that allows them to stand opposite it. Yet, whatever its plausibility as a reading of the *Critique* in other respects, this streamlined conception of objects omits a crucial dimension on which critical realist readings in particular insist. Far from being simply the appearance of something on hand within the subject's horizon, an object as such belongs to nature as an objective realm determined by synthetic *a priori* principles. Perhaps Heidegger's realization of his neglect of this dimension explains his admission that he is guilty in *KPM* of "overinterpreting" the *Critique of Pure Reason*.

In any case, this overinterpretation has exercised considerable hold on several philosophers on the European continent. Merleau-Ponty, Foucault, and Deleuze all have their differences with Heidegger, yet each of them invokes the interpretation that he gives of the Kantian subject in *KPM*;[44] similarly, Derrida draws on this interpretation to defend Heidegger from Levinas's objections (as well as to advance his

44 Maurice Merleau-Ponty, *Phénoménologie de la perception* (Paris: Gallimard, 1945), 482, 487; Jean-Pierre Faye, "Philosophie le plus ironique" in Yannick Beaubatie (ed.), *Tombeau de Gilles Deleuze* (Tulle: Mille sources, 2000), 91: "Dès l'an 50 nous [Faye and Deleuze] évoquions ensemble le grand profond livre heideggerien de 1929, *Kant et le problème*

own objections to aspects of Heidegger's own thinking)[45]; a critical commentary on *KPM* plays a crucial role in Jean-Luc Nancy's account of images and imagination.[46] Indeed, at least for this stripe of thinkers, *KPM* has become something of a canonical reading of the *Critique of Pure Reason*, perhaps explaining the relative dearth among them, as mentioned at the outset, of comparable studies of the *Critique*.[47]

de la métaphysique, alors non traduit, – et ses trois 'ek-stases' du temps";
Gilles Deleuze, *Différence et répétition* (Paris: Presses Universitaires de France, 1976), 260n1; Gilles Deleuze, *Foucault*, tr. Seán Hand (Minneapolis: University of Minnesota Press, 1989), 107–119, 129f.

[45] Jacques Derrida, *L'écriture et la différence* (Paris: Éditions du Seuil, 1967), 199, 206f ; *Marges de la philosophie* (Paris: Les editions de Minuit, 1972), 34, 49, 54.

[46] Jean-Luc Nancy, *The Ground of the Image*, tr. Jeff Fort (New York: Fordham University Press, 2005), 23f, 80–99.

[47] Perhaps a further reason contributing to this dearth among philosophers on the Continent is the fact that many (for example, Emanuel Levinas, Paul Ricoeur) find more critical inspiration in the *Critique of Practical Reason* and others (for example, Jean-François Lyotard, Hannah Arendt, Gilles Deleuze) in the *Critique of the Power of Judgment* than in the *Critique of Pure Reason*.

17 Kant's *Critique of Pure Reason* and Analytic Philosophy

I. INTRODUCTION

This chapter considers three key works of analytic Kantianism: Clarence Irving Lewis, *Mind and the World Order* (1929); Sir Peter Strawson, *The Bounds of Sense* (1966); and Wilfrid Sellars, *Science and Metaphysics: Variations on Kantian Themes* (1968). We begin with some characteristics of early analytic philosophy that framed analytic philosophers' views of Kant's *Critique of Pure Reason*.[1]

Early Anglophone analytic philosophy came to focus on language. Ordinary language analysis contends that philosophical problems arise from decoupling terms or phrases from their ordinary contexts of use, in which alone they have definite use and meaning; it tends to a therapeutic approach to philosophy. What may be called "ideal language" analysis (broadly speaking) contends that philosophical problems arise through the use of the "material" mode of speech – that is, ordinary speech about persons, things, or events, to formulate philosophical problems; diagnosing and solving or dissolving these problems requires ascending to a constructed "formal" mode of speech, which restates those issues meta-linguistically as

This chapter is dedicated to the late Jay Rosenberg, with whom I dearly wished to have discussed these matters, at least once more.

I thank Graham Bird, Bob Scharff, and especially Bill deVries for helpful comments, and Paul Guyer for his kind invitation, his excellent suggested focus, and his editorial patience and assistance.

[1] Carnap's views are far more indebted to neo-Kantianism than to Kant. The other two philosophers most germane to the present topic are Moritz Schlick and Jay Rosenberg; see Bibliography, Articles cited in this volume. On McDowell's purported Kantianism, see Graham Bird, "McDowell's Kant: *Mind and World*," *Philosophy* 71.276 (1996), 219–43; and my "Contemporary Epistemology: Kant, Hegel, McDowell," *The European Journal of Philosophy* 14.2 (2006):274–302; repr. in J. Lindgaard, ed., *John McDowell: Experience, Norm and Nature* (Oxford: Blackwell, 2008), 124–51.

concerning sentences or statements.[2] Though such philosophy can be therapeutic, most versions tended to more ambitious, constructive philosophical analyses. A third, not necessarily exclusive strand of analytic philosophy holds that the sole purview of philosophy is conceptual analysis, all other legitimate inquiry belonging to natural science.[3]

In 1922, Russell declared, "I should take 'back to the eighteenth century' as a battle-cry, if I could entertain any hope that others would rally to it."[4] The pinnacle of Russell's eighteenth century was Hume's *Enquiry Concerning Human Understanding*, according to which we can only know analytic propositions ("relations of ideas") *a priori*, while synthetic propositions ("matters of fact") can only be known *a posteriori*. Three main strategies dominated analytic epistemology: ordinary language attempts to solve or dissolve apparent epistemological difficulties; proposals for a tenable empiricism that replaces the psychological dimensions of Hume's epistemology with purely logical analyses or constructions, centrally, of persons or physical objects out of sets of sense data; and proposals for tenable versions of meaning and verification empiricism.

From the outset, analytic philosophers rejected Kant's contention that some synthetic propositions can be known *a priori*. The anti-metaphysical bent of analytic philosophy opposed Kant's apparently metaphysical form of transcendental idealism. The anti-naturalism involved in pure conceptual analysis, especially within epistemology, opposed Kant's cognitive psychology. Powerful new logics developed by Frege, Russell and Whitehead, and modern algebra appeared to discredit Kant's understanding and use of logic in the first *Critique*. Einstein's use of Riemannian geometry within Relativity Theory appeared to discredit Kant's commitment to Euclidean geometry, its spatial constructions, and his Euclidian account of our spatial form of outer intuition. The strategy

---

[2] The distinction between the "material" and "formal" modes of speech is anachronistic, although it parallels well enough for present purposes the contrast between surface grammar and logical re-analysis central to Russell's pioneering work.

[3] For an account of philosophical sea-change wrought by analytic philosophy, see Graham Bird, *Philosophical Tasks: An Introduction to Some Aims and Methods in Recent Philosophy* (London: Hutchinson University Library (Hutchinson & Co.), 1972).

[4] Russell, "Dr. Schiller's Analysis of *The Analysis of Mind*," in J. Passmore, gen. ed., *The Collected Papers of Bertrand Russell* (London: Routledge, 1994), 9:39. Cf. Quine: "On the doctrinal side, I do not see that we are farther along today than where Hume left us. The Humean predicament is the human predicament," *Ontological Relativity and Other Essays* (New York: Columbia University Press, 1969), 72, cf. 74, 76.

of dividing, isolating, and resolving philosophical puzzles piecemeal opposed Kant's systematic approach. And especially in England, understanding of the *Critique* was hindered by serious misinterpretations promulgated in the nineteenth century.[5] The reception of Kant's *Critique* into analytic philosophy was fraught from the outset.

2. C. I. LEWIS; *MIND AND THE WORLD ORDER*

Lewis published *Mind and the World Order* before analytic philosophy took root in North America, within the context of American Philosophy, in the forms of Idealism (Royce), Critical Realism, and Pragmatism, especially Pierce and Dewey, though Lewis was current with work by, for example, Bergson, Russell, and Whitehead. Lewis was a logician, a pioneer in modal logic and in history and philosophy of logic.[6] Consequently, *Mind and the World Order* shows affinities with later analytic developments, though its distinctively pragmatic character remains a key virtue.[7] Like Peirce, Lewis studied Kant's *Critique* over many years. In view of his criticisms of Kant, Lewis's analysis and defense of his "conceptualistic pragmatism" shows many more points of close agreement than may be expected.

Understanding these agreements requires acknowledging Lewis's main misunderstanding of Kant's *Critique*. Lewis alleged that Kant uses "the term 'experience' as if experience and the phenomenally real coincide," thus precluding any Kantian account of dreams and ascribing phenomenalism to Kant (154, 214, 221).[8] Lewis's allegation rests upon his apparent difficulties identifying Kant's reasons for Transcendental

---

[5] See John Watson, *Kant and his English Critics: A Comparison of Critical and Empirical Philosophy* (Glasgow: Maclehose, 1881), and René Wellek, *Immanuel Kant in England: 1793–1838* (Princeton: Princeton University Press, 1931).

[6] See J. Corcoran, "C. I. Lewis: History and Philosophy of Logic," *Transactions of the Charles S. Peirce Society* 42.1 (2006):1–9.

[7] Lewis, Clarence Irving, *Mind and the World Order* (New York: Scribners, 1929). Cf. Lewis, "Logical Positivism and Pragmatism," in J. D. Goheen and J. L. Mothershead, Jr., eds., *Collected Papers of Clarence Irving Lewis* (Stanford: Stanford University Press, 1970), 91–112. Although Lewis's epistemology is often assimilated to familiar forms of foundationalism, this is erroneous; see Eric Dayton, "C. I. Lewis and the Given," *Transactions of the Charles S. Peirce Society* 31.2 (1995), 254–84; and William H. Hay, "Lewis' Relation to Logical Empiricism," in P. A. Schilpp, ed., *The Philosophy of C. I. Lewis* (LaSalle: Open Court, 1986), 309–27.

[8] L. W. Beck replied in "Did the Sage of Königsberg Have No Dreams?," in *idem., Essays on Kant and Hume* (New Haven: Yale University Press, 1978), 38–60.

404   KENNETH R. WESTPHAL

Idealism[9] and his misunderstanding of Kant's Transcendental Deduction. Lewis held that the key to Kant's Deduction is: "That which can not validly be thought under the categories can not be given in intuition" (214).[10] To the contrary, Kant's central problem in the Deduction is that appearances may satisfy the constraints of our forms of intuiting without for that reason also satisfying the constraints of our *a priori* categories of judgment (A 89–90/B 122–3). Attempting to prove the legitimacy of our use of our categories to judge appearances is a further, positive aim of the Deduction and indeed of Kant's entire Analytic of Concepts.[11]

Fortunately, our understanding of Kant's *Critique* has improved considerably, revealing how Kantian are many central features of Lewis's epistemology in *Mind*. Like Kant, Lewis too is impressed by the lesson of the scientific revolution, that "We must first be in possession of criteria which tell us what experience would answer what questions, and how, before observation or experiment could tell us anything" (259, cf. B xii–xiv); both take this lesson to indicate that *a priori* concepts and principles play fundamental roles in empirical, and especially in scientific, knowledge, which require philosophical examination. Both agree in rejecting non-conceptual "knowledge by acquaintance," indirect or representationalist theories of perception, and the skeptical egocentric predicament.[12] Both take perceptual judgment to be central to epistemology. Both distinguish linguistic or conceptual meaning from cognitive significance.[13] Both are fallibilists about empirical knowledge (213),[14] although Lewis neglected this feature of Kant's epistemology (227), perhaps because of his phenomenalist misreading. Both distinguish (though not in the same ways) between the *a priori* and the *a posteriori*, and between the analytic and the synthetic; both agree that the key question

---

More specifically, Lewis had difficulty identifying Kant's reasons for his transcendental idealist account of space and time and the attendant distinction between phenomena and noumena (*Mind*, 215–6).

In §§2–4, otherwise unattributed parenthetical page references are to the main work discussed in each section.

Various sections of Kant's *Critique* mentioned here are discussed in relevant contributions to this volume.

Mind, 117–8, 166. The ascription of these views to Kant is complex; I summarize the main points in "Consciousness and its Transcendental Conditions: Kant's Anti-Cartesian Revolt," in S. Heinämaa, V. Lähteenmäki, & P. Remes, eds., *Consciousness: From Perception to Reflection in the History of Philosophy* (Dordrecht: Springer, 2007), 223–43.

Collected Papers, 96; cf. A 239–41/B 299–300, and the end of §4.

The fallibilist strands in Kant's epistemology are a central topic of my *Kant's Transcendental Proof of Reason* (Cambridge: Cambridge University Press, 2004), they converge in §63.

is the *quid juris* about the respective roles of these four aspects of human knowledge and experience (A 37–8/B 116). Both hold that our explicit awareness, judgment, and knowledge is possible only on the basis of basic, pervasive, implicit judgmental cognitive activity;[15] hence they reject Cartesian "transparency of consciousness" theses. Both argue that experience is only possible for us if the world presents us with similarities and contrasts among the *qualia* or the objects presented to us that we can recognize by using our *a priori* categories (360). Lewis learned from Kant's Second Analogy that central to analyzing and justifying empirical knowledge is determining that, and how we can properly discriminate between merely subjective forms of apparent succession from objective forms of actual succession, so that we can identify spatio-temporal objects and events.[16] Both agree that identifying objective states of affairs requires time, anticipation, and bodily behavior (175, 195, 288). Although Kant only briefly notes bodily comportment in the Second Analogy, namely, we identify the concurrent existence of various parts of a house in part by how we choose to glance in one direction or another (A190, 192–3/B 235, 237–8, 275), Arthur Melnick has argued cogently that bodily comportment is fundamental to Kant's theory of perceptual judgment.[17] Lewis and Kant both argue that ascribing sensory appearances to objective states of affairs requires conceptually structured perceptual judgment.[18] Indeed, Lewis contends, "Every criterion of classification is [a] criterion of reality of some particular sort. There is no such thing as reality in general; to be real, a thing must be a particular sort of real" (263), echoing Kant's reasons for denying that being is a real predicate (A 598/B 626).

These substantial points of agreement highlight Lewis's four central disagreements with Kant's *Critique*. Lewis contends, first, that there are no *a priori* structures of our human forms of spatial and temporal intuiting (198, 214). Modern algebra shows that geometry can be developed purely formally, without appeal to spatial constructions, and can be developed consistently in both Euclidean and non-Euclidean forms (241, 298). Einstein's Theory of Relativity rejects the requirement of simultaneity embedded in Kant's account of spatial and especially geometrical construction (253). Moreover, none of Kant's *a priori* grounds for constructing Euclidean geometrical figures and proofs can address

---

[15] *Mind*, 19, 84, 88, 89, 134–5, 140, 196, 236, 285–9, 290–1, 332, 341.

[16] *Mind* 138–9, cf. 151, 175; A 182–4, 189–97/B 225–7, 234–42.

[17] See Arthur Melnick, *Space, Time, and Thought in Kant* (Dordrecht & Boston: Kluwer, 1989), 1–26, 36–50, 189–204, 466–81; cf. Paul Guyer's review, *Kant-Studien* 85 (1994):477–82.

[18] *Mind* 133; A 247/B 304, cf. B 309, 342–3.

the application of geometry to physical objects (295–8). Lewis contends that "we most certainly *could* have an experience in which Euclidean-appearing things should, upon further examination, turn out to have non-Euclidean properties" (299). Hence the remaining question is which system of geometry is most successfully applicable to any empirical domain (298).

Lewis contends, second, that the lesson of the algebratization of geometry holds for conceptual systems generally. "Inference," Lewis contends, "is analytic of systems, not of propositions in isolation."[19] The inferential relations that explicate and define any formal, conceptual system are developed and defined independently of any applicability of that system. The variety of such systems, the variety of bases for developing equivalent systems, the historical record of presumed axiomatic truths being exposed as false, and the change of concepts associated with the same term all show, Lewis contends, that there are no fixed categories such as Kant's, and that the traditional ideal of justification solely by deduction from self-evident first premises (*scientia*) is false, in both formal and non-formal domains (84, 198, 202–5, 233–4).

Lewis further contends, third, that these general points about formal, conceptual systems hold equally of the conceptual systems we use, implicitly or explicitly, to identify objects, events, and natural regularities, including all natural-scientific systems of classification. All such systems have a formal truth in terms of logical implication within the system, independent of any reference to particular domains of application. Hence, Lewis argues, the "only knowledge *a priori* is purely analytic; all empirical knowledge is probable only" (309). Hence, he concludes, there is no synthetic *a priori* knowledge. The central case for Lewis's view concerns our extrapolation from past and present regularities to likely future regularities. (Its centrality is explained shortly.) Especially in this case, philosophers have sought a synthetic principle, such as the uniformity of nature, to "bridge the gap between abstract ideas in the mind and the reality presented in experience" (309). Yet in this case, too, Lewis argues (in the final 100 pages) that "for the validity of empirical generalizations as ... knowledge of probabilities[,] no *a priori* truth other than the merely analytic is required" (310).

Finally, Lewis develops a much simpler deduction of the categories, which (if sound) renders Kant's Transcendental Deduction otiose (37–8, 219). Indeed, the clues to Lewis's simpler deduction are supplied by Kant. According to Lewis, "the deduction of the categories consists at bottom in this: that without the validity of categorial principles no experience is possible" (320). Indeed, "in some passages of the 'subjective deduction'

[19] *Collected Papers*, 10.

the argument turns precisely upon the consideration that the only alternative to a categorized and orderly experience is a meaningless flux of mere *schwärmerei*" (321).[20]

Regarding the *a priori* origin of our concepts, Lewis was more radical than Kant. Lewis argued that all concepts are *a priori* because they are all classificatory inventions of the mind. Experience only provides us sensory presentations or *qualia*; it is entirely up to us to classify these effectively as objective, subjective, or illusory within any one of our conceptual classifications of the real (x, 13–14, 197, 222–5). Sensory presentations or *qualia* simply occur; they are not themselves representations and involve no knowledge because they involve no concepts, judgments, nor any distinction between truth and error (44, 46, cf. 275). Our categories rule nothing in or out of experience. Instead, our categories provide various specific classifications of various ways in which something can be real: "whatever is denominated 'real' must be something discriminated in experience by criteria which are antecedently determined" (x). In this sense, some sensory presentation or *quale* may be or belong to a real mirage, or a real spurious perceptual misjudgment, or a veridical perception of a real physical object; the question "real or not?" can only be answered for specific classifications of phenomena (here using the term "phenomena" in a neutral sense). Accordingly, "*A priori principles of categorial interpretation are required to limit reality; they are not required to limit experience*" (222, italics original; cf. 231). Because all classification involves ascription of reality of one or another kind, it involves expectations of future experiences; no single sensory presentation or *quale* suffices to verify any such classification. Moreover, which future experiences eventuate depends in part on our own decisions about how to act (356–7). Hence the *a priori* "represents the activity of mind itself; it represents an attitude in some sense freely taken" (196–7). More fully, Lewis states:

The necessity of the *a priori* is its character as legislative act. It represents a constraint imposed by the mind, not a constraint imposed upon the mind by something else.

And the *a priori* is independent of experience ... precisely because it prescribes *nothing* to the content of experience. That only can be *a priori* which is true *no matter what*. What is anticipated is not the given but our attitude toward it; it formulates an uncompelled initiative of the mind, our categorial ways of acting. Truth which is *a priori* anticipates the character of the *real*; ... The real, however, is not the given as such, but the given categorically interpreted. In determining its

---

[20] By the "subjective deduction," Lewis apparently intends the A Deduction; see A 112, although a parallel passage occurs in the Second Analogy (A 200–2/B 246–7). Also see below on the transcendental affinity of the sensory manifold.

own interpretation – and only so – the mind legislates for reality, no matter what future experience may bring. (197)

Lewis primarily emphasizes the *a priori* origin of all our concepts, although careful reading of *Mind* reveals that Lewis rejects both concept empiricism and verification empiricism, as he explicitly argues elsewhere. Accordingly, he holds that our concepts are *a priori* regarding their content as well.

Lewis's conceptualistic pragmatism analyzes the *a priori* in relation to experience because he argues that the independence of our *a priori* categories from experience is qualified: " ... what is *a priori* and of the mind is prior to the content of the given, yet in another sense not altogether independent of experience in general" (24, cf. 21). Although no experience or set of experiences can require us to change our conceptual classifications, our own interests in devising and improving useful, informative classifications lead us to devise new systems (or sub-systems) of classification and to abandon their predecessors or alternatives (232).

Because our conceptual classifications are, in part, embedded in our practical attitudes toward classifying experiences as they occur, because more than a few experiences are required to verify any classification, and because which experiences pertaining to that classification occur depends in part upon our chosen courses of action, Lewis's "question of the possibility of knowledge *a priori*" is: "How do we know in advance that if it does not conform to our principle it will not be veridical, or will not be real in the category which is in question?"[21] Lewis's answer is his alternative to Kant's Transcendental Deduction; it involves four main points. First, although perception is always relative to the perceiver and his or her behavior, this relativity does not entail that perception is inherently misleading or illusory (143, 160–4). The logic of relativity shows that something can have or exhibit relative characteristics only because it has its own intrinsic or "absolute" (non-relative) characteristics (167–73). Second, we could not discriminate among *qualia* nor anything else in an undifferentiated experiential field (59). Third, it is confused and misleading to formulate the problem of induction as Hume does, as if we experience and identify physical objects though we cannot know laws governing their behavior. To the contrary, though distinct, the issues of whether or how we identify physical objects or events and of whether or how we identify laws governing their behavior are correlative problems requiring conjoint solution (320).

Like Kant, Lewis argues, fourth, that we can only identify physical objects (and likewise events as objective successions) by discriminating

[21] *Mind* 224, cf. ix, 195, 308, 319.

regularities in their behavior that are partly manifest to us in how they appear to us, by distinguishing their regularities from those regularities in their appearances that depend upon our own chosen courses of action. Only because we are active beings can we at all distinguish between sensory presentations or *qualia* and the appearances of physical objects or other kinds of real occurrences (30–1, 130, 140–1). Making such distinctions requires that the order of sensory *qualia* be not fully predetermined or fixed; instead, that order is in part a function of our chosen courses of action (357–8). That these basic points hold is manifest in our experience and action; the only alternative is an experience consisting in the "mere flitting of meaningless presentations," perhaps approximated by "the experience of an oyster with the oyster left out" (378). Hence, "a world without law must likewise be a world without recognizable things. The recognition of objects requires the same kind of order or reliable relatedness which law also requires" (320).[22] Hence, if we have experience at all, the question is not whether there are physical objects, regularities governing their behavior, or any human knowledge of these, but rather to what extent can we identify and thereby come to know various kinds of things and the regularities governing their behavior (351, 353). Lewis concludes:

A certain minimal order is prescribed *a priori* in the recognition of the real. It is a regulative maxim of reason to seek further uniformities which may be stated in principles finally of maximal comprehensiveness and simplicity. But there neither is nor can be any prescription of the specific type of uniformity or correlation which is demanded in this interest of further intelligibility. (353)

Hence "we *do* know with certainty and *a priori* that if X is a physical thing, then it will conform to certain general principles which can be laid down in advance because they constitute criteria of the physical" (322). All of these points are, by design, compatible with both the possibility and the social and historical facts of significant, often sudden change in our systems of classificatory concepts.[23]

Lewis's alternative to Kant's Transcendental Deduction is indeed close to an important, if controversial analyisis of Kant's.[24] Kant identified and partly analyzed an important transcendental, formal, though material condition for the very possibility of self-conscious human

---

[22] Cf.: "*The determination of reality, the classification of phenomena, and the discovery of law, all grow up together*" (*Mind* 263, italics original).

[23] *Mind* 228, 237–8, 263, 265–6, 298–9, cf. 225, 271.

[24] Paul Guyer examines and rejects Kant's analysis of transcendental affinity in *Kant and the Claims of Knowledge* (Cambridge: Cambridge University Press, 1987), 132, 138–44, 379–83. Kant's analysis is reconstructed rather differently and defended in *Kant's Proof*, §§15–29.

experience, the transcendental affinity of the sensory manifold (A 113). According to this principle, unless the contents of one's sensations have a minimum, humanly recognizable degree of regularity and variety, they would not admit of perceptual synthesis, and so would provide no basis for even putative cognitive judgments using either a priori or empirical concepts.[25] Hence this affinity of the sensory manifold is transcendental because it is a necessary a priori condition of the possibility of self-conscious experience. It is formal because it concerns the orderliness of the matter of empirical sensations. However, ultimately it is satisfied neither by the a priori intuitive conditions of experience analyzed in the Transcendental Aesthetic nor by the a priori conceptual conditions ana-lyzed in the Transcendental Analytic. Kant recognizes that its satisfaction is due to the "content" or the "object" of experience.[26] Hence this transcen-dental condition is neither conceptual nor intuitive, but rather material.

Kant stresses that a complete sensibility and understanding, capable of associating perceptions, does not of itself determine whether any appearances to it or any of its perceptions are in fact associable. If they were not, there may be fleeting, random sensations – Lewis's flitting Schwärmerei – but there could be no unified, and hence no self-conscious, experience. In part, this would be because those irregular sensations would disallow reproductive synthesis; they would not admit of any psychological association, and so could not afford a basis for developing empirical concepts or for using categorial concepts to judge objects. There could be no schematism and hence no use of cate-gories in a world of chaotic sensations or appearances. In this regard, the necessity of the associability of the sensory manifold is a conditional necessity, holding between that manifold and any self-conscious human subject. Necessarily, if a human subject is self-consciously aware of an object or event via a sensory manifold, then the content of that manifold is associable. The associability of this content is its "affinity." The fact that such affinity is necessary for the possibility of self-conscious-experience entails that this affinity is transcendental, though we cannot determine a priori how much associability our finite cognitive minds require (A 653–4/B 681–2). Above this minimal level of regularity and variety, there is then a reflective issue about the extent to which we can systematize what we experience.

Kant's analysis of transcendental affinity is expressly tailored to our finite cognitive capacities. Accordingly, one might ask of Lewis, how much order among qualia suffices for human experience? Lewis answers optimistically that we can identify order even within "any apparently

[25] A 657/B 685, cf. A 90–1, 100–1, 108, 121–3, 653–4/B 122–3, 681–2.
[26] A 112–13, 653–54/B 681–82.

chaotic character of experience" and "reduce it to some kind of intelligible order," even if only to expect maximum novelty (226, 388). Lewis's optimism appears required to keep distinct the "equivalence of the *a priori*, the analytic, and the intensional, on the one hand, [and] of the *a posteriori*, the synthetic, and the extensional, on the other," which have too often been confused within logic (433). Yet recent epistemology stemming from cognitive science has made us more mindful of our computational finitude. Lewis notes that identifying order depends in part upon our degree of intelligence (351). Lewis considers a "perverse demon," whose sole purpose in feeding us *qualia* "is to mislead us and render knowledge impossible" (387). Even if there are reasons to suppose that human beings can only discriminate a finite number of distinct sensory *qualia* (363, 387, 431), so that the demon must eventually repeat some (387), it is far from obvious that such repetitions must fall within the scope of regularity comprehensible to (say) average human intelligence. In this regard, Kant's analysis, which appeals expressly to our cognitive limitations, better justifies the conclusion required by Lewis's analysis. However much Lewis's distinction is required in logic, this issue belongs to epistemology. How might Lewis respond?

According to Lewis, our intellect is active and embodied, otherwise it could not generate any conceptual classifications (21, 24, 27, 30-1, 92, 290-1). Any world in which our intellect can have sensory presentations is one that contains our own physical bodies and whatever physical things condition our sensory presentations (161, 286). Furthermore, "'The human mind' is distinctly a social product," due to our need to cooperate within our natural and social environment, and "our categories ... reflect that fact" (238-9), not least because our classifying together various sensory *qualia* "with similar appearances in the past is too swift and instinctive" to be explicit. Such rapid, implicit classification, Lewis presumes, is evolutionarily basic to human (and to animal) cognition (290-1, cf. 358). To the extent that the cognitive evolution of our species belongs to Lewis's epistemology, there are further grounds to support his claim that any world in which *we* can *be* is one in which we can identify relevant similarities and differences among presentations, such that we can identify relevant similarities and differences among presented objects and events. Conversely, Lewis surmises, "If we were jelly-fish in a liquid world, we should probably not add at all, because the useful purposes served by such conceptions would be so slight" (252).[27]

---

[27] Lewis's jelly-fish bear comparing with Russell's denizens of the Sun and with Wittgenstein's expandable rulers and objects; see my "Kant, Wittgenstein, and Transcendental Chaos," *Philosophical Investigations* 28.4 (2005):303-23.

Such appeals to our cognitive finitude strongly suggest that augmenting Lewis's alternative deduction in this way makes for a much more synthetic and perhaps even *a posteriori* analysis than suits either Lewis's liberal form of *a priori* conceptual analysis or even his broad model of a transcendental deduction. I close this section with three brief remarks. First, genuinely pragmatic epistemology can be combined coherently and constructively with genuinely transcendental analysis and proof.[28] Second, Lewis's rich, multi-faceted account of conceptual meaning in *Mind* compromises, if not undermines, the traditional (as well as many contemporaneous) distinctions between the *a priori* and the *a posteriori* and also the analytic and the synthetic. His conceptualistic pragmatism suggests that the relevant contrast here is not between the *a priori* and the *a posteriori*, but between the more formal and the more material. Third, those who would question Lewis's appeal to human nature as "externalist" factors in justification that would commit a *petitio principii* against the skeptic should consider carefully Lewis's criticism of the deductivist pretensions of *scientia*, which are far more central to skeptical hypotheses than their proponents typically realize. Lewis's *Mind and the World Order*, long since shunted aside by programmatic declarations by extensionalist logicians, awaits philosophical rediscovery.

3. PETER F. STRAWSON: *THE BOUNDS OF SENSE*

The Bounds of Sense (London: Methuen, 1966) occupies a uniquely influential position in the intersection of Kant's *Critique* and analytic philosophy. At the time of its publication, there was philosophically sensitive, textually scrupulous and in this sense "analytic" Anglophone research on Kant's *Critique* – for example, by A. C. Ewing, W. H. Walsh, Graham Bird, Manley Thompson, Charles Parsons, and Douglas Dryer. Such research, however, was regarded by mainstream analytic philosophers as a historical specialty. Hence, when a leading analytic philosopher emphatically proclaimed that Kant's Transcendental Deduction is "one of the most impressive and exciting [passages] in the whole of philosophy" (25), that "[n]o philosopher in any book has come nearer to achieving this strenuous aim [of thinking up to the limits of thought] than Kant himself in the *Critique of Pure Reason*" (44), and specifically that

Kant's genius nowhere shows itself more clearly than in his identification of the most fundamental of these conditions [of the possibility of self-consciousness] in

---

[28] Or so I argue in "Can Pragmatic Realists Argue Transcendentally?," in J. Shook, ed., *Pragmatic Naturalism and Realism* (Buffalo, NY: Prometheus, 2003), 151–75.

its most general form: *viz.* the possibility of distinguishing between a temporal order of subjective perceptions and an order and arrangement which objects of those perceptions independently possess – a unified and enduring framework of relations between constituents of an objective world. Almost equally important is his recognition that this distinction must be implicit in the concepts under which the contents of experience are brought, since there is no question of perceiving, as it were, the pure framework itself. These are very great and novel gains in epistemology, so great and so novel that, nearly two hundred years after they were made, they have still not been fully absorbed into the philosophical consciousness (29):

Mainstream analytic philosophers paid attention – although also because Strawson corroborated everything they disliked about Kant's *Critique* while promising to extract from Kant's text a philosophically respectable analysis.[29] Strawson's analysis was hailed as a "new and improved version of the central argument of Kant's Transcendental Deduction,"[30] and *Bounds* launched a new genre of analytic transcendental arguments.[31]

Strawson aimed to determine "how far Kant succeeds in establishing that certain features are, in the austere sense, *a priori* features of our conception of experience" (70). Strawson's positive reconstruction of Kant's analysis can be summarized in his own words. (This is important for reasons indicated later.) Strawson's main conclusion from Kant's Transcendental Aesthetic is:

[We] can conceive of no form of experience which does not involve a temporal ordering of the particular items of which we become aware ... (72). [Kant's Transcendental Deduction provides] reason for entertaining favourably an exceedingly general conclusion: viz. that any course of experience of which we can form a coherent conception must be, potentially, the experience of a self-conscious subject and, as such, must have such internal, concept-carried connectedness as to constitute it (at least in part) a course of experience of an objective world, conceived of as determining the course of that experience itself. (117, cf. 118, 121)

[Kant's Analogies of Experience and Refutation of Idealism] ... prove something important. Experience of the objective demands the possibility of determining

---

[29] The most comprehensive response to Strawson's criticisms of Kant's *Critique* is by Robert Greenberg, *Kant's Theory of A Priori Knowledge* (University Park: Pennsylvania State University Press, 2001).

[30] Quoted from the first sentence of Richard Rorty, "Strawson's Objectivity Argument," *Review of Metaphysics* 24.2 (1970):207–44.

[31] Unfortunately, it also swept from view Graham Bird's better book, *Kant's Theory of Knowledge* (London: Routledge & Kegan Paul, 1962). On "analytic transcendental arguments" see Thomas Grundmann, *Analytische Transzendentalphilosophie: Eine Kritik* (Paderborn: Schöningh, 1993), and Robert Stern, ed., *Transcendental Arguments: Problems and Prospects* (Oxford: Oxford University Press, 1999).

objective time-relations (132). ... [O]nly if it is possible to distinguish between the subjective time-order of perceptions and the time-relations of [perceived] objects ... is it possible to give content to the general notion of experience of an objective reality, hence to make intelligible the possibility of experience itself (140–1). ... [The] key notion in this problem is that of currently unperceived objects which are nevertheless objects of possible perception ... existing at the same time as objects of actual perception. If there were no such co-existence of objects of possible with objects of actual perception, there would be no effective distinction to be drawn between objective and subjective time-orders. ... [This distinction] is effectively employed only if we think of objects encountered in experience, objects which we actually perceive, as existing not only when we perceive them, but also at other times, when we perceive, not them, but other objects. ... This notion involves that of the possession by objects which we actually perceive of a relative permanence or persistence which our perceptions of them do not possess (141, cf. 132). ... We cannot ... characterize those perceptions themselves except with the help of concepts of persistent things which we perceive the objects of those perceptions as instances of. [Hence] ... we must conceive of such objects as *ordered in some system or framework of relations such as alone can give sense to the notion of particular identity of such objects*. ... [T]he most natural way, and perhaps the only way, for us to conceive of a possible framework or system of relations of the kind required is to conceive of it as spatial. [Hence] ... we must conceive of ourselves, as perceivers, as having at any moment a determinable position in the system of relations to which the perceiver belongs. For only under this condition can the subjective series of our experiences be conceived as a series of *perceptions* of objects existing independently and enjoying their mutual relations in the system (142).

Lack or possession of order-indifference on the part of our perceptions is ... our criterion – whether we reflectively realize the fact or not – of objective succession or co-existence (134). [Distinguishing] ... between objective and subjective time-determinations (143) [requires identifying] changes in perceptions which are attributable to changes in the viewpoint of the observer. [Such changes] ... exhibit a regular correlation with change of the observer's position and his sense-orientation-in relation to objects in the world. The possibility of this correlation in turn seems to depend upon changes and persistences in the world of objects being themselves subject to some kind and degree of order and regularity. (144)

[Hence] ... our concepts of objects, and the criteria of re-identification which they embody, must allow for changes in the objective world subject to the limitation that change must be consistent with the possibility of applying those concepts and criteria in experience. ... [T]his requirement [is] satisfied [because] our concepts of objects are linked with sets of conditional expectations about the things which we perceive as falling under them. For every kind of object, we can draw up lists of ways in which we shall expect it not to change unless ..., lists of ways in which we shall expect it to change if ..., and lists of ways in which we shall expect it to change unless ...; where, with respect to every type of change or non-change-listed, the subordinate clauses introduce further and indefinite lists of clauses each of which would constitute an explanatory condition of the change or absence of change in question. (145)[32]

The point is that in contradistinction to concepts of simple sensory *qualities*, and in contradistinction, too, to any concepts there may be of particular sensory *items* which are quite fully describable in terms of simple sensory qualities ('sense-data', perhaps, in one sense of the term), concepts of *objects* are always and necessarily compendia of causal laws or law-likeness, carry implications of causal power or dependence.[33] [These] must make up a great part of our concepts of any persisting and re-identifiable objective items. And without some such concepts of these, no experience of an objective world is possible. (145–6)

[Thus] ... we may suppose that while perceptions of the world may reveal *some* objective changes which we can characterize as inexplicable, quite unpredictable or utterly random, they can do so only against a background of persistence and alterations which we recognize as explicable, predictable, and regular. (144, *cf.* 101)

This summary of Strawson's positive analysis reveals some important though neglected characteristics of Strawson's enlistment of Kant into the program of descriptive metaphysics, "of determining the fundamental general structure of any conception of experience such as we can make intelligible to ourselves" (44, *cf.* 57, 146) through conceptual analysis.[34]

In advance of his analysis, Strawson proposes to show that a skeptic who challenges us to reconstruct a public world of physical objects and events on the sole basis of our private sense data "demonstrates his failure to have grasped the conditions of the possibility of experience in general" (19). This result is desirable, but Strawson's method is insufficient to this task. He contends that the various constraints Kant identifies as governing our possible experience "must somehow be reflected in the character of our concepts themselves" (144–5). Because his analysis focuses almost exclusively on our concepts and their interrelations, the strongest conclusion Strawson can justify pertains to how we must "conceive" or "think of" our experience, how we must "take" objects to be, or how we must perceive them "as" physical objects and events. This

[32] Here Strawson highlights a key point of Lewis's analysis; had Lewis better understood Kant's analysis of this point, he might have realized that Kant did not espouse phenomenalism.

[33] Strawson's analysis concurs here with Lewis's.

[34] "My book [*Bounds*] was, you might say, a somewhat ahistorical attempt to recruit Kant to the ranks of the analytical metaphysicians, while discarding those metaphysical elements that refused any such absorption" (Strawson, "A bit of Intellectual Autobiography," in H.-J. Glock, ed., *Strawson and Kant* [Oxford: The Clarendon Press, 2003], 1–14). For a thorough examination of Strawson's positive analysis, see Grundmann, *Analytische Transzendentalphilosophie*.

limitation results from his frequent, characteristic use of locutions such as those underscored here:

[The] distinction ... between objective and subjective time-orders ... is effectively employed only if we think of objects encountered in experience, objects which we actually perceive, as existing not only when we perceive them, but also at other times, when we perceive, not them, but other objects. (141)

... we must conceive of ourselves, as perceivers, as having at any moment a determinable position in the system of relations to which the perceiver belongs. For only under this condition can the subjective series of our experiences be conceived as a series of *perceptions* of objects existing independently and enjoying their mutual relations in the system. (142)

Such locutions pervade Strawson's analysis.[35] Perhaps Strawson's analysis may counter some sense data analyses,[36] but because it addresses only how we must *conceive* our experience, it cannot address the skeptic.[37] To address skepticism, Strawson's analysis would have to demonstrate not simply that we must *conceive of* ourselves, our experience, and the objects or events we purportedly experience in certain commonsense

[35] I invite the reader to identify each such locution and similar ones in the earlier summary of Strawson's version of the Deduction, and in the constructive passages of *Bounds*, Part II. Although some occurrences of terms such as "see" or "perceive" appear to be factive, suggesting veridical perception, nothing in Strawson's analysis justifies such connotations. Instead, if they are used in such senses, they occur as independent premises. Most directly, Strawson states: "We *perceive successively* objects which we nevertheless *know* to be *co-existent*" (141; italics original). If we do know this, then skepticism is a dead issue, though apparently for reasons Moore already had in hand. When Strawson immediately queries, "But how can we know this?" (141), his answer reverts to the kinds of locutions I emphasize.
[36] Grundmann notes difficulties identifying what sort of sense data analysis Strawson addresses (*Transzendentalphilosophie*, 135–40).
[37] Grundmann notes two passages that might suggest that Strawson aims to show that our conception of objectivity is linked to the world as it truly is (*Transzendentalphilosophie*, 132). Yet these passages too expressly concern how "[o]ur sensible experience may, and does in fact, exhibit that connectedness which enables us to employ empirical concepts of objects, to count our sensible representations as veridical perceptions" (*Bounds*, 92), or how "[w]hat is meant by the necessary self-reflexiveness of a possible experience in general could be otherwise expressed by saying that experience must be such as to provide room for the thought of experience itself. The point of the objectivity-condition is that it provides room for this thought" (*ibid.*, 107). Provision for having such thoughts, however, does not involve – not for any reasons Strawson provides – grounds for supposing these thoughts to be either true or justified.

ways, but that we *rightly*, *truly*, and indeed *justifiedly* so conceive them. This task belongs to normative epistemology, not to *descriptive* metaphysics; knowledge requires both truth and justification. Strawson's conceptual analyses are indeed necessary, but not sufficient, to answer basic questions in epistemology, as Kant already understood. This limit is built into Strawson's aims and method, and these limits have been repeatedly re-confirmed in the ensuing critical discussion of his analysis.

Strawson's analysis in *Bounds* remains within the ambit of Hume's skepticism in the *Treatise*. Strawson's analysis highlights issues of concept-possession and use – namely, their use to conceive of or to "take" ourselves, objects, and events in certain commonsense ways as indicated. In "Of Scepticism with regard to the senses" Hume acknowledges that we all *have* the concept of a physical object ("the idea of body") and that it is central to how we conceive our experience and what we experience, and he is at pains to account for the acquisition, definition, and use of this concept in accord with his concept-empiricism. Hume there argues that, however ineliminable it may be from our beliefs, the very idea of body, the very concept "physical object," is an utter fiction incapable of any *justifiable* cognitive role.[38]

Strawson's attention to the integration of a complex of conceptual resources within our commonsense realistic conception of experience exhibits the standard epistemological problem confronting coherence theories of justification, aired at the outset of Logical Positivism and recently re-learned by Laurence BonJour.[39] No matter how coherent or tightly integrated a set of beliefs, propositions, or concepts may be, coherence alone cannot justify their truth. Ironically, *Bounds* appeared only three years after Gettier demonstrated the insufficiency of conceptual analysis for epistemology.[40] Gettier's counterexamples to conceptual analyses of Justified True Belief models of empirical knowledge all highlight features of a person's actual cognitive processes and circumstances from which non-empirical conceptual analysis must prescind. Among much else, Gettier's article ushered in a return to more naturalistic approaches to epistemology attending to our actual cognitive processes and circumstances, including developments in cognitive science

[38] See my *Hegel, Hume und die Identität wahrnehmbarer Dinge* (Frankfurt am Main: Klostermann, 1998), §4.
[39] On the debate regarding Logical Positivism, see my *Hegel's Epistemological Realism* (Dordrecht: Kluwer, 1989), 56–7; on BonJour's coherence theory, see Laurence BonJour, "Haack on Justification and Experience," *Synthese* 112 (1997): 13–23, at pp. 13–4.
[40] Edmund Gettier, "Is Justified True Belief Knowledge?," *Analysis* 23 (1963): 121–3.

and epistemological interest in artificial intelligence, including the excellent works on relevant aspects of Kant's cognitive functionalism by, for example, Patricia Kitcher and Andrew Brook.[41]

Strawson recognized deficiencies in *Bounds* regarding both Kant's *Critique* and the core issues. He points especially to "Kant's New Foundations of Metaphysics" and "The Problem of Realism and the *A Priori*" as significantly improving his view.[42] To these I would add "Imagination and Perception" and "Perception and its Objects," which attend to central issues of perceptual judgment.[43] When Paul Guyer later argued that Kant's transcendental psychology examines basic constraints on any cognitive system that synthesizes information over time, Strawson granted the point and acknowledged that his castigating "the imaginary subject of transcendental psychology" (32) was "somewhat rude."[44]

Kant recognized that conceptual analysis alone is insufficient to his epistemological tasks in the *Critique* (A 216–18/B 263–65). Even when conceptual analysis is as liberal as Strawson's, Kant's point stands. Kant knew that disregarding our basic cognitive capacities and attendant incapacities grants the field to skeptics. Strawson's tantalizing sketch inspired many philosophers to seek more detail in and more ambitious results from Kant's *Critique*. The present volume and comparable recent works are, *inter alia*, continuing testimony to his riveting reconstruction of Kant's Deduction.

[41] Respectively, *Kant's Transcendental Psychology* (New York: Oxford University Press, 1990) and *Kant and the Mind* (Cambridge: Cambridge University Press, 1994).

[42] Both essays appear in P. F. Strawson, *Entity and Identity – And Other Essays* (Oxford: Oxford University Press, 1997), 233–44, 246–51, respectively; Strawson singles them out in "Autobiography," 9.

[43] These essays appear, respectively, in P. F. Strawson, *Freedom and Resentment and Other Essays* (London: Methuen, 1974), 45–65; and in G. F. MacDonald, ed., *Perception and Identity* (Ithaca: Cornell University Press, 1979), 41–60. The Kantian pedigree of these essays is revealed by comparison with Bella K. Milmed, "'Possible Experience' and Recent Interpretations of Kant," in L. W. Beck, ed., *Kant Studies Today* (LaSalle: Open Court, 1969), 301–21; and with Sellars, "The Role of the Imagination in Kant's Theory of Experience," in H. Johnstone, ed., *Categories: A Colloquium* (University Park: Pennsylvania State University Press, 1978), 231–45.

[44] See Guyer, "Psychology and the Transcendental Deduction," in E. Förster, ed., *Kant's Transcendental Deductions* (Stanford: Stanford University Press, 1989), 47–68; and Strawson, "Sensibility, Understanding, and the Doctrine of Synthesis: Comments on Henrich and Guyer," *ibid.*, 69–77.

The lack of epistemological import of Strawson's analysis in *Bounds* poses a choice: either produce a much-improved version of Kant's "descriptive metaphysics," engage in normative epistemology, or make the most possible of Hume's observation that skepticism is a creature of one's study. In *Scepticism and Naturalism*, Strawson chose this latter option, yet in so doing he did not renege on his apparently more Kantian analysis in *Bounds*.[45]

4. WILFRID SELLARS, SCIENCE, AND METAPHYSICS: VARIATIONS ON KANTIAN THEMES

Unlike other analytic empiricists, Sellars realizes that issues about perceptual judgment are subtle and crucial. Sellars takes conceptual explication to be an essential, though not sufficient, strategy for understanding and resolving substantive philosophical issues. Within analytic philosophy, the important shift is from "analysis" to "explication."[46] Conceptual analysis seeks explicit, *a priori* (certainly non-empirical), exhaustive specifications (definitions or "analyses") of key terms, claims, or principles. In contrast, conceptual "explication" is the partial and provisional specification of key terms (etc.) *in use*, so that explications, unlike analyses, are tied by actual linguistic practices to their relevant domains of thought and inquiry – and thus also to intellectual and cultural history. Like the classical Pragmatists, Sellars explicates our concepts-in-use to gain theoretical understanding (for example, 96, 98, 110).

Influenced by Carnap, a cornerstone of Sellars's philosophy is semantic ascent to a constructed formal meta-language: All abstract entities are to be defined in and confined to the meta-language. Recourse to the formal mode of speech does not justify nominalism, though adopting it requires nominalism. Yet why expect philosophically significant confusions not to infect the formal mode of speech? This neglected issue was addressed by Sellars upon Aristotle's advice: because these issues are so complex, elusive, and easily obscured by incautious phrasing, one must consult carefully the opinions of the many and the wise. Sellars found the wise throughout philosophical history, from the pre-Socratics to the present day,[47] because core issues regarding the logical forms of thought and the connection of thought with things are perennial, arising in

[45] London: Methuen, 1985.
[46] Carnap, *Logical Foundations of Probability* (Chicago: University of Chicago Press, 1950; 2nd rev. ed. 1962), 1–18.
[47] Parmenides is mentioned thrice (62, 71, 77); the contemporary counterparts of Heraclitus are radical sense-datum theorists and causal process time-slicers, heirs to Hume all.

distinctive, paradigmatic forms in each era (67–9). One result of Sellars's expansive research is a catalog and critical assessment of philosophical locutions – that is, of the "ordinary language" of philosophers. Only by examining these can one find the most suitable, least misleading formulations of issues, specific theses, distinctions, and their relations. Sellars knew that the anti-systematic, piecemeal method of analytic puzzle-solving was doomed in its own terms by 1950 when Carnap adopted a moderately holistic semantics in "Empiricism, Semantics, and Ontology."[48] Thus, even when cast in the formal mode of speech, philosophy must be systematic. The interconnection among philosophical issues provides another check against inapt formulations.

Recourse to a meta-language has a further implication, also characteristic of Sellars's views and method. Valid inferences within any language are specified in its meta-language. Hence 'proofs', as Lewis acknowledged, are neither more nor less than deductions which accord with the rules instituted by the meta-meta-language (for example, Carnap's L- and P-rules). Accordingly, the "basic concepts and distinctions" of any philosophical account "are to be tested or 'proved' by the illumination they provide, and the coherence of the story they make possible" (1).

These features of Sellars's method appear prominently in *Metaphysics*. Like Lewis, Sellars develops a distinctive conceptual pragmatism; unlike Lewis, Sellars expressly defends "synthetic necessary truths," necessary truths that depend upon their subject matter (68–9).[49] Like Kant and Lewis, Sellars argues that standard empiricist views of perception and sensory evidence are irreparably flawed.[50] Unlike them, Sellars seeks to turn this critique to the advantage of an improved, decidedly

---

[48] See Warner Wick, "The 'Political' Philosophy of Logical Empiricism," *Philosophical Studies* 2.4 (1951): 49–57. Sellars and Herbert Feigl founded this journal the previous year. Carnap's classic essay first appeared in *Revue International de Philosophie* 4 (1950), and with revisions in Carnap, *Meaning and Necessity* (Chicago: University of Chicago Press, 1956), 205–221.

[49] Wilfred Sellars, *Science and Metaphysics: Variations on Kantian Themes* (London: Routledge and Kegan Paul, 1968). This formulation replaces Sellars's previous defense of the "synthetic *a priori*" in *Science, Perception and Reality* (London: Routledge & Kegan Paul, 1963; hereafter: '*Perception*'), 293–4, 298–320. There Sellars notes how his view converges with and diverges from Lewis's (ibid., 293–4, 300–01).

[50] See Sellars, "Empiricism and the Philosophy of Mind" (*Perception*, 127–96), on which see Willem deVries and Timm Triplett, *Knowledge, Mind, and the Given: Reading Wilfrid Sellars's "Empiricism and the Philosophy of Mind"* (Cambridge, MA.: Hackett Publishing Co., 2000). On Kant's critique of empiricism, see Chapter 2 of this volume by Kenneth Winkler.

Kantian empiricism. Sellars regards Kant's Transcendental Deduction not as a *proof* but rather as a sophisticated theory of judgment that would resolve both skepticism and much of epistemological debate because both depend upon seriously inadequate analyses and pictures of the mind, nature, and their relations.[51] Rectifying these deficiencies requires a cogent philosophy of mind that dispels skeptical and epistemological quandaries. In addition to Kant's Transcendental Analytic, such a philosophy of mind requires Sellars's non-relational account of "meaning" and "aboutness" (ix) and his account of "picturing."

Here we consider how *Science and Metaphysics* consists in *Variations on Kantian Themes*: Sellars agrees with Kant that our commonsense world is phenomenal because it only exists in our experiencings, and that appearances to us are caused by noumena. However, Sellars contends that these noumena are the objects of the ultimate, Peircean science and are thus in principle knowable rather than unknowable.[52] Kant defines as transcendental "all cognition ... that is occupied not so much with objects but rather with our mode of cognition of objects, insofar as this [mode] is to be possible *a priori*" (A 11–2/B 25). Although Sellars demurs about its *a priori* status, *Metaphysics* is an exercise in transcendental philosophy (147) that aims to identify and to justify various synthetic necessary truths (68), including those that form the core of our cognitive use of concepts (cf. 100). Chapter I and the Appendix aim to correct Kant's Transcendental Aesthetic; like Lewis and Strawson, Sellars rejects Kant's equation of space and time with our forms of intuiting. The three chapters on "The Conceptual and the Real" (60–150) form a contemporary counterpart to Kant's Transcendental Analytic. *Metaphysics* develops a distinctive form of transcendental idealism; its final chapter addresses fundamental principles of Kant's moral theory, as does Kant in parts of the

---

[51] See Sellars's 1976 Lectures on Kant's *Critique* in P. V. Amaral, ed., *Kant and Pre-Kantian Themes: Lectures by Wilfrid Sellars* (Atascadero: Ridgeview Publishing Co., 2002), 1–179, 278. Graham Bird, in *The Revolutionary Kant* (LaSalle., IL: Open Court, 2006) develops a much improved "descriptive metaphysics" (the first option mentioned at the end of §3) by, in effect, developing this point from Sellars.

[52] For a synopsis, see Jay Rosenberg, "Wilfrid Sellars," in the *Stanford Encyclopedia of Philosophy*, then see Willem deVries, *Wilfrid Sellars* (Chesham, Bucks, UK: Acumen, 2005), James O'Shea, *Wilfrid Sellars* (Cambridge: Polity, 2007), and then Johannes Haag, *Erfahrung und Gegenstand* (Frankfurt am Main: Klostermann, 2007) and Jay Rosenberg, *Wilfrid Sellars: Fusing the Images* (Oxford: Oxford University Press, 2007). Cf. deVries' review of Haag, *Erfahrung*, in *Internationales Jahrbuch des Deutschen Idealismus* 5 (2007): 368–75.

Transcendental Dialectic.[53] Transcendental philosophy requires what Kant calls "transcendental reflection,"[54] which, Graham Bird notes, "ascribes concepts to sense or understanding, [and] is concerned with the relation between concepts and their objects, and with the distinction between objects of the senses ... and objects of understanding or reason."[55] Transcendental reflection also considers how various sensory or conceptual representations ought to be related in cognitive judgments.[56] These are central issues in *Metaphysics*.

Sellars stresses the normativity of conceptual systems.[57] The considerations Sellars brings to bear on his topics must be neutral between the commonsense or "manifest" image we have of ourselves in our everyday world (analyzed pre-eminently by Aristotle and Strawson; 15, 170-1) and the natural-scientific image of nature we have developed since Galileo; it must also be neutral between knowledge and morality. To assess neutrally the judgmental resources of each of these domains, Sellars's overarching transcendental standpoint cannot be an outgrowth of any one of these (sub)domains, though it must be deeply informed within each and by them all. Where Kant examines our cognitive – specifically sensory, conceptual, and judgmental – capacities to form legitimate cognitive judgments and to distinguish these from illegitimate forms, Sellars examines specific sorts of propositions, all of which express the content of various kinds of judgment. In their respective ways, Kant and Sellars both examine the logical forms of thought, the feeling for which Sellars finds, prior to Kant, in Ockham's disciples and in Leibniz, although it is "almost totally lacking in Descartes and his British successors" (35). Sellars's critique of philosophical and of commonsense locutions serves both as a phenomenology of various domains of human experience, as reflected in our talk within and about them, and as a basis for identifying the canonical forms of propositions (or forms of judgment) within each. This aspect of Sellars's endeavor is a sustained examination and regimentation of forms of *classification*, through which he defends intensions and their roles in our acts of representing and our claims to truth. Both Kant and Lewis are committed to intensions and to their roles in classifications and true judgments; Sellars shows how central such systems are to human thought and how they can be defended against recent extensionalist

---

[53] The transcendental character of Sellars's philosophy is highlighted by Haag, *Erfahrung*, esp. 52–60, 359–422.

[54] A 261–3, 269, 295/B 317–9, 325, 351.

[55] *Revolutionary*, 540, cf. 540–3.   [56] *Kant's Proof*, §§1.2, 1.3.

[57] See O'Shea, *Sellars*, 176–90; cf. deVries, *Sellars*, index under "normative" and "norms."

dogma (77, 110).[58] Sellars's transcendental analytic in the three chapters on "The Conceptual and the Real" lacks the strong *a priori* character of Kant's, yet his frequent and incisive explications of common philosophical confusions are exercises in impure *a priori* analyses of propositions, a neglected theme central to Kant's *Critique*.[59] Because Sellars's critique includes our concepts of sensing and sensation, it assumes some of the role of Kant's Amphiboly and catalogs many dialectical fallacies. If Kant's target in the Transcendental Dialectic is traditional metaphysics, Sellars's target is traditional and contemporary philosophy of mind; both areas purport to be non-empirical philosophical domains, and Kant's Paralogisms contribute significantly to anti-Cartesian philosophy of mind.

Although highly formalized, Sellars's transcendental logic is not formalist for four key reasons: It uses conceptual explication rather than analysis; its synthetic necessary truths are deeply informed by empirical inquiry and scientific methodology; its formal notion of truth, "S-assertability," means "*correctly* assertible" in accord with "the relevant semantical rules, and on the basis of such additional ... information as these rules may require" (101), where such information is often empirical; and Sellars insists on the mutual *irreducibility* of the orders of being, of knowing (including picturing, representation, method, and explanation), and of obligation (145, 147, 164, 172). These non-formalist features of Sellars's analysis align it significantly with Kant's Transcendental Logic.

The key to Sellars's transcendental logic is Kant's "thesis of the primacy of judgmental content and judgmental form," that judgmental content is irreducible to non-judgmental content (61). (Sellars speaks of "logical contents" to distinguish between logical operators and their counterpart occurrences as configurations of elements within pictures; 60–1, 121.) Sellars's list of judgmental contents implicitly follows Kant's

58 Quine's "Two Dogmas of Empiricism" assumed rather than proved extensionalist logic was the only tenable logical point of view, despite both Lewis's detailed criticisms of *Principia Mathematica*'s extensionalism and Carnap's non-Platonist intensions, "meaning postulates." "The analytic-synthetic distinction" is not a definite description because there are distinct analyses of "the analytic," each of which provides a distinctive contrast with "the synthetic." That so few of Quine's readers noticed his *petitio principii* deserves both historical and philosophical reflection. See Jay Rosenberg, "Sellars and Quine: Compare and Contrast," in *Fusing the Images*, 33–46.

59 See Konrad Cramer, *Nicht-reine synthetisch Urteile a priori: Ein Problem der Transzendentalphilosophie Immanuel Kants* (Heidelberg: Winter, 1985).

Table of Judgments; it includes logical connectives, quantifiers, subject-predicate connections, and modalities such as "necessary"; "the content *true*," Sellars suggests, may appear in Kant's Table "under the guise of 'actuality'" (93n). In the contemporary context, Sellars cannot begin with a Table of Judgments,[60] but he argues in detail that "extensions are limiting cases of intensions and cannot be understood apart from them. Thus classes, in the logistic sense, cannot be understood apart from properties, nor truth apart from propositions" (77, cf. 110, 113). Within recent philosophy of language and semantics, these are decidedly Kantian theses.

One key question of Kant's *Critique* concerns intentionality: how (if at all) are we able to be aware of objects or events without the mind?[61] This is Sellars's key question about "The Conceptual and the Real," which he addresses in three stages: intentionality, truth, and picturing. The first key to intentionality is intensions pertaining to individuals, universals, and states of affairs (64). The key to intensions is "a dualism of two modes of *in-esse*, the *in-esse* of attributes in representings and the *in-esse* of attributes in things" (92). Sellars contends that the actual existence of individuals and their characteristics in the world can be recognized or otherwise thought about because our sensory states, our thoughts, and our language are structured by functional *counterparts* to individuals, their attributes, and our experiences of them (25-6). In their respective ways, conceptual episodes and linguistic episodes stand for their senses "by virtue of the patterns they make ... with other designs, with objects (in a suitably broad sense) and with actions" (76). Sellars takes seriously Wittgenstein's notion of language games, likening these patterns to moves of pieces in a game, such as chess: the material constitution of the piece is secondary to its role or function and its actual moves or uses (79, 94, 107-8).[62]

Within Sellars's metalanguage, attributes are treated as classifications of characteristics of things; individuals are treated as instances of various characteristics. Our classificatory intensions function something like Fregean senses (literally, "ways of being given," "*Arten des Gegebenseins*"), within actual or possible acts of representing (63-5). To

---

[60] Long-standing criticisms of Kant's Table of Judgments have been answered by Michael Wolff, *Die Vollständigkeit der kantischen Urteilstafel* (Frankfurt am Main: Klostermann, 1995), *Abhandlung über die Prinzipien der Logik* (Frankfurt am Main: Klostermann, 2004, rev. ed. 2009), and in a series of intervening articles.

[61] A 197/B 242; to Herz, 21 Feb. 1772, 10:130.

[62] To make this point, Sellars alludes to the Texas version of chess, a joke in which the counties of Texas serve as the chess board, the pieces are a rich Texan's Cadillacs, and a move involves driving a Cadillac to another county.

characterize these counterpart functions, Sellars treats abstract singular terms (for example, "the pawn," "the triangle") as distributive singular terms (80–1, 95–6). He introduces dot quotes to abstract from differences among natural languages, thus highlighting the logical forms of *thought* at a transcendental level. This approach affords a flexible, functional account of logical operators (which have senses though not intensions) as well as other abstract singular terms, the senses of which are intensions. Thus any occurrence of "not" in English, "*nicht*" in German, or "*niet*" in Russian (and so on), is an occurrence of 'the •neg•' (81), where "the criteria for the application of dot-quoted expressions ('This is a •not•', 'This is a ·triangular·') consist in being subject to the same semantical correctnesses as the expressions within the dot quotes" (87). This strategy affords perspicacious contrasts between such fraught notions as "stands for," "connotes," "denotes," "refers to," and "names" (81). Sellars summarizes retrospectively:

> The general strategy was to construe the *in-esse* of contents in representings on the model of *standing for* as a relation between linguistic expressions and their senses. Intensions were construed to be a sub-class of senses, consisting of those which can meaningfully be contrasted with *extensions*, as triangularity can be contrasted with the class of triangular things. ... in addition to intensions, in this technical sense, the class of senses includes the items which were originally introduced as 'logical contents' and, perhaps, ... 'contents' pertaining to practical thought. (93)

"Extensions" are individuals who or which exemplify characteristics classified in intensions. Sellars seeks to provide a functional role semantics that relieves the explanatory itch or the apparent queerness of how properties of things exemplify various kinds (classifications) we identify, in part by obviating the search for "objects" which are supposed to *be* attributes (103, 104–5, 110). This too is part of Sellars's clarificatory philosophy of mind regarding judgment. He contends that exemplification, like truth, "is a matter of the semantical correctness of a certain performance – roughly the de-quoting of a quoted expression" (110).

Sellars replaces the concept of truth with "S-assertibility," according to which a proposition is "*correctly* assertible ... in accordance with the relevant semantical rules, and on the basis of such additional ... information as these rules may require" (101). S-assertibility is universal in scope, although it takes specific forms depending upon the semantical rules governing different types of propositions (101, 116). Thus, in brief, does Sellars defend the "primacy of classification and the truth performance" (113) against competing contemporary views that seek to eliminate them or reduce them to other functions.

Because Sellars's analysis of truth is intensional and semantic in these regards, it does not itself pertain directly to relations between our representations and the world of individuals who or which are the extensions of all the intensions so far considered. To account for factual truth, Sellars further explicates S-assertability (107n) in terms of "picturing." His account of picturing is a subtle elaboration of Wittgenstein's insight in the *Tractatus* that "one can only say of two objects that they stand in a certain relation by placing the corresponding referring expressions in a counterpart relation" (108). In accord with the irreducible primacy of judgmental form, the relations among pictured elements cannot themselves be represented *as elements within* the picture (*cf.* 121). Instead, the elements within a picture must stand in counterpart relations to the relations among the elements of whatever is pictured. Picturing is thus a relation between two relational structures, such as some worldly situation (137) and our linguistic, perceptual, or conceptual representing of it. Subject to the normative constraints of proper picturing, this affords either correct or incorrect picturing. Accordingly, referring expressions are ineliminable (109) and the primary concept of factual truth is truth as correct picture (119). Very roughly, atomic statements constitute "'linguistic pictures' of the world" (119, cf. 124). Sellars subtly elaborates this basic model, though details must be omitted here, except to note Sellars's emphatic claim that "Wittgenstein's insight [about picturing] provides the keystone that can keep philosophical semantics from collapsing ever anew into a ruble of fruitless discussion" (110).

This brief sketch of the structure of Sellars's analysis of intentionality shows its Kantian character in several of Sellars's results. One of these is his distinguishing between existential quantification and definite descriptions (124) because referring expressions function within semantical uniformities that are tied to an agent's activities regarding relevant referents; this requires propositions that describe the relative mutual locations of these referents and of the agent that suffice to identify the location "here and now" of those referents (125-6). This view is tantamount to Kant's semantics of singular cognitive reference. Briefly, Kant recognized through his critique of Leibniz in the Amphiboly that descriptions, no matter how specific, cannot themselves determine whether they are empty, definite, or ambiguous. Hence, however useful for semantics of meaning, definite descriptions are insufficient for *cognitive* reference; to be even a candidate for knowledge, a description, proposition, or judgment must be referred to a particular or particulars localized by the subject within space and time through singular sensory presentation.[63] Kant thus anticipates Gareth Evans's analysis in "Identity and

[63] Essentially the same account of Kant's semantics of singular cognitive reference is ascribed to Kant by Westphal, *Kant's Proof*, §§7, 8, 63.2, and by Bird, *Revolutionary*, 255-6, 267-8, 525-30.

Predication,"[64] although he also supercedes it by analyzing its rich epistemological implications. Kant's semantics provides excellent grounds for rejecting verificationist theories of meaning,[65] while insuring that genuine cognitive claims about particulars require locating them in time and space. In one stroke, Kant refutes the transcendent cognitive pretensions of rationalism and theology, "knowledge by acquaintance," description theories of reference, and deductivist models of justification (*scientia*) in empirical domains, and proves the cognitive irrelevance of merely logical possibilitities to the justificatory status of empirical claims (fallibilism).

Like Kant, Sellars holds a sensationist account of (outer) sensations, according to which sensations themselves are not objects of self-conscious awareness; instead, they are components of acts of awareness, typically of particulars in our surroundings (cf. 10). Kant, Lewis, and Sellars are direct realists about our perception of spatio-temporal-particulars and critical realists about perceptual knowledge.[66]

Because synthetic necessary connections can be either statistical or universal, Sellars's attention to legitimate *versus* illicit forms of judgment and inference reveals that "the sceptic, when he is not arguing invalidly from the absence of contradiction to physical possibility, is arguing invalidly from the consistency of 'exceptions' with statistical necessity to the consistency of the latter with a hypothetical 'universal exception'" (69n). Not only Kant's modal theory in the Postulates, but his entire Critical method, predicated on the insufficiency of conceptual analysis for substantive epistemology, rejects any conflation of logical with physical possibility, just as the Transcendental Analytic blocks generalizing from the universal possibility of perceptual error to possibility of universal perceptual error.

Sellars's account of the distinction between conceptual and non-conceptual (sensory) states of consciousness (10) and his basic model of counterpart functional roles that partially constitute the content of overt speech and of both conceptual and sensory episodes (18–9, 26–7, 63) are

---

[64] *Journal of Philosophy* 72.13 (1975):343–63.

[65] Including the verificationist "Principle of Significance" Strawson ascribes to Kant (*Bounds* 16).

[66] See Rolf George, "Kant's Sensationism," *Synthese* 47.2 (1981):229–55; and William Harper, "Kant on Space, Empirical Realism, and the Foundations of Geometry," *Topoi* 3.2 (1984):143–61. Sellars's preoccupation with Kant's account of empirical intuitions appears to have occluded from him Kant's account of sensations and their synthesis-guiding *Merkmale* (B 33, A 320/B 376–77, cf. *Judgment* 5:484.13–18). When Strawson attends to perceptual judgment, he too espouses direct realism and critical realism.

directly indebted to Kant's distinction between forms of sensibility and forms of judgment, between empirical intuitions and spatio-temporal-forms of intuiting, and between phenomenal space and time and a logically possible noumenal counterpart duration and presence (38, citing A 770–1/B 149, 798–9). His observation that "basic factual predicates come in families of competing predicates, one or other of which must be satisfied by every object that *can* satisfy a predicate of that family" (119–20), reflects Kant's account of disjunctive and infinite negative judgments (A 71–4/B 97–9), which are central to Kant's discriminative account of causal judgments.[67] Even Sellars's Ryleans who can only think by speaking aloud echo Kant, who in the *Anthropology* (7:332) highlights our human moral character by contrasting us with extra-terrestrial rational beings who can only think by speaking aloud.

More significantly, Sellars's meta-linguistic analysis of modality reflects Kant's thesis that the modal categories only concern the cognitive value of a judgment's copula, not the content of the judgment (A 74–6/B 99–101). Sellars's nominalism places all modality in the meta-language. Both the commonsense and the scientific images of the world are rife with modal discourse, all of which accordingly must be transcendentally ideal, even though, Sellars contends, increasingly accurate natural science can correctly identify physical particulars and their spatio-temporal relations. Accordingly, much of the conceptual framework of final science is transcendentally ideal, though its objects are transcendentally real and known in and through that framework.

Sellars agrees with Kant that our commonsense spatio-temporal world of physical objects and all their perceptual qualities, delightful or unpleasant as they may be, are transcendentally ideal phenomena, though not due to Kant's idealist account of our spatio-temporal forms of intuiting. Sellars holds that ultimately commonsense physical objects do not exist *as* they are conceived within the manifest, commonsense image of the world; as thus conceived, commonsense objects and events exist only in our actual or potential representings of them (42, 48, 49, 53, 56n). The final science, should we survive to achieve it, presents us with a radically different, though far more accurate conception and specification of what we commonsensically take to be physical objects, and those scientifically described and certified particulars are the true causes of commonsense (though transcendentally ideal) appearances (49, 148, 150). Objects and events as described by the ultimate science are the genuine noumena, though they are ultimately knowable. *Science and Metaphysics* is deeply Kantian, much more so than Sellars's critique of Kant's transcendental idealism may suggest.

[67] See *Kant's Proof*, §36.3.

There are five truly great theories of particulars and universals, their relations and our knowledge of them. Four are those of Plato, Aristotle, Kant, and (do not be incredulous) Hegel.[68] As accounts of those issues, these theories converge very significantly, thus throwing their subtle and profound differences into illuminating relief. Historically, the fifth such theory would be Ockham's, although because Sellars is a modern philosopher deeply concerned with the relations of mind and world, rendered so problematic by the rise of natural science, Sellars's nominalism is the fifth such theory. Anyone seeking to ascertain the cogency of an interpretation of the *Critique*, not only philosophically but also textually and historically, can do little better than consider how well it fares against Sellars's writings on and through Kant's philosophy.[69]

5. CONCLUSION

Scholarship on Kant's *Critique of Pure Reason*, when conjoined with historical sensitivity and textual scruple, has certainly benefitted from engagement with analytic philosophy and has often produced findings with broad philosophical significance to analytic philosophy.[70] Some themes from Kant's thinking are abroad in analytic philosophy, though they tend to be rather bland appeals to framework principles for structuring inquiry or analysis, notions more neo-Kantian than Kantian.[71] Regrettably, the philosophical results of Kant's *Critique* do not appear even yet, as Strawson notes, to have been "absorbed into the

---

[68] See my "Hegel's Phenomenological Method and Analysis of Consciousness," in K. R. Westphal, ed., *The Blackwell Guide to Hegel's Phenomenology of Spirit* (Oxford: Wiley-Blackwell, 2009), 1–36.

[69] For example, Haag, *Erfahrung*, argues that Kant's theory of intentionality is superior to Sellars's.

[70] Two excellent examples of such research are Robert Howell, *Kant's Transcendental Deduction* (Dordrecht: Kluwer, 1992), and Jay Rosenberg, *Accessing Kant: A Relaxed Introduction to the Critique of Pure Reason* (New York: Oxford University Press, 2005). My remarks should not be misunderstood to suggest that the great historical works on Kant's *Critique* have become irrelevant, nor that non-analytic scholarship on the *Critique* has not progressed. This chapter has a specific scope; for a balanced account of recent scholarship see Paul Natterer, *Systematischer Kommentar zur Kritik der reinen Vernunft: Interdisziplinare Bilanz der Kantforschung seit 1945* (Berlin: de Gruyter, 2003).

[71] See, for example, Strawson, "Echoes of Kant," *Times Literary Supplement* 4657 (3 July 1992):12–13; Graham Bird, "Kantian Themes in Contemporary Philosophy II," *Proceedings of the Aristotelian Society*, Supp. vol. 72 (1998): 131–51.

philosophical consciousness" (*Bounds* 29). Barry Stroud observes, "it is not easy to incorporate the depth and power of Kant's transcendental deduction into present-day philosophical attitudes and preconceptions."[72] Indeed so: Kant delivered what he promised, an "alterted method of our way of thinking" (B xviii).[73] Understanding, appreciating, and assessing Kant's *Critique* certainly requires a changed way of thinking. For historical reasons, self-critical methodological reflection on one's own way of philosophizing has been subdued in much of analytic philosophy. Consider Comte's primary use of his cyclical three-stage law of human intellectual development (mythological, theological, and scientific eras) to prompt reflection on one's own historical and philosophical position within one of those stages. In Comte's case, this meant reflecting on why the proper scientific outlook is positivist. In contrast, Mill always took positivism for granted. Thus was Comte's rich kind of philosophical reflection lost to the Anglophone tradition in their correspondence.[74] Consequently, few analytic philosophers recognize how firmly Russell planted the analytic tradition back into the eighteenth-century-framework of Hume's first *Enquiry*. Likewise, few discussants recognize how deeply Cartesian is Stroud's apparently innocuous presentation of global perceptual skepticism – a feature thrown sharply into relief by Kant's widely neglected anti-Cartesianism.[75]

[72] "Transcendental Arguments and 'Epistemological Naturalism'," *Philosophical Studies* 31 (1977): 105–15, 105.
[73] See Adrian Moore's contribution to this volume, Chapter 13.
[74] See Robert Scharff, *Comte after Positivism* (Cambridge: Cambridge University Press, 1995).
[75] *Kant's Proof*, §63.

Bibliography

I.SELECTED EDITIONS OF THE *CRITIQUE OF PURE REASON*

Kant, Immanuel. *Critik der reinen Vernunft*. Riga: Johann Friedrich Hartknoch, 1781.
Kant, Immanuel. *Critik der reinen Vernunft. Zweyte hin und wieder verbesserte Auflage*. Riga: Johann Friedrich Hartknoch, 1787.
Kant, Immanuel. *Kant's gesammelte Schriften*. Herausgegeben von der Königlich Preußischen (subsequently Deutschen, then Berlin-Brandenburgischen) Akademie der Wissenschaften. 29 vols. Berlin: Georg Reimer (subsequently Walter de Gruyter & Co.), 1900–.
Band III, *Kritik der reinen Vernunft, Zweite Auflage 1787*. Herausgeber: Benno Erdmann. Berlin: Georg Reimer, 1911.
Band IV, *Kritik der reinen Vernunft, 1te. Auflage 1781, bis Von den Paralogismen der reinen Vernunft*. Herausgeber: Benno Erdmann. Berlin: Georg Reimer, 1911.
Kant, Immanuel. *Kritik der reinen Vernunft*. Herausgegeben von Ingeborg Heidemann. Stuttgart: Philipp Reclam Jun., 1966.
Kant, Immanuel. *Kritik der reinen Vernunft*. Herausgegeben von Jens Timmermann, mit eine Bibliographie von Heiner Klemme. Hamburg: Felix Meiner Verlag, 1998.
Kant, Immanuel. *Theoretische Philosophie: Texte und Kommentar. Band I: Kritik der reinen Vernunft*. Herausgegeben von Georg Mohr. Frankfurt am Main: Suhrkamp Verlag, 2004.

2.SELECTED TRANSLATIONS OF THE *CRITIQUE OF PURE REASON*

Kant, Immanuel. *Critick of Pure Reason*. Second edition with notes and explanation of Terms. Translated by Francis Haywood. London: William Pickering, 1848.
Kant, Immanuel. *Critique of Pure Reason*. Translated by John Miller Dow Meiklejohn. London: Henry G. Bohn, 1855. Revised and expanded translation based on Meiklejohn, edited by Vasilis Politis, London: J. M. Dent, 1993.
Kant, Immanuel. *Critique of Pure Reason*. Translated by F. Max (Friedrich Maximilian) Müller. London: Macmillan, 1881. Translated, edited, and with an Introduction, based on the translation by Max Müller, by Marcus Weigelt. London: Penguin Group, 2007.
Kant, Immanuel. *Critique of Pure Reason*. Translated by Norman Kemp Smith. London: Macmillan, 1929. Second impression with corrections, London: Macmillan, 1933.

Kant, Immanuel. *Critique of Pure Reason: Unified Edition.* Translated by Werner S. Pluhar, Introduction by Patricia Kitcher. Indianapolis and Cambridge: Hackett Publishing Co., 1996.
Kant, Immanuel. *Critique of Pure Reason.* Translated and edited by Paul Guyer and Allen W. Wood. Cambridge: Cambridge University Press, 1998.

3.SELECTED TRANSLATIONS OF OTHER WORKS BY KANT

The Cambridge Edition of the Works of Immanuel Kant in English Translation. Paul Guyer and Allen W. Wood, General Co-Editors. 13 vols. to date. Cambridge: Cambridge University Press, 1992–. Volumes of specific relevance include:
Kant, Immanuel, *Theoretical Philosophy, 1755–1770.* Translated and edited by David Walford in collaboration with Ralf Meerbote. Cambridge: Cambridge University Press, 1992.
Kant, Immanuel, *Theoretical Philosophy after 1781.* Edited by Henry Allison and Peter Heath, translated by Gary Hatfield, Michael Friedman, Henry Allison, and Peter Heath. Cambridge: Cambridge University Press, 2002.
Kant, Immanuel. *Notes and Fragments.* Edited by Paul Guyer, translated by Curtis Bowman, Paul Guyer, and Frederick Rauscher. Cambridge: Cambridge University Press, 2005.
Kant, Immanuel. *Correspondence.* Translated and edited by Arnulf Zweig. Cambridge: Cambridge University Press, 1999.
Also:
Kant, Immanuel. *Lectures on Philosophical Theology.* Translated by Allen W. Wood and Gertrude M. Clark. Ithaca: Cornell University Press, 1978.

4.THE EARLY REVIEWS OF THE *CRITIQUE*

Landau, Albert, editor. *Rezensionen zur Kantischen Philosophie 1781–87.* Bebra: Albert Landau Verlag, 1991.
Gesang, Bernward, editor. *Kants vergessener Rezensent: Die Kritik der theoretischen und praktischen Philosophie Kants in fünf frühen Rezensionen von Hermann Andreas Pistorius.* Kant-Forschungen, Band 18. Hamburg: Felix Meiner Verlag, 2007.
Sassen, Brigitte, editor. *Kant's Early Critics: The Empiricist Critique of the Transcendental Philosophy.* Cambridge: Cambridge University Press, 2000.

5.SURVEYS OF KANT'S THOUGHT AND ITS DEVELOPMENT (SINGLE- AND MULTI-AUTHOR)

Adickes, Erich. *Kant als Naturforscher.* 2 volumes. Berlin: Walter de Gruyter & Co., 1924.
Ameriks, Karl. *Interpreting Kant's Critiques.* Oxford: Clarendon Press, 2003.
Bauch, Bruno. *Immanuel Kant.* Third, enlarged edition. Berlin: De Gruyter, 1923.
Beck, Lewis White. *Early German Philosophy: Kant and His Predecessors.* Cambridge, MA.: Harvard University Press, 1969.
Bird, Graham, editor. *A Companion to Kant.* Oxford and Malden: Blackwell Publishing, 2006.
Brandt, Reinhard. *Die Bestimmung des Menschen bei Kant.* Hamburg: Felix Meiner Verlag, 2007.

Buchdahl, Gerd. *Metaphysics and the Philosophy of Science: The Classical Origins Descartes to Kant.* Oxford: Basil Blackwell, 1969.

Caird, Edward. *The Critical Philosophy of Immanuel Kant.* 2 vols. London: Macmillan, 1889.

Carl, Wolfgang. *Der schweigende Kant: Die Entwürfe zu einer Deduktion der Kategorien vor 1781.* Göttingen: Vandenhoeck & Ruprecht, 1989.

Cassirer, Ernst. *Das Erkenntnisproblem in der Philosophie und Wissenschaft der neueren Zeit.* 3 volumes. Berlin: Bruno Cassirer, 1906–1920. (vol. II)

Cassirer, Ernst. *Kants Leben und Lehre* (1918). *Gesammelte Werke,* vol. 8, edited by Birgit Recki. Hamburg: Felix Meiner Verlag, 2001. Translated as: *Kant's Life and Thought.* Translated by James Haden. New Haven: Yale University Press, 1981.

Delekat, Friedrich. *Immanuel Kant.* Second edition. Heidelberg: Quelle & Meyer, 1966.

Deleuze, Gilles. *Kant's Critical Philosophy.* Translated by Hugh Tomlinson and Barbara Habberjam. Minnneapolis: University of Minnesota Press, 1993.

De Vleeschauwer, H.-J. *La Déduction Transcendentale dans l'oeuvre de Kant.* 3 vols. Antwerp, Paris, and The Hague: De Sikkel, Champion, and Martinus Nijhoff, 1934–37.

De Vleeschauwer, H.-J. *The Development of Kantian Thought: The History of a Doctrine.* Translated by A. R. C. Duncan. London, Edinburgh: Thomas Nelson and Sons, 1962.

Dietzsch, Steffen. *Immanuel Kant: Eine Biographie.* Leipzig: Reclam Verlag, 2003.

Fulda, Hans-Friedrich, and Jürgen Stolzenberg, editors. *Architektonik und System in der Philosophie Kants.* Hamburg: Felix Meiner Verlag, 2001.

Gerhardt, Volker. *Immanuel Kant: Vernunft und Leben.* Stuttgart: Reclam, 2002.

Gerhardt, Volker, and Friedrich Kaulbach. *Kant.* Erträge der Forschung, Band 105. Darmstadt: Wissenschaftliche Buchgesellschaft, 1979.

Guyer, Paul. *Kant's System of Nature and Freedom: Selected Essays.* Oxford: Clarendon Press, 2005.

Guyer, Paul. *Kant.* London: Routledge, 2006.

Guyer, Paul. *Knowledge, Reason, and Taste: Kant's Response to Hume.* Princeton: Princeton University Press, 2008.

Guyer, Paul, editor. *The Cambridge Companion to Kant.* Cambridge: Cambridge University Press, 1992.

Guyer, Paul, editor. *The Cambridge Companion to Kant and Modern Philosophy.* Cambridge: Cambridge University Press, 2006.

Guylga, Arsenij. *Immanuel Kant: His Life and Thought.* Translated by Marijan Despalatovic. Boston, Basel, Stuttgart: Birkhauser, 1987.

Haering, Theodor. *Der Duisburg'sche Nachlaß und Kants Kritizismus um 1775.* Tübingen: J. C. B. Mohr, 1910.

Heidemann, Dietmar H., and Kristina Engelhard, editors. *Warum Kant Heute? Systematische Bedeutung und Rezeption seiner Philosophie in der Gegenwart.* Berlin and New York: Walter de Gruyter & Co., 2004.

Heintel, Peter, and Ludwig Nagl, editors. *Zur Kantforschung der Gegenwart.* Damrstadt: Wissenschaftliche Buchgesellschaft, 1981.

Höffe, Otfried. *Immanuel Kant.* Translated by Marshall Farrier. Albany: State University of New York Press, 1994.

Irrlitz, Gerd. *Kant Handbuch.* Stuttgart: Verlag J. B. Metzler, 2002.

Kemp, John. *The Philosophy of Kant.* London: Oxford University Press, 1968.

Klemme, Heiner F. *Immanuel Kant*. Frankfurt am Main: Campus Verlag, 2004.
Körner, Stephan. *Kant*. Harmondsworth: Penguin Books, 1955.
Kuehn, Manfred. *Kant: A Biography*. Cambridge: Cambridge University Press.
Külpe, Oswald. *Immanuel Kant*. Third edition. Leizpig: Teubner, 1912.
Longuenesse, Béatrice. *Kant on the Human Standpoint*. Cambridge: Cambridge University Press, 2005.
Neiman, Susan. *The Unity of Reason: Rereading Kant*. New York: Oxford University Press, 1994.
Oberer, Hariolf, and Gerhard Seel, editors. *Kant: Analysen – Probleme – Kritik*. 3 vols. Würzburg: Königshausen & Neumann, 1988, 1996, 1997.
Rickert, Heinrich. *Kant als Philosoph der modernen Kultur: Ein geschichtsphilosophischer Versuch*. Tübingen: J. C. B. Mohr, 1924.
Ritzel, Wolfgang. *Immanuel Kant: Eine Biographie*. Berlin: Walter de Gruyter & Co., 1985.
Schönecker, Dieter. *Kants Begriff transzendentaler und praktischer Freiheit*. Berlin: Walter de Gruyter & Co., 2005.
Sidgwick, Henry. *Lectures on the Philosophy of Kant*. London: Macmillan, 1905.
Simon, Josef. *Kant: Die fremde Vernunft und die Sprache der Philosophie*. Berlin: Walter de Gruyter & Co., 2003.
Stolzenberg, Jürgen, editor. *Kant in der Gegenwart*. Berlin: Walter de Gruyter & Co., 2007.
Velkley, Richard L. *Freedom and the End of Reason: On the Moral Foundation of Kant's Critical Philosophy*. Chicago: University of Chicago Press, 1989.
Vorländer, Karl. *Immanuel Kant: Der Mann und das Werk*. 2 vols. Leipzig: Felix Meiner Verlag, 1924.
Vorländer, Karl. *Immanuel Kants Leben*. Fourth edition. edited by Rudolf Malter. Hamburg: Felix Meiner Verlag, 1986.
Walker, Ralph C. S. *Kant*. London: Routledge & Kegan Paul, 1978.
Ward, Andrew. *Kant: The Three Critiques*. Cambridge: Polity Press, 2006.
Watson, John. *Kant and his English Critics: A Comparison of Critical and Empirical Philosophy*. Glasgow: Maclehose, 1881.
Wellek, René. *Immanuel Kant in England: 1793–1838*. Princeton: Princeton University Press, 1931.
Werkmeister, W. H. *Kant's Silent Decade: A Decade of Philosophical Development*. Tallahassee: University Presses of Florida, 1979.
Werkmeister, W. H. *Kant: The Architectonic and Development of His Philosophy*. LaSalle: Open Court Publishing Co., 1980.
Werkmeister, W. H., editor. *Reflections on Kant's Philosophy*. Gainesville: University Presses of Florida, 1975.
Wolff, Robert Paul, editor. *Kant: A Collection of Critical Essays*. Garden City: Doubleday Anchor, 1967.
Wood, Allen W. *Kant*. Oxford and Malden: Blackwell Publishing, 2005.
Wood, Allen W., editor. *Self and Nature in Kant's Philosophy*. Ithaca: Cornell University Press, 1984.
Wundt, Max. *Kant als Metaphysiker: Ein Beitrag zur Geschichte der deutschen Philosophie im 18. Jahrhundert*. Stuttgart: Ferdinand Enke, 1924.
Wundt, Max. *Die deutsche Schulphilosophie im Zeitalter der Aufklärung*. Tübingen: J. C. B. Mohr, 1945.

6.COMMENTARIES ON THE *CRITIQUE OF PURE REASON*

Adorno, Theodor W. *Kant's Critique of Pure Reason.* Edited by Rolf Tiedemann, translated by Rodney Livingstone. Stanford: Stanford University Press, 2001.

Allison, Henry E. *Kant's Transcendental Idealism: An Interpretation and Defense.* Revised edition. New Haven: 2004.

Altman, Matthew C. *A Companion to Kant's* Critique of Pure Reason. Boulder: Westview Press, 2008.

Aschenbrenner, Karl. *A Companion to Kant's Critique of Pure Reason: Transcendental Aesthetic and Analytic.* Lanham: University Press of America, 1983.

Bennett, Jonathan. *Kant's Analytic.* Cambridge: Cambridge University Press, 1966.

Bennett, Jonathan. *Kant's Dialectic.* Cambridge: Cambridge University Press, 1974.

Bird, Graham. *The Revolutionary Kant: A Commentary on the* Critique of Pure Reason. Chicago and LaSalle: Open Court Publishing Co., 2006.

Broad, C. D. *Kant: An Introduction.* Edited by C. Levy. Cambridge: Cambridge University Press, 1978.

Buroker, Jill Vance. *Kant's* Critique of Pure Reason: *An Introduction.* Cambridge: Cambridge University Press, 2006.

Collins, Arthur. *Possible Experience: Understanding Kant's Critique of Pure Reason.* Berkeley and Los Angeles: University of California Press, 1999.

Dicker, Georges. *Kant's Theory of Knowledge: An Analytical Introduction.* New York: Oxford University Press, 2005.

Dryer, Douglas P. *Kant's Solution for Verification in Metaphysics.* London: George Allen and Unwin, 1966.

Erdmann, Benno. *Kants Kriticismus in der ersten und in der zweiten Auflage der Kritik der reinen Vernunft.* Leipzig: Leopold Voss, 1878.

Ewing, A. C. *A Short Commentary on Kant's* Critique of Pure Reason. Chicago: University of Chicago Press, 1938.

Fischer, Kuno. *A Commentary on Kant's Critick of Pure Reason.* Translated by John Pentland Mahaffy. London: Longmans, Green & Co., 1866.

Gardner, Sebastian. *Kant and the Critique of Pure Reason.* London: Routledge, 1998.

Guyer, Paul. *Kant and the Claims of Knowledge.* Cambridge: Cambridge University Press, 1987.

Heimsoeth, Heinz. *Transzendentale Dialektik: Ein Kommentar zu Kants Kritik der reinen Vernunft.* 4 vols. Berlin: Walter de Gruyter & Co., 1966–71.

Höffe, Otfried. *Kants Kritik der reinen Vernunft: Die Grundlegung der modernen Philosophie.* Munich: C. H. Beck, 2003.

Kemp Smith, Norman. *A Commentary to Kant's 'Critique of Pure Reason'.* Second edition. London: Macmillan, 1923.

Kitcher, Patricia. *Kant's Transcendental Psychology.* New York: Oxford University Press, 1990.

Longuenesse, Béatrice. *Kant and the Capacity to Judge.* Princeton: Princeton University Press, 1998.

Luchte, James. *Kant's* Critique of Pure Reason: *A Reader's Guide.* London: Continuum, 2007.

Martin, Gottfried. *Kant's Metaphysics and Theory of Science.* Translated by P. G. Lucas. Manchester: Manchester University Press, 1955.

Mohr, Georg, and Marcus Willaschek, editors. *Immanuel Kant: Kritik der reinen Vernunft.* Berlin: Akademie Verlag, 1998.

Natterer, Paul. *Systematischer Kommentar zur Kritik der reinen Vernunft: Interdisziplinäre Bilanz der Kantforschung seit 1945.* Kant-Studien Ergänzungsheft 141. Berlin: Walter de Gruyter & Co., 2003.

Paton, H. J. *Kant's Metaphysics of Experience: A Commentary on the First Half of the Kritik der reinen Vernunft.* 2 vols. London: George Allen & Unwin, 1936.

Pippin, Robert. *Kant's Theory of Form: An Essay on the Critique of Pure Reason.* New Haven: Yale University Press, 1982.

Prichard, H. A. *Kant's Theory of Knowledge.* Oxford: Clarendon Press, 1909.

Rosenberg, Jay F. *Accessing Kant: A Relaxed Introduction to the* Critique of Pure Reason. Oxford: Clarendon Press, 2005.

Savile, Anthony. *Kant's Critique of Pure Reason: An Orientation to the Central Themes.* Oxford: Blackwell Publishing, 2005.

Schultz, Johann. *Exposition of Kant's Critique of Pure Reason.* Translated by James C. Morrison. Ottawa: University of Ottowa Press, 1995.

Strawson, P. F. *The Bounds of Sense: An Essay on Kant's Critique of Pure Reason.* London: Methuen, 1966.

Tetens, Holm. *Kant's "Kritik der reinen Vernunft": Ein systematischer Kommentar.* Stuttgart: Philipp Reclam jun., 2006.

Vaihinger, Hans. *Commentar zu Kant's Kritik der reinen Vernunft.* 2 vols. Stuttgart: W. Spemann and Union Deutsche Verlagsgesellschaft, 1881–92.

Van Cleve, James. *Problems from Kant.* Oxford: Oxford University Press, 1999.

Walsh, W. H. *Kant's Criticism of Metaphysics.* Edinburgh: Edinburgh University Press, 1975.

Watkins, Eric. *Kant's Critique of Pure Reason: Background Source Materials.* Cambridge: Cambridge University Press, 2009.

Weldon, T. D. *Kant's Critique of Pure Reason.* Second edition. Oxford: Clarendon Press, 1958.

Wilkerson, T. E. *Kant's Critique of Pure Reason: A Commentary for Students.* Oxford: Clarendon Press, 1976.

Wolff, Robert Paul. *Kant's Theory of Mental Activity: A Commentary on the Transcendental Analytic of the Critique of Pure Reason.* Cambridge, Mass.: Harvard University Press, 1963.

7. OTHER MONOGRAPHS AND SINGLE-AUTHOR COLLECTIONS ON THE *CRITIQUE OF PURE REASON*

Abela, Paul. *Kant's Empirical Realism.* Oxford: Clarendon Press, 2002.

Adickes, Erich. *Kant und das Ding an sich.* Berlin: Pan Verlag, 1920.

Adickes, Erich. *Kants Lehre von der doppelten Affektion des Ich als Schlüssel zu seiner Erkenntnistheorie.* Berlin: Pan Verlag, 1924.

Al-Azm, Sadik. *The Origins of Kant's Arguments in the Antinomies.* Oxford: Clarendon Press, 1972.

Allison, Henry E. *The Kant-Eberhard Controversy.* Baltimore: Johns Hopkins University Press, 1973.

Allison, Henry E. *Idealism and Freedom: Essays on Kant's Theoretical and Practical Philosophy.* Cambridge: Cambridge University Press, 1996.

Ameriks, Karl. *Kant's Theory of Mind: An Analysis of the Paralogisms of Pure Reason.* Oxford: Clarendon Press, 1982; new edition, 2000.

Ameriks, Karl. *Kant and the Fate of Autonomy: Problems in the Appropriation of the Critical Philosophy*. Cambridge: Cambridge University Press, 2000.

Ameriks, Karl. *Interpreting Kant's Critique*. Oxford: Clarendon Press, 2003.

Aquila, Richard E. *Representational Mind: A Study of Kant's Theory of Knowledge*. Bloomington: Indiana University Press, 1983.

Aquila, Richard E. *Matter in Mind: A Study of Kant's Transcendental Deduction*. Bloomington: Indiana University Press, 1989.

Banham, Gary. *Kant's Transcendental Imagination*. Basingstoke: Palgrave Macmillan, 2006.

Baum, Manfred. *Deduktion und Beweis in Kants Transzendentalphilosophie: Untersuchungen zur "Kritik der reinen Vernunft."* Königstein: Athenäum Verlag, 1986.

Bayne, Steven M. *Kant on Causation: On the Fivefold Routes to the Principle of Causation*. Albany: State University of New York Press, 2004.

Beck, Lewis White. *Studies in the Philosophy of Kant*. Indianapolis: Bobbs-Merrill, 1965.

Beck, Lewis White. *Essays on Kant and Hume*. New Haven: Yale University Press, 1978.

Beck, Lewis White. *Selected Essays on Kant*. Edited by Hoke Robinson. Rochester: University of Rochester Press, 2006 (contains selections from previous two volumes).

Bird, Graham. *Kant's Theory of Knowledge: An Outline of One Central Argument in the Critique of Pure Reason*. London: Routledge & Kegan Paul, 1962.

Birken-Bertsch, Hanno. *Subreption und Dialektik bei Kant: Der Begriff des Fehlers der Erschleichung in der Philosophie des 18. Jahrhunderts*. Stuttgart-Bad Canstatt: Fromann-Holzboog, 2006.

Brandt, Reinhard. *The Table of Judgments: Critique of Pure Reason A 67–76/B 92–101*. Translated and edited by Eric Watkins. North American Kant Society Studies in Philosophy, Volume 4. Atascadero: Ridgeview Publishing Company, 1995.

Brittan, Gordon. *Kant's Theory of Science*. Princeton: Princeton University Press, 1978.

Brook, Andrew. *Kant and the Mind*. Cambridge: Cambridge University Pres, 1994.

Buchdahl, Gerd. *Kant and the Dynamics of Reason: Essays on the Structure of Kant's Philosophy*. Oxford: Blackwell, 1992.

Buroker, Jill Vance. *Space and Incongruence: The Origin of Kant's Idealism*. Dordrecht: D. Reidel Publishing Co., 1981.

Butts, Robert E. *Kant and the Double Government Methodology: Supersensibility and Method in Kant's Philosophy of Science*. Dordrecht: D. Reidel Publishing Co., 1984.

Caranti, Luigi. *Kant and the Scandal of Philosophy: The Kantian Critique of Cartesian Scepticism*. Toronto: University of Toronto Press, 2007.

Carl, Wolfgang. *Die Transzendentale Deduktion der Kategorien in der ersten Auflage der Kritik der reinen Vernunft: Ein Kommentar*. Frankfurt am Main: Vittorio Klostermann, 1992.

Coffa, J. Alberto. *The Semantic Tradition from Kant to Carnap: To the Vienna Station*. Cambridge: Cambridge University Press, 1991.

Cohen, Hermann. *Kants Theorie der Erfahrung*. First Edition: Berlin: F. Dümmler, 1871. Second edition. Berlin: F. Dümmler, 1885.

Collingwood, R. G. *An Essay on Metaphysics*. Revised edition. Edited by Rex Martin. Oxford: Clarendon Press, 1998.

Cramer, Konrad. *Nicht-reine synthetische Urteile a priori: Ein Problem der Transzendentalphilosophie Immanuel Kants*. Heidelberg: Carl Winter Universitätsverlag, 1985.

Dickerson, A. B. *Kant on Representation and Objectivity*. Cambridge: Cambridge University Press, 2004.

Edwards, Jeffrey. *Substance, Force, and the Possibility of Knowledge: On Kant's Philosophy of Material Nature*. Berkeley and Los Angeles: University of California Press, 2000.

Englehard, Kristina. *Das Einfache und die Materie: Untersuchungen zu Kants Antinomie der Teilung*. Kantstudien Ergänzungsheft 148. Berlin: Walter de Gruyter & Co., 2005.

Enskat, Rainer. *Kants Theorie des geometrischen Gegenstandes*. Berlin: Walter de Gruyter & Co., 1978.

Ewing, A. C. *Kant's Treatment of Causality*. London: Routledge & Kegan Paul, 1924.

Falkenburg, Brigitte. *Die Form der Materie: Zur Metaphysik der Natur bei Kant und Hegel*. Frankfurt am Main: Athenäum, 1987.

Falkenburg, Brigitte. *Kants Kosmologie: Die wissenschaftliche Revolution der Naturphilosophie im 18. Jahrhundert*. Frankfurt am Main: Vittorio Klostermann, 2000.

Falkenstein, Lorne. *Kant's Intuitionism: A Commentary on the Transcendental Aesthetic*. Toronto: University of Toronto Press, 1995.

Findlay, J. N. *Kant and the Transcendental Object: A Hermeneutic Study*. Oxford: Clarendon Press, 1981.

Forster, Michael N. *Kant and Skepticism*. Princeton: Princeton University Press, 2008.

Friedman, Michael. *Kant and the Exact Sciences*. Cambridge, MA: Harvard University Press, 1992.

Garnett, Christopher Browne, Jr. *The Kantian Philosophy of Space*. New York: Columbia University Press, 1939.

Gram, Moltke S. *Kant, Ontology, and the A Priori*. Evanston: Northwestern University Press, 1968.

Gram, Moltke S. *The Transcendental Turn: The Foundations of Kant's Idealism*. Gainesville and Tampa: University Presses of Florida, 1984.

Greenberg, Robert. *Kant's Theory of A Priori Knowledge*. University Park: Pennsylvania State University Press, 2001.

Greenberg, Robert. *Real Existence, Ideal Necessity: Kant's Compromise, and the Modalities Without the Compromise*. Kantstudien Ergänzungsheft 157. Berlin: Walter de Gruyter & Co., 2008.

Grier, Michelle. *Kant's Doctrine of Transcendental Illusion*. Cambridge: Cambridge University Press, 2001.

Haag, Johannes. *Erfahrung und Gegenstand: Das Verhältnis von Sinnlichkeit und Verstand*. Frankfurt am Main: Vittorio Klostermann, 2007.

Hanna, Robert. *Kant and the Foundations of Analytic Philosophy*. Oxford: Clarendon Press, 2001.

Hanna, Robert. *Kant, Science, and Human Nature*. Oxford: Clarendon Press, 2006.

Heidegger, Martin. *Kant und die Frage nach dem Ding: zu Kants Lehre von den transzendentalen Grundsätzen*. Tübingen: Max Niemeyer, 1962. Translated as: *What is a Thing?* Translated by W. B. Barton, Jr. and Vera Deutsch. Chicago: Henry Regnery, 1967.

Heidegger, Martin. *Kant und das Problem der Metaphysik*. Edited by Friedrich-Wilhelm von Herrmann. Heidegger, *Gesamtausgabe*. Band 3. Frankfurt am Main: Vittorio Klostermann, 1991.

Heidegger, Martin. *Kant and the Problem of Metaphysics*. Fifth edition, enlarged. Translated by Richard Taft. Bloomington: Indiana University Press, 1997.

Heidegger, Martin. *Phänomenologische Interpretationen von Kants Kritik der reinen Vernunft.* Edited by Ingtraud Görland. *Gesamtausgabe,* Band 25, second edition. Frankfurt am Main: Klostermann, 1987. Translated as: *Phenomenological Interpretation of Kant's Critique of Pure Reason.* Translated by Parvis Emad and Kenneth Maly. Bloomington: Indiana University Press, 1997.

Heidemann, Dietmar H. *Kant und das Problem des metaphysischen Idealismus.* Berlin: Walter de Gruyter & Co., 1998.

Henrich, Dieter. *The Unity of Reason: Essays on Kant's Philosophy.* Edited by Richard Velkley. Cambridge, Mass.: Harvard University Press, 1994.

Hindrichs, Gunnar. *Das Absolute und das Subjekt: Untersuchungen zum Verhältnis der Metaphysik und Nachmetaphysik.* Frankfurt am Main: Vittorio Klostermann, 2008.

Hinsch, Wilfried. *Erfahrung und Selbsbewußtsein: Zur Kategoriendeduktion bei Kant.* Hamburg: Felix Meiner Verlag, 1986.

Hintikka, Jaakko. *Logic, Language-Games, and Information: Kantian Themes in the Philosophy of Logic.* Oxford: Clarendon Press, 1973.

Hintikka, Jaakko. *Knowledge and the Known: Historical Perspectives in Epistemology.* Dordrecht: D. Reidel Publishing Co., 1974.

Holzhey, Helmut. *Kants Erfahrungsbegriff.* Basel: Schwabe, 1970.

Horstmann, Rolf-Peter. *Bausteine kritischer Philosophie.* Bodenheim bei Mainz: Philo Verlag, 1997.

Hossenfelder, Malte. *Kants Konstitutionstheorie und die Transzendentale Deduktion.* Berlin: Walter de Gruyter & Co., 1978.

Howell, Robert. *Kant's Transcendental Deduction: An Analysis of Main Themes in His Critical Philosophy.* Dordrecht: Kluwer, 1992.

Kaulbach, Friedrich. *Die Metaphysik des Raumes bei Leibniz und Kant.* Kant-Studien Ergänzungsheft 79. Bonn: Bouvier Verlag, 1960.

Klemme, Heiner F. *Kants Philosophie des Subjekts: Systematische und entwicklungsgeschichtliche Untersuchungen zum Verhältnis von Selbstbewußtsein und Selbsterkenntnis.* Kant-Forschungen, Band 7. Hamburg: Felix Meiner Verlag, 1996.

Klotz, Christian. *Kants Widerlegung des problematischen Idealismus.* Göttingen: Vandenhoeck & Ruprecht, 1993.

Koriako, Darius. *Kant's Philosophie der Mathematik: Grundlagen – Voraussetzungen – Probleme.* Kant-Forschungen, Band 11. Hamburg: Felix Meiner Verlag, 1999.

Lachièze-Rey, Pierre. *L'idéalisme Kantien.* Deuxième Édition. Paris: J. Vrin, 1950.

Langton, Rae. *Kantian Humility: Our Ignorance of Things in Themselves.* Oxford: Clarendon Press, 1998.

Malzkorn, Wolfgang. *Kants Kosmologie-Kritik: Eine formale Analyse der Antinomienlehre.* Kant-Studien Ergänzungsheft 134. Berlin: Walter de Gruyter & Co., 1999.

Martin, Gottfried. *Arithmetik und Kombinatorik bei Kant.* Berlin: Walter de Gruyter & Co., 1972.

Melnick, Arthur. *Kant's Analogies of Experience.* Chicago: University of Chicago Press, 1973.

Melnick, Arthur. *Space, Time, and Thought in Kant.* Dordrecht: Kluwer, 1989.

Melnick, Arthur. *Themes in Kant's Metaphysics and Ethics.* Studies in Philosophy and the History of Philosophy, Volume 40. Washington, D.C.: Catholic University Press of America, 2004.

Melnick, Arthur. *Kant's Theory of the Self.* London: Routledge, 2009.

Milmed, Bella Kussy. *Kant and Current Philosophical Issues: Some Modern Developments of His Theory of Knowledge.* New York: New York University Press, 1961.

Mosser, Kurt. *Necessity and Possibility: The Logical Strategy of Kant's* Critique of Pure Reason. Washington, D.C.: Catholic University of America Press, 2008.

Nagel, Gordon. *The Structure of Experience: Kant's System of Principles.* Chicago: University of Chicago Press, 1983.

Parsons, Charles. *Mathematics in Philosophy: Selected Essays.* Ithaca: Cornell University Press, 1983.

Powell, C. Thomas. *Kant's Theory of Self-Consciousness.* Oxford: Oxford University Press, 1990.

Prauss, Gerold. *Erscheinung bei Kant: Ein Problem der "Kritik der reinen Vernunft."* Berlin: Walter de Gruyter, 1971.

Prauss, Gerold. *Kant und das Problem der Dinge an sich.* Bonn: Bouvier Verlag, 1974.

Reich, Klaus. *The Completeness of Kant's Table of Categories.* Translated by Jane Kneller and Michael Losonsky. Stanford: Stanford University Press, 1992.

Rescher, Nicholas. *Kant and the Reach of Reason: Studies in Kant's Theory of Rational Systematization.* Cambridge: Cambridge University Press, 2000.

Rosefeldt, Tobias. *Das logische Ich: Kant über den Gehalt des Begriffes von sich selbst.* Hamburg: Philo, 2000.

Rotenstreich, Nathan. *Experience and Its Systematization: Studies in Kant.* Second edition. The Hague: Martinus Nijhoff, 1972.

Rousset, Bernard. *La Doctrine Kantienne de l'objectivité.* Paris: J. Vrin, 1967.

Sacks, Mark. *Objectivity and Insight.* Oxford: Clarendon Press, 2000.

Schneeberger, Guido. *Kants Theorie der Modalbegriffe.* Basel: Schwabe, 1952.

Schwyzer, Hubert. *The Unity of Understanding: A Study in Kantian Problems.* Oxford: Clarendon Press, 1990.

Seeberg, Ulrich. *Ursprung, Umfang, und Grenzen der Erkenntnis: Eine Untersuchung zu Kants transzendentaler Deduktion der Kategorien.* Hamburg: Philo, 2008.

Sellars, Wilfrid. *Science and Metaphysics: Variations on Kantian Themes.* London: Routledge & Kegan Paul, 1968.

Sellars, Wilfrid. *Kant and Pre-Kantian Themes: Lectures by Wilfrid Sellars.* Edited by Pedro Amaral. Atascadero: Ridgeview Publishing Co., 2002.

Sellars, Wilfrid. *Kant's Transcendental Metaphysics: Sellars' Cassirer Lecture Notes and Other Essays.* Edited by Jeffrey F. Sicha. Atascadero: Ridgeview Publishing Co., 2002.

Senderowicz, Yaron M. *The Coherence of Kant's Transcendental Idealism.* Dordrecht: Springer, 2005.

Shabel, Lisa A. *Mathematics in Kant's Critical Philosophy: Reflections on Mathematical Practice.* London: Routledge, 2003.

Smith, A. H. *A Treatise on Knowledge.* Oxford: Clarendon Press, 1943.

Smith, A. H. *Kantian Studies.* Oxford: Clarendon Press, 1947.

Smyth, Richard. *Forms of Intuition.* The Hague: Martinus Nijhoff, 1978.

Stapleford, Scott. *Kant's Transcendental Arguments: Disciplining Pure Reason.* London: Continuum, 2008.

Stepanenko, Pedro. *Categorías y autoconocienca en Kant.* México (D.F.): Instituto de Investigaciones Filosóficas, Universidad Nacional Autónoma de México, 2000.

Strawson, P. F. *Entity and Identity and Other Essays.* Oxford: Clarendon Press, 1997.

Sturma, Dieter. *Kant über Selbstbewußtsein: Zum Zusammenhang von Erkenntniskritik und Theorie des Selbstbewußtseins.* Hildesheim: Georg Olms Verlag, 1985.

Svare, Helga. *Body and Practice in Kant.* Dordrecht: Springer, 2006.

Szrednicki, Jan T. *The Place of Space and Other Themes.* The Hague: Martinus Nijhoff, 1983.

Thöle, Bernhard. *Kant und das Problem der Gesetzmäßigkeit der Natur.* Berlin: Walter de Gruyter & Co., 1991.

Tonelli, Giorgio. *Kant's Critique of Pure Reason within the Tradition of Modern Logic.* Edited by David H. Chandler. Hildesheim: Georg Olms Verlag, 1994.

Warren, Daniel. *Reality and Impenetrability in Kant's Philosophy of Nature.* London: Routledge, 2004.

Watkins, Eric. *Kant and the Metaphysics of Causality.* Cambridge: Cambridge University Press, 2005.

Waxman, Wayne. *Kant's Model of the Mind: A New Interpretation of Transcendental Idealism.* New York: Oxford University Press, 1991.

Waxman, Wayne. *Kant and the Empiricists: Understanding Understanding.* New York: Oxford University Press, 2005.

Westphal, Kenneth. *Kant's Transcendental Proof of Realism.* Cambridge: Cambridge University Press, 2004.

Wike, Victoria S. *Kant's Antinomies of Reason: Their Origin and Resolution.* Washington, D.C.: University Press of America, 1982.

Winterbourne, A. T. *The Ideal and the Real: An Outline of Kant's Theory of Space, Time, and Mathematical Construction.* Dordrecht: Kluwer, 1988.

Wolff, Michael. *Der Begriff des Widerspruches: Eine Studie zur Dialektik Kants und Hegels.* Meisenheim: Verlag Anton Hain, 1981.

Wolff, Michael. *Die Vollständigkeit der kantischen Urteilstafel.* Frankfurt am Main: Vittorio Klostermann, 1995.

Zöller, Günter. *Theoretische Gegenstandsbeziehung bei Kant: Zur systematischen Bedeutung der Termini "objektive Realität" und "objektive Gültigkeit" in der "Kritik der reinen Vernunft."* Berlin: Walter de Gruyter, 1984.

8. MULTI-AUTHOR COLLECTIONS ON THE *CRITIQUE OF PURE REASON*

Beck, Lewis White, editor. *Kant Studies Today.* LaSalle: Open Court Publishing Co., 1967.

Bieri, Peter, Rolf-Peter Horstmann, and Lorenz Krüger, editors. *Transcendental Arguments and Science: Essays in Epistemology.* Dordrecht: D. Reidel, 1979.

Butts, Robert E., editor. *Kant's Critique of Pure Reason, 1781–1981. Synthese* 47, nos. 2 and 3 (1981).

Chadwick, Ruth, and Clive Cazeaux, editors. *Immanuel Kant: Critical Assessments.* 4 vols. London: Routledge, 1992. (vols. I and II)

Förster, Eckart, editor. *Kant's Transcendental Deductions: The Three 'Critiques' and the 'Opus postumum'.* Stanford: Stanford University Press, 1989.

Forum für Philosophie Bad Homburg, editors. *Kants transzendentale Deduktion und die Möglichkeit von Transzendentalphilosophie.* Frankfurt am Main: Suhrkamp, 1988.

Garber, Daniel, and Béatrice Longuenesse, editors. *Kant and the Early Moderns.* Princeton: Princeton University Press, 2008.

Glock, Hans-Johann, editor. *Strawson and Kant.* Oxford: Clarendon Press, 2003.

Gram, Moltke S., editor. *Interpreting Kant.* Iowa City: University of Iowa Press, 1982.

Gram, Moltke S., editor. *Kant: Disputed Questions.* Chicago: Quadrangle Books, 1967.

Kitcher, Patricia, editor. *Kant's* Critique of Pure Reason: *Critical Essays.* Lanham: Rowman & Littlefield, 1998.

Klemme, Heiner F., and Manfred Kuehn, editors. *Immanuel Kant.* 2 vols. Aldershot: Ashgate/Dartmouth, 1999. (vol. I: *Theoretical Philosophy*)

Kopper, Joachim, and Rudolf Malter, editors. *Materialen zu Kants "Kritik der reinen Vernunft."* Frankfurt am Main: Surhkamp, 1975.

Mohanty, J. N., and Robert W. Shahan, editors. *Essays on Kant's Critique of Pure Reason.* Norman: University of Oklahoma Press, 1982.

Parrini, Paolo, editor. *Kant and Contemporary Epistemology.* Dordrecht: Kluwer, 1994.

Penelhum, Terence, and J. J. MacIntosh, editors. *The First Critique: Reflections on Kant's Critique of Pure Reason.* Belmont: Wadsworth, 1969.

Posy, Carl J., editor. *Kant's Philosophy of Mathematics: Modern Essays.* Dordrecht: Kluwer, 1992.

Robinson, Hoke, editor. *The Spindel Conference 1986: The B-Deduction. Southern Journal of Philosophy* 25, Supplement (1987).

Schaper, Eva, and Wilhelm Vossenkuhl, editors. *Bedingungen der Möglichkeit: 'Transcendental Arguments' und transzendentales Denken.* Stuttgart: Klett-Cotta Verlag, 1984.

Schaper, Eva, and Wilhelm Vossenkuhl, editors. *Reading Kant: New Perspectives on Transcendental Arguments and Critical Philosophy.* Oxford: Basil Blackwell, 1989.

Stern, Robert, editor. *Transcendental Arguments: Problems and Prospects.* Oxford: Clarendon Press, 1999.

Tuschling, Burkhard, editor. *Probleme der "Kritik der reinen Vernunft": Kant-Tagung Marburg 1981.* Berlin: Walter de Gruyter & Co., 1984.

Van Cleve, James, and Robert E. Frederick, editors. *The Philosophy of Right and Left.* Dordrecht: Kluwer, 1991.

Walker, Ralph C. S., editor. *Kant on Pure Reason.* Oxford: Oxford University Press, 1982.

Watkins, Eric, editor. *Kant and the Sciences.* Oxford: Oxford University Press, 2001.

9. ARTICLES CITED IN THIS VOLUME

Adickes, Erich. "Die bewegenden Kräfte in Kants philosophischer Entwicklung und die beiden Pole seines Systems." *Kant-Studien* 1 (1896–97).

Adickes, Erich. "Die bewegenden Kräfte in Kants philosophischer Entwicklung und die beiden Pole seines Systems." *Kant-Studien* 1 (1896–97).

Ameriks, Karl. "Kant's Deduction of Freedom and Morality." *Journal of the History of Philosophy,* **19** (1981): 53–79.

Ameriks, Karl. "The Critique of Metaphysics: The Structure and Fate of Kant's Dialectic." In *The Cambridge Companion to Kant and Modern Philosophy.* Edited by Paul Guyer. Cambridge: Cambridge University Press, 2006.

Anderson, R. Lanier. "It Adds Up After All: Kant's Philosophy of Arithmetic in Light of the Traditional Logic." *Philosophy and Phenomenological Research* **69** (2004): 501–40.

Anderson, R. Lanier. "Containment Analyticity and Kant's Problem of Synthetic Judgment." *Graduate Faculty Philosophy Journal* **25** (2004): 161–204.

Anderson, R. Lanier. "Neo-Kantianism and the Roots of Anti-Psychologism." *British Journal for the History of Philosophy* **13** (2005): 287–323.

Anderson, R. Lanier. "The Wolffian Paradigm and its Discontents: Kant's Containment Definition of Analyticity in Historical Context." *Archiv für Geschichte der Philosophie* **87** (2005): 22–74.

Beck, Lewis White. Review of Martin Heidegger, *Kant and the Problem of Metaphysics*. *Philosophical Review* **72** (1963): 396–398.

Beck, Lewis White, "Lewis' Kantianism." In: *idem.*, *Studies in the Philosophy of Kant* (Indianapolis: Bobbs-Merrill, 1965), 108–124; also published as: "The Kantianism of Lewis," in: P. A. Schilpp, ed., *The Philosophy of C. I. Lewis* (LaSalle.: Open Court, 1986), 271–85.

Beiser, Frederick. "Emil Lask and Kantianism." *Philosophical Forum* **39** (2008): 283–95.

Bird, Graham. "McDowell's Kant: *Mind and World*." *Philosophy* **71**(1996): 219–43.

Bird, Graham. "Kantian Themes in Contemporary Philosophy II." *Proceedings of the Aristotelian Society*, Supplementary vol. **72** (1998): 131–51.

BonJour, Laurence. "Haack on Justification and Experience." *Synthese* **112** (1997): 13–23.

Bullard, Alice. "Kant in the Third Republic: Charles Renouvier and the Constructed Self." *Proceedings of the Western Society for French History* **25** (1998): 319–28.

Carson, Emily. "Kant on Intuition in Geometry." *Canadian Journal of Philosophy* **27** (1997): 489–512.

Carson, Emily. "Kant on Arithmetic and the Conditions of Experience." unpublished ms., McGill University.

Caruthers, Paul, "Conceptual Pragmatism." *Synthese* **73** (1987): 205–24.

Cassirer, Ernst. "Hermann Cohen und die Erneuerung der Kantischen Philosophie" (1912). In *Gesammelte Werke*. Vol. 9. Edited by Birgit Recki. Hamburg: Felix Meiner Verlag, 2001, 119–38.

Cassirer, Ernst. "Zur Theorie des Begriffs. Bemerkungen zu dem Aufsatz von G. Heymans" (1928). In Cassirer, *Gesammelte Werke*. Vol. 17. Edited by Birgit Recki. Hamburg: Felix Meiner Verlag, 2004, pp. 83–91.

Cassirer, Ernst. "Bemerkungen zu Martin Heideggers Kant-Interpretation." *Kant-Studien* **35** (1931): 1–26.

Chignell, Andrew. "Belief in Kant." *Philosophical Review* **116** (2007): 323–360.

Chignell, Andrew. "Neo-Kantian Philosophies of Science: Cassirer, Kuhn, and Friedman." *Philosophical Forum* **39** (2008): 253–62.

Chignell, Andrew. "Causal Refutations of Idealism." *Philosophical Quarterly* (forthcoming).

Cohen, Hermann. "Zur Controverse zwischen Trendelenburg und Kuno Fischer." *Zeitschrift für Völkerpsychologie und Sprachwissenschaft*. Band 7. Edited by M. Lazarus and H. Steinthal. Berlin: F. Dümmler, 1871, pp. 249–96.

Corcoran, J. "C. I. Lewis: History and Philosophy of Logic." *Transactions of the Charles S. Peirce Society* **42** (2006): 1–9.

Couturat, Louis. "La Philosophie des Mathématiques de Kant." *Revue de Métaphysique et de Morale* **12** (1904): 321–83.

Crawford, Patricia. "Kant's Theory of Philosophical Proof." *Kant-Studien* **53** (1961–62).

Dahlstrom, Daniel. "Heidegger's Kantian Turn: Notes to his Commentary on the *Kritik der reinen Vernunft*." *Review of Metaphysics* **45** (1991): 329–361.

Dayton, Eric. "C. I. Lewis and the Given." *Transactions of the Charles S. Peirce Society* 31 (1995): 254–84.

de Jong, Willem. "Kant's Analytic Judgments and the Traditional Theory of Concepts." *Journal of the History of Philosophy* 37 (1995): 613–41.

Deligiori, Katerina. "Kant, Hegel, and the Bounds of Thought." *The Bulletin of the Hegel Society of Great Britain* 45/46 (2002).

deVries, Willem. Review of of Johannes Haag, *Erfahrung und Gegenstand*. *Internationales Jahrbuch des Deutschen Idealismus* 5 (2007): 368–75.

Dicker, Georges. "Kant's Refutation of Idealism." *Nous* 42:1 (2008): 80–108.

Dillon, M. C. "Apriority In Kant and Merleau-Ponty." *Kant-Studien*, 78 (1987): 403–423.

Divers, John. "Kant's Criteria of the A Priori." *Pacific Philosophical Quarterly* 80 (1999): 17–45.

Eberhard, J. A. "Ueber die Unterscheidung der Urtheile in analytische und synthetische." *Philosophische Magazin* I (1789): 307–32. Hrsg. J. A. Eberhard. Halle: J. J. Gebauer.

Edel, Geert. "Transzendentale Deduktion bei Kant und Cohen." In *Kant im Neukantianismus: Fortschritt oder Rückschritt?* Edited by Marion Heinz and Christian Krijnen. Würzburg: Königshausen & Neumann, 2007, pp. 25–36.

Emundts, Dina. "Kant über die innere Erfahrung." In Uwe Kern, editor. *Was ist und was sein soll: Natur und Freiheit bei Immanuel Kant*. Berlin: Walter de Gruyter, 2007. pp. 189–205.

Emundts, Dina. "Emil Lask on Judgment and Truth." *Philosophical Forum* 39 (2008): 263–81.

Faye, Jean-Pierre. "Philosophie le plus ironique." In Yannick Beaubatie, editor. *Tombeau de Gilles Deleuze*. Tulle: Mille sources, 2000.

Ferrari, Massimo. "Cassirer, Schlick und die Relativitätstheorie. Ein Beitrag zur Analyse des Verhältnisses von Neukantianismus und Neopositivismus." In *Neukantianismus: Perspektiven und Probleme*. Edited by Ernst Wolfgang Orth and Helmut Holzhey. Würzburg: Königshausen & Neumann, 1994, pp. 418–41.

Ferrari, Massimo. "Ist Cassirer methodisch gesehen ein Neukantianer?" In *Der Neukantianismus und das Erbe des deutschen Idealismus: die philosophische Methode*. Edited by Detlev Pätzold and Christian Krijnen. Würzburg: Königshausen & Neumann, 2002, pp. 103–21.

Flach, Werner. "Das Problem der transzendentalen Deduktion: seine Exposition in der Kritik der reinen Vernunft und seine Wiederaufnahme im Neukantianismus der Südwestdeutschen Schule." In *Materialien zur Neukantianismus-Diskussion*. Edited by H.-L. Ollig. Darmstadt: Wissenschaftliche Buchgesellschaft, 1987. pp. 150–62.

Förster, Eckart. "Kant's Refutation of Idealism." In A. J. Holland, editor. *Philosophy, Its History and Historiography*. Dordrecht: D. Reidel Publishing Company, 1985, pp. 295–311.

Friedman, Michael. "Causal Laws and the Foundations of Natural Science." In *The Cambridge Companion to Kant*, ed. P. Guyer. Cambridge: Cambridge University Press, 1992, pp. 161–199.

Friedman, Michael. "Geometry, Construction and Intuition in Kant and his Successors." In Gila Sher and Richard Tieszen, editors, *Between Logic and Intuition: Essays in Honor of Charles Parsons*. Cambridge: Cambridge University Press, 2000, pp. 186–218.

Friedman, Michael. "Ernst Cassirer and the Philosophy of Science." In *Continental Philosophy of Science*. Edited by Gary Gutting. Malden: Blackwell, 2005, pp. 71–83.

Friedman, Michael. "Ernst Cassirer and Thomas Kuhn: The Neo-Kantian Tradition in History and Philosophy of Science." *Philosophical Forum* **39** (2008): 239–52.

Gabriel, Gottfried. "Windelband und die Diskussion um die Kantischen Urteilsformen." In *Kant im Neukantianismus: Fortschritt oder Rückschritt?* Edited by Marion Heinz and Christian Krijnen. Würzburg: Königshausen & Neumann, 2007, pp. 91–108.

George, Rolf. "Kant's Sensationism." *Synthese* **47** (1981): 229–55.

Gettier, Edmund. "Is Justified True Belief Knowledge?," *Analysis* **23** (1963): 121–23.

Giovanelli, Marco. "Kants Grundsatz der 'Antizipationen der Wahrnehmung' und seine Bedeutung für die theoretische Philosophie des Marburger Neukantianismus." In *Kant im Neukantianismus: Fortschritt oder Rückschritt?* Edited by Marion Heinz and Christian Krijnen. Würzburg: Königshausen & Neumann, 2007, pp. 37–55.

Gochnauer, Myron. "Kant's Refutation of Idealism." *Journal of the History of Philosophy* **12** (1974): 195–206.

Guyer, Paul. "Kant on Apperception and *A Priori* Synthesis." *American Philosophical Quarterly* **17** (1980): 205–12.

Guyer, Paul. Review of Arthur Melnick, *Space, Time, and Thought in Kant*. *Kant-Studien* **85** (1994): 477–82.

Guyer, Paul. "The Unity of Reason: Pure Reason as Practical Reason in Kant's Early Conception of the Transcendental Dialectic." In Paul Guyer, *Kant on Freedom, Law, and Happiness*. Cambridge: Cambridge University Press, 2000, pp. 60–95.

Guyer, Paul. "Space, Time, and the Categories: The Project of the Transcendental Deduction." In Ralph Schumacher, editor. *Idealismus als Theorie der Repräsentation?* Paderborn: Mentis, 2001. pp. 313–38.

Harper, William. "Kant on Space, Empirical Realism, and the Foundations of Geometry." *Topoi* **3** (1984): 143–61.

Hatfield, Gary. "Kant on the Perception of Space (and Time)" in Paul Guyer, editor, *The Cambridge Companion to Kant and Modern Philosophy* (Cambridge: Cambridge University Press, 2006).

Hay, William H. "Lewis' Relation to Logical Empiricism." In Paul Arthur Schilpp, editor. *The Philosophy of C. I. Lewis*. LaSalle: Open Court Publishing Co., 1986, pp. 309–27.

Heidegger, Martin. "Das Problem der Realität in der neuzeitlichen Philosophie." In *Frühe Schriften*, ed. Friedrich-Wilhelm von Herrmann, Gesamtausgabe, Band 1 (Frankfurt am Main: Klostermann, 1978), 1–15.

Heidegger, Martin. "Kants These über das Sein" (1961). In Heidegger, *Wegmarken, 1919–1958*. Edited by Friedrich-Wilhelm von Herrmann. *Gesamtausgabe*. Band 9. Frankfurt am Main: Vittorio Klostermann, 1996; Translated as "Kant's Thesis about Being," in Heidegger, *Pathmarks*. Edited by William McNeill. Cambridge: Cambridge University Press, 1998, pp. 337–363.

Heidelberger, Michael. "Kantianism and Realism: Alois Riehl (and Moritz Schlick)." In *The Kantian Legacy in Nineteenth-Century Science*. Edited by Michael Friedman and Albert Nordmann. Cambridge, MA: MIT Press, 2006, pp. 227–47.

Heimsoeth, Heinz. "Metaphysische Motive in der Ausbildung des kritischen Idealismus." *Kant-Studien* **29** (1924): 121–159.

Helmholtz, Herman Ludwig von. "Über das Sehen des Menschen" (1855). Reprinted in Helmholtz, *Vorträge und Reden*. Fourth edition. Braunschweig: Vieweg, 1896. Vol. 1, pp. 85–117.

Helmholtz, Hermann Ludwig von. "Die Thatsachen in der Wahrnehmung" (1878). Reprinted in Helmholz, *Vorträge und Reden*. Fourth edition. Braunschweig: Vieweg, 1896. Vol. 2, pp. 213–47. Translated as: "The Facts of Perception." In Herman Helmholtz. *Science and Culture: Popular and Philosophical Essays*. Edited by David Cahan. Chicago: University of Chicago Press, 1995, pp. 342–80.

Hendricks, Christina. "Foucault's Kantian Critique: Philosophy and the Present." *Philosophy & Social Criticism*, **34** (2008): 357–382.

Henrich, Dieter. "The Proof-Structure of the Transcendental Deduction." *Review of Metaphysics* **22** (1969): 640–59.

Hogan, Desmond. "How to Know Unknowable Things in Themselves." *Noûs* **43** (2009): 49–63.

Hogan, Desmond. "Three Kinds of Rationalism and the Non-Spatiality of Things in Themselves." *Journal of the History of Philosophy* **47** (2009): 355–82.

Holzhey, Helmut. "Zu Natorps Kantauffassung." In *Materialien zur Neukantianismus-Diskussion*. Edited by H.-L. Ollig. Darmstadt: Wissenschaftliche Buchgesellschaft, 1987, pp. 134–49.

Horstmann, Rolf-Peter. "Hermann Cohen on Kant's Transcendental Aesthetic." *Philosophical Forum* **39** (2008): 127–38.

Husserl, Edmund. "Kant und die Idee der Transzendentalphilosophie" (1924). In Husserl, *Erste Philosophie (1923/24)*. Edited by R. Boehm. The Hague: Martinus Nijhoff, 1956.

Jacquette, Dale. "The Uniqueness Problem in Kant's Transcendental Doctrine of Method." *Man and World* **19** (1986): 425–38.

Janiak, Andrew. "Kant's Views on Space and Time," *Stanford Encyclopedia of Philosophy*, http://plato.stanford.edu/kant-spacetime/ September 14, 2009.

Kitcher, Philip. "Kant and the Foundations of Mathematics." *Philosophical Review* **84** (1975): 23–50.

Kitcher, Philip. "Projecting the Order of Nature." In Robert Butts, editor. *Kant's Philosophy of Science*. Dordrecht: D. Reidel, 1986, pp. 201–35.

Kitcher, Philip. "'A Priori.'" In Paul Guyer, ed. *The Cambridge Companion to Kant and Modern Philosophy*. Cambridge: Cambridge University Press, 2006. pp. 28–60.

Krijnen, Christian. "Das konstitutionstheoretische Problem der transzendentalen Ästhetik in Kants ' Kritik der reinen Vernunft' und seine Aufnahme im südwestdeutschen Neukantianismus." In *Kant im Neukantianismus: Fortschritt oder Rückschritt?* Edited by Marion Heinz and Christian Krijnen. Würzburg: Königshausen & Neumann, 2007, pp. 109–34.

Langley, Raymond. "Kantian Continuations in Jaspers." In *Karl Jaspers*. Edited by Joseph Koterski, and Raymond Langley. Amherst: Humanities, 2003, pp. 193–204.

Longuenesse, Béatrice. "The Transcendental Ideal and the Unity of the Critical System." In *Proceedings of the Eighth International Kant Congress*. Edited by Hoke Robinson. Milwaukee: Marquette University Press, 1995. Vol. 1, part 2, pp. 521–38.

Maaß, J. G. "Ueber den höchsten Grundsatz der synthetischen Urtheile; in Beziehung auf die Theorie von der mathematischen Gewissheit." *Philosophisches Magazin* II, 2, 2 (1789–90): 186–231. Hrsg. J. A. Eberhard. Halle: J. J. Gebauer.

Malter, Rudolf. "Heinrich Rickert und Emil Lask." *Materialien zur Neukantianismus-Diskussion*. Edited by H.-L. Ollig. Darmstadt: Wissenschaftliche Buchgesellschaft, 1987, pp. 87–104.

Marx, Wolfgang. "Die philosophische Entwicklung Paul Natorps im Hinblick auf das System Hermann Cohens." In *Materialien zur Neukantianismus-Diskussion*. Edited by H.-L. Ollig. Darmstadt: Wissenschaftliche Buchgesellschaft, 1987, pp. 66–86.

Milmed, Bella K. "'Possible Experience' and Recent Interpretations of Kant." In L. W. Beck, editor. *Kant Studies Today*. Lasalle: Open Court Publishing Co., 1969, pp. 301–21.

Natorp, Paul. "Über objective und subjective Begründung der Erkenntniss (Erster Aufsatz)." *Philosophische Monatshefte* **23** (1887): 257–86.

Natorp, Paul. "Kant und die Marburger Schule." *Kant-Studien* **17** (1912): 193–221.

O'Shea, James R ., "Conceptual Connections: Kant and the Twentieth Century Analytic Tradition." In G. Bird, ed., *The Blackwell Companion to Kant* (Oxford: Blackwell, 2007), 513–27.

Parsons, Charles. "The Transcendental Aesthetic." In Paul Guyer, ed., *The Cambridge Companion to Kant*. (Cambridge: Cambridge University Press, 1992).

Parsons, Charles. "Kant's Philosophy of Arithmetic." In Parsons, *Mathematics and Philosophy*. Ithaca: Cornell University Press, 1983, pp. 110–49.

Parsons, Charles. "Infinity and Kant's Conception of the Possibility of Experience." *Philosophical Review* **78** (1964): 182–97; reprinted in *Mathematics and Philosophy*, pp. 95–109.

Politis, Vasilis. "Invoking the Greeks on the Relation between Thought and Reality: Trendelenburg's Aristotle – Natorp's Plato." *Philosophical Forum* **39** (2008): 191–222.

Pollok, Konstantin. "Sedimente des Wissens – Kants Theorie der Naturwissenschaft und ihre Dynamisierung bei Michael Friedman." *Oldenburger Jahrbuch für Philosophie* **1** (2007): 51–82.

Pollok, Konstantin. "'An Almost Single Inference' – Kant's Deduction of the Categories Reconsidered." *Archiv für Geschichte der Philosophie* **90** (2009): 323–45.

Quine, W. V. O. "Two Dogmas of Empiricism." In Quine, *From a Logical Point of View*. Cambridge, MA: Harvard University Press, 1953, pp. 20–46.

Rauscher, Frederick. "A Second Look at the Second Step of the B-Deduction" (forthcoming).

Richardson, Alan. "'The Fact of Science' and Critique of Knowledge: Exact Science as Problem and Resource in Marburg Neo-Kantianism." *The Kantian Legacy in Nineteenth-Century Science*. Edited by Michael Friedman and Albert Nordmann. Cambridge, MA.: MIT Press, 2006, pp. 211–26.

Rickert, Heinrich. "Zwei Wege der Erkenntnistheorie. Transzendentalpsychologie und Transzendentallogik." *Kant-Studien* **14** (1909).

Rickert, Heinrich. "Alois Riehl." *Logos* **13** (1924–25).

Rorty, Richard. "Strawson's Objectivity Argument." *Review of Metaphysics* **24** (1970): 207–44.

Russell, Bertrand. "Dr. Schiller's Analysis of *The Analysis of Mind*." In J. Passmore, general editor. *The Collected Papers of Bertrand Russell*. London: Routledge, 1994), 9: 39.

Schlick, Moritz. "Gibt es ein materiales Apriori?" *Wissenschaftlicher Jahresbericht der Philosophischen Gesellschaft an der Universität zu Wien für das Vereinsjahr 1930/31*, rpt. in: *idem.,Gesammelte Aufsätze 1926–1936* (Wien: Gerold, 1938), 19–30.

Sedgwick, Sally. "Hegel on Kant's Antinomies and the Distinction between General and Transcendental Logic." *Monist* **74** (1991): 403–20.

Sellars, Wilfrid. "Empiricism and the Philosophy of Mind." In *Minnesota Studies in the Philosophy of Science*. Vol. 1. Edited by Herbert Feigl and Michael Scriven. Minneapolis: University of Minnesota Press, 1956, pp. 253–329. Reprinted in Sellars, *Science, Perception, and Reality*. London: Routledge & Kegan Paul, 1963, 127–96; reprinted with an introduction by Richard Rorty and a study guide by Robert Brandom. Cambridge, MA: Harvard University Press, 1997.

Sellars, Wilfrid. "The Role of the Imagination in Kant's Theory of Experience." In H. Johnstone, editor. *Categories: A Colloquium*. University Park: Pennsylvania State University Press, 1978, pp. 231–45.

Shabel, Lisa. "Kant on the 'Symbolic Construction' of Mathematical Concepts." *Studies in History and Philosophy of Science* **29** (1998): 589–621.

Shabel, Lisa. "Kant's 'Argument from Geometry.'" *Journal of the History of Philosophy* **42** (2004): 195–215.

Shabel, Lisa. "Apriority and Application: Philosophy of Mathematics in the Modern Period." In Stewart Shapiro, editor. *The Oxford Handbook of Philosophy of Mathematics and Logic*. Oxford: Oxford University Press, 2005. pp. 29–50.

Shin, Sun Joo. "Kant's Syntheticity Revisited by Peirce." *Synthese* **113** (1997): 1–41.

Smith, Daniel W., "Deleuze and Derrida, Immanence and Transcendence." In *Between Deleuze and Derrida*. Edited by Paul Patton and John Protevi. London: Continuum, 2003.

Stevenson, Leslie. "Opinion, Belief or Faith, and Knowledge." *Kantian Review* **7** (2003): 72–101.

Strawson, P. F. "Echoes of Kant." *Times Literary Supplement* 4657 (3 July 1992):

Stroud, Barry. "Transcendental Arguments and 'Epistemological Naturalism'." *Philosophical Studies* **31** (1977): 105–15.

Sutherland, Daniel. "Kant's Philosophy of Mathematics and the Greek Mathematical Tradition." *Philosophical Review* **113** (2004): 157–201.

Sutherland, Daniel. "Kant on Fundamental Geometrical Relations." *Archiv für Geschichte der Philosophie* **87** (2005): 117–158.

Sutherland, Daniel. "Kant on Arithmetic, Algebra, and the Theory of Proportions." *Journal of the History of Philosophy* **44** (2006): 533–58.

Warren, Daniel. "Kant and the Apriority of Space." *The Philosophical Review* **107** (1998): 179–224.

Watkins, Eric. "Kant on Rational Cosmology." In Watkins, *Kant and the Sciences*, pp. 70–89.

Watson, Stephen. "Regulations: Kant and Derrida at the End of Metaphysics." In *Deconstruction and Philosophy*. Edited by John Sallis. Chicago: University of Chicago Press, 1987. pp. 71–86.

Westphal, Kenneth R. "Can Pragmatic Realists Argue Transcendentally?" In J. Shook, editor. *Pragmatic Naturalism and Realism*. Buffalo: Prometheus, 2003, pp. 151–75.

Westphal, Kenneth R. "Kant, Wittgenstein, and Transcendental Chaos." *Philosophical Investigations* **28** (2005): 303–23.

Westphal, Kenneth R. "Contemporary Epistemology: Kant, Hegel, McDowell." *The European Journal of Philosophy* **14** (2006): 274–302; reprinted. in J. Lindgaard, editor. *John McDowell: Experience, Norm and Nature*. Oxford: Blackwell, 2008, pp. 124–51.

Westphal, Kenneth R. "Consciousness and Its Transcendental Conditions: Kant's Anti-Cartesian Revolt." In S. Heinämaa, V. Lähteenmäki, and P. Remes, editors. *Consciousness: From Perception to Reflection in the History of Philosophy*. Dordrecht: Springer, 2007, pp. 223–43.

Westphal, Kenneth R. "Hegel's Phenomenological Method and Analysis of
Consciousness." In Kenneth R. Westphal, editor. *The Blackwell Guide to Hegel's
Phenomenology of Spirit*. Oxford: Wiley-Blackwell, 2009. pp. 1–36.
Wick, Warner. "The 'Political' Philosophy of Logical Empiricism." *Philosophical
Studies* 2 (1951): 49–57.
Windelband, Wilhelm. "Kuno Fischer und sein Kant." *Kant-Studien* 2 (1897–98): 1–10.
Windelband, Wilhelm. "Otto Liebmanns Philosophie." *Kant-Studien* 15 (1910), iii–x.
Zöller, Günter. "Review Essay: Main Developments in Recent Scholarship on the
Critique of Pure Reason." *Philosophy and Phenomenological Research* 53 (1993):
445–66.

10.OTHER WORKS CITED

Adam of Wodeham. *Treatise on Indivisibles*. Edited and translated by Rega Wood.
Dordrecht: Kluwer, 1988.
Ameriks, Karl, editor. *The Cambridge Companion to German Idealism*. Cambridge:
Cambridge University Press, 2000.
Arnauld, Antoine and Pierre Nicole. *Logic or the Art of Thinking*. Edited by Jill Vance
Buroker. Cambridge: Cambridge University Press, 1996.
Bauch, Bruno. *Die Idee*. Leipzig: Reinicke, 1926.
Baumgarten, Alexander Gottlieb. *Meditationes philosophicae de nonnullis ad poema
pertinentibus/Philosophische Betrachtungen über einige Bedingungen des
Gedichtes*. Translated and edited by Heinz Paetzold. Hamburg: Felix Meiner
Verlag, 1983.
Baumgarten, Alexander Gottlieb. *Ästhetik*. Translated and edited by Dagmar Mirbach.
2 vols. Hamburg: Felix Meiner Verlag, 2007.
Beiser, Frederick C. *German Idealism: The Struggle against Subjectivism, 1781–1801*.
Cambridge, MA.: Harvard University Press, 2002.
Beneke, Friedrich Eduard. *Kant und die philosophische Aufgabe unserer Zeit: Eine
Jubeldenkschrift auf die Kritik der reinen Vernunft*. Berlin: Mittler, 1832.
Bird, Graham. *Philosophical Tasks: An Introduction to Some Aims and Methods in
Recent Philosophy*. London: Hutchinson University Library, 1972.
Bristow, William. *Hegel and the Transformation of Philosophical Critique*. Oxford:
Oxford University Press, 2007.
Cantoni, Carlo. *Emanuele Kant*. 3 vols. Milan: Brigola, 1879–1884.
Carnap, Rudolf. *Meaning and Necessity*. Chicago: University of Chicago Press, 1956.
Carnap, Rudolf. *Logical Foundations of Probability*. Second revised edition. Chicago:
University of Chicago Press, 1962.
Cassirer, Ernst. *Substanzbegriff und Funktionsbegriff: Untersuchungen über die
Grundfragen der Erkenntniskritik* (1910). *Gesammelte Werke*, vol. 6. Edited by
Birgit Recki. Hamburg: Felix Meiner Verlag, 2000. Translated in: *Substance and
Function and Einstein's Theory of Relativity*. Translated by William Curtis Swabey
and Mary Collins Swabey. LaSalle: Open Court Publishing Co., 1923.
Cassirer, Ernst. *Zur Einsteinschen Relativitätstheorie. Erkenntnistheoretische
Betrachtungen*. Berlin: Bruno Cassirer, 1921. Translated in: *Substance and Function
and Einstein's Theory of Relativity*. Translated by William Curtis Swabey and Mary
Collins Swabey. LaSalle: Open Court Publishing Co., 1923.
Cassirer, Ernst. *Philosophie der symbolischen Formen*. 3 vols. Berlin: Bruno Cassirer,
1923, 1925, 1929. In *Gesammelte Werke*, vols. 11–13. Edited by Birgit Recki.

Hamburg: Felix Meiner Verlag, 2002. Translated as *Philosophy of Symbolic Forms*. Translated by Ralph Manheim. 3 vols. New Haven: Yale University Press, 1953–57.

Cohen, Hermann. *Das Princip der Infinitesimal-Methode und seine Geschichte: ein Kapitel zur Grundlegung der Erkenntnisskritik*. Berlin: F. Dümmler, 1883.

Cohen, Hermann. *Logik der reinen Erkenntnis*. Second edition. Berlin: Bruno Cassirer, 1914.

Crusius, Christian August. *Entwurf der notwendigen Vernunftwahrheiten*. Leipzig: Gleditsch, 1745.

Crusius, Christian August. *Weg zur Gewißheit*. Leipzig: Gleditsch, 1747.

Deleuze, Gilles. *Différence et répétition*. Paris: Presses universitaires de France, 1976.

Deleuze, Gilles. *Foucault*. Translated by Seán Hand. Minneapolis: University of Minnesota Press, 1989.

Deleuze, Gilles. *Negotiations, 1972–1990*. Translated by Martin Joughin. New York: Columbia University Press, 1990.

Derrida, Jacques. *Dissemination*. Translated by Barbara Johnson. Chicago: University of Chicago Press, 1981.

Derrida, Jacques. *L'écriture et la difference*. Paris: Éditions du Seuil, 1967.

Derrida, Jacques. *Marges de la philosophie*. Paris: Les editions de Minuit, 1972.

Descartes, René. *Oeuvres de Descartes*. Edited by C. Adam, and P. Tannery. 13 vols. Paris: L. Cerf, 1879–1913.

Descartes, René. *The Philosophical Writings of Descartes*. Vols. I-II translated by John Cottingham, Robert Stoothoff, and Dugald Murdoch; vol. III translated by Cottingham, Stoothoff, Murdoch, and Anthony Kenny. Cambridge: Cambridge University Press, 1985–91.

deVries, Willem. *Wilfrid Sellars*. Chesham, Bucks: Acumen, 2005.

deVries, Willem and Timm Triplett. *Knowledge, Mind, and the Given: Reading Wilfrid Sellars's "Empiricism and the Philosophy of Mind."* Indianapolis and Cambridge, Mass.: Hackett Publishing Co., 2000.

Dickson, M. and Mary Domski, editors. *Discourse on a New Method: Reinvigorating the Marriage of History and Philosophy of Science*. Chicago and LaSalle: Open Court Publishing Co., forthcoming.

Djaballah, Marc. *Kant, Foucault, and Forms of Experience*. London: Taylor & Francis Group, 2008.

Dummett, Michael E. *The Logical Basis of Metaphysics*. Cambridge, Mass.: Harvard University Press, 1991.

Dummett, Michael E. *Thought and Reality*. Oxford: Oxford University Press, 2006.

Fichte, Johann Gottlieb. *Gesamtausgabe der Bayerischen Akademie der Wissenschaften*. Edited by Reinhard Lauth et. al. Stuttgart-Bad Canstatt: Fromann-Holzboog, 1962–2007.

Fichte, Johann Gottlieb. *The Science of Knowledge*. Edited and translated by Peter Heath and John Lachs. Cambridge: Cambridge University Press, 1982.

Fichte, Johann Gottlieb. *Foundations of Natural Right*. Edited by Frederick Neuhouser, translated by Michael Baur. Cambridge: Cambridge University Press, 2000.

Fichte, Johann Gottlieb. *The System of Ethics*. Translated and edited by Daniel Breazeale, and Günter Zöller. Cambridge: Cambridge University Press, 2005.

Fischer, Kuno. *System der Logik und Metaphysik oder Wissenschaftslehre*. Second edition. Heidelberg: Bassermann, 1865.

Förster, Eckart. *The Twenty-Five Years of Philosophy*. Cambridge, MA.: Harvard University Press, forthcoming.

Foucault, Michel. *Essential Works*. Translated by Robert Hurley and others. Volume One. New York: New Press, 1997.

Franks, Paul. *All or Nothing: Systematicity, Transcendental Arguments, and Skepticism in German Idealism*. Cambridge, MA.: Harvard University Press, 2005.

Friedman, Michael. *Reconsidering Logical Positivism*. Cambridge: Cambridge University Press, 1999.

Friedman, Michael. *A Parting of the Ways: Carnap, Cassirer, and Heidegger*. Chicago and LaSalle: Open Court Publishing Co., 2000.

Friedman, Michael. *Dynamics of Reason: The 1999 Kant Lectures at Stanford University*. Stanford: Center for the Study of Language and Information, 2001.

Grundmann, Thomas. *Analytische Transzendentalphilosophie: Eine Kritik*. Paderborn: Schöningh, 1993.

Gutting, Gary. *Michel Foucault's Archaeology of Scientific Reason*. Cambridge: Cambridge University Press, 1989.

Hanewald, Christoph. *Apperzeption und Einbildungskraft: Die Auseinandersetzung mit der theoretischen Philosophie Kants in Fichtes früher Wissenschaftslehre*. Berlin: Walter de Gruyter & Co., 2001.

Hegel, Georg Wilhelm Friedrich. *Werke in zwanzig Bänden (Theorie-Werkausgabe)*. Edited by Eva Moldenhauer and Karl Markus Michel. Frankfurt am Main: Suhrkamp, 1970.

Hegel, Georg Wilhelm Friedrich. *Faith and Knowledge*. Translated and edited by W. Cerf and H. S. Harris. Albany: State University of New York Press, 1977.

Hegel, Georg Wilhelm Friedrich. *Encyclopedia Logic*. Translated by T. F. Geraets, W. A. Suchting, and H. S. Harris. Indianapolis and Cambridge: Hackett Publishing Co., 1991.

Heidegger, Martin. *Nietzsche*. 2 vols. Pfullingen: Neske, 1961.

Heidegger, Martin. *Der Satz vom Grund*. Pfullingen: Neske, 1978.

Heidegger, Martin. *Prolegomena zur Geschichte des Zeitbegriffs*. Edited by Petra Jaeger. *Gesamtausgabe*, Band 20. Frankfurt am Main: Vittorio Klostermann, 1979.

Heidegger, Martin. *Metaphysische Anfangsgründe der Logik*. Edited by Klaus Held. *Gesamtausgabe*, Band 26, second edition. Frankfurt am Main: Vittorio Klostermann, 1990.

Heidegger, Martin. *Zur Bestimmung der Philosophie*. Edited by B. Heimbüchel. *Gesamtausgabe*, II. Abteilung: Vorlesungen, vol. 56/57. Frankfurt am Main: Vittorio Klostermann, 1999.

Henrich, Dieter. *Between Kant and Hegel: Lectures on German Idealism*. Edited by David S. Pacini. Cambridge, Mass.: Harvard University Press, 2003.

Herbart, Johann Friedrich. *Psychologie als Wissenschaft, neu gegründet auf Erfahrung, Metaphysik und Mathematik*. In *Sämtliche Werke*. Edited by K. Kehrbach and O. Flügel. 19 vols. Langensalza: Beyer, 1887–1912; in vol. 5, 1890.

Hogan, Desmond. *Rationalism and Causal Realism in Kant's Metaphysics*. Unpublished Ph.D. Dissertation. Yale University, 2005.

Holbach, Baron d'. *Système de la nature* (1770) (Paris, 1821) 2: 155.

Horstmann, Rolf-Peter. *Die Grenzen der Vernunft: Eine Untersuchung zur Zielen und Motiven des Deutschen Idealismus*. Third edition. Frankfurt am Main: Vittorio Klostermann, 2004.

Hume, David. *Dialogues Concerning Natural Religion*. Edited by Richard Popkin. Indianapolis: Hackett Publishing Co., 1983.

Hyder, David. *Kant and Helmholtz on the Physical Meaning of Geometry.* Berlin: Walter de Gruyter & Co., 2009.

Jacobi, Friedrich Heinrich. *Werke.* Edited by Friedrich Roth and Friedrich Köppen. 6 vols. Leipzig: G. Fleischer, 1812–25.

Jacobi, Friedrich Heinrich. *The Main Philosophical Writings and the Novel Allwill.* Edited by G. di Giovanni. Montreal: Queens-McGill University Presses, 1994.

Jaspers. Karl. *The Great Philosophers.* Translated by Ralph Manheim. New York: Harcourt, Brace & World, 1962.

Jaspers, Karl. *Philosophy.* Translated by E. B. Ashton. 3 vols. Chicago: University of Chicago Press, 1969.

Kern, Iso. *Husserl und Kant. Eine Untersuchung über Husserls Verhältnis zu Kant und zum Neukantianismus.* The Hague: Martinus Nijhoff, 1964.

Köhnke, Klaus Christian. *Entstehung und Aufstieg des Neukantianismus: Die deutsche Universitätsphilosophie zwischen Idealismus und Positivismus.* Frankfurt am Main: Suhrkamp, 1986. Translation (without notes): *The Rise of Neo-Kantianism: German Academic Philosophy between Idealism and Realism.* Translated by R. J. Hollingdale. Cambridge: Cambridge University Press, 1991.

Kripke, Saul A. *Naming and Necessity.* Cambridge, MA.: Harvard University Press, 1980.

Krois, John Michael. *Cassirer. Symbolic Forms and History.* New Haven: Yale University Press, 1987.

Kusch, Martin. *Psychologism: A Case Study in the Sociology of Philosophical Knowledge.* London: Routledge, 1995.

Lange, Friedrich Albert. *Geschichte des Materialismus und Kritik seiner Bedeutung in der Gegenwart.* Edited by A. Schmidt. Frankfurt am Main: Suhrkamp, 1974. Translated as: *History of Materialism and Criticism of Its Present Importance.* Translated by Ernest Chester Thomas. 3 vols. London: Trübner, 1877–81.

Lask, Emil. *Die Logik der Philosophie und die Kategorienlehre: Eine Studie über den Herrschaftsbereich der logischen Form.* Tübingen: J. C. B. Mohr, 1911.

Lask, Emil. *Die Lehre vom Urteil.* Tübingen: J. C. B. Mohr, 1912.

Leibniz, Gottfried Wilhelm. *Theodicy.* Translated by E. M. Huggard. New Haven: Yale University Press, 1952.

Leibniz, Gottfried Wilhelm. *Philosophical Papers and Letters.* Edited by Leroy E. Loemker. Dordrecht: D. Reidel, 1969.

Leibniz, Gottfried Wilhelm. *New Essays on Human Understanding.* Edited by Peter Remnant and Jonathan Bennett. Cambridge: Cambridge University Press, 1981.

Leibniz, Gottfried Wilhelm. *Philosophical Essays.* Edited and translated by Roger Ariew and Daniel Garber. Indianapolis and Cambridge: Hackett Publishing Co., 1989.

Lewis, Clarence Irving. *Mind and the World Order: Outline of a Theory of Knowledge.* New York: Charles Scribner's Sons, 1929.

Lewis, Clarence Irving. *Collected Papers of Clarence Irving Lewis.* Edited by John D. Goheen and John L. Mothershead, Jr. Stanford: Stanford University Press, 1970.

Liebmann, Otto. *Kant und die Epigonen: Eine kritische Abhandlung.* Edited by Bruno Bauch. Berlin: Reuther & Reichard, 1912.

Locke, John. *An Essay Concerning Human Understanding.* Edited by P. H. Nidditch. Oxford: Clarendon Press, 1975.

Lyotard, Jean-François. *The Postmodern Condition.* Translated by Geoff Bennington and Brian Mssumi. Minneapolis: University of Minnesota Press, 1984.

Maimon, Salomon. *Versuch über die Transzendentalphilosophie.* Berlin: Christian Friedrich Voß und Sohn, 1790. Modern edition edited by Florian Ehrensperger. Hamburg: Felix Meiner Verlag, 2004.

McDowell, John. *Mind and World.* Revised edition. Cambridge, MA.: Harvard University Press, 1996.

Meier, Georg Friedrich. *Auszug aus der Vernunftlehre.* Halle: Rengerische Buchhandlung, 1752.

Merleau-Ponty, Maurice. *Phénoménologie de la perception.* Paris: Gallimard, 1945. Translated as: *Phenomenology of Perception.* Translated by Colin Smith. London: Routledge & Kegan Paul, 1962.

Moore, A. W. *Points of View.* Oxford: Oxford University Press, 1997.

Nancy, Jean-Luc. *The Ground of the Image.* Translated by Jeff Fort. New York: Fordham University Press, 2005.

Natorp, Paul. *Platos Ideenlehre: Eine Einführung in den Idealismus.* Leipzig: Dürr, 1903.

Natorp, Paul. *Logik: Grundlegung und logischer Aufbau der Mathematik und mathematischen Naturwissenschaften in Leitsätzen zu akademischen Vorlesungen* (1904). Second, revised edition. Marburg: Elwert, 1910.

Natorp, Paul. *Die logischen Grundlagen der exakten Wissenschaften.* Second edition. Leipzig: Teubner, 1921.

O'Shea, James. *Wilfrid Sellars.* Cambridge: Polity, 2007.

Pippin, Robert. *Hegel's Idealism: The Satisfaction of Self-consciousness.* Cambridge: Cambridge University Press, 1989.

Quine, Willard Van Orman. *Ontological Relativity and Other Essays.* New York: Columbia University Press, 1969.

Rawls, John. *Lectures on the History of Moral Philosophy.* Edited by Barbara Herman. Cambridge, MA.: Harvard University Press, 2000.

Reinhold, Karl Leonhard. *Versuch einer neuen Theorie des menschlichen Vorstellungsvermögen.* Prague and Jena: C. Widtmann and I. M. Mauke, 1789.

Renouvier, Charles. *Essais de Critique Générale.* 3 vols. Paris: Ladrange, 1854–64.

Rickert, Heinrich. *Der Gegenstand der Erkenntnis: Einführung in die Transzendentalphilosophie.* Sixth edition. Tübingen: J. C. B. Mohr, 1928.

Rickert, Heinrich. *Die Heidelberger Tradition in der Deutschen Philosophie.* Tübingen: J. C. B. Mohr, 1931.

Riehl, Alois. *Der philosophische Kriticismus und seine Bedeutung für die positive Wissenschaft.* 3 vols. Leipzig: Engelmann, 1887.

Rosenberg, Jay. *Wilfrid Sellars: Fusing the Images.* Oxford: Oxford University Press, 2007.

Rufus, Richardus. *In Physicam Aristotelicum.* Edited by Rega Wood. Oxford: Oxford University Press, 2003.

Russell, Bertrand. *The Problems of Philosophy.* New York: Henry Holt and Co., 1912.

Russell, Bertrand. *Our Knowledge of the External World.* London: George Allen & Unwin, 1914.

Sartre, Jean-Paul. *Being and Nothingness.* Translated by Hazel Barnes. New York: Philosophical Library, 1956.

Sartre, Jean-Paul. *The Transcendence of the Ego.* Translated by Forrest Williams and Robert Kirkpatrick. New York: Noonday, 1957.

Scharff, Robert. *Comte after Positivism.* Cambridge: Cambridge University Press, 1995.

Schelling, Wilhelm Friedrich Joseph. *Werke.* Edited by Manfred Schröter. 6 vols. Munich: Beck, 1927.

Schelling, Wilhelm Friedrich Joseph. *The Unconditional in Human Knowledge: Four Early Essays (1794–1796).* Edited by Fritz Marti. Lewisberg: Bucknell University Press, 1980.

Schopenhauer Arthur. *The World as Will and Representation.* Trans. E. J. F. Payne. 2 vols. Indian Hills: The Falcon's Wing Press, 1958.

Sedgwick, Sally, editor. *The Reception of Kant's Critical Philosophy: Fichte, Schelling, and Hegel.* Cambridge: Cambridge University Press, 2000.

Sellars, Wilfrid. *Science, Perception and Reality.* London: Routledge & Kegan Paul, 1963.

Sherover, Charles. *Heidegger, Kant and Time.* Bloomington: Indiana University Press, 1971.

Stang, Nicholas. *Kant's Modal Metaphysics.* Unpublished Ph.D. Dissertation. Princeton University, 2008.

Stern, Robert, editor. *Transcendental Arguments: Problems and Prospects.* Oxford: Oxford University Press, 1999.

Strawson, P. F. *Individuals: An Essay in Descriptive Metaphysics.* London: Methuen, 1959.

Strawson, P. F. *Freedom and Resentment and Other Essays.* London: Methuen, 1974.

Tiedemann, Dietrich. *Geist der spekulativen Philosophie.* 6 vols. Marburg: Neue Akademische Buchhandlung, 1791–97.

Tennemann, Wilhelm Gottlieb. *Geschichte der Philosophie.* 11 vols. Leipzig: J. A. Barth, 1798–1819.

Tlumak, Jeffrey. *Classical Modern Philosophy.* New York: Routledge, 2007.

Vorländer, Karl. *Geschichte der Philosophie.* Second edition. 2 vols. Leipzig: Dürr, 1908.

Westphal, Kenneth R. *Hegel's Epistemological Realism.* Dordrecht: Kluwer, 1989.

Westphal, Kenneth R. *Hegel, Hume und die Identität wahrnehmbarer Dinge.* Frankfurt am Main: Vittorio Klostermann, 1998.

Windelband, Wilhelm. *Präludien: Aufsätze und Reden zur Philosophie und ihrer Geschichte* (1884). Ninth edition. Tübingen: J. C. B. Mohr, 1924.

Wolff, Christian. *Vernünfftige Gedancken von Gott, der Welt und der Seele des Menschen* [German Metaphysics]. Halle: Rengerische Buchhandlung, 1719.

Wolff, Christian. *Philosophia rationalis sive logica.* Frankfurt and Leipzig: Libraria Rengeriana, 1740.

Wolff, Michael. *Abhandlung über die Prinzipien der Logik.* Frankfurt am Main: Vittorio Klostermann, 2004.

Wood, Allen W. *Kantian Ethics.* Cambridge: Cambridge University Press, 2008.

Index

For EU product safety concerns, contact us at Calle de José Abascal, 56–1°, 28003 Madrid, Spain or eugpsr@cambridge.org.

www.ingramcontent.com/pod-product-compliance
Ingram Content Group UK Ltd.
Pitfield, Milton Keynes, MK11 3LW, UK
UKHW020345140625

459647UK00019B/2311

* 9 7 8 0 5 2 1 7 1 0 1 1 4 *